THE MAN AND THE STATESMAN

The Collected Works of Frédéric Bastiat

Jacques de Guenin, General Editor

The Man and the Statesman: The Correspondence and Articles on Politics

"The Law," "The State," and Other Political Writings, 1843–1850

Economic Sophisms and "What Is Seen and What Is Not Seen"

Miscellaneous Works on Economics: From "Jacques-Bonhomme" to Le Journal des Économistes

Economic Harmonies

The Struggle Against Protectionism: The English and French Free-Trade Movements

Frédéric Bastiat

THE MAN AND THE STATESMAN

The Correspondence and Articles on Politics

FRÉDÉRIC BASTIAT

Translated from the French by
Jane Willems and Michel Willems
with an introduction by
Jacques de Guenin and Jean-Claude Paul-Dejean

Annotations and Glossaries by
Jacques de Guenin, Jean-Claude Paul-Dejean,
and David M. Hart

Translation Editor
Dennis O'Keeffe

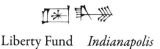

Liberty Fund   *Indianapolis*

This book is published by Liberty Fund, Inc., a foundation established
to encourage study of the ideal of a society of free and responsible individuals.

𒂼𒄄

The cuneiform inscription that serves as our logo and as the design motif
for our endpapers is the earliest-known written appearance of the word "freedom"
(*amagi*), or "liberty." It is taken from a clay document written about 2300 B.C.
in the Sumerian city-state of Lagash.

C 10 9 8 7 6 5 4 3 2 1
P 10 9 8 7 6 5 4 3 2 1

Image of the village of Mugron, France, the town where Bastiat spent most of his
adult life, from a postcard at www.communes.com/www.notrefamille.com.

Library of Congress Cataloging-in-Publication Data

Bastiat, Frédéric, 1801–1850. [Selections. English. 2011]
The man and the statesman: the correspondence and articles on politics /
Frédéric Bastiat; translated from the French by Jane Willems and Michel Willems,
with an introduction by Jacques de Guenin and Jean-Claude Paul-Dejean;
annotations and glossaries by Jacques de Guenin and David M. Hart.
p. cm. — (Collected works of Frédéric Bastiat)
Includes bibliographical references and index.
ISBN 978-0-86597-786-0 (hc.: alk. paper)—ISBN 978-0-86597-787-7 (pbk.: alk. paper)
1. Bastiat, Frédéric, 1801–1850—Political and social views.
2. Bastiat, Frédéric, 1801–1850—Correspondence.
3. France—Politics and government—1830–1848.
4. France—Politics and government—1848–1852. I. Title.
HB105.B3A25 2011
320.944—dc22   2010033541

LIBERTY FUND, INC.
8335 Allison Pointe Trail, Suite 300
Indianapolis, Indiana 46250-1684

Contents

General Editor's Note, xi

Note on the Translation, xv

Note on the Editions of the *Œuvres Complètes,* xix

Acknowledgments, xxi

General Introduction, by Jacques de Guenin and
    Jean-Claude Paul-Dejean, xxiii

Frédéric Bastiat Chronology, xxxvi

Map of France Showing Cities Mentioned by Bastiat, xxxviii

Map of Southwestern France, xxxix

PART 1: *Correspondence*

    Introduction to the Correspondence, by David M. Hart, 3

    Correspondence, 11

PART 2: *Articles and Addresses*

  SECTION 1: *Articles of Biographical Interest*

    1. Two Articles on the Basque Language, 305

    2. Reflection on the Question of Dueling, 309

    3. On the Bordeaux to Bayonne Railway Line, 312

    4. Draft Preface for the *Harmonies,* 316

    5. Anglomania, Anglophobia, 320

    6. Proposition for the Creation of a School for Sons of
       Sharecroppers, 334

  SECTION 2: *Political Manifestos*

    1. To the Electors of the *Département* of the Landes, 341

    2. To the Electors of the District of Saint-Sever, 352

    3. On Parliamentary Reform, 367

4. To the Electors of the Landes, 387

5. Letter to a Group of Supporters, 387

6. Political Manifestos of April 1849, 390

7. Letter on the Referendum for the Election of the President of the Republic, 395

Section 3: *Electoral Principles*

1. Electoral Sophisms, 397

2. The Elections, 404

3. Fragment, 410

4. Letter to a Candidate, 410

5. Letter to Roger Dampierre, 412

Section 4: *Articles on Politics*

1. On a New Secondary School to Be Founded in Bayonne, 415

2. Freedom of Teaching, 419

3. Freedom of Trade, 421

4. The Parisian Press, 425

5. Petition from an Economist, 426

6. Article in *La République française,* 429

7. The Scramble for Office, 431

8. Impediments and Taxes, 432

9. Freedom, 433

10. Laissez-faire, 434

11. Under the Republic, 435

12. On Disarmament, 437

13. The Kings Must Disarm, 439

14. Articles in *La République française* on the Political Situation, 440

15. To Citizens Lamartine and Ledru-Rollin, 444

16. Report Presented to the 1849 Session of the General Council of the Landes, on the Question of Common Land, 446

17. National Assembly, 451

18. Parliamentary Conflicts of Interest, 452

19. Parliamentary Reform, 457

20. Letter to an Ecclesiastic, 463

21. On Religion, 466

22. On the Separation of the Temporal and Spiritual
Domains, 468

23. The Three Pieces of Advice, 471

Glossaries
Glossary of Persons, 477
Glossary of Places, 509
Glossary of Subjects and Terms, 511

Appendix: List of the Correspondence by Recipient, 521
Bibliography of Primary Sources, 525
Index, 535

General Editor's Note

The Collected Works of Frédéric Bastiat will be the most complete edition of Bastiat's works published to date, in any country or in any language. The main source for this translation is the *Œuvres complètes de Frédéric Bastiat,* published by Guillaumin et Cie. in the 1850s and 1860s.[1] The additional sources used in this edition are the following: *Lettres d'un habitant des Landes, Frédéric Bastiat,* collected by Mme Cheuvreux (Paris: Quantin, 1877); articles published in *La Chalosse,* a local newspaper of the Landes, an area, or *département,* in southwestern France where Bastiat spent most of his life; articles published in *La Sentinelle des Pyrénées,* a newspaper printed in Bayonne; and various unpublished letters or articles gathered by the historian Jean-Claude Paul-Dejean, a Bastiat scholar, who has also collaborated in writing the introduction to this volume and the notes of the whole edition.

Although the Guillaumin edition was generally chronological, the volumes in this series have been arranged thematically:

> *The Man and the Statesman: The Correspondence and Articles on*
> *Politics*
> *"The Law," "The State," and Other Political Writings, 1843–1850*
> *Economic Sophisms and "What Is Seen and What Is Not Seen"*
> *Miscellaneous Works on Economics: From "Jacques-Bonhomme" to Le*
> *Journal des Économistes*
> *Economic Harmonies*
> *The Struggle Against Protectionism: The English and French*
> *Free-Trade Movements*

---

1. For a more-detailed description of the publication history of the *Œuvres complètes,* see "Note on the Editions of the *Œuvres Complètes*" and the bibliography.

The initial Guillaumin edition of the *Œuvres complètes,* published shortly after Bastiat's death, comprised six volumes. Later on, Prosper Paillottet, Bastiat's editor and executor, inherited a number of unpublished letters and articles, some of which were drafts, sometimes not even complete, but always meaningful enough to be of interest. After due consultation with Bastiat's intellectual friends, including Richard Cobden, Paillottet decided to publish everything in a seventh volume. The drafts themselves were regrouped under the heading *ébauches* (drafts), and this volume contains some of them.

There are three kinds of notes in this edition: footnotes by the editor of the Guillaumin edition (Prosper Paillottet), which are preceded by "(Paillottet's note)"; new editorial footnotes to this edition, which stand alone (unless they are commenting on Paillottet's notes, in which case they are in square brackets following Paillottet's note); and source notes, which are given in the last line of the heading for each letter or article. For those items taken from the *Œuvres complètes,* which constitutes the source for the majority of the items, the source note consists of the volume number and the beginning page number[2] plus any additional source information if the item has been previously published in a journal or similar publication.

In the text, Bastiat (and Paillottet in the notes) makes many passing references to his works, for which we have provided an internal cross-reference if the work is found in this volume. For those works not in this volume, we have provided the location of the original French version in the *Œuvres complètes* (indicated in a footnote by "*OC,*" followed by the Guillaumin volume number, beginning page number, and French title of the work).

In addition, we have made available two online sources[3] for the reader to consult. The first source is a table of contents of the seven-volume *Œuvres complètes* and links to PDF facsimiles of each volume. The second source is our "Comparative Table of Contents of the Collected Works of Frédéric Bastiat," which is a table of contents of the complete Liberty Fund series. Here, the reader can find the location of the English translation of the work in its future Liberty Fund volume. These contents will be filled in and updated as the volumes come out and will eventually be the most complete comparative listing of Bastiat's works.

---

2. See the bibliography for a complete listing of the *Œuvres complètes,* as well as a listing of other works cited in this volume.

3. These two sources can be found at http://oll.libertyfund.org/person/25.

In order to avoid multiple footnotes and cross-references, three glossaries have been provided for the identification of the persons, places, and subjects and terms mentioned in the text that were important to Bastiat in his time. The glossaries also provide historical context and background for the reader as well as a greater understanding of Bastiat's work. If a name as it appears in the text is ambiguous or is in the Glossary of Persons under a different name, a brief footnote has been added to the text to identify the name as it is listed in the glossary.

It should be remembered that when the Guillaumin edition was issued a number of people who knew Bastiat personally were still alive. The ellipses added by Paillottet, which precede or end some letters and which signal the omission of expressions of politeness or affection, have been reproduced in this edition. Ellipses are also used to indicate either a missing portion of the drafts or a deliberate cut by Paillottet when he thought that the passage in question was too private in nature. Finally, original italics as they appear in the Guillaumin edition have been retained.

Jacques de Guenin
Saint-Loubouer, France

Note on the Translation

In this translation we have made a deliberate decision not to translate Frédéric Bastiat's French into modern, colloquial American English. Wherever possible we have tried to retain a flavor of the more florid, Latinate forms of expression that were common among the literate class in mid-nineteenth-century France. Bastiat liked long, flowing sentences, in which idea followed upon idea in an apparently endless succession of dependent clauses. For the sake of clarity, we have broken up many but not all of these thickets of expression. In those that remain, you, dear reader, will have to navigate.

As was the custom in the 1840s, Bastiat liked to pepper his paragraphs with exclamations like "What!" and aphoristic Latin phrases like *Quid leges sine moribus?* (What are laws without customs?). We have translated the latter and left most of the former as a reminder that this was written in a bygone age when tastes were very different. We have also kept personal names, titles of nobility, and the like in their original French if the persons were French; thus, "M." instead of "Mr."; "Mme" instead of "Mrs."; "Mlle" instead of "Miss"; and "MM" instead of "Messrs."

Because Bastiat was a political theorist and an economist, he used many technical terms and expressions in his writings, some of which need explanation as they have no exact translation into today's speech. One example is *liberté,* which could be translated as either "liberty" (if one wanted to retain a more eighteenth-century flavor) or "freedom" (if one wanted a more modern sense). We have used both depending on the context and how it sounded to our ears. Another is *pouvoir,* which we have variously translated as "power," "government," or "authority," again depending on the context. A third example consists of the words *économie politique* and *économiste.* In both French and English throughout the eighteenth, and for most of the nineteenth, centuries, the term *political economy* was used to describe what we now call "economics." Toward the end of the nineteenth century as economics became more mathematical, the adjective "political" was dropped and not replaced. We have preferred to keep the term *political economy* both because it was still current when Bastiat was writing and because it better describes the state of the discipline, which proudly mixed an interest in moral philosophy, history, and political theory with the main dish, which was economic analysis; similarly, with the term *économiste*. Today one can be a free-market economist, a Marxist economist, a Keynesian economist, a mathematical economist, an Austrian economist, or whatever. The qualifier before the noun is quite important. In Bastiat's day it was assumed that any "economist" was a free-market economist, and so the noun needed no adjectival qualifier. Only during the 1840s, with the emergence of socialist ideas in France and Germany, did there emerge a school of economic thinking that sharply diverged from the free market. But in Bastiat's day this had not yet become large enough to cause confusion over naming. Even in 1849, when Gustave de Molinari published his charming set of dialogues, *Les Soirées de la rue St. Lazare,* between three stock characters—the socialist, the conservative, and the economist—it was perfectly clear who was arguing for what, and that the economist was of course a laissez-faire, free-market economist.

A particularly tricky word to translate is *industrie,* as is its related term *industriel.* In some respects it is a "false friend," as one is tempted to translate it as "industry" or "industrious" or "industrial," but this would be wrong because these terms have the more narrow modern meaning of "heavy industry" or "manufacturing" or "the result of some industrial process." The meaning in Bastiat's time was both more general and more specific to a particular social and economic theory current in his day.

In the eighteenth century *industry* had the general meaning of "productive" or "the result of hard work," and this sense continued to be current in the early nineteenth century. *Industry* also had a specific meaning, which was tied to a social and economic theory developed by Jean-Baptiste Say and his followers Charles Comte and Charles Dunoyer in the 1810s and 1820s, as well as by other theorists such as the historian Augustin Thierry. According to these theorists there were only two means of acquiring wealth: by productive activity and voluntary exchanges in the free market (i.e., *industrie*—which included agriculture, trade, factory production, and services) or by coercive means (conquest, theft, taxation, subsidies, protection, transfer payments, or slavery). Anybody who acquired wealth through voluntary exchange and productive activities belonged to a class of people collectively called *les industrieux,* in contrast to those individuals or groups who acquired their wealth by force, coercion, conquest, slavery, or government privileges.

The latter group were seen as a ruling class or as "parasites" who lived at the expense of *les industrieux*.

Bastiat was very much influenced by the theories of Say, Comte, and Dunoyer and adopted their terminology regarding *industry*. So to translate *industrie* in this intellectual context as "production" (or some other modern, neutral term) would be to ignore the resonance the word has with the social and economic theory that was central to Bastiat's worldview. Hence, at the risk of sounding a bit archaic and pedantic, we have preferred to use *industry* in order to remain true to Bastiat's intent.

When Bastiat uses an English word or phrase, we have mentioned this in a footnote, with one exception: Bastiat frequently writes such terms as "free trade" and "free trader" in English, especially in his correspondence with Richard Cobden, and thus we have not noted these occurrences.

A final note on terminology: in Bastiat's time, the word *liberal* had the same meaning in France and in America. In the United States, however, the meaning of the word has shifted progressively toward the left of the political spectrum. A precise translation of the French word would be either "classical liberal" or "libertarian," depending on the context, and indeed Bastiat is considered a classical liberal by present-day conservatives and a libertarian by present-day libertarians. To avoid the resulting awkwardness, we have decided by convention to keep the word *liberal*, with its nineteenth-century meaning, in the translations as well as in the notes and the glossaries.

Note on the Editions of the Œuvres Complètes

The first edition of the *Œuvres complètes* appeared in 1854–55, consisting of six volumes.[1] The second edition, which appeared in 1862–64, was an almost identical reprint of the first edition (with only minor typesetting differences) but was notable for the inclusion of a new, seventh volume, which contained additional essays, sketches, and correspondence.[2] The second edition also contained a preface by Prosper Paillottet and a biographical essay on Bastiat by Roger de Fontenay ("Notice sur la vie et les écrits de Frédéric Bastiat"), both of which were absent in the first edition.

Another difference between the first and second editions was in the sixth volume, which contained Bastiat's magnum opus, *Economic Harmonies*. The first edition of the *Œuvres complètes* described volume 6 as the "third revised and augmented edition" of *Economic Harmonies*. This is somewhat confusing but does have some logic to it. The "first" edition of *Economic Harmonies* appeared in 1850 during the last year of Bastiat's life but in an incomplete form. The "second" edition appeared in 1851, after his death, edited by La Société des amis de Bastiat (most probably by Prosper Paillottet and Roger de Fontenay) and included the second half of the manuscript, which Bastiat had been working on when he died. Thus the edition that appeared in the first edition of the *Œuvres complètes* was called the "third" edition on its title page. This practice continued throughout the nineteenth century, with editions of *Economic Harmonies* staying in print as a separate volume as

---

1. *Œuvres complètes de Frédéric Bastiat, mises en ordre, revues et annotées d'après les manuscrits de l'auteur* (Paris: Guillaumin, 1854–55). 6 vols.: vol. 1, *Correspondance et mélanges* (1855); vol. 2, *Le Libre-échange* (1855); vol. 3, *Cobden et la Ligue ou L'agitation anglaise pour la liberté des échanges* (1854); vol. 4, *Sophismes économiques. Petits pamphlets I* (1854); vol. 5, *Sophismes économiques. Petits pamphlets II* (1854); vol. 6, *Harmonies économiques* (1855). [Edited by Prosper Paillottet with the assistance of Roger de Fontenay, but Paillottet and Fontenay are not credited on the title page.]

2. Vol. 7: *Essais, ébauches, correspondance* (1864).

well as being included as volume 6 in later editions of the *Œuvres complètes*. By 1870–73, therefore, when the third edition of the *Œuvres complètes* appeared, the version of *Economic Harmonies* that appeared in volume 6 was titled the "sixth" edition of the work.

Other "editions" of the *Œuvres complètes* include a fourth edition, 1878–79, and a fifth edition, 1881–84. If there was a sixth edition, the date is unknown. A seventh edition appeared in 1893, and a final edition may have appeared in 1907. (For a complete listing of the editions of the *Œuvres complètes* that were used in making this translation, see the bibliography.)

Acknowledgments

The Man and the Statesman is the first volume of an English-language edition of the complete works of Frédéric Bastiat. The translation and editorial matter in this book and in the forthcoming volumes are the result of the efforts of a Franco-American team whom I have had the honor to coordinate and whose work I have reviewed at every step.

Jane Willems and Michel Willems were the initial translators; Jean-Claude Paul-Dejean, a historian of Bastiat, his epoch, and his surroundings, prepared the initial drafts of the notes and glossaries. The notes were adapted and translated by me; my English was reviewed by Diana Dupuy, of English origin, who in 2001 translated "To the Electors of the District of Saint-Sever" for the Foundation for Economic Education to commemorate the two-hundredth anniversary of the birth of Bastiat. Dr. Dennis O'Keeffe, Professor of Social Science at the University of Buckingham and Senior Research Fellow at the Institute of Economic Affairs in London, carefully read the translation and made very helpful suggestions at every stage. Dr. David Hart, Director of the Online Library of Liberty Project at Liberty Fund, further reviewed the translations. As an expert in eighteenth- and nineteenth-century European economists, he considerably enriched the notes related to the said economists and provided much of the scholarly apparatus. Aurelian Craiutu, Professor of Political Science at Indiana University, Bloomington, reviewed the final translations with Dr. Hart and contributed his considerable knowledge of nineteenth-century French politics to the review of the translation. Last but not least, Dr. Laura Goetz, Senior Editor at Liberty Fund, my constant correspondent on the other side of the Atlantic, organized and coordinated with me the various aspects of the project from its inception through to final manuscript.

This volume has thus all the strength and weaknesses of a voluntary, collaborative effort. We hope Bastiat would approve, especially as no government official was involved at any stage.

Jacques de Guenin
General editor, founder, and president
of the Cercle Frédéric Bastiat

General Introduction

As in the title of his last publication, *What Is Seen and What Is Not Seen,* Bastiat's life contains both "seen" and "unseen" elements. What was readily "seen" by his contemporaries was the arrival in 1844 of a somewhat rustic inhabitant from the provinces into the circle of the sophisticated and urbane Parisian free-market economists. In just a few short years, before his early death in 1850, Bastiat had made a profound impact on French intellectual and political life as a theoretician, a pamphleteer, a journalist, and a deputy (member of Parliament). What is not so readily apparent, either to his contemporaries or to modern readers, is the history of the man before his sudden arrival in Paris.

The present volume, most of which has never been translated into English before, attempts to fill that gap in our understanding—from exploring how Bastiat's origins in a small French country village shaped his self-image to discovering how the economic turmoil of the Napoleonic wars adversely affected his family's fortunes; how his early education contributed to the development of his uniquely inquiring mind; how his discovery of the ideas of Jean-Baptiste Say in the early Restoration period and the English Anti–Corn Law League in the early 1840s led him to become the leading advocate of free trade in France; and how a gentleman farmer became a politician on the national stage during the 1848 revolution.

THE "UNSEEN" BASTIAT: LIFE IN THE PROVINCES (1801–44)

The Bastiat family came from Laurède, a small village in the county of Mugron in an area of the *département* of the Landes called La Chalosse. Bastiat's great-grandfather, who had been a landowner, settled in Mugron in order to open a trading business. Around 1760 Pierre Bastiat, Frédéric's grandfather, following in the family footsteps, also established a trading house, this time in Bayonne, with his son, also named Pierre, and his son-in-law Henri Monclar. The business benefited from the franchise granted to the port of Bayonne in 1784 that enabled merchants to supply French and Spanish wines to Holland and to trade wool with Spain and Portugal.

Like many constitutionally minded liberals of the time, Pierre Bastiat initially approved of the events of the early stage of the French Revolution but came to oppose the Terror. Nevertheless, he took advantage of the forced sale of aristocratic property to purchase his own estate, in 1794, acquiring a domain called Sengresse, near Mugron, with a manor house and twelve sharecropping farms, thus strengthening the economic position of the Bastiat family in the Chalosse region. In 1800 Pierre *fils* married a young woman from Bayonne with whom he had two children: a son, Frédéric, in 1801, and later a daughter who died soon after birth.

But their economic prosperity was short-lived. Napoléon's continental blockade (1806), which was designed to bring England to its knees by preventing British goods from being sold in Europe; the naval war between Britain and France; the French invasion and occupation of Spain (1808); and the British counterattack through Portugal all severely disrupted Bayonne's commerce, with its close ties to England and Spain, and created serious problems for the Bastiat–Monclar family trading business. To compound the family's economic crisis, Frédéric's parents caught tuberculosis. His mother and grandmother both died in 1808, when he was only seven. His grandfather left the management of the family business to Henri Monclar and retired with his daughter Justine to the Mugron house, taking with him young Frédéric and his father, who died soon after. So, by the age of nine, Frédéric had lost both his mother and his father. He was subsequently brought up by his grandfather and his aunt Justine, a kind, intelligent, and devoted woman, who became his surrogate mother.

Bastiat's Childhood

Frédéric was a lively child, precocious and gifted, at ease in every circumstance. Perhaps to ensure that his talents were not left undeveloped, Justine decided that he should have an excellent education. She sent him first to the high school in nearby Saint-Sever; however, upon discovering that the education there was mediocre, she sent him in 1814 to one of the most prestigious schools of the time, the high school of Sorèze, near Carcassonne, in the *département* of Le Tarn. In 1791 the school, a former royal military school, privatized during the Revolution, came under the management of two brothers, François and Raymond-Dominique Ferlus, who introduced

educational reforms from which Bastiat was to benefit greatly. The first reform was to enroll pupils from different social, religious, geographical, and
cultural backgrounds in order to create a truly cosmopolitan and tolerant
environment for learning. Pupils came from several European countries and
even as far away as the United States. This is not surprising given the strong
connections between the new American republic and France, typified by
Thomas Jefferson's love of French literature and political and economic
thought. In addition, by employing a Catholic as well as a Protestant chaplain to minister to students of both denominations, the school exemplified
in a day-to-day practical manner the notion that different religious groups
could flourish and learn side by side.

The second educational reform at Bastiat's school was the "moderniza-
tion" of the curriculum to include the study of modern languages. Latin
and Greek, so-called dead languages, were minimized in favor of English,
German, Italian, and Spanish. Science, mathematics, and accounting introduced the students to practical economic reasoning; the vigorous and open
debate of philosophical matters encouraged students to debate ideas while
respecting others and developing intellectual agility. Sports and music were
also part of the curriculum—Bastiat excelled at sprinting and riding; he also
studied the cello, which he continued to play throughout his life. In sum,
Bastiat was exposed to a rounded and truly "liberal" education.

The third educational reform was the innovative method of teaching. For
example, pupils were encouraged to engage in collaborative learning, which
led to Bastiat and his friend Victor Calmètes jointly winning first prize in
poetry in 1818.

Unfortunately, Bastiat was unable to complete his education and to grad-
uate with a baccalaureate. At the age of seventeen he was forced to leave
Sorèze in order to return to Bayonne to help his uncle, Henri Monclar, with
the family business. Nevertheless, his experience at the school, which exposed him to a cosmopolitan, tolerant, and business-oriented environment,
profoundly affected him throughout his life.

Bastiat's Discovery of Political Economy

During his nearly seven years in Bayonne, Bastiat continued to broaden
his intellectual horizons. He studied business law and read the works of the
economists Adam Smith and Jean-Baptiste Say and the philosopher Pierre
Laromiguière. The ideas of Say were especially important at this time and,
furthermore, had a personal relevance for Bastiat. Bayonne, a once-thriving

port, was in decline in part because of the protectionist regime established by the restored monarchy after 1815. Like Bastiat, Say had started out as a businessman (a textile manufacturer) and, like Bastiat, had experienced the effects of protectionism under the continental blockade and the disruptions of the Napoleonic wars. Say's major work, *Traité d'économie politique* (*Treatise of Political Economy*), first published in 1803, was expanded and a new edition was published in 1814, in time to influence a rising generation of post-Napoleonic French liberals like Bastiat. For example, lawyer Charles Comte and journalist Charles Dunoyer both used Say's ideas to develop a theory of "industrialism," whereby a new era of unfettered commerce and industry was about to supplant the era of protectionism and warfare, which they believed had passed away with the fall of Napoléon.

At this time Bastiat also joined a Masonic lodge, La Zélée, which promoted ideals of virtue, tolerance, and liberalism similar to those he had encountered in Sorèze. He also acquired many contacts at the lodge, such as the banker Jacques Laffitte, who became a friend of the family and later minister of finance and prime minister under Louis-Philippe.

In 1824, when Bastiat was twenty-four, his grandfather died, and Bastiat inherited three of the sharecropping farms of Sengresse. Chalosse was a region of mixed farming, in which the only commercial activities were the sale of wine and a few head of cattle. Like many reform-minded landowners before him, Bastiat hoped to increase output and thus profits by replacing the traditional three-year crop rotation (wheat was grown on a third of the land, corn on another third, and the last third was left as fallow) with a two-year rotation, by leaving out the year of fallow. He devoted twenty-five acres to the experiment and engaged the help of the most gifted of his sharecroppers' sons. His experiments were not successful, however, and he eventually abandoned his efforts, leaving the sharecroppers to cultivate his land in their own traditional way.

When he was not engaged in agricultural reform, Bastiat spent much time with his friend Félix Coudroy reading not only the works of Comte and Dunoyer but also those of Benjamin Franklin and Antoine Destutt de Tracy, and discussing their ideas during long walks in the countryside. Bastiat was deeply influenced by Comte's work, in particular, the *Traité de législation* (*The Treatise of Legislation*) (1827; rev. ed., 1835), which he described as "the book that tells you the most, and makes you think most." One can only wonder at the directions taken in the animated conversations between the two friends as they walked about Bastiat's recently acquired estate.

Bastiat's First Foray into Politics

With the downfall of King Charles X in the revolution of July 1830, Bastiat inserted himself into the political turmoil on the side of the constitutional monarchy. He traveled to Bayonne to try to win over the garrison to the cause of the revolution. He asserted that "our cause is triumphing, the nation is admirable, people are going to be happy." Although he was a supporter of democracy and sought the return of a republic, Bastiat eventually rallied behind the constitutional monarchy of Louis-Philippe, the July Monarchy, which would last from 1830 until its overthrow in yet another revolution in 1848.

Following the 1830 revolution, Bastiat felt confident enough in the future to increase the size of his estate and to begin a new career as justice of the peace. In 1831 he purchased four sharecropping farms, which increased the size of the Sengresse estate by some 25 percent. Because Bastiat did not have the money to pay for the farms on his own, he married Clotilde Hiard, a wealthy heiress.[1]

In the same year, at the age of twenty-nine, Bastiat was appointed justice of the peace for the county of Mugron, a post he retained until 1846. He carried out his duties with considerable skill, showing common sense, an eye for the quick and efficient solution of disputes, and surprising competence for someone who did not have any formal legal training. His reputation was such that litigants from outside his geographical, or even legal, jurisdiction sought him out to resolve their disputes.

His success as justice of the peace led to further activities that cemented his growing reputation as one of the leading citizens of Mugron. In 1833 he was elected general counselor of the county of Mugron, a position to which he was reelected three times until his death in 1850. He showed an interest in everything likely to favor the economic development of the area, in particular a project for a canal alongside the Adour River, about which he published a number of articles. He also fought against the excessive taxation of wine and spirits, which he believed was causing a crisis in the wine

---

1. Bastiat never mentions his wife in his long and detailed correspondence. It appears as if his marriage to her was one strictly of convenience, to finance his estate. Love was expected to come later, as was often the case at the time, but it did not materialize. After their marriage, he apparently had no intimate life with her; and, although he took care of her financially, he left her in the custody of his Aunt Justine.

industry in the Chalosse region, and against protectionism, which impeded the export of wine.

Other activities that engaged Bastiat during this period included membership in the local Landes agricultural society, the creation of a school for sharecroppers' children (which was ultimately unsuccessful), the organization of the local wine growers, and the writing of articles for the local press. Between 1843 and 1845, he wrote many articles in the Bayonne press that foreshadowed the main themes on free trade that were later to make him famous as the leading advocate of free trade in France.[2]

Bastiat Discovers Richard Cobden and the Anti–Corn Law League

In Bastiat's time, Mugron was a busy port on the Adour River with a population of twenty-two hundred. The relative prosperity and cosmopolitan nature of the town was reflected in its educated bourgeoisie, who enjoyed gathering at "The Academy," a popular club, to discuss various philosophical, political, and economic subjects. Not surprisingly, Bastiat and Coudroy were frequent visitors. One day, in 1844, one of the more anglophobic members of the club furiously brandished a newspaper under Bastiat's nose, showing translated extracts from a recent speech by Sir Robert Peel, the British prime minister, to Parliament. The translation ended thus: "We will not adopt this measure. If we did, we would fall, like France, to the lowest rank of all the nations." Bastiat was so surprised that a British prime minister would make such a gratuitous statement about France in Parliament that he bought a subscription to the English newspaper, the *Globe and Traveller,* in order to see for himself. Some time later, Bastiat was able to read Peel's speech in the original English and discovered that the words "like France" were not there. It had been a mistranslation into French by a perhaps hostile, anti-British newspaper editor. It was while tracking down this mistranslation of Peel's speech that Bastiat came across reports in the English press of Richard Cobden's rapidly growing, popular free-trade movement, the Anti–Corn Law League, a movement that was largely ignored by the French press.

For Cobden and his associates in the Anti–Corn Law League, the aim of the campaign was to abolish the protectionist laws that prevented the free

---

2. These articles, which have never been republished, were not included in the *Œuvres complètes* but will be reproduced for the first time in the final volume of this edition, *The Struggle Against Protectionism: English and French Free Trade Movements.*

import of "corn" (wheat)[3] and to introduce a regime of free trade. One of the driving forces behind the free-trade movement was the inadequate harvest of 1844, which had left many poor people short of food, even starving. The British landowning aristocracy, wishing to maintain high domestic prices for wheat, did not want to open the borders to cheaper foreign wheat. Bastiat's family had personally suffered under protectionism, and he had read and discussed the ideas of the leading economic theorists on the benefits of free trade, but reading about the success of Cobden's popular movement against protectionism in the British press had galvanized Bastiat. He wished to emulate the Anti–Corn Law League in France.

He began by writing a long article, "On the Influence of French and English Tariffs on the Future of the Two Peoples." The conclusion was clear to Bastiat: England, on the verge of setting up free trade, was going to enjoy increasing prosperity, while France, constrained by protectionism, was going to decline hopelessly. He sent the article to the leading French economics journal, *Le Journal des économistes,* without much hope that it would be published. However, it was published and became an instant success in the circle of free-market economists in Paris.[4] Bastiat was immediately invited to Paris by the foremost French economists of the time, who recognized in him one of their peers.

THE "SEEN" BASTIAT (1844–50)

So Bastiat moved to Paris. "I must quit Mugron. I must separate myself from those I love," wrote Bastiat to Coudroy. "But there is life in Paris only, and one vegetates elsewhere." In addition to his association with the economists, he became friends with the Cheuvreux family, who hosted a salon. We have an amusing description of the newly arrived provincial Bastiat by Mme Cheuvreux, who carefully notes the un-Parisian cut of his clothes:

> There I saw Bastiat fresh from the Great Landes present himself at M. Say's[5] home. His attire was so conspicuously different from those sur-

---

3. The term *corn,* as mentioned here and elsewhere throughout this book, is used in the British context, meaning grain, especially wheat.

4. *Le Journal des économistes* 9 (August–November 1844): 244. (*OC,* vol. 1, p. 334, "De l'influence des tarifs français et anglais sur l'avenir des deux peuples.")

5. Jean-Baptiste Say (1767–1832) was the leading political economist in the first third of the nineteenth century. His son, Horace Say (1794–1899), was a businessman active

rounding him that the eye, however distracted, could not help but stare at him for a moment. The cut of his garments, due to the scissors of a tailor from Mugron, was far away from ordinary designs. Bright colors, poorly assorted, were placed next to one another, without any attempt at harmony. Floss-silk gloves covering his hands, playing with long white cuffs; a sharp collar covering half his face; a little hat, long hair; all that would have looked ludicrous had not the mischievous appearance of the newcomer, his luminous glance, and the charm of his conversation made one quickly forget the rest. Sitting in front of this countryman, I discovered that Bastiat was not only one of the high priests of the temple, but also a passionate initiator. What fire, what verve, what conviction, what originality, what winning and witty common sense! Through this cascade of clear ideas, of these displays, new and to the point, the heart was shown, the true soul of man revealed itself.[6]

Once settled in Paris, Bastiat directed his newly found passion for free trade into a campaign, modeled on that of the British Anti–Corn Law League, to enlighten the French public about the benefits of free trade and the steps being taken to achieve this on the other side of the Channel. Before he began the campaign in earnest, he wished to bring himself up to date with the latest developments in Britain. So he traveled to England, attended public meetings of the Anti–Corn Law League, and talked with its principal leaders, in particular Cobden, with whom he was to establish a lasting, trustful, and friendly relationship. The documentation he collected on that trip was summarized and translated in the book *Cobden and the League*, which was published in 1845.

In Paris Bastiat felt very much at home among the circle of the free-market economists, or "Les Économistes," as they called themselves. He began sending out a stream of vigorous articles full of corrosive wit and telling economic insights to the major Parisian and provincial newspapers. Many of these articles appeared individually in *Le Journal des économistes* and were soon republished in book form as *Economic Sophisms*. Their impact was con-

---

in liberal circles in the 1840s and 1850s. Horace's son, Léon Say (1826–96), was a banker, a successful politician in the Third Republic, and editor of *Le Nouveau dictionnaire d'économie politique* (1891). For more detailed information on the Says, see the Glossary of Persons.

6. *Lettres d'un habitant des Landes*, Frédéric Bastiat, pp. 3–4.

siderable, and they were quickly translated into English, German, Italian, and Spanish.

Toward the end of 1845 the Bordeaux Chamber of Commerce sought advice from Bastiat about the possibility of creating a movement to push for a customs union between France and Belgium. In a series of articles published in *Le Mémorial bordelais,* Bastiat argued that their energies would have greater impact if they campaigned more broadly for free trade, along the lines of the Anti–Corn Law League, rather than for a bilateral commercial treaty. The chamber took his advice and on 23 February 1846 (the same month in which the British Parliament voted to abolish the Corn Laws) a Bordeaux free-trade association was created, the first such association to be founded in France. A similar association was soon founded in Paris in July 1846, the Association pour la liberté des échanges, headed by François-Eugène Harcourt (duc d'Harcourt).

Bastiat was very much the driving force behind this national free-trade association. He served as its general secretary; he was the editor of *Le Libre échange,* the association's weekly paper; and he authored the association's manifesto,[7] which stated in the clearest possible terms that "exchange is a natural right, like property." It was, however, a difficult task to emulate the success of the British Anti–Corn Law League. Bastiat followed the League's strategy of organizing public meetings in Paris and some of the major towns, such as Lyons and Marseilles, but after a promising start the association's membership began to stagnate and by the end of 1847 it was clear that the movement was not flourishing. In a letter to Cobden, Bastiat wrote that in France "instructing the masses is an impossible task, because they have neither the civic right, the habit, nor the liking for grand rallies and public discussion. This is one more reason for me to aim to gain contact with the most enlightened and influential classes *through* becoming a deputy."[8] This statement indicated a shift in Bastiat's strategic thinking about the best way to campaign for free trade. If the grassroots approach, which had proven so successful in England, did not work in France, Bastiat was prepared to try something else, in this case standing for election to the Chamber of Deputies.

---

7. *OC,* vol. 2, p. 1, "Déclaration des principes."
8. See Letter 46, pp. 75–76.

Bastiat's Political Career

At the legislative elections of 1846, Bastiat ran against the government-supported candidate, Marie Gustave Larnac. In his "profession of faith," or election manifesto,[9] written to explain his position to the voters, Bastiat outlined his basic political and economic ideas: a government limited strictly to providing only justice, law-enforcement, and defense services; international free trade; freedom of education;[10] and protection of property rights. He also criticized the tendency for governments to expand and spend, the excessive number of civil servants in parliament, and the frequent changes of government to satisfy the ambition of some members of parliament to become ministers. But in spite of the clarity and logic of his pamphlet, he was not elected.

Another opportunity appeared after the revolutionary days of February 1848, which resulted in the downfall of the July Monarchy and the establishment of the Second Republic. Bastiat was elected in 1848 as deputy of the Landes to the Constituent Assembly and reelected in 1849 to the Legislative Assembly. For the next thirty months, in spite of declining health and family concerns, he worked feverishly as a member of parliament, a pamphleteer, and a theoretician. His parliamentary activities, especially as vice president of the finance committee, enabled him to work with many leading figures, such as the poet and historian Alphonse Lamartine, the novelist Victor Hugo, the political theorist and writer Alexis de Tocqueville, the anarchist and socialist Pierre-Joseph Proudhon, the Catholic priest and orator L'Abbé Jean-Baptiste-Henri Dominique Lacordaire, the future emperor Louis-Napoléon Bonaparte, and the socialist Louis Blanc.

Bastiat's desire was to help build a truly liberal republic, one that would avoid the utopian interventionism of the socialists on the "left" (such as the make-work schemes of the National Workshops) and the authoritarian tendencies of the conservatives of the "right" (who were encouraged by the election of Louis-Napoléon to the presidency of the Republic). Bastiat did not belong to any political party because, in the words of Léon Say, "He had too strong a personality to be a complete politician." Bastiat chose to fight

---

9. See "To the Electors of the District of Saint-Sever," p. 352.

10. Education was a state monopoly. Bastiat felt that education should belong to the private sphere, with the state taking on a supervisory role.

errors, especially economic errors, from wherever they came. Finding that both the left and the right often made serious errors concerning economic policy, Bastiat did not spare either side when it came to upholding his principles. "This is why on some occasions I had to vote with the left and on others with the right; with the left when it defended liberty and the Republic, with the right when it defended order and security."[11]

Although elected vice president of the finance committee—an important position at a time of severe budgetary difficulties for the new government— Bastiat played a modest role, as he was not a naturally gifted public speaker. He was not quick at repartee, and his voice, which was weakened by the illness[12] that would soon kill him, did not carry well in the often heated arguments that ensued.

Bastiat gave speeches on such diverse subjects as postal reform and taxes, the repression of strikes, and conflicts of interest that result when civil servants or government officials also sit in parliament. He voted against such issues as the reintroduction of imprisonment for debt, the legal suits against Louis Blanc, and the 1.2-million-franc credit asked for by the executive for the purpose of sending a military expedition to Rome (supposedly to free the pope but in fact aimed at destroying the newly created Roman republic).

If Bastiat's true talents did not lie in public speaking, they did indeed lie in the brilliant essays and books that flowed from his pen in the last few years of his life. Among the most influential pamphlets were *Protectionism and Communism; Capital and Rent; Peace and Freedom or the Republican Budget; Parliamentary Conflicts of Interest; Damned Money; Free Credit; Baccalaureate and Socialism; The State; Plunder and Law; The Law;* and *What Is Seen and What Is Not Seen.* In these and other essays and pamphlets he fought the interventionist economic ideas of Adolphe Thiers, Joseph Proudhon, and Victor Considérant, among others. He also defended his own ideas on the natural organization of society; on the freedom to work, to exchange, and to seek an education; on the need for the limitation of public expenditure and the reduction of the state to its essential functions; on the adoption of a peaceful foreign policy based on disarmament of the

11. See "Political Manifestos of April 1849," p. 393.

12. The exact nature of Bastiat's illness is not known with certitude. It is thought that it was most likely tuberculosis, which killed his parents, or cancer of the larynx.

navy and army; and on the possibilities of real social progress. By the latter he explained that "I sincerely hope to see the sufferings of the workers reduced to a minimum, but the more the state gets involved in their fate, the more their sufferings will increase."

Bastiat's Views on Free Trade and Peace

Like Cobden, Bastiat was convinced that free trade and peace were integrally connected. Both men agreed that free trade would lead to greater international cooperation and would lessen economic conflict among nations. The growth of international economic interdependence brought about by the advancement of free-trade policies would create in each nation a strong domestic lobby for peace; and the elimination of tariffs and subsidies would reduce the power and influence of the vested interests that push for war. It was for these reasons that Bastiat eagerly participated in the burgeoning organized peace movement, which began to hold annual meetings to discuss the issues and to promote peace among nations. The first Peace Congress was held in London in 1843 (the year the Anti–Corn Law League was founded), and a second was held in Brussels in 1848. Bastiat also opposed colonization schemes for much the same reasons. He criticized the idea behind the French colonization of Algeria and the method by which it was carried out, not to mention its exorbitant cost.

The outpouring of essays in this period enabled Bastiat to touch upon a number of points of economic theory in a sometimes novel but desultory fashion. He had dreamed for some time of writing his magnum opus, to be titled *Economic Harmonies,* which would be followed by another volume titled *Social Harmonies.* Although absorbed by urgent assignments, pressured by time, and consumed by illness, Bastiat wrote an incomplete draft of his book in barely three months. The writing obviously suffers from this haste, and the reviews were mixed as a result. *Economic Harmonies* received a favorable review abroad and a somewhat mixed one at home. For example, Bastiat's ideas on value and on the role of natural factors on production, rent, and population did not conform to the orthodox views held by the reviewer in *Le Journal des économistes.* After Bastiat's death, in 1850, the controversy over his book continued, with the American economist Henry C. Carey accusing Bastiat of plagiarism.[13]

---

13. Reported in Letters 204, 206, and 209 of the correspondence section of this volume.

During the last year of his life, Bastiat found the energy to write two of his best-known pieces: *What Is Seen and What Is Not Seen* and *The Law*. Unfortunately his health deteriorated rapidly, and he suffered from a ceaseless cough. On the advice of his doctor, he went to Italy to enjoy the warmer climate and relieve his symptoms. Upon reaching Rome, exhausted, Bastiat died on 24 December 1850 at the age of forty-nine. France had lost one of its greatest defenders of the free market.

Jacques de Guenin and
Jean-Claude Paul-Dejean

Frédéric Bastiat Chronology

1801   Born in Bayonne, 30 June.

1808   Death of mother. Moves to Mugron with father, grandfather, and Aunt Justine.

1810   Death of father.

1814–18   Attends school at Sorèze.

1819–25   Works in Bayonne for his Uncle Monclar.

1825   Death of grandfather. Inherits part of his estate.

1830   The "three glorious days," 27–29 July. Louis-Philippe becomes "king of the French."

1831   Appointed county judge.

1833   Elected to the General Council of the Landes.

1840   Travels to Spain and Portugal.

1844   *On the Influence of French and English Tariffs on the Future of the Two Peoples.*

1845   Travels to Paris and London.
        Cobden and the League.
        Economic Sophisms (first series).

1846   Monitors the Association pour la liberté des échanges.
        To the Electors of the District of Saint-Sever.
        Founds weekly journal *Le Libre échange.*

1847   *Economic Sophisms* (second series).

1848   Revolution, 22–24 February. The republic is proclaimed.
        Elected to the Constituent Assembly, 23 April.
        Founds *La République française* and *Jacques Bonhomme.*
        Property and Law.
        Justice and Fraternity.
        Property and Plunder.
        The State.
        Louis-Napoléon elected president of the republic, 10 December.

1849   Elected to the Legislative Assembly, 13 May.
        Protectionism and Communism.
        Capital and Rent.
        Peace and Freedom, or the Republican Budget.
        Parliamentary Incompatibilities.
        Damned Money.
        Free Credit.
1850   *Economic Harmonies.*
        Plunder and Law.
        The Law.
        Baccalaureate and Socialism.
        What Is Seen and What Is Not Seen.
        Departure for Rome, September.
        Dies in Rome, 24 December.

Map of France Showing Cities Mentioned by Bastiat

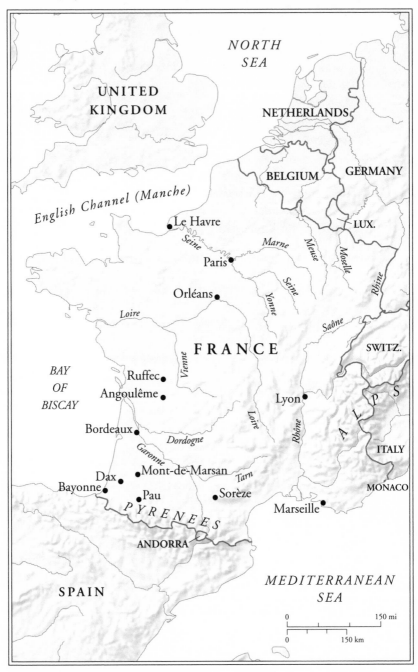

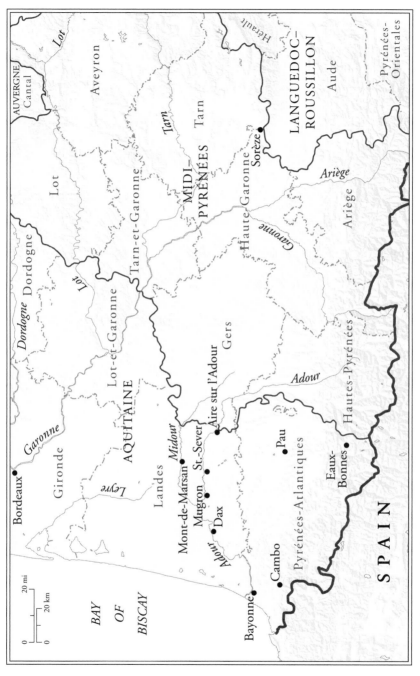

Map of Southwestern France

Cartography by Mapping Specialists, Madison, Wisconsin.

Part 1

Correspondence

Introduction to the Correspondence

THE MAN WHO EMERGES FROM THE CORRESPONDENCE

The Man and the Statesman, the first volume of Liberty Fund's Collected Works of Frédéric Bastiat, contains 208 letters Bastiat wrote during the period from September 1819 to just a few days before his untimely death, on Christmas Eve 1850, from a serious illness, most likely tuberculosis or throat cancer, or possibly a combination of both. The letters in this volume are taken primarily from volume 7 of the Guillaumin edition of his complete works, edited by Prosper Paillottet and published from 1854 to 1855.[1] Additional letters were published in 1877 in a collection by Mme Cheuvreux, a close friend,[2] or have been discovered in recent times by the Bastiat scholar Jean-Claude Paul-Dejean.

For those who are familiar only with Bastiat the author of provocative and thoughtful essays on economics and politics, such as the masterful "What Is Seen and What Is Unseen" or the incomplete treatise *Economic Harmonies,* the letters will reveal another Bastiat, unknown, more complex, and even conflicted. The Bastiat in these letters is the shy, unsophisticated, and somewhat gauche provincial magistrate who tries to make an impression in the metropole of Paris; the budding economic theorist who is welcomed into the ranks of the Société d'économie politique, attending their monthly dinners and writing articles for their main organ, *Le Journal des économistes;* the ardent supporter of peace and free trade who valiantly endeavors to mimic the political success of his hero and friend Richard Cobden; the courageous deputy who is involved in fighting on the barricades to defend the new republic during the revolution of February 1848 in Paris; the loyal friend of those he

---

1. *Œuvres complètes de Frédéric Bastiat.* See also the General Editor's Note, note 1; and the bibliography.

2. *Lettres d'un habitant des Landes, Frédéric Bastiat.*

3

left behind in Mugron, the provincial town to which he longs to return in order to escape the noise, turmoil, and frustrations of Paris; the companion of a number of successful and sophisticated bourgeois families, the women especially, who provide him with a family life and a personal intimacy that his own family could not or did not supply; the humorous and witty observer of the foibles of the "cold economists" who took themselves very seriously; and the pitiful sufferer of a long, painful, and ultimately fatal disease, which hampered his efforts to complete his magnum opus, *Economic Harmonies.*

The letters also tell us much about the intellectual, political, and social life of France during the 1840s, a time when France was experiencing considerable economic and social change, the beginnings of industrialization, the rise of socialism, the collapse of the July Monarchy, the 1848 revolution and the creation of a new republic, and the rise of Louis-Napoléon, who would eventually install himself as emperor. When Bastiat is sent to represent his province in the Constituent Assembly, he becomes a minor player in the revolution, serving on a finance committee because of his economic expertise. In the background of his correspondence we see the shadows of major players like Cavaignac, Guizot, Lamartine, and even Louis-Napoléon, filtered through the eyes of someone very new to the capital and very critical of the ability of any political party, whether left or right, socialist or legitimist, to solve the underlying political and economic problems that France faced.

As a laissez-faire, classical liberal, Bastiat was practically alone in the Assembly in arguing that the state should introduce free trade along the lines of the United Kingdom, deregulate the economy, and massively retrench the size of the military and public sector, thus allowing equally massive cuts in taxation in order to benefit the working class. Of course, Bastiat was surrounded on all sides by political groups and vested interests, which opposed these policies. It is surprising how long Bastiat was able to remain optimistic in the face of this opposition before he realized that he could better serve the cause of liberty by returning to writing. Unfortunately a premature death cut him down before he could achieve this goal.

For contemporary classical liberals Bastiat's letters provide a marvelous window into a long-forgotten world where opposition to war and colonialism went hand in hand with support for free trade and economic deregulation. Bastiat's numerous letters to Richard Cobden, a successful English businessman, a member of Parliament, and the leader of the British Anti–Corn Law League, are full of insights into how Cobden was able to organize a mass movement that succeeded in abolishing the most important restrictions on the free importation of grain into Britain. The letters also reveal Bastiat's repeated pleas that Cobden pressure the British government into reducing the size of its army and navy, a move that would encourage the French government to do likewise. Intertwined with these matters were discussions about the various international peace congresses held in 1848, 1849, and 1850, which Cobden and Bastiat either attended or wanted to attend.

In addition, Bastiat's letters provide information about the activities of the radical liberal economists in Paris who were members of the Société d'économie politique. Bastiat had learned much of his economics from reading the works of Jean-Baptiste Say and Charles Comte, who were the towering figures of early-nineteenth-century French classical liberal economic thought. Although both had passed from the scene by the time Bastiat arrived in Paris (Say in 1832 and Comte in 1837), a second generation of economists was active in the 1840s: Charles Dunoyer (Comte's long-time colleague), Horace Say (Say's son), Adolphe Blanqui, Gilbert Guillaumin, Joseph Garnier, Gustave de Molinari, and many others. Bastiat wrote several important articles for *Le Journal des économistes,* which showed his considerable skill as a writer who could make complex ideas come to life for all levels of readers. Whenever he could, he attended the monthly dinners held by the Société, and his letters are often filled with amusing anecdotes of what transpired at these functions.

THE RECIPIENTS OF BASTIAT'S CORRESPONDENCE

A closer examination of the 208 letters we have by Bastiat shows some interesting patterns. We do not have access to the original letters that were published by Guillaumin/Paillottet in 1854 and Mme Cheuvreux in 1877. It is clear that Paillottet took liberties with the letters, cutting out sections that were "too personal" or including incomplete drafts of letters found among Bastiat's effects. This was done both to enhance the reputation of a much-honored man and to protect the privacy of the recipients of his letters who were still alive. In spite of these handicaps, enough of the personal and private Bastiat comes through to be interesting to modern readers.

The letters were written to twenty-three individual recipients over a period of thirty years. Ten recipients received only one letter; another five recipients received only two or three letters each. The bulk of the letters was sent to seven recipients. It might be useful to divide Bastiat's correspondence into four main groups: friends and colleagues from his provincial home;

Richard Cobden and the free-trade group in England; his adopted families, the Cheuvreux family and the Schwabes; and the political economists in Paris.

The largest number of letters (fifty-one) was sent to Félix Coudroy, who trained as a lawyer and lived in the town of Mugron. He became a close friend of Bastiat's, and Bastiat commented that they agreed on everything they ever discussed on the many long walks they took together through the countryside. Bastiat repeatedly pours out his soul to Coudroy about his homesickness for Mugron, his uncertainties about his career, and his move to Paris. Another Mugron inhabitant, the mayor, Bernard Domenger, also received a large number of letters from Bastiat (seventeen). He was both a friend and a colleague while Bastiat was a magistrate. Their correspondence involves mainly local affairs. Bastiat wrote letters (fourteen) to an old school friend, Victor Calmètes, who later became a judge in Montpellier. Calmètes is interesting because of his involvement in liberal circles independently of Bastiat. He joined the society "Aide toi, le ciel t'aidera" (help yourself, heaven will help you), which had been organized by Guizot and included prominent liberal members such as La Fayette and Benjamin Constant.

The second-largest number of letters (forty-four) was sent to Richard Cobden. Bastiat was inspired by the success of the Anti–Corn Law League in mobilizing a popular movement that succeeded in pressuring the British government into abolishing the Corn Laws in 1846, and he wanted to emulate its successes in France by starting his own free-trade movement. In his letters to Cobden, Bastiat asks for advice, provides his own observations on the balance of forces either supporting or opposing free trade in Britain and France, and, toward the end of his life, discusses their collaboration in the international peace movement. Bastiat traveled to Britain several times to meet with Cobden and other members of the free-trade and peace movements and seemed to very much enjoy the company of Cobden and his family.

The third-largest number of letters (forty) was sent to the Cheuvreux family, which consisted of Mme Cheuvreux (Hortense), M. Cheuvreux (Casimir), and their daughter Louise. Casimir was a successful businessman whose wealth enabled the family to spend much time attending spas and traveling about Europe. Bastiat frequently visited their home or met them on their travels. He wrote most of the letters (thirty-five) to Mme Cheuvreux, who seems to have adopted the lonely Bastiat as a member of the family. They gave each other advice about family matters, illnesses, places to visit, and the trivia of bourgeois life. There is not a great deal of intellectual content in these letters, but they do show the personal, familial side of Bastiat. There are no letters to members of Bastiat's own family extant—a strange fact that suggests considerable alienation on his part and a strong psychological need to attach himself to a substitute family, such as the Cheuvreux. Another family of whom Bastiat was very fond was the Schwabes, who were English friends of the Cheuvreux family. He visited them when he went to England to see Cobden, and they visited him when they were traveling in Europe. He wrote eleven letters, mostly to Mrs. Schwabe, and they are similar in tone and content to the letters he wrote to Mme Cheuvreux.

Bastiat also wrote to a number of important liberal figures, such as Horace Say (seven); Charles Dunoyer, one of the leading liberal intellectuals of the first half of the nineteenth century (one); the poet and statesman Alphonse de Lamartine (one); the Italian economist Giovanni Arrivabene (two); and Prosper Paillottet, who was to be Bastiat's legal executor and editor of his papers after his death (eleven).

THEMES IN BASTIAT'S CORRESPONDENCE

Although Bastiat's letters are numerous and their recipients diverse, it is worth noting that several recurring themes appear throughout the letters, as well as some contradictions in his thought.

There are many references to the idea of justice, which might seem surprising for an economist, as we have come to expect modern economists to be "scientific" and dispassionate. Nineteenth-century political economists, however, were different. For example, Bastiat refers in his letters to issues of justice regarding ordinary working people, and there is a surprising recognition of the possibility that his own family fortune might have been based upon the unjust acquisition of church property during the Revolution. His strong sense of justice is also reflected in his acts of personal courage on the barricades in Paris during the 1848 revolution, suggesting an activist side to his political and economic philosophy. At times he even doubts the morality and efficacy of serving as a politician and expresses ambivalence about his choice of career versus that of working outside politics as a writer.

Bastiat's enigmatic and conflicting relationships with, and views of, women can be detected in many of his letters. His sentiments range from the never-mentioned and absent "wife"[3] to his close relationships with Mme Cheuvreux and Mrs. Schwabe and his considerable fondness for their children, despite having no children of his own. Further, in apparent contradiction to his distant and essentially nonexistent relationship with his wife, he did favor women's rights in general and in particular acknowledged the considerable contribution of women to modern literature.

Bastiat was also conflicted over where he felt truly at home: the countryside of the Landes, his birthplace, or the metropolitan city of Paris. This sentiment is evident in the great delight he took in sending and receiving letters of all kinds and from all people. The letters of course were very useful in maintaining personal relationships, but he always seems to be wishing he were somewhere other than where he was at any given moment.

The issues of mortality and religion that appear in many of the letters offer yet another dimension to Bastiat's complex personality. Given the fact that he lost both parents at an early age to tuberculosis, it is not surprising that Bastiat was aware of his own mortality. He was afraid of cholera and other diseases, he suffered a painful and debilitating illness, and he knew that this illness would likely end his life far too early. The letters in which these thoughts and feelings are apparent are very touching. Bastiat did not seem to take any solace from religion, however. His letters contain scattered remarks about religion, some fairly critical, especially of its formalism and emptiness. As someone from a small town who "made it big" in the metropolis of Paris, Bastiat, not unsurprisingly, occasionally reveals in the privacy of his letters his insecurity concerning his provincialism, clothes, and accent.

In spite of these curiosities and perhaps contradictions, Bastiat should also be remembered for his sense of humor and wit. A few examples should suffice. Although Bastiat never finished his magnum opus, *Economic Harmonies,* which took as its theme the central role played by the idea of "harmony" in his social theory, he was not above making puns on the word *harmony* at his own expense. To take another example, Bastiat was keen to mix in the circles inhabited by "Les Économistes" of Paris; at the same time he could see the humor in their preference for wearing somber black cloaks.[4] Finally there is the gentle teasing that Bastiat gave his aunt's chambermaid,

---

3. See also "General Introduction," note 1.

4. See Letter 148. In this letter, Bastiat makes fun of economists' self-importance, recounting how, at a dinner party he was attending, "the hall embellished with a number of black, white, and pink cloaks showed that there were not only economists present."

who happened to be an ardent supporter of free trade—perhaps one of the very few in France—and Bastiat could definitely see the humor, perhaps somewhat black, in this situation.

It is hoped that these letters will provide the reader with a new perspective on the life of Bastiat and will fill in some of the gaps in our knowledge about his activities as an economist, writer, free-trade activist, politician, friend, and family man. The letters should also provide the personal and political background needed to help us better understand the essays and books that will be published in subsequent volumes of the Liberty Fund edition of the Collected Works.

David M. Hart

Correspondence[1]

1. Letter to Victor Calmètes
   Bayonne, 12 September 1819   [vol. 1, p. 1]

. . . .

My friend, we are in the same boat. Both of us are attracted to intellectual activity rather than the kind to which duty calls us, the difference being that the reflection which takes our fancy is closer to that of a lawyer than to that of a trader.

You know that I mean to go into commerce. When I entered the world of business, I conceived of business as purely mechanical and thought that six months would be enough to make me a trader. This being so, I did not think it necessary to work very hard and I concentrated in particular on the study of philosophy and politics.

I have since lost any illusions I had on this point. I now recognize that the science of commerce is not enclosed within the limits of routine. I have learned that a good trader, in addition to knowing his merchandise and where it comes from, and knowing the worth of what he can exchange, and bookkeeping, all of which experience and routine can teach in part, must also study the law and broaden his knowledge of *political economy*, which is not part of routine and requires constant study.

These considerations caused me considerable perplexity. Should I continue to study philosophy, which I like, or should I plunge into finance,

1. (Paillottet's note) Among the letters of F. Bastiat which we are publishing here, many, especially the first, are of autobiographical interest only. Others relate to economic matters and the history of the free-trade movement of which Bastiat was the promoter and effective leader in France. We consider that his correspondence with R. Cobden, which reveals the essential agreement in the views of these two illustrious men and their reciprocal influence on each other, is genuinely important as a collection of historical documents.

which I dread? Should I sacrifice my duty to my inclination or my inclination to my duty?

Having decided to put my duty before everything, I was about to start my studies when I thought of taking a look at the future. I weighed up the wealth I might hope to gain and balanced it against my needs and ascertained that whatever small happiness commerce might afford me, I might, while still a young man, free myself of the burden of work that would not make for my happiness. You know my tastes, you know whether, if I were able to live happily and peacefully, however little my wealth exceeded my needs, I would choose to impose the burden of a boring job on myself for three quarters of my life in order to possess a pointless surplus for the rest of my life.

. . . So now you know. As soon as I have acquired a certain prosperity, which I hope will be soon, I will be giving up business.

---

2. Letter to Victor Calmètes

Bayonne, 5 March 1820   [vol. 1, p. 2]

. . . I had read the *Treatise on Political Economy* by J. B. Say, an excellent and highly methodical work. Everything flows from the principle that *riches are assets and that assets are measured according to utility*. From this fertile principle, he leads you naturally to the most far-flung consequences so that, when you read this work, you are surprised, as when reading Laromiguière,[2] at the ease with which you go from one idea to the next. The entire system passes before your eyes in its various forms and gives you all the pleasure that a sense of the obvious can provide.

One day when I was in quite a large gathering, a question of political economy was discussed in conversation, and everyone was talking nonsense. I did not dare to put my opinions forward too much, since they were so diametrically opposed to the conventional wisdom. However, as each objection forced me to go up a notch to put forward my arguments, I was soon driven to the core principle. This was when M. Say made it easy for me. We started from the principle of political economy, which my adversaries admitted to be just. It was easy for us to go on to the consequences and reach that which was the subject of the conversation. This was the point at which I perceived

---

2. Bastiat is possibly making a reference to Laromiguière, *Leçons de philosophie sur les principes de l'intelligence*.

the full merit of the method and I would like it to be applied to everything. Do you not agree with me?

———————

3. Letter to Victor Calmètes

Bayonne, 18 March 1820 [vol. 1, p. 3]

I entered into the world one step at a time, but I did not rush into it, and, in the midst of its pleasures and pains, when others, deafened by so much noise, forget themselves, if I can put it like that, in the narrow circle of the present, my vigilant soul was always looking over its shoulder, and reflection prevented it from letting itself be dominated. What is more, my taste for study has taken up a great deal of my time. I concentrated so much on it last year that this year I was forbidden to continue with it, following the painful complaint it caused me. . . .

———————

4. Letter to Victor Calmètes

Bayonne, 10 September 1820 [vol. 1, p. 4]

. . . .

One thing that occupies me more seriously is philosophy and religion. My soul is full of uncertainty and I cannot bear this state. My intellect rejects *faith* while my heart hankers after it. In fact, how can my intellect reconcile the great ideas about the Divine with the puerility of certain dogmas; and on the other hand, how can my heart not want to find rules of conduct in the sublime moral code of Christianity? Yes, if paganism is the mythology of the imagination, Catholicism is the mythology of sentiment. What could be more likely to interest a sensitive heart than the life of Jesus, the morality of the Gospels, and meditation on Mary? How touching all this is. . . .

———————

5. Letter to Victor Calmètes

Bayonne, October 1820 [vol. 1, p. 4]

I must admit, my dear friend, that the subject of religion fills me with hesitation and uncertainty, which is beginning to become a burden. How can I not see the dogmas of our Catholicism as mythology? And in spite of it all, this mythology is so beautiful, so consoling, so sublime that error is almost preferable to truth. I have a feeling that if I had one spark of faith in my heart, it would shortly become a flame. Do not be surprised at what

I am saying to you here. I believe in God and the immortality of the soul, that virtue is rewarded and vice chastised. This being so, what a huge difference there is between a religious person and an unbeliever! My state is unbearable. My heart burns with love and gratitude to God and I do not know how to pay him the tribute of homage I owe Him. He occupies my thoughts only vaguely, while a religious man has before him a career that is fully marked out for him to pursue. He prays. All the religious ceremonies keep him constantly occupied with his Creator. And then this sublime reconciliation between God and man, this redemption, how sweet it must be to believe it! What an invention it is, Calmètes, if it is one!

Apart from these advantages, there is another which is no less important. The skeptic has to work out a moral code for himself and then follow it. What perfect understanding, what force of will he must have! And who is there to reassure him that tomorrow he will not have to change the ideas he holds today? A religious man, on the other hand, has his route fully mapped out before him. He takes nourishment from a moral code that is always divine.

----

6. Letter to Victor Calmètes

Bayonne, 29 April 1821   [vol. 1, p. 5]

For my part, I think that I am going to settle irrevocably on religion. I am tired of searches that lead and can only lead nowhere. There, I am sure of finding peace and I will not be tormented by fears, even if I make mistakes. What is more, it is such a beautiful religion that I can imagine that you can love it to such an extent that you obtain happiness in this life.

If I manage to make up my mind, I will take up my former pleasures again. Literature, English, and Italian will take up my time as in the past. My spirit has been numbed by books on controversy, theology, and philosophy. I have already reread a few tragedies by Alfieri. . . .

----

7. Letter to Victor Calmètes

Bayonne, 10 September 1821   [vol. 1, p. 5]

I want to let you have a word on my health. I am changing my way of life, I have abandoned my books, my philosophy, my devotion, my melancholy, in a word my spleen, and I am all the better for it. I am getting out in the world and it is singularly amusing. I feel the need for money, which makes me keen to earn some, which gives me a taste for work, which leads me to spend the day quite pleasantly in the store, which, in the last analysis, is extremely beneficial to my mood and health. However, I sometimes regret the sentimental enjoyment to which nothing can be compared, the love of poverty, the taste for a retired and peaceful life, and I think that by indulging in a little pleasure, I have wanted only to wait for the moment to abandon it. Enduring solitude in society is a misconception and I am thankful that I have understood this in good time....

8. Letter to Victor Calmètes

Bayonne, 8 December 1821   [vol. 1, p. 6]

I was away, my dear friend, when your letter arrived in Bayonne, which has made my reply somewhat late. How pleased I was to receive this dear letter! The longer the time of our separation recedes from us the more tenderly I think of you and prize having a good friend all the more. I have found no one here to replace you in my heart. How fond we were of one another! For four years, we were not parted from one another for an instant. Often the uniformity of our way of life and the perfect harmony of our feelings and thoughts did not allow us to talk much. With any other, silent walks of such length would have been unbearable; with you, however, I was never tired and they left me nothing to want for. I know people who love one another just to show off their friendship, while we loved each other unobtrusively and frankly; we realized that our friendship was remarkable only when someone brought it to our attention. Here, dear friend, everyone loves me but I have no friend....

... So, here you are, my friend, in your robes and mortarboard. I find it difficult to know whether you have the disposition for the task you have chosen. I know that you have a great deal of justice and sound judgment, but that is the least of your requirements. You also need ease of speech, but is it pure enough? Your accent is not likely to have improved in Toulouse nor got any better in Perpignan. Mine is still dreadful and will probably never change. You love studying and quite like discussion. I therefore think that you should now concentrate on the study of law, as these are notions that can be learned only by working, like history and geography, and later on the physical aspects of your profession. Grace, and noble and easy gestures, a certain veneer, the kind of glances and gestures of the hand, that indefinable something that will attract, warn, and carry people along. That is halfway to success. Read the letters by Lord Chesterfield[3] to his son on this subject. It is a book whose moral code I am far from approving, attractive as it is, but a true mind like yours will easily be able to set aside what is bad and profit from what is good.

For my part, it is not Themis[4] but blind fortune that I have chosen or which has been chosen for me as a lover. However, I must admit, my ideas on this goddess have changed a great deal. This *base metal* is no longer so base in my eyes. Doubtless, it was a fine thing to see the Fabricii and Curii[5] remaining poor when the only reward of robbery and usury was wealth, and doubtless Cincinnatus did well to eat broad beans and radishes, since he would have had to sell his inheritance and honor to eat more delicate dishes. But times have changed. In Rome, wealth was the fruit of chance, birth, and conquests; today, it is the reward only of work, industry,[6] and economy. In these circumstances, it is nothing if not honorable. Only a real fool taken from secondary school would scorn a man who knows how to acquire assets with honesty and use them with discernment. I do not believe that the world is wrong in this respect when it honors the rich; its error is to honor indiscriminately the honest rich man and the rich scoundrel. . . .

––––––––––

9. Letter to Victor Calmètes

Bayonne, 20 October 1822 [vol. 1, p. 8]

Everyone pursues happiness, everyone situates it in a certain condition of life and aspires to it. The happiness you attach to a retired life has perhaps no other merit than to be perceived from a great distance. I have loved solitude more than you have, I have sought it with passion and have enjoyed it, but if it had lasted a few months longer, it would have led me to the grave. Men, and especially young men, cannot live alone. They grasp things with too much ardor, and if their thought is not spread over a thousand varied objects, the one that absorbs them will kill them.

I would like solitude, but I would want to have it with books, friends, a

3. Philip Stanhope.
4. Greek goddess of justice.
5. Caius Fabricius Licinius (282–178 B.C.); Manius Curius Dentatus (?–270 B.C.): Roman consuls, known for their honesty.
6. Normally the French word *l'industrie* would be translated as "production"; however, Bastiat is referring to a specific concept developed by Comte and Dunoyer in their theory of industrialism. See also "Note on the Translation," pp. xvi–xvii.

family, and material *interests*. Yes, interests my friend, do not laugh at this word; they bind people together and generate work. You may be sure that a philosopher, even if he were interested in agriculture, would soon be bored if he had to cultivate someone else's land free of charge. It is interest that embellishes an estate in the eyes of its owner, which puts a value on the inventory, makes Orgon happy, and makes the Optimist say:

> The chateau de Plainville is the most beautiful chateau in the world.

You appreciate that when I speak of returns or of interests, I do not mean that sentiment that is close to egoism.

To be happy, I would like, therefore, to own an estate in a lively country, especially in a country where old memories and long-standing habits would have given me a link with everything there. This is when you enjoy everything, this is the *via vitalis*.[7] I would like to have as my neighbors or even as coinhabitants friends like you, Carrière, and a few others. I would like an *estate* which was not so large that I would be able to neglect it, nor so small that it would give me worries and deprivations. I would like a wife.... I am not going to draw her portrait, I rather feel that I would be incapable of doing it and I would myself be (I have no false modesty with you) my children's teacher. They would not be bold as in towns, nor uncouth as in lightly populated areas. It would take too much time to go into the details, but I assure you that my plan has the supreme merit, that of not being romantic....

---

10. Letter to Victor Calmètes

    Bayonne, December 1822   [vol. 1, p. 9]

. . . .

    Yesterday, I was reading a tragedy by Casimir Delavigne entitled *The Pariah*.[8] I am no longer used to making critical analyses, so I will not discuss this poem with you. What is more, I have abandoned the general tendency of French readers to look for transgressions of the rules in what they read rather than pleasure. If I enjoy what I read, I am not very critical of the work, since the interest is the most important of its attractions. I have noticed that the weak point of all modern tragedians is dialogue. In my view, M. Casimir

---

7. The "vital way."

8. The work referred to is Delavigne's *Le Paria: Tragédie en cinq actes, avec des cœurs.*

Delavigne, who is better at this than Arnault and Jouy, is far from being perfect. His dialogues are not short enough nor sufficiently consistent, but rather tirades and speeches which do not even relate to one another, and this is a fault that readers forgive the least easily since the work thus becomes less true to life and less plausible. I seem rather to be present at a discussion between two preachers or the advocacy of two barristers than listening to a sincere, lively, and unaffected conversation between two people. Alfieri excels in dialogue, I think, and Racine's is also very simple and natural. For the rest, carried along by a lively interest (which perhaps is not sufficiently often suspended) I rather skimmed than read *The Pariah*. Its versification seemed to me to be fine and rather too metaphorical if the characters were not Eastern. But the disaster was rather too easy to predict and from the beginning the reader is not in suspense.

---

11. Letter to Félix Coudroy[9]

Bayonne, 15 December 1824 [vol. 1, p. 14]

I note with pleasure that you are fervently studying English, my dear Félix. As soon as you have overcome the initial difficulties, you will find in this language a font of resources because of the great number of works it possesses. Apply yourself above all to translation and fill your storehouse with words and the rest will follow. At school I had a notebook and folded the pages in two; on one side I wrote all the English words I did not know and on the other the corresponding French ones. This method enabled me to stamp the words more effectively in my head. When you have finished *Paul et Virginie*,[10] I will send you some other things; in the meantime I will note here a few lines of Pope to see if you can translate them. I must confess that I doubt this, since it was a long time before I reached this stage.

I am not surprised that studying is so attractive to you. I would also like it a lot if other uncertainties did not torment me. I am still like a bird on the

---

9. (Paillottet's note) It is with M. Coudroy that, through twenty years of study and conversation, Bastiat prepared himself for the brilliant and all too short role of the last six years of his life. When he sent him *Economic Harmonies* from Paris, Bastiat wrote on the flyleaf of the volume, "My dear Félix, I cannot say that this book is a gift from *the author;* it is as much yours as mine." This message is fine praise. See the biographical introduction. [*OC,* vol. 1, p. lx, "Notice sur la vie et les écrits de Frédéric Bastiat."]

10. The tragic story of two children raised in the wild, published in 1787 by Bernardin de Saint-Pierre (1737–1814).

branch, since I do not want to do anything to displease my parents, but as long as this continues I will be setting aside any ambitious projects and will continue with solitary study.

> Let us (since Life can little more supply
> Than just to look about us, and to die)
> Expatiate free o'er all this scene of man.[11]

I should not be afraid that study will not be enough to quench my ardor, since I will stop at nothing less than acquiring knowledge of politics, history, geography, mathematics, mechanics, natural history, botany, four or five languages, etc., etc.

I must tell you that, since my grandfather became subject to attacks of fever, his mind is disturbed and consequently he does not want to see any member of his family go too far away. I know that I would worry him considerably if I went to Paris, and this being the case I can see that I will abandon the idea since the last thing in the world I wish to do is to cause him pain. I am fully aware that this sacrifice is not that of a fleeting pleasure but one affecting the usefulness of my entire life, but in the end I am determined to make it to avoid hurting my grandfather. On the other hand, I do not, just for a few business reasons, wish to continue the type of life I live here, and consequently I am going to suggest to my grandfather that I settle permanently in Mugron. There again I fear a snag, that people will want me to take over part of the administration of the estate, which means that I will find in Mugron all of the disadvantages of Bayonne. I am not at all suited to sharing administration. I want to do it all or none of it. I am too gentle to dominate and too vain to be dominated. But in the end I will lay down my conditions. If I go to Mugron, it will be to concentrate only on my studies. I will drag along as many books as I can, and I do not doubt that after a little time I will come to take a great deal of pleasure in this type of life.

---

12. Letter to Félix Coudroy

Bayonne, 8 January 1825 [vol. 1, p. 16]

I am sending you the preceding pages, my dear Félix, which will be a constant proof that I am not neglecting to reply to you but merely to for-

---

11. This excerpt is in English in the original. From Alexander Pope's "An Essay on Man," Epistle 1 (1733).

ward the letter. I have this unfortunate fault resulting from my untidy habits which means that I believe that I have done my duty to my friends when I write to them, without thinking that the letter itself has to be sent.

You talk to me about political economy as though I knew more about it than you. If you have read Say carefully, as you appear to have done, I can assure you that you will have left me far behind, since I have read only the following four works on this subject, Smith,[12] Say, Destutt, and *Le Censeur.* What is more, I have never studied M. Say in depth, especially the second volume, which I have just glanced through. You have given up hope that sane ideas on this subject will ever penetrate public opinion, but I do not share your despair. On the contrary, I believe that the peace that has reigned in Europe for the last ten years has spread them a great deal, and it is a good thing perhaps that this progress is slow and imperceptible. The Americans in the United States have very sound ideas on these matters, although they have set up customs stations in retaliation. England, which is always at the head of civilization in Europe, is now giving a good example by gradually giving up the system that hampers it.[13] In France, commerce is enlightened but owners are less so, and manufacturers work just as hard to retain their monopolies. Unfortunately, we do not have a chamber capable of ascertaining the true state of the nation's understanding. The seven-year period[14] is also detrimental to this slow and upward drift of ideas from public opinion which partly rejuvenates the legislature. Finally, a few events and above all the incorrigible French character that enthuses about anything new and is always ready to treat itself to a few fine words will prevent the truth from triumphing for a short while. But I do not despair. The press, necessity, and financial interest will end up by achieving what reason still cannot. If you read *Le Journal du commerce,* you will have seen how the English government tries to enlighten itself by *officially* consulting the most enlightened traders and manufacturers. The conclusion then agreed is that the prosperity of Great Britain is not the product of the system it has followed but the result of many other

12. Adam Smith.

13. (Paillottet's note) Thus, twenty years before his first publication, Bastiat was already concerned with the beginnings of customs reform started in our neighbor's country by Huskisson.

14. The law of 5 February 1817 had organized the election of one-fifth of the Chamber of Deputies every year. Following the success of ultralegitimists in February 1824, the government, in order to keep the majority, extended the term of office to seven years, with an election of one-seventh of the chamber each year.

causes. It is not enough for two facts to exist at the same time to conclude that one is the cause and the other the effect. In England, trade restrictions and prosperity certainly relate to each other through coexistence and contiguity, but not through causation. England has prospered not because of, but in spite of, countless taxes. This is the reason I find the language of ministers so ridiculous when they say to us each year, "You see how rich England is, it pays a billion!"

I think that if I had more paper, I would continue this abstruse chatter. Farewell, with my fondest good wishes.

---

13. Letter to Félix Coudroy

Bordeaux, 9 April 1827   [vol. 1, p. 18]

My dear Félix, as I have not yet decided when I will be returning to Mugron, I want to break the monotony of my absence with the pleasure of writing to you and I will begin by giving you a few items of literary news.

First of all, I will tell you that MM Lamennais and Dunoyer (whose names are not habitually linked in this way) are still at the same point, that is to say, the former at his fourth volume and the latter at his first.[15]

In a newspaper entitled *Revue encyclopédique,* I read a few articles which I found interesting, including a very short study on the work of Comte[16] (a study limited to a short expression of praise), considerations on insurance and in general on the applications of the calculation of probabilities, a speech by M. Charles Dupin on the influence of public education, and lastly an article by Dunoyer entitled "A Study of Popular Opinion," to which the name of *industrialism*[17] has been given.[18] In this article, M. Dunoyer does not go back further than MM B. Constant and J. B. Say, whom he quotes as being the first political writers to have observed that the purpose of social activity is industry. To tell you the truth, these authors have not perceived the use that might be made of this observation. The latter has considered such industry only in the light of the production, distribution, and consumption of wealth and in his introduction he even defines politics as *the science of the*

---

15. Possibly references to Lamennais, *Essai sur l'indifférence en matière de religion;* and Dunoyer, *L'Industrie et la morale considérée dans leurs rapport avec la liberté.*

16. A reference to Comte, *Traité de législation.*

17. See "Note on the Translation," p. xvi–xvii.

18. A reference to Dunoyer, "Esquisse historique des doctrines auxquelles on a donné le nom industrialisme."

organization of society, which seems to prove that, like eighteenth-century authors, he sees politics only as concerning the forms of government and not as the basis and purpose of society. As for M. B. Constant, after being the first to have proclaimed this truth, that the aim of society's activity is to secure industry, he is so far from having made it the basis of his doctrine that his major work[19] covers only forms of government, the checks and balances of political power, etc. etc. Dunoyer then moves on to an examination of *Le Censeur européen*, whose authors, once they had taken over the isolated observations of their predecessors, have made from them an entire corpus of doctrine which is discussed with care in this article. I cannot analyze an article for you that is itself just an analysis. I will tell you, however, that Dunoyer seems to me to have reformed a few of the opinions that were predominant in *Le Censeur*. For example, I think that he is now giving the word *industry* a more extended meaning than before, since he includes in this word any work that tends to improve our faculties; thus any useful and legitimate work counts as industry and any man who takes part in it, from the head of the government to an artisan, is a producer.[20] From this it follows that Dunoyer continues to think as before that, in the same way that hunting peoples select their most skillful hunter to be their leader, and warlike peoples the most intrepid warrior, industrious peoples should also summon to the helm of public affairs those men who have most distinguished themselves in industry. However, he thinks that he has made a mistake in individually naming the branches of production from which the choice of rulers should be made and in particular, agriculture, commerce, manufacturing, and banking, for although these four sectors doubtless cover the majority of the huge circle of industry, they are not the only ones through which men hone their faculties by means of work and several others appear even more suited to training legislators, such as those of jurist and man of letters.

I have discovered a real treasure in a slim volume containing a mixture of moral and political writings by Franklin.[21] I am so keen on this that I have started to use the same means as he to become as good and happy as he.

---

19. Bastiat is referring to Constant's *Principes de politique;* however, his most detailed discussion of economic matters is found in his *Commentaire sur l'ouvrage de Filangieri.*

20. Bastiat and Dunoyer have used the term *industrieux,* which is translated here as "producer." See also "Note on the Translation," pp. xvi–xvii.

21. Bastiat is probably referring to a French translation of a selection of Franklin's writings, *La Science du Bonhomme Richard.*

However, there are some virtues that I will not even seek to acquire since they appear to be quite unattainable in my case. I will bring you this small work.

I have also come across by chance a very detailed article on beet sugar. Its authors have calculated that it would cost the manufacturer ninety centimes a pound, where cane sugar sells at one franc ten centimes. You can see that, assuming total success, it would leave not much of a margin. What is more, to devote oneself with pleasure to this type of work and perfect it, you would need a knowledge of chemistry, which unfortunately is totally foreign to me. Be that as it may, I was bold enough to write a letter to M. Clément. Lord only knows whether he will reply.

For the sum of three francs a month, I am attending a course in botany three times a week. We cannot learn much there, as you can see, but apart from passing the time, it is useful in putting me in touch with the people who are concerned with science.

This is just chatter; if it did not cost you so much to write, I would ask you to *reciprocate by return*.

---

14. Letter to Félix Coudroy

Bayonne, 3 December 1827.   [vol. 1, p. 20]

. . . You are encouraging me to carry out my project, and I do not think I have ever in my life been so determined. From the start of 1828, I will use my time in removing the obstacles, the most considerable of which are pecuniary. Going to England, renovating my house, purchasing the livestock, instruments, and books I need, organizing the financing for wages and seed, all for a small sharecropping farm (because I want to start with just one), I feel will carry me a bit far. It is clear to me that in the first two or three years, my agriculture will not produce much, both because of my inexperience and because the crop rotation I propose to adopt will show its full effect only in due course. However, I am very happy with my situation since, if I did not have enough to live on and a bit more from my little property, it would be impossible to undertake such an enterprise; for as I can sacrifice the income from my property, if need be, nothing prevents me from doing what I want. I read books on agriculture and nothing equals the beauty of this working life, because it has everything, but it requires knowledge that is foreign to me, such as natural history, chemistry, mineralogy, mathematics, and many other things.

Farewell, my dear Félix, good luck and return soon.

15. Letter to Victor Calmètes

Mugron, 12 March 1829   [vol. 1, p. 40]

. . . .

On this subject, do you know that I am intending to go into print in my lifetime? What, I can hear you say, Bastiat an author? What is he going to give us? A collection of ten or twelve tragedies? An epic? Or perhaps some madrigals? Will he follow in the footsteps of Walter Scott or Lord Byron? None of these things, my friend; I have limited myself to gathering together the heaviest forms of reasoning on the heaviest of questions. In a word, I am dealing with our system of trade restrictions. See if that tempts you, and if so I will send you *my complete works,* once, of course, they have been given the honor of being printed. I wanted to tell you more about this, but I have too much else to say to you. . . . [22]

---

16. Letter to Victor Calmètes

Mugron, July 1829   [vol. 1, p. 40]

. . . I am pleased to see that we have nearly the same opinion. Yes, as long as our deputies want to further their own business and not that of the general public, the public will remain just *the tail end* of the people in power. However, in my opinion, the evil comes from further afield. We easily surmise (since it suits our amour propre) that all evil results from power; on the contrary, I am convinced that its source is the ignorance and inertia of the masses. What use do we make of the rights given to us? The constitution tells us that we will pay what we consider appropriate and authorizes us to send our representatives to Paris to establish the amount which we wish to hand over in order to be governed; we then give our power of attorney to people who are beneficiaries of taxation. Those who complain about the prefects are themselves represented by them. Those who deplore the wars of sympathy[23] we are waging in the east and the west, sometimes in favor of freedom for a people, sometimes to put another into servitude, are themselves represented by army generals. We expect prefects to vote for their own

22. (Paillottet's note) This work was not printed.
23. On 1 January 1820, a revolt against the absolutist and feudal regime of Ferdinand VII of Spain forced the king to reestablish the liberal constitution of 1812. In 1823, France, mandated by the Congress of Verona, mounted a military intervention resulting in the restoration of the previous regime.

elimination and men of war to become imbued with pacifist ideas![24] This is a shocking contradiction. But, men will say, we expect from our deputies *dedication* and *self-renunciation,* virtues from classical times which we would like to see resurrected in our midst. What a puerile illusion! What sort of policy can be based on a principle distasteful to human organization? At no time in history have men ever renounced themselves, and in my view it would be a great misfortune if this virtue took the place of personal interest. If you generalize self-renunciation in public opinion, you will see society destroyed. Personal interest, on the other hand, leads to individuals bettering themselves and consequently the masses, which are made up solely of individuals. It will be alleged, pointlessly, that the interest of one man is opposed to that of another; in my opinion this is a serious, antisocial error.[25] And, if we may progress from general notions to their application, if taxpayers are themselves represented by men with the same interests as they, reforms will occur by themselves. There are some who fear that the government would be destroyed by a spirit of economy, as though each person did not feel that it was in *his interest* to pay for a force responsible for the repression of evildoers.

I embrace you warmly.

---

17. Letter to Félix Coudroy[26]

Bayonne, 4 August 1830   [vol. 1, p. 21]

My dear Félix, I am so over the moon I can scarcely hold my pen. It is not a question here of a slave revolt, *the slaves* indulging in greater excesses, if that is possible, than their oppressors. It is enlightened men who are rich

24. See "On Parliamentary Reform," p. 367.

25. (Paillottet's note) In this passage, the basic idea that Bastiat was to develop so masterfully twenty years later in the *Harmony of Interests* can be seen. ["Harmony of Interests" was Bastiat's incomplete major work and was published posthumously as *Economic Harmonies.*]

26. The following letters of 4 and 5 August, to Félix Coudroy, describe the repercussions in Bayonne of the "three glorious days" (27, 28, 29 July 1830). On 26 July 1830, Jules Armand Polignac (prince de Polignac), prime minister of Charles X, promulgated four ordinances modifying the electoral law and restricting freedom. During the three following days, about fifty thousand people defeated the regular troops led by Marshall Marmont. Charles X abdicated and fled to England. Louis-Philippe, duc d'Orléans, was appointed king by the parliament. Bayonne had learned of the "three glorious days" by 3 August.

Bayonne was a fortified town dominated by a fortress, with thirty-three hundred troops, and close to the Spanish border.

and prudent who are sacrificing their interests and their lives to establishing order and its inseparable companion, freedom. Let people tell us after this that riches weaken courage, that enlightenment leads to disorganization, etc., etc. I wish you could see Bayonne. Young people are carrying out all forms of service in the most perfect order; they are receiving and sending out letters, mounting guard, and are acting as local, administrative, and military authorities all at once. Everyone is working together, townsmen, magistrates, lawyers, and soldiers. It is an admirable spectacle for anyone who is capable of seeing it, and if I used to be only half committed to the Scottish persuasion,[27] I would be doubly so today.

A provisional government[28] has been set up in Paris, made up of MM Laffitte, Audry-Puiraveau,[29] Casimir Périer, Odier, Lobeau, Gérard, Schonen, Mauguin, and La Fayette as the commander of the National Guard, which is more than forty thousand men. These people could make themselves dictators; you will see that they will do nothing to enrage those who have no belief in either good sense or virtue.

I will not go into detail on the misfortunes which the terrible Praetorian guards, known as royal guards, have inflicted on Paris. Sixteen regiments of these men, greedy for power, roamed the streets, cutting the throats of men, children, and old men. It is said that two thousand students lost their lives there. Bayonne is mourning the loss of several of its sons; on the other hand, the gendarmerie, the Swiss mercenaries, and bodyguards were crushed the next day. This time, the regular infantry, far from remaining neutral, fought vigorously for the nation. However, we still have to mourn the loss of twenty thousand brothers who died to secure liberty[30] and benefits for us which they will never enjoy. I heard the hope for these frightful massacres expressed in our circle;[31] the person who expressed it must feel satisfied.

The nation was led by a crowd of deputies and peers of France, includ-

27. (Paillottet's note) In Bastiat's thought, political economy and politics were inseparable. Here he is linking liberal ideas with the teachings of Adam Smith, the illustrious professor at Glasgow University.

28. Bastiat is mistaken here. There was no provisional government but a municipal commission of five people, appointed to keep the peace in Paris.

29. Audry de Puyravault.

30. (Paillottet's note) Bastiat exaggerates the losses; in fact, seven hundred troops and two thousand insurgents were killed.

31. He is talking about the circle in Mugron.

ing generals Sémélé, Gérard, La Fayette, Lobeau, etc., etc. Despotism had entrusted its cause to Marmont, who, it is said, has been killed.

The École polytechnique has suffered greatly and fought bravely.

At last, calm has been restored and there is no longer a single soldier in Paris; this great town, following *three consecutive days and nights* of massacres and horror, is governing itself and governing France, as if it were in the hands of *statesmen*. . . .

It is fair to proclaim that the regular troops supported the national will everywhere. Here, a hundred and forty-nine officers met to deliberate. One hundred and forty-eight swore that they would break their swords and tear off their epaulettes rather than massacre a people just because they do not wish to be oppressed. In Bordeaux and Rennes, their conduct was the same, which reconciles me somewhat to the law of recruitment.

The National Guard is being organized everywhere and three major advantages are expected. The first is to prevent disorder, the second to maintain what we have just acquired, and the third to show other nations that while we do not wish to conquer others, we are ourselves impregnable.

Some believe that to satisfy the desires of those who consider that France can exist only as a monarchy the crown will be offered to the duc d'Orléans.[32]

For my part, my dear Félix, I was pleasantly disappointed; I came looking for danger, I wanted to conquer with my fellow men or die with them, but I found only laughing faces and, instead of the roar of cannon, I heard only outbursts of joy. The population of Bayonne is admirable for its calm, energy, patriotism, and unanimity, but I think I have already told you that.

Bordeaux has not been so fortunate. There were a few excesses. M. Curzay seized the letters of office.[33] On the 29th or 30th, of the four young men who were sent to claim them back as a sacred property, one was run through by his sword and he wounded another. The two others threw him to the crowd, who would have massacred him had the constitutionalists not pleaded for him.

Farewell, I am tired of writing and must be forgetting many things. It is midnight and for the last week I have not slept a wink. At least today, we can indulge ourselves in sleep.

---

32. Louis-Philippe.

33. M. Curzay, a senior official, intercepted the mail to keep the Bordeaux people ignorant of what was going on in Paris.

There is talk of a movement of four Spanish regiments on our border. They will be well received.

Farewell.

———————

18.　Letter to Félix Coudroy

Bayonne 5 August 1830　　　　　　　　　　　　　　　　[vol. 1, p. 24]

My dear Félix, I will not talk any more about Paris to you as the newspapers will inform you of all that is going on. Our cause is triumphing, the nation is admirable, and the people will be happy.

Here the future appears to be darker. Fortunately, the question will be decided this very day. I will scribble the result for you in the margin.

This is the situation. On the 3rd, many groups were gathered in the square and were discussing, with extraordinary exaltation, whether we should not immediately take the initiative of displaying the tricolor flag. I moved about without taking part in the discussions, as whatever I said would have had no effect. As always happens, when everyone talks at once, no one does anything and the flag was not displayed.

The following morning, the same question was raised. The soldiers were still well disposed to let us act, but during the hesitation, dispatches arrived for the colonels and obviously cooled down their zeal for the cause. One of them even cried out in front of me that we had a king and a charter and that we ought to be faithful to them, that the king could not do wrong, that his ministers were the only guilty ones, etc., etc. He was replied to roundly . . . but this repeated inaction gave me an idea which, by dint of my turning it over in my mind, got so ingrained there that since then I have not thought till now of anything else.

It became clear to me that we had been betrayed. The king, I said to myself, can have one hope only, that of retaining Bayonne and Perpignan; from these two points, he would raise the Midi and the west and rely on Spain and the Pyrenees. He could foment a civil war in a triangle whose base would be the Pyrenees and the summit Toulouse, with the two angles being fortresses. The country it comprises is the very home of ignorance and fanaticism; one side of it touches Spain, the second the Vendée, and the third Provence. The more I thought about it, the clearer this project became. I told my most influential friends about it but they, inexcusably, had been summoned at the citizens' pleasure to take charge of various organizations and no longer had time to think of serious matters.

Other people had had the same idea as I, and by dint of shouting and repetition it became general. But what could we do when we were unable to deliberate and agree, nor make ourselves heard? I withdrew to reflect and conceived several projects.

The first, which was already that of the entire population of Bayonne, was to display the flag and endeavor, through this movement, to win over the garrison of the chateau and the citadel. This was done yesterday at two o'clock in the afternoon, but by old people who did not attach the same significance to it as Soustra, I, and a lot of others, with the result that this coup failed.

I then took my papers of authorization to go to the army encampment to look for General Lamarque. I was relying on his reputation, his rank, his character as a deputy and his eloquence to win over the two colonels and, if need be, on his vigor to hold them up for two hours and present himself at the citadel in full military dress, followed by the National Guard with the flag at their head. I was on the point of mounting my horse when I received word that the general had left for Paris, and this caused the project, which was undoubtedly the surest and least dangerous, to fail.

I immediately had a discussion with Soustra, who unfortunately was occupied with other cares, telegraphic dispatches, the soldiers' encampment, the National Guard, etc., etc.; we went to find the officers of the 9th, who have an excellent spirit, and suggested that they seize the citadel; and we undertook to lead six hundred resolute young men. They promised us the support of their entire regiment, after having, in the meantime, deposed their colonel.

Do not say, my dear Félix, that our conduct was imprudent or frivolous. After what has happened in Paris, what is most important is that the national flag should fly over the citadel in Bayonne. Without that, I can see civil war in the next ten years, and, although I do not doubt the success of the cause, I would willingly go so far as to sacrifice my life, an attitude shared by all my friends, to spare our poor provinces from this fearful scourge.

Yesterday evening, I drafted the attached proclamation to the 7th Light, who guard the citadel, as we intended to have it delivered to them before the action.

This morning, when I got up, I thought that it was all over; all the officers of the 9th were wearing the tricolor cockade, the soldiers could not contain their joy, and it was even being said that officers of the 7th had been seen wearing these fine colors. An adjutant had even shown me personally the positive order, given to the entire 11th division, to display our flag. However, hours went by and the banner of liberty was still not visible over the citadel.

It is said that the traitor J—— is advancing from Bordeaux with the 55th regulars. Four Spanish regiments are at the border, there is not a moment to lose. The citadel must be in our hands this evening or civil war will break out. We will act with vigor if necessary, but I, who am carried along by enthusiasm without being blind to the facts, can see that it will be impossible to succeed if the garrison, which is said to be imbued with a good spirit, does not abandon the government. We will perhaps have a few wins but no success. But we should not become discouraged for all that, as we must do everything to avoid civil war. I am resolved to leave straight away after the action, if it fails, to try to raise the Chalosse. I will suggest to others that they do likewise in the Landes, the Béarn, and the Basque country; and through famine, wiles, or force we will win over the garrison.

I will keep the paper remaining to me to let you know how this ends.

The 5th at m idnight

I was expecting blood but it was only wine that was spilt. The citadel has displayed the tricolor flag. The military containment of the Midi and Toulouse has decided that of Bayonne; the regiments down there have displayed the flag. The traitor J—— thus saw that the plan had failed, especially as the troops were defecting on all sides; he then decided to hand over the orders he had had in his pocket for three days. Thus, it is all over. I plan to leave immediately. I will embrace you tomorrow.

This evening we fraternized with the garrison officers. Punch, wine, liqueurs, and above all, Béranger contributed largely to the festivities. Perfect cordiality reigned in this truly patriotic gathering. The officers were warmer than we were, in the same way as horses which have escaped are more joyful than those that are free.

Farewell, all has ended. The proclamation is no longer useful and is not worth the two sous it will cost you.

---

19. Letter to Victor Calmètes

Bayonne, 22 April 1831   [vol. 1, p. 12]

I am annoyed that a property qualification for eligibility[34] should be an obstacle to your election or at least to your standing as a candidate. I have always thought that it was sufficient to require guarantees from electors, and

34. To be eligible to be a candidate at legislative elections one had to pay a minimum amount of direct taxes.

that that required from candidates is a disastrous duplication. It is true that deputies should be remunerated, but that is too close to the knuckle, and it is ridiculous that France, which pays everybody, should not remunerate *its businessmen.*

In the district in which I live, General Lamarque will be elected outright for the rest of his life. He has talent, probity, and a huge fortune. This is more than what is required. In the third district of the Landes, a few young people who share the opinions of the left have offered me the opportunity of being a candidate.[35] As I have no remarkable talents, fortune, influence, or relations, it is certain beyond doubt that I would have no chance, especially as the movement is not very popular around here. However, as I have adopted the principle that the post of deputy should be neither solicited nor refused, I replied that I would not involve myself in it and that whatever the post my fellow citizens called on me to undertake, I was ready to devote my fortune and life to them. In a few days they should be holding a meeting at which they will decide on their choice of a candidate. If their choice falls on me, I admit that I would be overjoyed, not for myself, since apart from the fact that my definite nomination is impossible (if it occurred it would ruin me), but because I hanker today only for the triumph of principles, which are part of my existence, and that if I am not certain of my means, I am of my vote and my ardent patriotism. I will keep you informed. . . .

Your devoted friend,

---

20. Letter to Félix Coudroy

Bordeaux, 2 March 1834   [vol. 1, p. 17]

. . . I have spent a little time getting to know a few people and will succeed in doing so, I hope. But here, on every face to which you are polite you see written "What is there to gain from you?" It is discouraging. It is true that a new newspaper is being founded. The prospectus does not tell you very much and the editor still less, since the first has been written with the pathos that is all the fashion and the second, assuming that I am a man of the party, limited himself to making me feel how inadequate *Le Mémorial*[36] and *L'Indicateur* were for patriots. All that I was able to obtain was a great deal of insistence that I should take out a subscription.

---

35. Bastiat was a candidate at the legislative elections of 1831. He obtained only 6 votes of 250.

36. *Le Mémorial bordelais.*

Fonfrède[37] is perfectly in line with Say's principles. He writes long articles which would be very good in a sustained work. I will take the risk of going to visit him.

I believe that a series of lectures would succeed here and I am tempted. I think that I would have the strength to do it, especially if one could start with the second session, since I admit that I could not answer at the first or even be able to read fluently, but I cannot thus abandon all my business affairs. We will see about it nevertheless this winter.

A teacher of chemistry has established himself here already. I dined with him without knowing that he gave classes. If I had known, I would have found out how many pupils he had, what the cost was, etc. I would have found out whether, with a history teacher, a teacher of mechanics, and a teacher of political economy a sort of *Athenaeum* could be formed. If I lived in Bordeaux, it would have been very unfortunate if I did not manage to set it up, even if I had to bear all the costs myself, since I am convinced that if a library were added, this establishment would succeed. Learn history, therefore, and we will perhaps try one day.

I will stop now; thirty drummers are practicing under my window and I cannot hear myself think.

Farewell.

---

21. Letter to Félix Coudroy[38]

Bayonne, 16 June 1840   [vol. 1, p. 29]

My dear Félix, I am still about to leave; we have booked our seats three times already and finally they have been booked and paid for Friday. We have been out of luck, for when we were ready, the Carlist General Balmaceda blocked the roads and it is to be feared that we will have difficulty in getting through. But you must not say anything so as not to worry my aunt,

37. Henri Boyer-Fonfrède.

38. Historical background for the following four letters, related to Bastiat's trip to Spain: In 1840, Spain brought to an end a civil war that had started in 1833. At the death of Ferdinand VII, two individuals fought for the throne: his brother, Don Carlos, and his widow, Maria Christina. The supporters of the former wanted to go on with absolute monarchy, while those of the latter wanted to introduce a constitutional monarchy. After some initial successes, the Carlists were defeated and forced to give up. Don Carlos went into exile. One of the victorious generals, Espartero, nicknamed "Duke of Victory," supported by Great Britain, emerged as the strong man of the regime.

who is already only too ready to fear the Spanish. For my part, I find that the business that is propelling us toward Madrid is worth taking a few risks for. Up to now, it has shown itself in a very favorable light. We would find the capital required here if we limited ourselves above all to founding just a Spanish company.[39] Will we be stopped by the sluggishness of this nation? In this case, I will have to bear my traveling costs and will be compensated by the pleasure of having seen at close quarters a people whose qualities and faults distinguish it from all the others.

If I note anything of interest, I will take care to keep it in my wallet to let you know.

Farewell, my dear Félix.

---

22. Letter to Félix Coudroy

Madrid, 6 July 1840 [vol. 1, p. 29]

My dear Félix, I have received your letter of the 6th. From what you tell me of my dear aunt, I see that for the moment she is in good health but she has been somewhat unwell; for me that is the reverse side of the coin. Madrid today is a theater that is perhaps unique in the world, which Spanish laziness and lack of interest are handing over to foreigners who, like me, have some knowledge of the customs and language of the country. I am certain that I could do excellent business here, but the idea of being away from my aunt at an age when her health is starting to become delicate, prevents me from thinking of announcing my exile.

Since I have set foot in this singular country, I have meant to write to you a hundred times. But you will excuse me for not having had the energy to do this when you learn that we devote the morning to business, the evening to an essential walk, and the day to sleeping and gasping under the weight of heat that is uncomfortable more because it is continuous than by reason of its intensity. I have forgotten what clouds look like, since the sky is perfectly clear and the sun fierce. You can rest assured, my dear Félix, that it is not through negligence that I have delayed writing to you, but I am really not suited to this climate and I begin to regret that we did not postpone our departure by two months. . . .

I am surprised that the aim of my trip is still a secret in Mugron. It is no longer one in Bayonne and, before my departure, I wrote about it to

---

39. (Paillottet's note) It was a matter of founding an insurance company.

Domenger to commit him to taking an interest in our business. It is really excellent, but will we succeed in founding it? I cannot yet say; the bankers in Madrid are a thousand miles away from organized opposition and any idea imported from abroad is welcomed by them with suspicion. They are also very difficult on questions relating to people, with each one saying to you, "I am taking no part in the business if such and such a house is taking part." The fact is, they earn so much money with supplies, loans, monopolies, etc., that they do not bother much with anything else. There are a lot of obstacles to overcome, and it is all the more difficult because they do not give you the opportunity of seeing them in more relaxed surroundings. Their houses are as barricaded as fortresses. We have found two classes of bankers here; the first, Spaniards of old families, are the most difficult to persuade, but they are also the ones who can give the most consistent support to the enterprise. The others, who are bolder and more European, are more approachable but have less standing. They form the old and new Spain. We had to choose and have knocked on the door of pure Spain, and I fear that it will refuse and that, in addition, by this very act, we will have the door of modern Spain slammed in our faces. We will abandon the quest only when we have exhausted all the means to success and we have reason to believe that the solution will not be long in coming.

This business and the heat are so absorbing me that I really do not have the energy to apply my powers of observation to anything else. I am not taking any notes, in spite of the fact that I am not short of subjects. I am in a position to see how things work and, if I had the strength and talent to write, I think I would be able to write letters as interesting as those of *Custine*[40] and perhaps more true to life.

To give you an idea of how easy I would find it to live here, apart from the business being done and in which I might take part, I have been given an opportunity of involving myself in court proceedings taken by Italian houses against the Spanish nobility, which would give me enough to live on without undertaking other work, but the thought of my aunt has made me reject this offer. It smiled on me as being a way of prolonging my stay and studying this theater, but my duty obliges me to refuse it.

My friend, I very much fear that Catholicism will suffer the same fate here as in France. There is nothing more beautiful, dignified, solemn, and

---

40. The work to which Bastiat here refers is Custine's *L'Espagne sous Ferdinand VII* (1838).

imposing than religious ceremonies in Spain, but other than that I cannot see in what respect this people is more spiritual than others. This is, moreover, a subject we will discuss at length on my return, when I have had the opportunity of observing it better.

Farewell, my dear Félix, please visit my aunt and give her my news. I assure you of my deepest friendship.

---

23. Letter to Félix Coudroy

    Madrid, 16 July 1840   [vol. 1, p. 32]

My dear Félix, I thank you for your fine letters dated 1st and 6th July; my aunt also took the trouble to write to me so that, up to now, I have received news often and I need it. I cannot say that I am bored, but I am so unused to living far from home that I am happy only on the days I receive letters.

You are doubtless curious to know where we are with our insurance company. I am now almost certain that we will succeed. A great deal of time is necessary to win over the Spaniards whose names we need, and then much more is required to operate such a huge machine with inexperienced people. But I am convinced that we will reach our goal. The share that Soustra and I should be having in the profits, as the founders, has not been settled. It is a delicate matter to which we are not referring, since neither of us is very bold in this connection. This being so, we will defer to the decision of the Board of Directors. For me, this will be a subject on which to gain experience and make observations. Let us see whether the Spanish, who are so suspicious, so reserved, and so unapproachable, are honest and great when they know people. Apart from this matter, our business is progressing slowly but surely. Right now, we have the key to the whole matter, nine names from which to form a board, and names that are so well known and honorable that it seems impossible that anyone will think of competing with us. This evening there will be a meeting to examine the statutes and conditions and I hope that at the first round the company's articles of association will be signed. When this is done, perhaps I will return to France to see my aunt and attend the session of the General Council. If I can do this at all, I will. But I will then have to return to Spain, because the company will give me the opportunity to make a complete journey *free of charge.* Up to now, I cannot say that I have traveled much. With my two companions, I have not entered a single Spanish house, apart from the stores. The heat has canceled all public meetings, balls, theater performances, and bullfights. Our room and a few offices, the French restaurant and the walk to the *Prado* form the circle from which we do not stray. I would like to take my revenge soon. Soustra leaves on the 26th as he is needed in Bayonne. Read all of this to my aunt, whom I embrace fondly.

The most marked characteristic of the Spanish nature is its hatred and suspicion of foreigners. I think this is a genuine vice, but it must be said that it is encouraged by the self-conceit and trickery of many foreigners. They blame and ridicule everything; they criticize the cooking, the furniture, the rooms, and all the customs of the country because in fact the Spanish pay little attention to life's comforts. However, we who know, my dear Félix, to what extent individuals, families, and nations can be happy without enjoying these types of material comforts will be in no hurry to condemn Spain. These foreigners will arrive with their pockets full of plans and absurd projects, and because people do not rush to acquire their shares they become annoyed and cry ignorance and stupidity. This rush of *swindlers* at first did us a great disservice and will continue to do so to any good business. For my part, I am pleased to think that Spanish suspicion will prevent the nation from falling into the trap, since the foreigners, once they have brought their plans, if they want them to succeed, will be forced to bring in capital and in many instances French workers.

Please give me news of Mugron from time to time, my dear Félix; you know how much homesickness overcomes us when we are far away.

Farewell, my dear Félix; please remember me to your sister.

---

24. Letter to Félix Coudroy

Madrid, 17 August 1840   [vol. 1, p. 34]

. . . You have asked me a question I cannot answer: How can the Spanish people allow the monks to be chased away and killed?[41] I ask myself this often, but I do not know the country well enough to explain this phenomenon to myself. What is probable is that the era of monks is finished everywhere. Their uselessness, rightly or wrongly, is a generally established belief. Assuming that there were forty thousand monks in Spain, involving as many families with five members, that would only make two hundred thousand

---

41. The Spanish clergy had considerable influence, legal powers, and wealth. From 1835 to 1837, a number of monasteries were confiscated by law and sold to help pay off the ever-increasing public debt. The law was applied in a very brutal way.

inhabitants compared with ten million. Their immense riches may have tempted many people from the prosperous class, and the prospect of being relieved from a host of fiscal impositions may have tempted many people from the ordinary class. The fact is that the power of the monks is finished; but certainly no measure, assuming it is necessary, has ever been conducted with as much savagery, as much lack of foresight and political tact.

The government was in the hands of the moderates who wanted monasteries to be abolished but did not dare to set about it. Financially, the hope was, with the product of the national property, to pay Spain's debts, end the civil war, and restore the state of the finances. Politically, through the division of the lands, they wanted to reconcile a considerable part of the people to the revolution. I think that this aim has been unsuccessful.

As they did not dare to act legally, an agreement was reached with the fanatics. One night, the fanatics broke into the monasteries. In Barcelona, Malaga, Seville, Madrid, and Valladolid they cut the throats of the monks or chased them away. The government and the public forces remained impassive witnesses of these atrocities for three days. When the uprising ran out of steam, the government intervened and the minister Mendizabal issued a decree confiscating the monasteries and monastic property. This is now being sold; but you will have the measure of this government. Some individual or other declares that he wants to tender for an item of national property. The state has it valued and this valuation is always very low because the acquirer is in league with the assessor. Once this is done, the sale is processed publicly. Agreement is also reached with the notaries to avoid publicity, and the property is yours for a low price. You have to pay a fifth in cash and the other four-fifths in eight installments over eight years. The state receives in payment rent from various sources which is traded on the stock exchange at a loss ranging from 75 to 95 percent, that is to say, that with twenty-five francs and even with five, you pay one hundred francs.

Three things result from this: first, the state receives almost nothing, you can even say nothing; second, it is not those from the provinces who are buying, since they are not at the stock exchange to barter paper; and third, this mass of land sold all together for a pittance has depressed the price of other properties. In this way, the government, which has made scarcely enough to pay the army, will not be paying back the debt.

The property will be divided up only when the speculators sell it on.

The farmers have simply changed masters, and instead of paying farm rents to the monks, who, it is said, were very accommodating owners who did not stick to the rules and who lent seed and even renounced income in bad years, they will be paying on the nail to Belgian and English companies which, uncertain as to the future, will be aiming to repay the state with produce from the land.

The simple peasant, in calamitous years, will no longer be given soup at the monastery door.

Lastly, humble owners will be able to sell their lands only for a pittance. This, it seems to me, will be the result of this disastrous operation.

More capable men had suggested that advantage be taken of an existing custom in use here: leases of fifty and even one hundred years. They wanted to lease farms to peasants at a moderate rate for fifty years. With the income, the annual interest on the debt would have been paid and Spain's credit would have been raised, and at the end of fifty years the peasants would have had an immense capital, probably more than doubled through security and hard work. You will see at a glance the political and financial superiority of this arrangement.

Be that as it may, there are no more monks. What has become of them? Probably some died in the monasteries in the service of Don Carlos, and others would have succumbed to starvation in the gutters and attics of towns. A few may have found refuge with their families.

As for the monasteries, they have been converted into cafés, public dwellings, theaters, and most of all into barracks for another group of predators, rather cruder than the others. Several were demolished to widen streets and construct squares; on the site of the most beautiful of all, one that was considered to be a masterpiece of architecture, a passageway and a hall that clashed in style were built.

Nuns are no less to be pitied. In the event, those who wished to return to the world were thrashed; the others were enclosed in two or three convents, and because their property, which represented the dowries they had brought to their order, had been seized, they should have been paid a pension. However, since this is not paid, you can often see on convent gates this simple notice, *Pan para las pobres monjas* (bread for the poor nuns).

I am beginning to think, my dear Félix, that our M. Custine had really not seen Spain in its true light. Hatred for another civilization had made him seek here virtues which are not there. Perhaps he has on the contrary committed the same fault as the Spanish, who see nothing to criticize in

English civilization. It is with great difficulty that our prejudices allow us to see things as they are, let alone judge them well.

I am coming home, my dear Félix, and I have learned that tomorrow the law on *ayuntamientos* (local councils)[42] will be proclaimed. I do not know whether I have spoken of this matter with you but here at least is a summary.

The moderate government, which has just fallen, had appreciated that, to govern Spain, the central power had to be given a certain authority over the provinces. Here, from time immemorial, each province, each town, and each village governs itself. As long as the monarchical principle and the influence of the clergy compensated for this extreme dilution of authority, things went on more or less well, but now this state of things cannot last. In Spain, each locality nominates its *ayuntamiento, alcaldes, regidors,*[43] etc. These *ayuntamientos,* in addition to their municipal functions, are responsible for gathering taxes and raising troops. The result of this is that when a town has reason to be discontented, whether well founded or not, it limits itself to not collecting taxes or refusing to collect its share. What is more, it appears that these *ayuntamientos* are the centers of major abuses and that they do not hand over to the state half of the contributions they gather. The moderate party therefore wanted to undermine this power. A law has been proposed by the government, adopted by the chambers, and sanctioned by the queen, which stipulates that the queen will select the *alcaldes* from three candidates nominated by the people. The fanatics uttered loud cries, leading to the revolution in Barcelona and the intervention of Espartero's saber. However, what is seen only here, and what you have to be here to grasp, is that the queen, although obliged to change the government, has nominated another which is maintaining the law already voted and approved. Doubtless, since it came to power through a violation of the constitution, this government believed it had to show that it respected it by allowing a law that had received the sanction of the three powers[44] to be promulgated. This law will

42. The law, which was promulgated by Queen Maria Christina in July 1840, allowed the queen to appoint members of the local councils but met with violent opposition from General Espartero. (See Letter 21, note 38.) It took the abdication and exile of Maria Christina (15 July 1840) to unravel the situation.

43. *alcaldes:* mayors; *regidors:* aldermen.

44. The parliament, the senate, and the king.

therefore be proclaimed tomorrow. Will this pass off without disturbance? I scarcely dare to hope so. In addition, because France and our ambassador are considered to be at the root of this hoax, after the events in Barcelona it is to be feared that the rage of the fanatics will be directed against our fellow countrymen. I will therefore take care to write to my aunt in two days' time since the newspapers will not fail to talk about the insurrection being planned. It is none the less terrifying to think that, to keep order, there are just a few soldiers faithful to Espartero, who must be mortally offended by the manner in which his coup d'état has been thwarted.

But what a subject for discussion is Spain, which, to achieve liberty, is losing the monarchy and the religion that are so dear to her and, in order to achieve unity, has placed under threat the local freedoms which are the very fabric of her existence!

Farewell, your devoted friend. I do not have the time to reread this jumble; make of it what you will.

P.S. My dear Félix, the peace in Madrid was not disturbed for a minute. This morning, the members of the *ayuntamiento* met in public session to promulgate the new law which will bring down their institution. They had this ceremony followed by an energetic protest in which they said that they would all die rather than obey the new law. It is also being said that they paid a few men to shout the customary *vivas* and *mueras*,[45] but the people were no more moved than the peasants of Mugron would be, and the *ayuntamiento* succeeded only in showing the increasing necessity of the law. For when all is said and done would it not be a very sad spectacle to see a town in upheaval and the safety of its citizens compromised by the very people who are responsible for maintaining order?[o]

I have been assured that the fanatics did not agree among themselves; the most advanced (I do not know why credit has been given to this quotation by people's agreeing to adopt it) said:

> It is absurd to start a movement which fails to achieve a result. A movement can be decisive only if the people are involved; however the people do not want to take action for the sake of ideas. We therefore have to show them that there is a real possibility of pillage.

45. *vivas:* "long life" and [o] "down with."

And in spite of this terrible logic, the *ayuntamiento* has not given way to this initial provocation! Anyway, I am just relaying public gossip since for my part I was in the Royal Library and did not see anything.

———————

25. Letter to Félix Coudroy

Lisbon, 24 October 1840   [vol. 1, p. 39]

My dear Félix, it is a long time since I wrote to you. It is because we are so far apart and it takes such a long time to receive a reply from Mugron that I am never sure of receiving it here. Finally, I have more or less made up my mind, unless something unexpected happens, to bid farewell to the Peninsula a week from Monday. My intention is to go to London; I cannot, according to the advice you have sent me from my aunt, first go to Plymouth. The steamboat goes straight to London. I thought at first that I would embark for Liverpool. I would thus satisfy economy and my taste for ships, since navigation under sail is cheaper and more romantic than monotonous steam. But the season is so late that it would be reckless, and I would run the risk of spending a month at sea.

I was a little bored in Lisbon for the first few days. Now, apart from the very natural desire to return home, I am happy here, although I live a very uneventful life. But the climate is so gentle and fine, the plant life so rich, and I feel such well-being and unaccustomed good health that I attribute the absence of boredom to this.

This is a country that, I think, would suit you well: neither hot nor cold, with no fog nor damp. If it rains, the downpour lasts for a day or two; then the sky regains its serenity and the atmosphere its gentle warmth. There is a little water available everywhere; there are clumps of myrtle, orange trees, tufted trellised vines, and heliotropes that cover walls as convolvulus does at home. Now I understand the life of the Moors. Unfortunately, the people here are not a match for nature; they do not want to take the trouble the Arabs took to achieve such delights. Perhaps you think that these fervent Catholics scorn the freshness and scent of the orange trees and that they are devoted to the severe pleasures of thought and contemplation. Alas! I will be returning very disillusioned with the good opinion of Custine; he believed he saw what he wanted to see.

For me it will be curious to study England after studying the Peninsula. The comparison would be even more interesting if Catholicism were as fervent here as it is represented. But in the end I will be seeing a people whose religion lies in intelligence after having seen one for whom it lies in the senses. Here the pomp of ceremony, the candles, incense, magnificent vestments and statues, together with the most abject demoralization. There, on the other hand, family ties, men and women each with the duties of their sex, work ennobled by patriotic aim, faithfulness to the traditions of their ancestors, a constant study of the moral code of the Bible and the Gospels, with a religion which is simple, solemn, and close to pure deism. What a contrast! What differences! What a source of reflection!

This trip will also have produced an effect which I did not expect. It has been able to remove the habit we had adopted to observe ourselves, to hear ourselves think and feel, and to follow all the meanderings of our opinions. This self-study has many attractions, and amour propre gives it an abiding interest. But in Mugron, we were always in uneventful surroundings, and able to revolve only in the same circle; when you travel, unexpected situations give rise to new observations. For example, it is probable that the current events[46] have affected me very differently from the way they would have if I had been in Mugron; more fervent patriotism makes my thought more active. At the same time, the field in which it functions is wider, just as a man standing on a height sees a wider horizon. But the power of our gaze is a given quantity for each of us and this is not so for the faculty of thinking and feeling.

My aunt, on the occasion of the war, recommends prudence to me; I must absolutely not run any risks. If I sailed in a French ship and war was declared, I might fear corsairs, but in an English ship I will not run this risk, unless I fall into the hands of a French cruiser, which would not be very dangerous as it happens. According to the news received today, I note that France has taken the attitude of sentimental resignation, which is becoming grotesque. From here she appears to be very *embarrassed,* and making it a point of honor to *prove her moderation;* to each insult she replies by arguments to show that she has been insulted. She appears to believe that remorse will overcome the English and that, with tears in their eyes, they will stop pursuing their aim and ask our forgiveness. That reminds me of this quotation: "He struck me but I told him just what I thought of him."

46. A diplomatic crisis was shaking Europe in 1840. France alone supported the pasha of Egypt, Mehmet Ali, in his position on Syria—against Russia, Prussia, Austria, and Great Britain.

Send your letters to me in London, addressed to MM A. A. Gower, Nephew and Company.

----

26. Letter to Félix Coudroy

Lisbon, 7 November 1840 [vol. 1, p. 42]

My dear Félix, in spite of the strong desire I have to get back to France, I have been obliged to prolong my stay in Lisbon. A cold made me decide to postpone my departure by a week, and in this period papers have been found which I have to go through, which has made me stay even longer. But there will have to be very powerful reasons to keep me here after the 17th of this month. Finally, this delay has allowed me to get better, which would have been more difficult at sea or in London.

It was very unfortunate to be far from France at such an interesting time; you cannot imagine the patriotism that burns within us when we are in a foreign country. At a distance it is no longer the happiness nor even the freedom of our country that is foremost in our mind, but its grandeur, glory, and influence. Unfortunately I very much fear that France does not enjoy much of either the first or the last of these advantages.

I am sad to be without news nor to be able to forecast accurately when I will be receiving any; at least in London I hope to find a pile of letters.

Farewell, the time for collecting letters is approaching.

----

27. Letter to Félix Coudroy

Paris, 2 January 1841 [vol. 1, p. 43]

My dear Félix, I have been dealing with a plan for an *association for the defense of the interests of wine producers.*[47] However, as is my habit, I was hesitating over mentioning it to a few friends, because I could not see any half measures between success and ridicule, when M. Humann came to the chambers to present the expenditure and receipts budget for 1842. As you will have seen, the minister has found no better solution for making good the deficit caused by our policy than to add four new taxes on drinks. This emboldened me, and I went to visit several deputies to tell them about my project. They cannot become directly involved, because this would undermine the independence of their vote in advance. This is a reason for some

----

47. See "Wine and spirits tax" in the Glossary of Subjects and Terms.

and a pretext for others, but it is not a reason for the owners of vineyards to fold their arms in the face of the danger threatening them.

There is just one way not only of redirecting their new general protest but also of obtaining justice for previous grievances, and that is to *organize ourselves. Organization* for a *useful* aim is a guaranteed means of success. Each wine-producing *département* has to have a central committee and each committee a delegate.

I do not yet know to what extent I will be taking part in this organization. This will depend on my meetings with my friends. Perhaps it will be necessary for me to stop when passing through Orléans, Angoulême, and Bordeaux in order to work at founding the association. Perhaps I should limit myself to my *département,* and in any case because time is of the essence, you should see Domenger, Despouys, Labeyrie, and Batistant[48] and persuade them to go round the canton to prepare people for legal resistance that is strong and organized.

I do not need to describe in detail to you the power the association has, my dear Félix. Tell everyone your convictions. I hope to be in Mugron in a fortnight and we will work in tandem.

Farewell, your devoted friend.

---

28. Letter to Félix Coudroy

Paris, 11 January 1841 [vol. 1, p. 44]

Why are you not with me, my dear Félix, as this would remove many of my hesitations! I have told you about the new project I have thought of, but when I am alone and left to myself the difficulties of carrying it out terrify me. I feel that success is almost a certainty, but it requires a moral strength that your presence would give me and material resources that I do not know how to take it upon myself to ask for. I have felt the pulse of several deputies and found them cold. Almost all of them have *interests* to protect; you know that almost all of our men in the Midi are seeking government positions. As for the opposition, it would be dangerous to make it prominent in the association as it would make it an instrument, and this must be avoided. This being so and having weighed everything up, we must abandon founding the association from the *top down,* which would have been quicker and easier. What we have to secure is the base. If it is strongly constituted, it will carry

48. Wine growers.

everything along. The wine producers should be under no illusions; if they remain inert, they will be weakly defended here. I will try to leave here next Sunday. In one pocket I will have the draft statutes of the association and in the other the prospectus for a small newspaper intended initially to be the propagator and subsequently the mouthpiece of the association. With that, I will be able to find out whether this project is viewed sympathetically in Orléans, the Charente, and the Garonne basin. The outcome will depend on my observations. A sudden initiative would have been more to my taste. A few years ago, I might have attempted this; nowadays an advance of six to eight thousand francs makes me draw back, and I am truly ashamed of this since a few hundred subscribers would have relieved me of any risk. I lacked courage, there is nothing more to say.

I am obliged, my dear Félix, to make unceasing mention of my impartiality and philosophy in order not to become discouraged, in view of all the wretchedness I am witnessing. Poor France! Every day, I see deputies who, when spoken to individually, are opposed to fortifications in Paris but who nevertheless support them in the chamber, one in support of Guizot, another to avoid abandoning Thiers, and a third for fear that he will be branded a Russian or an Austrian. Public opinion, the press, and fashion carry them along, and many yield to still baser motives. Marshall Soult himself is personally opposed to this measure, and all he dares to do is to suggest that it be accomplished slowly, in the hope that public opinion will change and come to his support, when there will still be only about a hundred million swallowed up. It is much worse in external matters. It appears that all eyes are blindfolded and people run the risk of being mistreated if a single fact is put forward that contradicts the ruling prejudice.

Farewell, my dear Félix, I am looking forward to chatting with you again; we will not be short of subjects.

Farewell, my friend.

---

29. Letter to Félix Coudroy

Bagnères, 10 July 1844   [vol. 1, p. 45]

My dear Félix, a few days ago I received a letter from M. Laffitte from Aire, a member of the General Council, which embarrasses me a great deal. He tells me that General Durrieu is going to be raised to the peerage, that the government wishes to replace him in the Chamber by a secretary of the duc de Nemours. He adds that the electors of Aire are not willing to suffer this candidature, and finally he asks me if I would stand, in which case he thinks that I would have many votes in this canton, where I had only his at the last election.

As the legislature has only three sessions to sit, and thus I would be free to retire at the end of this term without causing an extraordinary meeting of the electoral college of Saint-Sever, I would be quite willing to enter the ring once more if I could count on some good fortune. But I must not blind myself to the damage that the schism which has taken place in the liberal party will do to me. If in addition I have once more to be opposed by the aristocracy of money and the bar, I prefer to remain peacefully in my corner. I would regret it a little, because I feel that I could have been useful to the cause of free trade, which is so vital for France and above all for our region.

But that is not a reason for me to put myself forward recklessly; I am therefore resolved to wait for serious overtures to be made by influential electors. I consider that the affair affects them closely enough for them not to leave candidates the task of taking care of it themselves.

I wanted to send my article to *Le Journal des économistes,* but have not had the opportunity. I will take the first that comes along. It has the fault, common to all the works of novices, of wanting to say too much. Such as it is, I think it is of some interest. I will take advantage of the opportunity to try to start a correspondence with Dunoyer.

----

30. Letter to Félix Coudroy

Eaux-Bonnes, 26 July 1844 [vol. 1, p. 46]

Your letter had a painful effect on me, my dear Félix, not because of the news you give me of the electoral prospects but because of what you tell me about yourself, your health, and the terrible struggle taken on by your body and spirit. I nevertheless hope that you wished to speak of the habitual state of your health and not a recurrence that has taken place since my departure. I understand your sufferings well, especially since to a lesser extent I experience them myself. These miserable obstacles that health, wealth, and shyness raise like a wall of brass between our desires and the theater in which they might be satisfied are an unutterable torment. Sometimes I regret having drunk at the cup of science, or at least not having limited myself to synthetic philosophy, and better still to religious philosophy. At least in these you can draw consolation for all types of situations in life, and we might still tolerably organize the rest of the time we have to spend here below. But a solitary existence in retirement is incompatible with our views (which nevertheless act on us with all the force of mathematical truths), since we know that truth has power only when it is diffused. From this arises the irresistible need to communicate it, broadcast it, and proclaim it. What is more, everything is so linked in our way of thinking that the opportunity and facility of revealing a link in the chain cannot content us; yet to reveal the total picture requires the conditions of talent, health, and position which we will always lack. What can we do, dear friend? Wait for a few more years to pass over our heads. I often count them and take a form of pleasure in noting that the more they accumulate, the faster they seem to go:

Vires acquirit eundo.[49]

Although we are conscious of knowing the truth, with regard to the mechanics of society and from a purely human point of view, we also know that it escapes us as far as the relationship of this life to future life is concerned, and what is worse, we believe that in this respect we cannot know anything with certainty.

We have here several very distinguished priests. Once every two days, they give instruction of the highest order, which I follow regularly. It is almost a repetition of Dabadie's[50] famous work. Yesterday the preacher said that in man there are two orders of disposition of which one is linked to the fall and the other to redemption. According to the second, man is made in the image of God, while the first led him to make God in man's image. He used this to explain idolatry and paganism and showed their terrifying agreement with corrupt nature. He then said that the fall had so far buried corruption in the heart of man that he still retained an affinity for idolatry which had thus insinuated itself right into Catholicism. I think he was referring to a host of practices and devotions which form such an obstacle for intelligent minds. But if they understand things in this way, why do they not attack these idolatrous doctrines openly? Why do they not reform them? Why, on the contrary, do we see them rushing to increase their number? I am sorry I have not been in contact with this ecclesiastic, who, I believe, is a professor of theology at the faculty in Bordeaux, to discuss this with him.

---

49. "[Fama] vires acquirit eundo": "Rumor acquires strength by going." (Virgil, *Aeneid,* bk. IV, line 175.)

50. Dabadie was a monk born in Saint-Sever. He was not well known outside his native town. The said "famous work" did not reach posterity.

This takes us far away from the elections. From what you tell me, I have no doubt that the man from the chateau will be nominated. I am surprised that our king, who is farsighted, does not understand that by peopling the chamber with toadies he is sacrificing the very principle of the constitution for a few short-term advantages. He is ensuring a vote for himself, but is placing an entire district beyond the boundaries of our institutions; and this maneuver, if extended to all of France, will succeed in corrupting our political customs, which are already primitive. On the other hand, abuses will increase in number because they will encounter no resistance; and when the cup is full, what remedy will a nation seek that has not learned to make an enlightened use of its rights?

For my part, my dear Félix, I do not feel strong enough to fight for a few votes. If they do not come on their own, let them follow their own course. I would need to go from canton to canton to organize the means of support for the struggle. This is more than I can do. After all, M. Durrieu is not yet a peer.

I have taken advantage of an opportunity to send *Le Journal des économistes* my article on English and French tariffs.[51] I think it includes points of view that are all the more important in that they do not appear to preoccupy anyone. I have met politicians here who have not the first idea of what is going on in England, and when I talk to them of the customs reform that is taking place in that country, they do not want to believe it. I have enough time to compose my letter to M. Dunoyer.[52] As for my work on the distribution of taxes, I do not have the materials at hand to give it its final polish.[53] The session of the general council will be a good opportunity to publish it.

Farewell, my dear Félix. If you learn anything new please let me know, but of all the news you could give me, the most pleasant would be to say that the depression which permeates your letter was due to a transitory indisposition. After all, my friend, and in the deep shadows that surround us, let us cling to the idea that a primary cause that is intelligent and merciful has subjected us for reasons beyond our comprehension to severe tests in life; this should constitute our faith. Let us wait for the day when it will consider it right to relieve us and to admit us to a better life; this should constitute our hope.

---

51. *OC*, vol. 1, p. 334, "De l'influence des tarifs français et anglais sur l'avenir des deux peuples."

52. See Letter 34.

53. *OC*, vol. 1, p. 283, "Mémoire sur la repartition de l'impôt foncier dans les Landes."

With these sentiments in our heart, we will be able to bear our afflictions and suffering. . . .

------

31. Letter to A. M. Laurence

Mugron, 9 November 1844   [vol. 7, p. 369]

Dear Sir and Colleague,

Thank you for your kind words in the letter you were good enough to write to me on the subject of my little work on the distribution of taxes.[54] I sincerely regret that it has not been more effective in changing your beliefs, since I acknowledge that in the arguments caused on occasion by neighborhood rivalry your noble spirit places you above the petty bias which others find it impossible to put aside. For my part, I can state that, if any error or exaggeration has infiltrated my text, it has been quite involuntary. I am far from envying for my area's sake the prosperity of yours, quite the contrary, and it is my firm conviction that neither of the two can prosper without the other benefiting. I even think that this solidarity embraces all nations. For this reason, I bitterly deplore the *national jealousies* that are the favorite theme of journalism. If I had, as you think, based my reasoning on the false premise that *the entire area of the sea pine plantations in the Landes*[55] *was equally productive,* I would retract on the spot. However, there is nothing in my writing that justifies this allegation. Nor have I mentioned hail, frost, or fires. These are circumstances which ought to have been taken into account when the current tax was applied to various crops. It is this tax, such as it is, which is my point of departure. Nor do I think that I attributed the distress of the wine-producing region to the improper distribution of the tax. But I said that the distribution of the tax should be adjusted as a result of this distress, since it is a principle that tax is raised on income. If the income of a county is reduced permanently, its contribution should also be reduced and consequently that of the other counties should increase. This is also an additional proof of the solidarity between all the parts of the territory, and the Greater Landes harmed itself when, through our colleague, M. Castagnède, it opposed the agricultural community's becoming the mouthpiece for our grievances to the authorities.

54. Ibid.

55. Before the nineteenth century, the part of the Landes *département* located north of the Adour River was covered with swamps. A huge forest of sea pines was successfully planted during the nineteenth century, and in time the swamps dried up.

You say that in Villeneuve[56] agriculture has made progress without the population increasing in number. This doubtless means that each individual and each family has become more prosperous. If this prosperity has not encouraged marriages and births and extended the average life expectancy, Villeneuve is, for a reason I cannot guess, beyond all the laws of nature which govern population phenomena.

Lastly, dear sir and colleague, you refer me to the evidence military recruitment affords. You say that it shows that the finest stock and the strongest men come from the areas that are most cultivated and which grow vines. However, please note that I do not go so far as to compare the population of the Landes to that of the Chalosse but only each of these populations *to itself* at different periods of time. For me, the question is not to determine whether the population of the Landes is as vigorous and dense as that in the Chalosse but whether, in the last forty years, one has made progress and the other regressed in these two respects. It was easy for me to check the numbers. With regard to the quality of the human stock, I would be willing to consult the recruitment tables, if they have them at the prefecture.

You can see that, like all the authors in the world, I do not readily admit to being mistaken. However, I must say that I have not sufficiently explained the scope of the passage in which I summarized in figures the various considerations scattered through my work. I am fully aware that population movement cannot be a good basis for distribution; my sole aim has been to make my conclusions understandable by using figures, and I sincerely hope that direct research by the authorities will produce results not far from those I have reached, because, in my view, there is a relationship that is, if not very tight, then at least of a notably approximate kind, between the progress of the population and that of income.

---

32. Letter to Richard Cobden

Mugron, 24 November 1844 [vol. 1, p. 106]

Sir,

Steeped in the schools of your Adam Smith and our J. B. Say, I was beginning to believe that this doctrine that was so simple and clear had no chance of becoming popular, at least for a long time, since, over here, it is com-

56. Villeneuve de Marsan, a city in the east of the Landes.

pletely stifled by the specious *fallacies*[57] that you refuted so well and which are disseminated by the Fourierist, communist, and other sects with which our country is for the moment infatuated, and also by the disastrous alliance of the *party newspapers* with those newspapers paid for by committees of manufacturers.

It was in this state of total discouragement in which these sad circumstances had cast me that, as I happened to have taken out a subscription to the *Globe and Traveller,*[58] I learned both of the existence of the *League* and the struggle between free trade and monopoly in England. As I am an enthusiastic admirer of your powerful and very moral association and in particular of the man who appears to give it such forceful and wise direction in the face of countless difficulties, I have been unable to contemplate this sight without wanting to do something for the noble cause of the liberation of work and commerce. Your honorable secretary, Mr. Hickin, was good enough to send me the issue of the *League,* dated January 1844, together with a number of documents relating to the *campaign.*

Equipped with these documents, I have tried to draw public attention to your *proceedings,* on which French newspapers have maintained a calculated and systematic silence. I have written articles in the newspapers of Bayonne and Bordeaux, two towns naturally positioned to become the cradle of the movement. In addition, recently I had published in *Le Journal des économistes* (issue no. 35, Paris, October 1844) an article which I recommend to you. What has been the result? Newspapers in Paris, on which our laws confer the monopoly of opinion, have considered discussion to be more dangerous than silence. They have therefore created *silence* around me, totally sure that these arrangements would reduce me to impotence.

In Bordeaux, I have tried to organize an association for *trade liberalization,* but I have failed because, although there are a few souls who *instinctively* would like freedom *to a certain extent,* there are none who understand it in principle.

What is more, an association functions only through publicity, and it needs money. I am not rich enough to endow it on my own, and asking for money would have created the insurmountable obstacle of suspicion.

I have thought of founding in Paris a daily newspaper based on these two concepts, free trade and the elimination of a partisan spirit. Here again, I

57. In English in the original.
58. An English newspaper. See "Anglomania, Anglophobia," p. 333.

have encountered money and other problems, which I will not go into. I will regret it for the rest of my life, because I am convinced that a newspaper like this, which fills a public need, would have a chance of success. (I have not given up on this.)

Lastly, I wanted to know whether I had any chance of being elected a deputy, and I have become certain that my fellow citizens would give me their vote, since I almost achieved a majority at the last elections. However, personal considerations prevent me from aspiring to this position, which I might have used to the advantage of our cause.

Obliged to limit my action, I began to translate your sessions[59] in *Drury Lane* and *Covent Garden*. Next May, I will submit this translation for publication. I expect it to have a good effect.

1. It will be necessary for France to become acquainted with the existence of the spirited campaign in England against monopolies.
2. It will be necessary for people to stop thinking that freedom is just a trap set by England for other nations.
3. The arguments in favor of free trade would perhaps have more effect if they were in the lively, varied, and popular form of your *speeches* rather than in the methodical works of economists.[60]
4. Your *tactic* that is so well directed downward to the people and upward to Parliament will teach us to act in the same way and inform us on the benefit we may gain from constitutional institutions.
5. This publication will be a forceful blow to the two major plagues of our time, *the partisan spirit and national hatreds.*
6. France will see that in England there are two entirely conflicting opinions and that, consequently, it is absurd and contradictory to envelop the whole of England in the same hatred.

In order for this work to be complete, I would have liked to obtain a few documents on the *origin and beginnings of the League.* A short history of this association would be a suitable preface to the translation of your speeches.[61] I have asked Mr. Hickin for these documents, but doubtless he has been too

59. For what became *Cobden and the League.*
60. Bastiat means those students of economic science who favor free markets (Les Économistes).
61. See this letter, note 59.

busy to reply to me. My documents go back only to January 1843; I would at least need the debate in Parliament on the 1842 tariff and in particular the speech in which Mr. Peel proclaimed the economic truth in the form that has become so popular, "We must be allowed to buy in the cheapest market, etc."

I would also like you to tell me which of your speeches, either at meetings or in Parliament, you think most appropriate to translate. Lastly, I would like my book to contain one or two *free-trade discussions* in the House of Commons and ask that you would be good enough to tell me which ones.

I would be most honored to receive a letter from the man of our time for whom I have the keenest and most sincere admiration.

---

33. Letter to Horace Say

Mugron, 24 November 1844   [vol. 7, p. 377]

Sir,

Please allow me to express to you the feeling of deep satisfaction I had on reading your kind letter of the 19th of this month. Without the sentiments contained in this most valued letter, how would we, men of solitude who are deprived of the useful warnings received through contact with the rest of the world, know whether or not we are in the group of dreamers, all too common in the country, who have allowed themselves to be obsessed by a single idea? Do not tell me, sir, that your approval can merely have limited value in my eyes. Since France and humanity lost your illustrious father, whom I also venerate as my intellectual father, what sentiments can be more precious to me than yours, especially when your own writings and the expressions of confidence which the population of Paris have heaped on you give such authority to your judgments?

Among the authors of your father's school whom death has respected, there is one above all whose agreement is of inestimable value to me, although I would not have dared to solicit it. I refer to M. Charles Dunoyer. His first two articles in *Le Censeur européen* ("On the Equilibrium Between Nations"),[62] together with those by M. Comte which precede them,[63] settled

---

62. Dunoyer, "Du système de l'equilibre des puissances européennes."
63. Comte, "Considérations sur l'état moral de la nation française"; and Comte, "De l'organisation sociale."

the direction of my thought and even my political actions a long time ago.[64] Since then the economist school[65] appears to have given way before the host of socialist sects which seek to achieve the universal good, not in the laws of human nature but in artificial organizations which are the products of their imagination. This is a disastrous mistake, which M. Dunoyer has been campaigning against for a long time with a perseverance that can almost be called prophetic. I therefore could not prevent the rise of a feeling almost of pride when I learned from your letter that M. Dunoyer has approved of the spirit of the text you have had the goodness to include in your esteemed collection.

You are kind enough, sir, to encourage me to send you a further text. I am now devoting the little time I have at my disposal to a work of patience, the usefulness of which I consider to be unquestionable, even though it consists only of simple translations. In England there is a major movement in support of free trade. This movement has been kept carefully hidden by our newspapers and where, from time to time, they are obliged to mention it, it is to distort its nature and influence. I would like to put documents relating to it before the French public and show that on the other side of the Channel there is a party with many members that is powerful, honest, judicious, ready to become the national party, and ready to direct the policy of England, and it is to this party that we should extend a hand of friendship. The public would then be capable of judging whether it is reasonable to envelop the whole of England in the wild hatred that the press is trying to whip up with such obstinacy and success.

I am expecting other benefits from this publication. Readers will find in it an attack on the very root of the *partisan spirit*, the undermining of the basis of *national hatred*, the theory of markets set out not methodically but using forms that are popular and striking, and finally, they will see in action the energy, the *demonstration tactics* which now mean that in England, when genuine abuse is attacked, it is possible to forecast the day it will be

---

64. In the hiatus between the forced closure of *Le Censeur* by the censors in 1815 and its reopening in 1817 under the name *Le Censeur européen*, Comte and Dunoyer discovered the work of Jean-Baptiste Say, which transformed their view of how societies functioned and the future course of their progress under the impulse of "industrialism." Bastiat was to adopt much of their social and economic theory as his own.

65. Bastiat uses the expression *l'école économiste* to refer to adherents of the free market, or the laissez-faire, school of economic thought (Les Économistes). It is worth noting that, in Bastiat's time, *economist* was systematically understood as "liberal economist."

abolished, just as our military engineers forecast the time at which besiegers will seize a citadel.

I am planning to come to Paris in April next to supervise the printing of this publication,[66] and if I had any hesitations in doing this your kind offer and the desire to make your acquaintance and those of the distinguished men whom you meet would be enough to persuade me.

Your colleague, M. Dupérier, was also good enough to write to me about my article. "It is good in theory," he said; and I am tempted to reply to him by your esteemed father's quip, "My God, what is no good in practice is good for nothing." M. Dupérier and I follow very different paths in politics. My esteem for him is all the higher for his frankness and the frankness of his letter. These days, there are very few candidates who tell their opponents what they think.

I forgot to say that if the time and my health permit, following your encouraging invitation I will send another article to *Le Journal des économistes*.[67]

I would be grateful, sir, if you would convey to MM Dussard, Fix, and Blanqui my thanks for their kindness and assure them that I wholeheartedly support their noble and useful work.

P.S. I am taking the liberty of sending you a text published in 1842 relating to the elections written by one of my friends, M. Félix Coudroy. You will see that the doctrines of MM Say, Comte, and Dunoyer have generated some green shoots in places on the arid soil of the Landes. I thought you would be pleased to learn that the sacred fire is not quite extinguished. As long as there is still a spark, we should not lose hope.

---

34. Letter to Charles Dunoyer, Member of the Institute[68]

Mugron, 7 March 1845   [vol. 7, p. 371]

Sir,

Of all the testimonials I might have hoped to receive, that which I have just received from you is certainly the most precious. Even allowing for kind-

---

66. *Cobden and the League.*

67. This letter was written in November 1844. The next article by Bastiat to appear in *Le Journal des économistes* was titled "Letter from an Economist to M. de Lamartine, on the Occasion of His Article Entitled 'The Right to Work.'" (*OC*, vol. 1, p. 406, "Un Économiste à M. de Lamartine.")

68. Institut de France.

ness in the very flattering references to me on the first page of your book,[69] I cannot help being certain that I have your vote, knowing how much you are in the habit of matching your utterances to your thought.

When I was very young, sir, a happy chance made me pick up *Le Censeur européen* and I owe the direction of my studies and outlook to this circumstance. In the time that has elapsed since this period, I am unable to distinguish what is the fruit of my own meditations from what I owe to your writings, so completely do they appear to have been assimilated. But if all that you had done were to reveal to me in *society* and its virtues (its views, ideas, prejudices, and external circumstances) the true elements of the good it enjoys and the evils it endures, if all you had taught me were to see in governments and their forms only the results of the physical and moral state of society itself, it would be none the less proper, whatever additional knowledge I had managed to acquire since then, to give you and your colleagues the credit for its direction and principle. It is enough to say to you, sir, that nothing could give me more genuine satisfaction than the reception you have given to the two articles I sent to *Le Journal des économistes* and the sensitive way in which you were kind enough to express it.[70] I will be devoting serious study to your book and gleaning much enjoyment from following the development of the fundamental distinction to which I have just referred.

---

35. Letter to Alphonse de Lamartine

Mugron, 7 March 1845[71]   [vol. 7, p. 373]

Sir,

Absence has prevented me from expressing to you earlier the deep gratitude I felt at the reception you deigned to give to the letter I took the liberty of addressing to you through *Le Journal des économistes.* The letter you have

---

69. Dunoyer, *De la liberté du travail.*

70. Probably a reference to the first two articles Bastiat had published in *Le Journal des économistes* on British and French tariffs and on Lamartine. (*OC,* vol. 1, p. 331, "De l'influence des tariffs français et anglais sur l'avenir des deux peuples" and "Un Économiste à M. de Lamartine.")

71. (Paillottet's note) The letter to which Bastiat is replying had been sent to him in connection with the article in *Le Journal des économistes* entitled "From an Economist to M. de Lamartine." [*OC,* vol. 1, p. 406, "Un Économiste à M. de Lamartine."]

been good enough to write to me is very precious to me and I will always keep it, not only because of the inimitable charm which pervades it but also and above all as an example of your kind readiness to encourage the first attempts of a novice who has not been afraid to point out in your admirable writings a few proposals which he considers to be errors that have escaped your genius.

Perhaps I have gone too far in asking you for that analytical rigor, that accuracy in dissection which explores the field of discovery but which cannot enlarge it. All human faculties have their mission; it is up to a genius to lift himself up to view new horizons and point them out to the crowd. At first these horizons are vague, and reality and illusion are confused in them; the role of analysts is then to come and measure, weigh, and distinguish them. This is how Columbus revealed a new world. Do we find out whether he had taken all the measurements and traced all the contours? Is it even important that he thought he had landed in Cathay? Others have come after, patient workers who have corrected and added to the work. Their names remain unknown while that of Columbus has resounded down the centuries. But, sir, is not a genius the king of the future rather than of the present? Can he claim immediate and practical influence? Do his powerful leaps forward into unknown regions have much in common with the activities of men of the present time or those of businessmen? This is a doubt that I am putting to you; your future will answer it.

You are good enough to acknowledge, sir, that I have traveled through the domain of liberty and you are urging me to rise to meet equality and still further to meet fraternity. How can I help but try, when the request is yours, to take new steps in this noble direction? Doubtless, I will not attain the heights to which you soar, since the habits of my mind no longer allow me to use the wings of imagination. But I will endeavor at least to direct the torch of analysis to a few corners of the huge subject you are suggesting that I study.

Permit me to end by saying, sir, that a few incidental disagreements do not prevent me from being the most sincere and fervent of your admirers, as I hope one day to be the most fervent of your disciples.

36. Letter to Richard Cobden

Mugron, 8 April 1845   [vol. 1, p. 109]

Sir,

Since you permit me to write to you, I will reply to your kind letter dated 12th December last. I have been discussing the printing of the translation I told you about with M. Guillaumin, a bookseller in Paris.

The book is entitled *Cobden and the League, or the Campaign in England in Favor of Free Trade.* I have taken the liberty of using your name for the following reasons: I could not entitle this work *The Anti–Corn Law League.* Apart from the fact that this would have a barbarous sound for French ears, it would have brought to mind just a limited conception of the project. It would have presented the question as purely *English,* whereas it is a humanitarian one, the most notably so of all those which have brought campaigning to our century. A simpler title, *The League,* would have been too vague and would have made people think of an episode in our national history. I therefore felt it necessary to make it clear by preceding it with the name of the person acknowledged to be the "driving force of this campaigning." You have yourself recognized that individual names were sometimes needed "to give point, to direct attention" and I am using this as my justification.

Fashion—individual names, acknowledged reputations—has so much influence here that I felt it necessary to make a further effort to bring it over to our side. I have written a letter to M. de Lamartine in the *économistes* (the February 1845 issue).[72] This illustrious writer, yielding to the tyrant fashion, had assailed economists in the most unjust and thoughtless manner, since, in the same text, he adopted their principles. I have reason to believe, from the reply he was good enough to send me, that he is not far from joining our ranks, and that would perhaps be enough to cause an unexpected swing in public opinion to us. Doubtless, such a swing would be fragile, but finally we would have, at least temporarily, an audience, and that is what we lack. For my part, I ask for one thing only, and that is that people do not deliberately cover their ears.

Permit me to recommend that you *peruse* the letter to which I refer, if you have the opportunity.

I am, sir, your faithful servant,

---

72. *Le Journal des économistes.* (*OC,* vol. 1, p. 406, "Un Économiste à M. de Lamartine.")

37. Letter to Félix Coudroy

Paris, May 1845 [vol. 1, p. 50]

My dear Félix, I am sure that you are waiting to hear from me. I, too, have a lot to tell you but I must be brief. Although at the end of each day it transpires that I have done nothing, I am always busy. In Paris, the way things are, until you are in the swing of things you need half a day to put fifteen minutes to good use.

I was given a good welcome by M. Guillaumin, who is the first *economist* I have seen. He told me that he would give a dinner, followed by a reception, to put me in contact with the men of our school; as a result I have not gone to see any of these people. This dinner was held yesterday. I was on the right of the host, clear proof that the dinner was in my honor, and Dunoyer was on his left. Next to Mme Guillaumin were MM Passy and Say. MM Dussard and Reybaud were also there. Béranger had been invited but he had other engagements. In the evening a crowd of other economists arrived: MM Renouard, Daire, Monjean, Garnier, etc., etc. Between you and me, my friend, I can tell you that I felt a keen satisfaction. There were none of these people who had not read, reread, and perfectly understood my three articles. I could write for a thousand years in *La Chalosse, La Sentinelle,* or *Le Mémorial*[73] without finding a genuine reader, except for you. Here, one is read, studied, and understood. I am sure of this since all or nearly all of them went into the greatest detail, which shows that politeness was not the only reason for this welcome; the only one I found a little cold was M. X. To tell you of the kindnesses I was covered with and the hope that appeared to be based on my cooperation is to make you understand that I was ashamed of my role. My friend, I am perfectly convinced today that, although our isolation has prevented us from equipping our minds sufficiently, it has, at least when it comes to particular questions, given them a strength and accuracy which many more educated and gifted men perhaps do not possess.

What gave me the most pleasure, because it proved that I have really been read with care, is that the last article, entitled "Sophism,"[74] was ranked above the others. This is the one in fact in which the principles are examined in the greatest depth, and I was expecting it not to have been tackled. Dunoyer

73. Newspapers from, respectively, the Landes, Bayonne, and the Pyrenees, which published articles by Bastiat. For the latter, see the glossary of subjects: *Le Mémorial bordelais.*

74. *Economic Sophisms.*

asked me to write an article on his work, to be included in the *Débats*.[75] He was kind enough to say that he thought me eminently suited to making his work appreciated. Alas! I can already see that I will not be able to maintain the far too lofty status which these kind men have accorded me.

After dinner, we discussed dueling. I gave a brief summary of your brochure. Tomorrow we are having another corporate dinner at Véfour; I will take it there and, as it is not long, I hope it will be read. If you could rewrite it, or at least modify it, I believe it might be included in the journal, but the rules prevent it from being quoted verbatim. Incidentally, *Le Journal des économistes* is not as lowly rated as I feared. It has five or six hundred subscribers and is gaining authority every day.

Repeating the conversation to you would carry me too far. What a world, my friend, and it can well be said "You live only in Paris and just vegetate elsewhere!" In spite of this, I already hanker after our walks and intimate conversations. I lack paper; farewell, dear Félix. Your friend.

P.S. I was mistaken. A dinner, even if it is with economists, is not an opportune occasion for reading a brochure. I gave yours to M. Dunoyer and will not know what he thinks for a few days. You will find in the 27 March issue of *Le Moniteur,* which should be in the library in my room, the indictment of dueling by Dupin.[76] Perhaps that will give you an opportunity to lengthen your brochure. I spent this evening with *Y.* He gave me the most cordial welcome and we discussed everything, even religion. I thought he was weak on this subject, since he respects it without believing in it.

It was only today that I went to pay my respects to M. Lamartine. I did not enter, as he was leaving for Argenteuil, but with his usual courtesy, he sent me a message to say that he wanted us to talk without constraint and gave me an appointment for tomorrow. How well will I do?

During our dinner, or more accurately after it, a major question was bandied about: "on intellectual property." A Belgian, M. Jobard, expressed new ideas which will astonish you. I am longing to discuss all this with you. The fact is, in spite of my successes of the moment, I feel that I am no longer

75. *Le Journal des débats.* Bastiat is referring to a review he wrote in that journal, "Sur l'ouvrage de M. Dunoyer. De la liberté du travail." (*OC,* vol. 1, p. 428, "Sur un livre de M. Dunoyer.")

76. The attorney general, Charles Dupin, modified the French legislation concerning dueling in order to reduce the number of fatalities. The law was in effect from 1837 to 1839. See also "Reflection on the Question of Dueling," note 3, pp. 309–10.

disposed to be entertained in this manner. This is water off a duck's back, and all things considered, life in the provinces might be made more pleasant than it is here if one just had a taste for studying and the arts.

Farewell, my dear Félix, until later. Write to me from time to time and keep busy on your work on dueling. Since the court has reverted to its strange legal posture, it is worth doing.

---

38. Letter to Félix Coudroy

Paris, 23 May 1845   [vol. 1, p. 52]

You are expecting a lot of details, my dear Félix, but you are going to be disappointed. Since my last letter, which I sent via Bordeaux and for which I have not yet received a receipt, we have been having weather that is discouraging me from making visits. I spend my mornings wasting time on mere trifles, shopping, and essential business and the evenings regretting this. My letter will therefore be rather arid though I hope you will be pleased with it because of the letter from Dunoyer that I enclose. You will see that he liked your piece on dueling. I have just left him and he repeated to me verbally what he has written in his letter. He praised the essence and style of your brochure and said that it was based on solid work that was on the right track. He expressed his regret that he could not discuss it further and his desire to come to my house to discuss the subject in greater detail. Tomorrow I will send it to M. Say, who is a really nice man because of his gentleness and grace, combined with very firm principles. He is the anchor of the economists' party. Without him, without his conciliating spirit, the group would soon be dispersed. Many of *my colleagues* are employed by newspapers which pay them much better than *Le Journal des économistes*. Others have political affairs to maintain. In a word, the whole thing is an accidental meeting of well-meaning men who like each other even though their opinions differ on many points; there is no firm, organized, and homogeneous party. For my part, if I had the time to remain here and the fortune to hold receptions at home, I would try to found a sort of League. But when you are only passing through, it is useless to embark on such a grand enterprise.

Anyway, I have arrived too soon; my translation is being printed only slowly.[77] If I had been able to hand out a few copies, they might perhaps have opened a few doors to me.

---

77. *Cobden and the League.*

I have not seen M. de Lamartine; he is away from Paris and I do not know when he will return.

Another nice man is M. Reybaud. The proof of his remarkably vigorous intellect is that he became an economist by studying the nineteenth-century reformers. He agreed with them when he began his work, but his good sense has triumphed.

I am trying to find out whether M. Guizot has written to you. It is to be feared that his many activities prevent him from reading your brochure. If he were just a man of letters, he would certainly reply to you, but he is a minister and member of the government. In any case, if anything arrives from that quarter, do let me know.

I have been somewhat occupied with public affairs, I mean departmental ones. It would take too long to tell you about it. But I believe that the Adour, that is to say, the lower Adour, from Hourquet to the Gave, will obtain 1.5 million francs. Chance put me in a position to give this a helping hand: it will always be an advantage if the steamboats reach Pontonx. As for the stretch between Mugron and Hourquet, one is dying to know what was responsible for its exclusion, but what can we do? There is just one thing that the general public does not want to become involved in, and that is public affairs.

I do not know whether I will write to my aunt today. In any case tell her that we are all well here. Farewell, my dear Félix; remember me to your sister.

---

39. Letter to Félix Coudroy

Paris, 5 June 1845   [vol. 1, p. 54]

My dear Félix, an opportunity has arisen for Bordeaux and I do not want to let it go without a few words of reply to your letter. Forgive me if I am too brief. I am ashamed to call myself busy since the days pass without my making use of them. This is something that can be explained only here. In any case, we will soon be able to talk about everything we find so interesting and that interests scarcely anyone but us.

You have not acknowledged receiving the letter from Dunoyer; I think that you received it only after the departure of Calon. You have seen his opinion of your brochure, and I am longing to hear that of M. Guizot—if he gives it to you—since people assure you that the sole occupation of men in power is to retain it. I have not yet sent it to M. Say, as he is in the country and I will not see him until Friday. He is a charming man and the one I prefer; I am due to dine with him at Dunoyer's and on the 10th at Véfour at the economists' banquet. We should be tossing around the question of inviting the government (always the government!) to set up chairs of political economy. I have been made responsible for preparing a few ideas on this, and this is a subject which would please me, but I will limit myself to mulling over my opinion since, there as elsewhere, there are egos and placemen who have to be handled with kid gloves. As for an association which would please me a great deal more, I will wait for my translation[78] to be published before speaking about it, since the translation may prepare people's minds for it. However, for an association, an agreed principle is needed, and I am very much afraid that it is lacking. I have never seen so much fear of *absolute conviction,* as though we should not be leaving our opponents the task of moderating our progress as necessary.

In Mugron, I will explain to you the reasons which prevent the journal from being modified. Besides, the Paris press is now based on advertising and, from the financial point of view, is established on bases of such a kind that *nothing new is possible.* This being so, it is only the association and the sacrifices that it alone can make that can get us out of this blind alley. I am coming to things that are personal to me and speak of them to you openly as to a bosom friend, with no false modesty. I believe that a lack of incomprehension is a characteristic which we have in common and I do not fear that you will find me too presumptuous.

My book will have thirty sheets,[79] and twenty have been printed. I hope that it will all be ready at the end of the month. I have changed nothing or very little of the introduction I read to you. About half will appear in the next issue of *Le Journal des économistes.*[80] Ignorance of affairs in England is such, even here, that this work should, I think, have an effect on studious people. I will tell you frankly what effect it has.

Each day I acquire proof that the previous articles have had some effect. The publisher has received several requests for subscription *giving reasons,* among which is a letter from Nevers that said "Two articles in *Le Moniteur industriel* have reached us which seek to refute an article in *Le Journal des économistes* entitled 'Sophisms.' All we know of this article are the quota-

---

78. Ibid.
79. The *sheets* ("feuilles" in French) are printer's sheets, which cover several pages.
80. Bastiat is referring to the introduction of *Cobden and the League.*

tions in *Le Moniteur* but they were enough to give us a high opinion of it. Would you please send it to us and give us a subscription?" Two subscriptions were requested from Bordeaux. But what gave me the most pleasure was a conversation I had with M. Raoul Duval, a counselor at the court of Rheims, a town that is essentially protectionist. He assured me that the article on tariffs had been read aloud and that at each instant the manufacturers said, "That is true, that is very true, that is what is going to happen to us, there is no answer to this." This scene, my dear Félix, signposts the route I should be following. If I could, I would now examine the real situation of our protected industries in the light of principles and go into the field of facts. M. Guillaumin wants me to review a dozen more *sophisms* to gather them together and, *at his expense,* to make them into a low-cost brochure that might reach a wide audience.

It needs to be you, my dear Félix, for me to recount these things which, as it happens, leave me as cold as if they concerned a third party. I was already set on my articles and your judgment was enough of a guarantee for me; I was only too happy that there were still other readers as I had given up hope of this.

I will tell you that I have almost decided to go to shake hands with Cobden, Fox, and Thompson; a personal acquaintance with these men may be useful to us. I have some hope that they will give me some documents, but in any case I will make a stock of a few good works, including speeches by Fox and Thompson on subjects other than free trade. If I stayed in Paris I would feel the need to devote myself to this specialty, and this would be indeed enough for my frail shoulders. But, in our gentle retreat, that would not be enough for us. Anyway, economics appears much finer when it is embraced in its totality. It is this harmonious whole that I would like to be able to master one day. You should indeed take the time to set out some of its traits.

If my small treatise, *Economic Sophisms,* is a success, we might follow it with another entitled *Social Harmonies.*[81] It would be of great use because it would satisfy the tendency of our epoch to look for organizations and artificial harmonies by showing it the beauty, order, and progressive principle in natural and providential harmonies.

I will take some works from here. My trip will at least serve to provide us with some fodder and knowledge of something of the spirit of the century.

---

81. No book with such a title was published by Bastiat. The title was later changed to *Economic Harmonies* (see note 189, p. 131, and note 336, p. 251).

Farewell, my dear Félix. I have not written to my aunt today; please tell her that I have received her letter with much pleasure after being so long without one.

---

40. Letter to Félix Coudroy

16 June 1845 [vol. 1, p. 57]

My dear Félix, I have to tell you that my *League* has been printed.[82] They are now working on the introduction and it cannot take longer than a week. It therefore appears that at the end of the month I will be free to go to London and that on 15 July I will have the pleasure of greeting you. Tomorrow, I dine at Dunoyer's with all of our group, Dussard, Reybaud, Fix, Rossi, and Say. I will seal my letter only after this, in case I have some news to tell you. On Sunday, an approach was made to me and perhaps this will be discussed tomorrow. There is so much for and against that I could never take a decision without you. It is to be the manager of *Le Journal des économistes*. From the financial point of view, it is a wretchedly low salary, a hundred louis per year, including editing. However, you will easily understand how close this position is to my inclinations. First of all, this journal, well managed, could have a great influence on the Chamber, and by extension the press. If the economist in situ establishes a reputation for superiority in his specialty, it would be impossible for him not to be feared to some extent by the protectionists and reformers, in a word, ignorant people of all sorts. Through the spoken word I will never get very far because I lack confidence, memory, and presence of mind, but my pen is sufficiently skilled in dialectics to put to shame certain of our statesmen.

Secondly, if I am managing the journal, my management will end up being exclusive since I will be surrounded by lazy people, and, to the extent that the shareholders allow, I will succeed in giving it the homogeneity that it lacks.

I will be in natural and necessary contact with all the eminent men, at least in the spheres of political economy and financial and customs affairs, and finally, I will be in their eyes the spokesperson of a public opinion that is conscientious and enlightened. I think that a role of this sort may be extended indefinitely, depending on the level of the person holding it.

As for the work, it is not of the type, like daily journalism, that would

---

82. *Cobden and the League.*

distract me from continuing my studies. Lastly (and this is only a distant prospect), if the manager of the journal is equal to his task, he might profitably join the ranks of candidates for a chair of political economy that falls vacant.

These are the points in favor. But it would mean leaving Mugron. I would have to leave the people I love and allow my aunt to progress in solitude into old age. I would need to lead a strict life here and see passions unfurl without sharing them. I would unceasingly witness the spectacle of ambition being satisfied without allowing this sentiment to approach my heart, since our entire strength lies in our principles and in the confidence we are able to inspire. In this respect, this is not what I fear. Simple habits are far from terrifying me.

------

41. Letter to Félix Coudroy

18 . . . [83]   [vol. 1, p. 59]

I left Dunoyer's this morning at one o'clock. The guests were those I mentioned, plus M. de Tracy.[84] Political economy was scarcely touched upon; these people dabble in it as amateurs. However, during dinner free trade was discussed a little. M. *X* said that the English were *putting on an act*. I did not think it appropriate to challenge this term, but I was very tempted to ask him if he believed in the principle of freedom or not. For in the end, if he believed in it, why did he not want the English to believe in it too? Because it is in their interest? I remembered your argument: if people formed a temperance society, should we denigrate it on the grounds that it is in people's interest to be temperate? If I write a sophism on this subject, I will slip this refutation into it. After dinner, I was drawn into a game of whist: a wasted evening. The entire editorial staff of the journal was there: Wolowski, Villermé, Blaise, Monjean, etc., etc. . . . another disappointment, I fear. *Z*—— is crazy about agriculture, and about protectionism. Truly, I am getting a close view of things and feel that I might do good and pay my debt to the human race.

Let us return to the journal. No one asked me for a definite commitment; now I will wait. I am discussing it with my aunt; I need to see what she thinks. She would certainly let me follow my inclination if she saw a financial future in it and, humanly speaking, she would be right; she cannot

83. No month given.
84. Antoine Destutt de Tracy.

comprehend the extent of the position I could be taking. If she speaks to you about it, let me know the effect that my letter has. For my part, I will tell you about the effect my *League* will produce. Will anyone read it? I doubt it. We are snowed under with reading matter here. If I told you that, except for Dunoyer and Say, none of my colleagues has read Comte! You already know that —— has not read Malthus. At dinner, Tracy said that the extreme poverty in Ireland[85] proved Malthus's doctrine wrong! I have heard it said to someone that there was *some good* in the *Treatise on Legislation*[86] and above all in the *Treatise on Property*.[87] Poor Comte! Say told me his sad story; persecution and his probity killed him.

You will, of course, not breathe a word on what I have told you about the management of the journal. You will appreciate that this news would cause an unfortunate stir.

I think that I have told you that the publisher of the *League* is also going to publish the *Sophisms*. This will be a small, low-cost book, but the title is not attractive. I am looking for another; please help me. The small book by Mathieu de Dombasle was entitled "*A Shaft of Common Sense,*" etc.

As I cannot cover all the sophisms in one small volume, if it sells well, I will write another.[88] It would be a good thing if, for your part, you dealt with a few. I would alternate them with mine and that would enable you at least to make the acquaintance of my colleagues and you could then, if you wanted, have yourself *published* at no cost, which is not a simple matter.

Farewell, my dear Félix; write to me.

───────────

42. Letter to Félix Coudroy

Paris, 3 July 1845 (eleven o'clock in the evening)   [vol. 1, p. 60]

. . . Like you, my dear Félix, I envisage the future with terror. Leaving my aunt, separating myself from those I love, leaving you alone in Mugron, without your friend, without books, is dreadful. And for my own part, I do not know whether solitary work, meditated on at leisure and discussed with you,

───────────

85. Ireland had 5.2 million inhabitants in 1801, 8.2 million in 1841—an increase of 58 percent in forty years, in spite of two million emigrants. The misery was due not to an excessive population increase but to the fact that an Ireland living mainly on potatoes found one-third of the harvest destroyed by blight in 1845 and the entire harvest destroyed in 1846.

86. Comte, *Traité de législation*.

87. Comte, *Traité de la propriété*.

88. *Economic Sophisms*.

would not be better. On the other hand, it is certain that there is a position here to be attained, the only one for which I have an ambition and the only one which suits me and for which I am suitable. It is now certain that I can have the manager's position at the journal and I do not doubt that I will be given six francs per subscription. There are five hundred subscribers, which makes three thousand francs. This is absolutely nothing, financially speaking, but we need to believe that strong management stamped on the journal will increase its membership and if we achieved a figure of one thousand, I would be satisfied. Then there is the prospect of a course of lectures; I do not know whether I told you that at our last dinner, we decided that an approach would be made to the government to found chairs of political economy[89] at the university. MM Guizot, Salvandy, and Duchâtel expressed approval of this project. M. Guizot said: "I am so well disposed to this that it was I who founded the chair that M. Chevalier occupies. Obviously, we are going down the wrong road and it is essential to disseminate healthy economic doctrines. However the major difficulty is to choose the right people." At this reply, MM Say, Dussard, Daire, and a few others assured me that, if they were consulted, they would designate me. M. Dunoyer would certainly be in favor of me. I have found out that the minister of finance was impressed with my introduction and he himself asked me for a copy of the work. I would thus have a good chance, if not of being called to the university, at least if Blanqui, Rossi, or Chevalier were nominated, of replacing one of these men at the Collège de France or the Conservatoire.[90] One way or another, I would be launched with an assured existence, and that is all I need.

But having to leave Mugron! Having to leave my aunt! What about my chest! What about the limited circle of my acquaintances! In sum, the long chapter of objections . . . Oh, why am I not ten years younger and in good health! Moreover, you will understand that this prospect is still distant but that the management of the journal would put a great deal of opportunity on my side. Therefore, instead of producing two *sophisms,* selected from those that are popular and anecdotal, in the next issue, I sense an opportunity to develop my ideas, and I am going to devote tomorrow to rewriting two or

89. Apart from conferences and private education, political economy was taught only in the Conservatoire national des arts et métiers, by Auguste Blanqui, and at the Collège de France, by Michel Chevalier.

90. Conservatoire national des arts et métiers.

three of the most important. This is why I cannot write to you at length as I would like and am forced to speak about myself instead of replying to your affectionate letters.

M. Say wants to entrust to me all his father's papers; there are some curious things in them. What is more, it is an expression of confidence that touches me. Hippolyte Comte, the son of Charles, will also be letting me go through the notes of our favorite author, who is totally unknown right here. . . . But I do not want to fail in what I owe to the men who are showering me with proofs of their friendship.

You see, dear Félix, that there are so many reasons for and against; I really must decide soon. Oh! I really need your advice, and above all for you to tell me what my poor aunt thinks.

Although I scarcely answer your letters, I nevertheless must tell you that the work of Simon is very rare and extremely expensive. There are only four copies, of which two are in the public libraries. Bossuet had the entire edition destroyed.

Farewell, my dear Félix; excuse the haste with which I write.

---

43. Letter to Félix Coudroy

London, July 1845   [vol. 1, p. 62]

My dear Félix, I arrived here yesterday evening. Knowing how much you are interested in our cause and in the role that chance has given me, I will tell you everything that happens, especially since I have no time to take notes and, this being so, my letters will be useful later in reminding me of my memories so that I can give you more details face to face.

After I settled in at the hotel (at ten shillings a day), I started to write six letters to Cobden, Bright, Fox, Thompson, Wilson, and the secretary who sends me the *League*. Then I wrote six dedications in six of my books and went to bed. This morning, I took my six copies to the League's office with the request that they be given to the people concerned. Someone told me that Cobden was leaving the same day for Manchester and that probably I would find him in the throes of making his preparations (preparations for an Englishman consist in swallowing a steak and stuffing two shirts into a bag). I ran to Cobden's; I did in fact meet him and we chatted for two hours. He understands French well and speaks it a little and anyway I understand his English. I described to him the state of opinion in France, the effect I expect this book to have, etc., etc. He told me how sorry he was to be leaving

London and I saw that he was on the point of canceling his trip. He then told me, "The League is like a Masonic lodge, except for the fact that everything is public. Here is a house that we have rented to receive our friends during the Bazaar. It is now empty, so you must move in." I demurred, to which he replied, "This may not be convenient to you, but it is useful for the cause since Messrs. Bright, Moore, and other members of the League spend their evenings there and you must always be in their midst." However, because it was subsequently decided that I would go to join him in Manchester the day after tomorrow, I did not think it necessary to move for two days. He then took me to the Reform Club, a magnificent establishment, and left me in the library while he took a bath. After this, he wrote two letters to Bright and Moore and I accompanied him to the station. In the evening, I went to see Bright, still at the same hotel, although these people do not live there; his welcome was not quite as cordial. I noticed that he did not approve of my including Cobden's name in the title of my book. In addition, he appeared surprised that I had translated nothing by M. Villiers. His own contribution in the book is small, although he deserves greater recognition as he has the gift of an attractive eloquence. However, all this was sorted out during the conversation. As I was obliged to speak slowly to make myself understood and was discussing subjects with which I was familiar with men of exactly the same mind, I was certainly in the most favorable of circumstances. He took me to Parliament, where I have remained up to now, since they were discussing a question which included education and religion. I left at eleven o'clock and then started to write to you. Tomorrow I have an appointment with him, and the day after tomorrow I am going to see Manchester and meet my friend Cobden again. He is to arrange my accommodation and leave me in the hands of Mr. Ashworth, the rich manufacturer who put across such a good argument to demonstrate to farmers that the export of manufactured objects implied the export of the things included in them and that, consequently, restrictions on trade would hit them in the face. This brusque departure, I fear, will prevent me from seeing Fox and Thompson before my return, as well as Mill and Senior, for whom I have letters.

This is a short account of my first day. I will thus enter Manchester and Liverpool in circumstances which few Frenchmen could hope to enjoy. I will be there on a Sunday. Cobden will take me to the Quakers and the Wesleyans. We will at last know something, and as for factories, nothing will be hidden from me. What is more, all the operations of the League will be unveiled to me. There was a vague suggestion of a second edition of my book on a wider scale. We will see.

Let us not forget Paris. Before leaving, I spent an hour with Hippolyte, the son of Charles Comte, who showed me all of his father's papers. There are two or three courses of lectures given in Geneva, London, and Paris, all of which doubtless supplied material for the *Treatise on Legislation,* but what a gold mine to open up!

Farewell, I must leave you. I still have three letters to write to Paris and it is already tomorrow, since it is past midnight.

---

44. Letter to Richard Cobden

London, 8 July 1845   [vol. 1, p. 110]

Sir,

At last I have the pleasure of presenting you with a copy of the translation about which I have spoken to you on several occasions. In carrying out this work, I was convinced that I was rendering a genuine service to my country, both by popularizing sane economic doctrines and unmasking the guilty men who concentrate on maintaining disastrous national restrictions. I was not mistaken in my expectations. I distributed about a hundred copies in Paris and they have had the best possible reception. Men who, through their position and the subject of their study, ought to know what is happening in your country were surprised on reading it. They could not believe their eyes. The truth is that everyone in France is unaware of the importance of the campaign in your country, and people still suspect that a few manufacturers are seeking to propagate ideas of freedom abroad through pure British Machiavellianism. If I had confronted this prejudice directly, I would not have vanquished it. By leaving the *free traders* to act and allowing them to speak, in a word, by *translating* you, I hope that I have dealt it a blow from which it will not recover, provided that the book is read. *That is the question.*[91]

I hope, sir, that you will be good enough to grant me the honor of having a short discussion with you and expressing my gratitude, fellow feeling, and profound admiration to you personally.

Your most humble servant.

91. In English in the original.

45. Letter to Mr. Paulton

Paris, 29 July 1845   [vol. 7, p 374]

My dear sir, as I told you, I am sending you four copies of my translation which I ask you to forward to the editors of the *Times*, the *Morning Chronicle*, etc., etc. I would consider myself happy if the English press gave a favorable welcome to a work I consider useful. This would compensate me for the indifference with which it has been received in France. All those to whom I have given it continue to show surprise at the serious facts revealed in it, but no one is buying it, and this is not surprising since no one knows the subject with which it deals. Our newspapers, moreover, appear to have decided to bury the question under a veil of silence. It will cost me dear to have attempted to open my country's eyes, but what is worse is not having succeeded.[92]

When I arrived here, I found a letter from Sir Robert Peel. As he wrote it before having read the book, he did not have to give his opinion on it. He also avoided quoting its title (*Cobden and the League*). If that is through diplomacy, the latter must be a deep-seated habit of your prime minister for him to use it on such an insignificant occasion. This is a copy of his note.

> Whitehall, 24 July
> Sir Robert Peel presents his compliments to M. Bastiat, and is most obliged to M. Bastiat's attention in transmitting for the acceptance of Sir Robert Peel a copy of his recent publication. Sir Robert hopes to be enabled to profit by it, when he shall have leisure from the present severe pressure of parliamentary business.[93]

This letter is unsigned. I would be curious to know if it is written in Sir Robert's own handwriting.

I found other letters, including two of not inconsiderable importance. One was from M. Passy,[94] a peer of France and an ex-minister of trade. He gives his unalloyed approval of the principles contained alike in the introduction and in your work.

The other letter is from M. de Langsdorf, our chargé d'affaires in the Grand Duchy of Baden. He tells me that he has read the book with enthusi-

---

92. See "Anglomania, Anglophobia," p. 320.
93. In English in the original.
94. Hyppolite Passy.

asm and learned for the first time what is happening in England. At the moment, there is a meeting in Karlsruhe of officers from all of the Zollverein[95] who are determined to plug the tiniest loophole through which foreign trade might come to infiltrate the great *national market*. What he tells me about this supports Mr. Cobden's idea of having the history of the League translated into German, together with a selection of your speeches. Could not England, which has had the Bible translated into three or four hundred languages, also have this excellent course of practical political economy translated at least into German and Spanish?[96] I know the reasons which prevent you from seeking to act on the foreign scene at present. But simple translations would prepare people's minds without your being liable to accusations of making propaganda.

If, later, the League is able to acquire a few copies of my translation without difficulty, I think this is the most useful purpose to which it might be put. This would be to take the same number of towns in order of their commercial importance and send a copy to each, addressed to the literary circle or chamber of commerce.

I will not attempt, sir, to convey to you all my gratitude for the fraternal welcome I received in your midst. I want only to have the opportunity of demonstrating it by my acts, and it would make me happy to meet members of the League in France. I have already paid two visits to Mr. Taylor without being able to meet him.

I forgot to tell you that, since the letter from M. de Langsdorf is confidential and comes from a man in the public eye, it must be clearly understood that his name cannot be quoted in any journal.[97]

I assure you, my dear sir, of my sincere friendship. Please remember me to all our comrades in work and hope.

95. The German Zollverein (or customs union) was created in 1833 and based on the low Prussian tariff.

96. A Spanish translation of *Cobden and the League* appeared quickly: *Cobden y la Liga: La agitación inglesa en favor de la libertad de comercio,* translated by Elias Bautista y Muñoz (Madrid: Grabado de Don Baltasar González, 1847).

97. (Paillottet's note) I think that I should have no scruple in revealing the name of M. de Langsdorf publicly now. What criticism could he encounter now for secret sympathies expressed in favor of free trade nineteen years ago?

46. Letter to Richard Cobden

Mugron, 2 October 1845 [vol. 1, p. 111]

Whatever the charm, my dear sir, that your letters have just brought to me in my solitude, I would not allow myself to provoke them by such frequent obtrusiveness. However, an unforeseen circumstance has made it a duty for me to write to you.

I have met a young man in Paris circles who seemed to me to be full of heart and talent, whose name is Fonteyraud, the editor of *La Revue britannique*. He has written to me to offer to continue my work by inserting a follow-up of the operations of the League in the collection he is editing.[98] With this in mind, he wants to go to England to see your fine organization for himself and has asked me for letters of introduction to you and MM Bright and Wilson.[99] The object he has in view is too useful for me not to be quick to agree and I hope that, for your part, you would be willing to satisfy M. Fonteyraud's elevated curiosity.

However, in a second letter, he tells me that he has yet another aim which, according to him, would require effective, in other words, financial support from the League. I have been swift to tell M. Fonteyraud that I could not speak to you about a project about which I knew very little. I made it clear to him, moreover, that, according to me, any action carried out on public opinion in France that appeared to be directed and financed by England would be counterproductive since it would strengthen the deep-rooted prejudices that many adroit men have vested interests in exploiting. If therefore M. Fonteyraud makes his journey, would you, together with Messrs. Bright and Wilson, assess his projects for yourselves and consider me to be totally outside the undertaking he is considering? I hasten to leave this subject to reply to your affectionate letter of 23 September.

I am sorry to hear that your health is suffering from your immense workload, both private and public. Certainly, it could not be undermined for a finer cause; each of your pains will remind you of noble actions, but that would be small consolation and I would not dare to voice it to other than you, since to understand it one would need to have your self-sacrifice and devotion to the public good. But at last your work is reaching its target, you do not lack workers around you, and I hope that you will at last seek strength in repose.

---

98. Fonteyraud and Garnier, *Mélanges d'économie politique.*

99. Bastiat refers to two Wilsons in his correspondence. Here, Bastiat is most likely referring to George Wilson.

Since my last letter, a movement of which I had given up hope has started in the French press. All the Paris newspapers and very many provincial newspapers have reported on the demonstration against the Corn Laws, to mark my book. It is true that they have not understood its full implications, but at last public opinion has been woken up. This was the essential point, the one I was hoping for with my whole heart and it is a question now of not allowing it to fall back into indifference, and if there is anything I can do about it, that will not happen.

Your letter arrived the day after we had an election. It was a courtier who was elected.[100] I was not even a candidate. The electors are imbued with the idea that their votes are a precious gift, an important and personal service. This being so, they expect their vote to be personally solicited. They do not wish to understand that a parliamentary mandate is their own affair, that they will suffer the consequences of trust that is well or badly placed and consequently it is up to them to give it with discernment, without waiting for it to be solicited or wrested from them. For my part, I had taken the decision to stay in my corner and, as I expected, I was left there. Probably, in a year, we will have general elections in France. I doubt whether in the intervening period the electors will have come round to more appropriate ideas. However, a considerable number of them appear to have decided to support me. My efforts in favor of our wine-producing industry will give me an effective name of which I can make use. For this reason, I am pleased to see that you were willing to second the views I set out in the letter that the *League* has quoted.[101] If you could arrange for this journal to support the principle of ad valorem rights to be applied to wine, this would give my candidature a solid and honorable base. In fact, in my circumstances, being a deputy is a heavy charge, but the hope of contributing to the formation of a nucleus of *free traders* within our parliament comes before all personal considerations. When I think that, in our two chambers, there is not a single man who dares to acknowledge the principle of free trade, who understands its full significance, or who is capable of supporting it against the sophisms of monopoly, I must admit that, in the depths of my heart, I want to win the empty seat I see in our legislative body, although I do not want to do anything that would increasingly distort the dominant ideas relating to elections. Let us try to be worthy of their confidence and not to gain it by surprise.

Thank you for the judicious advice you have given me by indicating the

---

100. Marie Gustave Larnac. See "On Parliamentary Reform," p. 367.

101. *OC*, vol. 1, p. 387, "De l'avenir du commerce des vins entre la France et la Grande-Bretagne."

procedure for disseminating economic doctrines you think would be best suited to the situation in our country. Yes, you are right, I can see that here light has to be diffused from top to bottom. Instructing the masses is an impossible task, because they have neither the civic right, the habit, nor the liking for grand rallies and public discussion. This is one more reason for me to aim to gain contact with the most enlightened and influential classes *through* becoming a deputy.

I am very pleased to hear that you have good news from the United States.[102] I was not expecting this. America is lucky to speak the same language as the League. It will not be possible for its monopolists to withhold your arguments and work from the knowledge of the general public. I would like you to tell me, when you have the opportunity to write to me, which American journal is the most faithful representative of the economist school.[103] The circumstances of this country are analogous with ours and the *free-trade* movement in the United States could not fail to produce a good and strong impression in France if it were widely known. To save time, would you please take out a one-year subscription for me and ask M. Fonteyraud to reimburse you? It would be easier for me to reimburse him than to send it to you.

I accept with great pleasure your offer to *exchange* one of your letters for two of mine. I consider that you are sacrificing here again the *fallacy* of *reciprocity,* since I will certainly be the winner and you will not receive *equal value*. In view of how busy you are, I would have been ready to undertake to write to you three times. If ever I become a deputy, we will renew the bases of our contract.

---

47. Letter to [D.] Potonié[104]

Mugron, 24 October 1845   [From the private collection of Jean-Claude Paul-Dejean]

Dear Sir,

The most kind letter that you have been good enough to write to me has revived in me old projects and hopes, which cost me a great deal to abandon. Long before I knew of the existence of the English League, I had conceived

102. The tariff of 1842 was heavier than that of 1832. It was reduced in 1846.
103. *Les Économistes.*
104. The only Potonié that the editor could find is D. Potonié, who wrote *Note sur l'organisation facultative des débouchés de l'industrie parisienne.*

the idea of forming an association against protectionism, this absurd system which, apart from the direct harm it causes, causes so many ancillary calamities, national hatreds, wars, standing armies, navies, taxes, restrictions, plunderings, etc. As I needed a fulcrum to set up my lever, I thought of our wine-producing population, which seemed to me to be the most likely to embrace the cause of free trade. I tried to form it into an organization, as you will see from the brochure which it is my pleasure to enclose with this letter. My mistake was to address this call to a single class only, and the class that is probably the least political, the most dispersed, and the most difficult to organize. I ought to have called together all the consumers and in addition all the producers who felt they were sufficiently strong and honest to reject all forms of protection and taxes, for however you look at them, protectionist duties are none other than the taxes we raise from one another.

This frustrated idea was just dormant in my mind, and you can doubtless guess with what joy and enthusiasm I welcomed the arrival of the English League, which pursues the same aim with an energy, a spirit of togetherness, a line of conduct and the talents, resources, and opportunities that I lacked.

I have now been happy to learn from your letter of the existence in Paris of elements which, when they are properly put into operation, may serve as the basis for a similar association to the League. The men who have devoted themselves to the setting up of what is known as "The Articles of Paris"[105] are certainly the most appropriate people to lay the foundations for this institution. At the heart of enlightened opinion, close to one another, and in a position to exert an influence on the press, on our political representatives, and on public opinion; more disposed than most to make well-judged sacrifices and more able to supervise the use made of them, they certainly have to offer quite different resources from the wine-producing population. Besides, these people would have only to glimpse this center of action to join it in full sympathy. I believe that we will soon also obtain the support of men in the government, as they receive fixed salaries that bear the weight of the protectionist regime without any possible compensation. I would say the same thing about bankers, traders, merchants, lawyers, doctors, and all the countless sectors of artisans whose work by its very nature is not likely to be protected by customs duties.

---

105. "The Articles of Paris" industry covered a wide range of luxury items, from leather goods to jewelry and fashion. They exported quite well.

I see from your letter that "The Articles of Paris" has already formed a general association divided into sections, one of the most important of which is under your chairmanship. If you consider, sir, that it is possible to find the seed of an energetic league in this institution, and if you think that my efforts and devotion can help in this great work, please write to me and you will find me ready to join you and your colleagues. I have already sounded out a few key figures, for in France they are necessary if one is to succeed in anything, and I know some who would be only too ready to welcome the honor of the initiative. For my part, I will join the combat at whatever level I am placed, for apart from the fact that I put our noble cause a thousand times higher than our little individual ideas, I have learned from Mr. Cobden, the one man in the world in whom I have the fullest confidence, that individual self-sacrifice is the soul and cement of any voluntary association. Let us, therefore, make ourselves small and give free rein to the conceit of others, and use this quotation from Danton as a commentary: "Let our memory perish and may freedom triumph."

As for a demonstration to the League, I do not see where this would lead. What would be genuinely and immediately useful would be for "The Articles of Paris" to have a representative in London while Parliament is sitting. In the midst of this collapse of duties which is taking place in England, a man who had the confidence of the members of the League who have great influence in these matters might perhaps obtain considerable advantages for "The Articles of Paris," especially since England is no longer asking for reciprocity or what are called concessions. We do have an ambassador, but it is not possible to deal with things like this officially, and this you will readily understand. . . . As Great Britain is accomplishing this reform without asking anything from foreigners, she cannot accept foreigners' attempts to influence her resolutions.

When I was in London and enjoying quite close relations with officers in the Board of Trade and members of the League, I sought to convince them that they would be acting shrewdly by encouraging the introduction of our wine into their country. The spirit of my lectures on this subject is set out in the brochures I am enclosing, and I had the pleasure of receiving letters from Cobden and other members of Parliament telling me that they were working hard to make my ideas succeed; what I said to them with regard to wine might equally apply to Parisian goods. England feels that if she opened her market to Parisian goods without France lowering her duties, Parisians would have trouble effecting purchases from England in return, and this would soon open their eyes to the inconsistency of our policy and foment in us the spirit of free trade. I do not doubt that she is aiming her reforms in this direction. For my part, sir (and I hope that you will not find this confidence out of place), I must say that I deeply regret that my financial situation does not allow me to spend time in London at this time. Something tells me that I could do some good there.

Allow me, sir, in ending this overlong letter, to thank you for your kind words both in your own name and that of your sons and colleagues.

I am, sir, your devoted servant.

---

48. Letter to Richard Cobden

Mugron, 13 December 1845 [vol. 1, p. 115]

My dear sir, I am greatly in your debt, since you were willing, in the midst of your noble and arduous work, to relax the agreement which I had gratefully accepted of "one letter for two," but I unfortunately have only too many excuses to invoke and while all your time is so usefully devoted to the public good, mine has been absorbed by the greatest and most personal grief that I might suffer on this earth.[106]

I was delaying writing to you to have news of M. Fonteyraud. I needed to know in what terms I should thank you for your welcoming him on my recommendation. I had total peace of mind in this, as I had heard indirectly that he was delighted with his trip and enthusiastic about the members of the League. I am pleased to learn that the members of the League were no less pleased with him. Although I did not know him very well, I considered that he had it in him to be his own recommendation. Doubtless, he has not had the opportunity to write to me yet.

On this subject, you have returned to my visit to you and the excuses you express to me leave me quite embarrassed. Except for the first two days when, for unforeseen reasons, I found myself alone in Manchester and when my morale was undoubtedly afflicted by the sad influence of your strange weather (an influence whose expression I allowed to emerge in the unfortunate note to which you refer), with the exception of these two days, as I have said, I was overwhelmed by the care and kindnesses expressed by you and your friends, Messrs. John and Thomas Bright, Paulton, Wilson,

---

106. (Paillottet's note) The death of a relative.

Smith,[107] Ashworth, Evans, and many more, and I would be truly ungrateful if, because there was an election in Cambridge during these two days, I remembered only this moment of *spleen*[108] and forgot those which you imbued with goodwill and charm. You can be sure, my dear sir, that our dinner in Chorley and your eminently instructive meeting with Mr. Dyer at Mr. Thomas Bright's have left indelible memories in my mind and heart. You want me to make another visit. That is not entirely impossible and this is how it might be arranged. It is probable that the big question will be settled this summer, and, like a valiant fighter, you will need to take a little rest and bind your wounds. Since words have been your principal arms, their means of expression in you will have suffered the most, and you have made reference to your state of health in your last letter. It so happens that in the Pyrenees over here there are marvelous springs to cure exhausted chests and larynxes. So come and spend a season as part of the family in the Pyrenees. I promise you either to come to collect you or to accompany you back, at your choice. This trip will not be detrimental to the cause. You will see our wine-producing population and will gain an idea of the spirit that animates it or rather that does not animate it. When we pass through Paris, I will introduce you to all our comrades in political economy and rational philanthropy. I like to think that this trip would leave its beneficial traces in your health and memories, and also in shifting French attitudes about freeing up trade. Bordeaux is also a town which it would interest you to see. People's minds there are quick and enthusiastic; just a spark will set them ablaze, and this might well come from your words.

Thank you, my dear sir, for the offer you made me regarding my translation. Permit me, however, not to accept it. It is a personal sacrifice which you wish to add to so many others and I must not agree to it.

I feel that the title of my book does not allow you to claim any influence on the part of the *League*. This being so, let us allow my poor volume to live or die by itself. However, I cannot be sorry that, in France, I attached your name to the history of this great movement. In doing this, I may have upset your worthy colleagues a little and this involuntary injustice gives me some cause for remorse. But truly, to arouse and catch attention here, it is necessary for a doctrine to be incarnated in an individual personality and for a great movement to be represented and summarized in an individual

107. John Benjamin Smith.
108. In English in the original.

name. Without the great figure of O'Connell, the Irish unrest would have taken place unnoticed in our newspapers. And look what has happened. The French press now uses your name to designate the orthodox principle in political economy. It is an ellipsis, a shorthand method of speaking. It is true that this principle is still the subject of much dispute, and even sarcasm. But it will grow and commensurately your name will grow with it. The human mind is made like this. It needs flags, banners, incarnations, and individual names, and in France more than elsewhere. Who knows whether your destiny will not arouse in our country the emulation of some man of genius?

I have no need to tell you with what interest and anxiety I follow the development of your *campaign.* I regret that Sir Robert Peel has let himself be overtaken. His personal superiority and position make him able to provide services to the cause that are more immediately achievable, perhaps, than those it can expect from Russell, and I fear that the arrival of a Whig government will result in the reassembly of a formidable aristocratic opposition which will prepare new conflicts for you.

You are good enough to ask me what I do in my solitude. Alas, dear sir, I am embarrassed to have to reply with this shameful word, *Nothing.* The pen tires me and speech even more so, to the extent that if a few useful thoughts ferment in my head I have no longer any means of revealing them externally. I sometimes think of our unfortunate André Chénier. When he was on the scaffold, he turned to the people and said, striking himself on the forehead, "It is a pity, I had something there." And I too think that "I have something there." But who is whispering this thought to me? Is it the consciousness of a genuine truth? Is it fatuous pride? For which idiotic hack today does not think he also "has something there"?

Farewell, my dear sir; permit me to shake your hand most affectionately across the distance that separates us.

P.S. I have frequent contact with Madrid and it would be easy for me to send a copy of my translation there.

---

49. Letter to Alcide Fonteyraud

Mugron, 20 December 1845   [vol.1, p. 194]

My dear M. Fonteyraud, I will not reply today to your letter, a letter that is so charming, so honest and interesting in terms of the subjects it discusses with me and the way it deals with them. This is just a simple acknowledgment, which I am entrusting to a person who is leaving in a few hours for Paris.

I received news of you through the journal of the League, from M. Guillaumin and Mr. Cobden, who speaks of you in terms that I will not repeat to you for fear of wounding your modesty.... However, I am changing my mind. Mr. Cobden will one day be sufficiently famous for you to be very happy to know the opinion he has uttered of you. Moreover, this judgment includes a piece of advice, and I have no right to stop it on its way, especially since you persist in giving me the title of *Master*. I will fulfill the functions of this role once, if not by giving you advice, at least by passing on to you that emanating from an authority regarded as very impressive by the disciples of *free trade*.

These then are the words of Mr. Cobden:

> "Let me thank you for introducing to us M. Fonteyraud, who excited our admiration not only by his superior talents, but by the warmth of his zeal in the cause of free trade. I have rarely met a young man of his age possessing so much knowledge and so mature a judgment both as respects *men* and *things*. If he be preserved from the temptations which beset the path of young men of literary pursuits in Paris" (whether Mr. Cobden is alluding to the schools of sentimentality or the traps of the partisan spirit, I do not know), "he possesses the ability to render himself very useful in the cause of humanity."[109]

As the rest concerns only your amour propre, permit me to omit it.

It is sweet and consoling to go through life supported by such a testimonial. There is really something deep in our heart which tells us of our own merit, but when we see the blindness of all men to this, how can we ever have the certainty that the awareness of our strengths is its true measure? In your case, you have been judged and consecrated; you have been dedicated to the cause of humanity. *Learn and disseminate* should be your motto; such is your destiny.

Oh! How my heart beat when I read your description of the great meeting in Manchester! Like you, I felt enthusiasm penetrate my every pore. Has anything like this, whatever Solomon said, been seen under the sun? We have seen major gatherings of men grow passionate for a conquest, a victory, an interest, or the triumph of brute force, but has anyone ever seen ten thou-

---

109. The parts of this paragraph in quotation marks are in English in the original.

sand men unite to ensure the triumph of a major principle of universal justice by peaceful means, through speech and sacrifice? Even if free trade were
an error or an illusion, the League would be no less glorious, for it has given
the world the most powerful and moral of all instruments of civilization.
How can we not see that this concerns not merely the liberation of trade
but in turn all the reforms and acts of justice and reparation that humanity
might carry out by means of these massive and vibrant organizations!

For this reason, with what happiness, I might almost say, with what outbursts of joy did I welcome the news you gave me at the end of your letter! France also will have her League! France will grow out of her eternal
adolescence, blush at the shameful puerility in which she is vegetating, and
become an adult! Oh! Let this day come and I will salute it as the finest in
my life. Will we never cease to attribute glory to the development of physical
force, to wish to settle all matters by the sword and glorify only that courage
shown on the battlefield, whatever its motives and works? Will we finally
understand that, since *public opinion is the monarch of the world,* it is public
opinion that we have to work on and to which we have to communicate the
enlightenment which shows it the right direction together with the energy
to take it?

But after enthusiasm comes reflection. I tremble lest some disastrous
germ infiltrate the beginnings of our League, for example a spirit of compromise, gradualness, procrastination, or caution. Everything will be lost if the
League does not espouse or stick closely to an *absolute principle.* How could
members of the League themselves agree if the League tolerated variable
principles in varying degrees? And if they did not agree among themselves,
what influence could they have outside?

Even if we should be only twenty, ten, or five, let that twenty, ten, or five
have the same goal, the same determination, and the same faith. You have
witnessed the campaign in England, I have myself studied it closely, and I
know (and this I ask you to convey clearly to our friends) that if the League
had made the slightest concession at any time in its existence, the aristocracy
would have made short work of it a long time ago.

Therefore, let an association be formed in France. Let it undertake to free
trade and industry from any monopoly. Let it devote itself to ensuring the
triumph of the principle and you may count on my support. By word, pen,
and purse, I will be its man. If it means legal proceedings, suffering persecution, or braving ridicule, I will be its man. Whatever role I am given, whatever rank I am allocated, on the hustings or in cabinet, I will be its man. In

enterprises of this kind, in France more than elsewhere, what is to be feared are rivalries based on amour propre; amour propre is the first sacrifice that we have to make on the altar of public good. I am mistaken; perhaps indifference and apathy are greater dangers. Since this project has been set up do not let it fail. Oh! Why am I not with you?

I was going to end my letter without thanking you in advance for what you will be saying about my publication in *La Revue britannique.* A simple translation cannot be worth such fulsome praise. Be that as it may, praise and criticism are welcome when they are sincere.

Farewell, your affectionate friend.

---

50. Letter to Richard Cobden

Mugron, 13 January 1846   [vol.1, p. 118]

My dear sir, what gratitude do I not owe you for having been good enough to think of me in the midst of such pressing occupations, ones so conducive to absorbing your interest so compellingly? You wrote to me on the 23rd, the very day of that astonishing meeting in Manchester, which certainly has no precedent in history. May the people of Lancashire be honored! It is not only *free trade* that the world will owe them, but also the enlightened, moral, and devoted art of campaigning. Humanity will at last recognize the *instrument* of all reform. At the same time I received your letter, the issue of the *Manchester Guardian* with an article on this session arrived. As I had seen the report of your first meeting in Manchester a few days previously in *Le Courrier français,* I thought that public opinion had now been awakened in France, and I did not think it necessary to translate *the report of your proceedings.* I am now annoyed that I did not do so, since I see that this *major event* has not produced an impression commensurate with its importance here.

How I congratulate you a thousandfold, my dear sir, for having refused an official position in the Whig cabinet.[110] This is not to say that you would not be very capable and worthy of power. It is not even that you could not render considerable service. But in the century in which we are, we are so imbued with the idea that whoever appears to devote himself to the public good is in fact working for his own benefit. There is so little understanding of devotion to a principle that no one can believe in disinterestedness, and you will certainly do more good through this example of selflessness and the moral effect it will have on people's minds than you would have been able to

---

110. Vice president of the Board of Trade.

do on the ministerial bench. I would have liked to embrace you, my dear sir, when you taught me, through this conduct, that your heart is equal to your intelligence. Your noble actions will not go unrewarded; you are in a country in which public probity is not discouraged through ridicule.

Since we are talking about devotion, this will lead me on to the other part of your good letter. You advise me to go to Paris. I, myself, feel that at this decisive moment I should be at my post. My own interest as well as that of the cause requires this. For the last two months, our newspapers have been serving up a pile of nonsense on the League, which they would not be able to do if I were in Paris, as I would not let one of these escape without battling with it. On the other hand, since I am better informed than many others on the influence of your movement, I would acquire a certain authority in the eyes of the public. I can see all this, but I languish in a village in the *département* of the Landes. Why? I think I have mentioned this in one of my letters. I have an honorable and uneventful, although modest situation here.[111] In Paris, I could earn my living only by my pen, something I do not criticize in others but to which I have an inexpressible aversion. I therefore have to live and die in my corner, like Prometheus on his rock.

Perhaps you will have some idea of the mental suffering I am experiencing when I tell you that we tried to organize a *League* in Paris. This attempt has failed and was bound to fail. The proposal was put forward during a dinner with twenty people at which two ex-ministers were present. You can imagine how much success that was likely to have! Among the guests, one wanted ½ freedom, another ¼ freedom, yet another ⅛ freedom, and perhaps three of four were ready to request freedom *in principle*. Just try to make a united and fervent association out of that! If I had been in Paris, a mistake like that would never have been made. I have made too close a study of what constitutes the strength and success of your organization. A vital League cannot spring up from a group of men gathered together randomly. As I wrote to M. Fonteyraud, let us be ten, five, or even two if necessary, but let us raise the flag of absolute freedom and absolute principle, and let us wait for those with the same faith to join us. If chance had caused me to be born with a more consistent fortune, with an income of ten to twelve thousand francs, there would have been a League in France right now, doubtless more than somewhat weak but bearing within it the two mightiest principles of truth and dedication.

On your recommendation, I have offered my services to M. Buloz. If he

---

111. Justice of the peace in the county of Mugron.

had made me responsible for an article to be included in *La Revue des deux mondes,* I would have continued the absorbing story of the *League* up to the end of the ministerial crisis. But he did not even send me a reply. I very much fear that these newspaper editors see the most important events only as an opportunity to satisfy the curiosity of their *subscribers,* ready to shout, depending on the event, "Long live the king, long live the League!"

The Chamber of Commerce of Bordeaux has just raised the banner of free trade. Unfortunately, it has taken a text, *Customs Union between France and Belgium,* that is in my view too restricted. I will send them a letter in which I will endeavor to show them that they would have much more power if they espoused the cause of the *principle* and not that of a special application to this or that treaty. It is the *fallacy* of reciprocity which paralyzes the efforts of this chamber. Treaties smile on it because it sees the possible stipulation of *reciprocal benefits, reciprocal concessions,* and even *reciprocal sacrifices.* Under this liberal veneer, the disastrous thought still lies hidden that imports are an evil in themselves and should be tolerated only when foreigners have been persuaded to tolerate our *exports* in their turn. As a model to be followed, I would enclose with my letter a copy of the famous deliberation of the *Chamber of Commerce* of Manchester on 13th and 20th December 1838.[112] Why does the Chamber of Commerce of Bordeaux not take the generous initiative in France that the Chamber of Commerce of Manchester took in England?

As I know how extensive your commitments are, I scarcely dare to ask you to write to me. Nevertheless, please remember from time to time that your letters are the most effective balm for soothing the boredom of my solitude and the torments arising from my feeling of uselessness.

---

51. Letter to Richard Cobden

Mugron, 9 February 1846   [vol. 1, p. 122]

My dear sir, when you receive this letter you will be in the *line of fire*[113] of the discussion. I hope, however, that you will find a moment for our country, France, for in spite of the interesting things you tell me about the state of

112. At the 13 December 1838 meeting, the president of the chamber of commerce, Mr. Wood, criticized the Corn Laws but wanted to let the Whig government of John Russell modify them. Instead, Cobden was in favor of a total and immediate repeal.

113. Discussion of the Corn Bill in the Commons.

affairs in your country, I will not discuss them. I would have nothing to say about them and would waste precious time in expressing feelings of admiration and happiness of which you have no doubt. Let us therefore discuss France. But before we do, I want to put an end to the English question. I have seen nothing in your *Peel's measure* that relates to wine. This is certainly a major fault in terms of political economy and public policy. A final vestige *of the policy of reciprocal treaties* is to be found in this omission, as well as that in the case of *timber*. This is a stain on Sir Robert Peel's project, and it will detract hugely from the moral effect of the whole, precisely on the classes, in France and in the north, who were the most disposed to accept this elevated teaching. This omission and the sentence "We shall beat all other nations" are fuel for the game of prejudice; they will feast on them for a long time. They will see in them the secret and Machiavellian ideas of *perfidious Albion*. Please, put forward an amendment. However great the absolutism of Sir Robert Peel, he could not resist your arguments.

I have now returned to France (from which I have scarcely departed). The more I reflect, the more I have reason to congratulate myself on one thing that at first caused me some anxiety. It is having included your name in the title of my book. Your name has now become popular in my country, and with your name, so has your cause. I am snowed under with letters. I am asked for details, newspapers open their columns to me, and the Institut de France has elected me a corresponding member with MM Guizot and Duchâtel voting for me. I am not blind enough to attribute this success to myself; I owe it to the relevance of the case and to the fact that the right time has come, and I appreciate it, not for my own sake but as a means of being useful. You will be surprised that all of this has not persuaded me to take up residence in Paris. This is the reason. Bordeaux is preparing a major demonstration, too large in my opinion, as it will include a great many people who think they are *free traders* and who are no more free traders than Mr. Knatchbull. I consider that my role at this time is to put to good use my knowledge of the methods of the *League,* and to ensure that our association is based on solid foundations. Perhaps you will be sent the issue of *Le Mémorial bordelais* in which I have included a series of articles on this subject.[114] I insist and will continue to insist to the end that our League, like yours, be devoted to an absolute principle and if I do not succeed in doing this I will abandon it.

---

114. *OC,* vol. 7, p. 30, "Projet de ligue anti-protectioniste" and the following two essays.

This is what I am afraid of. In demanding a *wise* freedom and *moderate* protection, we are sure to gain a great deal of sympathy in Bordeaux and that will please the founders. But where will all this lead? To the Tower of Babel. It is the actual principle of protection that I wish to breach. Until this business is settled, I will not go to Paris. I have been told that a meeting of forty to fifty traders will be taking place in Bordeaux. It is there that the bases for a league will be established, on which I have been invited to give my opinion. Do you remember that we have searched in vain for your *rule* in the *Anti–Bread Tax Circular?* How I regret now that we were not able to find it! If Mr. Paulton could spend an hour looking for it, the time would not be wasted, for I fear that our League might adopt shaky founding principles. After this session, there will be a grand *meeting* at the Exchange to raise a *League fund.* The mayor of Bordeaux has taken up his position at the head of the movement.

I have heard about the address you received from the Société d'économie politique[115] but I have not read it. I hope it is worthy of you and our cause!

I beg your pardon for talking at such length about France, but you will understand that the weak cries it utters are almost as interesting to me as the virile accents of Sir Robert.

Once the business in Bordeaux is settled, I will go to Paris. The hope that you will visit has made my decision for me.

I will draw up a plan for the distribution of fifty copies of my translation.

----

52. Letter to Richard Cobden

Bordeaux, February 1846 [vol. 1, p. 124]

My dear sir, you will doubtless be interested to learn that a demonstration is taking place in Bordeaux in favor of *free trade.* The association has now been constituted. The mayor of Bordeaux has been appointed its president. Before long, the subscription list will be opened and we hope that this will produce about a hundred thousand francs. This is a fine result. I dare not hold out a great deal of hope and fear that our somewhat timid beginnings may raise obstacles for us later. We did not dare set out the principle boldly. We limit ourselves to saying that the association demands the abolition of

115. Cobden's address (to a banquet held in his honor) can be found in *Annales de la Société,* vol. 1, 1846–53.

protectionist dues *as quickly as possible.* In this way, the question of gradual progress has been retained and your *total and immediate* could not be passed. In view of people's lack of intellectual development in this respect, it would have been useless to insist, and it is to be hoped that the association, whose aim is to enlighten others, will have the effect of enlightening itself.

When this matter has been settled, I am determined to go to Paris. I have received several letters, which give me to understand that the huge sector of industry entitled "Articles of Paris"[116] is ready to start a movement. I thought that my duty lay in setting aside any personal reasons I had for staying in my corner. I assure you that I am making a sacrifice to the cause whose merit lies in its lack of visibility.

In the last month, my book[117] has had an extraordinary success in Bordeaux. The prophetic tone with which I announced the reform has given me a reputation that I scarcely merit, since all I have had to do is be the echo of the League. I am taking advantage of it nevertheless, for advertising purposes. When I am in Paris, I will take advice to see whether it would not be appropriate to produce a second edition in a *low-cost* format. I am sure that the association in Bordeaux will come to my aid if need be. You would spare me a great deal of work if you would suggest two speeches by MM Bright, Villiers, and others after consulting them. This would avoid my having to reread the three volumes of the *League.* I need these men to indicate the speeches in which they dealt with the question from the highest and most general point of view, and where they refuted the most universally held *fallacies,* especially *reciprocity.* I will add comments, statistical information, and portraits. Lastly, I also need you to indicate a few parliamentary sessions, especially the stormiest ones, in which *free traders* were attacked the most relentlessly. A work like this, sold for three francs,[118] will do more than ten treatises on economics. You cannot imagine the good that the first edition did in Bordeaux.

I cannot help deploring the fact that your *prime minister* let slip the opportunity of arousing astonishment in Europe. If, instead of saying, "I need new subsidies to increase our army and navy forces," he had said, "Since we are adopting the principle of free trade, there can no longer be any question

116. See Letter 47, note 105.
117. *Cobden and the League.*
118. The sale price of *Cobden and the League* was 7.5 francs; *Economic Sophisms* was 4 francs.

of *outlets* and colonies. We will give up Oregon[119] and even perhaps Canada. Our disputes with the United States will disappear and I am proposing that we reduce our army and navy." If he had said this, the effect would have been as great a difference between this speech and the treatises on economics, which we are still reduced to producing, as between the sun and treatises on light. Europe would have been converted within a year and England would have won on *three* fronts. I will not list them as I am overcome by tiredness.

---

53. Letter to Félix Coudroy

Bordeaux, 19 February 1846   [vol. 1, p. 65]

My dear Félix, I had promised to write to you about the events in Bordeaux. I have been so interrupted by visits, meetings, and other annoying incidents that the time for postal collections always arrives before I have been able to honor my promise; what is more, there is not much to tell you. Things are happening very slowly. We floundered about a great deal while settling the first stages of a *constitution*. Finally a makeshift version emerged from the discussion, and today it is being offered for the approval of seventy to eighty founding members. The final board will be installed with the mayor[120] at its head as president, and in two or three days a grand meeting will take place to open the subscription list. It is thought that Bordeaux will raise one hundred thousand francs.[121] I am longing to see it. You understand that it is only from today, when the board has been installed, that attention can be paid to a plan, since it is the board that should take this initiative. What will the plan be like? I do not know.

As for my personal contribution, it is limited to being present at the sessions, writing a few articles for newspapers,[122] paying and receiving visits, and dealing with economic objections of all kinds. It has been made very clear to me that the level of education in this matter is not sufficient to keep the institution going and I would be leaving with no hope if I did not count on the institution itself to enlighten its own members.

---

119. In 1818, under the "Indivision Treaty," in Oregon, British and American citizens had the same hunting, fishing, navigation, and circulation rights. The treaty was renewed in 1827 and canceled in 1846.
120. Martin Duffour-Dubergier.
121. It raised fifty-six thousand francs.
122. Articles published in *Le Mémorial bordelais* of 8, 9, 10, and 11 February.

Here I found my poor *Cobden* all the fashion. A month ago, there were only two copies, the one I gave Eugène[123] and the copy at the bookseller's; today, it is to be found everywhere. I would be embarrassed, my dear Félix, to tell you what an opinion has been formed of the author. Some suppose that I am a first-rate scholar, and others that I have spent my life in England studying its institutions and history. In short, I am very embarrassed at my position, since I know full well the difference between what is true and what is exaggerated in this current view. I do not know whether you will see today's *Mémorial*[124] (the 18th); you will understand that I would not have used this tone if I had not had a clear view of what I could achieve.

It has almost been decided that, when this organization is fully on its feet, I will go to Paris to try to rally Parisian industry, which I know is well disposed toward us. If this is successful, I foresee one difficulty, and that is to persuade the people in Bordeaux to send their money to Paris. It is certain, however, that Paris is the center from which everything must radiate, since, on the basis of the same expenditure, the Paris press has ten times more influence than the provincial press.

When you write to me (as soon as possible, please) tell me about your personal situation.

---

54. Letter to Victor Calmètes

Bayonne, 4 March 1846   [vol. 1, p. 13]

My good, long-standing friend, your letter warmed my heart, and reading it, it seemed to me that there were twenty-five years fewer hanging around my neck. I was drawn back to those happy days when our being arm in arm reflected our cordial relationship. Twenty-five years! Alas! The weight of them has quickly made itself felt again.

.   .   .   .

I think that in itself, my appointment as a corresponding member of the Institute[125] is of little importance, and I greatly fear that many mediocre people have been able to adorn themselves with this title. However, the particular circumstances leading to my nomination do not allow me to refuse your friendly congratulations. I had published only one book, and in this

123. Eugène de Monclar.
124. *Le Mémorial bordelais.*
125. Institut de France.

book only the preface was my work. Once I had returned to my solitude, this preface worked in my favor, unknown to me, since the same letter, which informed me of my appointment, announced my candidature. Never in my life had I thought of this honor.

This book is entitled *Cobden and the League.* I am sending it to you with this letter, which spares me from having to tell you about it. In 1842 and 1843, I endeavored to attract attention to the subject it covers. I sent articles to *La Presse, Le Mémorial bordelais,* and other newspapers. They were refused. I saw that my cause had been utterly destroyed by a *conspiracy of silence* and I had no other solution but to produce a book. This is how I came to be an author without knowing it. Now I have embarked on a career and I sincerely regret it; although I have always liked *political economy,* it is at a cost to myself to give it all my attention, which I like to allow to roam freely over all the subjects of human knowledge. What is more, in this economic science, just one question sweeps me along and will be absorbing me: the freedom of international relations; for perhaps you have seen that I have been assigned a role in the association that has just been formed in Bordeaux. Such is our century; you cannot become involved without being strangled in the bonds of specialization.

. . . I forgot to tell you about the elections. The electors in my region are thinking about me but we are snubbing one another. I claim that their choice is their affair and not mine, and that consequently I have nothing to ask them for. They absolutely insist that I should go and canvas their votes, doubtless in order to gain some right over my time and services, with personal aims. You can see that we do not agree and therefore I will not be nominated.

Farewell, dear Calmètes;
your devoted friend.

---

55. Letter to Richard Cobden

Paris, 16 March 1846 [vol. 1, p. 126]

My dear sir, I have waited a few days to reply to your fine and instructive letter. It is not because I did not have a great deal to tell you, but I had no time; even today, I am writing only to let you know that I am arriving in Paris. If I had had any hesitation in coming, the hope you give me of seeing you there soon would have been enough to persuade me.

Bordeaux is really in a state of uproar. It has been *fashionable* to be associated with this work and I have found it impossible to follow my plan, which was to limit the association to the *converted*. I was overwhelmed by the *furia francese*. I can see that this will be a significant obstacle in the future, since already, when we wanted to petition the chambers to establish our claims, deep divisions came to the fore. In spite of this, we read and study, and that is a great deal. I am counting on the uproar itself to enlighten those who are creating it. Their aim is to educate others, and they will end by educating themselves.

As I arrived yesterday evening, I cannot give you any news in this letter. I would prefer a thousandfold to form a core of deeply persuaded men than generate a noisy demonstration like that in Bordeaux. I know that people are already talking about *moderation, gradual reforms,* and *experiments.* If I can, I will advise those people to form an association among themselves on these lines and leave us to form another in the domain of the abstract and absolute principle of *no protection,*[126] as I am deeply convinced that ours will absorb theirs.

----

56. Letter to Félix Coudroy

Paris, 22 March 1846   [vol. 1, p. 66]

My dear Félix, I hope that you will not delay giving me your news. God willing, an arrangement has been found: I scarcely hope for it and want it desperately. Once you are free from this painful preoccupation, you will be free to devote your time to useful things, for example, your article in *Le Mémorial,*[127] which I have had the time to read only quickly, but which I will reread tomorrow at my uncle's. It is extremely lively and provides excellent and vivid arguments. On Monday, I will read it to the assembly, which will be quite numerous. When I am slightly better settled, I will tell you the name of the newspaper in Paris to which you should send it; at that stage, however, you should, as far as possible, refrain from mentioning wine. I have just mentioned that we were having an assembly on Monday. Its aim is to set up the board of the association. We have the duc d'Harcourt as president, and he accepted with a resolution which I liked. The other members will be MM Say, Blanqui, and Dunoyer. However, Dunoyer does not much like being in the spotlight, and I will be proposing in his place

126. In English in the original.
127. *Le Mémorial bordelais.*

M. Anisson-Duperron, a peer of France, whom I found compelling in that he is firm on the basic idea. As treasurer, we will have the baron d'Eichthal, a rich banker. Finally, a secretary, who obviously will be called upon to bear the brunt of the work, will join the management. No doubt you can foresee that these functions will fall on my shoulders. As always, I am hesitating. It will be hard work binding myself to such an arduous and assiduous task. On the other hand, I think I can be useful by devoting myself entirely to this business. Between now and Monday I must make an irrevocable decision. Besides, I hope that we will not lack subscribers. Peers, deputies, bankers, and men of letters will flock to us in sufficient numbers, and even a few major manufacturers. It seems clear that there has been a significant change in public opinion and success is perhaps not as far off as we first supposed.

Here, people very much want me to be nominated as a deputy; you cannot imagine how much credit I received for the quasi-prophecy contained in my *introduction*.[128] It confuses and embarrasses me, as I am certain that I do not match up to my reputation, but I have very little hope with regard to becoming a deputy, since the events in Bordeaux and Paris have very little echo in Saint-Sever. And, incidentally, this would perhaps be a further reason for keeping me at a distance. Dear old Chalosse[129] does not appear to understand the importance of the enterprise to which I have devoted my efforts; if this were not the case, it is probable that it would want to join in by increasing my influence in its own interest. I do not bear it any grudge; I love it and will serve it to the end, however indifferent it is.

Today, I made my entry into the Institut,[130] where they discussed the question of education. University professors, led by Cousin, monopolized the discussion. I am very sorry I have left my work on the subject in Mugron, as I can see that no one considers it from our point of view.

Try from time to time to write articles to maintain the sacred flame in Bordeaux. Later we can doubtless make them into a collection to be distributed in large numbers. In my next letter to my aunt, I will add a note to tell you what they thought of your last article in the Assembly.

I am expecting our friend, Daguerre, in order to be introduced to M. de Lamenais, whom I hope to convert to *free trade*. M. de Lamartine has an-

---

128. To *Cobden and the League*.
129. Bastiat is referring affectionately to the Chalosse region of the Landes.
130. Institut de France.

nounced his membership, as has our good Béranger. We will be bringing in M. Berryer as well, as soon as the association is sufficiently strongly established not to be diverted by political passions. The same is true for Arago; you see that the leading minds of our time will be on our side. I have been assured that M. de Broglie will agree to be president. I must admit that I go in some fear of the diplomatic approach, which is bound to be his habit. His presence will doubtless have a prodigious effect from the start, but we must look to the future and not be dazzled by transitory brilliance.

---

57. Letter to Richard Cobden

Paris, 25 March 1846 [vol. 1, p. 127]

My dear sir, as soon as I received your letter, I handed over your reply to the address from our Société d'économie politique to M. Dunoyer. I have just translated it, and it appeared to contain nothing that might have unfortunate consequences if it were published. The only thing is that we do not have any clear idea on where we should publish this precious document. *Le Journal des économistes* will not be published until about 20 April. This is rather late. A significant number of newspapers are committed to the monopoly, many others to anglophobia, and many others again are worthless. An approach will be made to *Le Journal des débats*. I will tell you the result in a postscript. Certainly, there is nothing but pure, noble, true, and cosmopolitan sentiments in your letter, as in your heart. But our nation is so susceptible to, and also so imbued with, the idea that free trade is good for you but not for us, and that you adopted it *in part* through Machiavellianism and to inveigle us down this path; these ideas, as I say, are so prevalent and popular that I do not know whether the publication of your address will not be inopportune at the time we are forming an association. People will not fail to say that we are the dupes of perfidious Albion. Men who know that if *two and two are four* in England they do not make *three* in France laugh at these prejudices. However, I think it prudent to dissipate rather than confront them. This is why I will be submitting the question of publication to a few enlightened men whom I am meeting this evening and I will let you know tomorrow the result of this consultation.

I stressed the words *in part* for this reason: our principal point of support for the campaign is the commercial class, the traders. They earn their living by trade and they want as much of it as possible. They are also used to conducting business. Under this twin heading, they are our best auxiliaries. However, they support monopoly in one respect, the maritime aspect, protection for the national fleet, in a word, what is known as the *surtax*.[131]

However, it so happens that our shipowners are all taken with the idea that, in his financial plan, Sir Robert Peel has not amended your Navigation Act and that he has left the full force of protection on this; I leave you to imagine the consequences they are drawing from this. I seem to remember that Huskisson amended your Navigation Act. I have your tariff, and I do not see anywhere that goods carried by foreign ships are subject to differential taxes. I would like to be sure of this question, and if you do not have time to enlighten me, could you not ask Mr. Paulton or Mr. James Wilson to write a fairly detailed letter to me on this subject?

I will now tell you a little about our association. I am beginning to be a little discouraged by the difficulties, even physical ones, of doing anything in Paris. Distances are huge, you waste a lot of time in the streets, and in the ten days I have been here I have put only two hours to good use. I would decide to abandon the enterprise if I did not see some elements of usefulness. Peers, deputies, bankers, men of letters, all of whose names are well known throughout France, have agreed to join our society, but they do not want to take the first step. Even supposing we succeeded in bringing them together, I do not think we would be able to count on a very active contribution from people who are so busy, so carried away by the whirlwind of business and pleasure. But the sole mention of their names would have a considerable effect in France and would make it easier for similar and more practical associations to be founded in Marseilles, Lyons, Le Havre,[132] and Nantes. This is why I am resolved to waste two months here. What is more, the Paris society would have the advantage of giving a little courage to *free-trade* deputies, who, rejected by public opinion up to now, have not dared to admit their principles.

I have incidentally not lost sight of what you told me one day, that the movement, which was constructed from the bottom up in England, should be constructed from the top down in France, and for this reason I am delighted to see such major figures join us as Harcourt, Anisson-Dupéron, Pavée de Vandœuvre, and perhaps de Broglie among the peers; Eichthal,

131. An extra tax levied on goods imported into France on foreign ships.
132. Free-trade associations were effectively established in Marseilles (17 September 1846), Lyons (13 October 1846), and Le Havre (28 November 1846).

Vernes, Ganneron, and perhaps Rothschild among the bankers; and Lamartine, Lamenais, and Béranger among the men of letters. I am certainly far from believing that all these illustrious people have fixed opinions. It is instinct rather than a clear vision of the truth that guides them, but the very fact of their adhesion will commit them to our cause and oblige them to examine it. This is why I hold the cause dear, since without it I would prefer a wholly homogeneous association of a dozen followers who are free from commitments and unbound by the considerations that a name in politics imposes.

What factors sometimes make events great! Certainly if an opulent financier became devoted to the cause, or what would amount to the same thing, if a man who was profoundly persuaded and devoted had a huge fortune, the movement would quickly make progress. Today, for example, I know twenty prominent people who are watching each other, hesitating, and restrained only by the fear of tarnishing the brilliance of their name. If, instead of running from one to the other, on foot, mud spattered on my back, to meet one or two a day only and to obtain only evasive or dilatory replies, I could gather them round my table, in a sumptuous dining room, what difficulties would be overcome! Believe me, it is neither my spirit nor my heart that is failing. But I feel that this superb Babylon is not my place and I must make haste to return to my solitude and limit my contribution to a few articles in newspapers and some writing. Is it not strange that I should have reached the age at which hair goes gray, be a witness of the progress of luxury and repeat like the Greek philosopher,[133] "How many things there are that I do not need!" and that I should feel overwhelmed by ambition at my age? Ambition! I dare to say that this ambition is pure, and if my poverty makes me suffer, it is because it is an invincible obstacle to the progress of the cause.

Forgive me, my dear sir, for these outpourings from my heart. I am talking about myself when I should be discussing only public affairs with you.

Farewell; I remain always your affectionate and devoted servant.

---

58. Letter to Richard Cobden

Paris, 2 April 1846   [vol. 1, p. 130]

My dear sir, as I told you, your reply to the address of the Société d'économie politique will appear in the next issue of *Le Journal des écono-*

---

133. Socrates (469–399 B.C.E.).

mistes.[134] I hope it will produce a good effect. However, in view of the extreme susceptibility of our fellow citizens, it was deemed appropriate not to publish it in the daily press and to wait until our Paris association was on a firmer footing.

What we lack above all is a mouthpiece, a special journal, like the *League*. You will tell me that this must be a product of the association. However, I firmly believe that, to a certain extent, it is the association that will be the *product* of the journal; we do not have the means of communication and no accredited journal can provide us with one.

For this reason, I have thought about creating a weekly journal entitled *Libre échange.* I received the estimate for it yesterday evening. It can be established for an expenditure of 40,000 francs for the first year and receipts, based on one thousand subscribers at 10 francs, would only be 10,000 francs; a loss of 30,000 francs.

Bordeaux will, I hope, agree to bear part of this. But I must envisage covering the total cost. I thought of you. I cannot ask England for an open or secret subsidy as this would result in more disadvantages than benefits. But could you not obtain for us one thousand subscriptions at half a guinea? This would mean receipts of 500 pounds sterling or 12,500 francs, or 10,000 francs net once postage charges have been deducted. I think that London, Manchester, Liverpool, Leeds, Birmingham, Glasgow, and Edinburgh would be enough to take these thousand copies in *genuine* subscriptions, which your agents would facilitate. There would then be no subsidy, but faithful encouragement, which could be acknowledged openly.

When I see the timidity of our so-called *free traders* and how little they understand the necessity of adopting hard and fast principles, I consider it essential—as I will not hide from you—to take the initiative of starting this journal and managing it, for if, instead of *preceding* the association, it *follows* it, and is obliged to take on its spirit instead of creating it, I fear that the enterprise will be still-born.

Please reply as soon as you can and give me your frank advice.

59. Letter to Richard Cobden

Paris, 11 April 1846   [vol. 1, p. 131]

My dear sir, I hasten to tell you that your reply to the address of the economists will appear in this month's journal, which will be published between the 15th and 20th. The translation is a little weak, as the person to whom it was mainly addressed thought it more appropriate to soften a few expressions in order to humor the susceptibility of our general public. This susceptibility is genuine, and what is more, it is cleverly manipulated. Just recently, while reading a few proofs in a printing works, I came across a book in which we were positively accused of having been bribed by England or rather by the League. As I knew the author, I persuaded him to withdraw this absurd allegation, but it made me realize the increasing danger of having any financial link with your society. I find it impossible to see anything reprehensible in the few subscriptions you may take in our writings in order to distribute them in Europe, and yet from now on I will refrain from calling on your sympathy and, independently of the reasons you give me, this is enough to make me resolve to conform to the national prejudice in this regard.

Although the movement in Bordeaux was rather impressive, I fear that it will create a great many obstacles precisely for that reason. No one dares do anything in Paris, for fear of not doing as much as Bordeaux. Right from the beginning, I predicted that an association, unnoticed at first but made up of men that were totally united and persuaded, would have a better chance than a grand demonstration. Finally, we have to act using the elements we have to hand, and one of the benefits of the association, if ever it spreads, will be *to train*[135] the members themselves. They certainly need it. They cannot perceive the distinction between *revenue-raising* duties and *protectionist* duties. That means that they do not understand the very principle of the association, the only thing that can give it strength, cohesion, and longevity. I have developed this thesis in today's issue of *Le Courrier français,* and will continue to do so.

Whatever happens, there has been incontrovertible progress in this country. Six months ago, no newspaper would support us. Today, we have five in Paris, three in Bordeaux, two in Marseilles, one in Le Havre, and two in Bayonne. I hope that a dozen peers and as many deputies will join our League and draw from it, if not enlightenment, at least courage.

135. In English in the original.

60. Letter to Félix Coudroy

Paris, 18 April 1846   [vol. 1, p. 68]

My dear Félix, I am totally deprived of your letters and it is true that I myself have been very negligent. You cannot believe that I have no time, but this is nevertheless true; when you are living as though so to speak "camping in Paris," the availability of time is so bad that you end up doing nothing.

I will not tell you very much about myself. I have so many people to see that I see no one; this may seem paradoxical but it is true. I have been only once to Dunoyer's, once to Comte's, once to Mignet's, and so on. I am able to have contact with the newspapers; *La Patrie, Le Courrier français, Le Siècle,* and *Le National* have opened their columns to me. I have not been able to sign up with the *Débats.*[136] M. Michel Chevalier has offered to include my articles in it, but I want to have entry to their actual offices to avoid cuts and changes.

The association is moving forward at the speed of a tortoise; I will not have my position settled until Sunday week, when there will be a meeting. Here are the names of some of the members: Harcourt, Pavée de Vandœuvre, Admiral Grivel, Anisson-Duperron, Vincens de Saint-Laurent, peers.

Lamartine, Lafarelle, Bussières, Lherbette, de Corcelle, and a few other deputies.

Michel Chevalier, Blanqui, Wolowski, Léon Faucher, and other economists. D'Eichthal, Cheuvreux, Say, and other merchant bankers.

The difficulty is to gather together these figures who are borne along in the political whirlwind. Behind them, there are young people who are more fervent and who must be contained at least provisionally, so as not to lose the advantage of having the support of these well-known and popular names.

In the meantime, we have had a meeting of the traders and manufacturers in Paris. Our aim was to prepare them; I was very *ill prepared* myself and I had not devoted more than one hour to thinking about what I would have to say. I drew up a very simple plan in which I could not go wrong and was happy to find that this method was not beyond my powers. By starting very simply and in a conversational tone, without seeking to be either witty or eloquent, but only to be clear and convincing, I was able to talk for half an hour without either fatigue or shyness. Others were more brilliant. We will

136. *Le Journal des débats.*

be having another, larger meeting in a week's time and then I will try to enthuse the Latin Quarter.

I have seen the minister of finance[137] in the last few days. He approved of all I am doing and asks for nothing more than to see public opinion molded.

Farewell; time is running short and I am even afraid that I am late.

---

61. Letter to Félix Coudroy.

Paris, 3 May 1846 [vol. 1, p. 70]

My dear Félix, I have learned that there is an opportunity to send this letter and, although I am not at my best (as I have been holding my pen for seven hours), I do not want to let it pass without giving you my news.

I mentioned a meeting tomorrow to you and this is its subject. The addition of famous figures has buried our modest association. These people wanted to start everything again *ab ovo*[138] and we therefore have to construct a program and draw up a manifesto, and this I have been working on all day. But there are four others who are doing the same thing. Whether we want to choose or combine, I can see a long, fruitless discussion ahead, because there are many men of letters, many theorists, and then there is the matter of ego. I would therefore not be surprised if it were referred to yet another commission where the same difficulties will arise, since everyone except me will defend his work and will come to be judged by the Assembly. This is a pity. The manifesto will be followed by the statutes, an organization that complies with these, and subscriptions, and it is only after all this that I will be confirmed. Sometimes I feel the urge to give up, but when I think of the beneficial effect that the simple manifesto with its forty signatures will produce, I cannot summon up the courage to do so. Perhaps when the manifesto has been issued, I will go to Mugron to wait for my summons, since the thought of spending months on end coping with simple formalities without doing anything useful appalls me. Besides, the electoral battle may require my presence. M. Dupérier sent me a message to say that he had formally withdrawn, and even added that he had burned his boats and written to all his friends that he had abandoned his candidature. Since this is so, if other candidates do not come forward, I may find myself confronting M. de

---

137. Jean-Pierre Lacave-Laplagne.
138. "From scratch."

Larnac alone, and this combat does not worry me because it will be a conflict of doctrines and opinion. What amazes me is not to receive any letters from Saint-Sever. It appears that Dupérier's communication ought to have attracted a few overtures to me. If you hear anything, please let me know.

---

62. Letter to Félix Coudroy

Paris, 4 May 1846 [vol. 1, p. 71]

Yesterday evening a manifesto was discussed and adopted. The discussion was serious, interesting, and profound, and that in itself is a very good thing, since many people who undertake to enlighten others enlighten themselves. All executive powers were entrusted to a commission made up of MM Harcourt, Say, Dunoyer, Renouard, Blanqui, Léon Faucher, Anisson-Duperron, and me. On the other hand, this commission will be transmitting to me, at least in practice, the authority it has received and will limit itself to a controlling function; in these circumstances, could I possibly abandon a role that might fall into other hands and compromise the entire cause? I am unhappy at leaving Mugron and my accustomed ways, whimsical work, and our conversations. This is a desperate wrench, but have I any right to step back?

Farewell, my dear Félix; your
friend.

---

63. Letter to Félix Coudroy

Paris, 24 May 1846 [vol. 1, p. 72]

My dear Félix, I have run around so much this morning that I cannot hold my pen properly and my writing is all trembling. What you have told me concerning the usefulness of my presence in Mugron is a constant preoccupation. But, my friend, I am almost certain that, if I left Paris, our association would collapse, and we would have to start all over again. You will make up your own mind about this; this is the position we are in: I think I told you that a commission had been appointed with full powers, but just when we were about to issue our *manifesto,* several of the commissioners wanted us to obtain *prior authorization.*[139] A request was made for this and the minister agreed, but the days go by and nothing seems to come. In the meantime, the manifesto is in our files. It was certainly a mistake to request *authorization;*

---

139. No association of more than twenty persons could be formed without prior authorization from the government.

we should have limited ourselves to a simple *declaration*. Our faint-hearted commissioners thought they were being accommodating to the minister but I think they caused him embarrassment since, especially with the elections coming shortly, he will be afraid of upsetting the manufacturers.

Nevertheless, M. Guizot has declared that he will give the authorization, M. de Broglie has made it understood that he would come over to us immediately afterward and this is why I am still being patient, but if there is any more delay I will complain loudly at the risk of demolishing everything, so as to start on another course and with other people.

You see how difficult it is to leave the field at this time. It is not that I do not want to, for, my dear Félix, Paris and I are not made for one another. There is too much to say on this subject, so we will leave it for another day.

Your article in *Le Mémorial*[140] was excellent. Few people have read it, as it arrived only at the end of our meetings for the reason which I have told you, but I have sent it to Dunoyer and Say as well as to a few others, and everyone thought it was sufficiently lively and clear to absorb the reader and oblige him to agree. The "I will no longer be involved" could not fail to please Dunoyer a great deal; unfortunately the current view is leaning to an appalling degree in the other direction: "Involve the state in everything." We will shortly produce a second edition of my *Sophisms*.[141] We could include this article and a few others in this, if you write them. I can certainly tell you that this small book is destined to be circulated widely. In America, they are offering to distribute it widely, and the English and Italian newspapers have translated it almost in its entirety.[142] But what annoys me a little is to see that the three or four pleasantries that I have slipped into this volume have been highly successful while the serious part has been widely overlooked. For this reason, you also should try a few *buffa*.[143]

I must end here. I have just learned that an opportunity has occurred with regard to Bordeaux and I want to take advantage of it.

---

140. *Le Mémorial bordelais.*

141. *Economic Sophisms.*

142. The first English translation was *Popular Fallacies Regarding General Interests. Being a Translation of the Sophismes économiques,* by M. Frédéric Bastiat, with notes by G. R. Porter (London: J. Murray, 1846). Also appearing was an American edition: *Sophisms of the Protective Policy,* translated from the second French edition by Mrs. D. J. McCord, with an introductory letter by Dr. Francis Lieber (New York: Geo. P. Putnam; Charleston, S.C., 1848). An Italian edition also quickly appeared: *Sofismi economici,* translated by Antonio Contrucci (Florence: C. P. Onesti, 1847).

143. Opera buffa, or comic opera.

64. Letter to Richard Cobden

Paris, 25 May 1846   [vol. 1, p. 133]

It is quite a few days since I last wrote to you, dear Mr. Cobden, but finally I could not have found a more appropriate opportunity to atone for my negligence, since I am pleased to introduce to you the mayor of Bordeaux, the worthy and jovial president of our association, M. Duffour-Dubergié. I do not think I need add anything to assure him of the most cordial welcome on your part. Knowing the close union which binds all the members of the League, I am even dispensing with the duty of writing to Messrs. Bright, Paulton, etc., as I am sure that, on your recommendation, M. Duffour will be admitted to your circle as a member of this great confraternity which has arisen in support of the freedom and union of peoples. And who is more worthy of your friendship than he? He it was who, through the authority of his position, his wealth, and his character, carried Bordeaux along and caused the little that has occurred in Paris to happen. He has not procrastinated and hesitated like our diplomats in the capital. His resolution has been sufficiently prompt and forceful for our government itself not to have the time to hinder the movement, even supposing it had the intention of doing so.

Please, therefore, welcome M. Duffour as the true founder of the association in France. Others will seek and maybe gain the glory for this one day. This is quite normal, but, for my part, I will always give the credit to our president in Bordeaux.

In the midst of the uproar and excitement which must be surrounding your affairs, perhaps you sometimes wonder how our small league in Paris is getting on. Alas, it is in a period of the doldrums, which is very annoying for me. As French law requires associations to be authorized, several of our most prominent members stipulated that this formality should precede the release of any information outside. We therefore submitted our request, and since then we are dependent on the goodwill of the ministers. They have indeed promised authorization, but they have not issued it. Our colleague, M. Anisson-Dupéron, is devoting to this matter a zeal for which he should be praised. He combines the vigor of a young man with the maturity of a peer of France. Thanks to him, I hope we will succeed. If the minister stubbornly refuses to authorize us, our association will be dissolved. All the faint-hearted will leave, but there will always remain a certain number of members with greater resolve and we will constitute an organization on different lines. Who knows whether in the long run this sorting out will not be an advantage to us?

I must admit that I will regret having to abandon fine, well-known names. These are needed in France, since our laws and customs prevent us from doing anything with and through the people. We can scarcely act with just the enlightened classes and, since this is so, men who have acquired a reputation are excellent auxiliaries. But, as a last resort, it is better to do without them than not to do anything at all.

It would appear that the protectionists are preparing a desperate defense in England. If you have a moment, I would be grateful if you would give me your views on the outcome of the struggle. M. Duffour will witness this great conflict. I envy him his good fortune.

---

65. Letter to Mr. Richard Cobden

Mugron, 25 June 1846   [vol. 1, p. 134]

It is not for you to apologize, my dear sir, but for me, for you are making great and noble use of your time while I, who am wasting mine, ought not to have waited so long without writing to you. You are at the end of your work. The hour of triumph has sounded for you. You can give yourself the testimonial that you have left a deep imprint of your passage on this earth and humanity will bless your name. You have led your huge campaign with the vigor, comprehensiveness, prudence, and moderation that will be an eternal example for all future reformers and, I say this most sincerely, the perfection you have brought to the *art of campaigning* will be a greater benefit for the human race than the specific purpose of your efforts, however great that is. You have taught the world that genuine strength lies in public opinion and shown it how to put this strength to work. I take it upon myself, my dear Cobden, to award you the palm of immortality and anoint your forehead with the mark of a great man.

As for me, you will see from the date of my letter that I have deserted the battlefield, not because of discouragement but temporary disgust. It must be said; the task in France is more specialized and less likely to make inroads in public sympathy. The material and moral obstacles are also huge. We have neither the *railways* nor the *penny postage*.[144] We are not accustomed to sub-

---

144. In English in the original.

scriptions; French minds are impatient with all hierarchy. We are capable of discussing the details of a regulation or the formalities of a meeting for a year. Lastly, our greatest misfortune is that we have no genuine *economists*. I have not met two who are capable of supporting the cause and its doctrine in a comprehensive and correct fashion, and we see the most gross errors and concessions infiltrating the speeches and writings of those known here as *free traders*. *Communism* and *Fourierism* absorb all the young minds, and we will have a host of outer ramparts to destroy before being able to attack the heart of the fortress.

If I turn my gaze on myself, I can feel tears of blood coming to my eyes. My health does not allow me to work assiduously and ... but what use are complaints and regrets!

The September Laws[145] which oppose us are not greatly to be feared. On the contrary, the government is doing us a favor by placing us in this posture. It offers us the means of stiffening the public fiber a little and melting the ice of public indifference. If it wanted to counter the rise of our ideas, it could not have gone about it in a worse way.

You make no mention of your health. I hope it is a little stronger. I would be very sorry if you came to Paris and I did not have the pleasure of doing you the honors there. It is doubtless an instinct for contrast that incites you to go to Cairo, *contraria contrariis curantur*.[146] You wish to escape the fog, liberty, and unrest in Britain by seeking refuge under the sun, despotism, and political inertia of Egypt. Oh that I might, in seven years' time, go to seek rest from the same weariness in the same place!

You are thus going to dissolve the League! What an instructive and imposing prospect! What is the abdication of Scylla compared with such an act of selflessness? This is the time for me to rewrite and complete my *History of the League*. But will I have the time? The flow of affairs takes up all my waking hours. I also need to produce a second edition of my *Sophisms* and I would very much like to write a small book entitled *Economic Harmonies*. It will make a pair with the other; the first demolishes and the second would build.

145. Laws restricting liberties promulgated in September 1835, following an attempted assassination of Louis-Philippe.
146. "Opposites are balanced by opposites."

66. Letter to Richard Cobden

Bordeaux, 21 July 1846   [vol. 1, p. 136]

My dear and excellent friend, your letter found me here in Bordeaux, where I have come to attend a meeting following the return of our president, M. Duffour-Dubergié. This meeting will take place in a few hours' time; I am to speak at it and this is exercising my mind to such an extent that you must excuse the confusion and incoherence of this letter. Nevertheless, I do not want to put off writing to you since you have asked me to reply by return.

I do not need to tell you how pleased I was to learn of the conclusion of your great and glorious enterprise. The keystone has fallen, and the entire monopoly structure will crumble, including the *colonial system,* which is linked to the protectionist system. This above all is what will have a strong influence on public opinion in Europe and dissolve the truly disastrous and profound prejudices in this country.

When I entitled my book *Cobden and the League,* no one had told me that you were the soul of this powerful organization and that you had communicated to it all the qualities of your mind and heart. I am proud that I sensed this and that I foresaw, if not anticipated, public opinion throughout England. For the love of man, please do not reject the acknowledgment the country wishes to give you. Allow the people to express their gratitude freely and nobly. England is honoring you and is honoring herself even more through this great act of justice. Be sure that she is investing the hundred thousand pounds sterling at a high rate of interest, since as long as she knows how to reward its faithful servants well she will be well served.[147] She will never lack great men. Here in France, we also have fine minds and noble hearts, but their potential remains unrealized because the country has not yet learned this important but oh, so simple lesson: *honor what is honorable and despise what is despicable.* The gift they are preparing for you is the glorious culmination of the most glorious enterprise that the world has ever seen. Leave these great examples to reach future generations in their entirety.

147. Cobden had severe financial difficulties in 1845 that continued into 1846, the result of his increased activities with the Anti–Corn Law League and subsequent neglect of his family business. His friends and colleagues organized a public fund-raising campaign, which enabled him to pay off most of his debts. Most likely Bastiat is here referring to this campaign.

I will be going to Paris at the beginning of August. It is not likely that I will be arriving there as a deputy. The same cause is still forcing me to wait for this mandate to be *imposed* on me, and in France, this wait can be long. But, like you, I think that the work I have to do is outside the legislative perimeter.

I have just left the meeting, at which I did not speak.[148] But, with reference to election as a deputy, an extraordinary thing has happened to me. I will tell you about it in Paris. Oh, my friend, there are countries in which you have to have a truly great spirit to concern yourself with the public good, so great an effort is deployed to discourage you!

---

67. Letter to Félix Coudroy

    Bordeaux, 22 July 1846   [vol. 1, p. 73]

My dear Félix, I wrote to you the day before yesterday and would not be surprised if my letter went astray, since for the last month I have been going from one misunderstanding to another. I would need a ream of paper to tell you all that has happened to me. They are not pleasant things but they do have the advantage of letting me make great strides in acquiring knowledge of the human heart. Alas! Perhaps it would be better to retain the few illusions we should have at our age.

First of all, I have found out that the delay in sending out my brochure is the result of intrigue. My letter to M. Duchâtel[149] offended him, but it forced out of him the authorization that so many highly placed figures were pursuing for the last three months. And do you think the association in Bordeaux was grateful? Not at all. There has been a complete change of opinion against me here, and I have been *branded* a *radical;* my brochure was the final straw. M. Duchâtel has written to the prefect, the prefect summoned the manager of *Le Mémorial*[150] and hauled him over the coals, and the manager has atoned for his fault by delaying my brochure. In spite of this, right now, the four hundred copies should have reached you.[151]

As for what is happening with regard to the elections, it would take too

---

148. See Letter 67.
149. The letter to M. Duchâtel, minister of the interior, was published on 30 June 1846 by *Le Mémorial bordelais*. The authorization was granted in July.
150. *Le Mémorial bordelais.*
151. See "To the Electors of the District of Saint-Sever," p. 352.

long and I will tell you when we meet. The result is that I will not be supported anywhere, except perhaps in Nérac.[152] However, I see this as a mere show of opposition and not as a serious candidature, unless the *unexpected* happens on election day.

Yesterday we had a meeting of the association in Bordeaux. The way I was begged to speak made me *beg* to refuse.

I presume that right now all the electors of Saint-Sever have received my brochure. This is all I have to offer them with my devotion to duty. Distributing it must be giving you much work. If there are four of you, however, the task will be lighter. I hope to have returned to Mugron by the 28th or 29th, just in time to vote.

Farewell, my dear Félix, I will not seal this letter until this evening, in case I have anything to add.

P.S. I have just had an important interview, which I will tell you about. But the result is that Bordeaux will not be supporting me; they want an economist who is right in the center. The minister has recommended *Blanqui*.

---

68. Letter to Richard Cobden

Paris, 23 September 1846 [vol. 1, p. 138]

Although I have not a great deal to tell you, my dear friend, I do not want to let any more time go by without writing to you.

We are still in the same situation, with a great deal of trouble bringing an *organization* to birth. I hope, nevertheless, that next month will be more productive. First of all, we will have a headquarters. That is a good start; it is the *embodiment*[153] of the League. Next, several *leading men*[154] are returning from the country, among whom is the excellent M. Anisson, whom I have been missing.

In the meantime, we are preparing for a second meeting on the 29th. This is perhaps a little dangerous, since a *fiasco* in France tends to be deadly. I am offering to speak at it and I will reread your lesson on eloquence several times between now and then. Could I obtain this from a better source? I assure you that I will have at least two precious, although negative, qualities

152. Town in the *département* of Lot et Garonne.
153. In English in the original.
154. In English in the original.

in the absence of others, simplicity and brevity. I will not try to make people laugh or cry, but to elucidate a difficult point of economic science.

There is one point on which I do not agree with you, that is, on *public speaking*. I think it is the most powerful instrument of propagation. Is it nothing to have several thousand listeners who understand you much better than if they were reading you? Afterward, the next day, everyone wants to know what you said and the truth goes on its way.

You know that Marseilles has issued its pronunciamento; the people there are already richer than we. I hope they will help us, at least in founding the journal.

Brussels has just formed its association. And what is surprising, the association has just published the first issue of its journal. Alas! The Belgians probably do not have a law on stamps and another on surety.[155]

I am impatient to know whether you have visited our marvelous Pyrenees. The mayor of Bordeaux wrote to tell me that my desolate Landes appeared to you to be the land of lizards and salamanders.[156] And yet deep affection can transform this frightful desert into an earthly paradise! But I hope that our Pyrenees will have reconciled you to the south of France. What a shame that all the provinces that surround Pau, the Juranson, the Béarn, the Tursan, the Armagnac, and the Chalosse cannot carry out trade that would be so natural with England![157]

Let us return to the subject of associations. One is being formed of *protectionists*. This is the best thing that could have happened to us, as we really need a *stimulus*. It is said that another is being formed in favor of free trade in *raw materials* and the *protection of factories*. That one, at least, does not pretend to be based on a *principle* and take account of justice. It thus considers itself to be eminently *practical*. It is clear that it cannot stand alone and that it will be absorbed by us.

155. Before the postal reform of 1848, the price of mail depended on distance and was paid by the recipient. The surety was a deposit that the editor of a periodical had to make to provide for any future fine.

156. After the dissolution of the League, Cobden undertook a tour around Europe, traveling to France, Spain, Italy, Prussia, and Russia. From Bordeaux, he went to Spain through the Landes and the Pyrenees.

157. All these areas, which produced wines and spirits, were handicapped by difficult communications with Bayonne and tariffs.

69. Letter to Richard Cobden

Paris, 29 September 1846 [vol. 1, p. 140]

My dear friend, I have been to visit M. de Loménie,[158] who has come to my lodgings though we still have not met. But I am meeting him tomorrow and will make available to him all my documents and those of Fonteyraud. In addition, I will offer him my cooperation, either for translating or, if need be, giving his article a veneer of economic orthodoxy. I have at the forefront of my memory the passage from your closing speech in which you make an excursion into the future and from there open up to your listeners a horizon that is wider and finer than that offered to you from the Pic du Midi. This speech will be translated and sent to M. de Loménie. He might well also use your excerpt on emigration, which is really eloquent. In short, let me have some information on it. The only thing is that I have to tell you that very little is said here about this *gallery of famous men*. I am assured that this type of work is a speculation on the amour propre of those who aspire to celebrity. But perhaps this insinuation arises from the jealousies of authors and publishers, *irritabile genus,*[159] the vainest species of men I know after fencing masters.

I have just received your nice letter. Has it reached me in time? I have incorporated the text you indicate quite naturally in my speech. How could I not have thought of asking for your advice? This doubtless is because I have a head full of arguments and felt that I was *rich.* But I thought only of the *subject* and you have made me think of the *audience.* I now understand that a good speech must be supplied to us by the audience rather than by its subject. Running through mine in my head, I think that it is not too philosophical and that it combines economic science, appropriateness, and parables in proper proportion.[160] I will send it to you and you will let me know your view of it for my edification. You will understand, my dear Cobden, that any tact would do me a disservice. I have as much amour propre as the next man and no one fears ridicule more than I, but that is precisely why I want good advice and good criticism. One of your remarks might spare me a thousand in the future that is opening out before me and carrying me along. A great many things will be decided tonight.

158. Louis Léonard de Loménie, writer and professor of literature.
159. "The grumbling tribe."
160. *OC*, vol. 2, p. 238, "Second discours, à Paris."

I am expected in Le Havre. Oh! What a burden is an *exaggerated* reputation! There, I will have to discuss the *shipping interest.* I remember that you had good things to say on this subject in Liverpool or in Hull. I will do some research, but if you have any good ideas relating to Le Havre, please let me have them for charity's sake or rather, *through me,* bestow this charity on the fearful shipowners who are counting on the *small number of trading operations to increase the number of transport facilities.* What blindness! What a distortion of human intelligence!

> And I am astonished when I think of this,
> To what depths the human spirit can sink.

I will not post my letter until tomorrow, so that I can tell you about an event that I am sure will interest you as much as if it were personal.

I was forgetting to tell you that your previous letter arrived too late. I had already booked two separate apartments, one for the association and the other for me, but in the same house. We have to accept our fate with the motto that consoles Spanish people in all circumstances: *no hay remedio!*[161] As for my health, do not worry, it is better. I believe that Providence will give me enough to see me through. I am becoming superstitious; is it not good to be this way just a little?

But here my letter is arriving at the *square yard.* It will pay heavy duties. This would probably not happen if the post office adopted the *ad valorem duty.* I am leaving some space for tomorrow.

Midnight.

The session[162] has just ended. Anisson chaired it. The audience was larger than the previous time. We had five *speeches* including two from professors who thought they were giving classes. Very much more than I, they thought about their subject more than their audience. M. Say had a great success; he spoke with warmth and was roundly applauded. I am pleased about that, since how can one fail to like this excellent man? M—— made *three* excellent speeches in one. His only fault was length. I was the fifth to speak, with the disadvantage of having a harassed audience. Notwithstanding this, I had as much success as I wished. What was funny is that the only emotion I felt was in my *calves.* I now understand Racine's line:

161. "There is no cure."
162. The second public meeting of the Association pour la liberté des échanges.

And my trembling knees are buckling beneath me.

The 30th.

I have seen only one newspaper, *Le Commerce*. This is what it says: "Mr. Bastiat succeeded in having his economic parables accepted through an unpretentious delivery that was accompanied by a thoroughly southern eloquence." This scant praise is enough for me and I want no more, since God preserve me from arousing envy in my colleagues!

---

70. Letter to Félix Coudroy

> Paris, 1 October 1846   [vol. 1, p. 74]

My dear Félix, I have had no news of you and consequently do not know how you are progressing in your court case. May you be close to a solution and success! Give me news of your good sister; were the baths at Biarritz beneficial for her? I am sorry you were not able to accompany her; I think Mugron must be becoming sadder and more monotonous for you with each passing day.

People in Bordeaux have written to tell me that several of our articles are being reprinted as a brochure. This is why I am in no hurry to produce a second volume of *Sophisms;* this would be duplication. Just writing my correspondence takes me as much time as I can devote to writing. My friend, I am not only part of the association, I am the association in its entirety, not because I lack enthusiastic and devoted colleagues when it comes to speaking and writing. As for organizing and administering this vast machine, however, I am on my own, and how long will this last? On the 15th of this month, I am taking possession of my place of work. I will then have staff. Until then, I cannot undertake any intellectual work.

I am sending you an issue of the journal that reports on our public session yesterday. I made my debut on the Paris stage in extremely unfavorable circumstances. There was a large audience and for the first time there were women in the public gallery. It had been arranged that five speakers would be heard and that each would speak for half an hour. This already made the session last for two and a half hours. I was to speak last; of my four predecessors, two were faithful to the rules and two others spoke for more than an hour; they were professors. I therefore stood up in front of an audience harangued by three hours of economics and in a hurry to leave. I myself was very tired by such an extended wait. I stood up with the terrible foreboding that my head would let me down. I had prepared my speech carefully but without writing it down. You can imagine how terrified I was. How was it that I did not have a moment of hesitation or feel any worry or emotion, except in my legs? I cannot explain it. I owe it all to the modest tone with which I started. After warning the audience that they should expect no eloquence, I felt perfectly at ease and I must have succeeded since the newspapers report only this speech. This is a great test I have passed. I tell you all this frankly, as you can see, persuaded that you will be delighted both for me and the cause. My dear Félix, I am sure that we will triumph. In a short time, my fellow countrymen may trade their wines for anything they want. The Chalosse will come back to life. This is the thought that sustains me. I will not have been totally without use to my country.

I presume that I will be going to Le Havre in two or three months to organize a committee. The prefect in Rouen has warned M. Anisson "that he should take care to come at night if he does not wish to be stoned."

I am assured that yesterday evening there was a large protectionist meeting in Rouen. If I had known this, I would have gone incognito. I would congratulate myself if these people did as we do; that would goad us on. And incidentally it is a safety valve; as long as they defend themselves through legal channels, there will be no fear of collision.

Farewell, my dear Félix. Write to me from time to time; put your solitude to good use and do something worthwhile. I very much regret not being able to undertake anything for true glory. If you think of a good way of doing so, let me know of it. I am assured that parables and jokes have greater success and more effect than the best treatises.

---

71. Letter to Richard Cobden

Paris, 22 October 1846   [vol. 1, p. 142]

My dear friend, I was beginning to worry about your silence. At last I have received your letter dated . . . and I am delighted to learn that you and Mrs. Cobden are enjoying being in Spain. What will happen when you see Andalusia! As far as I was able to see, in Seville and Cadiz there was an air of equality in the manners between classes which was balm to the soul. I am enchanted to learn that there are good *free traders* beyond the Pyrenees. Perhaps they will put us to shame. Dear friend, I think we have in common that we are free of personal jealousy. But do you have national jealousy? For my part, I scarcely feel any. I would like my country to give a good example, but failing that, I would prefer even more that it receive good example rather than wait a century to take the lead. And yet . . . I cannot refrain from uttering a philosophical thought. Nations take great pride in having a great musician, a good painter, or a skillful captain, as though that added something to their own merit. It is said that "the French invent, the English encourage." For heaven's sake! Would you not agree that invention is a personal *fact* and encouragement a *national fact?* Bentham said of science, "What propagates it is more valuable than what advances it." I say the same of virtues.

But whither am I wandering? To the view that it matters little whether progress reaches us *from the dusk or the dawn,* provided that it comes.

Your speech will appear in two Paris newspapers. It was not I who translated it. I noted that you were able to give advice to more places than just Paris. Moreover, you did this with perfect propriety and I very much approve of your having told the Castilians that it is not necessary to kill people in order to teach them how to live.

Here we are moving slowly but we are moving. Our most recent meeting was good and the public is clamoring for another. I went to Le Havre. An association has been formed there but it did not think it necessary to adopt our title. I fear that these people have not understood the importance of rallying round a single principle. They are demanding *trade reform and a reduction in consumption taxes.* How much there would be to say! Trade reform! They did not dare utter the word *freedom,* because of shipping. A reduction in taxes! Into what topics of discussion will this draw them?

On the subject of shipping, I inserted an article in the Le Havre journal, which had a good *local* effect.[163] M. Anisson thinks that it is at the expense of the principle. I do not think so, but it pains me to disagree with the most enthusiastic and enlightened of my colleagues. I would very much like you to be close to us to be able to settle this disagreement. But truly, a debate by letter would take too long.

I do not know whether it is to my shame or glory but I have read nothing *about the marriage.*[164] Our journal, the *Courrier,*[165] has been speaking

---

163. Bastiat wrote three letters in Le Havre which were published in *Le Mémorial bordelais.* (*OC,* vol. 7, p. 131, "Aux négociants du Havre.")

164. Marriage of the young queen of Spain, Isabella II. Palmerston pushed for a candidate favored by the English, Leopold of Saxe-Coburg; and Guizot, for a son of Louis-Philippe. But the queen preferred her cousin Francisco.

165. *Le Courrier français.*

of nothing else for the last two months. I have told it that it would do just as well to print under its title *"Journal of a Spanish Coterie."* It has lost its subscribers and is blaming it on *Libre échange*.[166] What a shame! I really am homesick for my Landes. There, I *imagined* human turpitude, but it is much sadder to see it.

Farewell, my brother in arms, take care of your health and that of Mrs. Cobden, to whom I send my best regards. Be careful of the Spanish climate, which is very treacherous and destroys the lungs without appearing to affect them.

---

72. Letter to Richard Cobden

     Paris, 22 November 1846   [vol. 1, p. 144]

My dear friend, I thank you for having made it possible for me to follow you in your travels in the newspapers of Madrid, Seville, and Cadiz. The expressions of friendship that you receive everywhere reach our fine cause, *through you*.[167] It makes me happy to see that people's tributes are finally reaching the right target instead of being diverted, as is customary, toward the actions that, for whatever reason, inflict the most obvious evils on the poor human race. At the same time I am very glad to learn that you are enjoying good health and that Mrs. Cobden has not suffered from such a long journey.

I share your opinion on Spain and the Spanish. However, are you not cherishing a few illusions on the degree of prosperity enjoyed by this country? I know that everyone always talks about its fertility, but the absence of rivers, canals, roads, and trees creates obstacles whose significance you should appreciate. By isolating people, they obstruct both moral and social development and the accumulation of wealth. Spain needs someone to invent a means of enabling trains to cross the mountains.

Because I have little time and scarcely enough to keep up with correspondence with my family, I will go straight to the question of *free trade* in France. At present we are overwhelmed. The protectionists are campaigning in depth and in the English style. Newspapers, contributions, calls to the workers, and threats to the government are all being used. When I say

---

166. Bastiat's journal, on the verge of publication.
167. In English in the original.

English style, I mean that they are using a great deal of energy and a true understanding of campaigning.

In this respect, our provinces in the north are much further advanced than our *départements* in the south. In addition, a more pressing interest is goading them on. In twenty-four hours they have founded a journal, while we ... would you believe that we still do not know whether Bordeaux is willing to help us or not? Marseilles and Le Havre are isolating themselves and their only reason for this is that they do not think we are practical enough, as though we had something other to do than destroy a public error. But I was expecting all this and even worse.

I have not been able to escape the need to take on the physical work myself. Lack of money on the one hand and the commitments of my colleagues on the other leave me with no alternative but to abandon everything or drink deep from this chalice. I have seen in the protectionist journal and in democratic broadsheets the strangest *fallacies*[168] without having the time to refute them, and it is even impossible for me to gather together the material for a second volume of *Sophisms,* although I have them in sufficient number. The only thing is that they are all of the *buffa*[169] type, and I would like to intersperse them with a few *seria.*[170] As for another, more complete edition of *Cobden and the League,* I am not even thinking about it.

What a difference it would make, my dear friend, if I could go from town to town speaking and writing!

Be that as it may, public opinion has been awoken and I entertain hope.

It has almost been decided that we will be publishing our first issue in the first few days of December, without knowing how we will be able to continue. However, should not good causes be able to rely on Providence? I will send you a copy as often as I can contact you in your wanderings. I also hope that you will be able to gain us subscribers abroad. We have worked out that at twelve francs we need five thousand subscribers to cover our costs. We would then be able to do without Marseilles and Le Havre. In spite of the fact that we have to be very circumspect with regard to foreigners, and especially the English, I do not think there will be any disadvantages in your fellow countrymen helping us to increase the circulation of our journal in those countries in which French is widely spoken.

168. In English in the original.
169. Opera buffa, or comic opera.
170. Opera seria, or serious opera.

I have just received a letter from Bordeaux. It gives me hope that we will receive help. The mayor is working on this with good heart.

Another piece of good fortune has just happened to me. The *workers* have committed me to going to meet them and reach an agreement with them. If I won them over, they would carry along the democratic party. I will devote all my efforts to this.

---

73. Letter to Richard Cobden

Paris, 25 November 1846 [vol. i, p. 147]

My dear friend, yesterday evening we held our third public session. The Montesquieu Hall was full and many people could not enter, which is, in Paris, the most favorable circumstance for attracting people. New classes of people appeared in the audience. I had sent tickets to workers and students at the law school. The public was admirable and, although the speakers sometimes forgot the rule of wisdom and prudence which was of course in their own interest too, *stop talking!* the audience listened with religious attention where they were not carried away with enthusiasm. Our speakers were MM Faucher, who commented with great emphasis and pertinence on an official letter from the protectionists to the council of ministers; Peupin, a worker, who would have been a perfect model of verve and simplicity if he had kept to his subject, from which he was rather too eager to wander; and Ortolan, who gave an eloquent speech and considered the question from a totally new point of view. This speech roused the audience and stiffened the French fiber. Lastly, Blanqui, who was as energetic as he was witty. Our worthy president opened the session with a few graceful words imbued with the fine tone that our nominal aristocracy still retains. I will send you all of this.

Speaking in public has an irresistible attraction for French people. It is therefore probable that we will be overwhelmed with requests and, as for me, I have decided to wait to be asked to speak. This makes it possible that I will have a long wait; be that as it may, it will not bother me to be ready if need be. Therefore, if you have any new ideas or a thought that, when developed, might serve as a text for a good speech, please let me have them. If my health cannot cope with the amount of internal work that has fallen upon me, I will request a holiday and take advantage of it to go to Lyons, Marseilles, Nîmes, etc. Therefore, please send me anything that you consider would be relevant for these various towns. You might write these thoughts down on scraps of paper as they come to mind, and enclose them in your letters. I will mix the drink using the flavorings you have given me.

In particular, I would like to examine in depth the question of *wages*, that is to say, the influence that freedom and protectionism have on them. It would be no trouble at all for me to deal with this major question in economic terms, and if I had to write a book on this, I would perhaps produce a satisfactory result. But what I lack is one of the clear, striking reasons that are ready to be put before the workers themselves and which, in order to be understood, do not need all the previous notions of *value, currency, capital, competition,* etc.

Farewell, my dear friend, write to me in Barcelona. I think I am slightly feverish and have subjected myself to doing nothing today. This is why I am stopping, assuring you once more of my friendship.

---

74. Letter to Richard Cobden

Paris, 20 December 1846 [vol. 1, p. 148]

My dear friend, I had lost track of you for a while and am glad to know that you are in France, in the most delightful country on earth, if it had common sense. Ah! My friend, I was expecting our opponents to exploit blind popular passions against us, including the hatred of foreigners. But I did not think that they would succeed so well. They have once more bribed the press and the word is out to treat us as traitors and agents of *Pitt*[171] *and Coburg.* Would you believe that, in my own region, this calumny has made inroads? I have had letters from Mugron to say that people dare to speak of me only within the family, so fiercely has public opinion been aroused against our enterprise. On the 29th of this month, I am due to speak in the Montesquieu Hall[172] and I plan to refer to this delicate subject and develop the idea that "the English oligarchy has borne down hard upon the world, and it is this that explains the universal distrust with which anything that is done across the Channel is met. But there is a country on which it has borne down harder upon than on any other and that is England itself. This is why there is in England a class that stands up to the oligarchy and is gradually stripping it of its dangerous privileges. This is the class that has in succession achieved Catholic emancipation, electoral reform, the abolition of slavery,

---

171. William Pitt the Younger.
172. At the fourth meeting of the Association pour la liberté des échanges.

and free trade, and that is on the point of achieving the liberation of the colonies. It is therefore working in our direction, and it is absurd to envelop it in the same hatred that we should be reserving for the domineering classes in all countries."

That is the text. I think I will be able to dress it up sufficiently to have it accepted.[173]

How much I would have to tell you, my dear friend, but I do not have enough time. I am sending you the first four issues of our journal. I have marked what I have written. I was constrained, under pain of having the enterprise fail, to mention my name and now I can no longer accept the responsibility for everything that is said in it. This is going to lead to a crisis, because I need to be able to produce the journal in the way I want or else someone else must give it his signature.

Of all the sacrifices I have made to the cause, this is the greatest. Carrying on the fight in my own way was more suited to my character, sometimes writing serious and lengthy articles and at others going to Lyons or Marseilles, in short being guided by my native sensibility. Here I am, on the contrary, chained to daily polemics. However, in our country, that is the scope of usefulness.

You have no need of an introduction to M. Rossi; your reputation will open all doors to you. However, since you want one, I will send you a letter from M. Chevalier or from someone else.

Now, I believe that our efforts should be directed to the distribution of our journal, *Le Libre échange*. Rest assured that, as soon as we are free of the inevitable tensions accompanying a launch, this journal will be produced with a good spirit and may give considerable service, *provided that it is read*. Devote yourself, therefore, during your travels, to finding subscribers to it and ensure that the borders of Italy are not closed to it. Underline that it does not attack any political institution or religious belief. Italy is the country which provided the most subscribers to *Le Journal des économistes*. It should provide even more to *Libre échange,* which will appear every week and cost only twelve francs. That is not all. I think you ought to write to London or Manchester, because, after all, *the cry*[174] against England does not prevent us from finding subscribers there. Subscriptions are a matter of *life and death* for us. My dear Cobden, after having directed the movement in

---

173. This speech was never made.
174. In English in the original.

England from such a height, please do not disdain the humble mission of a subscription broker.

I am truly ashamed to send you this letter written in fits and starts and not really knowing what I am saying. I will find the time to write to you in more relaxed fashion, either tonight or tomorrow night.

---

75. Letter to Richard Cobden

Paris, 25 December 1846 [vol. 1, p. 151]

My dear friend, I communicated your letter to Léon Faucher. He says that "you do not know France." For my part, I am convinced that we can succeed only by awakening a sentiment of justice and that we would not even be able to mention the word *justice* if we accepted the shadow of *protection.* We have tried it, and the only time we wanted to make overtures to a town, it laughed in our faces. It is this conviction and the certitude I have that it is not sufficiently shared that principally committed me to accepting the management of the journal. Not that it is a very real management; there is an editorial committee, which has full authority, but I hope nevertheless to give some clear color to the spirit of this broadsheet. What a sacrifice, my friend, to accept the job of a journalist and put my name at the foot of a medley! But I am not writing to you to air my complaints.

Marseilles does not appear, any more than Bordeaux, to understand the need to concentrate the action in Paris. This is weakening us. Our opponents have not made this mistake, and although their association is harboring the countless germs of division, they are containing these germs through their skill and self-sacrifice. If you have the opportunity of seeing the leaders in Marseilles, please explain the situation to them clearly.

The cry[175] against England is stifling us. Formidable prejudices have been aroused against us. If this hatred for *perfidious Albion* were just a fashion, I would wait patiently for it to blow over. However, it has deep roots in people's hearts. It is universal, and as I have told you, I think that in my village people no longer dare to talk of me outside the family. What is more, this blind passion serves protected interests and political parties so well that they exploit it in the most shameless fashion. As an isolated writer, I might refute them energetically, but, as a member of an association, I must act with more prudence.

175. In English in the original.

Besides, it must be said that events do not favor us. On the very day that Sir Robert Peel accomplished *free trade,* he asked for a credit of twenty-five million for the army, as though to proclaim his lack of faith in his work and as though to throw our best arguments back in our faces. Since then, the policy of your government has always been imbued with a spirit of teasing which irritates the French people and makes it forget what might remain to it of impartiality. Ah! If I had been prime minister of England, on the occasion of Krakow[176] I would have said, "The 1815 treaties have been broken. France is free! England fought the principle of the French Revolution up to Waterloo. Now it has another policy, that of nonintervention to its full extent. Let France recover its rights, like England in eternal neutrality." And fitting action to words, I would have dismissed half of the army and three-quarters of the sailors. But I am not the prime minister.

---

76. Letter to Richard Cobden

Paris, 10 January 1847   [vol. 1, p. 152]

My dear friend, I received your two letters written in Marseilles almost at the same time. I agree with your merely passing through this town, as God alone knows how a longer visit would have been interpreted. My friend, the obstacle that will be constructed against us by national prejudices is much more serious and will last for longer than you appear to believe. If the monopolists had whipped up anglophobia *for the needs of the cause,* this strategic maneuver could easily be countered. In any case, France would have discovered the trap in a very short time. But they are exploiting a sentiment that already existed, which has deep roots in people's hearts, and—shall I tell you?—although mistaken and exaggerated, can be explained and justified. There is no doubt that the English oligarchy has borne down painfully upon Europe, and that its pendulum policy of sometimes supporting the despots in the north to repress freedom in the south and sometimes whipping up liberalism in the south to contain the despotism in the north, must have generated an inevitable reaction everywhere. You will tell me that you should never confuse peoples with their governments. That is fine for thinkers. But

---

176. After the Vienna Congress of 1815, Krakow had been a free town under the joint protection of Prussia, Russia, and Austria. Following an upheaval in 1846, Krakow was invaded by troops of the three countries and annexed to the Austrian empire. France and England protested in the name of the 1815 treaty.

nations judge each other by the external action they carry out against each other. And then, I must admit, this distinction is a bit subtle. Peoples stand by their governments to a certain extent and let them act even if they do not actively help them. The constant policy of the British oligarchy has been to involve the nation in its intrigues and enterprises in order to generate in it a hostile feeling against the human race and thus keep it in a state of dependence. Now this general hostility is coming to the surface; it is a just punishment for past sins and it will survive long after these same sins disappear.

Thus the national sentiment of which the monopolists are making use is very real. In addition, it serves the parties admirably. The democrats, the republicans, and the opposition on the left all exploit it as best they can, some for making the king unpopular, others for overthrowing M. Guizot. You will agree that the monopolists have discovered in this a very dangerous power.

To outwit this maneuver, I had the idea of beginning by acknowledging the Machiavellianism and invasive policy of the British oligarchy and then saying, "Who has suffered more than the English people themselves?" revealing the sentiment of opposition that it has encountered in England from time immemorial and showing this sentiment resisting the war against American independence in 1773 [*sic*] and the war against the French Revolution in 1791. This sentiment was then repressed but not stifled; it still lives, it is growing and has become *public opinion*. This is what extracted Catholic emancipation, the extension of electoral suffrage, and the abolition of slavery from the oligarchy, and more recently, the destruction of monopolies. It will also extract the liberation of trade with the colonies. And on this subject, I will show that the liberation of trade will lead to political liberation. Therefore, *invasive politics* will have ceased to exist, since we do not give up invasions that have been achieved to run after new forms of invasion.

Following this, through translations of writings by you, Fox, and Thompson, I will show that the League is the mouthpiece and outward expression of the sentiment which harmonizes with that in Europe, etc., etc.; you can guess the rest. But I will need time and strength and I have neither. As I cannot write, this will be the text for the end of my next speech in the Montesquieu Hall. For the rest, I will not say anything I do not think.

How lucky you are to be under Italian skies! When will I also see the fields, the sea, and the mountains! *O rus! Quando ego te aspiciam!*[177] And above all, when will I be in the midst of those who love me! You, yourself,

---

177. "O countryside! When shall I look upon you!"

have made sacrifices, but they were done in order to build the foundation of civilization. In all conscience, my friend, is the same selflessness expected of someone who can bring only a grain of sand to the monument? However, I needed to think of this before; now the sword has been drawn from its scabbard. It will never return. The monopoly or your friend will go to *Père Lachaise*[178] before it does.

---

77. Letter to Félix Coudroy

    Paris, 11 March 1847   [vol. 1, p. 76]

My dear Félix, your letter arrived just in time to remove the anxiety caused by your one of the previous day. However, I had the premonition that you would give me better news and my confidence was precisely based on my aunt's somnolence, which caused you to worry, for on two occasions I was able to ascertain that it is rather a good sign where she is concerned. However, the constitution of our physical bodies is so strange that I was not very reassured by it. I was therefore waiting impatiently for your letter and unfortunately fate decreed that it was delayed for several hours today because of snow. I have it at last and am at peace. What a torment for us it is, my dear Félix, when uncertain circumstances combine with the state of uncertainty of our minds. Abandoning my poor aunt at this time when she is ill and without a relative at her side! That thought is frightful. On the other hand all the threads of our enterprise are in my hands: the journal,[179] correspondence, and the accounts, and can I leave the whole structure to collapse? There was a committee meeting in which I spoke of my need to absent myself and was given to understand to what extent I was committed. However, a friend has offered to do the journal in my absence. This is a great help, but how many other obstacles remain! In the end, my aunt is feeling better. This will be a lesson to me and I will arrange to be able to take at least a few days, if I need to. For your part, my dear Félix, please keep me fully up to date.

Your white cottage beckons me. I admire and congratulate you for situating your castles in the air, where only you can attain them. Two adjoining sharecropping farms; a proper combination of fields, vineyards, pastures; a few cows; two patriarchal families of sharecroppers; two servants, who do

---

178. Famous cemetery in Paris.
179. *Le Libre échange.*

not cost much in the country; proximity to the presbytery; and above all, your good sister and your books. There is really enough there to vary, fill, and sweeten your autumn days. Perhaps one day I also will have a cottage close to yours. Poor Félix! You think that I am pursuing fame. If it were my destiny, as you say, it would escape me here, where I am doing nothing worthwhile. I can feel a new dissertation on economic science in my head and it will never emerge! Farewell, it is perhaps already too late for the post.

---

78. Letter to Richard Cobden

Paris, 20 March 1847 [vol. 1, p. 155]

My dear friend, I was filled with anxiety and even surprised not to receive news of you. I asked myself, "Has the *free-trade* atmosphere in Italy made him forget our protectionist region?" I thought every day of writing to you, but where would I find you, where should I address my letters? At last, I have received yours of the 7th. After my pleasure at hearing that both you and Mrs. Cobden were in good health, I have another cause for satisfaction, that of knowing Italy to be so far advanced in the right doctrine. Thus, my poor France, so far in advance of other nations in many respects, is being left behind in political economy. My national pride should be suffering, but I will whisper low in your ear, my friend, that I have little patriotism of this sort and if my country is not the one shining the light, I at least want it to shine in other skies. *Amica patria, sed magis amica veritas,*[180] and I say to peace, the happiness of mankind, and the brotherhood of nations, in the words of Lamartine to enthusiasm:

Come from the dusk or the dawn.

I am writing to you, my dear Cobden, two hours before my departure for Mugron, to which the serious illness of the old aunt, who has been like a mother to me since I had the misfortune in childhood of losing mine, is summoning me urgently. How will our journal fare during my absence? I do not know and yet my name will remain affixed to it! It is truly a difficult enterprise, as you cannot make the slightest mention of passing events without the risk of upsetting the political susceptibilities of one or another colleague. This assiduous care to avoid anything that might annoy the political parties (since all are represented in our association) deprives us of three-quarters

180. "Our native country is friendly but truth is more friendly."

of our strength. What immense good our journal might do if it contrasted the inanity and danger of current policy with the grandeur and security of free-trade policies! Before the journal was founded, I had a plan to publish a small book each month in the same mold as the *Sophisms,* in which I would have free rein. I really think it would have been more useful than the journal itself.

Our campaigning is not very active. We still need a *man of action.* When will he appear? I do not know. I should be that man, I am propelled forward by the unanimous confidence of my colleagues, *but I cannot.*[181] My character is not suited to this and all the advice in the world cannot turn a reed into an oak. In the end, when the question will preoccupy people's minds, I very much hope a Wilson will appear.

I am sending you the five or six latest issues of *Le Libre échange.* It is not very widely distributed, but I have been assured that it was not without some influence on a few of our *leading men.*[182]

It appears that this year our government will not dare to put forward a customs law that introduces significant changes into the current legislation. This is discouraging a few of our friends. As for me, I do not even want the current amendments. Down with the laws that precede the advance of public opinion! And I want not so much *free trade* itself as the spirit of *free trade* for my country. *Free trade* means a little more wealth; the spirit of *free trade* is a reform of the mind itself, that is to say, the source of all reform.

You tell me about Naples, Rome, Sardinia, and the Piedmont. But you say nothing about Tuscany. However, this region must be very curious to see. If you come across any good book on the state of this region, please try to send it to me. I would not be displeased to have a few of the oldest Italian economists, for example, *Nicolò Donato,* in my humble library. I think that, if fame were not somewhat capricious, Turgot and Adam Smith, while continuing to be acknowledged as great men, would lose their reputation as inventors.

---

79. Letter to Richard Cobden

Paris, 20 April 1847   [vol. 1, p. 157]

My dear friend, your letter of the 7th, written from Rome, found me at my post. I spent three weeks with a sick relative. I hoped that this journey

181. In English in the original.
182. In English in the original.

would also restore me to health, but this has not been so. Influenza has degenerated into a stubborn cold and I am currently spitting blood.[183] What astonishes and frightens me is to see how far a few drops of blood expelled from the lungs can weaken our poor bodily system, especially the head. I find it impossible to work and very probably I will be asking the council for a further leave of absence. I will take advantage of this to go to Lyons and Marseilles, to strengthen the links with our various associations, which are not as closely in agreement as I would wish.

I have no need to tell you how much I share your views on the *political* results of free trade. We are being accused within the democratic and *socialist* party of being devoted to the cult of *material* interests and of bringing everything down to questions of *wealth*. I must admit that when it concerns the masses I do not share this stoic disdain for wealth. This word does not mean having a few écus more; it means bread for those who are hungry, clothing for those who are cold, education, independence, and dignity. But after all, if the sole result of free trade were to increase public wealth I would not spend any more time on it than on any other matter relating to agriculture or industry. What I see above all in our campaigning is the opportunity to confront a few prejudices and to have a few just ideas penetrate the consciousness of the general public. This is an indirect benefit that outweighs the direct benefits of free trade a hundredfold, and if we are experiencing so many obstacles in spreading our *economic argument,* I believe that providence has put these obstacles in our path precisely so that the indirect benefits can be felt. If freedom were to be proclaimed tomorrow, the general public would remain in its present rut with regard to other considerations, but initially I am obliged to deal with these ancillary ideas with extreme caution so as not to upset our own colleagues. For this reason, I am concentrating my efforts on clarifying the economic problem. This will be the starting point for more advanced views. I only hope that God will allow me three or four years of strength and life! Sometimes I tell myself that if I worked alone and for my own account, I would not have to take such precautions and my career would have been more useful.

During the three weeks I was away, a few disagreements broke out within

183. This is the first explicit reference to the disease that eventually killed Bastiat. His coughing up of blood suggests that he was suffering from tuberculosis or consumption. In his last letters he also mentions a painful larynx, which might have been a symptom of throat cancer.

our associations. These concerned the difficult shade of meaning between revenue-raising duties and protectionist duties.[184] A few of our colleagues have resigned, and it so happens that these are the most industrious. They wanted to set aside the question of raising revenue, even with respect to wheat. The majority wanted total exemption for subsistence products and raw materials. This is an initial cause of dissent. There is another relating to our finances, which are far from being adequate. This is the reason why I want to travel to the Midi, but I will not leave without warning you.

I knew about the Naples reform; M. Bursotti was good enough to send me some documents on this. I gave them to Garnier, my colleague, who has doubtless lost them since he has not returned them to me. If you have the opportunity to see M. Bursotti again, please convey my good wishes and regards to him. This also applies to MM Pettiti, Scialoja, etc.

You mention the state of our newspapers, but you probably do not know the extent and depth of the problem. The art of writing is so debased that a gang of young twenty-year-olds is dictating to the entire world through the press before they have themselves studied or learned anything. But this is not the worst. The leaders are all linked to politicians and any matter becomes a ministerial question in their hands. If only God allowed the problem to stop there! There is also *venality,* which knows no bounds. Prejudice, errors, and calumny are priced at so much a line. One person has sold himself to the Russians, another to protectionism, a third to the university, and yet another to the banks, etc. And we call ourselves civilized! I truly believe that at the very most we have a foothold in the path of civilization.

Will you allow me, my dear friend, to acknowledge with some reservations the accuracy of this axiom, "Trade is the exchange of the superfluous for the essential"? When two men, in order to carry out more work in the same time, agree to share the work, can it be said that one of the two or even neither of the two is making a superfluous contribution? Is the poor devil who works twelve hours a day to earn his bread making a superfluous contribution? Trade, in which I believe, is no more than the separation of occupations or the division of labor.

It would be desirable for the pope[185] to make his views on economics

---

184. In the absence of an income tax, state revenue in the nineteenth century largely depended on indirect taxes and import duties. Revenue-raising duties would be a low rate of tax applied to all goods. Protectionist duties would be much higher and applied only to those goods that would protect domestic vested interests.

185. Pius IX.

known, even though he cannot carry them out. This would encourage part of the clergy in France, who are not very informed about our cause but who are not opposed to it either, to support us.

---

80. Letter to Richard Cobden

Paris, 5 July 1847 [vol. 1, p. 159]

My very dear friend, the details you tell me about Italy and the state of knowledge on economics in that country were of great interest to me. I received the precious collection[186] which you were good enough to send me. Alas! When will I have the time to look at them? At least I will have them available for all my friends so that, one way or another, your generous intentions will not be fruitless.

You are good enough to ask after my health. I have an almost constant cold, and if this is the case in July, what will it be like in December? But what worries me the most is the state of my brain. I do not know what has happened to the ideas which it used to produce in such abundance in the past. Now I am running after them and I cannot catch them. This worries me. I feel, dear friend, that I ought to have remained outside the association and retained the freedom to go at my own pace, to write and speak when I wished and how I wished. Instead of this, I am bound by the most indissoluble bonds by my home circumstances, the journal, finance, administration, etc., etc., and the worst of it is that this is irremediable, given that all my colleagues are otherwise occupied and can barely give their minds to our affairs during the rare meetings we have.

My friend, the ignorance and indifference in this country with regard to political economy are well beyond anything I could have imagined. This is not a reason for becoming discouraged; on the contrary, it is a reason for us to sense the usefulness and even urgency of our efforts. But I have now understood one thing, which is that free trade is a goal that is too far ahead of us. It will be fortunate if we manage to remove a few obstacles from the path to it. The greatest of these obstacles is not the protectionist party but *socialism,* with its many ramifications.[187] If monopolists were the only ad-

---

186. Bastiat is referring to the fifty-volume collection *Economisti classici italiani,* which contained works by many authors, including Cesare Beccaria, 1738–94; Gaetano Filangieri, 1752–88; Ferdinando Galiani, 1728–87; and Pietro Verri, 1728–97.

187. Socialism became an organized intellectual and political movement during the 1840s in France. It had a number of different schools of thought: the Fourrierists, the

versaries, they would not be able to handle the debate. However, socialism comes to their rescue. It accepts free trade in principle but postpones its implementation until the time when the world is organized in accordance with the design of Fourier or some other inventor of social order. And what is amazing is that, in order to prove that free trade would be harmful before that, they take up all the arguments put forward by monopolists, the balance of trade, the export of specie, the superiority of England, etc., etc.

This being so, you will answer that confronting the monopolists is to combat the socialists. No. Socialists have a theory of the *oppressive nature of capital,* which they use to explain the inequality of the condition and all the suffering of the poverty-stricken classes. They call upon the passions, sentiments, and even the best instincts of men. They attract young people, highlight the evil, and claim to have its remedy. This remedy consists of an artificial social order of their invention which will make all men equal and happy without their needing any enlightenment or virtue. Provided always that all socialists were in agreement on this social order, we might hope to shoot it down in people's minds. But you will understand that, in this realm of ideas, and as soon as it is a question of molding a social order, each person forges his own design and each morning we are assailed by new inventions. We therefore have to combat a hydra which grows ten heads as soon as we cut off one.

The unfortunate thing is that this method is powerfully attractive to the young. They are shown suffering and through this their hearts are initially touched. Then they are told that anything can be cured through the use of a few artificial schemes, and in this way their imagination is brought into the campaign. How difficult it is for them subsequently to listen to you when you come forward to disillusion them by setting out the beautiful but severe laws of social economics and say to them: "To eradicate evil from this world (and just that part of evil over which human action has some power), the procedure takes longer; vice and ignorance have to be eradicated first."

Being struck by the danger in the path along which the young were rushing headlong, I took the initiative of asking young people to listen to me. I gathered together students from the schools of law and medicine, i.e., the

followers of the anarchist Proudhon, and the Saint-Simonians. They were a major target for the classical liberals, especially given their influence in the 1848 revolutions. See the long article, with accompanying bibliography, Reybaudin, "Socialistes, socialisme," in vol. 2 of *Dictionnaire de l'économie politique,* pp. 629–41.

young men who, in a few years' time, will be governing the world, or France at least. They listened to me with goodwill and friendliness but, as you will readily understand, without understanding me very well. No matter; since the experiment has been started I will continue it to the end. You know that I am still considering the plan of a small work entitled *Economic Harmonies.* This is the *positive* point of view, whereas the *Sophisms* are *negative.* To prepare the ground, I distributed the *Sophisms* to these young people. Each one received a copy. I hope that this will unblock their minds a little, and at the end of the holidays I plan to set out the harmonies methodically.

You will now understand, my friend, what store I set by my health! Oh, may God allow me at least one year more of strength![188] May He allow me to set out to my young fellow citizens what I consider to be the true social theory in the following twelve chapters: "Needs," "Production," "Property," "Competition," "Population," "Liberty," "Equality," "Responsibility," "Solidarity," "Fraternity," "Unity," and "The Role of Public Opinion," and I will place my life in His hands without regret, indeed with joy.[189]

Farewell, my friend. Please thank Mrs. Cobden for her good wishes; I send you both every good wish for your happiness.

---

81. Letter to Félix Coudroy.

Paris, August 1847   [vol. 1, p. 78]

. . . I am sending you the latest issue of the journal. You will see that I have taken the plunge with regard to the school of law. The breach has been made. If my health stands up to it I will certainly continue and, from next November, I will be giving a course to these young people, not on pure political economy but on social economics, using this phrase in the meaning we have given it, the "Harmony of Social Laws." Something tells me that this course, intended for young people who have logical minds and warmth in their souls, will not be totally without use. I think that I will generate conviction, and following this I will at least indicate the correct sources to them.

---

188. Bastiat was aware that he did not have long to live and worried that he would not finish his book *Economic Harmonies* (he did not). He had in fact another two years and five months to live when he wrote this letter.

189. The final structure of the book (unfinished after his death but edited by Paillottet) contained twenty-five chapters. A first volume was published during Bastiat's lifetime, and it contained only ten chapters.

Finally, if God will allow me only one more year of strength, my time spent on earth will not have been in vain. Is it not better to have managed a journal and given a course to the young people in schools than to be a deputy?

Farewell, my dear Félix;

your friend.

---

82. Letter to Horace Say

Mugron, Monday, October 1847 [vol. 7, p. 380]

... Our country is in great need of instruction in economics. Ignorance in this respect is so great that I am in great fear for the future. I fear that governments will one day bitterly repent having hidden their light under a bushel. The experience I have just gained from this journey has shown me that our books and newspapers are not enough to spread our ideas. Apart from the fact that they have very few subscribers, most of these subscribers do not read them. I have seen *Le Journal des économistes* still as untouched in the bookstores as the day it was published by our good friend Guillaumin, and *Libre échange* piled on counters still encircled by its band. Is this not discouraging? I think that oral teaching must come to the aid of written teaching. Among those who attend a session, there are always a few who conceive a desire to study the question. Committees should be organized in towns and lecturers should then be sent around constantly. But how many of these do we have who are able to devote themselves to this work? For my part, I would do it willingly if I were given a completely free hand. I am tempted to try the experiment in Bordeaux. Without this, we can do but little....

---

83. Letter to Richard Cobden

Paris, 15 October 1847 [vol. 1, p. 162]

My dear friend, I learned of your return to London in this morning's journals with a great deal of pleasure. I have not had any news of you for so long! I hope that you will not neglect to write to me as soon as you are rested a little from your fatigue and that you will tell me about the reactions you have had to our program in northern Europe.

Here progress is very slow, where there is any progress at all. The crisis over subsistence products and the financial crisis have managed to put our doctrines in the shade. It appears that Providence is accumulating problems at the start of our work and is taking pleasure in making it more difficult. Perhaps it is part of the divine plan to make success dearly bought and to allow no objection to remain unheard, in order that freedom should become part of our laws only after it has become firmly embedded in public opinion. With this in mind, I will not view the delays, difficulties, obstacles, and trials as misfortunes for our cause. By prolonging the struggle, these will enable us to clarify not only the principal issue but also a great many ancillary matters which are equally as important. Success in legislation is receding, but public opinion is maturing. I would therefore not complain if we were equal to our task. We are, however, very weak. Our militant members have been reduced to four or five stalwarts, almost all of whom are very busy in other spheres. I myself lack practical education; my type of approach, which is to examine principles, makes me unfit to debate events when they accumulate, as I should. What is more, I lose intellectual strength when my physical strength fails. If I could negotiate with nature and exchange ten years of sickly life for two years of vigor and health, the bargain would be quickly struck.

We are also encountering major obstacles from your side of the Channel. My dear Cobden, I must speak frankly to you. In adopting free trade, England has not adopted the policies which logically result from it. Will it do so? I do not doubt this, but when? That is the question. The position that you and your friends will be adopting in Parliament will have an immense influence on our undertaking. If you repudiate your diplomatic policy with energy and if you manage to reduce the size of your naval forces we will be strong. If not, what sort of figure will we cut in the eyes of the public? When we forecast that free trade will lead English policy down the path of justice, peace, economy, and colonial independence, will France be bound to take our word for it? There is an inveterate distrust of England here, which I would go so far as to call a feeling of hostility, which is as old as the very names *French* and *English*. Well then, this feeling is excusable. Its mistake is to disapprove globally of all your parties and fellow citizens. But should not nations judge each other by their external acts? It is often said that nations should not be confused with their governments. This adage is both true and false, and I dare say that it is false with regard to those peoples who have constitutional means of influencing *public opinion.* Bear in mind that France is not educated in economics. Whenever the French read history, therefore, and when they note the succession of invasions by England, when they study the diplomatic means which led to these invasions, when they see a centuries-old system followed assiduously whether the Whigs or the

Tories are at the helm of state, and when they read in your newspapers that England currently has thirty-four thousand sailors on warships, how do you expect them to trust in the strength of a principle, which incidentally they do not understand, to bring about a change in your policy? Something else is needed, namely deeds. Restore free trade to your colonies, repeal your Navigation Act,[190] and above all disband your naval forces and retain only those that are essential for your security, and in so doing reduce your overheads and debts and relieve your population, cease to threaten other peoples and the freedom of the seas, and then, you may be sure, France will pay attention.

My dear Cobden, in a speech I gave in Lyons, I dared to forecast that this legislature, which has seven years more to run, would bring your political and economic systems into harmony. "Before seven years are up," I said, "England will have reduced its army and navy by half." Do not make me tell a lie.[191] I met only with incredulity. I am being blamed for being a prophet; I am taken for a fanatic with short-term views who fails to understand British wiles. I, for my part, have confidence in two forces, the force of truth and the force of your true interests.

I do not have a detailed knowledge of what is happening in Athens and Madrid. What I can tell you is that Palmerston and Bulwer inspire universal mistrust. You will answer that if Mr. Bulwer is scheming in Madrid, M. Glucksberg[192] is doing the same. So be it. But if the former is acting against the interests of France as the latter is doing against the interests of England, there is nevertheless this difference, that England boasts that it knows where its interests lie. We are still imbued with our old ideas. Is it surprising that our actions reflect this? You, on the other hand, who have shed these ideas, should now reject the acts that go with them. Repudiate Palmerston and Bulwer. Nothing would do more to place us, free traders, in an excellent position in the public's eyes. What is more, I would like you to tell me the position you intend to take on this matter in Parliament. I will start to influence public opinion here.

---

190. The Navigation Act was repealed in 1849 by the cabinet of John Russell.

191. Of course, this prediction did not come true. A couple of years after his death the Crimean War broke out (1854–56), and by the end of the century Britain had the largest navy and the most extensive empire in the world.

192. Louis Charles Decazes.

I must admit, my dear friend, that, although I am against any form of charlatanism, if you have a majority and are in a position to bring in a new policy in accordance with the principles of *free trade,* I would like you to do this with some pomp and ceremony. If you reduce your navy, I would like you to link this measure specifically to *free trade* and proclaim loudly that England had gone down the wrong path and that, because her current purpose is diametrically opposed to that it has pursued up to now, its means need to be the opposite as well.

I will not talk to you about wine. I see that your financial situation does not allow you to pursue major tax reform. However, is it too much to ask for a moderation in the dues which will not be harmful to your revenues? I would like it to be you personally who puts forward this proposal, and I will tell you why some other time. I have room only to assure you of my friendship.

---

84. Letter to Richard Cobden

Paris, 9 November 1847   [vol. 1, p. 166]

My dear Cobden, I read with great interest your account of your journey and I hope to gain as much pleasure as instruction from the articles you plan to send to *Le Journal des économistes.*[193] M. Say has already written to you about this. He is always eager to seize an opportunity to enhance this compilation which he founded and supports. Your letters are a welcome advantage to him. I urge you most sincerely to devote part of your available time to this. The cause we serve is not bounded by the borders of a nation. It is universal and will find its solution only in its acceptance by all peoples. For this reason, you can do nothing more useful than to increase the reputation and circulation of *Le Journal des économistes.* I am not totally satisfied with this review; I am now sorry that I did not take over its management. Philosophical argument of this sort would have suited me better than daily polemics.

The difficulties surrounding us are increasing; we do not have only *vested interests* against us. Public ignorance is now becoming manifest in all its sorry extent. What is more, the *parties* need to destroy us. Following a series

---

193. *Le Journal des économistes* lists many speeches and letters by Cobden in the general table of contents for the years 1841–65.

of circumstances which would take too long to recount here, they are all against us. All have the same goal, *tyranny*. They differ only on the question of knowing in whose hands the despotism will be placed. This is why the thing they fear most is a spirit of true freedom. I assure you, my dear Cobden, that, if I were twenty years younger and in good health, I would take common sense as my armor and truth for my lance, and I would be sure to win. Alas, however, the spirit cannot do anything without the body, in spite of its noble origin.

What grieves me above all, I who am so devoted to the democratic sentiment in all its universality, is to see French democracy in the vanguard of opposition to free trade. This echoes warlike ideas, an exaggerated sense of national honor and passions which seem to grow green again at each revolution; 1830 has *manured*[194] them. You tell me that we let ourselves fall too easily into the trap set by the protectionists and that we ought to have ignored their *anglophobic* arguments. I think you are mistaken. Doubtless it is useful to eradicate protection, but it is even more useful to eradicate national hatred. I know my country; she has a lively attitude in which truth and falsehood are mixed. France sees an England that is capable of crushing all the world's navies and moreover knows that it is directed by an unscrupulous oligarchy. This fact is blocking its vision and prevents France from understanding free trade. I would go even further and say that even were she to understand it, she would want none of it for its purely economic benefits. What we need to show France above all is that free trade would cause the military dangers she fears to disappear. For my part I would prefer to fight on for a few years more and overcome national prejudice as well as economic ones. I am not worried that the protectionists have selected this field of battle. My intention is to publish in our journal the debates held in Parliament and in particular the speeches by *free traders*.

The 15th.

My friend, I will not hide from you that I am terrified by the vacuum that is forming around us. Our opponents are full of daring and ardor. Our friends, on the other hand, are becoming discouraged and losing interest. What good is it to be right a thousandfold if we cannot make ourselves heard? The protectionists' tactics, greatly supported by the newspapers, are to let us be right all on our own.

194. In English in the original.

85. Letter to Félix Coudroy

Paris, 5 January 1848 [vol. 1, p. 78]

My dear Félix, while writing to Domenger, I am taking advantage of the opportunity just to wish you a better year than the previous ones.

I am ashamed to publish the second volume of my *Sophisms;* it is just a ragbag of what has already been printed in journals. A third volume will be needed to lift me up; I have material in rough form for it.[195]

However, I would much more like to publish the course I am giving to young students in the schools.[196] Unfortunately, I have the time only to jot a few notes down on paper. This infuriates me, since I can tell you, and you know this already, that we see political economy from a slightly new angle. Something tells me that it can be simplified and more closely linked to politics and moral values.

Farewell; I must leave you as I am reduced to counting each minute.

---

86. Letter to Mrs. Schwabe

Paris, 17 January 1848 [vol. 7, p. 420]

Madam,

I am very pleased to learn that Mr. Schwabe has had a pleasant journey and that he found the situation in England improving.

Thank you for having thought of sending me *Punch.* Perhaps I will find something in it for *Le Libre échange,* after which I will pass it on to M. Anisson or will bring it back to you myself.

I enclose five copies of the last issue of *Le Libre échange.* I wrote the first article on *armaments* in the hope that it may have some influence in England. I am very pleased to learn therefore that you will be ensuring that it gets there.

195. Two series of the *Sophisms* were published (as *Economic Sophisms*), but a third never appeared.

196. The notes Bastiat refers to have not survived, but his address "To the Youth of France" (*OC,* vol. 6, p. 1, "À la jeunesse française"), which prefaces *Economic Harmonies,* might give some idea of what he said to the students in his course.

87. Letter to Félix Coudroy

Paris, 24 January 1848 [vol. 1, p. 78]

I can write you a few words only as I am suffering from the same illness I had in Mugron and which, among other disagreeable characteristics, has deprived me of all my strength. It is impossible for me to think, let alone write.

My friend, I would have liked to discuss our campaign with you but I am not capable of this. I am not at all happy with our journal; it is weak and anemic like anything that comes out of an association. I am going to ask for total power, but alas, I will not be given health with power.

I am not receiving *Le Mémorial*[197] (from Bordeaux), and consequently I have not seen your article "Anglophobia."[198] I am sorry about this. I might perhaps have drawn a few ideas from it, or we might have reprinted it.

---

88. Letter to Mrs. Schwabe

Paris, 27 January 1848 [vol. 7, p. 420]

Please receive the homage of a small volume which I have just had published. It is not a weighty work; it just contains some of the trifles that have already appeared in journals. I have been assured that this superficial format is useful in its way, and this is what has decided me to continue down this path which is not at all to my taste.[199]

---

89. Letter to Félix Coudroy

Paris, 13 February 1848 [vol. 1, p. 79]

My dear Félix, I have had no news of you and do not know how your trial is going. I presume that the decree has not been issued, since you would have told me if it had. Please God that the court is properly inspired! The more I think about this matter, the more I think that the judges cannot make conjectures against common law; if this is in doubt, the eternal law of justice (and even the Code) should take precedence.

Politics are stifling our program somewhat. Besides, there is a very fla-

---

197. *Le Mémorial bordelais.*
198. Bastiat himself wrote an essay called "Anglomania, Anglophobia." See p. 320.
199. (Paillottet's note) This refers to the second series of *Economic Sophisms.*

grant conspiracy of silence which began with our journal.[200] If I could have foreseen this, I would not have founded it. Reasons of health have obliged me to give up the management of this broadsheet. It must be added that I did not take pleasure in my involvement in view of the small number of our readers, and the divergence of political opinions of our colleagues did not allow me to stamp a sufficiently democratic management style on the journal; the finest aspects of the question had to be kept in the dark.

If there had been a greater number of subscribers, I would have been able to make this broadsheet my own property, but the state of public opinion stands in the way of this, and in addition my health is an invincible obstacle. Now I will be able to work with a little more latitude.

I am continuing to give my course to law students. My audience is not very numerous but its members come regularly and take notes; the grain is falling on fertile ground. I would have liked to have been able to write up this course, but I will probably leave only confused notes.

Farewell, my dear Félix. Write to me, tell me how your affairs and health are doing; it is not out of the question that I will come and see you before too long. Please remember me with affection to your good sister.

---

90. Letter to Mrs. Schwabe

Paris, 16 February 1848   [vol. 7, p. 421]

I am very grateful for all the kindnesses you shower on me. I have received your excellent syrups which have succeeded in curing me. I therefore hope to go to a concert this evening, but rather late as I am dining with M. de Lamartine, and you will understand what it costs to abandon the music of his words even for that of Chopin. However, as the concert starts late, I will tear myself away from the charming conversation of our great poet.

---

91. Letter to Richard Cobden

Paris, 25 February 1848   [vol. 1, p. 168]

My dear Cobden, you already know our news. Yesterday we were a monarchy and today we are a republic.[201]

---

200. *Le libre échange.*
201. Louis-Philippe abdicated on 24 February 1848, thus bringing the July Monarchy to an end.

I have not the time to tell you about it, I simply want to put before you a point of view of the utmost importance.

France wants and needs peace. Her expenses are going to increase, her income to decrease, and her budget is already in deficit. She therefore needs peace and a reduction in her military undertakings.

Without this reduction no serious savings are possible, and therefore no financial reform and no abolition of odious taxes. And without these, the revolution will fall out of favor.

But France, as you will understand, *cannot take the initiative of disarming.* It would be absurd to ask her to do so.

You see the consequences. Because she does not disarm, she cannot reform anything; and because she does not reform anything, she will be killed by her finances.

The sole fact that foreigners are *retaining their forces* is obliging us to perish. But we do not wish to perish. Therefore, if foreign nations do not put us in a position to disarm by disarming themselves, if we have to keep three or four hundred thousand men in a state of readiness, we will be drawn into a war of words. This is inevitable. For in this case, the only means of being able to draw breath here would be to create embarrassment for all the kings of Europe.

If, therefore, foreigners understand our situation and its dangers, they will not hesitate to give us this proof of confidence by disarming *significantly.* In this way, they will put us in a position to do likewise, rebuild our finances, relieve the people, and accomplish the work which has been thrust upon us.

If, on the other hand, foreigners consider it prudent to remain armed, I do not hesitate to say that this so-called prudence is the greatest imprudence, since it will reduce us to the extremity which I have already mentioned.

Please heaven that England understands this and makes it understood. It would save the future of Europe. If she follows the traditions of old-style politics, I challenge you to tell me how we can escape the consequences.

Think carefully about this letter, dear Cobden, and weigh all its statements. See for yourself whether everything I have said to you is not inevitable.

If you remain armed, we will remain armed with no evil intentions. But because we remain armed, we will be overcome by the weight of unpopular taxes. No government could survive this. Governments can change as much as they like. Each will encounter the same problem and the day will come when it will be said, "Since we cannot send the soldiers back to their homes, we will have to dispatch them to arouse the people."

If you disarm to a significant extent and if you unite closely with us to advise Prussia to follow the same policy, under these conditions a new era may and will spring into being on 24 February.

---

92. Letter to Richard Cobden

Paris, 26 February 1848 [vol. 1, p. 170]

My dear Cobden, I would give a great deal of money (if I had it) to have M. de Lamartine as our minister of foreign affairs for a moment. But I cannot reach him.

I wanted to go to London, but not without having seen him, since I need to submit to him the ideas I have to communicate to you.

England can do an immense amount of good without damaging herself in the slightest. She can replace France's disastrous prejudices with a sincere affection. She has only to will this. For example, why does she not quite freely abandon her veiled opposition to our sad conquest of Algeria? Why does she not quite freely abandon the dangers arising from the right of inspection?[202] Why does she allow the idea that she wishes to humiliate us to take root here? Why wait for events to poison these matters? What a magnificent spectacle it would be if England said: "When France has chosen a government, England will make haste to recognize it, and as proof of her friendship she will also recognize Algeria as French and renounce the right of inspection, of which she moreover acknowledges the ineffectualness and drawbacks!"

Tell me, my dear Cobden, what would such acts cost your country if they were freely carried out as I describe?

Over here, we cannot divest ourselves of the idea held by the French that the English covet Algeria. This is absurd, but this is how it appears.

We cannot efface from people's minds that the right to inspect is part of your policy. This is also absurd, but this is how it appears.

In the name of peace and humanity, bring about these great measures! Let us carry out popular diplomatic policies and let us do it in good time.

---

202. As part of the British campaign against the slave trade, British vessels would inspect foreign ships on the high seas to see if they were carrying slaves.

Write to me. Tell me frankly if a journey to London with this in mind, under the auspices of M. de Lamartine, would have any chance of bringing about a result. I will show him your letter.

---

93. Letter to Marie-Julienne Badbedat (Mme Marsan)

27 February 1848 [From the private collection of Jean-Claude Paul-Dejean]

My dear lady,

You must be anxious. I would like to reassure you. My cold has almost disappeared and in this respect I am in my normal state, with which you are familiar. On the other hand, the revolution has left me safe and sound.

As you will see in the newspapers, on the 23rd everything seemed to be over. Paris had a festive air; everything was illuminated. A huge gathering moved along the boulevards singing. Flags were adorned with flowers and ribbons. When they reached the Hôtel des Capucines, the soldiers blocked their path and fired a round of musket fire at point-blank range into the crowd. I leave you to imagine the sight offered by a crowd of thirty thousand men, women, and children fleeing from the bullets, the shots, and those who fell.[203]

An instinctive feeling prevented me from fleeing as well, and when it was all over I was on the site of a massacre with five or six workmen, facing about sixty dead and dying people. The soldiers appeared stupefied. I begged the officer to have the corpses and wounded moved in order to have the latter cared for and to avoid having the former used as flags by the people when they returned, but he had lost his head.

The workers and I then began to move the unfortunate victims onto the pavement, as doors refused to open. At last, seeing the fruitlessness of our efforts, I withdrew. But the people returned and carried the corpses to the outlying districts, and a hue and cry was heard all through the night. The following morning, as though by magic, two thousand barricades made the insurrection fearsome. Fortunately, as the troop did not wish to fire on the National Guard, the day was not as bloody as might have been expected.

All is now over. The Republic has been proclaimed. You know that this is good news for me. The people will govern themselves. I am convinced that for a long time they will govern themselves badly, but they will learn from

203. Fifty-two people were killed by the military.

experience. Right now, ideas I do not share have the upper hand. It is fashionable to expand the functions of the state considerably, and I think they should be restricted. For this reason, I am outside the movement, although several of my friends are very powerful in it. Two friends and I produced a leaflet to inject some of our ideas into the intellectual to and fro.[204]

Do not worry about the sequel. My age and health have extinguished in me any taste for street campaigning. As for a situation, I will not be seeking one, and will wait until I am considered useful.

I am writing you just a hasty note. I still have repose in view, since age and duties are piling up.

Julie is not giving me as good news as I would like.

Please ask her to write to me from time to time. I embrace both her and her children warmly.

Farewell, my dear lady.

---

94. Letter to Félix Coudroy

Paris, 29 February 1848   [vol. 1, p. 80]

My dear Félix, in spite of the shabby and ridiculous conditions you have been given, I will wholeheartedly congratulate you if you reach a settlement. We are getting old; a little peace and tranquillity in our later years is the happy condition to which we should lay claim.

Since, dear friend, I cannot give you either consolation or advice on this sad outcome, you will not be surprised if I immediately tell you about the major events which have just occurred.

The February revolution has certainly been more heroic than that of July.[205] There is nothing so admirable as the courage, order, calm, and moderation of the people of Paris. But what will the results be? For the last ten years, false doctrines that were much in fashion nurtured the illusions of the working classes. They are now convinced that the state is obliged to provide bread, work, and education to all. The provisional government has made a solemn promise to do so; it will therefore be obliged to increase taxes to endeavor to keep this promise, and in spite of this it will not keep it. I have no need to tell you what kind of future lies ahead of us.

204. Bastiat wrote a number of articles in February 1848 for *La République française* on these events.

205. The revolution of February 1848 brought an end to the July Monarchy, which in turn had come to power by revolution in 1830.

There is one possible recourse, which is to combat the error itself, but this task is so unpopular that it cannot be carried out safely; I am, nevertheless, determined to devote myself to this if the country sends me to the National Assembly.

It is clear that all these promises will succeed in ruining the provinces to satisfy the population of Paris, since the government will never undertake to feed all the sharecroppers, workers, and craftsmen in the *départements* and, above all, in the countryside. If our country understands the situation, I say frankly that she will elect me; if not, I will carry out my duty with greater safety as a simple writer.

The scramble for office has started, and several of my friends are very powerfully placed. Some of them ought to understand that my special studies may be useful, but I do not hear them mentioned. As for me, I will set foot in the town hall only as an interested spectator; I will gaze on the greasy pole but not climb it. Poor people! How much disillusionment is in store for them! It would have been so simple and so just to ease their burden by decreasing taxes; they want to achieve this through the plentiful bounty of the state and they cannot see that the whole mechanism consists in taking away ten to give it back eight, not to mention the true freedom that will be destroyed in the operation!

I have tried to get these ideas out into the street through a short-lived journal[206] which was produced in response to the situation; would you believe that the printing workers themselves discuss and disapprove of the enterprise? They call it *counterrevolutionary.*

How, oh how can we combat a school which has strength on its side and which promises perfect happiness to everyone?

My friend, if someone said to me, "You will have your idea accepted today but tomorrow you will die in obscurity," I would agree to it without hesitation, but striving without good fortune and without even being listened to is a thankless task!

What is more, as order and confidence are the supreme aims at present, so we must refrain from any criticism and support the provisional government at all cost, making allowances even for its errors. This is a duty that obliges me to make an infinite number of allowances.

Farewell, the elections will take place shortly, and we will see what hap-

---

206. *Jacques Bonhomme.*

pens then. In the meantime, let me know if you come across any attitudes favorable to me.

---

95. Letter to Bernard Domenger in Mugron

Paris, 4 March 1848 [vol. 7, p. 385]

My dear Domenger,

You are quite right to remain calm. Apart from the fact that we will all need it, the tempest would need to howl furiously before it was felt in Mugron. Up to now, Paris is enjoying the most perfect peace, and this spectacle is in my view just as imposing in its way as courage in battle. We have just witnessed the funeral ceremony.[207] I think that the entire universe was out in the street. I have never seen so many people. I have to say that the population appeared to be friendly but cold. Nothing can bring it to utter cries of enthusiasm. This is perhaps all to the good and appears to prove that time and experience have matured us. Are not unbridled demonstrations something of an obstacle to the proper management of affairs?

The political aspect of the future is not being given much attention. It seems that universal suffrage and other rights of the people are so unanimously agreed upon that they are given no further thought. But what is darkening our prospects are economic matters. In this respect, ignorance is so profound and widespread that severe experiences are to be feared. The idea that there is a scheme yet unknown but easy to find, which is bound to ensure the well-being of all by reducing work, is the dominant theme. As it is adorned with such fine terms as *fraternity, generosity,* etc., no one dares attack these wild illusions. Besides, no one would know how to do so. People instinctively fear the consequences which may arise from the exaggerated hopes of the working classes, but between this and being in a position to determine the truth there is a wide gap. For my part, I continue to think that the fate of the workers depends on the speed with which capital is built up. Anything that can, directly or indirectly, damage property, undermine confidence, or weaken security is an obstacle to the accumulation of capital and has an unfavorable effect on the working classes. This is also true for all taxes and irritating governmental interference. What should we therefore

---

207. The ceremony that took place on Saturday, 4 March, organized by the provisional government in honor of the citizens who died for the Republic during the days of 23 and 24 February.

think of the systems in fashion today which have all these disadvantages at once? As a writer, or in another capacity, if my fellow citizens call upon me, I will defend my principles to the last. The current revolution is not changing them any more than it is changing my behavior.

Let us say no more about the statements attributed to F——. This is far behind us. Frankly this meretricious program could not be sustained. I hope that people will be satisfied with the choices made in our *département*. Lefranc is a courageous and honest Republican who is incapable of making life difficult for anyone without serious and just reasons.

---

96. Letter to Richard Cobden

Mugron, 5 April 1848 [vol. 1, p. 171]

My dear friend, here I am, all alone. Why can I not bury myself here forever and work peacefully on the economic synthesis[208] I have in my head and which will never leave it! For, unless there is a change in public opinion, I am going to be sent to Paris with the responsibility of the awe-inspiring mandate of a representative of the people. If I had health and strength, I would accept this mission with enthusiasm. But what can my weak voice and my sickly and nervous constitution do in the midst of the revolutionary whirlwind? How much wiser it would have been to devote my final days to examining in silence the great problem of society and what the future holds in store for it, especially since something tells me that I would have found the answer. Poor village, the humble dwelling of my fathers, I am about to bid you an eternal farewell; I am going to leave you with the foreboding that my name and life, lost in the midst of storms, will not have even the modest usefulness for which you prepared me!

My friend, I am too far from the theater of events to tell you about them. You will learn about them before I do, and at the time I am writing to you, it may be that the facts on which I might base my reasoning are past history. If the overthrown government had left us finances in good order, I would have total faith in the future of the Republic. Unfortunately the treasury has been destroyed and I know enough about the history of our first revolution to realize the influence of financial chaos on events. An urgent measure leads to an arbitrary one, and it is above all in this situation that fate

---

208. Bastiat is referring here to his posthumously published *Economic Harmonies*.

exercises its power. At present, the people are behaving admirably, and you would be surprised to see how well *universal suffrage* is working right from the start. But what will happen when taxes, instead of decreasing, increase, when there is a shortage of jobs, and when bitter reality succeeds brilliant hopes? I had perceived a lifeline, on which it is true I scarcely placed much hope, since it presupposed wisdom and prudence in kings; this was the simultaneous disarmament of Europe. If this happened, finances would have been restructured everywhere, nations relieved and restored to order, industry would have developed, the number of jobs increased, and peoples would have waited calmly for the gradual development of administrative institutions. Monarchs, however, have preferred to *stake their all* or rather they were unable to assess present or future situations. They are pressing against a spring, without understanding that as their strength weakens that of the spring increases proportionately.

Imagine that they had disarmed everywhere and reduced taxes accordingly, and had, also, given to their nations institutions that are, moreover, not to be gainsaid. France, burdened with debt, would make haste to do likewise, only too happy to be able to found the Republic on the solid basis of a genuine relief of the burden on the people. Peace and progress would go hand in hand. However, the opposite has happened. People are arming everywhere, public expenditure (and taxes and hindrances) is increasing everywhere, when the taxes that exist are precisely what is causing revolutions. Will not all of this end in a terrible explosion?

What is wrong? Is justice so difficult to exercise and prudence so difficult to understand?

Since my arrival here, I have not seen an English newspaper. I do not know what is happening in your Parliament. I would have hoped that England would take the initiative in rational politics and would take it with the energetic boldness which she has shown so often in the past. I would have hoped that she would want *to teach mankind how to live,*[209] by disarming, abandoning expensive colonies, ceasing threatening behavior, protecting herself from any possibility of being threatened, removing unpopular taxes, and presenting the world with a fine spectacle of union, strength, wisdom, justice, and security. But, alas! Political economy has not yet sufficiently pervaded the masses, even in your country.

209. In English in the original.

97. Letter to Horace Say

Mugron, 12 April 1848 [vol. 7, p. 381]

My dear friend, I constantly look for your name in the newspapers, but they are not yet discussing the elections. They are probably too busy reporting on the political clubs. This is the only explanation I can give of the silence of the Paris press. Perhaps Paris is too stormy a theater, given your character and the life you are used to. I now regret that you have not considered moving to one of the *départements*. Socialist folly has whipped up such terror that because of your well-known antecedents you would have had wonderful opportunities there. Your candidature has the advantage of giving you the opportunity of putting about sane ideas. This is a great deal but not enough for our cause. For this reason, make a supreme effort, abandon your customary reserve for a few days, start something of a campaign, and leave no stone unturned to enter the Constituent Assembly. I sincerely believe that the salvation of the country depends on our principles gaining a majority.

If there is no change in public opinion here, my election is assured. I even think that I will gain all the votes except for those of a few traders in resin who are terrified of free trade.

All the committees[210] in the cantons support me.

Next Sunday, we will be having a general central meeting. I would have to make a huge mess of things to change the attitudes of electors toward me.

A very strange fact is the ignorance of socialist doctrines of the people in this country. There is a horror of communism. But communism is seen only as the sharing out of land. Last Sunday, during a large public meeting, a general murmur arose when I said that communism was not a threat in this respect. People seemed to deduce from these words that I was only very tepidly opposed to this form of communism. The rest of my speech removed this impression. It is really very dangerous to speak before an audience that is so little informed. You risk not being understood. . . .

I must admit to you that I am very worried about the future. How can industry revive when it is accepted in principle that the scope for regulation

---

210. Candidates to the elections of deputies were heard, then nominated, by county committees who then gathered to establish a list of candidates for the district. Each district would then discuss its candidates with the other districts in order to arrive at a single list for the *département*.

is unlimited? When every minute a decree on earnings, working hours, the cost of things, etc., can upset all economic decision making?

Farewell, my dear M. Say. Please remember me to Mme Say and M. Léon.

P.S. The central meeting of delegates took place yesterday; I do not know why it was brought forward. After answering questions, I withdrew and this morning learned that I have all of the votes except two. Having forgotten to post my letter before leaving, I have opened it to tell you this result which may please you. Try to make a supreme effort, my dear friend, to ensure that political economy, which is lifeless in the Collège de France,[211] is represented in the Chamber by M. Say. Shame to the country, if it excludes a name of this eminence that is so nobly borne!

---

98. Letter to Richard Cobden

Paris, 11 May 1848   [vol. 1, p. 173]

My dear Cobden, it is impossible for me to write to you in any length. Besides, what would I say to you? How can I foretell what will come out of an assembly of nine hundred people who are not restricted by any rule or precedent, who do not know one another, who are under the sway of so many errors, who have to satisfy so many just and illusory hopes, and who, in spite of this, have difficulty in listening to each other and debating because of their numbers and the huge size of the hall? All that I can say is that the National Assembly has good intentions. A democratic spirit reigns there. I would have liked to say as much of the spirit of peace and nonintervention. We will know the outcome on Monday. This is the day set for discussions on Poland and Italy.

In the meantime, I will go straight to the subject of my letter.

You know that a workers' commission used to meet at the Luxembourg Palace under the chairmanship of M. Louis Blanc. The presence of the National Assembly dispersed it, but it was quick to set up a commission responsible for carrying out an inquiry on the situation of industrial and agricultural workers and suggest ways of improving their lot.

This is a huge task, which the current illusions are making very hazardous.

I have been called upon to take part in this commission. I was fairly nom-

---

211. (Paillottet's note) The chair occupied by M. Michel Chevalier had been withdrawn and not yet reinstated.

inated, after I set out my doctrines frankly, but above all from the point of view of property rights. I am having printed what I said, which succeeded in having me nominated, in an article entitled *Property and Law,* which will be appearing in the next issue of *Le Journal des économistes.* Please read it.[212]

I now want to use this inquiry to bring truth out into the open. Whether I am right or wrong, we need the truth. In France, we do not have much experience of the *machinery* known as a *parliamentary inquiry.* Do you know of any work which describes the art of organizing these inquiries so as to reveal the truth? If you know of one, please let me know, or better still send it to me.

Anti-British prejudices are still far from being extinguished here. People think that the English are devoting themselves on the continent to countering the republican policy of France and I would not put this past your aristocracy. For this reason, I will be following with great interest your new campaign in favor of political and economic reform, which may reduce the foreign influence of the *squirearchy.*[213]

---

99. Letter to Mrs. Schwabe

Paris, 17 May 1848   [vol. 7, p. 421]

You must think me a very badly brought up Frenchman to have taken so long to thank you and your husband for the many gestures of affection you both showered on me during your stay in Paris. I certainly have not forgotten them. The memory of them will never be effaced from my heart, but you know that I made a journey to the Pyrenees I hold so dear. What is more, I did not know where to address my letters; this one will be sent in the hope it will be lucky.

The National Assembly has met. What will come out of this blazing furnace? Peace or war? Fortune or misfortune for the human race? Up to now, it has been like a child who stutters before speaking. Can you imagine a hall as big as the Place de la Concorde? In it, there are nine hundred members debating and three thousand onlookers. To have the opportunity of making yourself heard and understood, you have to utter high-pitched shouts accompanied by very emphatic hand movements, which rapidly result in an outburst of unreasonable fury in whoever is speaking. That is how we are conducting our internal proceedings. This takes up a lot of time and

---

212. *OC,* vol. 4, p. 275, "Propriété et loi."
213. That is, the nobility and the gentry. In English in the original.

the general public does not have the common sense to understand that this waste of time is inevitable.

You will have learned from the newspapers of the events of the 15th. The Assembly was invaded by a horde of the populace. The pretext was a demonstration in favor of Poland. For four hours, these people endeavored to wrest from us the most subversive votes. The Assembly bore this tempest calmly, and to do justice to our population and our century I have to say that we cannot complain of any personal violence. The result of this outrage has been to make known the wishes of the entire country. It enables the executive power to take prudent measures to which it cannot have recourse if there is no provocation. It is very fortunate that things were taken so far. Without this, the aims of the seditionists would never have been so clearly seen. Their hypocrisy brought them followers. They no longer have any; they have been unmasked, and once again the finger of Providence has been seen. There were ten thousand chances that things would not turn out so well.

I assume you are calling on Mrs. Cobden. Please convey to her the admiration I feel for her, following all you have said about her.

Farewell, dear lady. Can you not give me some hope of seeing you again? Your children do not know enough French and one of your daughters is a citizen of the Republic.[214] She must be made to breathe the air of her fatherland.

I shake the hand of Mr. Schwabe with great affection.

---

100. Letter to Richard Cobden

Paris, 27 May 1848   [vol. 1, p. 175]

My dear Cobden, thank you for having given me the opportunity of making the acquaintance of Mr. Baines.[215] I regret only having had just an instant to talk to such a distinguished man.

Forgive me for having caused you the trouble of writing to me on the subject of inquiries and their format. I have abandoned our working committee for the one on finance. When all is said and done, this is where all the questions and even all the utopian ideas will end up. Unless the country renounces the use of reason, it will need to subordinate even its foreign

---

214. One of the daughters of Mrs. Schwabe was born in Paris shortly after the Revolution.

215. Edward Baines.

policy to financial stringency to some extent. If only we can make the policy of peace triumph! For my part, I am convinced that, after the present war, nothing is more disastrous for my country than the system inaugurated by our government, which it calls "armed diplomacy." From whatever point of view it is considered, a system of this sort is unjust, wrong, and ruinous. I am saddened to think that just a few simple notions of political economy would be enough to make it unpopular in France. But how do we manage this when the vast majority thinks that the interests of nations and even interests in general are at root naturally antagonistic? We must wait for this prejudice to dissipate, and this will take a long time. As far as I am concerned, nothing can change my belief that my role was to be a country magistrate as in the past or, at the very most, a teacher. It should not be my fate to have been born in an age in which my place is on the stage of active politics.

What would be apparently simpler than convincing France and England to agree to disarm simultaneously? What would they have to fear? How many genuine, imminent, and pressing difficulties would they then be capable of resolving? How many taxes could be reformed! How many sufferings could be relieved! How much popular affection could be gained! How many troubles and revolutions could be averted! But we will not achieve this. The physical impossibility of collecting taxes will not suffice, in either of our countries, to have disarmament accepted, even though this is advisable as the simplest of prudent measures.

However, I have to say that I was pleasantly surprised to find the most favorable attitudes in our committee, made up of sixty members. May God enable the spirit animating it to be first diffused upon the Assembly and subsequently upon the general public. But alas! Out of fifteen committees there is one, responsible for ways and means, which has attained concepts of peace and economy. The other fourteen committees are preoccupied only with projects, all of which will lead to new expenditure; will they withstand the torrent?

I believe that at the present time you are enjoying the company of Mrs. Cobden and Mr. and Mrs. Schwabe. Please convey to them my affectionate good wishes. Since the departure of Mr. Schwabe, the Champs-Élysées seems to me to be a desert; before, I thought that they lived up to their name.[216]

---

216. Bastiat is making a play on words with the name of the Schwabes. In German, *der Schwabe* is a Swabian and *schwabenstreich* means "tomfoolery." Perhaps he is hinting that the Schwabes threw good parties.

101. Letter to Félix Coudroy

Paris, 9 June 1848   [vol. 1, p. 82]

My dear Félix, it has indeed been a very long time since I wrote to you; you must forgive me as I do not know which way to turn. This is how I live; I get up at six o'clock, dress, shave, have breakfast, and scan the newspapers, which takes me up to seven or half past seven. Around nine o'clock I have to leave, as the session of the finance committee[217] to which I belong starts at ten. This lasts up to one o'clock and then the public session begins and lasts until seven. I return home for dinner, and it is very rare that after dinner there is not a meeting of subcommissions responsible for special matters.

The only time at my disposal is therefore between eight and nine in the morning, and this is also when visitors arrive. All of this means that not only do I have no time for my correspondence but I cannot study anything just at the time when, now that I am in contact with the practical side of matters, I realize that I have everything to learn.

For this reason, I am profoundly disgusted with this job and what is happening is not conducive to raising my spirits. The Assembly[218] is certainly excellent from the point of view of its intentions; it has plenty of goodwill and wants to do good, but it cannot, first of all because it has no knowledge of the principles and secondly because there is no initiative anywhere. The executive commission is totally self-effacing; no one knows whether the members composing it agree with one another, because they emerge from their inertia only to express the most strangely incoherent of views. It is useless for the Chamber to express repeatedly its confidence in order to encourage them to act; it would appear that they have taken the decision to leave us to our own devices. Imagine what an assembly of nine hundred people responsible for debating and acting is like and add to this a huge hall in which one cannot be heard. For having wanted to say a few words today,[219] I have left with a cold, which is why I am not going out and can write.

But other symptoms are much more terrifying. The dominant notion, the one that has permeated every class of society, is that the state is respon-

217. Bastiat was vice president of the finance committee of the Constituent Assembly. On 9 May the Assembly elected the five members of an executive commission, a sort of joint presidency, above the ministers. General Cavaignac was nominated minister of war on 17 May.

218. Constituent Assembly.

219. On 8 June a proposition was made to raise by 5 percent the export subsidy of woollen cloth. The following day, Bastiat argued against the proposal.

sible for providing a living for everyone. This has caused a general rush in which the workers have finally become involved. They are blamed, feared; and what do they do? What every class up to now has done. The workers have a better case; they say, "Give us bread in exchange for work." Monopolists were and still are more demanding. But where will this lead us in the end? I dread to think.

Naturally the finance committee is resisting this, as its mission makes it thrifty and economical; it has therefore already become unpopular. "You are standing up for capital!" We are being killed by this word, since you ought to know that here "capital" is seen as a devouring monster.

Far from being dead, Duprat is not ill.

"The people you are killing off are in quite good health."

In the riots of the 15th,[220] I was neither struck nor threatened; I would even add that I did not feel the slightest emotion, except for the moment I thought that a public gallery was about to collapse under the feet of the seditionists. Blood would have flowed in the hall and then....

Farewell, my dear Félix.

---

102. Letter to Félix Coudroy

Paris, 24 June 1848   [vol. 1, p. 84]

My dear Félix, the journals will have told you of the frightful state of our sad capital. Cannon and rifle fire are the sounds that predominate; civil war has begun and with such ferocity that no one can foretell the outcome. While this sight distresses me as a man, you can only imagine what I am suffering as an economist; the real cause of the evil is certainly the false ideas of socialism.

You will perhaps be surprised, and many here are surprised that I have not yet set out our doctrine on the rostrum. They would doubtless forgive me if they were to cast a glance at this huge hall, in which you cannot make yourself heard. What is more, our Assembly is undisciplined; if a single word shocks a few members, even before the sentence is completed a storm breaks out. In these circumstances, you will understand my aversion to speaking. I

220. A demonstration had been organized on 15 May in order to support Poland, but it degenerated into a revolt against the government elected by the Assembly. The rioters invaded the Assembly, proclaimed its dissolution, and "formed" a revolutionary government. They were dispersed the same evening, and their leaders were arrested.

have concentrated my insignificant action on the committee of which I am a member (the finance committee), and up to now this has not been wholly unsuccessful.

I wanted to be able to give you the news of the outcome of the terrible battle that is raging around us. If the party of order wins, how far will reaction to this go? If the party of the riots wins, how far will its pretensions extend? We tremble to think. If this were some random struggle, I would not be discouraged. But the thing afflicting society is a manifest error, which will run its course to the end, since it is more or less shared by the very people who combat its exaggerated manifestations. May France never become like Turkey!

---

103. Letter to Richard Cobden

Paris, 27 June 1848   [vol. 1, p. 176]

My dear Cobden, you have learned of the huge catastrophe that has just afflicted France and which is afflicting the world. I believe you will be glad to have news of me but I will not go into many details. It is really too distressing for a Frenchman, even for a cosmopolitan Frenchman, to have to describe these dreadful scenes to an Englishman.

Allow me therefore to leave the task of giving you the facts to our journals. I will just say a few words about the causes. In my opinion, they are all rooted in socialism. For a long time our rulers have prevented a knowledge of economics from being widespread as far as they could. They have gone further. Out of ignorance, they have prepared people's minds to accept the errors of socialism and false republicanism, since this is the obvious trend in classical and university education. The nation has been infatuated with the idea that fraternity can be established by law. The state has been required to provide for the welfare of its citizens directly. But what has been the outcome? Because of the natural leanings of the human heart, each person has begun to claim a greater share of the welfare for himself from the state. This means that the state or the public treasury has been plundered. Every class has demanded from the state the means of subsistence, as of right. The efforts made by the state to provide this have led only to taxes and restrictions and an increase in deprivation, with the result that the demands of the people have become more pressing. In my view, a protectionist regime has been the first manifestation of this disorder. Owners, farmers, manufacturers, and shipowners have called upon the law to intervene to increase their share of wealth. The law has been able to satisfy them only by creating distress in the other classes, especially the working classes. These therefore raised a clamor, and instead of demanding that this plundering should cease, they demanded that the law should allow them to take part in the plundering as well. It has become general and universal. It has led to the ruin of all forms of industry. The workers, who are more deprived than ever, began to think that the dogma of fraternity had not been designed for them and took up arms. You know the rest: a frightful slaughter which, for four days, desolated the capital of the civilized world and which has still not been ended.[221]

It seems to me, my dear Cobden, that I am alone in the National Assembly to perceive the cause of the evil and consequently its remedy. However, I am obliged to keep quiet, for what is the use of speaking if I am not understood? I therefore sometimes ask myself if I am not a crank, like so many others, submerged in my old errors; but this thought cannot be right since I know too much, I think, about the problem in all its details. Besides, I tell myself: "In the end, what I am asking for is that the very harmonious and simple laws of Providence should triumph. Or are we to take it that Providence is in error?

I now profoundly regret that I accepted the mandate entrusted to me. I am not good for anything there, whereas, as a simple political writer, I might have been useful to my country.

---

104. Letter to Julie Marsan (Mme Affre)

Paris, 29 June 1848   [From the private collection of
Jean-Claude Paul-Dejean]

My dear Julie,

Cables and newspapers will have told you all about the triumph of the republican order after four days of bitter struggle.

I shall not give you any detail, even about me, because a single letter would not suffice.

I shall just tell you that I have done my duty without ostentation or temerity. My only role was to enter the Faubourg Saint-Antoine after the fall

221. Bastiat is referring to the so-called June Days, when, after the government attempted to close the national workshops, an uprising took place in Paris between 21 and 26 June. This was brutally crushed by the army under General Cavaignac, whose troops killed fifteen hundred workers.

of the first barricade, in order to disarm the fighters. As we went on, we managed to save several insurgents whom the militia wanted to kill. One of my colleagues displayed a truly admirable energy in this situation, which he did not boast about from the rostrum.

Your own letter arrived this morning precisely at the time the government was changed. I do not know M. ——, on whom the fate of Romain[222] depends, but I got together with Duprat to try to prevent the creation of the position. This is the best hope there is for the time being, subject to something better turning up.

I am happy to learn that the health of your mother is improving.[223] I hope that, as the children grow, her pain will be eased somewhat, because she is more and more attached to them. As far as I am concerned, I am longing to get acquainted with little Eugénie.

Mlle Marsan has been often writing to me in the last days. Her letters give such a picture of her. She tells me for example: "Three lines every three months, this is how you are treating me!" When I wrote to you, I wrote to her as well to tell her that I was not in any danger, and I added, "I tell you this to prevent any flights of fancy on your part." In her answer, she resorts to the word "flights" five or six times.

I am very sorry indeed about what you tell me of your financial position, my dear Julie, all the more so given that mine is not so brilliant that I could help you at this moment.

On 1 September, M. Lagelouze and Co. will remit me 650 francs that I shall put at the disposal of your mother.

---

105. Letter to Mr. Schwabe

Paris, 1 July 1848 [vol. 7, p. 423]

My dear Sir,

I thank you for the affectionate interest that made you think of me on the occasion of the terrible events which have afflicted this capital city. Thank heaven the cause of order and civilization won the day. Our excellent friends MM Say and Anisson were in the country, the first in Versailles and the sec-

---

222. Romain Affre, Julie's husband, had a temporary position as the head doctor at the Biarritz *bains de mer*. The position was to be made permanent for a candidate supported by political connections.

223. Her health had deteriorated following the death of her husband, Julie's father.

ond in Normandy. Their sons took part in the combat and came through with honor and unscathed.

It was false socialist ideas that caused our brothers to take up arms. It also has to be said that deprivation was a major contributor, but deprivation itself can be attributed to the same cause since, from the time we wished to make fraternity a legal obligation, capital no longer dares to show its face.

This is a very good time to preach the truth. During the entire time of the troubles, I have been able to consult widely with the National Guard, trying to show that each person should call upon his own forces to provide his means of existence and expect the state to provide only justice and security. I assure you that, for the first time, this doctrine was well received and a few friends gave me the means of expounding it in public, which I will be starting to do on Monday.

You will perhaps ask me why I am not fulfilling this mission within the National Assembly, whose rostrum echoes widely. This is because the hall is so huge and the audience so impatient that any demonstration is impossible.

This is very unfortunate, since I believe that there has never been in any country an assembly with better intentions, that is more democratic, a more sincere advocate of good, and more devoted. It is an honor to universal suffrage, but it has to be said that it shares the dominant preconceived ideas.

If you glance at the map of Paris, you will see that the insurrection has been graver than you appear to think. When it broke out, Paris had troops of no more than eight thousand men which, in accordance with good tactics, had to be kept together, since their number was insufficient to carry out operations. For this reason, the riot quickly overcame the suburbs and in a matter of two hours later would have overrun our street. From another direction, it was attacking the Town Hall and through the Gros-Caillou[224] was threatening the National Assembly to the extent that we also were reduced to erecting barricades. However, after two days, reinforcements reached us from the provinces.

You ask me whether this insurrection will be the last. I dare to hope so. We now have a government with determination and unity. The Chamber is imbued with a spirit of order and justice, but not vengeance. Today, our greatest enemy is deprivation and the lack of work. If the government reestablishes security, business will regenerate and this will be our salvation.

224. An area of Paris, then semiagricultural, near the Invalides.

You should not doubt, my dear sir, the enthusiasm with which I would accept your and Mrs. Schwabe's kind invitation, if I could. Two weeks spent with you in discussion, walks, music making, and playing with your lovely children would be true happiness for me. However, it very much appears that I will have to refuse myself this pleasure. I very much fear that our session will last a long time. You may be sure at least that, if I am able to get away, I will not fail to do so.

---

106. Letter to Richard Cobden

Paris, 7 August 1848   [vol. 1, p. 178]

My dear Cobden, I have left the Assembly to reply in a few lines to your letter of the 5th. I hoped to see our ministers to discuss your communication with them, but they did not come. While we are waiting for further details, this is what I know.

For 1848, we are facing a deficit that is impossible to make good through taxes. The minister of finance took the decision to solve this through a loan and to organize the budget in 1849 so as to balance the income and expenditure without having to call upon credit once again. The intention is good; what is needed is to remain faithful to it.

With this in mind, he acknowledged that ordinary income could meet expenditure in 1849 only if this was reduced by a rather significant amount. He therefore declared to all his colleagues that they set about making a reduction to be shared among all the departments. The Ministry of the Navy was targeted for thirty million of the proposed reduction and, since this department has sections that it is impossible to touch, such as expenditure on colonies, convict prisons, living expenses, salaries, etc., it follows that the reduction will bear only on the production of new armaments.

This resolution is not immutable. It does not come from a determination to reduce our military forces. However, it is certain that the government and Assembly would be strongly encouraged to continue down this road if England offered to follow us, and above all to precede us to a reasonable extent. It is to this that I shall be drawing Bastide's attention.

Right now, rumors about Italy are circulating which are likely to foil the good intentions of the minister of finance. I very much fear that peace in Europe cannot be maintained. Please God that at least our two countries walk in step!

Farewell, my dear Cobden; I will write to you shortly.

107. Letter to Richard Cobden

Paris, 18 August 1848   [vol. 1, p. 179]

My dear Cobden, I have received your letter and the fine speech by Mr. Molesworth. If I had enough time at my disposal I would have translated it for *Le Journal des économistes.* But I do not have the time and, what is more, the strength. This is slipping away from me and I must admit that I am now seized with the obsession of all writers. I would like to devote the little health left to me, first of all to set out the true principles of political economy as I see them, and then to show their links with all the other moral sciences. This is still my chimera of *Economic Harmonies.* If this work had been completed I think that it would draw to our cause a host of fine minds whose hearts are being drawn to socialism. Unfortunately, in order for a book to survive and be read, it has to be short, clear, accurate, and as full of feeling as of ideas, all at the same time. This means that it must not contain a single word that has not been weighed. It has to be formed drop by drop like crystal, and in silence and obscurity, also like crystal. This makes me sigh greatly for my beloved Landes and Pyrenees.

It has not yet seemed the right time to make overtures to Cavaignac on the subject of your letter.[225] The time seems to me badly chosen. We must wait until the situation in Italy is clearer. Nothing would be more unpopular now than a reduction of the army. All the parties would unite in condemning it, the politicians because of the state of Europe and owners and traders because of demagogic passion. The French army is a model of devotion and discipline. For the moment, it is our anchor of salvation. Its most popular leaders are in power and would not accept anything that would alienate the affection felt for it.

As for the navy, it is not likely that France will enter into negotiations on the subject of proportional reduction. England would need to go further and I very much fear that it is not prepared for this. I would at least like to know what we might hope to obtain.

The spirit of the public on this side of the Channel makes negotiations of this kind extremely difficult, especially with England alone. We must endeavor to expand it to include all the powers.

This is why I have not dared to compromise success by asking Cavaignac

---

225. (Paillottet's note) This refers to a simultaneous reduction of armaments by France and England.

for an ad hoc audience. I will endeavor to sound out his ideas from time to time and will let you know.

It is impossible to set oneself a nobler aim. I was pleased to see that *La Presse* is going down this road. I will try to get the *Débats*[226] to join in as well. The difficulty, however, will be in involving the popular journals, although I have not lost all hope of this.

Farewell, I must leave you now.

---

108. Letter to Félix Coudroy

Paris, 26 August 1848   [vol. 1, p. 85]

My dear Félix, I am very sorry to see that despite my wishes our correspondence is languishing. It would be very pleasant for me to continue by letter this exchange of feelings and ideas which, for so many years, was sufficient to maintain our happiness. Besides, your letters would be just what I need. Here, in the midst of events and the tumult of passions, I can feel the clarity of principles becoming blurred because of the compromises life demands. I am now convinced that the carrying out of business excludes the possibility of producing a work that is truly scientific, and yet I do not hide from you that I still have this old elusive fancy of writing my *Social Harmonies,* and I cannot suppress the idea that, had I remained in your company, I would have succeeded in coming up with a useful idea for the world. For this reason, I am longing to go into retirement.

This morning, we concluded the major inquiry which weighed so heavily on the Assembly and on the country. A vote by the Chamber authorized proceedings against Louis Blanc and Caussidière for the part they played in the uprising on 15 May.[227] People will perhaps be surprised in our region that this time I voted against the government. It was once my aim to explain to my electors the reason for my votes. Lack of time and strength is the only reason I would fail in this duty, but this vote is so serious that I would like to explain what determined it. The government believed that the proceedings against these two colleagues were necessary. People went so far as to say that the support of the National Guard could be counted on only on this condition. I did not feel I had the right, even for this reason, to gag the

226. *Le Journal des débats.*

227. Caussidière was active in the revolutions of 1830 and 1848. He was accused, with Louis Blanc, of being an agitator in the "conspiracy" of 15 May.

voice of my conscience. You know that perhaps in the whole of France there is no more determined an opponent of the doctrines of Louis Blanc than I. I have no doubt that these doctrines will have a disastrous influence on the attitudes of the workers and, consequently, on their actions. But were we being called upon to express an opinion on doctrines? Anyone who holds a belief must consider as disastrous a doctrine that contradicts this belief. When the Catholics had the Protestants burned, it was not because Protestants were in error but because this error was deemed to be dangerous. On this principle we would all kill each other.

We therefore needed to investigate whether Louis Blanc had really been guilty of the *offenses* of conspiracy and insurrection. I did not think so and anyone who read his defense could not think so. In the meantime, I cannot forget the situation in which we are: a state of siege[228] is in force, ordinary justice is suspended, and the press is muzzled. Could I hand over two colleagues to political opponents at a time when no rule of law was assured? This was an act with which I could not associate myself, a first step which I did not wish to take.

I do not blame Cavaignac for having temporarily suspended all forms of freedom; I believe that this sad necessity was as painful for him as it is to us and it may be justified by what justifies everything, public safety. However, does public safety require two of our colleagues to be handed over? I did not think so. Quite the contrary, I believed that such an act could only sow discord among us, inflame hatred, and deepen the abyss between the parties, not only in the Assembly but also in the whole of France. I considered that in the face of the current internal and external circumstances, when the country is suffering and needs order, confidence, governing institutions, and unity, it was an ill-chosen moment to sow the seeds of discord among the representatives of the nation. I think that we would do better to forget our grievances and causes of bitterness in order to work for the good of the country, and I considered myself fortunate that there were no detailed charges against our colleagues, since it was because of this that I was spared the duty of handing them over.

The majority thought otherwise. I hope it is not mistaken! I hope this vote is not the death knell of the Republic.

228. The state of siege was decreed on 4 June. A proposal to repeal it was discussed at the Assembly on 2 September. It was rejected by 529 deputies against 140. Bastiat was among the 140. The state of siege was repealed only on 19 October.

If you consider it apposite, I authorize you to send an extract of this letter to the local journal.

---

109. Letter to Bernard Domenger

Paris, 3 September 1848 [vol. 7, p. 386]

Tomorrow we are starting to debate the constitution. However, whatever you say, this work will always carry within its heart an all-devouring canker, since it will be debated in an atmosphere of siege and in the absence of freedom of the press. As for us, the representatives, we feel that we are totally free, but that is not enough. The parties will exploit the abnormal nature of our situation to undermine and discredit the constitution. I therefore voted against the state of siege yesterday. I believe that Cavaignac is making the common and very natural mistake of sacrificing the future to the present. As disposed as I am to lending strength to this honest and well-intentioned government we have put in place, I cannot go beyond this. Here I am then, voting yet again with the Red Republic, but it is not my fault. People should not look at *with whom* one votes, but *why*.

I presume that a new effort will be attempted in favor of freedom of the press. I will join this; above all I want the constitution to be respected. If in Paris there are such great ferments of disorder that the rule of law cannot be maintained, I would prefer the combat to be renewed and the country to learn to defend itself.

All the rumors are of legitimist plots. I cannot believe them! The legitimists who were powerless in '89 hope to be strong in 1848? May God prevent them from reawakening the beast of revolution! If you chance to see them, tell them clearly that they should be under no illusion. They are opposed by all the workers, all the socialists, all the republicans, and all the people, with leaders capable of prolonging events right up to the limit. Above all, the clergy should be circumspect. Men of *principle* who, like me, have faith in the power of truth ask only for a free debate and accept in advance the triumph of public opinion, *even if* (except for changing it) these men are few in number. Those who accept the struggle elsewhere, on the battlefield, are countless and determined to take things right to the end. Let the legitimists and clergy not give the signal for action; they would be overrun. Legitimists know that their principles have had their day, and as for the clergy, while they are not totally blind, they cannot ignore their vulnerable side. Let a degree of popular irritation arising from the industrial crisis and financial problems not inspire dangerous and wild hopes in them, unless they want to play their *trump card* once and for all.

Use your influence to safeguard our beloved *département* from the consequences of a desperate struggle. God knows that I do not want to deprive anyone of the right to express and put across his ideas! But we should carefully avoid anything that might resemble a conspiracy.

---

110. Letter to Félix Coudroy

Paris, 7 September 1848   [vol. 1, p. 87]

My dear Félix, your letter did not leave me the choice of the course of action I had to take. I have just sent in my resignation as a member of the General Council; I have not resigned as a representative and you know the reason why. In the end, it was not a few people from Mugron who bestowed this title on me. When all is said and done, the people from Mugron who bestowed this title on me were not few in number.

I would like to know how many there are of those who blame me who have read the defense of Louis Blanc in the *Moniteur*,[229] and, if they have not read it, it must be said that they are extremely presumptuous in speaking out.

It is said that I gave way to fear; fear was completely on the other side. Do these men think that less courage is needed in Paris than in the *départements* to confront the passions currently raging? We were threatened with the fury of the National Guard if we rejected the plan to start legal proceedings. This threat came from the sector that controls the might of the army. It was possible therefore for fear to influence the black balls but not the white ones.[230] You need to be uncommonly absurd and foolish to believe that it is an act of courage to vote in favor of might, the army, the National Guard, the majority, the passions of the moment, and the government.

Have you read the inquiry? Have you read the deposition of Trélat, an ex-minister? It says, "I went to Clichy but did not see Louis Blanc and did not hear that he went there; but I recognized traces of his passage in the attitudes, gestures, facial expressions, and even the utterances of the workers."

229. *Le Moniteur industriel.*
230. In order to vote yes or no to a specific question, the deputies dropped white or black balls into a ballot box.

Have you ever seen such passions expressed by more dangerous trends? And three-quarters of the inquiry is in this vein!

In short, in all conscience, I believe that Louis Blanc has done a great deal of harm in conjunction with all the socialists, and there are many of these who are, without even knowing this, among those who are making an outcry against him. However, I do not think that he took part in the outrages of May and June and I have no other reasons to give as to my conduct.

Thank you for having made me aware of the state of people's minds. I am too familiar with the human heart to blame anyone. From their point of view, those who blame me are right. May they be long preserved from this plague of socialism! I feel relieved of a great weight since I posted my letter to the prefect. The country will see that I want it to be represented as it wishes. When the by-election occurs, please ask M. Domenger urgently not to support my candidature. By accepting it, I was drawn by the desire to see my region once again; this was an entirely personal feeling and I have been punished for it. Now I want nothing more than to be rid of a mandate that is most painful.

III. Letter to Mr. Schwabe

Dover, 7 October 1848   [vol. 7, p. 425]

I do not want to leave the soil of England, my dear sir, without expressing the gratitude I feel and also without asking your pardon for all the trouble my stay with you caused. You will perhaps be surprised to see the date on this letter. While I was looking for Mr. Faulkner at Folkestone, the steamer was impolite enough to sail, leaving me on the quay, undecided as to whether I should jump on board. Twenty years ago, I would have tried. But I just watched it and, learning that another steamer was leaving this evening from Dover, I came here and do not regret the misadventure, since Dover is well worth staying an extra day in England for. This is what I would do even if I were not without all my luggage. Finally, I was able to deliver your message to Mr. Faulkner without any hurry.

... The two days I spent with Mr. Cobden were very pleasant. His temporary unpopularity has not changed his joyful and equitable temper. He says, and I believe he is right, that he is closer to disarmament today than he was to free trade when he founded the League. He is a great man and I recognize it for this reason: that his own interests, his reputation and glory are never weighed in the balance against the interests of justice and humanity.

I remain, etc.

---

112. Letter to Mr. Schwabe
    Paris, 25 October 1848   [vol. 7, p. 426]

. . . .

I thank you for your kind offers. One never leaves such good friends without planning to see them again. It would be too cruel not to nurture this hope. Alas, however! It is often just an illusion, as life is very short and Manchester very far away. Perhaps it will be given to me to do you the honors of my beloved Pyrenees. I often dream that your family, Cobden's family, Say's family, and I will all gather together in one of my cool valleys. These are plans which men would certainly carry out if they really knew how to live.

Paris continues to be calm. The boulevards are gay and sparkling, there are shows and spectacles to attract the crowds, and the French character is manifest in all its carefree lightness. This is a hundred times better than London, and if the revolutions in Germany continue[231] I do not abandon the hope of seeing Paris become an asylum for those fleeing political storms. What do we lack that stops us from becoming the most fortunate of nations? A grain of common sense. I think that this is not very much.

I can see why cholera[232] terrifies you, since you are surrounded by such a lovely and numerous family. The happier we are in our affections, the more we risk danger. He who is alone is vulnerable only through his least sensitive point, which is himself. Fortunately this dreadful scourge appears to be totally embarrassed by its impotence, like a tiger without teeth and claws. Because of my friends on the other side of the Channel, I rejoice to see from the journals that the most dreadful characteristic of cholera is its name and that, in fact, it causes less havoc than a head cold.

Farewell, etc.

---

231. Revolution broke out in February 1848 in France and in March in the German states. These uprisings resulted in the formation of the Frankfurt parliament and an attempt to create a liberal constitution, which ultimately failed.

232. In autumn 1848 there was an epidemic of cholera in Paris, but it was less severe than the epidemic of 1832.

113. Letter to Mme Cheuvreux

   Paris, November 1848   [*Lettres d'un habitant des Landes*, p. 8]

Madam,

At the Hôtel Saint-Georges, there are three forms of health that are so involved in each other that should one decline, the others are threatened. Allow me to ask how you are. At Mugron, at nine o'clock in the morning we have news of all of our friends. You know, provincial monotony has its compensations.

If you have to hand the name of the learned pharmacist who has discovered the art of making cod-liver oil palatable, please send it to me. I would also love it if this valued alchemist could teach me the secret of producing a pared-down version of political economy; this is a remedy that our sick society is very much in need of, but it refuses to take the smallest teaspoonful, so repulsive does it find the stuff.

   Your devoted servant,
   F. Bastiat

----

114. Letter to Mrs. Schwabe

   Paris, 14 November 1848   [vol. 7, p. 427]

Madam,

If my thoughts, guided by the memory of such pleasant and cordial hospitality, often turn to Crumpsall House and Manchester, they did so with still more emphasis yesterday evening, because *Sonnambula*[233] was being played at the Italiens and I could not stop myself from disobeying the doctor's orders and going to see this production. Each scene and each tune took me back to England, and either through emotion or the weakness of my constitution, I felt my eyes constantly brimming with tears. Who can explain the intimate nature of music! While I listened to the very touching duet and the splendid finale of the first act, it seemed to me that several months had been swept away and that, with the two performances blending into one, I was experiencing one and the same emotion. However, I must tell you, without wishing to criticize your singers, the work was infinitely better performed here, and although your first tenor was as good as ours, Madame

233. *La Sonnambula* (The Sleepwalker), an opera by Vincenzo Bellini (1801–35).

Persiani infinitely surpasses your prima donna. And also the Italian language was invented and specially made for music. When I heard Madame Persiani cry out, "Sono innocente" in the recitative, I could not help remembering the singular effect produced by the rhythmic translation of this sentence, "I am not guilty."

What can you do? The language of business, the sea, and political economy can never be that of music.

———————

115. Letter to Félix Coudroy

Paris, 26 November 1848   [vol. 1, p. 88]

My dear Félix, you must all have been expecting me in Mugron. My initial plan was to go there; when I agreed to join the General Council, I must admit to my shame that I was somewhat influenced by the prospect of this journey. The air of my birthplace has always had such great attraction! And I would so liked to have shaken your hand. At that time, there was one thing that was taken for granted, that the Assembly would be prorogued during the Council session. Since then, things have changed; it was considered dangerous to dissolve the only authority standing in our country and, as I shared this opinion, I had to remain at my post. It is true that I have been ill and often confined to my room, sometimes even to my bed, but at least I was in Paris, ready to do whatever circumstances required, to the extent of my strength.

This deterioration in my health, which is revealed mostly by weakness and apathy, has come at a bad time. To tell you the truth, my friend, I believe I might have been useful. I always note that our doctrines provide us with the solution to the difficulties that arise and, what is more, that when these solutions are set out simply, they are always well received. If a wider and more witty version of political economy had found an outlet in the Assembly, it would have been a real force since, no matter how often it is said, while this Assembly may lack enlightenment, there has never been one with more goodwill. Errors and the most strange and threatening theories have been advocated from the rostrum, as though to construct a counterpedestal to political economy and put its light in the shade. I was there, a witness glued to my seat, I felt within me what was needed to rally the intelligent minds and even the sincere hearts, and my wretched health condemned me to silence. What is worse, in the committees, commissions, and offices, I had to be very careful to keep my counsel in the certainty that if I had to take the stage I would not have been able to play my role. This is a cruel test. For this reason, I have to renounce public life and my total ambition is now to have three or four months of peace before me to write my *Economic Harmonies*. They are in my head but I am very much afraid that they will never come out.

Today's journals will tell you about yesterday's session. It went on until midnight. It was awaited with anxiety and even unease. I hope that it will produce a good effect on public opinion.

You ask my opinion on the forthcoming elections. I cannot understand how, with identical principles, the milieu in which we live is enough to make us see things from such different points of view. What journals or information do you receive for you to say that Cavaignac is leaning toward La Montagne?[234] Cavaignac was put where he is to support the Republic and he will do this conscientiously. Would people like it better if he betrayed it? At the same time as he wants the Republic, he understands the conditions under which it will survive. Let us go back to the time of the general elections. What was the almost generally held feeling? There were a certain number of *true and honest republicans* and also a huge multitude that until then had been divided, neither requesting nor wanting the republic but whose eyes had been opened by the February revolution. They understood that the monarchy had outlived its time and wanted to join the new order, letting it prove its worth. I dare to say that this was the dominant feeling, as the result of the election shows. The masses have chosen their representatives from the republicans of whom I have spoken, and this is why we may consider these two categories as making up the nation. However, above and below this huge body, there are two parties. The one above is known as the *Red Republic* and is made up of men who make exaggerated assaults when they need to flatter popular passions, while the one below is known as *Reaction*. This gathers together all those who aim to overthrow the Republic, set traps for it, and shackle its progress.

This was the situation in the early days of May, and to understand what came after, you should not forget that power was then held by the Red Republic, still dominated by the most extreme and violent parties.

What point have we reached through time, patience, and many perils? We have succeeded in making the power homogeneous with this huge mass,

234. "The Mountain," a reference to "the Left." During the French Revolution, the deputies from the "Left" had been sitting on the top rows of the Assembly, "the mountain."

which forms the nation itself. In effect, whence has Cavaignac drawn his government? Partly from the honest republicans of yesteryear and partly from the men who rallied to him sincerely. Note that he could not neglect any of these elements, nor could he ascend as far as the Montagne nor descend as far as the Reaction. This would have been to lack sincerity and a proper policy. He has taken enough open republicans for no one to doubt the Republic, and from the men of another age he chose those whose proclaimed loyalty prevented them from being considered suspect, like Vivien and Dufaure.

In this downward progression toward the exact point which coincides with public opinion and the stability of the Republic, we have offended the party of exaggerations, which conveyed to us the level of its discontent on 15 May and 23 June and we have disappointed the reactionaries, who are taking revenge through their choice. . . .

Now, if this huge multitude, which had rallied the government, breaks up and abandons the aim it set itself, forgetting the difficulties that the Assembly has encountered, I do not know any longer where we will be going. If it continues to be loyal, it must prove this by nominating Cavaignac.

The Reds, who at least have the merit of being consistent and sincere, are giving their votes to Ledru-Rollin and Raspail. . . . What ought we to do? I defer to your wisdom.

Except for the days in June when, like all my colleagues, on returning from the barricades, I went to tell the leader of the executive power what I had seen, I have never spoken to Cavaignac. I have never been in his circles, and he very probably does not know that I exist. But I listen to his words, I have observed his acts, and although I have not approved of them all, while I have often voted against him, in particular each time I considered that the exceptional measures arising from the requirements of June were being continued for too long, I am able to say, at least in my soul and conscience, that I believe Cavaignac to be honest. . . .

---

116. Letter to Félix Coudroy

    Paris, 5 December 1848   [vol. 1, p. 92]

My dear Félix, I am taking advantage of a reply I am sending Hiard to write you a couple of lines.

The elections are approaching. I have written a letter to the newspapers in the Landes. I do not know whether it has been published. In my own interest it would have been more prudent to keep quiet, but I considered that I ought to make my views known. If I am not nominated again, I will easily be consoled.

Up to now, we have had no news of the pope.[235] This is a major question that has been raised. If the pope wishes to agree to become the first among bishops, Catholicism may have a great future. Whatever Montalembert[236] says, temporal power is a major problem. We are no longer in an age in which it is possible to say, "All peoples will be free and will give themselves the government they wish, except for the Romans, because this suits us."

Farewell.

---

117. Letter to the Count Arrivabene[237]

Paris 21 December 1848 [vol. 7, p. 416]

My dear Sir,

The doubt you have expressed is very natural. It is possible that in pushing terms a little far I have gone beyond my ideas. The words, *by anticipation,* inserted in the passage you quote tell you that I intend to discuss the matter in detail. In a future article, I will cover *exchange* and then set out what I was bold enough to call *my theory of value.* I ask you to be kind enough to suspend your judgment until then. You may be sure that after this I will welcome your comments gratefully as they will enable me to explain better or to correct as needed.

You will acknowledge, I hope, that what appears to divide us is not very serious. I believe that *value* lies in the *services* exchanged and not in the things. *Materials* and *physical forces* are provided *free of charge* in nature and move free of charge from hand to hand. However, I do not say that two items of work, considered to be equal in intensity and duration, should be equally remunerated. He who is positioned to render a *service* that is more precious because of the materials or forces at its disposal is better remunerated; his work is more intelligent, more fortunate if you wish, but the value is in this work and not in things. The proof of this is that the same phenomenon occurs even where there is no physical object to mislead us and appear to take on value. In this way, if I feel the desire to hear the finest voice in the

---

235. Pius IX.
236. Charles Forbes.
237. (Paillottet's note) The letter from the Count Arrivabene, to which Bastiat is replying, relates to a passage in chapter 3 of the *Harmonies,* published in December 1848 in *Le Journal des économistes. [OC,* vol. 6, p. 73, "Des besoins de l'homme."]

world and am willing to make exceptional sacrifices to do this, I would call upon Jenny Lind. As she is the only one in the world who could render me this *service,* she could ask whatever price she wants. Her work would be better remunerated than that of another; it would have greater *value,* but this value lies in the *service.*

I believe that this is also true where a physical object is involved, and if we give it a *value,* it is through pure *metonymy.* Let us take one of your examples. A man grinds his wheat between two stones. Later he takes advantage of his situation on a hill exposed to wind and builds a mill. I request from him the *service* of grinding my wheat. Many others do likewise, and, as he disposes of a great force, he is able to render a great number of similar *services.* He is highly remunerated. What does this prove? That his intelligence is being rewarded, that his work is fortunate, but not that the value lies in the wind. Nature never receives any remuneration; I remunerate only a man and I do so only because he has rendered me a *service.* I appreciate this service because it would cost me more to do it for myself or to ask it from others. The value, therefore, lies in a comparative appreciation of a variety of services exchanged.

This is so true that, if competition is involved, the miller will lower his price; the service offered in future would have less value, even though the action of the wind remains the same and retains all of its *usefulness.* It is I, the consumer, who will profit freely from this decrease. It is not the usefulness of the wind that has changed, it is the value of the service.

You see that basically it is a quarrel of words. What does it matter, you tell me, if the value lies in a natural force or in the service rendered to me, by means of this force, by the person who has harnessed it? The result is the same for me.

I cannot tell you here what consequences, which according to me are very important, will result from this distinction. I sincerely believe that if I manage to put across my thesis I would have crushed all the socialist, communist, and other arguments, just as I would have removed many errors that have escaped economists with regard to property, income, credit, etc. It is perhaps an illusion of authorship, but I admit that it has taken over my entire being, and I regret that I have only a few moments to devote to this study.

I remain, my dear sir,

your devoted servant.

118. Letter to Mrs. Schwabe

Paris, 28 December 1848   [vol. 7, p. 428]

I acknowledge your kindness and that of Mr. Schwabe in insisting on inviting me a second time to experience the hospitality of *Crumpsall House*. You must know that I do not need any other persuasion than that of my heart, even though you might not be offering me the happy prospect of shaking Cobden's hand or hearing the great artist, Jenny Lind. But Manchester is really too far away. This is perhaps not a very gallant thing for a Frenchman to say, but at my age I can at least speak from reason. Please accept at least my deep gratitude.

Has Jenny Lind developed a *hatred* for my dear country? According to what you say, this vile sentiment must be foreign to her heart. Oh, let her come to Paris! She would be surrounded with tributes and enthusiasm. Let her come to cast a ray of joy over this desolate town, which so delights in anything that is generous and beautiful! I am sure that Jenny Lind would make us forget our civil discord. If I dared to express my thoughts in full, I can predict the finest palm that she could collect. She might be able to arrange things so as to bring back, if not a great deal of money, at least the sweetest memories of her life. Just appearing in two concerts and choosing for herself the benefits to spread around. What pure glory and what a noble way of avenging herself, if it is true, as it is said, that she was not acknowledged there! See, my good Mrs. Schwabe, if this great singer can be won over by this appeal to her heart. I will wager my head on this success.

We are approaching a new year. I formulate the wish that it will spread joy and prosperity over you and all those who surround you.

―――――――――

119. Letter to Mme Cheuvreux

Paris, January 1849   [*Lettres d'un habitant des Landes*, p. 10]

Madam,

I have just been told that tomorrow, Tuesday, at two o'clock, some very curious music will be played in the Church of Saint Louis d'Antin. It consists of thirteenth-century songs found in the archives of the Sainte Chapelle, which are imbued with all the naiveté of the time. Other people say that these songs cannot be old, since in the thirteenth century the art of writing music down was unknown.

Be that as it may, the solemnity will be of great interest; this is a question that is less difficult to assess by impression than by erudition.

Yesterday evening, I again took this dreadful brew, not without a terrible struggle between my stomach and my willpower. Is it possible for something so horrible to do good, and are not medical practitioners making fun of us?

On the whole, all remedies are unpleasant.

What does my dear Mlle Louise need? A little more physical exercise and a little less mental exercise, but she does not want this. What does her mother need? To seek a little less drawing room martyrdom, but she does not want this. What am I prescribed? Cod-liver oil? Decidedly, the art of being in good health is the art of doing what you really don't like.

F. Bastiat

---

120. Letter to Félix Coudroy

Paris, 1 January 1849 [vol. 1, p. 92]

My dear Félix, I want to give myself the pleasure of benefiting from the postal reform,[238] since I also contributed to it. I wanted it to be radical and we have only the mere beginnings; as it stands, it will at least allow the effusions of friendship.

Since February, we have experienced difficult days, and I believe that the future has never been darker and very much fear that the election of Bonaparte will not solve the problems. At first, I was happy with the majority which raised him to the presidency. I voted for Cavaignac, because I am sure of his total loyalty and intelligence, but although voting for him I felt that power would be a heavy burden for him. He has faced up to a terrible storm, drawn inextinguishable hatred to himself, and the party of disorder will never forgive him. If it was an advantage to be a man whose republicanism was assured and who at the same time could not enter into pacts with the Reds, on the other hand this very history created major difficulties for him. For a moment, I hoped that the appearance on the scene of a new personality with no links to the parties might inaugurate a new era. . . . Be that as it may, I and all the other sincere Republicans have taken the decision of

238. This reform, inspired by the English reform dating back to 1840, introduced a single payment in the form of a twenty-centime stamp for a standard letter for the whole of the country, plus Algeria. Previously, a fee had been paid by the addressee.

supporting this product of universal suffrage. I have not seen the slightest sign of systematic opposition in the Chamber. . . .

On the other hand, though they may well later begin to fight among themselves, the supporters of fallen dynasties start by demolishing the Republic. They know full well that the Assembly is the anchor of our salvation; they are therefore striving with all their might to have it dissolved and are putting forward petitions to do this. A coup d'état is imminent. Where will it come from? What will it bring? What is worse is that the masses prefer the president to the Assembly.[239]

For my part, my dear Félix, I am keeping away from all these intrigues. As far as my strength permits, I am occupying my time with advocating my program. You know its general outlines. This is the practical plan: to reform the post and the taxes on salt and wine and spirits; hence, a deficit in the income budget reduced to 1.2 or 1.3 billions; require the government to adjust the expenditure budget accordingly. Declare to it that we will not allow it to spend a penny more, thus obliging it to abandon any *interventions* abroad and all the *socialist utopian* measures at home; in a word, require these two principles and obtain them out of *necessity,* since we have not been able to obtain them from public *reason.*

I am putting this project forward everywhere. I have spoken to ministers who are my friends about it, but they scarcely listened to me. I have preached it in meetings of deputies. I hope that it will prevail. The first two acts have already been accomplished; there remains the tax on wine. Credit will suffer for a while, the stock exchange is in turmoil, but we must not retreat. We are faced with a gulf which is growing ever larger; we cannot hope to close it without someone suffering. The time for compromise is past. We will lend our support to the president and all ministers but we want these *three reforms,* not so much for themselves, but as the sure and sole means of achieving our motto, *peace and freedom.*

Farewell, my friend; I send you my good wishes for the New Year.

239. In January 1849 Bastiat seems to be foretelling the coming of a dictatorship. Louis-Napoléon seized power in a coup d'état in December 1851 and was made emperor in December 1852.

121. Letter to George Wilson, Chairman of the
Anti–Corn Law League[240]

Paris, 15 January 1894   [Vol 7, p. 412]

Dear Sir,

Please express to your committee my warmest gratitude for the kind invitation you have sent me in its name. I would have had much pleasure in attending as, sir, I say this loudly and clearly, nothing greater has been accomplished in this world in my opinion than this reform you are preparing to celebrate. I have the most profound admiration for the men I would have met at this banquet, George Wilson, Villiers, Bright, Cobden, Thompson, and so many others who have achieved the triumph of free trade or, rather, have given this great cause its initial and decisive impetus. I do not know which I admire more, the greatness of the aim you have pursued or the morality of the means you have used. I hesitate when I compare the direct good you have done with the indirect good for which you have prepared the ground, when I seek to assess on the one hand the actual reform you have carried out and on the other the art of pursuing all the reforms within the law and peacefully, a priceless art for which you have provided both the theory and the model.

I appreciate the benefits of free trade as keenly as anyone in the world.

---

240. (Paillottet's note) Here is the text of the invitation to which Bastiat is replying. [The following letter is in English in the original.]

BANQUET TO CELEBRATE THE FINAL REPEAL OF THE CORN LAWS
Newall's Buildings, Manchester, 9 January 1849

My dear Sir,

The act for the repeal of our corn laws will come into operation on the 1st February next, and it has been resolved to celebrate the event by a banquet in the Free Trade Hall in this City on the 31 January.

The prominent part you have taken in your own country, in the adversary of the principles of commercial freedom, and the warm sympathy you have always manifested in our movement, has induced the Committee to direct me respectfully to invite you to be present as a guest.

In conveying this invitation, permit me to hope that you may be able to make it convenient to make one among us at our festival.

Believe me, dear sir,

Your faithful and obedient servant,
George Wilson, Chairman

Even so, I am unable to limit the hopes that humanity should place on the triumph of your campaigning to this question alone.

You have not been able to demonstrate the right to trade without debating and consolidating the right of property at the same time. And perhaps England owes to your discourse that it is not, unlike the continent, permeated at this time with the false communist doctrines which, like protectionism, are only the negation of the right of property in a variety of forms.

You have not been able to demonstrate the right to trade without shedding a bright light on the legitimate functions of the government and the natural limits of the law. However, once these functions have been understood and these limits set, the people governed will no longer expect prosperity, well-being, and absolute good fortune but equal justice for all from their governments. Once this is so, governments will have their ordinary action circumscribed, will no longer repress individual energy, will no longer dissipate public assets as they build up, and will themselves be freed from the illusionary hopes pinned on them by their peoples. They will not be overthrown at each inevitable setback and the principal cause of violent revolution will be eliminated.

In sum, you have not been able to demonstrate the doctrine of free trade from the economic point of view without removing from people's minds the sad and disastrous aphorism, "The good of one person is at the expense of another." As long as this odious maxim was an article of faith around the world, there was radical incompatibility between the simultaneous prosperity of nations and peace between them. Proving that vested interests can be in harmony is thus preparing the way to universal fraternity.

I am convinced that in its more immediately practical aspects your trade reform is just the first link in a long series of reforms that will be even more valuable. For example, can it fail to extricate Great Britain from the violent, abnormal situation into which protectionism had drawn it, which is antagonistic to other peoples and consequently full of danger? The notion of monopolizing consumers had led you to pursue domination over the entire globe. Well then! I have no doubt that your colonial system is on the point of undergoing a most fortunate transformation. I do not dare forecast that you will come round to divesting yourself voluntarily of your colonies in your own interests, although I think you should, but even if you retain them, they will open up to world trade and will no longer reasonably be a source of jealousy and envy for anyone.

When this happens, what will happen to this famous vicious circle of an argument, "You need a navy to have colonies and you need colonies to have a navy." The English nation will become tired of paying *alone* the costs of its numerous possessions, in which it will have no more privileges than it has in the United States. You will reduce the size of your armies and fleets, as, once the danger has been removed, it would be absurd to retain the expensive precautions that this danger alone justifies. This would be a double and firm guarantee of world peace.

I will stop there; my letter would take on unseemly proportions if I wanted to list all the benefits of which free trade is the seed.

I would have liked to take an active part in promoting this great cause in my country as I am persuaded of its fruitfulness. Nowhere else are there such lively minds, nowhere else are hearts so inflamed with the love of universal justice, absolute good, and ideal perfection. France was enthusiastically in favor of greatness, morality, simplicity, and true free trade. All that was needed was to overcome a preconceived idea that was purely economic; to establish a proper commercial accounting, if one may put it that way; and to prove that trade, far from damaging the *national labor force,* always expands as long as it is beneficial and ceases, by its very nature and by virtue of its own law, when it starts to do harm, from which it follows that it does not need artificial, legal obstacles. It was an exceptional opportunity, in the midst of the shock of conflicting doctrines in this country, to raise the flag of freedom here. It would certainly have rallied all hopes and persuasions to it. It was at this moment that it pleased Providence, whose decrees I nevertheless applaud, to withdraw what little health and strength I had been granted. It will therefore fall to another to accomplish the work of which I dreamed, and may he come forward soon!

It is this reason of health, as well as my parliamentary duties, that obliges me to refrain from being present at the democratic and solemn occasion to which you are inviting me. I deeply regret this, as it would have been one of the highlights of my life and a precious memory for the rest of my days. Please present my apologies to the committee and allow me, in closing, to associate myself in my heart with your festivity through this toast:

To free trade among peoples! To the free circulation of men, things, and ideas! To universal free trade and all its economic, political, and moral consequences!

I am, sir, your obedient servant.

---

122. Letter to Bernard Domenger

Paris, 18 January 1849   [vol. 7, p. 388]

We are almost all agreed here on the need to disband.[241] However, a very large number (and were it not for fear of the elections, it would be all of us) would not want to bow to violent and artificial pressure. Many also fear for the very existence of the Republic. If there were only one pretender, it would be a matter of a revolution (from which God preserve us); but since there are several,[242] it is a question of civil war. We have every right to hesitate.

---

123. Letter to Mme Cheuvreux

Paris, February 1849   [*Lettres d'un habitant des Landes*, p. 11]

Madam,

I have just sent Faucher a reminder with regard to your protégé; he had lost touch with him, alas! How much compassion can he retain in a mind responsible for the destiny of the Republic! However, he has promised.

I did not see M. Say, Léon, or M. Cheuvreux at the Italiens yesterday; have you been ill? Was Mlle Louise tired of singing or writing letters? Or is it purely and entirely a matter of her fancy, such being the goddess, it is said, of Parisian women? Besides, the show was horribly gloomy; Alboni *heavy,* Ronconi out of tune, Bordogni[243] useless, costumes dreadful, etc., etc.

Please would you let me know if on Sunday you would like to pay a brief visit to the Auxerrois gate and then the Sainte Chapelle? I think that Mlle

---

241. The Assembly had been elected to draw up a constitution. It was voted on 4 November. On 10 December, Louis-Napoléon Bonaparte was elected president of the Republic and formed a new government. There was no reason to maintain the Constituent Assembly. Finally, in late January, the Assembly set the date for the election of the new Legislative Assembly provided for in the constitution for 19 May 1849.

242. There were three groups of pretenders to the restoration of the monarchy, or empire: the Legitimists (for the descendant of Charles X), the Orleanists (for the descendant of Louis-Philippe), and the Bonapartists.

243. Marietta Alboni, Giorgio Ronconi, Giulio Marco Bordogni: opera singers.

Louise, who loves everything that is beautiful, would like this monument. In my view it reaches the extreme point achieved by art in substituting the ethereal for the solid and daylight for stone, an art which appears to have been lost, judging from modern architecture.

Your devoted servant,

F. Bastiat

---

124. Letter to Mme Cheuvreux

Paris, February 1849   [*Lettres d'un habitant des Landes*, p. 12]

Madam,

It is with some confusion that I inform you of the result, closely resembling a fiasco, of my application to Faucher, but what do you expect, given that I am the worst petitioner in the world; it is perhaps a good thing. With regard to petitions, if I were habitually successful, who knows where I would stop, since everyone knows that I have no self-control.

M. Ramel may be granted 150 francs from the ministry of the interior. The administrative conventions require this to be given the name of assistance and not pension!

Yesterday evening's music ran through my head all night: "Io vorrei saper perche" and other delightful songs.

Farewell, Madam; I remain your devoted servant and that of Mlle Louise.

F. Bastiat

---

125. Letter to Bernard Domenger

Paris, 3 February 1849   [vol. 7, p. 388]

I am going to deal with the Le Peyrat farm[244] and the canal. For this reason, I will postpone speaking about this to you to another time.

My bad state of health coincides with the harsh exigencies of work. Since I hold, or think I do, a general view of the world of finance, I expounded it to my office colleagues. This was successful, since they almost unanimously nominated me to the budget commission. I wanted to perform the same demonstration again before this commission but, on the pretext of saving time, it forbade a general debate. It was thus necessary to discuss the details from the outset, which prevented an overall view being achieved. What would be your opinion of such a procedure in the face of a hopeless finan-

244. A candidate for the experimental farm mentioned in Letter 127.

cial situation, which could be saved only by a great theory if one were to be presented? For this reason, I felt it necessary to appeal to the Assembly and the general public by means of a brochure[245] on which I have been working yesterday and this morning.

I do not hide from myself that this is unlikely to succeed. Great assemblies lack initiative. Opinions are too wide ranging and nothing of worth can be achieved if the cabinet is inert. Ours is systematically inert: I sincerely believe that it is a public disaster. The current government might do some good. I have several friends in it, and I know that they are capable. Unfortunately, it came to power with the preconceived idea that it would not have the support of the Assembly and that it would have to maneuver in order to have it dismissed. I am absolutely sure that it is mistaken, and in any case was it not its duty to try? If it had come to the chamber to say, "The election on 10 December has put an end to the revolutionary period; now let us work together for the good of the people and administrative and financial reform," the chamber would have followed it enthusiastically, as it is passionately in favor of good and needs only to be guided. Instead of that, the government started by sulking. It presumed there would be disagreement, based on the sympathy shown by the Assembly to Cavaignac. But there is one thing that the Assembly prizes a thousand times above Cavaignac and that is the will of the people, as shown by universal suffrage. To show its absolute submission, it would have given its support to the head of the executive authority. How much good would have come of this! Instead of taking this course, the government retrenched itself in inertia and teasing. It proposes either nothing or else things that are unacceptable. Its tactic is to extend the stagnation of business through inertia, in the certainty that the nation will attack the Assembly for this. The country has lost a magnificent opportunity to move forward which it will not recover, since I very much fear that other storms are lying in wait for the next Assembly.

---

126. Letter to Bernard Domenger

Paris, 1849 [no month or day]   [vol. 7, p. 390]

As my unfortunate cold has prevented me from taking the rostrum, I sometimes have recourse to the pen. I enclose two brochures. One does not have a great deal of interest for the provinces. It is entitled *Capital and Rent*. My aim is to refute a preconceived idea, which has done much dam-

---

245. *OC,* vol. 5, p. 407, "Paix et liberté ou le budget républicain."

age among the workers and even among the young students at schools. This preconceived idea consists in thinking that interest from capital is theft. I therefore sought to demonstrate the intrinsic nature and raison d'être of interest. I might have made this brochure provocative, as the subject was conducive to this. However, I thought it best to refrain from this so as not to irritate those whom I wished to win over. The result has been that I have fallen into sluggishness and boredom. If ever I produce a second edition, I will rewrite it.

The other brochure is a draft budget or rather the fundamental idea that, in my view, must be at the base of the gradual reform of our financial system.[246] It shows the signs of having been written rapidly. There are portions that are too long, omissions, etc. Be that as it may, the prevailing idea is sufficiently highlighted.

I did not limit myself to writing down these ideas; I explained them in various workplaces and before the budget commission, of which I am a member. What I consider to be the most basic prudence was taken to be wild temerity. What is more, as the government is determined to remain inert, it is impossible for the commission to achieve anything worthwhile. A crowded meeting of men deprived of the resources provided by the administrative authority cannot pursue a systematic plan. Projects conflict with each other. General ideas are rejected as a waste of time, and they end up just dealing with details. Our budget for 1849 will be a fiasco. I believe that history will blame this on the Cabinet.

The elections are coming closer; I do not know what the Assembly will decide with regard to the notice period. Will I be able to come to see you? I would like to do so for various reasons: first of all, in order to breathe the air of my region and shake my friends' hands; second, to combat a few false notions which may have arisen concerning my actions in parliament; and lastly, to inform the electors of my views on the spirit in which they should make their choices. In my opinion, they could not do better than to remain faithful to the spirit which prevailed over them in April 1848. They do not think they produced a good Assembly. I maintain the opposite. It was slightly changed by the partial elections, which sent us both several revolutionaries and a large number of plotters. God preserve my country from having recourse in this way to the extreme wings of both parties! A

---

246. Ibid. Possibly a reference to the pamphlet *Paix et liberté; ou le budget républicain.*

violent clash would ensue. Doubtless, the country can nominate people only in accordance with its impressions and opinions of the moment. If it is reactionary, it will nominate reactionaries. But let it at least select new men. If it sends long-standing deputies with hearts full of bitterness and well versed in parliamentary intrigue, who are determined to overthrow everything, create traps for new institutions, and bring out as rapidly as possible all the faults that may sully our constitution, all will be lost! We already have the proof of this. Our constitution puts two equal powers into confrontation with each other without the means of settling any possible conflict. This is a great failing. And what has been the result? Instead of at least waiting for this failing to be revealed and for conflict to arise in due course, the government made haste to generate it needlessly. This is the thinking of a man in a hurry to derive criticism of our institutions from whatever happens. And why has this man acted in this way? Did he need to? No. But he is one of those who were deeply thwarted by the revolution and, without realizing it, he is taking pleasure in exacting his revenge at the expense of the country.

As for my personal fate, I do not know what this will be. The country might reproach me for not having done much! In effect, my health has been an invincible obstacle. It has paralyzed my physical and mental strength. I have thus disappointed my friends' expectations. But is this my fault? Whatever happens, if my mandate is withdrawn, I will resume with no bitterness the solitary habits that are so dear to me.

Farewell.

---

127. Letter to Bernard Domenger

Paris, 21 March 1849 [vol. 7, p. 392]

Your letter has reached me attached to that from M. Dup——.[247] The minister of trade had initially made me promises. Later, I learned that Dup—— had insisted with all his customary tenaciousness. Yesterday evening, I went to Buffet's house, taking Turpin with me. As he had been present at the General Council, he could testify as to what had happened and he did so in very formal terms. We met Dampierre there and he helped us.

247. On 3 October 1848, a decree established that there would be a farm school in each *département*. The General Council of the Landes decided that the school would be in the Chalosse. On 15 October, Aristide Dupeyrat declared his candidacy for the direction of the school. He was eventually chosen from among several candidates.

In spite of all this, I saw that the minister was uneasy; Duv——'s obsessions must have frightened him. He told us, "If I refuse Duv—— his farm, it will cause his death."

I had already written Buffet a closely reasoned letter and will write another, which I will end as follows: France wants administrative *decentralization*. If the minister believes he can overlook the wishes of all the regular mouthpieces of the *département* and act as he wishes, when it is a matter of determining where a farm will be set up, he may as well eliminate the institution of the general councils, as they will then just be a mirage.

I ask you, my dear D., to apologize on my behalf to M. Dup—— for not replying to him today. I will do so when I have further information. You see how the law regarding political associations[248] arouses Paris. The minister was very reckless to raise this matter. However, his unfortunate tactic is to disregard the Assembly, and I believe that he wished to have the law rejected in order to attribute full responsibility for the future to it.

No vote has ever cost me so dear as the one I cast yesterday. You know that I have always been in favor of *freedom except for the repression of* crime. I must admit that in the face of the political clubs this principle appears to have to give way. When I contemplate the fear they inspire in peace-loving people, the memories they resurrect, etc., etc., I tell myself that those who sincerely love the Republic must understand that they have to make it loved. It will be compromised if there is an intention to impose by force on the country an institution or even a liberty which appalls it. I therefore voted for the elimination of the clubs.

When I did this, I did not hide the disadvantages of this action. To succeed in politics, you have to join a party and, if possible, the strongest party. Voting according to your conscience with the right and the left according to the circumstances is to risk being abandoned by both. But before reaching this point, I had taken the decision only to consult my judgment and conscience and not *vote according to party lines*. This influenced the proposal I put forward. Systematic majorities and minorities are the death of representative government.

I believe that our government will make a considerable effort to avoid war. In previous times we might have feared that it would be carried along

248. Léon Faucher had submitted a law forbidding clubs of political orientation because some clubs were engaging in vigorous campaigning and fomenting trouble. The law was passed (404 votes for, 303 against).

by popular feelings in support of Italy, but things have changed a great deal. The disturbances in the peninsula have reduced this support. Charles Albert[249] will probably be defeated before we have the time to debate the opportunity of what should be done. But once the Austrians have reached Turin, all will not be lost, far from it. I am not even sure that it is only then that serious problems will begin. Oh, how difficult is it for men to get along together, when it might be so easy!

---

128. Letter to Mme Cheuvreux

Paris, Monday, March 1849   [*Lettres d'un habitant des Landes*, p. 13]

Madam,

I am quite positive that I have left something very precious at your house, something which men of my age should no longer leave behind, something which we should always feel when our hand strays to the left side of our chest, something whose loss reduces us to being scatterbrained or blind, in a word, my glasses.

If by any chance they have been found in your drawing room, please hand them to my messenger.

I am taking advantage of this opportunity to ask after the health of your Louisette, since this is the name you like to call her; I would be happy to learn that we will be able to hear her sweet voice tomorrow; admit that you are very proud of it.

Oh! You have good reason to be. I dare not repeat it too often, but I prefer a romantic song sung by her to an entire concert highlighted by musical trills and tours de force. After all, is it not good practice to judge things and especially the arts by the impression they give us? When your daughter sings, every heart pays attention and everyone's breath is held, from which I conclude that it is true music.

I am intrepidly protecting my health. I value it highly, being weak enough to believe that it still has some use.

Yesterday I went to see Mme de Planat. Through a few Germanic mists her mind shows traces of a deep source of common sense and original judgment, with just enough erudition for it not to be too much and perfect im-

---

249. On February 1849, in Rome, the Assembly decided to end the temporal authority of the papacy and proclaim the republic in Tuscany. The same year, Charles Albert, king of Sardinia, invaded Lombardy but was defeated by Austria and had to abdicate.

partiality; our unfortunate civil disturbances do not trouble the sureness of her opinions. She is a woman who thinks for herself and I would like you to meet her. However, she made me talk too much.

I have not visited Victor Hugo because I thought he lived in the Marais;[250] if I had known he lived in your district, then since the slope down to this area of Paris is easy, I would have made my entrance to his salon, which must be worth a visit.

Farewell. I shake the hands affectionately of those you call *the Trio* whom I love dearly.

F. Bastiat

---

129. Letter to Mrs. Schwabe

Paris, 11 March 1849 [vol. 7, p. 429]

I have been horribly negligent and horrible is the right word, since it is close to ingratitude. How can I excuse it after all the kindnesses with which I have been showered at Crumpsall House?

What is certain is that my activities exceed my strength. Perhaps I will be relieved of them soon. According to the opinions I am receiving from my region, I will not be *returned*. I was sent to uphold the Republic. I am now being reproached for being faithful to my mission. This will wound my feelings, as I have not deserved to be abandoned, and what is more we ought to weep for a country that discourages even honest action. What consoles me, however, is that I will be able to renew the ties of friendship and my work in solitude that is so dear to me.

It is with surprise and satisfaction that I learn of your forthcoming visit to Paris. I do not need to tell you with what pleasure I will shake your hand and that of Mr. Schwabe. My only fear is that this date coincides with that of our elections. If this is so, I will be two hundred leagues away, at least if I decide to subject myself to the risk of election. I have not yet made up my mind on this.

As you can well imagine, I am following the efforts of our friend Mr. Cobden with the keenest interest. I am even echoing it here. Yesterday, we obtained from our budget commission a reduction of two hundred thousand men in our armed forces. It is not very likely that the Assembly and the

---

250. District in the center of Paris.

government will accept such a radical change, but is this achievement with a commission nominated by the Assembly itself not a good sign?

. . . Farewell, madam, I am determined to write to you more regularly in the future. Today, I am busy with an important debate[251] which I have raised in the Assembly and which obliges me to carry out some research.

---

130. Letter to Félix Coudroy

Paris, 15 March 1849 [vol. 1, p. 94]

My dear Félix, your letters are really very infrequent, but they give me the pleasant feeling you experience when you see the steeple of your village church after a long absence.

It is a thankless task being a patriot and wanting to remain one of some consequence. Through some unknown optical illusion, the changes that occur around you are attributed to you. I have carried out my mandate in the spirit in which I received it; my country has the right to change and consequently to change its representatives, but it does not have the right to say that it is I who have changed.

You will have read in the newspapers that I proposed my motion. *Let representatives remain representatives,* I said, since if the law makes other prospects more appealing in their eyes, the mandate instantly becomes vitiated and exploited and, because it is the very essence of representative government, this entire system is undermined at its source and in its fundamental principles.

It was an extraordinary thing! When I mounted the rostrum I did not have ten supporters, and when I left it I had the majority. It is certainly not my powers of oratory that caused this phenomenon, but the power of common sense. The ministers and all those who aspired to become ministers were in ecstasy. They were just about to vote when the commission, with M. Billault at its head, evoked the amendment. It was sent back *as of right* to this commission. On Sunday and Monday there was a reaction in public opinion, which besides had had very little preparation, with the result that on Tuesday everyone said, "*Let representatives remain representatives!* But this is a frightful danger, it is worse than the Terror!" All the journals had cut, distorted, and deleted my words and put absurd notions into my mouth.

---

251. The debate concerned a potential conflict of interest when serving civil servants could also be elected to the Chamber of Deputies.

All the meetings in the rue de *Poitiers*,[252] etc., had emitted a cry of alarm; in a word all the usual means were employed.

In short, I was left with a minority made up of a few enthusiasts who no more understood me than the others, but one thing that is certain is that the impression was vivid and will be remembered for some time. More than one hundred members have told me that they were in favor of my proposal but voted against it for fear of making a mistake with such an important innovation on which they had not reflected sufficiently.

You know me well enough to think that I would not have liked to succeed through surprise. Later on, public opinion would have attributed all the calamities time would have brought on us to my amendment.

From a personal point of view, what is sad is the charlatanism that dominates newspapers.[253] There is a bias in favor of exalting certain men and deprecating others. What are we to do? It would be easy for me too to have a great number of friends in the press, but to do this I would need to make an effort, which I refuse, since the resulting chains would be too heavy.

As for the elections, I do not know whether I will be able to be present; I will go only when the Assembly has been dissolved. As a member of the budget commission, I have to remain at my post; let the country punish me if it wishes, I will have done my duty. I have one thing only I can reproach myself for, and that is not to have worked enough, and my excuse for this is my very poor health and the inability of my poor lungs to compete with the storms in parliament. Because I could not speak out, I took the course of writing. There is not a single question of burning importance which has not produced a pamphlet from me. It is true that I discussed the practical aspect less than the principles; in doing this I was obeying the character of my mind, which is to go back to the source of error, each person making himself useful in his own way. In the midst of all the heated emotions unleashed, I could not influence the effects, I just pointed out the causes. Have I really remained inactive?

In opposition to the doctrine of Louis Blanc, I wrote *Individualism and*

252. A group of deputies of the extreme right used to meet in a building on the rue de Poitiers.

253. For example, the following comment was made in *La Revue des deux mondes:* "M. Bastiat is keen to extend truths as far as paradoxes. This time, he has gone to the most paradoxical extreme of a false idea" (14 March 1843).

Fraternity.[254] When property was attacked, I wrote *Property and Law.* Income from land came under fire, so I wrote the five articles in the *Débats.*[255] The *practical* source of communism was revealed, so I wrote the pamphlet *Protectionism and Communism.* Proudhon and his followers preached *free credit,* a doctrine which spread like wildfire, so I wrote *Capital and Rent.* It was clear that a balanced budget would be sought through additional taxes, so I wrote *Peace and Freedom.*[256] We were faced with a law that encouraged parliamentary coalitions, so I wrote a pamphlet on *conflicts of interest.*[257] We were threatened with paper money, so I wrote the pamphlet *Damned Money.* All these pamphlets were distributed free of charge and in great numbers, which cost me a great deal; from this point of view the electors have nothing to reproach me for. From the point of view of action, I did not betray their trust either. On 15 May and during the days of June I played my part in the troubles. After this, let their verdict condemn me; I will perhaps feel it in my heart but not in my conscience.

---

131. Letter to Bernard Domenger

Paris, 25 March 1849 [vol. 7, p. 392]

The last time I wrote to you I did so in haste, and I believe I forgot to speak to you about the elections. The time is coming closer, and since you are determined to put me on your list, I would be grateful if you would inform me regularly of what is being said and done. I am certain that there is a great deal of prejudice in the region against me and that these sentiments are sustained and perhaps inflamed by candidates or someone in their midst. I am aware that discussions with my proposers would be useful, but I cannot leave the National Assembly before it is dissolved. For this reason, I will shortly be sending a report.

---

254. The pamphlet *Individualism and Fraternity* was written to refute Louis Blanc's socialist interpretation of the first French Revolution, *Histoire de la révolution française,* the first volume of which appeared in 1847. (*OC,* vol. 7, p. 328, "Individualisme et fraternité.")

255. *Property and Plunder.*

256. See Letter 126, note 246.

257. *OC,* vol. 5, p. 518, "Incompatibilités parlementaires."

I am sure that I will have little support from the district[258] that would be most necessary to me, that is, Saint-Sever. If a bargain is struck among the three districts and each puts forward two candidates, I will probably not be on the Saint-Sever list, and while the two other districts would regret this somewhat, these regrets would not go so far as to break the agreement. I will therefore be, as they say, *among three stools,* etc.

As I am convinced that I have done my duty, this failure will be hurtful initially. I hope that I will be rapidly consoled. I do not lack other work to do outside the legislature.

But, from the political point of view, I would consider it a great misfortune if the elections produced a result that differed significantly from that of 1848. If you assess it with impartiality you would acknowledge that the Assembly has carried out its mission, overcome the greatest physical and moral difficulties, and finally restored order to events and peace to people's minds, and that the most dangerous utopian ideas have been brought down before it, even though at the outset it was strongly imbued with illusionary hopes. This Assembly is on the right track. It would have accomplished for finance, if it had had the time, everything it was possible to do. Is it the right time to turn it out and replace it with different men imbued with a different spirit and with hearts full of bitterness? I can tell you that the government is very anxious about the future in this respect. Will we never cease to embark on adventures? I therefore think that, if there were anything better to do, it would be to continue in the electoral spirit of 1848, except for the removal of a few men, on the right and the left, who have shown a disruptive spirit of unruliness.

In our *département,* this reproach can scarcely be made to our representatives. Only one of them, probably in good faith, has produced a dangerous proposal, that of progressive taxation and the taking over by the state of several private industries. Keeping the Republic honest has been the motto of the job of a deputy. The question should thus be asked: are we going to send back the same representatives or will we make new choices with new purposes in view?

Experience has proved to me that the struggle between the districts will be a very small affair if it breaks out. I can assure you that the district of Saint-Sever is the one that gives me the least work. I do not remember hav-

258. There are three electoral districts in the *département:* Mont de Marsan, Dax, and Saint-Sever.

ing received a single letter from the chief towns: Hagetmau, Amou, Geaune, or Aire. Even Mugron has sent me only three on matters that are not incompatible with the mandate of a deputy; Dax and Le Saint Esprit have sent me more. In all, I am edified to see just how far the spirit of lobbying has died out.

----

132. Letter to Bernard Domenger

Paris, 8 April 1849   [vol. 7, p. 396]

Your letters are always precious to me and it is a consolation to me to think that impartial and enlightened friends are not being influenced by the prejudices against me.

I have in fact spoken again to Buffet.[259] I put the argument most likely to produce an effect to him. I said, "If, when it is a question of pure locality to ascertain where a model farm may render the most service, the unanimous wishes of thirty general councillors are set aside, do not talk to us any further of decentralization." He replied, "I have made up my mind to give way to the wishes of the region in questions like these." In spite of this he has not taken a firm decision; he fears our tenacious and obstinate opponents. I have been assured that he is spreading invective against me. He is a very singular type of *liberal*.

I have received a letter from M. Dup——. He is asking me to send a note to the minister. I have already sent him a memorandum. You can be sure that we will neglect nothing in ensuring the triumph of the general council's note.

My friend, I would like to speak to you about the elections and politics. But in truth, there is so much to say that I do not dare start. The need for order, security, and confidence is dominant in the country. This is only natural. However, I am convinced that this is misleading the people with regard to the relationship between the government and the Assembly at the moment. I would very much like to go around the *département* to put right disastrous misunderstandings. The Assembly should be dissolved and thus allow the representatives to go out to explain themselves, not in their own interest but in the interest of the future. It is very important that the elections are not held under the influence of false preoccupations.

The current ministers are honest, well intentioned, and determined to

259. See Letter 127, pp. 183–84.

maintain order. They are my personal friends and I believe that they understand the meaning of true liberty. Unfortunately, they came into power
with the preconceived idea that the Assembly, which came out in support
of Cavaignac, would of necessity be opposed to Bonaparte. In my soul and
conscience this was a mistaken assessment, and it has had the most disastrous consequences. The ministers thought of nothing other than dismissing
the Assembly and, with this in view, discrediting it. They pretend to take
no note of its votes, even when it demands the execution of laws. They refrain from any initiatives. They give us free rein. They are present at debates
like strangers in the gallery. Since they feel that they are supported by the
wind of public opinion they generate strife because they think that it will
be advantageous to them in the eyes of the country. They thus accustom the
country to having a low opinion of the principal power of any representative
government. They go even further: they put forward unacceptable laws in
order to provoke their rejection. This is what happened with regard to the
clubs. You will say that my vote on this law will go some way to reconciling
me with the electors. Well then! I have to tell you that this vote is the only
one I have on my conscience, as it is contrary to all my principles, and if I
had had a few minutes in which to reflect calmly I would certainly not have
given it. What determined me to do this was this. I said to my neighbors, "If
we want the Republic to remain in place, we must make it loved, not make
it feared. The country is in fear of the clubs, it hates them, let us sacrifice
them." The results of the law have proved that it would have been better
to stick to our principles, provide all the possible means of control, but not
eliminate freedom. This law has done nothing other than organize secret
societies.

Since then, I have voted three times and always to my regret against the
government. I will be reproached for this in the region, but nevertheless
these votes were conscientious.

   1. The Italian question. Like La Montagne, I rejected the agenda
      which pressed for an invasion of the Piedmont,[260] but for
      the opposite reason. La Montagne did not find this agenda
      sufficiently warlike; I found it too much so. You know that I am

260. See Letter 127, note 249. After its victory over Charles Albert, the Austrian government spoke of reestablishing the principles prevailing in Europe after the treaty of
Vienna, in 1815. That was interpreted in France as a threat to the Republic, and a military
intervention "of solidarity with the Italian republic" was decided on.

against intervention and this explains my vote. Besides, I do not approve of the diplomacy carried out in parliament. Foolhardy undertakings are entered into which subsequently prove to be an embarrassment. I preferred the pure and simple agenda for which I voted.

2. The question of the prefects.[261] If the government had made a frank admission, I would have overlooked it. However, it wished to claim that forty prefects became ill on the same day. Subtleties like this disgust common sense.

3. The Changarnier affair.[262] The same reason. If the government had demanded that a state of affairs contrary to the law should be prolonged, on the premise of the requirements of order, we might have agreed. However, it came to us to say, "We are asking for something arbitrary *and the National Assembly is no judge of the length of time this arbitrary state should last!*" The greatest despot in the world could not ask for anything different. I could not agree to this.

As for the elections, they will be what the good Lord wants them to be. If I have to fall, I have taken steps in advance and I have much work to do outside parliament. I have a work in my head and fear that I will not be able to deliver it. If the electors give me some leisure, I will console myself by working on this book, which is my chimera. My only wish is that they do not replace me in too unworthy a manner. There are some who, if put in my place, would not bring honor to the *département*.

---

133. Letter to Félix Coudroy

Paris, 25 April 1849 [vol. 1, p. 97]

My dear Félix, the elections may well be approaching, but I am not receiving any direct news of them. A nice, affectionate letter from Domenger is the sum of my pittance. I may presume that I am the only representative in this situation, and this gives me a premonition of my fate. Besides this, I have received a few bits of indirect information through Dampierre. He has left

261. Some prefects, retired for reasons of illness or infirmity, were recalled because of their hostility to the Republic.
262. Refers to Nicolas Anne Theodule Changarnier (1793–1877).

me in no doubt that the region has formed a movement, which implies that the confidence it placed in me has been withdrawn. I am neither surprised nor upset by this, *as far as I am concerned.* We are in an age in which you have to fling yourself into one of the extremist parties if you wish to succeed. Whoever casts a cool eye on the exaggerations of the parties and combats them remains abandoned and crushed in the center. I am afraid that we are moving toward a social war, a war of the poor against the rich, which may be the dominant event of the end of this century. The poor are ignorant, violent, and riddled with illusionary and absurd ideas, and the movement which is carrying them along is unfortunately justified to a certain extent by *genuine claims,* since indirect taxes are a reverse form of *progressive taxation* for them. As this is so, I could have only one plan, to combat the errors of the people and anticipate *well-founded complaints,* in order never to leave justice on their side. This has given rise to the eight or nine pamphlets I have written and my votes for all the financial reforms.

However, it has happened that, taking advantage of the need for security, which is the salient characteristic of public opinion, the rich are exploiting this need to the benefit of their own injustice. They remain cold and selfish, and they weaken any effort made to save them, their sole dream being the restoration of the small number of abuses brought down by the Revolution.

In this situation a clash appears inevitable to me, and it will be terrible. The rich are counting a great deal on the army, but experience of the past should make them rather less confident in this regard.

As for me, I ought to have been out of favor with both parties for the very reason that I was more concerned with combating their errors than enrolling myself under their banner; I and all the other men of *scientific* good will, that is to say, that which is based on justice as explained by science, will remain on the sidelines. The new Chamber, which ought to have been the same as the present one without the extremes, will on the contrary be made up of the two extreme camps, and intermediate prudence will be banished from it.[263] If this does happen, there is just one thing left for me to say: may God protect France! My friend, by remaining in obscurity, I would have reasons with which to console myself if at least my somber predictions fail to materialize. I have my theory to write down and I am receiving powerful encouragement just at the right time. Yesterday I read these words in an English review: in

263. Bastiat's prediction was right: the extreme right got 53 percent of the seats; the extreme left, 35 percent; and the moderate republicans, 9.3 percent.

political economy, the French school has gone through three phases encapsulated by the following three names, Quesnay, Say, and Bastiat.[264]

Of course, it is premature for me to be assigned this rank and role, but it is clear that I have a new, fertile idea that I believe to be true. This idea is one that I have never developed methodically. It has come through almost accidentally in a few of my articles, and since this has been enough to catch the attention of learned men, since it has already been given the honor of being considered as a *milestone* in science, I am now certain that when I produce the complete theory it will at least be examined. Is this not all I could wish for? With what ardor will I use my retirement to set out this doctrine, in the certainty that it will be scrutinized by judges who understand and who are waiting for it!

On the other hand, professors of political economy are trying to teach my *Theory of Value*[265] but are no more than feeling their way. It has made an impression in the United States, and yesterday in the Assembly a delegation of Americans presented me with a translation of my works.[266] The preface shows that they are waiting for the fundamental *idea* which up to now has rather been outlined than formulated. This situation is also true for Germany and Italy. It is true that all this is happening in the closed circle of professors, but it is through them that ideas make their entrance into the wider world.

I am therefore ready to accept with resolution the naturally very hard life that will be allocated to me. What gives me courage is not Horace's "non omnis moriar,"[267] but the thought that perhaps my life will not have been pointless for the human race.

Right now, where will I base myself in order to carry out my task, in Paris or in Mugron? I have not yet taken any decision but I feel that in your company the work would be better formulated. Having just one concept and subjecting it to an enlightened friend is certainly the best recipe for success.

264. That is, the physiocrats, the Smithians, and now the followers of Bastiat.

265. Bastiat could be referring to chapter 5 of *Economic Harmonies,* "On Value." (*OC,* vol. 6, p. 140, "De la valeur.")

266. An example of an American translation of one of Bastiat's works is an 1848 translation of *Economic Sophisms,* titled *Sophisms of the Protective Policy.* See Letter 63, note 142.

267. "All of me shall not die."

134. Letter to Bernard Domenger

Paris, 29 April 1849   [vol. 7, p. 399]

I have been very dilatory in replying to your letter of the 14th, but what could I do? Nature has riddled me with the oddest afflictions and I appear to become increasingly inert just when I need to be most active. So, since the question of elections has arisen, I have become absorbed and fascinated by a purely theoretical work, which takes up all my waking hours.

The very rare items of news reaching me give me no doubt as to the result of the vote concerning me; I have lost the confidence of the region. Let me explain; my mistake, and this is only a personal point of view, has been to perceive the two conflicting exaggerations and associate myself with neither. My friend, they are leading us toward civil war, a war of the poor against the rich. The poor demand *more* than is just; the rich do not want to grant *even* what is just. This is the danger. *Taxes that increase with wealth* have been rejected, and this is right, but *taxes that increase with deprivation* have been maintained, and this has provided good arguments to the people. No one knows better than I how many absurd claims they are making, but I also know that they have *well-founded complaints.* Therefore simple prudence, in the absence of equity, traced out the line of conduct for me to follow: resist the illusionary demands of the people and acknowledge their legitimate claims. But alas! The notion of justice has been *distorted* in the minds of the poor and the sentiment of justice has been *extinguished* in the hearts of the rich. I have therefore had to alienate myself from both classes. All that is left to me is to be resigned to my fate.

I hope that I am a false prophet! Before February, I said: "*Increasing resistance* in the government and an increasingly active *movement* in the opposition could result only in a wrenching division. Let us seek out the point at which justice occurs as this will save us." I was not mistaken. Both parties persisted in their ways and the result was a revolution.

Today, I say: The poor are demanding too much and the rich not granting enough; let us seek justice; this is where conciliation and security reside. But the parties persist, and we will have social war.

This will occur, I fear, in unfortunate conditions, as the more we refuse what is just to the populace the greater moral and material strength we give to its cause. This is why it is making terrifying progress. This progress is veiled by a transitory reaction, one determined by the general need for security, but it is genuine. The explosion will be delayed, but it will occur.

I had reached this point in my letter when I received one from our friends in Mugron. I left my letter to you to reply to them and naturally I repeated what I said above, since I can say only what is filling my heart. They are pressing me to return to the region, but what would I do there? Are people ready to organize major meetings? Without this, how could I make contact with such a large number of electors?

I received your letter of the 27th on the 30th. I will be going later to the Assembly and will see whether I can obtain leave of absence without any problem. I am very disinclined to do this just at the time when the budget for war will be debated and I will perhaps be called upon to defend it.

Everyone wants *economy* in general. But everyone resists each individual *economy* in particular.

---

135. Letter to Mme Cheuvreux

Paris, 3 May 1849   [*Lettres d'un habitant des Landes,* p. 16]

Madam,

Please allow me to send you a copy of my letter to the electors. This is certainly not to have your political opinion on it, but these documents are above all a matter of tact and delicacy. You have to talk about yourself a lot in them and how do you avoid either false modesty or outrageous vanity? How do you show yourself to be sensitive to ingratitude without falling into the ridiculous category of being *misunderstood*? It is very difficult to reconcile dignity with the truth. I think that a woman is above all suitable for pointing out any faults of this nature, provided that she is frank enough to say so. It is for this reason that I am sending you this piece of *homework* in the hope that you will be willing to read it and help me to avoid improprieties if they occur. I have learned that you are starting your salons again this evening. If I can escape from a meeting in which I will be kept a little late, I will come to receive your advice. Is this not a strange mission I am giving you and an opportunity to say with Faucher that "You really have to come from the wide Landes to be gallant in this style."

Have you had the patience to read last night's session?[268] What a sad conflict! In my opinion, an act of more than doubtful morality would have

---

268. The discussion in the Chamber on the subject of a telegram sent by Léon Faucher, minister of the interior, to the prefects a few days before the elections on 18 May 1849.

become excusable by a simple admission, especially as the responsibility for it lay with Faucher's predecessors. It is the system of defense that is pitiful. And then the representatives who hope to become ministers came to inflame and exploit the fault. Ah, madam! Am I condemned to go from one setback to another? Will it be necessary for me, who left the region as a believer, to return to it as a skeptic? It is not my faith in humanity that I fear to lose, that is unshakeable, but I need also to believe in a few of my contemporaries, in the people I see and who surround me. Faith as a general principle is not enough for me.

Here is a pamphlet on Biarritz; I am sure that when you read it you will say, "*That is where we ought to go*[269] to give my beloved Louise a strong constitution."

The author of this pamphlet wanted me to hand it over to one of my friends in a position close to the president of the Republic (always this Proteus of lobbying); I could not carry out this commission because of the word *Prince,* clumsily deleted in front of the name Joinville; this author,[270] a doctor, had also asked me to write a preface in the form of an apology. "But I do not know anything about medicine," I said to him. "Well then, hide your science behind your feelings." I then set about it. This introduction has no other merit than a certain sobriety of description, which is not very fashionable. As I am very fond of Biarritz, I am trying to do some advertising for it.

What a long letter this is! I will be outdoing M. Blondel.

> Farewell, Madam.
> Your devoted servant,
> *F. Bastiat*

---

136. Letter to Bernard Domenger

Paris, 1849[271]   [vol. 7, p. 401]

My election,[272] which I learned of two days ago, will make me busier after it than before, for while I was able to neglect it a little, I must not at least forget to express my total gratitude to my friends, not for the service they

---

269. Quotation from *Mignon* by Goethe.
270. Romain Affre.
271. Most probably 15 or 16 May 1849.
272. Bastiat, who was the deputy representing the Landes in the Constituent Assembly of 1848, was reelected in 1849 to the Legislative Assembly.

have rendered me, but for the devotion and confidence that they have demonstrated. You are in the front rank of these and I am most touched by the zeal you devoted to this, especially as it must have cost you a great deal. I know that you dislike electioneering and that for a long time you wished to take only a purely personal part in it. On the other hand, you must have put yourself into conflict with very many of your friends. I want you to know that these circumstances taken together have made me appreciate your devotion all the more.

What will be the fate of the new Assembly? People are pinning high hopes on it. God willing, these will not be pure illusions. It will certainly not be better intentioned than the one that has just passed on. But what do intentions achieve? Like *La Presse,* I think that the best assembly is good only for preventing evil. To do good, you need the initiative of a more concentrated power; we have had the proof of this for the last five months. The government has limited its role to arousing and sustaining a conflict, and the Chamber, with all its good intentions, was unable to do anything about this.

What makes the future fearful is ignorance. The poor classes are becoming regimented and are marching as one man to a senseless war, without the slightest premonition that they are committing suicide, since after they have destroyed capital and the very motive that builds it up, what will be their fate?

Fundamentally, the matter of taxation alone should stand between the two classes. Achieving proportional taxes is all that justice requires; beyond this, there is only injustice, oppression, and misfortune for all. But how do we put this across to men who combat the very principle of ownership?

I will tell you that in my head there is a thought that is absorbing me, distracts me from my work, and makes me neglect my friends. This is a new explanation of these two words: *property* and *community.*[273] I think that I can show in the most obvious way that the natural order of society bases on ownership itself the most beautiful, wide-ranging, and progressive community. This may appear paradoxical to you, but I have *total certitude* in my mind. I am anxious to be able to put this thought to the general public as I think that it will reconcile sincere men in all schools of thought. It will doubtless not draw the leaders of sects, but it will prevent the young people

---

273. Chapter 8 of *Economic Harmonies* deals with that very subject. (*OC,* vol. 6, p. 256, "Propriété, communauté.")

in schools from going to enroll themselves under the flag of communism. Am I in the coils of an illusion? This is possible, but the fact is that I am consumed with the desire to publish my idea. I am still afraid that I will not have the time, and when cholera was decimating the Assembly I said to God, "Do not take me from this world before I have accomplished my mission."

---

137. Letter to Mme Cheuvreux

Brussels, Hôtel de Bellevue, June 1849   [*Lettres d'un habitant*
                                                des Landes, p. 19]

Madam,

You wanted me to send you my traveler's impressions noted pell-mell on paper; do you not know that the diary has its dangers? It resembles memoirs in which you talk only about yourself. Oh, how much I would prefer to talk to you about yourself and your beloved Louise, about her occupations, her interests, her views, La Jonchère, and also a little about Le Butard; *there, all is poetry,* which cannot be said of the Brabant, this classic land of work, order, economy, and full stomachs. Besides, I can talk about it only through *hearsay,* as I arrived only yesterday evening and have seen it only through the window; in all truth this is serving me well, since it lays out before my gaze the king's palace. Thus, a few hours ago I was breathing air infected by republicanism, and now I have been plunged into an atmosphere of monarchy. Well then, would you believe that I have not even noticed the transition? The last word I heard on the other side of the frontier was the same as I heard on this side, "your passport." Alas, I did not have one. For a moment, I hoped that I would be sent back to Paris and my heart beat faster, but everything is becoming civilized, even gendarmes and customs officers, and in short I was allowed to pass with the recommendation that I should declare myself to the ministry of justice since, as the gendarme added, "We have been caught out several times, and only recently we nearly allowed M. Proudhon to escape." "I am not surprised," I replied, "that you have become so careful, and I will certainly go to make a declaration in order to encourage the gendarmerie to continue acting in this way."

But let us take things to a higher level. On Saturday, when I left the session (you see that I am writing a conscientious diary), I mentioned the word *Brussels.* "I am going there tomorrow at half past eight," said Barthélemy Saint-Hilaire; "let us go together." Accordingly I went to the rue La Fayette, thinking that I was arriving at the agreed time, but the convoy had left and

I had to wait for the one at midday. What was I to do in the interval? The Butte Montmartre is not far and the view from it is boundless. Around five o'clock, we crossed from France into Belgium and I was surprised not to feel any emotion. This was not so when I crossed our frontier for the first time; then I was eighteen and I was entering Spain! It was at the time of the civil war, I was riding a superb steed from Navarre, and, ever a *man of caution,* I had put a pair of pistols in my portmanteau, since Iberia is the land of great adventures, distractions that are unknown in Belgium. Might it be true that good social order kills poetry? I can still remember the impression made on me by the proud Castilians when I met them on the road on horseback and equipped with a blunderbuss apiece. They seemed to be saying: "I am not paying anyone to protect me; I protect myself." Among all races, it seems that civilization raises the level of the masses and lowers the value put on individual character. I fear that this country will confirm this observation.

It is impossible not to be struck by the appearance of comfort and well-being offered by Belgium. Huge factories that you meet at every step trumpet a happy confidence in the future to the traveler. I wonder if the industrial world, with its monuments, comfort, railways, steam, electric telegraphs, floods of books and journals, achieving the ubiquity, unpriced character, and common availability of material and intellectual goods, does not also have its own form of poetry, a collective form of poetry, of course. Does the ideal exist only in biblical, warlike, or feudal manners? Should we, in this respect, mourn the passing of wildness, barbarism, and chivalry? In this case, it is in vain that I seek harmony in civilization, since harmony is incompatible with the prosaic. However, I believe that what makes the past appear to us in such poetic colors, the Arab's tent, the grotto of the anchorite, or the keep of the lord of the manor, is distance, an optical illusion. We admire what contrasts with our habits and life in the desert moves us, while Abd el-Kader goes into ecstasy over the marvels of civilization. Do you think that there has ever been as much poetry in one of the heroines of antique times as in a woman of our era? Or that their minds were as cultured, their feelings as delicate, and that they had the same tenderness of heart and grace of movement and language?

Oh, let us not denigrate civilization!

Forgive me, mesdames, for this essay, but you asked for this in requesting me to write freely about things as they occurred to me. This is what I am doing, and I have to give my mind free rein, since two sources of ideas are closed to me: my eyes and my heart. My poor eyes do not know how to see as nature has refused them length of vision and rapidity; I cannot therefore describe towns or landscapes. As for my heart, it has been reduced to loving an abstraction, becoming passionate about humanity and science; others direct their aspirations toward God. This is not superfluous with respect to either; this is what I thought a short time ago when I left an asylum run by nuns devoted to caring for sick children, the mentally deficient, the deformed, and the scrofulous. What devotion! What selflessness! And after all, this life of sacrifice must not be full of suffering, since it leaves such expressions of serenity on their faces. Some economists deny the good done by these saintly women; what cannot be doubted is the influence for good that such a sight produces. It touches, induces tenderness, and raises the spirit; we feel ourselves to be better and capable of a faint imitation of this at the sight of such sublime and modest virtue.

I am running out of paper; otherwise you would not escape a lengthy dissertation on Catholicism, Protestantism, the pope, and M. de Falloux.

Please give me news of M. Cheuvreux; I hope he finds in the waters health and moral peace, so disturbed by the unrest caused by our miserable politics! Unlike me, he is not an isolated person without responsibility. He is thinking of you and his Louise; I understand his irritation at those causing trouble and reproach myself for not always having respected this sufficiently.

Farewell, I present my homage to both mother and daughter.

Your devoted servant,
F. Bastiat

---

138. Letter to Mme Cheuvreux

Brussels, June 1849   [*Lettres d'un habitant des Landes*, p. 25]

Madam,

The absence of your brother-in-law[274] will have a bad effect on those in favor of peace;[275] they are expecting a reception which they are not going to receive. M. Say is one of those who signed the invitation. On the basis of this circular several hundred foreigners are going to come to Paris, some crossing the Channel and others the ocean, and they will be expecting to find ardent zeal over here. What a disappointment they will have when they see that the cause of peace in France is represented by Guillaumin, Garnier, and Bastiat.

274. Horace Say.
275. The peace congress held in Paris, starting on 22 August 1849.

In England, it arouses entire populations, men and women, priests and the laity; does my country always have to be left behind?

I will be returning to Paris via Ghent and Bruges. I would like to arrive two days before the conference in order to find out what practical arrangements have been made since, I must admit, I am anxious about this. At the very least, I must carry out my duty of hospitality to Cobden, and to do this I may have to call on your boundless good nature; I will ask your permission to introduce to you one of the most remarkable men of our time. If I succeed, as I hope, in reaching Paris on Saturday, I will take the liberty of going to La Jonchère on Sunday. Will I find that nothing has changed there?

Will Mlle Louise be in full possession of her health and voice? It is a very pleasant although imperative habit to be informed as to what is interesting day by day and it makes even the shortest absence difficult.

Taking everything into account, mesdames, allow me not to take advantage of your indulgence and to hold back the telling of my tale of Antwerp. What is the use of sending it to you and giving you the trouble of reading it when I can shortly replace it with a few minutes of conversation? Besides, on rereading these notes, I see that they talk about everything except Antwerp. I have found the Belgians to be very proud of the common sense they have shown in the last two years of European troubles. They have hastened to put an end to their disagreements by mutual concessions; the king has set the example, and the Chamber and people have followed him. In short, they are all delighted with each other and with themselves. However, socialist and communist doctrines have continued their underground work and I think this is somewhat frightening for the people. This has brought to my mind a project that I will tell you about, but what in fact are projects? They resemble tiny bubbles, which appear and disappear on the surface of rough water.

Farewell, madam. Do not think that feelings act in the same way as projects. The affection I feel for you and your family is too deep and too solidly anchored not to last as long as my life and I hope beyond it.

F. Bastiat

---

139. Letter to Mme Cheuvreux

Notes taken in Antwerp, June 1849 　　　　　　[*Lettres d'un habitant des Landes,* p. 27]

The extremes have met. This is what you feel on the railways; the extreme multiplicity of impressions cancels them out. You see too many things to see any one thing. This is a singular way of traveling: you do not speak, your ears and eyes fall asleep, and you are wrapped in your thoughts in solitude. The present, which ought to be everything, is nothing. But also, with what tenderness does the heart turn back to the past and with what eagerness does it leap forward toward the future. "A week ago . . . in a week's time." Are these not well-chosen texts for meditation when, for the first time, Vilvorde, Malines, and Brabant fly past under a gaze that does not see them!

This morning I was in Brussels, this evening at five o'clock I was once more in Brussels; in the intervening period I saw Antwerp, its churches, its museum, its port, and its fortifications. Is this really traveling? What I call traveling is to enter into the society you are visiting, finding out the state of people's minds, their tastes, their occupations, their pleasures, the relationships between the classes, the moral, intellectual, and artistic level they have attained and what we can expect from them for the advancement of the human race. I would want to ask questions of their statesmen, their merchants, their laborers, their workers, their children, and above all their women, since it is the women who prepare future generations and control manners.

Instead of that, I am shown a hundred paintings, fifty confessionals, twenty steeples, I do not know how many statues in stone, marble, and wood, and I am told, "This is Belgium."

To tell you the truth, there is just one resource for the observer and that is the dinner table. It gathered around it today sixty diners not one of whom was Belgian. You could see five Frenchmen and five long beards; the five beards belonged to the five Frenchmen or rather the five Frenchmen to the five beards, since the principal should never be taken for the accessory.

This being so, I asked myself this question, "Why do the Belgians, English, Dutch, and Germans shave? And why do the French not shave?" In each country, men like to have it thought that they possess the qualities that are the most highly prized. If fashion turned to blond wigs, I would say to myself that these people are effeminate; if I noticed in portraits an exaggerated development of the forehead, I would think that these people had dedicated a cult to intelligence; and when savages disfigure themselves to make themselves look frightening, I conclude that they prize brute force above all. This is why I experienced a dreadful feeling of humiliation today when I saw all the efforts of my fellow countrymen to make themselves look ferocious. Why did they have these beards and moustaches? Why this military tattooing? Whom do they want to terrify and why? Fear! Is this the tribute that my country is bringing to civilization?

It is not only traveling salesmen who are indulging in this ridiculous travesty; should it not be up to women to fight it? But is this all I have brought back from Antwerp? It was worth the trouble to travel for miles without end or purpose. I saw paintings by Rubens in their own country; you can well imagine that I sought in living nature the models for these ample studies in flesh tints that the master of the Flemish School reproduced with such pleasure. I did not find them since in truth I think that the Brabant race is inferior to the Norman race. I am told I should go to Bruges; I would go to Amsterdam if this was my type of attraction but this red flesh is not my ideal. Sentiment and grace, this characterizes woman or at least the type of woman worthy of the paintbrush.

---

140. Letter to Bernard Domenger

Paris, Tuesday, 13 ... (Summer 1849)[276]   [vol. 7, p. 403]

You ask me to give you some news. Do you know that I might well ask you for some? For the last few days I have made myself into a hermit and what has happened to me is like a dream. I was tired and ill; in short, I had decided to ask for a leave of absence and I am spending it at the lodge at Le Butard. What is Le Butard? It is this:

Do you know the area which extends from Versailles to Saint-Germain and which includes Bougival, La Celle-Saint-Cloud, Vaucresson, Marly, etc.? It is the most delightful, hilly region and one that is certainly the most wooded in the world after the forests in America. This is why, as he did not have a sufficiently extended view at Versailles, Louis XIV had the chateau de Marly built and why immediately Mesdames de Montespan, Maintenon, and later Dubarry[277] had the delightful villas built at Louveciennes, Malmaison, La Jonchère, Beauregard, etc.

Today, these are all lived in by people I know. Near the center, in the middle of a thick forest, isolated like an eagle's nest, there is the lodge of Le Butard, which the king sited at the convergent point of a thousand avenues as a hunting lodge. It takes its name from its elevated position.

However, a *reactionary,* who has known for a long time that I wanted to enjoy this picturesque and untamed place and that I was thinking about

276. No month given.
277. Madame de Montespan, mistress of Louis XIV; Madame de Maintenon, second wife of Louis XIV; and Madame Dubarry, mistress of Louis XV.

producing something on *property,* allowed me to camp in his lodge at Le Butard, which he had rented from the state with the surrounding hunting rights. Here I am then, all alone, and I am enjoying this way of life so much that when my leave of absence is over I am proposing to go to the Chamber and return here every day. I read, go for walks, play the bass, write, and in the evening I go down one of the avenues which leads me to a friend. This is how I learned yesterday of the death of Bugeaud. He is a man who will be missed. His military frankness inspired confidence and in particular sorts of potential situations he might have been very useful to us.

I have come to Paris. There I have found things in a very sorry state. The senseless audacity of —— exceeds any belief. These men amuse themselves by trampling underfoot all the rules of representative government, constitution, laws, and decrees. They do not see that they are even making the monarchy they dream about impossible! What is more, they are playing with the honor, word, and even the security of France; they are compromising what she stands for and are drowning justice in blood. It is worse than madness.

Under these circumstances, I will be forced to leave my lodge in Le Butard or at least spend part of my days on the main roads. I will also have to interrupt the work I had begun to sketch out and which I had decided to publish, even in its rough form.

---

141. Letter to Prosper Paillottet

Paris, 14 July 1849 [vol. 7, p. 436]

My dear Paillottet, I am very grateful that you remembered me in our Pyrenees and at the same time I am proud of the impression they made on you. How happy I would have been to accompany you on your outings! We would perhaps have brought a chill and a touch of vulgarity to these fine landscapes by adding political economy to them. Actually, no, since social laws have their *harmonies* just like the laws governing the physical world. This is what I am trying to demonstrate in the book that I am currently working on—I have to admit that I am not happy with it.[278] I had a magnificent subject to which I have not done justice and have no time to rewrite, since the first pages are being printed. Perhaps this fiasco is not my fault. It is a difficult if not impossible thing to talk appropriately about social harmonies to an audience that is ignorant of, or which contests, the most ele-

---

278. *Economic Harmonies.*

mentary notions. Everything has to be proved, right up to the legitimacy of interests, etc. It is as if Arago wished to demonstrate the harmony of the movement of the planets to people who know nothing of arithmetic.

What is more, I am ill disposed and do not know to what to attribute this given that I am in good health. I am living at Le Butard where I hoped to find inspiration; instead of this, inspiration has fled.

It is being said that the Assembly will be prorogued from 15 August to 1 October. Please God that this is so! I will try to retrieve myself in my second volume in which I will be drawing the consequences of the first with regard to our current situation. A social problem—a French problem. . . .

Political economy owes a great deal to you as do I for your zeal in recommending *us*. Please continue to do so. One convert produces others. The country has a great need of this science, which will be its savior.

> Farewell, your very devoted
> servant,

---

142. Letter to Félix Coudroy

Paris, 30 July 1849   [vol. 1, p. 99]

My dear Félix, you have seen that the prorogation for six weeks has been passed with just a small majority. I am planning to leave on the 12th or 13th. I leave you to imagine with what happiness I will see Mugron, my relatives, and friends again. Please God that I will be left alone throughout this time! With your help perhaps I will finish the first part of my work.[279] I care very much about this. It got off to a bad start; it is too controversial; it is too labored, etc., etc.; I am longing to present it to the world, but I am determined not to play any parliamentary role before it is able to provide me with support. The other day, M. Thiers put out a challenge to those who believed they had the solution to the social problem. I was on tenterhooks on my seat but felt myself to be anchored to it because of the impossibility of making myself understood. Once the book has been published, I will have a resource to which I can refer the men of little faith.

Since we should be having the joy of seeing each other and continuing our delightful conversations, there is no point my replying to the political part of your letter. We are of one mind regarding principles; it is simply impossible for us to have differed on the facts themselves and on people.

279. Ibid.

I will bring the books you have asked me for, and perhaps also those that I need. Would you please do me the service of telling my aunt that I am in excellent health and that I am preparing to leave?

———————

143. Letter to Mme Cheuvreux

Mont-de-Marsan, 30 August 1849   [*Lettres d'un habitant*
des Landes, p. 31]

Madam,

Organizations that are somewhat ethereal are unfortunate in that they are highly sensitive to tiresome trials and disappointments, but how sensitive are they too to unexpected good fortune when it happens to them! Who would have told me that today I would receive news from La Jonchère? Space has the effect of time, and because I am many leagues away from my beloved Butard, I feel that I am also distant from it by many days both past and in the future. You and Mlle Louise, who are so indulgent, will forgive my outpourings on this subject; perhaps it is because I feel profoundly disgusted by political and social sentimentality that I have become somewhat sentimental in my affections. What can you do! The heart needs revenge; and also, I do not know how you, both mother and daughter, do it, but you have the gift and art of making all those who come into contact with you so content and happy that they can be excused for showing it a little. I was sure that M. Cheuvreux would be sorry not to have been able to join you in the fine welcome given to Cobden *at his house.* But I am happy to hear this. Would he not have found my manner of dispensing hospitality somewhat indiscreet? I wanted France and England to appear to each other in their best light. With the Cheuvreux ladies I was proud of Cobden; with Cobden I was proud of the Cheuvreux ladies. These insular peoples ought to know that each of the two countries has something to envy the other for.

It is a good sign that M. Cheuvreux is extending his stay at the spa; this proves that it is doing him good.

The journey ought to have tired me more. Two coaches always went together, with ours behind, that is to say in a cloud of dust. My traveling companions were dreary; thank God I talk to myself and imagination is enough for me; it has produced a plan that is the finest and most useful to humanity that you could imagine. It has only to be written down, but once again I will just have to rely on *good intentions.* If God takes account of this, I will be saved!

Just think, mesdames, how amusing I must find it to be kept here by the General Council, knowing that my aunt and friend[280] are expecting me in Mugron. And that is not all: I am enduring the weight of my fame; had they not held back all the most troublesome matters in order to do me the honors of the session? It was a question of being modest and a Gascon; I was both of these and to relieve myself of this strange form of courtesy I spoke of my fatigue. I took the opportunity, however, of producing a little *economiste* propaganda, given that our prefect has just infected his speech with socialism; this leprosy is getting everywhere. Tomorrow I will know which of the two schools will gain the majority in the Council. My fellow citizens are first-rate in support of me, they do have some small peccadilloes with which to reproach me, but they treat me like a spoiled child and appear to understand that I must be left to act, work, and vote capriciously.

I would like to bring Mlle Louise back a souvenir from our Landes, but what? Shall I go to Bayonne to find a few very tender romances set in restoration times, or else some Spanish boleros?

Mesdames, take pity on a poor exile; is it not strange to be *an exile* when one is *at home*? At this, you will say that I love paradoxes and that is a genuinely felt truth. For this reason, please write to me from time to time; I do not greatly dare to ask this sacrifice of Mlle Louise.

Please remain assured, both of you, of my fondness.

F. Bastiat

---

144. Letter to Mme Cheuvreux

Mugron, 12 September 1849   [*Lettres d'un habitant des Landes,* p. 34]

Madam,

It seems to me that twenty deliveries of letters have passed without bringing me any letters. Has time, like my watch, stopped since my return here? Or has Mlle Louise taken me at my word? However, a careful calculation which I have redone a hundred times tells me that it is not a week since my letter has gone. It is not your dear daughter who is in the wrong but my impatience. I would like to know whether M. Cheuvreux has returned to you in full health, if you yourself have recovered from your unpleasant insomnia, and in short if there is as much joy at La Jonchère as it deserves and

---

280. Félix Coudroy.

as I would wish. What a good invention the electric telegraph will be when it is put to the service of friendship! Perhaps one day it will have a telescope, which will enable it to see at two hundred leagues. Distance would then be bearable; for example, I would now turn it toward your drawing room. Mlle Louise is at the piano. I can guess from her expression the romantic song she is singing. M. Cheuvreux and you are experiencing the sweetest joy you can experience on this earth and your friends are forgetting that the last coaches are about to leave. This picture is heartwarming. Would it be unseemly and too provincial to tell you that this portrait of virtue, happiness, and union of which your family has given me such an example has been an antidote for me to the skepticism that is fashionable and a protection against *anti-Parisian* prejudice. What does this reproach by Rousseau mean, "Paris, a town of mud, etc.".? Not long ago I came across a novel by Jules Janin.[281] What a dreary and disastrous portrait of society! "The stable and the church go together," he says, meaning that esteem is gained in Paris only through the horse on which you parade in the wood or through hypocrisy. Tell me, pray, that you have never met this man or rather that he has never met you. Because they present wealth and selfishness as being the two sides of the same coin, novelists like him have supplied the grounds for socialist ranting. For my harmonies,[282] I needed to be sure that wealth is not only compatible with the qualities of the heart but that it develops and perfects them. I am sure of this now and feel that I am *proof,* as the English say, against skepticism.

Right now, madam, do you want me to lend you my marvelous telescope for a minute? I would really like you to be able to see from behind the curtain the following scenes of provincial life. In the morning, Félix and I walk around my room reading a few pages of Madame de Staël or a psalm by David; when dusk falls I go to the cemetery to look for a tomb, *my foot recognizes it, here it is!* In the evening I spend four hours in intimate contact with my good aunt. While I am buried in my Shakespeare, she talks with the most sincere animation, being kind enough both to ask the questions and provide the answers. Here comes the chambermaid, however, who thinks that the hours are long and feels obliged to give them a bit of variety; she comes on the scene and tells us about her electoral tribulations. The poor girl has been giving me publicity; people have always challenged her on *free trade* and she

281. Possibly a reference to Jules Gabriel Janin (1804–74), the author of *Pictures of the French.*
282. *Economic Harmonies.*

has argued with them. Alas, what arguments! She proudly repeats them to me and while she is giving her speech in Basque dialect, patois, and French, I remember this quotation from Patru, "There is nothing like a bad advocate for ruining a good cause."[283] Finally, suppertime arrives; dogs and cats rush into the room, escorting the garbure.[284] My aunt becomes furious. "Dreadful animals," she cries. "You see how bold they become when M. Bastiat arrives!" My poor aunt! This great fury is just artful tenderness and can be translated thus: "See what a nice person Frédéric is." I do not say that this is true, but my aunt wants this to be believed.

I was rightly telling you, madam, that letters from villages are deadly things; we can find subjects to write about only in the environment in which we live or in our own selves.

What a milieu Paris is for someone who writes! The arts, politics, and news are all in abundance, but here the outside world is sterile. You have to have recourse to another world, the inner one. In a word, you have to talk about yourself, and this consideration ought to have made me choose the smallest of scales. Instead of this I am clumsily sending you an acre of chatter; what reassures me is that my indiscretion will find it impossible to exhaust your indulgence.

I think that the prorogation has calmed the political effervescence a little; this should be a good thing, and in this respect we should wish that it were not so near to the end of its term. On our return, I would like the government to deliver us a heap of laws on which to browse, to take up our time, and to distract us from discussions that are sterile, or rather fertile only in hatred and exaggeration.

Please convey to M. Cheuvreux and Mlle Louise the great pleasure that I will have when I meet them again soon. Perhaps I will be back at La Jonchère again on Sunday, 30th September.

If I am in Paris, I will offer to escort Mme Girard, happy to receive the confidence of her maternal joys and cares. As for the tourists, I will be writing shortly to M. Say.

Farewell, madam; allow me
to assure you of my respectful
affection.
F. Bastiat

283. Possibly a reference to Olivier Patru, a seventeenth-century author.
284. A local cabbage and bacon soup.

145. Letter to M. Cheuvreux

Mugron, 16 September 1849   [*Lettres d'un habitant des Landes,* p. 39]

You have probably returned from the spa, my dear M. Cheuvreux. I am somewhat surprised at being reduced to conjecture.

There are some dreary times in which disturbed imaginations are easily inflamed. Can anyone leave Paris without thinking that he has left cholera there? The silence of our friends, which is always hard, is now becoming difficult to bear.

The purity of the air at La Jonchère reassures me. However, you have many relatives in Paris, and are not you yourself kept there almost every day by your judicial duties? These ladies have doubtless not thought of sparing me this form of anxiety. I would like to attribute their silence to less-dismal causes: business matters, pleasurable activities, walks, visits, music, chats, etc., and they also have a great many correspondents! Everyone has to take his turn. However, I would be happy to learn that everyone in your house is in good health and that this is also true of M. Say, the Renouards, at Croissy, etc.

When I arrived here, I organized a shooting party. I am sharing the catch between the Hôtel Saint Georges and the rue Boursault.

Yesterday, to put this matter of the shoot in context, I spent the day in the countryside where I lived in the past, sometimes alone and sometimes with others. The countryside here is very similar to that in which you live, a chain of hills with a river at their foot and plains as far as the eye can see beyond. The village is on the top of the hill and my property on the opposite bank of the river. But if art has done more to the banks of the Seine, nature is more unspoiled on those of the Adour. It would be impossible for me to express to you the impression I felt when I saw these long avenues of old oaks, this house with its huge rooms with only memories for furniture, these peasants with clothing in clear colors who speak in a simple language which I cannot help associating with the pastoral life. In fact I always think that a man in an overall and cap who speaks French is not *really* a peasant, and then the benevolent relationship between an owner and his sharecropper seems habitually to me to be another essential condition in establishing the genuine countryside. What a sky! What nights! What shadows! What silence, broken only by the distant barking of dogs to each other or by the vibrant and prolonged note echoing through space of the melancholy voice of a belated cowherd! These scenes affect the heart more than the eyes.

But here I am, back at the village. The village! It has moved one step closer to Paris. They read the gazette. Depending on the weather, they discuss Tahiti, or Saint-Jean d'Acre, Rome, or Comorn.[285] I was counting on the holidays to calm the political effervescence a little, but see how the wind of passions is getting up. France is once more between two impossible choices. The Republic has been led by guile and violence onto a terrain on which legitimism will beat it quite logically. It is sad to think that M. de Falloux matters and that the France of the nineteenth century does not. The population is nevertheless endowed with common sense; it wants what is good and understands this, but it has forgotten how to act of its own accord. A few horseflies always succeed in provoking it into inextricable difficulties. But let us not talk about such a dreary subject.

I hoped to have made progress with my book here,[286] an additional disappointment. Besides, I am no longer in such a hurry as, instead of being a *work of current interest,* it has become a work of pure doctrine and can have an effect, if effect it has, only on a few theoreticians. The real solution of the social problem would need to be propagated by a journal while still being based on a major book. I have something of an idea of embarking on a monthly publication, such as those of Lamartine and Louis Blanc. I think that our doctrine would spread like a fire or rather like a light, since it is certainly not incendiary. Everywhere I have preached it, I have found minds marvelously disposed to receive it. I tried this out on my colleagues in the General Council. Two obstacles terrify me: my health and finding the down payment.[287] We will discuss this soon, as I hope to spend the day of 30th September with you.

Farewell, my dear sir; if you have an extra moment, please spare your ladies the trouble of writing to me. Please assure them that the regime of privation to which they are subjecting me has not made me forget their boundless benevolence.

F. Bastiat

285. A fortress in Hungary.

286. *Economic Harmonies.*

287. This may be a reference to the fact that Bastiat had to make a down payment to publishers to cover some of the costs of having his books and pamphlets published. See also Letter 68, note 155.

146. Letter to Horace Say

Mugron, 16 September 1849 [vol. 7, p. 382]

See how our holidays, which have scarcely started, are coming to an end, even if they are not shortened for us. Are we going to be recalled to put an end to the Catholic muddle? Alas! It is to be feared that all we will do is muddle it a bit more. We are really in a blind alley. The Republic, through the determination of the government and disregard of the National Assembly, has put itself at the service of the inquisition. It now has two choices: either it goes the whole way, becoming more Jesuitical than the Jesuits, or it backs down, acknowledging the position of the Constituent Assembly, destroying the government and the current majority, and running the risk of internal upheaval and universal war. Like honor, principles are:

> ... like an island with steep hills and no shores;
> You cannot go back to it once you have left it.[288]

And yet the political difficulties are what worry me the least. What is distressing for this country is to see the men in the public eye one after the other sacrificing every shred of moral dignity and all intellectual *consistency*. The result is that the people are losing all trust and yielding to the most irremediable of solvents, skepticism.

This is why I would like the solution to the social problem, as provided by the most severe form of political economy, that is to say *self-government*,[289] to have a special mouthpiece all to itself. This idea should be put before the general public: that the government should guarantee security to each person and that it should not concern itself with anything else. A monthly publication with this aim and which would be distributed like those of Louis Blanc and Lamartine at a cost of six francs a year might be a useful sharpshooter for *Le Journal des économistes*. We will discuss this soon as I am planning to leave Bordeaux on the 28th if I can get a seat on the mail coach. . . .

288. Source unknown.
289. In English in the original.

147. Letter to Mme Cheuvreux

Mugron, 18 September 1849   [*Lettres d'un habitant des Landes,* p. 43]

There is a note of sadness in your letter, madam, and this is very natural. You have just lost a childhood friend. In these circumstances, the initial feeling is one of regret, and then you look around your entourage with worry and end up looking in at yourself. Your mind asks questions of the great unknown and, on receiving no reply, panics. This is because there is a mystery there which is not open to the spirit but to the heart. *Can you have any doubts when facing a tomb?*

Madam, allow me to remind you that you have not got the right to mourn for very long. Your soul is a tuning fork for all those who love you and you have to be happy under pain of making miserable your mother, your husband, and the delightful child whom you love so much that you would force everyone to love her if she did not do so perfectly well on her own.

My ideas have taken the same road, since we too have our trials. Cholera has not visited this region but it has sent a distressing emissary: my aunt's chambermaid is gravely ill, but they hope to save her. This has made my aunt appear to have lost twenty years, as she is on her feet night and day. For my part, I bow before such devotion to duty and I will always maintain that you, ladies, are *worth* a hundred times more than we. It is true that I do not agree with other economists on the meaning of the word *value*.[290]

Are you making fun of me, madam, in reproaching me for not writing? Five letters in four weeks! But what has happened to the precious missive which you mention? I will be inconsolable if it is lost definitively.

What was M. Augier talking about for you to have the kindness to send me his work? I like this young poet's verses a great deal and will long remember the vivid impression we had at the reading of his drama.[291] In any case, this play will be obtainable; he has doubtless kept the text and he will be happy to send it to me.

However, are your letter and that of Mlle Louise lost forever? In this case, will you be able to tell me what was in them? You may be sure that I will ask you to do this.

290. Bastiat is referring to his chapter on value in *Economic Harmonies.* (*OC,* vol. 6, p. 140, "De la valeur.")
291. *Gabrielle.*

It is on Saturday that I am leaving for Bayonne; I have only four more days here. Although Mugron is monotony personified, I will miss this sojourn of peace, the total independence, and free disposal of my time and the hours that so resemble one another that they cannot be distinguished:

> The uniform habits
> that bind from day to day;
> Neither fame nor study,
> Nothing but solitude,
> Prayer and . . . [292]

I have not finished the line as my literature master taught me that reason should never be sacrificed to rhyme.

19th. In two hours I will myself be going to Tartas[293] to post the boxes containing ortolans.[294] They will be leaving on Thursday morning and will arrive in Paris on Saturday. If, by chance, they are not delivered to the Hôtel Saint-Georges, you will have to take the trouble to go to the post office as punctuality is essential for these small creatures.

I hope that my fellow countrymen will not let themselves be *corrupted* on the way and that you will not have to echo the quotation from Faucher with regard to the conflicts of interest:[295] "Can anything good come out of the Great Landes?" Our friend de Labadie is already a good contrary case; what do you think, Mlle Louise? Since I am addressing you, allow me to say that my poor ears are in a sort of vacuum here. They are hungering and thirsting for music. Please keep a pretty romantic song, the most *minor* possible, for me. Would you not also like to practice the "Tropical Night"? You will end up liking it.

From music to the *Harmonies* is a very tempting switch. But since it is a question of economic harmonies, it throws a bit of cold water on things. So I will not talk to you about it. I will simply admit that, because of developments into which I have been drawn, my book will no longer reach other people than those professionally engaged. I am therefore almost resolved, as

292. Source unknown.

293. A small town in the Landes.

294. A type of bird; a table delicacy.

295. Bastiat is mockingly comparing French political corruption with the potential spoiling of the Ortolans.

I said to M. Cheuvreux, to start a monthly publication. I will be calling on you to *place advertisements.* Where journals are concerned, *placing* advertisements is at least as important as *composition* of articles. This is what our colleagues are too apt to forget. You must interest women in this work.

Farewell, madam; please remember me to M. Cheuvreux. I am not surprised that he finds the air at La Jonchère is better than that at Vichy. I beg Mlle Louise to allow me the word *friendship.* One is always embarrassed faced with such charming creatures; homage is very respectful and affection is very familiar. There is a bit of all this here and I do not know how to express it. They will have to guess at it a little.

Your very devoted servant,
F. Bastiat

---

148. Letter to Mme Cheuvreux

Paris, 7 October 1849   [*Lettres d'un habitant des Landes,* p. 48]

I have received from my beloved Landes this morning a carton that I assume contains some ortolan buntings. I am sending it to you without opening it. Supposing it contains woolen stockings! Oh, I would be very embarrassed, but when all is said and done I would be the butt of a few jokes. Yesterday evening, in my haste and with characteristic tact, I arrived at M. Say's house right in the middle of dinner. To celebrate the reopening of the Monday gatherings, all our friends were there. The party was in full swing to judge from the bursts of laughter that reached me in the drawing room. The hall embellished with a number of black, white, and pink cloaks showed that there were not only economists present.

After dinner, I approached the sister-in-law of M. D—— and, knowing that she has just arrived from Belgium, I asked her if she had had a pleasant trip. This is what she answered: "Sir, I had the unspeakable pleasure of not seeing the face of a single Republican because I hate them." The conversation could not continue for long on this subject, so I spoke to the person next to her, who started to tell me about the pleasant impressions made on her by Belgian royalism. "When the king passes," she said, "everything is joyful: shouts of joy, heraldic figures, banners, ribbons, and lanterns." I see that in order not to displease the ladies too much, we must make haste to elect a king. The embarrassment is to know which one, since we have three in the wings and who will win (after a civil war)?

I was obliged to take refuge with groups of men, since to tell you the truth political passions are grimaces on women's faces. The men pooled their skepticism. They are splendid propagandists who do not believe a word of what they preach. Or rather, *they do not doubt, they just* pretend to doubt. Tell me which is worse, to pretend to doubt or to pretend to believe? Economists really must stop this playacting. Tomorrow, there will be many guests to dinner. I will ask about a journal intended to disseminate principled intellectual certainties. I regret that M. Cheuvreux cannot be with us. While I disagree with him on particular questions, opinions of people or circumstances, we agree on ideas and the fundamentals of things. He would support me.

> Farewell, madam; allow me to
> call myself the most devoted and
> respectful of your friends.
> *F. Bastiat*

---

149. Letter to Mme Cheuvreux

Paris, 8 October 1849   [*Lettres d'un habitant des Landes,* p. 50]

Madam,

Quite by chance the journal of the Landes has published the traditional recipe in the region for preparing ortolans; doubtless *Lord Trompette* would not be offended if I sent him, through you, so precious a document.

Yesterday, when I came to deliver my parcel at the rue Saint-Georges, M. Cheuvreux did not make an appearance, although it was an audience day. Today we had an appointment to visit the electric telegraph. He did not come; can he be ill?

The discussion on socialism has been very good, with Charles Dupin excelling himself. Dufaure was admirable and La Montagne violent, nonsensical, and ignorant. What a desolate arena the Chamber has become! How inferior it is, as far as intentions are concerned, to the Constituent Assembly! Then, the vast majority was passionately in favor of good. Now people just dream of revolution and the only thing that checks them is the choice. In spite of this, society is making *progress.* No one can be taken to task for individual accidents, and I am sorry that that upsets good Mme Alexandre, but it is clear that the general movement is toward order and security.

For you, mesdames, to meet any contingency, you have laid up resources of good fortune in the affection of those close to you and will not both mother and daughter always be angels of consolation for each other?

> Allow me also to hope that you give just a little value to the unshakeable devotion of your respectful friend,
> *F. Bastiat*

---

150. Letter to Mrs. Schwabe

    Paris, 14 October 1849   [vol. 7, p. 382]

Do not be afraid, madam, that your advice is untimely. Is it not based on friendship? Is it not the surest sign of this?

It is in vain that you predict late flowering happiness for me in the future. This cannot happen for me, even in the pursuit or the triumph of an idea that is useful to the human race since my health condemns me to hate the struggle. Dear lady, I have poured into your heart just a drop from the chalice of bitterness that fills mine. For example, just look at my difficult political position and you will see whether I can agree with the prospects you offer me.

I have always had a political idea that is simple, true, and can be grasped by all, and yet it is misunderstood. What was I lacking? A theater in which to expose it. The February revolution occurred. It gave me an audience of nine hundred people, the elite of the nation given a mandate by universal suffrage with the authority to put my views into practice. These nine hundred people were full of the best intentions. They were terrified of the future. They hesitated and cast about for some notion of salvation. They were silent, waiting for a voice to be heard and to which they could rally. I was there; I had the right and duty to speak. I was aware that my words would be welcomed by the Assembly and would echo around the masses. I felt the idea ferment in my head and my heart . . . and I was forced to keep silent. Can you imagine a worse form of torture? I was obliged to keep silent because just at this time it pleased God to remove from me all my strength, and when huge revolutions are achieved such as to afford me a rostrum, I am unable to mount it. I was not only incapable of speaking but also even of writing. What a bitter disappointment! What cruel irony!

Here I am, since my return, confined to my room for simply having wanted to write a newspaper article.

That is not all; I had just one last hope. It was to put this thought down on paper before disappearing from this world so that it did not perish with me. I know very well that this is a poor resource as people today read only well-known authors. Cold print certainly cannot take the place of a speech delivered to the leading political theater in the world. But at least the idea that torments me would have survived. What can one do? The strength to write down and organize a whole theoretical treatise is failing me. It seems as though my mind is becoming paralyzed in my head. Is this not a poignant affliction?

But why am I telling you all this? I have to beg your indulgence. It is because I have bottled up my troubles for so long inside myself that, when I am in contact with a compassionate heart, I find all my private feelings longing to escape.

I would like to send your dear children a small French work that is full of feeling and truth and which has delighted almost all the generations of French young people. It was my childhood companion and later, not very long ago on winter evenings, a woman, her two children, and I wept together on reading it. Unfortunately, M. Heron has left and I do not know how to send it. I will try to send it to Mr. Faulkner in Folkestone.

Farewell, dear lady, I must leave you. Although I am not well, I have to go to defend the cause of the blacks in one of our committees[296] and then return to my only friend, my *pillow*.

---

151. Letter to Richard Cobden

Paris, 17 October 1849 [vol. 1, p. 181]

My dear Cobden, you should not doubt my eagerness to attend the meeting on 30 October, if my parliamentary duties are not a total obstacle to this. To have the pleasure of shaking your hand and witnessing the progress of public opinion in England in favor of peace will be a double happiness

---

296. Slavery was abolished twice in France, once during the first revolution, when Haiti declared its independence from France. This was supported by leading abolitionists in Paris, such as the Abbé Grégoire and Brissot, through the Society of the Friends of the Blacks. Napoléon reintroduced slavery after a bloody repression of the Haitian revolution in 1802. Slavery was abolished a second time on 27 April 1848, during the 1848 revolution.

for me. It will also be very pleasant for me to thank Mr. B. Smith[297] for his gracious hospitality, which I accept with gratitude.

Be assured that I will do all in my power to bring our excellent friend, M. Say. I am afraid his duties in the Council of State may retain him. I am all the more anxious to have him as a traveling companion since he does not totally believe in the peace conference.[298] To witness your meetings will surely steel his confidence. I will be seeing him this evening.

My friend, nations, like individuals, are subject to the law of responsibility. England will have a great deal of trouble convincing people of the sincerity of her efforts for peace. For a long time, for centuries perhaps, it will be said on the continent that England is preaching moderation and peace, but it has fifty-three colonies and two hundred million subjects in India. This single sentence will neutralize many a fine speech. When will England be advanced enough to renounce voluntarily a few of its expensive conquests? This would be a fine means of propaganda.

Do you think it would be imprudent or out of place to touch on this delicate subject?

---

152. Letter to Richard Cobden

Paris, 24 October 1849 [vol. 1, p. 182]

My dear Cobden, Say must have written to you to say that we plan to leave on Sunday evening to be in London on Monday morning. He is bringing his son with him. As for Michel Chevalier, he is still in the Cévennes.

However, there is another thing. M. Say's brother-in-law, M. Cheuvreux, who was absent when we went to spend a day at his house in the country, and who very much regretted having missed this opportunity of making your acquaintance, is planning to join us. In addition, he very much wants to be present at the movement of English public opinion in favor of peace and disarmament. However, as I do not want to be separated from M. Cheu-

297. John Benjamin Smith.

298. It is not clear what peace conference Bastiat was referring to, possibly a domestic British conference. International peace congresses were held in Brussels in September 1848, Paris in August 1849, Frankfurt in August 1850, and London in July 1851. Classical liberals came from all over the world to discuss ways to disarm and cut taxes. See the *Report of the Proceedings of the Second General Peace Congress* and the *Report of the Proceedings of the Third General Peace Congress*.

vreux, I am obliged to write to Mr. Smith to express my deepest gratitude and explain to him the reasons which prevent me from taking advantage of his generous hospitality.

While I am writing this letter, the repeal of the laws of banishment is being debated. I am very afraid that our Assembly will not have the courage to open France's doors to fallen dynasties. In my opinion this act of justice would consolidate the Republic.

153. Letter to Mme Cheuvreux

Paris, November 1849   [*Lettres d'un habitant des Landes,* p. 52]

Madam,

Here is a document that will interest you. For my part, I have not been able to read it without being moved to tears (the nature of a mountain is not always a rocky nature). To whom could I turn to share my impressions if not you?

I will be obliged to contest the opinion of my friends and this costs me dearly. But some Greek, whose name I can't recall, has said: "I love Plato, but I love truth better." It seems a certainty now that political economy has opened its doors to communism and it is up to it to close them.

If you have five minutes to spare, may I dare to ask you to give me news of the trio?

Your devoted servant,
F. Bastiat

---

154. Letter to Bernard Domenger

Paris, 13 November 1849   [vol. 7, p. 404]

The High Court of Versailles has just rendered its verdict.[299] We do not yet have all the details of this; we know only that eleven of the accused, including a member of the Assembly, have been acquitted. All the other representatives have been condemned to be deported, as well as Guinard. I have not followed the discussions sufficiently closely to have an opinion on them.

---

299. On 13 June there was a demonstration against the Roman expedition. It was easily dispersed, but sixty-seven people were arrested for inciting civil war and were brought to the High Court in Versailles. The normal rights of the accused had not been entirely respected.

I bow to justice and regret only that the defense was limited as to its means. This is always a worrying precedent. The authority of the cause being judged is not enhanced by this.

You have doubtless heard about my short trip to England. I left on Monday evening after the session and was back on Saturday morning, and for four days I saw only great things and great men, at least in my view.

When I arrived, a sort of very courteous cartel of socialists came to see me. It was a question of detailed discussions before an audience of workers and against Proudhon on the question of whether interest on capital is legitimate, a question that is more difficult and dangerous than the one concerning property, in that it is more general. I believe that I did some good in accepting the contest.[300]

On this subject, I will tell you, my dear Domenger, that the electors in the Landes may well grow tired of my apparent inaction. It is true that my work is capricious; I have to be taken with all my faults. However, I sincerely believe that the current danger is neither from the authorities nor from the Assembly, but from the misguidedness of popular opinion. It is thus in this direction that I am devoting my weak efforts. I hope that the good sense of our fellow countrymen will make them understand that each person has his own mission in life and that I am fulfilling mine.

---

155. Letter to Félix Coudroy

Paris, 13 December 1849   [vol. 1, p. 100]

My dear Félix, it is sad that our correspondence has slowed down so much. Do not conclude from this, I beg you, that my long-standing friendship for you is cooling; on the contrary, it seems that time and distance, those two great poets, lend charm to the memory of our walks and conversations. I miss Mugron, its philosophical calm and fruitful leisure hours on many occasions. Here, life is worn out with our doing nothing, or at least producing nothing.

Yesterday I spoke during the debate on wines and spirits. As I rarely take the rostrum, I wanted to put forward our ideas. With a bit of perseverance, we will make them triumph. They must have been deemed worthy of examination, as the entire Assembly listened to them in silence, without anyone

---

300. Bastiat discusses this in his letters to Proudhon. (*OC,* vol. 5, pp. 94–335, "Gratuité du crédit.")

being able to attribute this rare phenomenon to talent or to the reputation of the speaker. But what is appalling is that these efforts are wasted as far as the public is concerned, because of the poor condition of the journals. Each cloaks me in its own ideas. If they limited themselves to disfiguring or ridiculing my thought, I would accept my lot, but they attribute to me the very heresies that I am combating. What am I to do? Incidentally, I enclose *Le Moniteur;* enjoy yourself making comparisons.

I did not say all I wanted to say, nor in the way I wished to say it. Our southern volubility is an oratorical plague. When a sentence has been finished, we think of how the sentence should have been phrased. However, with the help of gestures, intonation, and action, we make ourselves understood by our *audience.* But this discourse written in shorthand is just slovenly and I myself cannot bear to read it.

We are really *overworked*[301] here, as the English say. These long sessions, office meetings, and commissions weigh you down and do no good. They constitute ten wasted hours, which waste the rest of the day, since (at least for weak heads) they are enough to remove the faculty of work. This being so, when will I be able to write my second volume, on which I am relying far more for publicity than on the first? I do not know whether *La Voix du peuple* is available in Mugron. *Socialism* is today enclosed in a formula, *free credit.* It describes itself thus: I am this or I am nothing. For this reason, it is on these grounds that I have attacked it in a series of letters to which Proudhon is replying.[302] I think they have done a great deal of good in removing the illusions of a great many misguided followers. But here is something that will astonish you: the bourgeoisie is so blind, so intense, and so confident in its natural strength that it considers it correct not to support me. My letters are in *La Voix du peuple* and this is enough for them to be despised by these people, as though they might do good elsewhere. Well! When it is a question of reconverting the workers, is it not better to tell the truth in the journal that they read?

On Tuesday, I will be starting my lectures to the young people in the schools. As you can see, there is no shortage of work and, just to make life simple, I am undergoing a treatment for my chest that takes up two hours of my day every day. It is true that it is making me feel very well indeed.

I am talking only about myself, my dear Félix. Please follow this example

301. In English in the original.
302. *OC,* vol. 5, pp. 94–335, "Gratuité du crédit."

and tell me a lot about yourself. If you wanted to follow my advice, I would strongly commit you to doing something useful, like producing a series of small pamphlets, for example. They take a long time to penetrate the masses but they end up doing their work.

---

156. Letter to Bernard Domenger

Paris, 25 December 1849   [vol. 7, p. 405]

I can write you only a few words, as my cold has laid me low. I assure you that it makes my existence very hard to endure.

The hospice affair[303] is one of those that make me decide to venture into the labyrinthine world of government. Yesterday, I ascertained that approval of the exchange would not encounter any difficulty and the decree authorizing it was drafted in front of me. However, it can be taken to the Élysée for signature only after the Council of State has approved it. One of my friends has promised me to expedite this affair as quickly as possible.

As for the subsidy, you will have something, but not one thousand francs. The fund handling this has only three hundred thousand francs for the whole of France and needs are unlimited, to the extent that each year the allocation for the following year is gobbled up in advance. I continue to believe that it would be better for the government not to become involved with this, because it would require a lot of senseless administrative work.

And is it not perfectly ridiculous that Mugron and M. Lafaurie are unable to exchange their houses without the approval of the Council of State and permission from the prisoner of Ham?[304] Truly, France has created problems and obstacles, merely for the sake of generating additional costs.

It is impossible for me to send you my polemical exchanges with Proudhon, as I have not kept the issues of *La Voix du peuple* in which my letters were published; but I have been assured that they will be collected into a volume, which I will send to you. Anyway, they are rather boring.

303. To extend the size of Mugron's hospice, a M. Lafaurie had agreed to exchange his large house for the existing hospice building. This operation, however, required a government decree.

304. Louis-Napoléon Bonaparte. In 1840 he attempted to provoke a military uprising in Boulogne. It failed, and he was condemned to life in the fortress of Ham by the House of Peers. He escaped in 1846.

157. Letter to Richard Cobden

Paris, 31 December 1849   [vol. 1, p. 182]

My dear Cobden, I am delighted with the Bradford meeting[305] and congratulate you sincerely for having finally tackled the colonial question. I know that you have always considered this subject very delicate as it affects the most sensitive chords of patriotic hearts. Renouncing rule over a quarter of the globe! Never has such evidence of common sense and faith in science been displayed by any nation! It is surprising that you were allowed to finish your speech. For this reason, what I admired most about this meeting was not the orator (allow me to say this!) but the audience. What can you not achieve with a nation which cold-bloodedly analyzes its dearest illusions and allows, before its very eyes, investigations of the darker side of its glory?

I recall that I boldly intimated the advice to you in the past to direct your aim on the colonial regime, with which *free trade* is incompatible. You replied at the time that national pride is a plant that grows in all countries and especially in yours, that you should not try to rip it out roughly, and that free trade would gnaw gradually on its roots. I agreed with this good commonsense observation while deploring the necessity for you to keep quiet, since I was perfectly aware of one thing, which was that as long as England had forty colonies Europe would never believe the sincerity of her protestations. For my part, it was useless for me to say, "Colonies are a burden." This assertion appeared as paradoxical as "It is a great misfortune for a gentleman to have fine farms." Obviously it is necessary for the assertion and proof to come from England herself. Forward then, my dear Cobden, redouble your efforts, triumph, liberate your colonies, and you will have achieved the greatest thing that exists under the sun since it began to shed light on the follies and fine actions of mankind. The more Great Britain prides herself on her colonial colossus, the more you have to demonstrate the clay feet of this idol, which devours the substance of your workers. Do what is needed to enable England freely, maturely, and in full conscience of what she is doing to tell Canada, Australia, and the Cape, "Govern yourselves by yourselves."[306] Lib-

305. Bastiat and Cobden were both active members of an international association called the Friends of Peace. This association had a congress in Brussels in 1848, one in Paris (chaired by Victor Hugo) in 1849, and one in Frankfurt in 1850. Cobden organized follow-up meetings in London, Birmingham, Manchester, and Bradford, all of which Bastiat attended.

306. After a rebellion in 1837 the Durham Report of 1839 recommended that the Canadian provinces be granted responsible government, which was put into effect by

erty will have won its greatest victory and political economy in action will be taught to the entire world.

For it is essential for protectionists in Europe to have their eyes opened at last.

Initially, they used to say, "England allows manufactured articles to enter the country. What great generosity since she has uncontested superiority in this respect! But she will not remove protection from agriculture since, with regard to this, she cannot stand up to competition from countries where the soil and labor cost nothing." You have answered this charge by removing the duty from wheat, animals, and all agricultural products.

They then said, "England is playacting and the proof of this is that she is not changing her laws on navigation, since rule over the seas is her lifeblood." And you have reformed these laws, not in order to destroy your navy but to strengthen it.

Now they say, "England may well decree free trade and freedom of the seas since, with her forty colonies, she has taken control of all the outlets in the world. She will never lay a hand on her colonial system." Overturn the old system and I do not know behind what prophecy protectionists will take refuge. As to prophecy, I dared make one two years ago. It was in Lyons, before a large assembly. I said at the time, "In less than ten years, England will herself voluntarily dismantle the colonial regime." Do not let me pass here for a false prophet.

Economic matters are as fiercely controversial in France as they are in England, but in a different direction. The basics of economic science are being stirred up. *Property, capital,* everything is being called into question; and what is deplorable is that good reasons are not always on the side of rationality. This is because of the universal ignorance of these matters. Communism is being combated with communist arguments. But at last the extremely lively intelligence of this country is being put to work. What will be the result of this work? It will doubtless be good for humanity, but will this good not be dearly purchased? Will we have to endure bankruptcies and paper money issued against the security of state landholdings, etc.? *That is the question.*[307]

1849. Responsible government (i.e., the Westminster system) was also introduced a little later in the Australian colonies: Victoria (1855); New South Wales, South Australia, and Tasmania (1856). New Zealand was granted this right in 1856 as well. The Cape Colony followed in 1872.

307. In English in the original.

You will doubtless be surprised to see me publish a purely theoretical work right now and I imagine that you will not be able to bear reading it. Nevertheless, I believe that it would have been of some use in this country if I had thought of issuing it in a cheap edition, and especially if I had been able to produce the second volume. *Ma non ho fiato:* in both physical and moral meanings, I lack the breath to do it.

I have sent a copy of this book to Mr. Porter. My friend, our reputations are like our wines; both need to cross the sea to acquire their full flavor. I would therefore like you to give me the names of a few people to whom I might send my volume so that, with your good offices, they might review it in the journals. It is of course understood that I am not seeking praise but a conscientious appraisal from my judges.

---

158. Letter to Félix Coudroy

Paris, January 1850   [vol. 1, p. 102]

Never a day goes past, my dear Félix, on which I do not think of replying to you. Always for the same reason, my head is so weak that the slightest work wears me out. As soon as I am involved in one of these preemptive matters, the little time that I can devote to holding a pen is taken up, and I am forced to put off my correspondence day after day. But finally, if I have to seek indulgence somewhere, it ought to be from my friends.

In a previous letter you told me that you had a project that you would tell me about. I am waiting and very willing to give you support, but if it concerns newspapers, I have to warn you that I have very little contact with them, and you can guess why. It would be impossible to create ties to them without losing one's independence. I have taken the decision that, whatever happens, I will not be a party man. With our ideas, that would be impossible. I am well aware that in these times to isolate yourself is to remove any influence you may have, but I prefer that. If I had the strength I had in the past, this would be the right time to carry out a real campaign to win over public opinion and my distance from any faction would be an advantage to me. But I can see the opportunity slipping away and this is very sad. Not a day goes by on which I am not given the opportunity to say or write some useful truth. The agreement between all the points of our doctrine will end up by making a strong impression on people's minds, which have incidentally been made ready for this by the succession of deceptions with which they have been misled. I can see this. Many of my friends are pressing me to enter the ring and I cannot. I assure you that I am learning resignation, and when I need it I will have laid up a good stock.

The *Harmonies* have passed unnoticed here, except for about a dozen connoisseurs. I was expecting this; it could not have been otherwise. I do not even have the support of the customary zeal of our small church, which accuses me of heterodoxy; in spite of this I am confident that this book will gradually carve out a place for itself. In Germany, it was received quite differently.[308] It is examined, ploughed up, worked over, and examined for what is there and what is not. Could I have asked for anything better?

Now I would ask the heavens to grant me one year to write the second volume, which has not even been started, after which I will sing the "Nunc dimittis."

Socialism is spreading at a frightening rate, but like all contagious diseases it is weakening as it spreads, and it is even mutating. This will be the death of it. The name may survive but not the thing. Today, *socialism* has become synonymous with *progress;* anyone who wants *any form of* change is a socialist. If you refute Louis Blanc, Proudhon, Leroux, or Considérant, you are nonetheless a socialist if you do not demand the *status quo* in all circumstances. This leads to a strange situation. One day, everyone will meet wearing this label in his hatband, and since, for all that, people will not be in any closer agreement on the reforms to carry out, other names will have to be invented and war will be declared among the socialists. This is already the case and it is this that is saving France.

Farewell, my dear Félix; please tell my aunt that I am well.

---

159. Letter to Mme Cheuvreux

Paris, 2 January 1850   [*Lettres d'un habitant des Landes,* p. 51]

Madam,

I have been aroused from my slumbers to be handed three volumes, which you sent me without a single word of explanation; have I been so unfortunate as to displease you?

Yesterday, you gathered your family and a few friends around your table to see in the New Year. This meal should have been only a joyful and cordial feast. Alas! Politics crept into it and it is all too true that, without me, even

308. See Letter 133, note 265.

politics might not have been able to cast its somber shadow over it, as perhaps everyone would have been in agreement.

But am I guilty? Did I not keep silent for a long time and did I not treat as *general* comments what I might have taken as *personal* ones? Words that resembled provocation? What would happen to me, madam, if this reserve were not enough?

Isolated, scarcely retaining for work the remnants of a strength that is deserting me, must I also lose the sweetness of intimacy, the one delight that binds me to the world?

Between M. Cheuvreux and me, what does a difference of opinion matter, especially when this does not concern our aims or any fundamental principle, but only the means of overcoming momentary difficulties?

It is as much through respect for him as for you, madam, that I drank the chalice that these people put to my lips. And after all, are the opinions for which I am reproached in fact so extravagant?

I would like people to agree to consider me as a hermit, a philosopher, a dreamer, if you like, who does not wish to join a party but who examines them all in order to see where danger lies and whether it can be averted.

In France, I can see two major classes, each of which can be divided into two. To use hallowed although inaccurate terms, I will call them the people and the bourgeoisie.

The people consist of a host of millions of human beings who are ignorant and suffering, and consequently dangerous. As I said, they are divided into two; the vast majority are reasonably in favor of order, security, and all conservative principles, but, because of their ignorance and suffering, are the easy prey of ambitious sophists. This mass is swayed by a few sincere fools and by a larger number of agitators and revolutionaries, people who have an inborn attraction for disruption or who count on disruption to elevate themselves to fortune and power.

The bourgeoisie, it must never be forgotten, is very small in number. This class also has its ignorance and suffering, although to a different degree. It also offers dangers, but of a different nature. It too can be broken down into a large number of peaceful, undemonstrative people, partial to justice and freedom, and a small number of agitators. The bourgeoisie has governed this country, and how has it behaved? The small minority did harm and the large majority allowed them to do this, not without taking advantage of this when they could.

These are the moral and social statistics of our country.

Since I hold very little to and believe even less in various forms of politics, am I going to devote my efforts and speak out against the Republic or the monarchy? Plot to change the institutions which I consider to be of no importance? *No!* But when I have the opportunity to address the people, I tell them of their errors, illusions, and false aspirations, I seek to unmask the impostors who are misleading them, and I say to them: "Ask only for justice for only justice can be of some use to you."

And when I speak to the bourgeoisie, I tell them: "It is not raging and ranting which will save you. In all encounters you must grant the people what justice demands, in order to be strong enough to refuse everything which exceeds justice."

And this is why the Catholics tell me that I have a double-edged doctrine and why *Le Journal des débats* says that I have to become used to displeasing both parties. Goodness, would it not be easier for me to throw myself body and soul into one of the two camps, to espouse its hatreds and illusions, to make myself the toady either of the people or the bourgeoisie, and to affiliate myself to the evil elements of both armies?

---

160. Letter to Mme Cheuvreux

Paris, January 1850   [*Lettres d'un habitant des Landes,* p. 57]

Madam,

I have just met Commander Matta,[309] who claims that people will be ill tomorrow at the Hôtel Saint-Georges. I hope he is as bad a prophet as he is a brave soldier! Please be good enough to let me have the true state of affairs. You will not allow me to mention health without giving some news of mine. I am better and Charruau,[310] like Sganarelle,[311] declares that I must be *cured.* However, yesterday evening, a fatiguing coughing fit revealed the *red* symptom that is as terrifying in physiology as it is in politics.[312] In spite of this, I would still be strong enough to take on whatever is left of your Louisette's

---

309. An army medical officer.

310. A physician.

311. One of Molière's characters, borrowed from the Commedia dell'arte. He appears in particular in *Le Médecin malgré lui.*

312. Another reference to the fatal illness that would eventually kill Bastiat.

cough if that were possible, but affection cannot do this miracle; this is one harmony that this world is lacking.

Farewell, madam,

F. Bastiat

Saturday

---

161. Letter to Mme Cheuvreux

Paris, February 1850   [*Lettres d'un habitant des Landes*, p. 58]

Madam,

With some regret I am returning to you the speech delivered by M. de Boislembert to mark the unveiling of the bust of M. Girard, with the reminder that you had promised me a copy. I read it with enthusiasm and would like to reread it once a month to steep myself in it. This is a life of Plutarch proportions, in harmony with our century. How I admire a life so fine, so honorable, and so fulfilled! What a magnificent blend of all the qualities that most honor human nature: genius, talent, activity, courage, perseverance, unselfishness, greatness, and strength of character in adversity! Up to this point, however, the portrait is very impressive and reveals only pure but severe lines; we admire but do not yet love him. Shortly after this, though, we are totally won over when the author describes, perhaps with too much sobriety, the sparkling wit, gentle gaiety, and inexhaustible benevolence that M. Girard invariably brought to his home life, the most precious gifts of all from heaven, that your father has not carried with him to the tomb.

These noble figures, madam, make men appear very small and humanity very great.

F. Bastiat

---

162. Letter to Bernard Domenger

Paris, 18 February 1850   [vol. 7, p. 406]

The political future is still very somber. Unfortunately, much passion and artificial suspicion are mingled with genuine grievances; this is always the case in revolutions. I who see men from all parties can, as it were, measure what is false in their mutual accusations. But hatred, whether well founded or not, produces the same effects. I believe that the majority understands that the most prudent course is to retain the republic. Its mistake is not to come out with sufficient resolution on this side. What is the use of unceasingly belittling and threatening that which you do not want to change? For its part, the minority is seeking to seize power again by means which will create a very heavy burden for it. It raises hopes which it will not be able to satisfy.

In the meantime I do not despair as debate clarifies a great many questions. The main thing is to gain time.

---

163. Letter to Mme Cheuvreux

　　　Paris, March 1850　　　　　　　[*Lettres d'un habitant des Landes,* p. 59]

Madam,

How can you hope to get better? Your cold is the prey of all those whom it pleases to make you speak in spite of it, and the number of these is great.

From Saturday up to yesterday morning, I have had just one coughing fit. It lasted twelve hours. I cannot understand how the fragile envelopes of breathing and thought do not burst under these violent and prolonged shocks. At least I have nothing to reproach myself for; I am meekly obeying my doctor. I have been kept in these last two days, but I will have to go to M. Say's house this evening to join my coreligionists.[313] It will be an effort. You would not believe how vividly my indisposition has brought out in me my old solitary and provincial inclinations. A peaceful room full of sunlight, a pen, a few books, a close friend,[314] and warm affection; this is all I needed to live. Do I need more to die? This *little* was what I had in my village, and when the time comes in a great many years I will no longer find it.

I am sending Mlle Louise a few verses on *women,* which I liked. They are, however, by a poet who is an economist since he has been nicknamed *the free trade rhymer.*[315] If I had the strength I would do a free translation of this piece in *thirty pages* of prose; this would do well in Guillaumin's journal. Your sweet little tease (I do not forget that she possesses the art of teasing to a high degree, not only without wounding but almost caressing) does not greatly believe in poetry of production and she is perfectly right. It is what I ought to have called *Social Poetry,* which henceforth, I hope, will no longer take for the subject of its songs the destructive qualities of man, the exploits of war, carnage, the violation of divine laws, and the degradation of moral

313. The economists living in Paris met for a dinner once a month.
314. Félix Coudroy.
315. Ebenezer Elliot.

dignity, but the good and evil in real life, the conflicts of thought, all forms of intellectual, productive, political, and religious combinations and affinities, and all the feelings that raise, improve, and glorify the human race. In this new epic, women will occupy a place worthy of them and not the one given to them in the ancient *Iliad* genre. Was their role really to be included in the booty?

In the initial phases of humanity, when force was the dominant social principle, the action of woman was wiped out. She had been successively beast of burden, slave, servant, and mere instrument of pleasure. When the principle of force gave way to that of public opinion and customs, she recovered her right to equality, influence, and power, and this is what the last line of the small item of verse I am sending Mlle Louise expresses very well.

You see how dangerous and indiscreet the letters of poor recluses are. Please forgive me this chatter; all I ask for in reply is reassurance as to the health of your daughter.

F. Bastiat
Monday

---

164. Letter to Bernard Domenger

Paris, 22 March 1850   [vol. 7, p. 407]

I have reason to believe that the decree that authorizes the exchange of buildings for the hospice in Mugron will reach the prefecture of the Landes on the day this letter reaches you. I have been assured that the president of the Republic has signed it, that the secretariat of the ministry of the interior has given it authority, and that the office for hospices is ready to act. The rest is up to you.

It is already two or three days since I gave the order to my publisher to send you three copies of my debate with Proudhon and three of my speeches on education, which have degenerated into a pamphlet since my cold has become a loss of voice. It is certainly not that I wish to have you swallow these lucubrations *three times,* but I would like you to give a copy each from me to Félix and Justine.[316]

The newspapers save me the trouble of having to talk politics with you. I believe that reactionary blindness is our greatest danger at the moment; we are being led straight into a catastrophe. What occasion have they selected

---

316. Félix Coudroy and Justine Bastiat.

to carry out experiments of this nature? One in which the people appear to be becoming disciplined and giving up illegal means. The great party said to be in favor of order has met one hundred and thirty thousand opponents at the elections and has carried only one hundred and twenty-five thousand followers. What will be the result of the proposed laws? It will be to make forty or fifty thousand people on the right go over to the left and thus give the left greater strength and a feeling of being right and to concentrate this strength on a lesser number of newspapers, which will result in giving it greater homogeneity, continuity, and strategy. This appears to me to be pure folly. I predicted this on the day Bordeaux sent us Thiers and Molé, that is to say, enemies of the Republic. Today we are in the position we were just before 1830 and 1848: the same slope, the same wagon, and the same coachmen. But then people's minds could understand the content of a revolution; now, who can say what will succeed the Republic?

---

165. Letter to Mme Cheuvreux

Paris, Friday, April 1850   [*Lettres d'un habitant des Landes,* p. 62]

Very dear Mme Cheuvreux,

Please forgive this address, which has escaped in a moment of effusion. We who suffer, like children, need indulgence, since the weaker the body, the more the spirit grows soft and it seems as though life, at its final as at its initial sunset, instills in the heart the need to seek attachments everywhere. These involuntary expressions of tenderness are the effect of all moments of decline, the end of the day, the end of the year, the basilica half-days, etc., etc. I experienced this yesterday in the shadowy alleys of the Tuileries. However, you must not become alarmed at this elegiac effusion. I am not at all Millevoie, and the leaves that have scarcely opened are not about to fall. In short, I am not worse, on the contrary, but only weaker and I can scarcely retreat in the face of an order that I take a holiday. What is in prospect is a solitude that is even more solitary; in the past I liked it, I knew how to people it with reading, work of a whimsical sort, and political dreams with interludes of cello playing. Temporarily, all these old friends have deserted me, even the faithful companion of isolation, meditation. This is not because my thought is slumbering, it has never been so active; at every instant it is grasping new harmonies[317] and it seems as though the book of humanity is opening be-

---

317. Bastiat had plans for writing a book titled *Social Harmonies.*

fore it. However, this is just one more torment since I cannot continue to transcribe the pages of this mysterious book onto a more palpable book published by *Guillaumin*. I am therefore chasing away these dear phantoms and, like the grumpy drum major who said, "I am handing in my resignation, let the government do what it can," I too am resigning as an economist and let posterity get on with it if it can.

There it is, this is a lamentation to explain my tactlessness. It is said of misfortunes that they never come singly and this is truer still for actions lacking tact. How many words have I used to justify a *single one* which you would have pardoned without all these comments, since you would not hold it against me if, in this spate of idleness, my thoughts fly to the Hôtel Saint-Georges, where everyone is always so good to me. This dear house! It is now full of extremely serious preoccupations.[318] The future of your Louise is perhaps being decided and consequently yours and that of M. Cheuvreux. The idea that so much peace, union, and happiness will be put to the test of a decisive revolution is truly frightening. But take courage, you have so many favorable opportunities!

Truly, my letters exceed by a hundred cubits those of M. B——. I beg you, madam, to accept my apologies for this. The most valid of these is that I scarcely dare to appear at your house this evening; is it not very selfish to seek distraction at a place to which you can bring only inopportune *coughing fits*? Of course, I do not say this about my friends; that would be ungrateful. But is society standing shoulder to shoulder with your benevolence?

Farewell, madam, I am your
devoted servant,
F. Bastiat

Mrs. Schwabe has just arrived without her children. I would like to introduce her to you.

----

166. Letter to Mme Cheuvreux

Bordeaux, May 1850   [*Lettres d'un habitant des Landes,* p. 65]

Here I am in Bordeaux, plunged with delight in the atmosphere of southern France. Although I have left the bustle of Paris to find the peace of my family roof once more, I assure you that my thoughts throughout the jour-

318. Allusion to a plan of marriage for Louise Cheuvreux, which had no follow-up. See letters 166, 168, and 169.

ney returned to the past more often than they envisaged the future. I therefore made haste to open the traveling case which I owe to the thoughtful consideration of M. Cheuvreux.

To be reduced to making my health the subject of the first chapter of my letters humiliates me somewhat but your kindness requires it. I can understand this: illnesses which involve coughs have the disadvantage of worrying our friends too greatly. They carry with them an intrusive bell, which unceasingly asks the question: which will gain the upper hand, the cold or the cold-ridden patient? Instead of tiring me, the trip made me feel better; it is true that for three days I had at my disposition an excellent remedy, silence, as it was only from Ruffec[319] onward that I departed somewhat from your orders. My two companions, who took it in turn to move to the outside seat of the mail coach to savor the delights of a cigar, were curious enough to examine the travel document. It turned out that they were both keen followers of political economy, and when they resumed their seat, they made sure to let me know that they were familiar with my small works (since not even the title of the *Harmonies* had reached them), and so, taking advantage of the opportunity, the green grass, and probably prodded by some devil, I have clipped from this pasture (conversation) the width of my tongue.[320] I had no right to do this since I had been forbidden to. But I yielded to it and my larynx did not fail to punish me. Do not scold me, madam; is silence not a regime that would suit you sometimes as much as it suits me and yet it is the last thing you do?

Let Mme Girard,[321] who is now staying with you, assert her authority to sequester you; what good does it do you to remain in your room if you open its doors wide from ten o'clock in the morning? Could you not sacrifice a few moments of conversation to your health? However, you know that the sacrifice will fall on others and for this reason you do not wish to do this. As you can see, I know the old ploy, which is to scold first so as not to be scolded. After all, I can see that we all descend from our mother, Eve. Your daughter, herself, who is so reasonable, often allows herself to be caught in the trap of music. On the subject of music, it is a great mistake to think that a sound is stifled in the narrow space of a drawing room and a second; a note, or rather a cry from the heart which I heard on Saturday, has traveled

---

319. Small town in the *département* of La Charente, between Paris and Bordeaux.

320. Allusion to a well-known fable of La Fontaine, *Les Animaux malades de la peste.*

321. Mother of Mme Cheuvreux.

two hundred leagues with me. It is still vibrating in my ear, to say the very least.

Poor dear child, I think that I have guessed the thought with which she cloaked Pergolesi's sad song; was this touching voice whose final accents seem to be lost in a tear not saying farewell to the illusions of youth, the fine dreams of an ideal happiness? Yes, it seemed as though your dear Louise felt herself carried along by circumstances to this fatal and solemn boundary, which separates the land of dreams from the world of reality. May real life bring her at least a calm and solid although slightly solemn happiness. What does she need for this? A good heart and common sense in the man who will be responsible for her destiny, that is the first condition; men whose fiery and artistic imagination casts a bright glow provide opportunities that are often dangerous, but we should not doubt that the noble aspirations of your child will find satisfaction one day.

How are you going to spend next month? Will you be staying in Paris? Will you be going to Auteuil, Saint-Germain, or London? I would more readily cast my vote for England, as it is there that you will find a pleasant blend of peace and amusement. To tell you the truth, my *votes* are not in good odor although their conscientious aim is to turn away the misfortunes that you fear; but let us not slide down the slope of politics. There is so much that is unforeseen in your resolutions that I am anxious to know what you will decide. I am afraid that I might learn that you are leaving for Moscow or Constantinople. Please, let me find you comfortably installed close to Paris. France is like Frenchwomen; she may have a few caprices but at the end of the day she is the most lovable, gracious, and finest woman in the world and so the most loved.

Farewell, mesdames, let these two months of absence not efface me from your memories; a further farewell to M. Cheuvreux and Mlle Louise.

Your devoted servant,
F. Bastiat

---

167. Letter to Prosper Paillottet

Mugron, 19 May 1850 [vol. 7, p. 437]

My dear Paillottet, thank you for the interest you take in my health and in my journey. This was completed very well and with fewer incidents than you foresaw. There was no misunderstanding between my seat and me. On the way, from Tours to Bordeaux, I met some ardent enthusiasts for political economy, which gave me pleasure but which forced me to speak rather too much. At Bordeaux I could not avoid anything worse than simple conversation since reaction has reached such excesses there that you needed to be made of marble to listen coolly to such blasphemy. All this meant that my larynx arrived here rather tired and the outpourings of friendship, as delightful as they were, are not conducive to relieving it. However, taking things as a whole, I am feeling a little better; I have more physical and intellectual strength. This is certainly a long bulletin on my health; your friendship demanded it, so lay the blame on that.

Yesterday I received *Le Journal des économistes* at the same time as your letter and read my article[322] in it. I do not know how you managed it, but I found it impossible to identify the *reworkings,* so well did they blend in with the original. Might I just suggest that the dominant idea of this article has not been sufficiently highlighted. In spite of this, it should attract sympathetic minds, and if I had been in Paris I would have had five hundred copies printed separately to distribute them in the Assembly. As the article was not long, I consider that *La Voix du peuple* ought to print it in one of its *Monday* editions.[323] If you hear anything about this, please let me know what is being said.

Here you are, responsible for my public and private affairs. In any case, please do not devote any other than your spare moments to this. You are very eager for my poor *Harmonies* to acquire a reputation. You will find this difficult. Only time will succeed in this, if they are worth time taking any trouble over them. I have obtained all that I could reasonably want, that is to say, that a few young men of goodwill study the book. This is enough for it not to fall down if it deserves to remain standing. M. de Fontenay will have done a great deal for me if he succeeds in obtaining the insertion of an account of it in *La Revue des deux mondes*.[324] He will do even more in the future through the developments he will be able to make from the principal idea. There is an entire continent to clear. I am just a pioneer, starting out with instruments that are very imperfect. Improved cultivation will come later and I could not encourage de Fontenay too strongly to prepare himself for this. In the meantime, try to gain M. Buloz's favor through our friend Michel Chevalier.

322. *Plunder and Law.*
323. *La Voix du peuple* did not publish Bastiat's article.
324. The review did not publish any account of *Economic Harmonies.*

I have probably forgotten a great many things, but they will return, because you will, I hope, be willing to write to me as often as possible. As for me, I will continue to provide you with my writing to decipher.

---

168. Letter to Mme Cheuvreux

Mugron, 20 May 1850   [*Lettres d'un habitant des Landes,* p. 69]

How I thank you, madam, for thinking of the exile in the Landes in the middle of all your occupations; I would scarcely dare to ask you to continue this charitable work if I did not know how persevering in your goodness you are. Please be certain that there is no cordial nor chest remedy that can equal a few lines from Paris, and my health is more dependent on the postman than the pharmacist. It is true that the pen is a heavy and tiring machine; do not send me long letters but just a few words as often as possible, so that I know what is being done, thought, felt, and resolved at the Hôtel Saint-Georges.

Here, for example, is a change of situation that I cannot say is completely unexpected. A short note from M. Cheuvreux made me think it was coming. Poor M. D—— has been dismissed; I am sure that the heart of your Louise is greatly relieved and that is already a good thing. If my wishes were granted, she would go through life without all these trials.

After I wrote to you from Bordeaux, I made some visits. Fortunately several of my friends were absent, as I would not have been able to avoid talking and shouting a great deal. The ones I saw are in such a state of exaltation that calm conversation with them is not possible. These unfortunate people are convinced that for the last two years no one has dared open the shops in Paris. Having taken this idea to heart, they want to escape a situation like this at any cost and, to do this, they do not recoil even from the idea of a civil or foreign war. My *département* has seemed to be more moderate; our prefect[325] has devoted himself unceasingly to moderating public opinion and he was therefore discharged from office on the day I passed through Mont-de-Marsan. We are being sent one who will be better able to arouse the people.

I arrived on Friday. When I saw the church spire of my village I was surprised not to experience the vivid emotions that the sight of it never failed

---

325. Louis-Napoléon Bonaparte appointed his supporters to the highest military and administrative positions in the country.

to arouse in me in the past. Are we like plants, and do the strings of the heart become woody with age, or else do I now have two fatherlands? I remember that Mlle Louise predicted that country life would have lost a great deal of its charms for me.

In a family council made up of my aunt, her chambermaid, and me (and I might say, epitomized by her chambermaid), it was decided that Mugron was as good as Les Eaux-Bonnes and that, in any case, it was not yet warm enough for the Pyrenees. I am therefore staying in the Landes until further instructions. This being decided, our native of the Basque country began to unpack my trunk; we soon saw her return to the drawing room totally upset and crying out, "Mademoiselle, M. Bastiat's linen is completely *perrec, perrec, perrec!*" I am sorry that de Labadie is no longer with you to explain the strength of the word *perrec,* which combines the three notions of shreds, rags, and tatters. What profound scorn must the poor girl feel for Paris and its laundrywomen! It is enough to make one resign as a representative!

On Saturday I went to see the rest of my family in the country and came back tired. The coughing fits have come back so strongly that breathing could not cope; I thought of the description of whale fishing that your cousin gave you. "Everything is fine," he said, "when you can give a little line to the wounded animal." Coughing is equally not much of a problem as long as the lungs can give it *a little line,* after which the situation becomes uncomfortable.

Truly, madam, these details prove to you that I am yielding to the affection I feel for you and that I am counting on yours, as long as this does not, I beg you, go beyond what we call the trio.

The post has brought me a letter; how can I express my gratitude to you! Did you guess my wishes then? My aunt and I have started to have arguments about the north and the south; she praises the superiority of the south, doubtless in order to keep me here, while I claim that everything of any good comes from the north, even the sun (we are receiving light from the north today). It is sending me your good wishes, giving me some reassuring news about Mlle Louise and a few details on these pleasant scenes in the home which I have often witnessed and which I appreciate so much.

F. Bastiat

169. Letter to Mme Cheuvreux

Mugron, 23 May 1850   [*Lettres d'un habitant des Landes,* p. 71]

Dear Mme Cheuvreux, my last letter had scarcely reached the other end of the long line that separates us, when along comes a second, ready to start out on the same road. Is there no indiscretion or unseemliness in this haste? I do not know, since I am not yet well versed in worldly manners, but please be indulgent; even more, please allow me to write to you as the whim takes me, without much regard for the dates and under the sway of impulse, the law that governs weak natures. If you knew how empty and dreary Mugron is, you would forgive me for always directing my gaze toward Paris. My poor aunt, who is more or less all my company, has aged a great deal and is losing her memory. All she has become is a heart; it seems as though her faculties of affection gain what the other faculties lose and I love her more than ever for this, but in her actual presence I cannot prevent my imagination from wandering; am I not ill, after all?

What good are illnesses if they do not give us the privilege of having our fantasies tolerated? This being so, it is agreed, I will attribute my indiscretion to my alleged sufferings; this is a trick that will always take in a woman's heart, but this must not lead me to deceive you and present myself in the light of a dying man. This is my health report: my cough is less frequent and strength is returning. I can climb the stairs without becoming out of breath; I have found my voice again, which can hum a complete octave. The only thing that inconveniences me is a small pain in the larynx, but I do not think it will last four days. Lastly, although I am not yet ready to offer up my visage to the daunting and exacting gaze of Mlle Louise, I think I am looking better.

Here I am, at peace with my conscience and having obeyed your orders. With regard to Mlle Louise and the face in question, this dear child is always destined to be prey to a painful doubt for a young girl: not to know, in spite of her exquisite tact, if she is being sought for *her own merits.* This is one of the disadvantages of wealth, but what should reassure her is that if anyone were initially attracted by this wealth, very shortly she would be appreciated for herself. I have told you that goodness of the heart could replace all the other qualities, but I was mistaken; there is something that perhaps is worth even more and that is a sense of duty, a natural disposition to conform to the rule, which is something that goodness of heart does not always imply.

Whatever the number and merit of your friends, please keep me a place in your affections; for my part, I can say this to you, to the extent that time and death are breaking the links around me, to the extent that I am losing the ability to take refuge in politics or study, your benevolence and that of your family are becoming increasingly necessary to me. This is the last light that shines on my life and this is doubtless why it is also the gentlest, purest, and most penetrating. After it will come the night, and let this at least be the night of the tomb.

F. Bastiat

———————

170. Letter to Mme Cheuvreux

Mugron, 27 May 1850   [*Lettres d'un habitant des Landes,* p. 76]

I was confused about the calendar and now my exile has set things right; it is the 27th.

My holiday [326] dates from the 12th, which means that a quarter of the two months has passed. After three times as long as this I will see Paris again.

I have done another calculation, madam, which is less attractive; your last letter was date-stamped the 17th. It is ten days since you wrote it and eight since I received it, eight days! This is nothing for you who spend them surrounded by your family or walking along the banks of the Seine or the Marne, chatting almost always delightfully with your daughter and husband! If at least I could be sure that no cold is stopping you from writing!

Yesterday, a telegraphed dispatch arrived announcing the vote on article 1;[327] I thought that the telegraph might be better employed at least as far as I am concerned.

You have so many friends who, while recommending you to rest, pursue you from morning to night; how anxious I am to learn that you have put a few kilometers between their assiduity and your graciousness!

I have to admit, madam, that La Fontaine was right and that a good number of men are women when it comes to chattering; when I was coming to seek my health here I had not thought that I would find it totally impossible to avoid long conversations. The people of Mugron have nothing to do and so they do not take account of time, except for the times of lunch or dinner. They also resemble Pope a little; they are so many question marks. I

326. Bastiat had been given a two-month leave of absence for health reasons.

327. Article 1 of a law restricting universal suffrage, opposed by 197 deputies, including Bastiat. The law was approved by the majority on 31 May.

leave you to think of how many words you have to deliver. Through a clever maneuver, I lead them into the village gossips or on their pet subjects, their eccentric preoccupations. This gives me a small respite, but all in all, *frankly* I talk too much, and this has cost me a crisis, which fortunately had no aftermath. I am much better now and ready to leave for Les Eaux-Bonnes, when the sun is pleased to play its part, but it is lazy; we can see mountains covered with snow from here, which will not be habitable much before the month of June.

When I look at Mugron with what are now city dweller's eyes, I believe I would be ashamed to show it to you; I would blush for it with its smoke-filled houses, its single, deserted road, its patriarchal furniture and neglected civil administration. Its only charm lies in a rustic naiveté, poverty that does not seek to hide itself, a nature that is always silent and peaceful, a total absence of rowdiness, all things that are appreciated and understood only through habit. Nevertheless, if in this uniform existence you place two objects of affection, I maintain that it becomes general happiness, just as when these objects of affection are absent it becomes general boredom and nothingness.[328] There I found again the affection of Félix. It is impossible to say with what joy we started our interrupted conversations again and what pleasure is to be found in the communion of two spirits in harmony, two parallel minds born on the same day, cast in the same mold, fed on the same milk, and having the same opinion on all things, be they religion, philosophy, politics, or social economics. Everything is examined without our succeeding in finding on any subject the slightest difference of opinion between us. This identity of understanding is a great guarantee of certainty, especially since, only ever having just a few books, these are our own opinions which are in contact and not the opinion of a common master. However, in spite of the pleasantness of this company, there is an emptiness here; Félix and I are companions mainly through our minds, and something is lacking in feeling. Here I am, being totally egotistical. I am ashamed of myself, and as a punishment I will take leave of you until tomorrow.

28th. The mail has arrived empty-handed, for what is this pile of letters and journals? However, I recognize Paillottet's writing; what has he got to say to me? He does not know you and will not have met M. Cheuvreux. I now regret not having dared to introduce him to you as I had the presenti-

---

328. He is referring to his fondness for his Aunt Justine and his friend Félix Coudroy.

ment that he would be punctual and that he would be good for me. Oh! I do hope that nothing dreadful has happened at the Hôtel Saint-Georges.

Farewell, mesdames, I feel that I am beginning to write in f minor. I had better stop while assuring you of my respectful and devoted attachment.

F. Bastiat

---

171. Letter to Prosper Paillottet

Mugron, 2 June 1850   [vol. 7, p. 439]

... My cousin left for Paris yesterday.[329] He will arrive at just about the same time as this letter and will hand you more than half of the article I am writing to complete the pamphlet.[330] However, the article has taken on such dimensions that we can no longer use it for this purpose. There will be nearly fifty pages of my writing, that is to say, enough to make a new pamphlet if it so merits. This is a trial. You know that I have always had the desire to know what would happen if I refrained from rewriting. This has been written almost by improvisation. For this reason I am afraid that it will lack the detail required for a pamphlet. In a few days' time I will send you the rest. When you have the entire article, you will be able to decide.

---

172. Letter to Horace Say

Mugron, 3 June 1850   [vol. 7, p. 384]

My dear Friend,

Why have you confined the excellent letter you sent to the latest issue of *Le Journal des économistes* within such narrow limits? With regard to the events and causes, it is full of wisdom and reveals a level of business experience which we are often reproached for lacking, with some justification. Articles like this always satisfy readers and put forward principles without mentioning them. You ought to develop the thought that you indicate only at the end of your letter. Yes, because of the sluggishness of financial markets, the prices of cereals are lower than they ought to be, and it is inevitable that they will soon exceed the normal level. This is the general law of supply and demand. Busier trading would have brought the two extremes closer

---

329. Eugène de Monclar.

330. (Paillottet's note) This work, instead of being used as an addition to the pamphlet *Plunder and Law*, became a separate pamphlet titled *The Law*.

to the average. What is more, it would have lowered the average itself as it would have prevented waste and reckless exports. A work by you on this subject would be very useful from both the practical and the scientific points of view. From the latter aspect, it would dissipate the disastrous prejudices against middlemen and the *cornering of goods*. Please undertake this work.

Although I take little interest in politics, I have been able to convince myself, and painfully, that our great statesmen have succeeded only too well in the first part of their campaign plan, which is to spread disquiet in order to exploit it. Everywhere I have been I have seen a truly morbid terror reign. It seems that we are threatened with an agrarian law.[331] People think Paris is sitting on a volcano. They go so far as to talk about an imminent conflict or foreign invasion, not for perverse reasons but out of fear of the worst. The Republic, republicans, and even those who merely submit are cursed and the lower classes are insulted by a flood of outrageous epithets. In short, I believe that everything is being thrown to the wind, even caution. Please God that this paroxysm passes quickly! Where will it lead?

---

173. Letter to Louise Cheuvreux

    Mugron, 11 June 1850   [*Lettres d'un habitant des Landes*, p. 80]

Dear Demoiselle,

It was my resolution, firmly taken, to let a full week go by before I wrote to you, for one may well count on the benevolence of friendship, but it should not be abused. However, I think that my haste may be excused, for you tell me that your mother is unwell and I am at the end of the world; I cannot send my rustic maid from the Franche-Comté to the Hôtel Saint-Georges to ask for news.

Here you are at last, finally settled in Fontainebleau, far from any noise. We must hope that a week of retirement and silence will restore all those with damaged health; it was yesterday that I learned of your departure from M. Say. This news had a strange effect on me at first; it was as though a hundred leagues more had come to separate us. This is because, since I have never been to Fontainebleau, my imagination was turned upside down.

I cannot thank you enough, dear demoiselle, for your most affectionate

---

331. The rise of socialism during the 1848 revolution made this a serious problem for many classical liberals. See the article by Courcelle-Seneuil on "Lois agraires," in the *Dictionnaire de l'économie politique*.

words; you have sent me words that are so sweet that they resemble rec-
ollections of harmonies or perfumes which the senses sometimes suddenly
remember, mingled with a few childhood memories.

But I sense from your letter that you have not yet recovered your gaiety;
let us see if I am mistaken. You have such noble self-control that, when it is
necessary, you *overcome* your emotions, but you lack the carefree spirit that
makes people forget them. Your nature will always arouse sympathy and admiration, but it will find it hard in this world to come upon the calm which
gives rise to long-lasting gaiety. What do you think of my efforts in psychol-
ogy? Whether or not they are accurate, I will give them to you; please do not
try to change yourself, you will gain nothing from this.

I am leaving tomorrow for Les Eaux-Bonnes; this is just another excuse
for this letter. The name Eaux-Bonnes reminds me of the dreadful risk I am
running; who knows whether I will not leave it just at the time you arrive?
Who knows whether your post chaise will not pass the enormous vehicle
which will carry me to Paris in the other direction? You must allow that it
would be a big disappointment for me.

Oh, come to the Pyrenees! Come right now to breathe this pure and
always fragrant air. Come and enjoy this peaceful corner of nature, such
an impressive place. There you will forget the troubles of this winter and
politics. There you will avoid the heat of the summer. Every day you will
vary your walks and excursions; you will gaze on new marvels and combine
strength, health, and moral adaptability with physical exercise. You will have
the joy of seeing your father lose sight of all his uncertainties which are now
an inseparable part of life in Paris. Take the decision, then. I will take you to
Biarritz and Saint-Sebastian in the Basque country; compare the journeys;
is this not better than Belgium and Holland?

One writer has said that there are just two types of people in the world,
"those that drink beer and those that drink wine." If you want to know how
you earn money, go and see the people who drink beer; if you prefer to
see how they laugh, sing, and dance, come and visit the people who drink
wine.

I had adopted a few illusions about the effect of the air of my native region; although I am coughing less frequently, I have a slight fever every evening. However, fever and Les Eaux-Bonnes have never been compatible.

I would also like to be cured of a bout of low spirits which I cannot explain. Where has it come from? Is it the result of the doleful changes that
Mugron has undergone in the last few years? Is it because ideas fly from me

without my having the strength to write them down on paper, to the great detriment of posterity? Is it because . . . is it because? But if I knew, this sadness would have a cause and it does not . . . I will stop there, before starting the boring jeremiads of splenetic dispositions, misunderstood souls or blasé ones, geniuses without recognition or those seeking soul mates, a cursed race that I detest. I prefer that people simply tell me, like Bazile:[332] It is your fever, *buona sera.*

Farewell; tell your father and mother how much I appreciate their remembering me. Farewell; when will I see you all again? Farewell; I repeat this word which is never neutral, since it is the most painful or the most pleasant that can ever cross our lips.

Please be assured, dear demoiselle, of the tender attachment of your devoted servant,

F. Bastiat

---

174. Letter to Mme Cheuvreux

Les Eaux-Bonnes, 15 June 1850   [*Lettres d'un habitant des Landes,* p. 85]

My dear Mme Cheuvreux,

Having arrived yesterday evening in Les Eaux-Bonnes, I went this morning to the post office. Reason told me there would be nothing there, but I had the feeling there would be something; in fact, reason was wrong as often happens, in spite of its name.

Thus, thanks to your goodness, I feel a fundamental joy that had deserted me, and our delightful valley will lose nothing by my looking upon it in this light.

On Thursday I went to Pau at around seven o'clock. I was in the rue du Collège where I think I have identified the house where you lived. How joyful and impressive this view of Pau is; light clouds hid the mountain and you could enjoy the foreground only: the Gave, Gélos, Bizanos,[333] and the slopes and villas of Jurançon.

---

332. A character in Beaumarchais' plays *Le Barbier de Seville* and *Le Marriage de Figaro.*

333. The Gave de Pau River, running through Pau; Gélos, a small town in the vicinity of Pau; Bizanos, a small town in the vicinity of Pau.

If the star under which I was born had created me a poet instead of making me a cold economist, I would send you verses, as there was in me a little of *Lamartine;* have not you and your Louise distributed a great many smiles over this landscape and does it not appear to have kept the memory of these? But poetry enjoys a degree of license forbidden to prose.

In Les Eaux-Bonnes, I have taken a room at the junction of three roads, which is well ventilated and full of sunlight and with an admirable view. The first night, I slept for twelve hours to the murmur of the Valentin.[334] When I arose I already felt in a better mood when I received the wonderful surprise of your letter. I took it with me on my morning walk and now I feel better in both mind and body than I have felt for a long time. This should be a warning to my friends; you should never take too much notice of the lamentations of a man under stress.

Mesdames, you scold me for having been unfaithful to my beloved *Harmonies,* but have they not set me a bad example? What evidence have they given me of their affection? For the last six months the only word they have addressed to me has been through the good offices of M. Paillottet; *seriously,* I can see that this book, if ever it is to be useful, will have its use only in the far distant future, and perhaps even this assessment is just a refuge for my amour propre. As the opportunity has arisen to write a small pamphlet[335] that is more topical, I have taken it and have a second in my head: I would like to paint *the moral state of the French nation as* I see it; analyze and dissect the highly varied elements which make up our two major political movements, *socialism and reaction;* distinguish what is justifiable and reasonable in them from what is false, exaggerated, selfish, and reckless; and end it with a *solution* or view of what should be done or rather undone.

The elections will not take place until 1854; let us not look so far into the future. I know in what state of mind the electors nominated me and I have never strayed from this path. They have changed and that is their right. However, I am persuaded that they have been wrong to change. It had been *agreed* that the republican form of government, a form that I could personally live without if necessary, would be tried honestly, and perhaps this would not have stood up to the test, however *sincere.* In this case it would naturally have fallen under the weight of public opinion: instead

334. A mountain brook flowing through Les Eaux-Bonnes.
335. *The Law,* written in Mugron a few days earlier.

of this, people are trying to overthrow it by means of plots, lies, injustice, organized and calculated terror, and discredit. They are preventing it from working and imputing to it things for which it is not responsible, and in doing this they are acting contrary to agreements without having anything to replace it.

Would it not be singular if, after so many projects and hesitations, you quite simply returned to La Jonchère? This countryside has been somewhat denigrated; ask the gardener for her opinion. When all is said and done, you have spent a good summer there. I will go to see you as often as possible as M. Piscatore wishes to let me have Le Butard again.

Your next letter will tell me what has been decided. Do you know that, from this point of view, your letters are fearful? The previous one never lets me guess what the following will say; four days in Fontainebleau are all well and good, but I am afraid that you will end up writing to me from Rome or Spa.

Mlle Louise will have returned in time to enjoy the young cousins from whom she is unfortunately growing apart; why therefore does she not want to make sure of a closer, more direct, and permanent happiness in this connection? She must sometimes ask herself this simple question: what would my father and mother do if they did not have me?

In bidding you farewell, it is with great joy that I think this is not a farewell from a far distance or a farewell for several months; I will be in Paris when the holiday is over.

Your respectful and devoted friend,

F. Bastiat

---

175. Letter to Prosper Paillottet

Les Eaux-Bonnes, 23 June 1850   [vol. 7, p. 440]

. . . Here I am at the so-called source of health. I am doing things conscientiously, which means that I am doing very little work. As I am not inclined to start further work on the *Harmonies,* I am finishing the pamphlet *What Is Seen and What Is Not Seen* and will probably be able to send it to you in a few days' time.

Thank you for the article you had printed in *L'Ordre.* It has just been reprinted in the newspapers in my *département.* This is probably all that will ever be known about my book.

Another report has appeared in *Le Journal des économistes*.[336] I cannot understand how M. Clément has thought it apposite to criticize my *future* chapter on population. What has been printed offers enough to work on without dealing in advance with what has not yet appeared. It is true that I have announced that I will be trying to prove the following thesis: The density of the population is equivalent to an increasing production capacity. M. Clément will have to agree with this or deny the virtues of trade and the sharing of work.

The criticism he has made of the chapter on landed property makes me think that it might be useful to reprint as a pamphlet the four or five articles which have appeared in the *Débats*[337] entitled "Property and Plunder." Besides, this would be another weapon in the armory of our manifesto, which those who do not have the patience to read the *Harmonies* will need.

Please remember me to MM Quijano and de Fontenay.

---

176. Letter to Mme Cheuvreux

Les Eaux-Bonnes, 23 June 1850   [*Lettres d'un habitant des Landes,* p. 89]

You have just joined forces with Mlle Louise, madam, to make me endure absence. In the midst of the problems of setting up home, you have found the time to write to me and, what is more, you give me the presentiment that those who are absent will not lose out to your leisure activities at La Jonchère. Oh, how good women's hearts are! I know full well that I owe a great deal to my sickly health; do you remember that I once said that the moments I remembered with the greatest pleasure were those of suffering, because of the touching care it brought me from my good aunt. Truly, mesdames, you are such as could make one want to be ill, but I must not play the hypocrite here and, even if it delays your next letter by twenty-four hours, I really must admit that I am better. I take the waters cautiously, although without the assistance of a doctor, for what is their use? Spa doctors are like confessors; they always have the same remedy.

---

336. Bastiat published a short version of *Economic Harmonies* with only ten chapters in 1850. After Bastiat's death Paillottet and Fontenay went through his papers and put together a larger edition with twenty-five chapters. The shorter first edition was reviewed by Ambroise Clément in *Le Journal des économistes* 26 (April–July 1850).

337. *Le Journal des débats.*

However, do not take advantage of my confession, and if you do not write to me on account of my health, write to me to tell me about your family.

There you are at La Jonchère. Since you are boasting of being properly countrified, try to get up earlier in the morning and gain a few extra minutes each day. Go for many walks, read a little, the newspapers as little as possible, and do not attract to yourselves more than a small number of friends at a time. This is the result of my consultation; it snaps its fingers at M. Chaumel's as he has lost my confidence.

Les Eaux-Bonnes is beginning to be very crowded; my dinner table is, however, not as well composed as on my last journey. It may be that the effort to avoid politics cools the conversation. Today, two people arrived from Le Havre who quizzed me on the chapter about my solution to the social problem.[338] I took advantage of the opportunity to put abroad some *detailed* publicity, reciting almost an entire pamphlet, which I wrote in Mugron. It was very strange! Everyone kept saying: "That's right! That's right!" until I spoke of applications; there, I was on my own. It is to be deplored that the classes who make the laws are unwilling to be just whatever that might cost, since, if this were so, each person would want to make the law, whether he be a manufacturer, farmer, shipowner, family man, taxpayer, artist, or worker. In the event, each person is a socialist as far as he himself is concerned and claims a share in the injustice, after which people are quite willing to grant others *state charity,* and this is a second form of injustice. As long as the state is regarded in this way as a source of favors, our history will be seen as having only two phases, the periods of conflict as to who will take control of the state and the periods of truce, which will be the transitory reign of a triumphant oppression, the harbinger of a fresh conflict. But may God forgive me, I am thinking myself still at the dinner table; I will go to bed, as it is better to put down the pen than use it too much.

338. In his discussions of social problems in various places in his works, for example, in *The Law, Property and Law, Property and Plunder,* and *Economic Harmonies,* Bastiat often elaborated on those discussions by writing that liberty was "the solution to the social problem."

177. Letter to Mme Cheuvreux

Les Eaux-Bonnes, 24 June 1850   [*Lettres d'un habitant des Landes,* p. 92]

You have seen the Pyrenees in Paris; I for my part am finding Paris in the Pyrenees. There are only beautiful women, fine outfits, countesses, and marquises; this morning some children chased one of their comrades away because he had come dressed in twill: you are not smart enough! These were the expressions used. His father, a doctor, was mortified by this.

Recently, I have been to the village of Aas; you know, you have to go down into the valley and up on the other side. I visited the cemetery; it is full of monuments: young men and women who came to Les Eaux-Bonnes to seek an end to their suffering and succeeded far beyond their hopes. Should we envy their fate? Oh, no. Not yet. I met two women and came back with them. The daughter was weak, slim, thoughtful, and fearful of the ride she was taking on horseback; her mother was in good health and indefatigable. Add to this the purest of language, the most distinguished manners, and you will understand that this necessarily reminded me of an outing at La Jonchère.

Yesterday, Sunday, we had a few joys, but alas, all the local color is leaving; the mountain folk were making their rounds to the sound of violins and Spaniards danced the fandango in smocks: tambourines, castanets, striped jackets, and mantillas, what will become of you? Violins are invading everywhere, and as for smocks, *there are no more Pyrenees.*[339] Oh, the smock will become the symbol of the next century! But after all, is not what appears to us to be a profanation in fact progress? It is funny that we, civilized people, so proud of our arts and outfits, should want people elsewhere to preserve knickerbockers and the Provençal flute forever and ever, to entertain the tourists.

Did I read correctly, mesdames? You tell me that I must not return to Paris until I am cured, that I must spend the winter in Mugron! You must find my absence very pleasant then!

Ah, there is no point in your saying this. I take your words as evidence of interest since I am the most obliging interpreter in the world. I am therefore hoping to return to Paris on 20 July, unless the Chamber is prorogued; this will be an extension of a week to my holiday. It would be amusing if the

339. An allusion to a phrase of Louis XIV's uttered when the king of Spain, Charles II, decided to make Philippe d'Anjou (grandson of Louis XIV) his heir.

Assembly inflicted a penalty on me for having returned too late while you scolded me for returning too soon.

I am anxious to receive a letter from La Jonchère to know whether M. Cheuvreux has decided to take a little rest or if you were pursuing your projects alone? Solitude for three! That is a universe; and is not Croissy close at hand, and the Renouard and Say families and Mme Freppa? In all conscience, I cannot pity you your fate!

Goodness, how I am overusing M. Cheuvreux's fine writing desk; it has solved the problem of pens for me and I have never written such incommensurate letters!

Please persuade Mlle Louise to pardon me and please call what others might call indiscretion, friendship.

> Farewell, your devoted servant,
> F. Bastiat

---

178. Letter to Prosper Paillottet

Les Eaux-Bonnes, 28 June 1850 [vol. 7, p. 441]

. . . Here is the first part of the pamphlet entitled *The Law*.[340] I have added nothing to it. I suppose that the other part is on the way. This is very serious for a pamphlet. However, the experience has taught me that what you count on the least is sometimes the most successful and that the *mind* is harmful to the *idea*.

I wanted to send you *What Is Seen*[341] but I do not think it is very successful. I ought to have adopted a lighter tone instead of resorting to a serious tone and, what is worse, a geometric form.[342]

I will be delighted to receive Michel Chevalier's work.[343] While he does me the honor of borrowing a few points of view, he provides me with a great

---

340. (Paillottet's note) No longer in manuscript form but as a printed proof.

341. *What Is Seen and What Is Not Seen.*

342. (Paillottet's note) See the note on page 336 of vol. 5. [Paillottet is referring to a footnote he wrote to *What Is Seen and What Is Not Seen* in which he describes how Bastiat lost the original manuscript in a house move and had to rewrite it. See also the Glossary of Subjects and Terms, *What Is Seen and What Is Not Seen.*]

343. Bastiat could be referring to one of several books that Chevalier published in 1850: *Les Questions politiques et sociales; Cours d'économie politique fait au Collège de France: La Monnaie;* or *Lettres sur l'organisation du travail.*

many facts and examples; this is free trade. Our manifesto is in sore need of his pen.

---

179. Letter to Prosper Paillottet

    Les Eaux-Bonnes, 2 July 1850   [vol. 7, p. 441]

... Your comment on *The Law* is accurate. I have not proved that the self-ishness that distorts the law is *unintelligent*. However, there is now no time to do this. Besides, this proof is shown by all of the preceding pamphlets and will be shown even better by those that follow. People will see that the severe hand of providential justice will sooner or later weigh cruelly on these demonstrations of selfishness. I very much fear that the middle classes of our time will pay the penalty. This is a lesson that has not spared kings, priests, the various forms of aristocracy, the Romans, members of the National Convention, or Napoléon.

I would write to M. de Fontenay to thank him for his kind letter if he had not told me he was leaving for the country. This colleague is made of stern stuff. What is more, the young people of our time have a flexible style which they will use to surpass us. This is how the world goes and *should go*. I am happy that this is so. What good would it do for an author to make a discovery if others did not come along to fertilize it, correct it if necessary, and above all spread it widely?

I intend to leave here on the 8th and to arrive in Paris around the 20th. I will subject my health to your ruling.

---

180. Letter to M. de Fontenay[344]

    Les Eaux-Bonnes, 3 July 1850   [vol. 1, p. 204]

... Perhaps you are too ardently in favor of the *Harmonies* in the face of opposition from *Le Journal des économistes*. Middle-aged men do not easily abandon well-entrenched and long-held ideas. For this reason, it is not to them but to the younger generation that I have addressed and submitted my book. People will end up acknowledging that *value* can never lie in materials and the forces of nature. From this can be drawn the absolutely free characteristic of gifts from God in all their forms and in all human transactions.

344. See Letter 175, note 336.

This leads to the mutual nature of services and the absence of any reason for men to be jealous of and hate each other. This theory should bring all the schools together on a common ground. Since I live with this conviction, I am waiting patiently, since the older I become the clearer I perceive the slowness of human evolution.

However, I do not conceal a personal wish. Yes, I would like this theory to attract enough followers in my lifetime (even if only two or three) for me to be assured before dying that it will not be abandoned if it is true. Let my book generate just one other and I will be satisfied. This is why I cannot encourage you too strongly to concentrate your thinking on capital, which is a huge subject and may well be the cornerstone of political economy. I have no more than touched upon it; you will go further than I and will correct me if need be. Do not fear that I will take offence. The economic horizons are unlimited: to see new ones makes me happy, whether it was I that discovered them or someone else that is showing them to me.

... Yes, you are right. There is a complete avenue of science to be explored with regard to the dread word *consumption;* this is what I will be establishing at the start of my second volume. As for *population,* it is incomprehensible that M. Clément can attack me on a subject that I have not yet tackled! And basically, to deny the axiom that *the density of the population is an advantage for production* is to deny all the power of trade and the division of labor.[345] What is more, it is to deny facts that are blindingly obvious. Doubtless, populations naturally organize themselves so as to produce as much as possible, and to do this they divide or merge as circumstances require; they obey a double tendency to spread out and to concentrate, but the more they increase, ceteris paribus, that is to say, all virtues, forward planning, and dignity being equal, the more the services divide and are mutually rendered and the more each person is rewarded for the least of his particular qualities, etc. . . .

---

345. Bastiat seems to be anticipating an argument that would be taken up by Julian Simon in the twentieth century. Simon saw population as "the ultimate resource." See Julian P. Simon, *The Ultimate Resource* (Princeton, N.J.: Princeton University Press, 1981).

181. Letter to Mme Cheuvreux

   Les Eaux-Bonnes, 4 July 1850   [*Lettres d'un habitant des Landes*, p. 95]

At last I have a letter from La Jonchère, my dear madam, and I am now certain that you are somewhere definite. What is more, you tell me that your first few days in the country have been happy, that you are taking long walks in the woods, and that you are having some lovely visits, since today the Say family have come to call.

Just as I have your first letter from La Jonchère, this is, I think, my last from Les Eaux-Bonnes. I will be leaving on the 8th, unless in the meantime I learn that the Assembly is going on holiday. However, if there is any doubt, I will have to leave. It is not that I have been fundamentally cured; while my health has improved, my larynx stubbornly continues to suffer.

It is clear that in Les Eaux-Bonnes this year, ridicule of the gentlefolk has risen to such a height that it is ruining everything. People adopt accents, figures, and manners worthy of Molière's pen; the only person who continues to be unaffected here is Mme de Latour-Maubourg. If she is giving a lesson to the *précieuses* around her, this lesson has gone unnoticed. Of course, I do not frequent these circles overly much, since I have noticed that they welcome only those people who give them the opportunity of saying, "I was with M. de ——, we were on a walk with the Count of ——, etc." My company is made up of a very ill lieutenant, a young Spaniard who is at death's door, and a Parisian aged twenty-three, as ill as the two others.

I am surprised that this time of exile, whose end I have desired so ardently, has seemed so short: "Everything that has to end passes quickly." This saying is as true as it is sad. In fact, the provincial habits I rediscovered have had a certain charm. Independence, free time, work, and leisure at will, reading at odd times, thoughts that wander on impulse, solitary walks, scenery that is admirable, peace and quiet, this is what you can find in our mountains, and the power of a piece of music in *b,* a single piece in *b,* would make it a paradise. What else would you need, other than a drop of the ambrosia that perfumes all the details of life that is called *friendship*?

You have seen the success and ovations given to MM Scribe and Halévy in the newspapers. This will have pleased you and doubtless made you regret that you were not there to witness it. Mlle Louise had the feeling that pleasant amusements were awaiting her in London. We should congratulate ourselves on everything that brings peoples together and unites them: in this respect your friends' attempt will bear good fruit. It will increasingly encourage our neighbors to study French. Reciprocity would be very useful, for we have a lot to learn from the other side of the Channel. I was happy to see that Richard Cobden, in difficult circumstances which must have been a cruel test for him, neither slipped nor stumbled.[346] He has remained true to himself, but these are things that our newspapers do not notice.

Have you read the article by M. de Broglie on Chateaubriand in *La Revue des deux mondes*? I was not displeased to see this chastisement inflicted on vanity that is inflated to a childish level. With such exclusive selfishness of heart one can be a great writer, but do you believe one can be a great man? For my part, I detest these blind and proud men who spend their lives striking postures and attitudes, who put humanity on one side of the scales with themselves on the other and believe they win the day. I regret that M. de Broglie did not seek to appreciate the value of Chateaubriand's philosophy; he would have found that it was very slight. From the eleventh volume of his memoirs, I copied out this paradox, "The perception of good and evil is obscured in proportion to the enlightenment of the mind; the conscience shrivels in proportion to the expansion of ideas."

If this is so, the human race is condemned to fatal and irremediable degradation; the man who has written these lines is a soul condemned.

5 July

Here is another letter from La Jonchère, but one that does not confirm its predecessor. In the meantime, I have had news from M. Say and I thought that you were all in good health. I see that sleep is eluding you, that Mlle Louise is fatigued by the heat, and that M. Cheuvreux himself is unwell! What a well-organized *trio*! What upsets me considerably is that I will have no news of you from now until 20 July, unless you are good enough to write to me once more, if only a note to Mugron. I am definitely leaving Les Eaux-Bonnes repeating the chorus of our ballad:

> Aigues caoutes, aigues rèdes,
> Lou mein maou n'es pot guari.[347]

"Hot water, cold water, nothing can cure my ill." It is true that the good cavalier was doubtless speaking of some strange wound on which all the springs

---

346. Cobden was opposed to the foreign policy of Palmerston.
347. This is the Gascony dialect, which evolved from the langue d'oc, from which Catalan and Provençal also evolved.

of the Pyrenees had no effect. I was better placed to count on them for my larynx; it resisted them; what should I do?

I will probably have some strong battles to confront at Mugron to get any holiday there as well. But I will resist these assaults as I cannot allow myself not to be present at the Assembly.

Do you wish to visit Les Cormiers?[348] It is a place that is very peaceful, cool, and solitary. If I spend two months there, I will perhaps reach the stage of starting out in the world of the *Harmonies*. I have not done anything about them here; my publisher is pressing me and I tell him that the coolness of the public is cooling my ardor. In this respect, I am committing the sin of lying. Authors do not lose courage over so little. In these types of misadventures, the angel or demon of pride calls out to them, "It is the public which is mistaken, it is too scatterbrained to read you or too backward to understand you." "That is all very well," I say to my angel, "but in this case I can dispense with working for it." "It will appreciate you in a century and that is enough for fame," replies the stubborn tempter.[349]

Fame! Heaven is my witness that I did not aspire to it and if one of its stray rays, ever so weak, should fall on this book, I would be delighted for the advancement of the cause and also a little for the satisfaction of my friends; let them love me without this and I will not give it another thought.

Your devoted servant,
F. Bastiat

---

182. Letter to Horace Say.

Les Eaux-Bonnes, 4 July 1850   [vol. 1, p. 200]

My dear Friend,

... I have read the article by M. Clément on the *Harmonies*. If I thought a controversy useful, I would accept it, but who would read it? M. Clément appears to think that it is a lack of respect for our masters to go deeper into problems that they have scarcely touched on, because at the time they were writing these problems had not been raised. According to him, they have

348. Le Butard.

349. For most of the first half of the twentieth century the works of Bastiat lay forgotten. It was not until the Foundation for Economic Education published a translation of "La Loi" in 1950, the centenary of Bastiat's death, that his work became known to another generation.

said everything, seen everything, and have left us nothing to do. This is not my opinion and it was certainly not theirs. Between the first and last pages of your father there is too significant a degree of progress for him not to have seen for himself that he had not reached the horizon and that no one would ever reach it. For me, even if the *Harmonies* were ever completed to my satisfaction (which they will not be), I would still see them only as a point from which our successors will draw a whole new world. How can we make progress when we are obliged to devote three-quarters of our time to elucidating the simplest questions for a misguided public?

... If you write the article on *insurance* for Guillaumin's Dictionary,[350] please make it clear that it is not only the companies that join together in *association* but also and above all *those who are insured*. It is they that form, without suspecting this, *an association* which is no less real for being voluntary and something one enters and leaves at will.

---

183. Letter to Mme Cheuvreux

Mugron, July 1850   [vol. 7, p. 435]

... You had just lost a childhood friend. In these circumstances, your first feeling is one of regret. You then cast a worried look around you and end up looking introspectively into yourself. The mind asks questions of the *great unknown*, and, as it receives no reply, it becomes terrified. This is because there is a mystery that is not accessible to the mind, but only to the heart. *Can you doubt on a tomb?* ...

---

184. Letter to M. Cheuvreux

Mugron, 14 July 1850   [*Lettres d'un habitant des Landes,* p. 100]

Your kind letter, my dear M. Cheuvreux, has just been handed to me. A few hours later and it would have had to retrace its journey to Paris in the same mail coach as the person to which it was addressed, since I am prepar-

---

350. Horace Say did write the article on insurance in the *Dictionnaire de l'économie politique* (published in 1854). The Say family was very much involved in compiling the various dictionaries of political economy published by Guillaumin. In the first edition, of 1852, a number of articles carried the name "Jean-Baptiste Say" (obviously selected from his books, as Say had died in 1832); his son Horace contributed twenty-seven articles, and his grandson Léon also wrote some articles. A second version, the *Nouveau dictionnaire de l'économie politique,* which appeared in 1891 and 1900, was edited by Léon Say.

ing to leave tomorrow. I am doubtless making a mistake; this must be so since everyone says so and I have already endured countless verbal and epistolary assaults. I do not claim to be right in the face of everyone, although Mme Cheuvreux is calling me a *sophist* in advance. The truth is that I could scarcely excuse myself from putting in an appearance in the Chamber before the holidays; after this I admit that I am yielding a bit to caprice. For some time now, I have had a very local pain in the larynx that is unbearable because it is continuous. I think I will find relief by changing my environment.

Mlle Louise may fear that her letter has gone astray in the Pyrenees. Please reassure her, it was given to me here on my arrival. Truly, it would have been a great privation for me, since your dear child has the art (if art it is) of infusing her letters with her soul and goodness. She spoke to me of the impression English literature had on her and then deplores the loss of belief that characterizes ours.

I was getting ready to write an essay in reply, on this text, but I will spare her this. Since I am leaving tomorrow, I will take my revenge face to face.

You are quite right, my dear M. Cheuvreux, to encourage me to continue these elusive *Harmonies*. I too feel that I have the duty to complete them, and I will endeavor to devote my holidays to them.

The field is so vast that it terrifies me.

When I said that the laws of political economy are harmonious, I did not mean only that they harmonize with each other, but also with the laws of politics, the moral laws, and even those of religion (granted the making of generalizations as to the particular rules of each cult). If this were not so, what good would it be for a set of ideas to promote harmony if this set clashed with other sets no less essential?

I do not know whether I am deluding myself, but it seems to me that it is through this and *only* through this that the lively and fertile beliefs whose loss Mlle Louise deplores will be regenerated within the human race. Extinguished beliefs will no longer be revived, and the efforts made in times of terror and danger to give society this anchor are more meritorious than effective. I believe that an inevitable ordeal is lying in wait for Catholicism. Acquiescence in form alone, which each person requires from others and from which acquiescence each person allows himself dispensation, cannot be a permanent state of affairs.

The plan I had conceived required political harmony to be first of all brought down to rigorous certainty, since this is its basis. It appears that I have not established this certainty adequately, since it has not struck anyone, even professional economists. Perhaps the second volume will provide more consistency for the first. I am subjecting myself to your and Mme Cheuvreux's advice to stop me in the future from doing anything else.

This letter will precede me by so little that I find it almost incorrect to send it to you. However, I did not want to leave Mugron without thanking you for all the kindnesses that you and your family have shown me during this absence.

Farewell, my dear sir,
Your devoted servant,
F. Bastiat

---

185. Letter to Richard Cobden

Paris, 3 August 1850 [vol. 1, p. 185]

My dear Cobden, since the departure of our dear friends, the Schwabes, I no longer have the opportunity of talking about you. However, I have not altogether lost sight of you, and recently I noted with joy, but no surprise, that you had disassociated yourself from your friends in order to remain faithful to your convictions. I am referring to the vote on Palmerston.[351] The upsurge in British pride that characterized this episode is not in step with the natural sequence of events and the progress of public reasoning in England. You were right to resist this. It is this perfect coherence of all of your actions and votes that will in the future give your name and example an unassailable authority.

I have spent some time in my native region to see whether my poor lungs, which serve me in a highly unreliable fashion, might be cured. I have returned somewhat better but suffering from an ailment of my larynx coupled with a total loss of my voice. My doctor has ordered me to keep total silence. For this reason, I am going to spend two months in the country not far from Paris. There, I will endeavor to write the second volume of the *Economic Harmonies*. The first went almost unnoticed in scholarly circles. I would not be an *author* if I accepted this judgment. I call on the future to correct this

---

351. Palmerston got a vote of censure from the Lords for having blocked the harbor of Piraeus to defend the interests of a British citizen named Pacifico. A few days later, Palmerston made a speech to defend his position and won approval—but not from Cobden. See Letter 188.

for I am convinced that this book contains an important idea, a *core concept.* Time will prove me right.

Today, I wanted to say a few words in support of our colleague in political economy, A. Scialoja. You know that he was a professor in Turin. Events caused him to become a minister of trade in Naples for a few days. This was in the days of the constitution. When absolute authority was reinstated, Scialoja, thinking that a ministry of trade was not sufficiently political to compromise its holder, did not wish to flee. He was to regret this. He was arrested and imprisoned. For ten months now, he has been clamoring to be released or put on trial.

I have taken a few steps here to arouse the interest of our diplomatic service. (Let diplomacy be good for something for once in its life!) I received the reply that our embassy would do what it could but that it stood little chance. It is said that Scialoja would be much better protected by English goodwill. Could you therefore please obtain support for him from your ambassador in Naples?

Scialoja is asking to be put on trial! I would much prefer for him to be given a passport for London or Paris, since I do not think that a Neapolitan trial would guarantee much equity, even for the most shining innocence.

Will you be going to Frankfurt?[352] For my part, it is no good my attending the Congress, since I have become dumb, but I would be very pleased to see you when you pass through Paris and my apartment at 3, rue d'Alger is at your disposal.

------

186. Letter to Richard Cobden

Paris, 17 August 1850   [vol. 1, p. 187]

My dear Cobden, as you know about my poor health, you will not have been surprised at my absence from the Congress in Frankfurt, especially since you will not have attributed it to a lack of zeal. Apart from the pleasure of being one of your colleagues in this noble enterprise, it would have been very pleasant for me to meet in Frankfurt friends that I rarely have the occasion to see and to meet a host of distinguished men from these two excellent races, the Anglo-Saxon and the Germanic. In a word, I have been deprived of this consolation like many others. For a long time now, mother nature has

352. International peace congresses were held in Brussels in September 1848, Paris in August 1849, Frankfurt in August 1850, and London in July 1851.

gradually been making me accustomed to all sorts of deprivations, as though to familiarize me with the final one which includes them all.

As I have had no news of you, for a time I did not know whether you were going to the Congress; since it did not occur to me that you could go from England to Frankfurt without going through Paris, and since I did not think either that you would pass through our capital city without letting me know, I concluded that you yourself had been prevented from doing so. I have been told that this is not so and I am happy for the Congress. Try to deal a mighty blow to this monster of war, an ogre that is almost as voracious when digesting as it is when eating, for I truly believe that arms cause almost as much harm to nations as war itself. What is more, they hinder good. For my part, I constantly return to what seems to me to be as clear as daylight: as long as disarmament prevents France from restructuring her finances, reforming her taxes, and satisfying the just hopes of the workers, she will continue to be a nation in convulsion . . . and God alone knows what the consequences will be.

A man whom I would have liked to see because of all the interest he has shown in me is M. Prince Smith, from Berlin. If he is at the Congress, please convey to him my great desire to meet him personally. How happy I would be, my dear Cobden, if you decided to pass through Paris and if you persuaded M. Prince Smith to accompany you on this excursion! But I do not dare to formulate such hopes. Good fortune does not seem to be made for me. For a long time now, I have been endeavoring to take advantage of good things when they come but not to expect them.

I consider that a short stay in Paris must be of interest to politicians and economists. Come and see the profound peace we are enjoying here, whatever the newspapers might say. Certainly, internal and external peace in the face of such a tumultuous past and such an uncertain future is a phenomenon that shows great progress in public common sense. Since France has survived this, it will survive a great many other difficulties.

Say what you like, the human mind is making progress, interests in the best sense of the word are prevailing, disagreements are less profound, and long-lasting *harmony* is establishing itself.

187. Letter to the President of the Peace Congress in Frankfurt[353]

Paris, 17 August 1850   [vol. 1, p. 197]

Mr. President,

An ailment of the larynx would not have been enough to keep me away from the Congress, especially as my role would rather have been to listen than to speak, if I were not undergoing a treatment that obliges me to remain in Paris. Please convey my regret to your colleagues. Much taken as I am with all that is grand and new in the spectacle of men of all races and languages who have come from all corners of the globe to work together for the triumph of universal peace, I would have joined my efforts to yours in favor of such a holy cause with zeal and enthusiasm.

In truth, universal peace is considered in many places an illusion, and as a result the Congress is considered to be an honorable effort but with no far-reaching effect. Perhaps this feeling is more prevalent in France than elsewhere because this is a country in which people are more weary of utopias and where ridicule is the more to be feared.

For this reason, if it had been given to me to speak at the Congress, I would have concentrated on correcting such a false assessment.

There was doubtless a time when a peace congress would have had no chance of success. When men made war to acquire loot, land, or slaves, it would have been difficult to stop them by moral or economic considerations. Even various forms of religion have failed to do this.

But today, two circumstances have changed the question radically.

The first is that wars no longer have vested interest as their cause or even their pretext, since they are always contrary to the real interests of the masses.

The second is that they no longer depend on the whims of a leader, but on public opinion.

The result of the combination of these two circumstances is that wars are due to become increasingly rare and finally disappear through the force of events and independently of any intervention by the Congress, since an event that harms the general public and which depends on the general public is bound to cease.

What, therefore, is the role of the Congress? It is to hasten this inevitable

353. For the Peace Congresses, see Letter 157, note 305. The Frankfurt Congress took place on 22, 23, and 24 August 1850. Among the 600 delegates, 250 were British, 31 American, and 15 French.

result by showing, to those who do not yet perceive this, how and why wars and arms are harmful to the general interest.

What element of utopia is there in such a mission?

For the last few years, the world has experienced circumstances which, in other eras, would have caused long and cruel wars. Why have these been avoided? Because, although there is a party in favor of war in Europe, there are also those who love peace. Although there are men who are ever ready to make war, in whom a stupid form of education has imbued ancient ideas and barbaric prejudices and who attach honor to physical courage alone, seeing glory only in military exploits, fortunately there are other men who are more religious, more moral, more farsighted, and who can work things out better. Is it not only natural that this latter category should endeavor to gain recruits from the former? How many times has civilization, as in 1830, 1840, and 1848, been, so to speak, in suspense faced with this question: which of the war or peace parties will gain the upper hand? Up to now, the peace party has triumphed and, it must be said, it is perhaps less through fervor or numbers than because it had political influence.

So peace and war depend on public opinion and opinion is divided. There is therefore a constantly imminent danger. In these circumstances, is not the Congress undertaking something that is useful, serious, effective, and even, I dare say, easy by trying to gain support for those in favor of peace so as to give them at last a decisive weight?

What is utopian in this? Does it mean saying to the people, "We are coming to enjoin you to trample your interests underfoot, to act henceforward in accordance with the principles of devotion, sacrifice, and self-renunciation?" Oh, if this were so, the enterprise would indeed be risky!

But on the contrary, we are coming to tell them: "Do not consult only your interests in the next life, but those in this one. Examine the effects of war. See whether they are not disastrous for you. See whether wars and heavy arms do not lead to interruptions in work, crises of production, the loss of strength, crushing debt, heavy taxes, impossible financial situations, discontent, and revolutions, not to mention deplorable moral habits and reprehensible violations of religious law."

Are we not allowed to hope that this language will be heard? Take courage, then, you men of faith and devotion, have courage and confidence! The gaze and hearts of those who are now unable to join your ranks will be following you.

> I remain, Mr. President, your most
> respectful and devoted servant.

188. Letter to Richard Cobden

Paris, 9 September 1850[354]   [vol. 1, p. 188]

My dear Cobden, I am grateful for the interest you are good enough to take in my health. It is still shaky. At the moment I have a severe inflammation and probably ulcers on the two tubes that take air to the lungs and food to the stomach. The question is to know whether this disease will stop or whether it will get worse. In the latter case, there will no longer be any means of breathing or eating, *a very awkward situation indeed.*[355] I hope not to be subjected to this ordeal for which, however, I am not neglecting to prepare myself by practicing patience and resignation. Is there not an inexhaustible source of consolation and strength in these words, "Non sicut ego volo sed sicut tu"?[356]

One thing that distresses me more than these physiological prospects is the intellectual weakness whose progression I see so clearly. I will doubtless have to abandon the completion of the work I have started. But, at the end of the day, has this book as much importance as I like to give it? Will posterity not get along very well without it? And if one should combat the unseemly love of material possessions, is it not also good to stifle the upsurges of author's vanity that come between one's heart and the only thing worthy of one's aspirations?

Besides, I am beginning to think that the principal idea that I am seeking to disseminate is not lost; yesterday a young man sent me in a letter an article entitled "An Essay on Capital."[357] It included these sentences:

354. This letter was also contained in the book published by Mme Cheuvreux, preceded by the following note:

> After having left the Pyrenees in July, Bastiat settled in the vicinity of Paris. He spent his mornings alone at Le Butard, and his evenings at La Jonchère. But his very painful laryngitis worsened, and regular work became more and more difficult. His friends, who the year before saw him write several chapters of *The Harmonies* amid noise and movement in a corner of their living room, on a table edge, dipping his pen in a bottle of ink drawn from his pocket, caught him then pushing away his paper with an impatient gesture; idle and bowing his head, Bastiat kept silent until the moment when his ardent thinking erupted like a meteor in eloquent sentences. But his words quickly brought back the pain in his throat and forced him to be silent.
>
> On 9 September 1850, the sick man, with a stoical self-control, informed Richard Cobden about the dreadful consequences of his situation.

355. In English in the original.
356. "Not my will but Thine be done."
357. An unpublished paper by M. de Fontenay. See Letter 180.

"Capital is the characteristic sign and measure of progress. It is the sole and necessary vehicle for it, with the special mission of aiding the movement from priced goods to free ones. Consequently, instead of augmenting natural prices, as it is alleged, its unchanging role is to lower them persistently."

These sentences encompass and summarize the most fertile of the economic phenomena that I have endeavored to describe. They include a guarantee of the inevitable reconciliation between the property-owning and the proletarian classes. Since this point of view on social order has not been defeated, since it has been perceived by others who will set it out for all to see better than ever I could, I have not entirely wasted my time and I am able to sing my "Nunc dimittis," with slightly less distaste.

I have read the report on the Congress in Frankfurt. You are the only one to know how to give this work a practical character, an influence on the world of business. The other speakers limit themselves to well-worn commonplaces. But I continue to think that the association will end up having a significant indirect influence by awakening and molding public opinion. Doubtless, you will not obtain the official declaration of universal peace, but you will make wars more unpopular, difficult, rare, and odious.

However, we should not hide the fact that the affair in Greece[358] has dealt a body blow to the supporters of peace and they will need a great deal of time to recover. Which French deputy, for example, will be sufficiently bold to speak merely of partial disarmament in the presence of the international principle involved in this Greek affair, with the consent (and it is above all this that is serious) of the British nation? Disarm! Could this be their cry when a formidable power is openly acting according to the principle that when it considers itself in confrontation, however slight the grounds of complaint, with another government, it will not only employ force against this government but also seize the *private property* of its citizens? As long as such a principle remains standing, whatever its cost, we will need to remain armed to the teeth.

There was a time, my friend, when diplomacy itself tried to have respect for *individual property* prevail at sea in time of war. This principle has entered our military mores. In 1814, the English took nothing in the south of France without paying for it. In 1823, we made war in Spain under the same conditions, and however unjust this war was from the political point of view, it made an admirable distinction, now acknowledged, between the public

358. See Letter 185, note 351.

domain and personal property. M. de Chateaubriand tried at this time to have the elimination of *privateering and letters of marque*,[359] in a word, respect for private property, included in international law. He failed, but his efforts reveal great progress in civilization.

How far back into the past Lord Palmerston[360] is taking us! It is therefore now admitted that if England has a grievance against King Othon, no Greek can claim ownership of a bark or a keg of goods. For the same reason, if France has any complaint against Belgium, Switzerland, or Piedmont, it may send battalions to seize houses, harvests, cattle, etc. This is barbaric. I repeat, with a system like this, everyone will need to remain armed to the teeth and be ready to defend his property, for, my friend, men are not yet Quakers. They have not renounced the right to *personal defense,* and they will probably never renounce this.

If, moreover, everything was limited to the doctrines and acts of Lord Palmerston, this would be one more iniquity for which to reproach diplomacy, but that would be all. But what is serious and threatening is the unexpected approval given to this policy by the English nation. One hope is left to me: that this approval is not typical.

But while making politics, I am forgetting to tell you that, in order to obey my doctors' prescriptions, with no great belief in them, I am leaving for Italy. They have condemned me to spend this winter in Pisa in Tuscany. From there, I will doubtless visit Florence and Rome. If you have any friends there who are close enough for me to introduce myself to them, please let me know, without taking the trouble to send introductory letters. If I knew where to find Mr. and Mrs. Schwabe, I would warn them of this journey in order to take their instructions. When you have occasion to write to them, please tell them about this trip.

---

189. Letter to Félix Coudroy

Paris, 9 September 1850 [vol. 1, p. 104]

My dear Félix, I am writing to you on the point of starting a long journey. The illness which I had when I saw you has settled on my larynx and throat.

359. *Privateering* (*la course*) refers to the expeditions of the corsairs, or privateers. The *letter of marque* was a commission given by a country to a privateer, in time of war, to capture ships of the hostile nation.

360. During the blockade of the Piraeus, two hundred Greek soldiers were captured.

The constant pain and weakness it causes has made it a genuine torture. However, I hope that I will not lack resignation. My doctors have ordered me to spend the winter in Pisa and I am obeying, although these gentlemen have not habitually inspired trust in me.

Farewell, I must stop because my head is preventing me from writing any more. I hope that I will have more vigor during my journey.

---

190. Letter to Prosper Paillottet

Lyons, 14 September 1850 [vol. 7, p. 442]

I do not wish to start out on the second half of my journey without telling you that everything has gone quite well up to now. I became a little tired only during the stage between Tonnerre and Dijon, but that was almost inevitable. I think that it would have been better to sacrifice a night and take the mail coach. It is always the best way. Spending the night on the way always obliges you to take stage carts and old crocks or be cast in among drunken men, etc., and you arrive at a bad inn only to repeat the procedure the next day.

I have not told you, my friend, how much I appreciated the idea that occurred to you for a moment to accompany me to Italy. I am as grateful to you as if you had in fact carried out this project. But I could not have agreed to this. This would have deprived Mme Paillottet of one day seeing this beautiful country or at least have reduced her chances of doing so. Besides, as I cannot talk, all the delight of traveling together would have been lost. Either we would have often disobeyed orders, which would have caused us regret, or we would have obeyed them only after a difficult and constant struggle. Be that as it may, I thank you from the bottom of my heart, and if Mme Paillottet feels up to the journey, come and fetch me in the spring, when I will no longer be dumb.

Please remind M. de Fontenay of my advice or, to put it more strongly, my pressing invitation to have his *Capital* printed.

---

191. Letter to Louise Cheuvreux

Lyons, 14 September 1850 [*Lettres d'un habitant des Landes,* p. 107]

Dear Demoiselle Louise,

Here I am in Lyons since yesterday evening; at a stretch you might have had this letter twenty-four hours earlier, but on my arrival I hesitated between the writing desk and bed. My heart encouraged me to favor the first and my body the second; who would ever have told me that my body would win in a conflict of this kind? However, scarcely was I in bed than it fell victim to a high fever, which explains its victory and justifies me in my own eyes. However, do not worry about this fever; it was very temporary and has completely gone this morning.

On Tuesday, after leaving you, I went to the *Économistes* dinner. M. Say was in the chair. Following the fatigue I always suffer in the evening, I could not go to bid farewell to Mme Say, for which I am very sorry.

On Wednesday, I set out at half past ten. Up to Tonnerre, the journey went extremely well. We went so quickly that we were scarcely able to enjoy the scenery, with the result that since my eyes were fixed on a cloud probably visible from La Jonchère, I remembered that you were not very happy with the words set to the pretty melody by Félicien David.

I addressed other words to my cloud. Unfortunately they did not rhyme and therefore are not worth my copying them down here. From Tonnerre to Dijon, troubles of all sorts began. If you follow this route, as I hope you will, M. Cheuvreux must contact M. G—— in writing to procure mail coaches.

As I was responsible only for myself, I trusted to luck, which could have looked after me better. There were six of us in the seating space of a stage-coach made for four. Out of these six people, four were women, which meant that under our feet, on our knees, and up against our sides we had a multitude of parcels, bags, baskets, etc.; truly, women, who are such adorable models of self-sacrifice in domestic life, appear not to understand that they owe something to others, even people they do not know, when in public.

From Châtillon to Dijon, I was crowded onto the top deck as the four-teenth passenger. It was during this stage that we crossed the watershed, one side of which looks to the ocean, the other the Mediterranean. When this line is crossed, it seems as though you are leaving your friends for a second time, as you no longer breathe the same air and are no longer under the same sky. Finally, from Dijon to Châlon, you have only two hours on the train and from Châlon to Lyons there is a delightful excursion by water.

But can I say that I am traveling? I am going through a succession of landscapes, that is all. I have no communication with anyone, whether in coaches, in boats, or in hotels. The more attractive people's faces appear, the more I shun them. The chapter of random adventures or unforeseen meetings does not exist for me. I am going through space like a bale of goods, except for a few visual delights of which I am soon tired.

You told me, dear demoiselle, that poetic Italy would be a source of new emotions for me. Oh, I very much fear that it will be unable to extricate me from this numbness which is gradually taking over all of my faculties. You gave me a lot of encouragement and advice, but for me to be sensitive to nature and art, you would have needed to lend me your soul, the soul that longs to blossom with happiness, which so quickly becomes attuned to everything that is beautiful, graceful, sweet, and lovely and which has such great affinity with all that is harmonious in light, color, sound, and life. Not that this need for happiness reveals any selfishness in your soul; on the contrary, if it seeks, attracts, or desires it, it is to concentrate it in itself as in a hearth and from there radiate it around you in wit, a fine mischief, constant good deeds, consolation, and affection. It is with this disposition of the soul that I would like to travel, as there is no prism that embellishes external objects more. However, I am changing surroundings and skies under a totally different influence.

Oh, how fragile is the human frame! Here I am, the plaything of a tiny pimple growing in my larynx. It is the thing that is driving me from the south to the north and from north to south. It is the thing that makes my knees buckle and empties my head. It is the thing that makes me indifferent to the Italian landscapes of which you speak. I will soon have no thought or concentration for anything other than it, like the old invalids who fill their entire conversations and all their letters with one single idea. It seems as though I am well down this path already.

To escape this, my imagination has one route still open to me and that is to go to La Jonchère. I imagine that you are enjoying with delight the fine days that September stores up. Here you are, all together! Your dear father and M. Edouard[361] have returned from Cherbourg delighted with the magnificent things they have seen and full of tales to tell. Just the presence of Marguerite would be enough to make your mountain a charming place to stay. Here is one who might boast of having been caressed! I love to hear parents reproaching each other for spoiling their children, a very innocent small conflict, since the most spoiled, that is to say the most loved, are those that succeed the best.

Dear demoiselle, allow me to remind you that you should not sing for too long a time, especially with the windows open. Be careful of the autumn chills and avoid catching cold in this season. Remember that if you caught one through your own fault it would be as though you were making all those who love you ill. Be careful of returning from Chatou[362] at eleven o'clock at

361. Edouard Girard.
362. Small town on the Seine, near Paris, in which La Jonchère was located.

night. To combine care for your health and your love of music, might not your evenings be turned into mornings? Farewell, dear Mlle Louise.

> Allow me to express my
> deep affection,
> *F. Bastiat*

---

192. Letter to Mme Cheuvreux

 Lyons, 14 September 1850   [*Lettres d'un habitant des Landes*, p. 113]

Dear Mme Cheuvreux,

 I am leaving tomorrow for Marseilles. If you take the boat at eleven o'clock you have only the inconvenience of spending the night in Valence and this will not be inconvenient for me since I will have the pleasure of taking news to your brother, the captain.

 If you go to Lyons, do not fail to climb Fourvières! This is an admirable viewpoint from which you can see the Alps, the Cévennes, the mountains of Forez, and those of the Auvergne. What an image of the world Fourvières gives! Down below, there is work and its insurrections,[363] halfway up, cannons and soldiers, and at the top religion with all its sad excrescences. Is this not the story of the human race?

 Contemplating the theater of so many bloody conflicts, I thought that there is no more pressing need in man than that for confidence in a future that offers some stability. What troubles the workers is not so much how low their wages are but their uncertainty, and if men who have achieved wealth were prepared to take a look at themselves, seeing with what ardor they love security, they would perhaps be somewhat indulgent toward the classes which always, for one reason or another, have the specter of unemployment before them. One of the most beautiful of economic harmonies is the ever-increasing tendency for all classes in succession to achieve *stability*. Society achieves this stability as civilization is attained, through earnings, fees, rent, and interest, in short everything that the socialists reject; to such an extent that their plans bring the human race back precisely to its point of departure, that is to say the time when uncertainty is at its highest for everyone. There is a subject here for new research for political economy . . . But what shall I tell you about Fourvières! What poetry, heavens, for the delicate ear of a

---

363. Allusion to the revolts of 1830 and 1834 of the "canuts," the textile workers who lost their jobs because of the growing use of machinery. The revolts were severely repressed.

woman!... Farewell once more, forgive this torrent of words; I am taking revenge for my silence, but is it fair that you should be the victim?

F. Bastiat

---

193. Letter to M. Cheuvreux

Marseilles, 18 September 1850   [*Lettres d'un habitant des Landes,* p. 115]

My dear M. Cheuvreux,

It was painful for me to leave Paris without shaking your hand, but I could not delay my departure on pain of missing the mail boat here. In fact, I arrived here yesterday and have just one day to make all my arrangements, obtain a passport, etc.

It is not even certain that I will be embarking; I have learned that travelers who go by sea are welcomed in Italy by quarantine. Three days in a quarantine station is not very attractive!

When I arrived in Marseilles, my first visit was to the post office, as I hoped to find a letter there; to know that all three of you were enjoying good health at La Jonchère would have made me so happy! There was no letter. Thinking about it made me realize that I was being too demanding since it is scarcely a week since I left the dear mountain. Silence makes time seem so long that it is not surprising that I attach so much importance to receiving a letter.

How anxious I am to reach Pisa. How anxious I am to know whether this fine climate will make my head strong and give it two hours of work a day. Two hours! This is not too much to ask, and yet this is still a vanity.

Doubtless, like André Chénier and like all authors, I think I have *something there,* but this upsurge of pride scarcely lasts long. Whether I transmit to posterity two volumes or just one, the progress of human affairs will remain unchanged.

No matter, I claim my two hours, if not for *future generations,* at least in my own interest. For if the prohibition to work has to be added to so many others, what will become of me in this tomb of my anticipation? I spent the night of Sunday to Monday in Valence. In spite of the desire I had to see the captain and the efforts I made to do this, I was not able to do it.

The 19th. I am definitely leaving tomorrow and by land. Here I am embarked upon an adventure whose outcome I cannot see.

This morning I was still hoping for a letter; I would have left happier.

Now only the good Lord knows where and when I will have news of you all; will I have to wait two weeks?

Dear M. Cheuvreux, please remember me to both mother and daughter and assure them of my profound friendship. Do not forget to remember me also to M. Edouard and Mme Anna, who will allow me to embrace their delightful child, although from afar.

Farewell, dear M. Cheuvreux,
F. Bastiat

---

194. Letter to Mme Cheuvreux

Marseilles (on board the *Castor*),   [*Lettres d'un habitant*
22 September 1850   *des Landes*, p. 117]

Dear Mme Cheuvreux,

Before leaving France, allow me to send you a few lines. The date of this letter will surprise you; here is the explanation.

As you know, since I was determined to go by land, I allowed the boat on the 19th to leave. At the time, a day sooner or later was of little importance and I was not willing to leave Marseilles knowing that one of your letters was on the point of arriving. I waited and was right to do so, since I have at last received your very benevolent and affectionate encouragement, and what is more, I know the major decision that has been taken at La Jonchère.

In short, I should have been taking the coach yesterday, but I was perfectly aware that, to avoid the quarantine station, I would encounter other inconveniences, such as going through clouds of dust, going from inn to inn, cab to cab, and using my larynx to argue with porters; all this was scarcely an attractive prospect. At eleven o'clock, while reading the Marseilles journal, I saw that the *Castor* was leaving for Leghorn in the afternoon. Although you advised me to avoid making unplanned decisions, I booked and paid for a ticket, thinking that the quarantine would be swallowed at a gulp if I closed my eyes. In the evening, the sea was so rough that the boat did not leave, and this is how I come to be scribbling this epistle while they are raising the anchor.

Since my arrival on board, I have noticed that it is a great mistake to be the last to book your ticket. Instead of having a good single cabin, you have a bed in a joint cabin.

Oh, what an improvident man! You are going to cross the Mediterranean in the joint cabin of a packet-boat; you will die in the general ward of a hospital and will be thrown in the common grave of a Campo Santo! What difference does it make, if the happiness I have dreamed of in this world is waiting for me in the next? However, it is better to have a single cabin, and this is why I am writing to you so that you can take the necessary steps.

Your journey is worrying me. At first, I thought I had the answer (who does not seek answers today?). I thought that His Holiness, who subjects his infallibility to the protection of our bayonets, should spare his soldiers an insulting quarantine. If this were so, it would have been easy for M. Cheuvreux and M. Edouard Bertin to obtain passages on a state vessel going to Civitavecchia. It seems, however, that even our troops are subject to the health regulations (a bad solution). The final consideration, then, is that a journey across the Apennines seems to me to be a risky venture at the end of October.

I meant to write to Mlle Louise since, just as a good government is very willing to raise a great many taxes but distributes them evenly, I feel the necessity to divide the weight of my lamentations; alas, my letter would not have been very pleasant! On my journey, I have been able to see only the side of things that is reprehensible and can be criticized. I am fully aware that colors are not in objects but in ourselves. According to whether we are in a rosy or black mood, we see everything in rosy or black hues.

Farewell, I cannot hold the pen any longer under the vibration of the steam engine.

Your devoted servant,
F. Bastiat

---

195. Letter to Mme Cheuvreux

Pisa, 2 October 1850   [*Lettres d'un habitant des Landes*, p. 120]

My dear Mme Cheuvreux,

Doubtless, we are both complaining about each other, you of the flood of letters with which I am overwhelming you and I who am desolate at not receiving any. However, I am not accusing you of not writing; it is not possible that you have let all this time go by without writing to me. I attribute my disappointment to some mismanagement by the Italian postal service. This explanation is all the more likely since I am also without news of my family and Paillottet.

I do not know whether you are continuing to plan your journey, what route you will be taking, etc. I have been to Leghorn to find out about the conditions at the quarantine station. The large apartments lack furniture, but as soon as I am sure of the date of your arrival, I will see that two rooms are prepared. A decent caterer will supply food and then, if you permit, I will put myself with pleasure into quarantine . . . "and Phaedra in the labyrinth." Poor man! I am forgetting that I cannot speak and that my company will be only a *nuisance*.

If only you knew, madam, how your enterprise worries me with regard to Mlle Louise. It is not that it offers the slightest danger; I even hope for fine weather in October, since the wind blows in September, but I fear that you will both be unwell. I entreat the influence of the heavens and the sea to be favorable!

At last, a moment of pleasure! I have read your letter of the 25th, which arrived accompanied by a missive from my aunt and another from Cobden. I wish you could see me; I am no longer the same person.

Is it really dignified for a man to be so *wholly* dependent on an external event, an accident of the post? Are there no extenuating circumstances for me? My life is just one long deprivation. Conversation, work, reading, plans for the future, all this I find lacking. Is it surprising that I am becoming attached, perhaps too much so, to those who are willing to take an interest in this ghost of an existence? Oh, their affection is more astonishing than mine. So you are leaving on the 10th? If this letter reaches you, please reply immediately.

You advise me to speak to you as I would to a court, to speak the truth, the whole truth, and nothing but the truth; I am very willing to do this but it is impossible to know whether I am better or worse. The progress of this illness, whether it moves forward or back, is so slow, so imperceptible that you see no difference between the day before or the day after. You have to take points of comparison that are further apart. For example, how was I a year ago at Le Butard? How was I there this year and how am I now? Here are three periods, and I have to admit that the results of this examination are not good.

The departure of your brother and his family will have left a great emptiness in La Jonchère. It needs only one lovely child like Marguerite to fill an entire house.

Farewell, dear Mme Cheuvreux.

Come, and come soon, to bring a little life to the Italy that seems dead to me. When you are all here, I will appreciate more its sun, climate, and arts. Until then, I will follow your advice and just take care of my body, make it an idol, dedicate a cult to it, and prostrate myself in adoration before it. If only I might recover speech when you arrive, for, madam, *dumbness* is painful in your presence! You have a collection of paradoxes in whose defense you are highly skilled, but to which it is a pleasure for me to reply.

Farewell; M. Cheuvreux will not be the least busy of the three. Please accept my great and respectful affection.

Your devoted servant,
F. Bastiat

---

196. Letter to Bernard Domenger

Pisa, 8 October 1850   [vol. 7, p. 408]

Who would have told us on the last occasion, when I had the pleasure of seeing you, that my first letter would be dated in Italy? I have come here strictly on doctor's orders. In fact, I have no doubt that if there is still time for my throat to be helped by anything, it will be by the pure, warm air of Pisa. Unfortunately, this is just one aspect of the question. The finest climate in the world cannot alter the fact that, when you cannot talk, write, read, or work, it is very sad to be alone in a foreign country. This makes me miss Mugron and I think that I would prefer to shiver in Chalosse than be warm in Tuscany. I am experiencing all sorts of disappointments here. For example, it would be easy for me to have contact with all the distinguished men in this country. This is because, as political economy is included in the study of law, this science is cultivated by almost all educated men. Do you want a singular proof of this? In Turin, although the principal language spoken is Italian, more copies of my *Harmonies* (in the French edition)[364] have been sold than in *Marseilles, Bordeaux, Lyons, Rouen,* and *Lille* combined, and this is true of all works on economics. You see, my dear friend, in what a state of illusion we live in France when we think we are in the vanguard of intellectual civilization. This being so, I was able to gain access to all the leading figures and eminent people and was perfectly placed to study this country in depth. Unfortunately, my constant preoccupation is to see nobody and to avoid people I know. What is more, close friends are going to come to see me from Paris; they will be visiting Florence and Rome as genuine connoisseurs, as they appreciate the arts and know a great deal about them. In any other

---

364. (Paillottet's note) Two months later, I encountered in Leghorn the counterfeit Belgian edition, which was selling well.

circumstances or with any other illness this would be such a pleasant event! But *dumbness* is an abyss that isolates you, and I will be obliged to flee them. Oh, I assure you that I am learning patience very well.

Let us talk of Mesdames X. I have always noticed that customary devotion does nothing to change the way men act and I very much doubt that there is more probity, gentleness, or mutual respect and consideration among our highly devout populations in the south than among the indifferent populations in the north. Young and amiable people will attend the bloody sacrifice of their Redeemer every day and will promise Him a great deal more than simple equity, and every evening they will deck altars to Our Lady with flowers. At every instant they will repeat: deliver us from evil, lead us not into temptation, thou shalt not take away or keep what belongs to another, etc., etc., and then when the opportunity occurs, they take as much as they can from their father's inheritance at the expense of their brothers, just as the sinners do. Why not? Are they not quits with an act of contrition and a firm purpose of amendment? They do good work; they give a half farthing to the poor and thus gain absolution. So what do they have to fear? What do they have to reproach themselves for, since they have succeeded in making accomplices of the ministry of God and God Himself?

I seem to think that Mme D—— had the notion of spending Holy Week in Rome. If she carried out this plan, I would perhaps make my devotions in her company; her presence and consequently yours would be very pleasant for me, at least if I succeeded in articulating a few words. Otherwise, considering only myself, I would rather you stayed where you are, since knowing that you were close to me and being reduced to avoiding you would be just one extra torture.

––––––––––

197. Letter to Prosper Paillottet

Pisa, 11 October 1850   [vol. 1, p. 205; vol. 7, p. 443]

I feel the desire to live, my dear Paillottet, when I read your account of your anxiety at the news of my death.[365] Thank heaven, I am not dead, not even more seriously ill. This morning, I saw a doctor who is going to try to rid me, at least for a few minutes, of this pain in my throat, whose constancy is so distressing. But in any case, if this news had been true, you would have had to accept it and be resigned to it. I would like all my friends to acquire

365. An Italian newspaper had announced Bastiat's death.

the philosophy I have myself acquired in this respect. I assure you that I will yield my last breath with no regret and almost with joy, if I could be sure to leave behind me, to those who love me, no searing regrets but a sweet, affectionate, and slightly melancholic memory. When I am no longer ill, this is what I will prepare them for. . . .

I do not know how long the current legislation on the press and obligatory signatures will last.[366] In the meantime, here is a good opportunity for our friends to make an honorable name for themselves in the press. I have noted with pleasure the articles by Garnier, well thought out and carefully written, and in which you see that he does not want to compromise the honor of the teaching profession. I urge him to continue. From all points of view, the situation is opportune. He can establish a fine position for himself by disseminating a doctrine in favor of which public sympathy is ready to be aroused. Tell him from me that, if the occasion arises, he should not allow either M. de Saint-Chamans or anyone else to identify my position with that of M. Benoist d'Azy with regard to tariffs. There are three essential differences between us:

1. First, although it is true that I am driven by the love of my region, this is not the same thing as being driven by the love of money.
2. Everything I have inherited and all my worldly assets are *protected* by our tariffs. Therefore, the more M. de Saint-Chamans deems me to be *self-seeking,* the more he has to consider me sincere when I state that protectionism is a plague.
3. But what totally precludes the protectionists' position in the Assembly from being identified with that of the free traders is the abyss that separates their demands. What M. Benoist d'Azy is asking of the law is that it should fleece me for his benefit. What I ask of the law is that it should be neutral between us and that it should guarantee my property in the same way as that of the blacksmith.

From what *La Patrie* appears to say, Molinari is responsible for a party that is livelier and more salient. For heaven's sake, let him not treat it lightly. How much good might he not do by showing how many leaflets there are

366. A law of 8 June 1850 increased the postage cost, reestablished the surety (see Letter 68, note 155), and made the journalist's signature compulsory for all articles of political, philosophical, or religious discussion.

that are unknowingly steeped in socialism! How could he have let pass the article in *Le National* on the book by Ledru-Rollin and these sentences?[367]

"In England, there are ten monopolies stacked one on top of the other; therefore it is free competition that is doing all the harm."

"England is enjoying a precarious prosperity only because it is based on injustice. For this reason, if England returns to the ways of justice, as Cobden is proposing, her economic decline is inevitable."

And it is for having made these great discoveries that the *National* has awarded Ledru-Rollin the title of *Great Statesman!*

Farewell, I am tired.

---

198. Letter to Mme Cheuvreux

   Pisa, 14 October 1850   [*Lettres d'un habitant des Landes,* p. 124]

My dear Mme Cheuvreux,

   At last! If nothing has upset your plans, if there has not been a coup d'état in Paris, if Mlle Louise has not been overcome by some cursed indisposition or M. Cheuvreux by a migraine, if he has settled his affairs with his court, if . . . if you have now taken the first step, the most difficult one, the one that costs the most, you will be on the railway en route for Tonnerre. Each evening, I will be able to say: "There are fifty leagues fewer between us." Oh, how happy our descendants will be to have electric telegraphs which will tell them: "Departure took place one minute ago." And now, madam, why are wishes based on friendship totally useless? If mine could be heard, your journey would be just a series of pleasant impressions; you would have beautiful sunshine as a constant companion, not to mention pleasant meetings all along your way. Mlle Louise would feel her strength increasing hourly and her gaiety and friendly interest in everything would not flag for a minute. This disposition would be caught by her father and mother, and this is how you would reach Marseilles. There, you would find a mirror-like sea, quarantine waived, etc. But all the wishes in the world will not prevent your having chosen a date for your departure that greatly increases the difficulties of your journey. This is somewhat due to my bad reputation. You are so convinced, having constantly repeated it, that I do not know my left from my right, your convictions in this respect are so deeply rooted, that I am taken to be totally

---

367. Bastiat is possibly referring to Ledru-Rollin's work *De la décadence de l'Angleterre,* which was reviewed in *Le Journal des économistes,* August 1850, by Coquelin.

incapable of properly executing the slightest maneuver, let alone of advising others. This is why you have not read a single word of what I have written on this subject. From what you say, it is as clear as daylight that you have leaped with both feet over all the passages in my letters where I set myself up as an adviser. However, it is pointless going over this again, since this advice, presuming you take account of it, will arrive too late.

Instead of a good French mail boat, will you not have a small Sardinian boat, loaded with goods, crowded with all kinds of passengers subject neither to control nor discipline, where the second-class passengers invade the first-class seats and come to smoke under the noses of women? No complaint can be made, least of all to the captain, since he sets the example of breaking all the rules. At least, this pilgrimage is beginning by the grace of God and it has to end under the same auspices.

Very dear madam, how can I end this letter without begging a pardon of which I am in great need? I have complained loudly of your silence; I was very ungrateful and very unjust, since I have received more letters, not than I wished but than I dared to hope for. The only thing was that the first was delayed and was a little laconic, and this was the cause of all this noise. Please be indulgent toward the complaints of patients: people with your goodness pity and excuse them but do not become annoyed by them.

Farewell, your devoted servant,

F. Bastiat

---

199. Letter to Richard Cobden

Pisa, 18 October 1850   [vol. 1, p. 192]

My dear Cobden, thank you for the interest you take in my health. I cannot say whether it is better or worse. Its progress is so imperceptible that I scarcely know the fate to which it is leading me. All that I ask of the heavens now is that the tubes that go from my mouth to my lungs and stomach do not become more painful. I have never given thought to the immense role they play in our lives. Drinking, eating, breathing, talking, all pass through them. If they do not work, we die; if they work badly it is very much worse.

The first sight of Italy, and in particular of Tuscany, has not had the same effect on me as it had on you.[368] This is not surprising; you arrived here in

---

368. Cobden journeyed to Italy in 1847.

triumph after having made the human race take one of its most remarkable steps forward. You were welcomed and feted by all the most enlightened and liberal men in the country who love the public good; you saw Tuscany from the summit. For my part, I have entered it from the opposite extreme; all my contacts up to now have been with boatmen, coachmen, waiters in inns, beggars, and *facchini*,[369] who constitute the most rapacious, tenacious, and abject race of men you could ever meet. I often tell myself that we should not be quick to judge and that very probably my interior disposition clouds my view of things. It is true that it is very difficult for a man who cannot speak and who can scarcely stand upright not to be very irritable, and therefore unjust. However, my friend, I do not think I am mistaken in saying this: when men disregard their dignity, when they acknowledge no other law than carelessness, and when they refuse to submit to any form of order or voluntary discipline, there is no hope. Here men are very well disposed to one another, and this disposition is taken to such lengths that it becomes a fault and an insuperable obstacle to any serious attempt to achieve independence and freedom. In the streets, in steamboats, on the railway, you will constantly see rules being flouted. People smoke where it is forbidden to do so, second-class passengers invade first class, and those that have not paid take the places of those who have. These are accepted events that do not annoy anyone, not even their victims. They seem to say: he has dared to do this, he was right and I would do as much in his place. As for officialdom and police constables and captains, how can they ensure that the rules are respected when they are always the first to break them?

Nevertheless, my dear Cobden, do not take these words for more than the tirade of a misanthropist. In the evening of the day before yesterday, boredom took me to Florence. I arrived at three o'clock in the afternoon. As I had no other luggage than an overnight bag, no one wanted to allow me into his hotel. I was overcome with tiredness and could not explain my situation since my voice had gone. Finally, in a more hospitable inn, I was given a cold, dark room in the attic. For this reason, yesterday I was in a hurry to leave this city of *flowers,* which for me had been just a city of *worries.* However, I did have the pleasure of meeting the marquis de Ridolfi. We talked a great deal about you. Later, if my *vocal cords* recover some of their sound, I will return to reconcile myself with the city of the Medici.

369. "Porters."

200. Letter to Horace Say

Pisa, 20 October 1850 [vol. 1, p. 201]

My dear friend, we wrote to each other at almost the same time on the day of the monthly dinner, which made our letters cross between Paris and Pisa. Since then, I have noticed no change, either for better or for worse, in my illness. Only, the feeling of pain is wearing because of its constancy. Weakness, isolation, and boredom I could overcome, if only it were not for this cursed tearing in the throat which makes all the numerous and essential functions that pass through it so painful. Oh, how much I would like to have one day of respite! But all the invocations on earth are powerless. From the strange dreams I have and the perspiration that always follows sleep, I can see that I have a slight fever every night. However, since I do not cough any more than before, I think that this fever is rather an effect of my continuous state of indisposition than a symptom of a constitutional illness.

... I believe in fact that political economy is more widely known here than in France because it is included in the law. It is a great thing to give a gloss of this science to the men who are more or less closely concerned with the execution of the laws, since these men contribute greatly to their drafting and in addition they form the basis of what is known as the enlightened class. I have no hope of seeing political economy taking root in the school of law in France. In this connection, the blindness of governments is incomprehensible. They do not want us to teach the only approach to economic science that guarantees them durability and stability. Is it not typical that the minister of trade and the minister of education, by passing me from one to the other like a ball, have effectively refused me a location in which to give lectures free of charge?

Since you are our *cappoletto,* our leader, you ought to indoctrinate our friends Garnier and Molinari in order that they take advantage of this unique occasion of the signature[370] which, whatever people say, is giving dignity to the newspaper. It is up to them, I believe, to give *La Patrie* something it has never had, which is color and *character.* They will have to act with great prudence and circumspection, since the paper is not an *économiste* publication either with respect to its director, its shareholders, or its subscribers. Its cachet should become apparent only gradually. I believe that our friends should not act as though they were in an overtly *économiste* journal and one

---

370. Signatures of Garnier and Molinari, who started to write articles in *La Patrie.*

which displayed the flag. This would be to cross swords with our opponents. But in *La Patrie* the tactic should not be the same. First of all, questions of free trade should be discussed only now and then, in particular the most controversial (such as the laws on navigation). It would be better to deal with the question on a higher plane, one that embraces politics, political economy, and socialism at the same time, that is to say, *state intervention.* In my view, they should also not put forward *nonintervention* as a theory or set of principles. All they should do is draw the attention of the reader to it each time the opportunity arises. In order not to generate mistrust, their role is to show for each individual case the *advantages* and *disadvantages* of intervention. Why should we hide the advantages? There have to be some if this intervention is so popular. They will therefore have to admit that, when there is *good to be done* or an evil to be *combated,* a call for government enforcement appears at first to be the shortest, most economic and effective means. In this very respect, in their place, I would show myself to be very broad-minded and conciliatory to government supporters, since they are very numerous and it is less a question of refuting them than winning them over. But after having acknowledged the immediate advantages, I would draw their attention to later disadvantages. I would say: This is how new functions, new civil servants, new taxes, new sources of discontent, and new financial problems are created. Then, by substituting government enforcement for private activity, are we not removing the intrinsic value of individuality and the means of acquiring it? Are we not making all citizens into men who do not know how to act individually, take a decision, and repulse unexpected events and surprise attacks? Are we not preparing elements of society for socialism, which is nothing other than one man's thought taking the place of everyone else's will?

If the various special questions that may arise are discussed from this point of view with impartiality, with the arguments *for* and *against* being correctly made, I believe that the public would take a greater interest in them and would soon recognize the true cause of our misfortunes. M. Dumas' circulars provide a good text to start with.

Farewell, my dear friend, would you believe that I am tired from having scribbled these few lines? However, I still have the strength to ask you to remember me to Mme Say and Léon.

201. Letter to the Count Arrivabene

Pisa, 28 October 1850   [vol. 7, p. 419]

I was profoundly touched, my dear sir, by the quite unforced and tact-
ful interest you have shown me in sending me a letter of introduction to
Mme Primi. You accurately guessed what suits my position and, above all,
my character and I must admit that not only Tuscany but paradise as well
would have less attraction for me if I did not meet a friendly soul there. You
can therefore imagine with what enthusiasm I would have met Mme Primi.
Unfortunately, she is away on holiday and I very much fear that I will have
no further opportunity to pay her my respects as I am planning to move
my quarters to Rome for the coming winter. It is exactly the need for a few
friends that has persuaded me to do this. In Rome, I will meet one of my
relatives, an excellent priest, and M. Say's brother-in-law with his family.[371]
Not being able to frequent society and, what is much worse, not being able
to work, I would be faced with enforced isolation and idleness, unbearable
without a few friends willing to bear with me and my miseries.

All that you tell me about Mme Primi and her sister makes me very much
regret missing this opportunity of making their acquaintance. If I am better
in the spring, I will probably be going through Tuscany again on my return
to France, since you can scarcely avoid examining a region that has such
interesting institutions and history when you have undergone so much to
come here. In this case, I will compensate for the disappointment that my
sudden departure has given me today.

I remember that at our last meeting in Paris, you spoke to me of M.
Gioberti. I have been to see him and am in debt to him for some excellent
recommendations for which my gratitude extends to you.

> Farewell, my dear sir;
> your devoted servant,

371. Eugène de Monclar; Cheuvreux family.

202. Letter to Mme Cheuvreux

    Pisa, 29 October 1850   [*Lettres d'un habitant des Landes*, p. 127]

Dear Mme Cheuvreux,

How difficult your journey from Florence to Rome must have been![372] In spite of that philosophical strength with which you encounter setbacks, in spite of the good humor that each one of you will have brought to the company, it is not possible for you not to have suffered from such terrible weather, traveling on potholed roads and in a region with no resources. My imagination scarcely dares follow you in this odyssey; all M. Sturler's forecasts rise up before it. However, how I bless the happy inspiration that made you take the sea route in Marseilles on the 19th! Two days later, the crossing became dangerous as the Mediterranean became rough enough to disrupt all the services, and when the boat that followed you arrived in Genoa, it was not able to reach Leghorn. It abandoned the journey at La Spezzia, where it put its passengers ashore. You escaped these perils, thank heaven, and this idea comforts me a little in the face of your current deprivations which, fortunately, will end this evening. The sight of the Eternal City makes you forget everything. I am counting on arriving in this Eternal City on Saturday, 2 November. I will leave Leghorn by the state mail boat (*tempo permettendo*) and you will understand why I will not be stopping in Civitavecchia.

Dear madam, let us not talk about my health; this is a sonata which I will have ample time to deafen you with in Rome. When I think that you have come to provide your husband and especially your daughter with pleasures and amusements, I have some remorse in leaping into your midst like some killjoy, since I am fully aware that for a long time I have been turning to Victor Hugo and his "Last Days of a Condemned Man," which is not much fun for my friends. I still find Victor Hugo's hero very fortunate, since he could at least think and speak; he was in the same situation as Socrates, so why did he not have the same attitude to things?

This small book that I asked you for shows us this Athenian philosopher, condemned to death, speaking about his soul and future. Socrates, however, was a pagan and reduced to creating for himself uncertain hopes through a process of reason. A condemned man who is a Christian does not have to

---

372. After having spent two days with him in Pisa, Bastiat's friends went to Rome to wait for him.

go down this road. Revelation spares him this, and his point of departure is precisely this hope, become a certainty, which was a conclusion for Socrates. This is why Victor Hugo's condemned man is just a coward. Is it not better to have in front of one a single month of strength and health, one month of vigor in body and soul with hemlock at the end, rather than one or two years of decline, increasing weakness and distaste, during which every link breaks and nature no longer appears to do other than detach one from earthly existence? In fact, however, it is for God to ordain and for us to be resigned.

I really think that I am a little better; I have been able to spend quite long sessions with M. Mure and in addition I have received a great many visits.

Paillottet has written to me. He is always the same person, good, obliging, devoted, and, what is more, unaffected, which is rather rare in Paris. My family has also given me news of itself.

Farewell, dear Mme Cheuvreux, till Saturday or Sunday. In the meantime, please assure M. Cheuvreux and your daughter of my wholehearted friendship, not forgetting the captain, and please express my compliments and respects to M. Edouard and Mme Bertin.

F. Bastiat

---

203. Letter to Félix Coudroy

Rome, 11 November 1850 [vol. 1, p. 104]

If I put off writing to you from day to day, my dear Félix, it is because I always think that in a little while I will have the strength to indulge in a long chat. Instead of this, I am obliged to make my letters ever shorter, either because my weakness is increasing or because I am losing the habit of writing. Here I am in the Eternal City, my friend, unfortunately very little disposed to visit its marvels. I am infinitely better than in Pisa, surrounded by excellent friends who wrap me in the most affectionate solicitude. What is more, I have met Eugene again and he comes to spend part of the day with me. So, if I go out, I can always give my walks an interesting aim. I would ask for one thing only, and that is to be relieved of this piercing pain in the larynx; this constant suffering distresses me. Meals are genuine torture for me. Speaking, drinking, eating, swallowing saliva, and coughing are all painful operations. A stroll on foot tires me and an outing in a carriage irritates my throat; I cannot work nor even read seriously. You see the state to which I am reduced. Truly, I will soon be just a corpse that has retained the faculty of suffering. I hope that the treatment that I have decided to undergo, the remedies I am given, and the gentleness of the climate will improve my deplorable situation soon.

My friend, I will speak only vaguely about one of the subjects you have discussed with me. I had already thought about this, and among my papers there should be some outlines of articles in the form of letters addressed to you. If my health returns and I am able to write the second volume of the *Harmonies,* I will dedicate it to you. If not, I will insert a short dedication in the second edition of the first volume. In the second of these cases, which will imply the end of my career, I will be able to set out my plan to you and bequeath to you the mission of completing it.

Here we have trouble getting papers. I have come across an old one, from the time when people were enthusiastic about improving the lot of the working classes. The future of workers, the condition of workers, and the eternal virtues of workers formed the text of all the books, pamphlets, reviews, or journals. And to think that these are the *same writers* who shower the people with insults, committed as they are to one of the three dynasties that are fighting over our poor France, and who are wholly responsible for this bad situation. Can you think of anything more dismal?

Thank you for having sent some biographical information to M. Paillottet. My life is of no interest to the general public, except for the circumstances that drew me out of Mugron. If I had known that people were interested in this account, I would have related this interesting fact.

Farewell, my dear Félix; unless I am completely unable to travel or *completely cured,* I am counting on spending the month of April in Mugron, since I have been forbidden to return to Paris before May. I groan at not being able to fulfill my duties as a representative, but it is unfortunately clear that it is not my fault. In Italy as well as in Spain, we often see how little influence external devotion has on morals.

Please remember me to all our friends and give news of me to my aunt. Please assure your sister of my friendship.

204. Letter to Prosper Paillottet

Rome, 26 November 1850   [vol. 1, p. 206]

My dear Paillottet, each time I receive a letter from Paris, it seems to me that my correspondents are *Toinettes* and that I am *Argan:*[373]

The cheeky girl has claimed for an entire hour that I was not ill! You know, my love, what is really the case.

All of you are taking a friendly interest in my illness, but you then treat me as a healthy man. You plan things for me to do, you ask my opinion on various serious subjects, and then you tell me just to write you a few lines. I would have liked you to have included the secret of saying everything in a few words, along with your advice, in your letter. How can I discuss the *parliamentary conflicts of interest* with you, the corrections to be made to it, and the reasons that make me think that this subject cannot be combined, either in substance or form, with the speech on the tax on wines and spirits—all of this in a single line? And then I have to say something about Carey, since you are sending me his proofs here in Tuscany—and the *Harmonies,* since you tell me that the current edition is out of print.[374]

In your fine letter, which I received today, you express the fear that, at the sight of Rome, I will be overcome with enthusiasm and that this will undermine my healing by shattering my nerves. In this, you are still assuming that I am a healthy man. You should understand, my friend, that there are two reasons, which are just as strong as each other, that Rome's monuments do not trigger an outburst of dangerous enthusiasm in me. The first is that I do not see any of these monuments, since I am more or less confined to my room, surrounded by ashes and coffeepots; the second is that the source of enthusiasm has completely dried up in me, since all the strength of my concentration and imagination are centered on the means of swallowing a little food or drink and getting a little sleep between two coughing fits.

In spite of my writing to Florence, I have no news of Carey's proofs.[375] God alone knows when they will arrive.

---

373. *Toinettes* and *Argan,* characters from Molière's play *Le Malade imaginaire.*
374. Carey's book, *The Harmony of Interests, Agricultural, Manufacturing, and Commercial,* was sent to Bastiat as proofs in November 1850, before it appeared in print.
375. Ibid.

Farewell; I will end abruptly. I would have a thousand things to say to you for M. and Mme Planat, M. de Fontenay, and M. Manin. Shortly, when I am better, I will chat longer with you. Now, it is all I can do to reach this page.

---

205. Letter to Mr. Domenger

Rome, 28 November 1850[376]   [vol. 7, p. 410]

I am very happy to have come to Rome where I have found a degree of medical treatment as well as some medicines; I do not know how I would have got on in Pisa. My throat has become so painful that just eating and drinking has become a major operation. Special preparations have to be made for me, and for this my friends have been very useful to me. I cannot say whether I am better. I do not notice any change from one day to the other, but if I compare myself on a month to month basis, I cannot avoid noticing a definite gradual weakening. May I have the strength in February, my dear D., to return to Mugron! However much the virtues of the climate are praised, they cannot replace home. Besides, I envisage two outcomes for my illness, a cure or the final conclusion. If I have to die, I would like to be laid to rest in the common resting place in which my friends and parents lie. I would like our circle of friends to accompany me to this final resting place and our excellent parish priest in Mugron to say for me this sublime request: *"Lux perpetua luceat ei!"*[377] etc., etc. Also, if I can, I intend to take advantage of the fine days of February to go to Marseilles, where Justin can come to fetch me.

If ever I return home, it will be a very sharp disappointment to have spent several months in Rome and not seen anything. I have visited Saint Peter's only, because its temperature never changes. I limit myself to taking the sun every day on Mount Pincio, where I cannot stay very long because there are no benches. I will therefore have seen Rome only as the crow flies. In spite of this, you always gain some information through reading, conversation, and

---

376. (Paillottet's note) Here the exact date is important because of the political assessments which follow, and Bastiat left the day blank. However, the address carries the clear Sardinia date stamp of 1 December, from which it follows that the letter was probably written and posted in Rome on 28 November.

377. "May perpetual light shine on him."

the atmosphere. What strikes me the most is the solidity of the Christian tradition and the abundance of irrefutable evidence of this.

My friend, the recent political outcome has given me much pleasure, since it gives some respite to our France. It seems to have justified totally my line of conduct. At the first elections, I promised to give an honest Republic a loyal trial, and I am sure that this was the general wish. For one reason or another, priests, nobles, and plebeians were in agreement on this although with different expectations. The Legitimists and Orleanists disappeared completely as such. But what happened? As soon as they were able, they began to belittle, cheat, calumniate, and embarrass the Republic in favor of Legitimism, Orleanism, or Bonapartism. All of this has failed, and now they are doing what they promised to do, which is what I have done and from which they diverged for two years. They have caused commotion in France for no good reason.

I was very mistaken, I admit, to talk to you as I did about Mesdames X——. I was under the influence of the idea that devotion, when it takes charge of detailed practices, overlooks genuine morals, and I had striking examples of this in view. But it is certain that this was nothing to do with these ladies.

---

206. Letter to Prosper Paillottet

Rome, 8 December 1850 [vol. 1, p. 207]

Dear Paillottet, Am I better? I cannot say; I feel constantly weaker. My friends think that my strength is returning. Who is right?

The Cheuvreux family is leaving Rome immediately because of Mme Girard's illness. You can imagine my sorrow. I like to think that it is above all because of the sorrow of such very good friends, but certainly more selfish motives have the upper hand.

Quite providentially, yesterday I wrote to my family asking them to send me a sort of Michel-Morin, a man full of gaiety and also resourceful, a coachman, cook, etc., etc., who has often served me and who is totally devoted to me. As soon as he arrives, I will be free to leave whenever I like for France. For you have to know that the doctor and my friends have taken a solemn decision on this matter. They consider that the nature of my illness has created so many problems that all the advantages of the climate do not outweigh the care provided at home. Given these opinions, my dear Paillottet, you will not be coming to Rome to carry out works of mercy for me. The affection you have shown me is such that you will be annoyed by this, I am sure. But console yourself with the thought that, because of the nature of my illness, you would have been able to do very little for me other than coming to keep me company for two hours a day, something that is more pleasant than reasonable. I would have liked to be able to give you some explanation of this. But heavens above! To explain would require a great deal of writing and I cannot do this. My friend, in a multitude of ways I am undergoing the torture of Tantalus. Here is a new example: I would like to express my thoughts to you in detail and I have not the strength. . . .

What you and Guillaumin will have done for the conflicts of interest[378] will be well done.

As for the Carey matter,[379] I must admit that it seems a little odd to me. On the one hand, Garnier has announced that the journal has taken the side of *property and monopoly*. On the other, Guillaumin tells me that M. Clément is going to take part in the conflict. If *Le Journal des économistes* wants to punish me for having treated a question in economic science independently, it is not very generous of it to choose a time when I am on my sickbed, unable to read, write, or think and seeking to retain at least the ability to eat, drink, and sleep which is escaping me.

As I feel that I cannot take up the conflict, I have added to my reply to Carey a few considerations addressed to *Le Journal des économistes*. Let me know how they have been received.

Will Fontenay then never be ready to enter the arena? He must understand how much I would need his assistance. Garnier says, "We have the support of Smith, Ricardo, Malthus, J. B. Say, Rossi, and all the economists *except for Carey and Bastiat*." I very much hope that belief in the legitimacy

---

378. See Letter 204, note 374

379. In a letter sent on 31 August 1850 to *Le Journal des économistes*, Carey criticized Bastiat's use of the word *harmony* in the title of his book and accused Bastiat of having been influenced by his own works on harmonies of interests without acknowledging it. This event prompted a storm of debate in the journal and in the Société d'économie politique during the first half of 1851. Numerous articles appeared in *Le Journal des économistes* in the 28 (January–April) and 29 (May–August) issues.

Bastiat replied indirectly in a letter to the journal written on 8 December 1850 and published after his death, on 15 January 1851 (see Letter 209). The controversy continued after Bastiat's death. In June 1851, in *Le Journal des économistes,* Paillottet quoted some writings of Bastiat dating back to 1834, which showed the originality of Bastiat's ideas. An exchange of letters between Paillottet and Carey put an end to the debate, and Carey acknowledged Bastiat's honesty (13 January 1852).

of landed property will soon find other defenders and I am especially counting on Fontenay.

Please write to Michel Chevalier to tell him how grateful I am for his excellent article on my book. His only fault is to be too benevolent and to leave too little room for criticism. Tell Chevalier that I am waiting only for a little strength to return to convey to him myself my deep gratitude. I sincerely hope that he will inherit M. Droz's[380] chair; this would be no more than belated justice.

---

207. Letter to Mme Cheuvreux
Rome, 14, 15, and 16 December 1850 [*Lettres d'un habitant des Landes,* p. 132]

Very dear Mme Cheuvreux,

I hope to sit on occasion at this desk, adding one line to another to send you a souvenir.

I have never been so close to nothingness and I would like to be all-powerful in order to make the sea as calm as a lake.

What emotions and duties await you in Paris! My only consolation is for you to tell me that you are ready, with courageous energy, to go down the road that God will have prepared for you, however painful it is.

My health remains the same. If I started to speak about it, it would be through a series of small details only, which would not be of any importance the following day.

Basically, I think Doctor Lacauchy is right not to listen to a word I say.

I am very pleased to think that M. Cheuvreux will shortly be seeing our excellent, all too excellent friend, Paillottet, and will persuade him to abandon an act of devotion that is now totally unnecessary. I very much fear that his presence in Paris will be absolutely essential for me if the *Harmonies* are reprinted. I cannot be involved with this and everything will be on his shoulders.[381]

---

380. Droz was appointed to the Académie française in 1813 and to the Académie des sciences morales et politiques in 1833. His death on 9 November 1850 would have left the vacancy to which Bastiat is probably referring.

381. A shortened version of *Economic Harmonies* with ten chapters had been printed in Bastiat's lifetime. Bastiat was working on additional chapters when he died. Paillottet found these unfinished chapters in Bastiat's papers and edited them for a new, larger edition of the book.

Sunday, 15 December

Here you are in Genoa and with just a little more patience you will be in France. It is five o'clock, the time you used to come to see me. Then I knew what gallery Mlle Louise had visited, what ruin or painting had interested her. This was a ray of sunshine in my life. Everything is ended, I am alone for twenty-four hours a day, except for the two visits from my cousin, de Monclar. The time to which I am referring has become bitter because it used to be too sweet; you proved to me with the scientific approach of your father that I was right to be the most grumpy, stupid, irritable, and often the most unjust of men. Besides, I think that I am learning resignation and am acquiring a certain taste for it.

Monday, 16 December

When Joseph came to say goodbye, the poor man dissolved into thanks. Alas! No one owes me any thanks and I owe them to everyone, especially to Joseph, who has been such a help to me.

A new discovery! A sudden movement removed all breath from me. With one breath being unable to join another, the pain was unbearable. I have concluded that I will have to make all movements slowly like an automaton.

Tuesday, 17 December[382]

Paillottet has arrived. He has announced the dreadful news to me.[383] Oh! You poor woman, poor child! You have received the most terrible and unexpected blow of all. How can you have borne it with a soul so little made for suffering? Louise will be able to control her sorrow better. Throw yourself into the arms of this divine strength, the only strength that can sustain you in such times of trial. May this strength never desert you. Dear friends, I do not have the fortitude to continue these disconnected words and fractured thoughts.

Farewell; in spite of my state of prostration, I still find bright sparks of sympathy for the misfortune that has come upon you.

Farewell, your friend,
Frédéric Bastiat

382. This letter, the last he wrote, preceded his death by just eight days.
383. The death of Mme Cheuvreux's mother.

208. Letter from Prosper Paillottet to Mme Cheuvreux[384]

Rome, 22 December 1850   [*Lettres d'un habitant des Landes*, p. 135]

Madam,

I am settling a personal debt and carrying out the wishes of our friend in giving you news of him. You had few illusions when you left him, and yet you could not have imagined that his strength would have declined so rapidly. This decline is very noticeable since my arrival here. The poor invalid is aware of it and is pleased within himself, as though it were a favor from heaven to shorten his suffering.

At first he protested in word and gesture at what he called my folly. M. de Monclar and I had difficulty persuading him that this was the right thing to do. However, I soon realized that my presence was a consolation and I am infinitely grateful to you, madam, for having made it possible to give him this. "Since you have made this long journey, I am very glad that you are here," he said to me on the third day. Besides, he never fails to ask me when I leave: "At what time will I see you tomorrow?"

This is how M. de Monclar, whose agreement I naturally sought, and I have divided his days. M. de Monclar visits him in the morning and leaves when I arrive, at half past eleven. I keep him company up to five o'clock in the afternoon, and after supper M. de Monclar returns.

It is an extremely painful spectacle that I am witnessing, but I would be very sorry, both through affection and duty, if I were not there. Death is almost always the third person present in our talks. Both he and I refrain from mentioning his name; he in order not to upset me and I in order not to give him the example of breaking down and weeping when he is such an example of courage. He is dying in fact just as I have always thought he ought to die, staring death in the face with total resignation.

The subjects we discuss are absent friends, among whom you and yours have the pride of place, followed by his beloved science, political economy, for which he has done so much and for which he would have wanted to do still more. I have no need to tell you that these discussions are very short and that I put my ear close to his lips from time to time. The few sentences he pronounces are received by me with a religious respect.

Yesterday, we went on an outing that enchanted him. Leaving by the *Po-*

---

384. Although this letter is not by Bastiat, it is included because it is an essential piece for an understanding of his last days.

polo gate, we went to the *ponte Molle* and returned through the Angelica gate. The sites we saw were bathed in fine sunshine. He repeatedly said to me, "What a delightful outing! How successful we have been!" The serenity of the sky had entered his soul. He was expressing a final farewell to the splendors of nature, which had so often aroused his enthusiasm.

Since the 20th, he has made his confession. "I want," he told me, "to die in the religion of my forefathers. I have always loved it, even though I have not followed its external practices."

I am limiting myself to these few details and perhaps I should even apologize for sending them to you, when you are in the throes of the most legitimate affliction caused by the most cruel of losses.

I missed meeting you in Leghorn by a whisker, since it appears that we were there on the same day, as I later found out. Anyway, I was glad that this encounter did not take place, since you still had a shred of hope, which I would have found it difficult to remove from you.

Please convey, madam, my affectionate sentiments to M. Cheuvreux and I assure you and Mlle Louise of my homage and respectful devotion.

P. Paillottet

------

209. Letter to *Le Journal des économistes*[385]

[Undated] [vol. 1, p. 209]

My book is in the hands of the general public. I do not fear that it will encounter a single person who, after reading it, will say, "This is the work of a plagiarist." A slow assimilation, the fruit of lifelong meditation, is only too evident, especially if it is compared with my other writings.

But whoever mentions *assimilation* admits that he has not drawn all his material from his own resources.

Oh, yes! I owe a great deal to Mr. Carey; I owe something to Smith, J. B. Say, Comte, and Dunoyer; and I owe something to my opponents and something to the air I have breathed. I owe something to the intimate discussions I have had with a close friend, M. Félix Coudroy, with whom for twenty years I have investigated all these questions in solitude, without there appearing the slightest disagreement in our assessments and ideas, something

------

385. (Paillottet's note) After the death of Bastiat, it was easy for his friends to inform Mr. Carey of his total loyalty. However, we consider that this letter is worthy of preservation, especially since the postscript contains the elements of a major exposition.

that is very rare in the history of the human mind and very propitious to the enjoyment of the delights of certainty.

This means that I do not claim the title of *inventor* with regard to harmony. I even believe that it is the mark of a small mind, one that is incapable of linking the present to the past, to imagine that it invents principles. Sciences and academic disciplines *grow* like plants; they spread, grow, and become refined. But what successor owes nothing to those that went before him?

In particular, the "harmony of interests" could not be the invention of one person only. Is it not the presentiment and aspiration of the human race, the aim of its eternal evolution? How can a political writer dare to claim for himself the invention of an idea that is the instinctive belief of all men?

This harmony has been proclaimed by economic science from the outset. This is proved by the very title of the physiocrats' books. Doubtless, scholars have often demonstrated this badly, they have allowed a great many errors to creep into their works which, for the very reason that they were errors, contradicted their beliefs. What does that prove? That scholars make mistakes. However, by dint of much trial and error, the core idea of the harmony of interests has always shone over the economist school, like its pole star. The only proof I want of this is the motto it has been criticized for: *laissez-faire, laissez-passer.*[386] It certainly implies a belief that interests achieve justice among themselves, under freedom's dispensation.

That having been said, I do not hesitate to give justice to Mr. Carey. I have known his works for a short time only; I have read them very superficially because of my occupations, my illness, and especially because of the singular divergence that, both in fact and in method, characterizes the English and French minds. We make generalizations, which our neighbors disdain. They go into detail in thousands and thousands of pages, which our attention cannot cope with. Be that as it may, I acknowledge that we owe this great and consoling cause, *the conformity between the interests of the various classes,* to no one more than to Mr. Carey. He has pointed it out and proved it from a great many and varied angles in such a way that there can be no further doubt of the general law.

---

386. Bastiat wrote a short article titled "Laissez-faire" for the first issue of the short-lived journal *Jacques Bonhomme* in June 1848 (see "Laissez-faire," p. 434. Joseph Garnier discusses the origin of the expression in the work of the physiocrats Gournay and Turgot (see "Laisser-faire, laissez-passer," in *Dictionnaire de l'économie politique*).

Mr. Carey complains that I have not acknowledged him. This is perhaps a mistake on my part, but it is not intentional. Mr. Carey has been able to show me new views and supply me with arguments but he has not revealed any principle to me. I could not quote him in my chapter on *trade,* which is at the root of all, nor in those on *value, the progressive society,* or *competition.* The time to base myself on his authority would have been in connection with *landed property,* but in this first volume I treated the question through my own theory of *value,* which is not that of Mr. Carey. At this time, I was planning to write a special chapter on *rent from land,* and I firmly believed that my second volume would follow the first closely. It was in this that I would have quoted Mr. Carey, and not only would I have quoted him, but I would have given way to him to allow him the leading role on the stage; this was in the interest of the cause. In fact, on the question of land, Mr. Carey cannot fail to be a major authority. To study the primitive and natural development of property, all he has to do is open his eyes. To set it out, he has only to describe what he sees, more fortunate in this than Ricardo, Malthus, Say, and all of us European economists, who can see only a landed property that is subject to the thousand artificial combinations of conquest. In Europe, to go back to the principle of landed property you have to use the difficult process used by Cuvier to reconstruct a mastodon. It is not very surprising that most of our writers made mistakes in this attempt at analogy. In America, every career reveals its genuine mastodons; one has only to open one's eyes. Therefore, I had everything to gain, or rather the cause had everything to gain, from my quoting the evidence of an American economist.

Finally, I cannot prevent myself from observing to Mr. Carey that a Frenchman can scarcely do him justice without a great effort at impartiality, and, as I am French, I was far from expecting him to deign to concern himself with me and my book. Mr. Carey professes the deepest scorn for France and the French and a hatred that borders on frenzy. He has expressed these sentiments in a good third of his voluminous writings and has taken the trouble to gather together, with no discernment it is true, a number of statistical documents to prove that we scarcely rank above the Hindus in the scale of humanity. To tell the truth, in his book Mr. Carey denies this hatred.[387] But in denying it, he proves it, for how can such a denial be explained? What provoked it? It is Mr. Carey's own conscience, when he himself was surprised

---

387. In an article of 15 May 1851, Carey claimed that it was not France as such he hated but rather war, and according to him, France was the great warrior nation of Europe.

by all the proofs of hatred toward France that are accumulated in his book, that impelled him to proclaim that he did not hate France. How many times have I not told M. Guillaumin, "There are excellent points in Mr. Carey's works and it would be a good thing to have them translated. They would contribute to advancing political economy in our country." However, I was obliged to add, "Can we cast before the French general public diatribes like this against France and do we not risk missing our aim? Will the public not reject the good that is in these books because of what is wounding and unjust?"

May I be allowed to end with a reflection on the word *plagiarism,* which I used at the start of this letter? The people from whom I may have borrowed a view or an argument think that I am greatly in their debt. I am convinced of the contrary. If I had not allowed myself to be drawn into any controversy, if I had not examined any theory, if I had not quoted anyone's name, if I had limited myself to establishing these two proposals: *Services are exchanged for other services; value is the relationship between services exchanged,* if I had then used these principles to explain all the highly complicated categories of human transactions, I believe that the monument I sought to raise would have gained a great deal (too much, perhaps, for the period) in clarity, grandeur, and simplicity.

P.S. I am leaving the subject of Mr. Carey and addressing, perhaps for the last time, with feelings of deep-seated goodwill, our colleagues on the editorial staff of *Le Journal des économistes.* In the note by this journal that provoked the complaint from Mr. Carey, the management announces that, with regard to landed property, it is siding with Ricardo's theory. The reason it gives is that this theory has the authority of Ricardo himself, as well as Malthus, Say, and all the economists, "except for MM Bastiat and Carey." The epigram is sharp and it is certain that the American economist and I are humbled in this antithesis.

Be that as it may, I reiterate that the journal's management has passed a decisive resolution for its scientific authority.

Do not forget that Ricardo's theory can be summed up thus: "Landed property is an unjust but necessary monopoly whose effect is to render the rich inevitably richer and the poor ever poorer."

The first disadvantage of this formula is that its very enunciation arouses an invincible distaste and conflicts in people's hearts, not with everything I would call generous and philanthropic, but with what more simply and bluntly I would see as honest. Its second mistake is that it is based on incomplete observation and consequently runs counter to logic.

This is not the place to demonstrate the legitimacy of rent from land, but since I have to provide a useful aim for this text, in a few words I will set out how I understand it and how my opponents err.

You have certainly known traders in Paris whose profits increase annually without anyone being able to conclude that they are overcharging for their goods each year. They are far from doing this, and there is nothing more commonplace and more true than this proverb: *Compensate through quantity*. It is even a general law governing the flow of trade, that the greater it becomes, the greater the discount that the trader gives his customers, while at the same time making more profit. To persuade you of this, you have only to compare what a hatter in Paris and one in a village earn per hat. This is a well-known example of a case in which, when public prosperity grows, the sellers become ever richer and so does the buyer.

Now, what I say is that it is not only the general law of profit, but also the general law of *capital* and *interest,* as I have proved to M. Proudhon, and the general law of *land rents,* as I would prove if I were not exhausted.

Yes, when France prospers, there is a consequent general rise in land rents and "the rich become ever more rich." To this extent Ricardo is right. But it does not follow that each agricultural product is increased in price at the expense of the workers. It does not follow that each worker is reduced to giving a greater proportion of his work to acquire a hectoliter of wheat. In a word, it does not follow that "the poor become ever poorer." It is exactly the opposite that is true. As rent increases, through the *natural effect of public prosperity* it becomes *less and less* of a burden on products that are more abundant, exactly like the hatter who favors his customers all the more when he is in a milieu in which there is a greater demand.

Believe me, my dear colleagues, let us not incite *Le Journal des économistes* to reject these explanations lightly.

Lastly, the third and perhaps the greatest mistake, in terms of economic science, of the Ricardo theory is that it is belied by all the individual and general events that occur around the globe. According to this theory, for a century we should have seen industrial and commercial movable assets drawn into rapid and fatal decline compared with landed fortunes. We ought to have witnessed the onset in our towns of barbarous behavior, of darkness and filth, and of difficulties in the means of transport. What is more, with merchants, artisans, and workers reduced to giving an ever-increasing proportion of their work to obtain a given quantity of wheat, we ought to be seeing wheat used less or at least no one being able to allow himself the same level of consumption of bread without curtailing other things he enjoys. I ask you, my dear colleagues, does the civilized world show any evidence of such a situation?

And then, with what purpose would you endow the journal? Would it say to landowners: "You are rich because you are enjoying an unjust but *necessary* monopoly, and, since it is necessary, enjoy it without scruple, especially since it ensures you ever-increasing riches"? Then turning to workers of all classes, would you say: "You are poor; your children will be poorer than you and your grandchildren even more so, until you die of starvation. This is because you are subject to an unjust but necessary monopoly, and since it is necessary, resign yourselves wisely and let the ever-increasing riches of the rich console you"?

I certainly do not ask for my ideas to be adopted without examination, but I believe that *Le Journal des économistes* would do better to subject the matter to study rather than issue an opinion right now. Oh, let us not readily believe that Ricardo, Say, Malthus, and Rossi, such eminent and well-founded minds, are mistaken. But let us not, either, lightly admit a theory that leads to such monstrosities.[388]

388. The text of this letter up to the postscript was published as "Note de M. Bastiat," in *Le Journal des économistes* 28 (January–April 1851): 50–52. The "Note" was preceded by Carey's letter and followed by a reply by Ambrose Clément. The postscript, however, appeared only in the *Œuvres complètes*.

Part 2

Articles and Addresses

1. Two Articles on the Basque Language

[Articles published in *La Chalosse,* 1 and 8 April 1838.
From the private collection of Jean-Claude Paul-Dejean.]

ON THE BASQUE LANGUAGE[1]

A journal is addressed to all classes of readers, and because of this it should cover only subjects that are of interest to the majority. I therefore have some natural hesitation in sending you an article devoted to a grammatical dissertation that is as dull in its narrow limits as it is by nature; I hoped that the frequent contacts between the people of the Chalosse and the Basque people would provide me with a good excuse for this.

On our western boundary, there is a nation that is proud, gracious, and intrepid and whose origins are unknown. What distinguishes it above all is a language that in all its structures bears the stamp of extreme antiquity, a language that is so philosophical and rational that it appears to have arisen in perfect form from the brain of an expert grammarian, a language that shows no signs of the irregularities and successive modifications that are the effect and living proof of the mixing of races.

When I say that the Basque language has retained its primitive purity, I am talking only about its grammatical forms. Religion and civilization have enlarged its vocabulary, but its grammar has remained unchanged.

---

1. This article is the only one in Bastiat's writings treating such a subject. It reflects the immense culture and curiosity of a man who had studied some Latin and Greek and was fluent in English, Spanish, and Italian. It is believed that, as a child in Bayonne, he had a chance to practice Basque, the local language spoken at home by some of his school friends.

I therefore dare to hope that a few of my fellow citizens will take some interest in this essay on the structures of the Basque language. Although it is very short, it will be enough, I think, to establish its antiquity. This having been said, I will leave to those with reflective minds to explain how it happens that antiquity and perfection go hand in hand where language is concerned whereas it is totally the other way round where other human inventions are concerned.

Today, I will deal with declensions and conjugations in Basque. If this article is not too unsuitable for your journal, I will devote another to the roots and etymology of this language.

Basque has no genders. In effect there is nothing rational in the classification of nouns into masculine, feminine, and neuter genders; apart from the fact that it is not useful in principle, it is always arbitrary in its application. Words *name* things and do not *classify* them.

On the other hand, Basque distinguishes between a noun used generally and one used with a specific meaning. An article removes from the noun its indefinite meaning: *seme,* son; *semec,* the son. Old French had something similar; by the removal of the article, as in this sentence: "poverty is not vice," words were given a very wide-ranging meaning.

Beings have relationships between each other of dependence, generation, situation, etc. These relationships are expressed in French by the prepositions *de, à, pour,* etc., in Latin sometimes by cases and sometimes by the prepositions *in, ad, cum,* etc.; in Basque they are always expressed by cases. For example,

Mendia	the mountain
Mendiac	the mountain, as the subject of an active verb
Mendiaz	of, that is to say, by means of
Mendian	in
Mendiari	to
Mendiaren	of (as in the genitive)
Mendiarekin	with
Mendico	for
Mendetic	from (out of)
Menderat	toward, etc.

You would be very wrong to think that this system increases the difficulties of the language.

Latin has only six cases but it has five declensions, which makes, including plurals, sixty characteristics. There are as many for adjectives and as many for the eternal family of pronouns, *qui, his, ego, hic,* etc. Basque has fourteen or fifteen invariable cases in which all nouns, pronouns, and indefinite adjectives, singulars and plurals, all the infinitives, participles, and adverbs are declined.

This system is not only much simpler but much more rational. In effect the terms of a relationship may vary even though the relationship is identical. Reason refuses to accept that, in this case, the sign of the relationship should vary. Let us compare a Latin sentence and its translation into Basque:

In nomine patris, et filii et spiritus sancti
Altaren eta semearen eta espiritu sainduaren icenean.

Here we have two relationships in Latin, one expressed by case and the other by the preposition *in;* one identical relationship of generation characterized by *is, i, us;* one preposition, sufficient in itself for marking a relationship which nevertheless regulates a case arbitrarily; and finally the need to make the adjective agree with the noun, four rules that are complicated and useless, and which do not encumber the simple and logical progress of the Basque version.

But if Basque declension is better than Latin declension for its simplicity, regularity, and logic, it is above all in scope that its superiority is remarkable.

The limits of a weekly journal are too narrow for me to show you here how all the adverbs, pronouns, participles, and infinitives in Basque come under the yoke of declension. I will limit myself to two remarks.

We have seen that the article *a* is used to determine a word and make it a true substantive. From this it follows that in Basque we can make a substantive out of a group of ideas represented by a word. Thus, *semearen,* "of the son," *semearena,* "that of the son," and this compound word can be totally declined. Thus, *hintcen,* "you were"; *hintcena,* "the one who was"; *hintcenaren,* "of the one who was," etc.

This means that there is not one single case for substantives, and in verbs not one tense, number, mode, or inflection that cannot be used with an article, and consequently all the forms of the declension, which opens out a truly boundless horizon to it.

A dissertation on Basque verbs would doubtless weary the reader. However, I cannot prevent myself from saying a few words about them before stopping.

Any tense in a verb serves only to express that such and such an attribute agrees with such and such a subject, and to indicate the time at which this correlation existed. With the result, it is true to say, that we always have to find in a verb the entire proposition plus the relationship of time. "I shall fall," if the language is properly constructed, should encompass five ideas: the idea of *me,* the idea of a *fall,* the idea of *affirmation,* the idea of the relation between *falling* and *me,* and lastly the idea of the *future;* there is none of this in French, and even less in Latin. Both of these languages use a formula that owes its value just to chance and conventions. Let us analyze the Basque formula *erorico bainiz,* which means "I shall fall."

First of all, you need to know that *erorico* is a genuine noun in the destinative case. *Erortea,* "the fall," *erorico,* "for the fall," like *mendico,* "for the mountain." *Ni* is also a noun or pronoun that means "me." *Niz* is its mediative case and is the equivalent of "of me," like *mendiaz,* "of the mountain."

Thus in the formula *erorico bainiz* you will find: the subject *ni,* "me"; the attribute *erortea,* "fall"; the affirmation *bai,* which means "yes"; the expression that the affirmation is done to the subject by the meditative *z* and the future expressed by the destinative *co.* This is just as though you were saying, "Yes for me for the fall," a manner of speaking that may sound strange to us but which is no less in accordance with the true principles of any language.

Indeed the verb *to be,* when used to link the attribute to the subject, does not appear to have to differentiate itself from a simple affirmation. Our patois appears to have retained something of this principle. We will precede our entire conjugation with the word *que.* For example, *que marchi, que toumbes, qu'ets riches,* etc., as though this was an elliptic formula in which the affirmation is implied. "I say that," or "I affirm that."

I will stop there. Other details will become wearisome. I hope that a few glimpses of Basque etymology will provide the reader with greater variety and increased interest.

2. Reflection on the Question of Dueling (Report)[2]

[vol. 7, p. 10. Originally published in *La Chalosse*, 11 February 1838.]

Literary centralization has currently reached such a point in France, and the provinces are so brainwashed that in advance she scorns anything that is not printed in Paris. It seems that talent, wit, common sense, erudition, and genius cannot exist outside the walls of our capital city. Have we thus discovered a short time ago that the silent calm of our retreats is essentially harmful to meditation and intellectual work?

The text to which we are drawing attention is in our eyes an eloquent protest against this blind prejudice. On his debut, the author, a young, unknown man, who perhaps does not have the measure even of himself, attacks one of the most brilliant of literary and political celebrities, and yet if anyone at all impartially compares the famous charge of M. Dupin with regard to dueling and the *reflections* of M. Coudroy, he will find, we dare to say, that, from the point of view of sound philosophy, elevated reasoning, and glowing eloquence, it is not the attorney general who emerges victorious from the combat.[3]

---

2. (Paillottet's note) At that time, Bastiat and his friend, M. Félix Coudroy, the author of a pamphlet on dueling, both believed they were destined for obscurity. It was only seven years later that the former was called upon to demonstrate the qualities of his mind on the national stage. To follow in Bastiat's footsteps, M. Coudroy lacked only one thing, health. We can see Bastiat's opinion of his friend's merit in the letters included in this volume. Here is an additional letter written in 1845:

> My dear Félix,
>   Because of the difficulty of reading, I cannot properly judge the style, but my sincere conviction (you know that here I set aside the usual modesty) is that our styles have different qualities and faults. I believe that the qualities of yours are such that, when it is used, it shows genuine talent; I mean to say a style that is lively and animated with general ideas and glimpses that are luminous. Always make copies on small sheets; if one needs to be changed, it will not cause much trouble. When you are copying you will perhaps be able to add polish, but, for my part, I note that the first draft is always faster and more accessible to today's readers who scarcely go into anything in depth.
>   Do you not have an opinion of M. Dunoyer?

3. We have not been able to track down the two pamphlets mentioned by Bastiat. It appears that Bastiat and Coudroy opposed the criminalization of dueling by the state on the basis that the practice was a voluntary activity between consenting adults. See

M. Coudroy examines first of all the relationship of dueling with existing legislation and it seems to us that in this respect his refutation of M.
Dupin's position leaves nothing to be desired. By applying to suicide the line
of argument through which the attorney general has succeeded in subjecting
dueling to our penal laws, he shows in a sensitive way that this interpretation
is forced and is as antipathetic to common sense as it is to public awareness,
and one which has led the court to bracket dueling with voluntary and premeditated murder.

M. Coudroy then seeks to ascertain whether this legal interpretation is
not undermining our constitution. We think it is difficult not to be struck
by the relevance of this notion. Our constitution, in fact, acknowledges that
it is public opinion, through the agency of legislative power and in particular
of the elective chamber, which classifies actions in the category of crimes,
misdemeanors, and misdeeds. No one can be punished for an act that this
power has not made subject to a punishment. However, if instead of taking
it for granted that any such act must be covered by the punishment, the legal
power is able to bend the act to fit the punishment by declaring that this act,
hitherto regarded as innocent, *belongs to a class of acts covered by the law in
question,* I do not see how we can prevent the public attorney from substituting himself for the legislator and the civil servant chosen by the authorities
for the representative elected by the people.

Following these considerations, the author tackles the moral and philosophical question, and here, it has to be said, he fills the immense gap which
appears in M. Dupin's charge. In his superstitious reverence for the law, all
the efforts of this magistrate are devoted to proving that it entails the assimilation of dueling into a kind of murder. But what are the effects of dueling
on society; what are the evils it prevents and represses? What other remedy
to these evils could we substitute for it? What changes would we need to introduce into our legislation to create a safeguard for honor in law, if courage
is not an admissible one? How would we succeed in giving legal verdicts the
sanction of opinion and preventing the granting of damages from inflicting
another withering blow on the offended person? What would the results
be of the undermining of the sensitivity of all citizens to honor and to the
opinion of their peers? These are all serious questions which M. Dupin does

---

Kevin McAleer, *Dueling: The Cult of Honor in Fin-de-Siècle Germany* (Princeton, N.J.:
Princeton University Press, 1994), p. 248, note 36.

not appear to have taken into consideration and which have been discussed by our fellow countryman with signal excellence.

Among the deliberations which struck us the most in this very worthwhile discussion, we will quote the passage in which the author highlights the reason for the ineffectiveness of punishments as deterrents to attacks on personal honor. In ordinary crimes and misdemeanors, the courts ascertain and punish only base actions whose impure source is regarded with contempt by public opinion. Legal sanctions and popular sanctions are in harmony. However, in matters of honor these two sanctions go in opposite directions, and if the courts pronounce a punishment involving death, personal restraint, or penal servitude against the offender, public opinion would inflict, even more rigorously, a penalty of infamy on the offended person for having had recourse to law to make himself respected. These verdicts of opinion are so unanimous that they are embedded in the heart of the magistrate himself, whereas his lips are obliged to pronounce a quite different verdict. We know the story of the judge before whom an officer complained of a blow received. "What, sir!" he cried indignantly, "you have received a blow and you have come here . . . but you are right, you are obeying the law."

We will also point out the fine refutation of a passage from Barbeyrac quoted by M. Dupin, in which the author shows us how the circle of human punishment expands in accordance with the progress of civilization, without, however, its being able to exceed permanently the limit beyond which the disadvantages of repression exceed those of the misdemeanor. The law itself has recognized this limit, when, for example, it prohibited the search for paternity. It did not pretend that beyond its sphere of activity there were not actions condemned by religion and moral law, in relation to which, however, it should disclaim any authority. It is in this class of action that we need to include attacks on honor.

But it is impossible for us to follow the author in the intellectual path he has pursued. To analyze a line of argument that is so vigorous would be to destroy its force and progress. We will therefore return to the pamphlet itself, with the warning, however, that it needs to be read, as it was written, with awareness and reflection. It is the material of a large book reduced to a few pages. It differs in this from the majority of the writings published today, in that in these publications the number of pages seems to increase in proportion to the lack of ideas. M. Coudroy, on the other hand, is rich in penetrating insights and sober in his development of ideas. His text is more valuable for the thoughts he suggests than for those he expresses. This is the seal of true merit.

Perhaps one might even reproach the author for being too restrained. When you read him, you feel that there has been a constant struggle between his ideas—which want to see the light of day—and his determined wish merely to reveal only half of them. But then, not everyone can, like Cuvier, reconstruct an entire animal from the glimpse of a fragment. We are living in a century in which an author has to express his entire thought to his reader.

A man of wit wrote, "Please excuse the length of my letter, I have not enough time to be shorter." Could not the majority of readers also say, "Your book is too short, I have not enough time to read it"?

------

3. On the Bordeaux to Bayonne Railway Line

Letter addressed to a commission   [vol. 7, p. 103. Originally published in
of the Chamber of Deputies   *Le Mémorial bordelais* on 19 May 1846.]

Sirs,

It is pointless both for those favoring the *direct route* and those the *winding one* to lay any claim to virtue. Each side has only one serious argument. The first says, "Our line is shorter by twenty-nine kilometers." The second replies, "Ours services four times as many people." Or, aggressively, one party claims: "Your *winding* route makes transport more expensive for each end" while the other retorts, "Your direct route goes through uninhabited countryside and sacrifices all the interests of the region."

When the issue is put this way, we understand how very important it is for the supporters of the direct route to prove first that the uninhabited countryside is not as uninhabited as people suppose and secondly that the valleys are neither as rich nor as populous as is claimed.

This is the line of argument to which the commission of inquiry of the Basses Pyrénées had recourse, and in the candid account of his thinking by the minister of public works, it was reproduced in the following terms:

"It should be noted that, in the districts of the greater Landes, the population has constantly increased by an average of 50 percent in the last forty years, while in the valleys, it has remained stationary and *has even decreased* in a few locations."

I have reason to believe that the factual matter quoted was drawn from a memorandum I published on the *distribution of taxes* in the *département* of the Landes, one which probably, nay, inevitably, will be put before you. I should therefore be allowed to protest against the strange use people are trying to make of it. I do not presume to plead for or against either of the two rival routes, but I do claim the right to object to the way in which those who would keep the railway out of our valleys have recourse to any and all arguments, even the ones about their suffering.

Anyone who has been involved with the vast subject of population knows that it increases normally much faster in regions that are underpopulated than in those in which it has already become dense. To say that this is a reason to give preference to the former with regard to the railway is like saying that the railway is more useful in Russia than in England and in the Landes than in Normandy.

The argument then generalizes a local fact. It is not true that the population is decreasing in the valleys of the Garonne, the Midouze, and the Adour. It is growing slowly there, it is true, precisely because it is very dense.

What is true, and what I do not withdraw, is that in a small region known as the Chalosse, situated on the left bank of the Adour, and in particular in four or five wine-growing districts in this province, *the number of deaths in the last twenty years has regularly exceeded the number of births.*

This is a deplorable perturbation, a phenomenon unique to this century, one which is manifested nowhere else, not even in Turkey. To know what we should infer from it, it is not sufficient merely to identify it factually; we have to relate it to its cause.

The population has decreased, say the commissioners of inquiry. This sentence is easily said. Oh! They do not realize the magnitude of what they are implying! They were not present during the painful labor through which a revolution like this was achieved! They do not realize all the moral and physical suffering that it involves. I will tell them. It is a sad story, but one that is full of edification.

The Chalosse is one of the most fertile regions in France.

In former times, wines were produced and shipped down the Adour. Some of the wine was consumed around Bayonne; the rest was exported to northern Europe. This export trade occupied the activity and capital of ten or twelve very well-regarded houses in Bayonne, the names of which one of your colleagues, M. Chégaray, can quote if need be.

At that time, the wines sustained their value well. Prosperity was extensive in the region as was the population. The number of sharecropping farms was naturally restricted and the farms did not cover more than two or three hectares. Each of these small vineyards, worked like a garden, supplied a family with an assured means of existence. Owners' and sharecroppers' incomes provided a livelihood for a populous class of artisans, and you can imagine how dense the population became under these economic arrangements.

However, things have changed a great deal!

The commercial policy that prevailed between the nations closed off the external markets of the Chalosse. Exports were, I say, not just reduced but destroyed, indeed completely annihilated.

On the other hand, the system of indirect taxation considerably restricted its internal markets. By freeing the wine produced on his property from consumption tax in favor of the owner, this system altered the division of labor in wine production. It acted as would a law which stated, "Bread shall be subject to a tax, except for that made by individuals in their household." Obviously, such an arrangement would tend to destroy bakeries.

Finally, the Adour is gradually ceasing to be navigable. Authentic documents show that ships used to go upriver to Aire. Elderly inhabitants of the region have seen them go as far as Grenade and I myself have seen them load at Saint-Sever. Now they stop at Mugron, and in view of the difficulties they have in getting there it is easy to see that shortly they will not go further than the confluence of the Midouze.

I do not have to discuss the causes for all this. They exist, it is clear. What effects have they had?

First of all, they reduce the income of the owners. Secondly, they make the portion of the sharecropper inadequate to provide a living for him and his family. It was therefore necessary for the owner to take a considerable slice out of what was left of his income to provide the sharecropper with what was strictly necessary to keep him alive. One of them had to be ruined. In vain did he combat the attractions of luxury with which the century surrounded him on all sides. In vain did he impose on himself the hardest sacrifices, the most detailed parsimony. He could not escape the bitter suffering that accompanied his inevitable degradation.

The sharecropper was no longer a sharecropper; his payment in kind served only to diminish his debt, and he became a day laborer, given a daily ration of corn in lieu of cash payment.

In other words, it was acknowledged that the acreage of farms, which was adequate in other circumstances, was now too restricted, and at this moment a remarkable revolution is taking place in the agricultural constitution of the region.

Since wine no longer had any markets, two hectares of vines could no longer constitute a working farm. There is a clear tendency to organize property on other bases. Out of two sharecropping farms with vineyards, one is made that encloses a fair proportion of arable land. It can be seen that, under the effect of the causes described, two or three hectares can no longer provide a living for a family of sharecroppers; five or six are needed. Mergers are also being made here, but these mergers change people's economic conditions.

In the village in which I live, thirty sharecropper houses have been demolished, according to the land register, and more than one hundred and fifty in the district whose legal interests have been entrusted to me, and, mark this well, this means as many families that have been plunged into complete destruction. Their fate is to suffer, decline, and disappear.

Yes, the population has decreased in one part of the Chalosse and if this admission had to be leveled against the region, I would also add that, although this decrease in population is evidence of our distress, it is far from expressing its full measure. If you traveled through my unfortunate homeland, you would see how much men can suffer without dying and understand that one life less on your cold statistics is a symptom of incalculable torture.

And now our sufferings are being used as evidence against us! And in order to refuse us markets mention is being made of suffering that has been inflicted on us by the lack of markets! Once again, I am not voicing an opinion on the route of the railway. I know that the interests of the Chalosse will weigh very little in the balance. But, although I do not expect it to be an argument in favor of the route through the valleys, I do not want it to be used as an argument against, because such an argument is as false as it is cruel. Is it not, in fact, pitiless cruelty to say to us, "You have beautiful sunshine, fertile soil, cool valleys, hill slopes on which the work of your fathers spreads prosperity and happiness? Thanks to these gifts of nature and art, your population was as dense as that in our richest provinces. You lost all your markets suddenly, and distress followed prosperity, and tears, songs of joy. Now, while we have at our disposal an immense outlet, we do not yet know whether we will allocate it to uninhabited areas or put it within your reach. Your sufferings have made our decision for us. They clearly exist; the government itself has noted them in the following laconic phrases: *this is nothing, just a falling population.* There is no reply to this, and we have now firmly decided to redirect the route through the greater Landes. By casting all your towns into ruin, this decision will accelerate the depopulation that so saddens you, but is not the *opportunity* of peopling the uninhabited areas worth the *certainty* of decreasing the population in the valleys?"

Oh! Sirs, give the railway the route which in your wisdom you consider to be in the best general interest, but if you deny it to our valley, do not say in your *considerations,* as you are committed to doing, that it is its misfortunes *and its misfortunes alone* that have determined your decision.

---

4. Draft Preface for the *Harmonies*

[vol. 7, p. 303. According to Paillottet, this draft,
in the form of a letter to the author, was
roughed out by him toward the end of 1847.]

My dear Frédéric,

So the worst has happened; you have left our village. You have abandoned the fields you loved, the family home in which you enjoyed such total independence, your old books which were amazed to slumber negligently on their dusty shelves, the garden in which on our long walks we chatted endlessly *de omni re scibili et quibusdam aliis,*[4] this corner of the earth that was the last refuge of so many beings we loved and where we went to find such gentle tears and such dear hopes. Do you remember how the root of faith grew green again in our souls at the sight of these cherished tombs? With what proliferation did ideas spring to our minds inspired by these cypresses? We had barely given thought to them when they came to our lips. But none of this could retain you. Neither these good ordinary country folk accustomed to seeking decisions in your honest instincts rather than in the law, nor our circle so fertile in quips that two languages were not enough for them and where gentle familiarity and long-standing intimacy replaced fine manners, nor your cello which appeared to renew constantly the source of your ideas, nor my friendship, nor that absolute ruler over your actions and your waking hours: your studies, perhaps your most precious assets. You have left the village and here you are in Paris, in this whirlwind where as Hugo says:

. . . .

---

4. "About every knowable matter and certain other things."

Frédéric, we are accustomed to speaking to each other frankly. Very well! I have to tell you that your resolution surprises me, and what is more, I cannot approve of it. You have let yourself be beguiled by the love of fame, I do not go so far as to say glory and you know very well why. How many times have we not said that from now on glory would be the prize only of minds of an immense superiority! It is no longer enough to write with purity, grace, and warmth; ten thousand people in France do that already. It is not enough to have wit; wit is everywhere. Do you not remember that, when reading the smallest article, so often lacking in good sense and logic but almost always sparkling with verve and rich in imagination, we used to say to one another, "Writing well is going to become a faculty common to the species, like walking and sitting well." How are you to dream of glory with the spectacle you have before your eyes? Who today thinks of Benjamin Constant or Manuel? What has become of these reputations which appeared imperishable?

Do you think you can be compared to such great minds?

Have you undertaken the same studies as they? Do you possess their immense faculties? Have you, like them, spent your entire life among exceptionally brilliant people? Have you the same opportunities of making yourself known, or the same platform; are you surrounded when need arises with the same comradeship? You will perhaps say to me that if you do not manage to shine through your writings you will distinguish yourself through your actions. I say, look where that approach has left La Fayette's reputation. Will you, like him, have your name resound in the old world and the new for three quarters of a century? Will you live through times as fertile in events? Will you be the most outstanding figure in three major revolutions? Will it be given to you to make or bring down kings? Will you be seen as a martyr at Olmultz and a demigod at the Hôtel de Ville? Will you be the general commander of all the National Guard regiments in the kingdom? And should these grand destinies be your calling, see where they end: in the casting among nations of a name without stain which in their indifference they do not deign to pick up; in their being overwhelmed with noble examples and great services which they are in a hurry to forget.

No, I cannot believe that pride has so far gone to your head as to make you sacrifice genuine happiness for a reputation which, as you well know, is not made for you and which, in any case, will be only fleeting. It is not you who would ever aspire to become the great man of the month in the newspapers of today.

You would deny your entire past. If this type of vanity had beguiled you, you would have started by seeking election as a deputy. I have seen you stand several times as a candidate but always refuse to do what is needed to succeed. You used constantly to say, "Now is the time to take a little action in public affairs, where you read and discuss what you have read. I will take advantage of this to distribute a few useful truths under the cover of candidacy," and beyond that, you took no serious steps.

It is therefore not the spur of amour-propre that drove you to Paris. What then was the inspiration to which you yielded? Is it the desire to contribute in some way to the well-being of humanity? On this score as well, I have a few remarks to make.

Like you I love all forms of freedom; and among these, the one that is the most universally useful to mankind, the one you enjoy at each moment of the day and in all of life's circumstances, is the freedom to work and to trade. I know that making things one's own is the fulcrum of society and even of human life. I know that trade is intrinsic to property and that to restrict the one is to shake the foundations of the other. I approve of your devoting yourself to the defense of this freedom whose triumph will inevitably usher in the reign of international justice and consequently the extinction of hatred, prejudices between one people and another, and the wars that come in their wake.

But in fact, are you entering the lists with the weapons appropriate for your fame, if that is what you are dreaming of, as well as for the success of your cause itself? What are you concerned with, I mean totally concerned with? A proof, and the solution to a single problem, namely: Does trade restriction add to the profits column or the losses column in a nation's accounts? That is the subject on which you are exhausting your entire mind! Those are the limits you have set around your great question! Pamphlets, books, brochures, articles in newspapers, speeches, all of these have been devoted to removing this gap in our knowledge: will freedom give the nation one hundred thousand francs more or less? You seem very keen on keeping from the light of day any knowledge which does not directly support this preemptive postulate. You seem set on extinguishing in your heart all these sacred flames which a love for humanity once lit there.

Are you not afraid that your mind will dry up and wither with all this analytical work, this endless argumentation focused on an algebraic calculation?

Remember what we so often said: unless you pretend that you can bring about progress in some isolated branch of human knowledge or, rather, unless you have received from nature a cranium distinguished only by its imperious forehead, it is better, especially in the case of mere amateur philosophers like us, to let your thinking roam over the entire range of intellectual endeavor rather than enslave it to the solving of one problem. It is better to search for the relationship of branches of science to each other and the harmony of social laws than to wear yourself out shedding light on a doubtful point at the risk of even losing the sense of what is grand and majestic in the whole.

This was the reason our reading was so various and why we took such care in shaking off the yoke of conventional verdicts. Sometimes we read Plato, not to admire him according to the faith of the ages but to assure ourselves of the radical inferiority of society in antique times, and we used to say, "Since this is the height to which the finest genius of the ancient world rose, let us be reassured that man can be perfected and that faith in his destiny is not misguided." Sometimes we were accompanied on our long walks by Bacon, Lamartine, Bossuet, Fox, Lamennais, and even Fourier. Political economy was only one stone in the social edifice we sought to construct in our minds, and we used to say: "It is useful and fortunate that patient and indefatigable geniuses, like Say, concentrated on observing, classifying, and setting out in a methodical order all the facts that make up this fine science. From now on, intelligence can stand securely on this unshakeable base and lift itself to new horizons." How much did we also admire the work of Dunoyer and Comte, who, without ever deviating from the rigorously scientific line drawn by M. Say, mobilize these acquired truths with such felicity in the domains of morality and legislation. I will not hide from you that sometimes, in listening to you, it seemed to me that you could in your turn take this same torch from the hands of your ancestors and cast its light in certain dark corners of the social sciences, above all in those which foolish doctrines have recently plunged into darkness.

Instead of that, there you are, fully occupied with illuminating a single one of the economic problems that Smith and Say have already explained a hundred times better than you could ever do. There you are, analyzing, defining, calculating, and distinguishing. There you are, scalpel in hand, seeking out what there is of worth in the depths of the words *price, utility, high prices, low prices, imports, and exports.*

But finally, if it is not for you yourself, and if you do not fear becoming dazed by the task, do you think you have chosen the best plan to follow in the interest of the cause? Peoples are not governed by equations but by generous instincts, by sentiment and sympathy. It was necessary to present them with the successive dismantling of the barriers which divide men into mutually hostile communities, into jealous provinces, or into warring nations. It was necessary to show them the merging of races, interests, languages, ideas, and the triumph of truth over error, witnessed in the intellectual shock it effects, with progressive institutions replacing the regime of absolute despotism and hereditary castes, wars eliminated, armies disbanded, moral power replacing physical force, and the human race preparing itself through unity for the destiny reserved for it. This is what would have inflamed the masses, and not your dry proofs.

In any case, why limit yourself? Why imprison your thoughts? It seems to me that you have subjected them to a prison regime of a single crust of dry bread as food, since there you are, chewing night and day on a question of money. I love freedom of trade as much as you do. But is all human progress encapsulated in that freedom? In the past, your heart beat for the freeing of thought and speech which were still bound by their university shackles and the laws against free association. You enthusiastically supported parliamentary reform and the radical division of that sovereignty, which delegates and controls, from the executive power in all its branches. All forms of freedom go together. All ideas form a systematic and harmonious whole, and there is not a single one whose proof does not serve to demonstrate the truth of the others. But you act like a mechanic who makes a virtue of explaining an isolated part of a machine in the smallest detail, not forgetting anything. The temptation is strong to cry out to him, "Show me the other parts; make them work together; each of them explains the others. . . ."

––––––––––

5. Anglomania, Anglophobia

[vol. 7, p. 309. According to Paillottet, this outline dates from 1847. Bastiat had wished to make a chapter out of it for the second series of *Economic Sophisms*, published at the end of the year.]

These two sentiments stand face to face and it is hardly possible in this country to judge England impartially without being accused by anglomaniacs of anglophobia and by anglophobics of anglomania. It appears that public opinion, which in France goes beyond what was an ancient Spartan law,[5] condemns us to moral death if we do not rush headlong into one of these two extremes.

However, these two sentiments exist and are already of long standing. They therefore exist justifiably, for, in the world of sympathy and antipathy, as in the material world, there is no cause without an effect.

It is easy to verify that these two sentiments coexist. The great conflict between democracy and aristocracy, between common law and privilege, is continuing, both implicitly and openly, with more or less enthusiasm, with more or less opportunity, worldwide. However, nowhere, not even in France, does it resound as much as in England.

As I say, not even in France. Here, in fact, privilege as a social principle, was extinct before our revolution. In any case, it received its coup de grace on the night of 4 August.[6] The equal sharing of property constantly undermines the existence of any leisured class. Idleness is an accident, the transitory lot of a few individuals, and whatever we may think of our political organization, it is always the case that democracy is the basis of our social order. Probably, the human heart does not change; those who achieve legislative power seek hard to create a small administrative fiefdom for themselves, whether electoral or economic, but nothing in all that takes root. From one session to another, the slightest hint of an amendment can overturn the whole fragile edifice, remove a whole raft of political appointments, eliminate protectionist measures, or change the electoral districts.

If we cast an eye on other great nations, such as Austria and Russia, we will see a very different situation. There, privilege based on brute force reigns with absolute authority. We can scarcely distinguish the dull murmur of democracy laboring away underground, like a seed that swells and grows far from all human sight.

In England, on the other hand, the two powers are full of force and vigor. I will say nothing of the monarchy, a kind of idol on which the two opposing factions have agreed to impose a sort of neutrality. But let us consider a little how the elements of force with which the aristocracy and democracy do battle are constituted and what the quality of their arms is.

The aristocracy has on its side legislative power. It alone can enter the

---

5. In Sparta, every newborn child was examined by the elders. If he was judged fit, he was left with his mother; otherwise, he was thrown into a pit.

6. On the night of 4 August 1789, the National Assembly suppressed all the privileges of the nobility and the clergy, with their agreement, in a moment of great enthusiasm.

House of Lords[7] and it has taken over the House of Commons, without one's being able to say when and how it can be dislodged from it.

It has on its side the established church—all of whose positions have been taken over by the younger sons of great families—an institution unreservedly English or Anglican, as its name indicates, and unreservedly a political force, having the monarch as its head.

It has on its side the hereditary ownership of land and entails, which prevent the breaking up of estates. Through this, it is assured that its power, concentrated in a small number of hands, will never be dispersed and will never lose its characteristics.

Through its legislative power, it controls taxes, and its efforts naturally tend to transfer the fiscal burden onto the people while retaining the profit from them.

We thus see it commanding the army and the navy, that is to say, still wielding brute force. And the manner in which recruitment to these bodies is carried out guarantees that it will never transfer its support to the popular cause. We may further note that in military discipline there is something that is both energetic and degrading, which aspires to efface in the soul of the army any urge to share common human feelings.

By means of the wealth and material power of the country, the English aristocracy has been able successively to conquer all parts of the globe it considered to be useful for its security and policy. In doing this, it has been wonderfully supported by popular prejudice, national pride, and the *economic sophism* which attaches so many crazy hopes to the colonial system.

In a word, the entire British diplomatic corps is concentrated in the hands of the aristocracy, and as there are always sympathetic links between all the privileged groups and all the aristocratic classes around the world, since they are all based on the same social principles and what threatens one threatens the others, the result is that all the elements of the vast power I have just described are in perpetual opposition to the development of democracy, not only in England but all over the world.

This explains the War of Independence in the United States and the even more relentless war against the French Revolution,[8] a war carried out using

7. The House of Lords was composed of hereditary peers, twenty-six Anglican prelates, sixteen Scottish peers, and an indefinite number of peers appointed by the king.

8. Great Britain had been at war with France from February 1793 to March 1802, at the head of two European coalitions.

not only steel but also and above all gold, used either to bribe alliances or spent to lead our democracy into excesses, social disorder, and civil war.

There is no need to go into further detail, to show the interest the English aristocracy might have had in stifling, at the same time as the very idea of democracy, any accompanying hints of forceful action, power, or wealth, anywhere. There is no need for a historical exposition of the action it carried out with regard to peoples in this respect, a policy which became known as the *alternating balance of power,* to show that *anglophobia* is not a sentiment that is totally blind and that it has, as I explained at the beginning, its own raison d'être.

As for *anglomania,* if it can be explained as stemming from a puerile sentiment, from the sort of fascination constantly exercised on superficial minds by the spectacle of wealth, power, energy, perseverance, and success, this is not what concerns me. I wish to speak about the serious reasons for sympathy which England is able rightly to generate in other countries.

I have just listed the powerful props of the English oligarchy, the ownership of land, the House of Lords, the House of Commons, taxes, the church, the army, the navy, the colonies, and diplomacy.

The forces of democracy possess nothing so clear and firm of purpose.

Democracy has on its side the power of the spoken word, the press, associations, work, the economy itself, increasing wealth, public opinion, a good cause, and truth.

I think that the progress of democracy is manifest. Look at the major breaches it has made in the walls of the opposing camp.

The English oligarchy, as I have said, had ownership of the land. It still has. But what it no longer has is a privilege grafted on this privilege, the Corn Laws.[9]

It had the House of Commons. It still has, but democracy has entered Parliament through the breach of the *Reform Bill,*[10] a breach which is constantly widening.

It had the established church. It still has, but it is shorn of its exclusive

---

9. The Corn Laws were abolished in February 1846. The story leading up to this abolition is related in *Cobden and the League.*

10. The Reform Bill of 1832 put an end to the most unfair rules of the previous electoral law and permitted some elements of the middle class to vote for the first time. The franchise was further extended in 1867 and 1885.

ascendancy by the increase in number and popularity of dissident churches[11] and the *Catholic Emancipation Bill.*

It had control of taxation. It still has taxes at its disposal but, since 1815, all ministers, whether Whigs or Tories, have been constrained to go from reform to reform, and at the first financial difficulty, the provisional *income tax* will be converted into a permanent land tax.

It had the army. It still has, but everyone knows the avid concern of the English populace to be spared the sight of red uniforms.

It had the colonies. These provided its greatest moral authority, since it was with the illusory promises of the colonial system that it carried along a populace both swollen with pride and misled. And the people are breaking this link by acknowledging the chimerical nature of the colonial system.

Finally, I have to mention here another conquest the people have made, which is probably the greatest. For the very reason that the weapons of the people are public opinion, a good cause, and the truth, and for the additional reason that they possess in all its fullness the right of defending their cause in the press, through speeches and gatherings, the people could not fail to attract, and in fact they did attract, to their banner the most intelligent and honest of the aristocrats. For it should not be thought that the English aristocracy forms a compact unity, all of like mind. We see, on the contrary, that it is divided on all the major issues and, either through fear, social adroitness, or philanthropy, certain illustrious members of the privileged class are sacrificing part of their own privilege to the needs of democracy.

If those who take an interest in the ups and downs of this great struggle and the progress of the popular cause on British soil are to be called *anglomaniacs,* I declare that I am an *anglomaniac.*

For me there is just one truth and one justice, and equality takes the same form everywhere. I also think that liberty always produces the same results everywhere and that a fraternal and friendly link should unite the weak and oppressed in all countries.

I cannot fail to see that there are two Englands, since in England there are two bodies of sentiment, two principles, and two eternally conflicting causes.[12]

---

11. The Anglican faith was a national church, the Church of England, the religion of the state itself. All other churches, called dissenting, had been legally tolerated since 1689.

12. Bastiat wrote about "two Englands" in an article in *Le Libre échange,* 6 February 1848. (*OC,* vol. 3, p. 459, "Deux Angleterres.")

I cannot forget that, although the aristocratic interest wanted to bend American independence beneath its yoke in 1776, it encountered in a few English democrats such resistance that it had to suspend freedom of the press, habeas corpus, and trial by jury.

I cannot forget that, although the aristocratic interest wanted to stifle our glorious revolution in 1791, it needed to set its army rabble on its own soil against the men of the people who opposed the perpetration of this crime against humanity.

I call those who admire the acts and gestures of the two parties without distinction *anglomaniacs*. I call those who envelop both in a blind, senseless disapproval, *anglophobes*.

At the risk of attracting to this little volume the hammer blows of unpopularity, I am forced to admit that this great, unending, and gigantic effort by democracy to burst the bonds of oppression and attain its rights in full, offers in my view particularly encouraging prospects in England which are not available in other countries, or at least not to the same degree.

In France, the aristocracy fell in '89, before democracy was ready to govern itself. The latter had not been able to develop and perfect in all their aspects those qualities, robustness, and political virtues which alone could keep power in its hands and constrain it to make prudent and effective use of them. The result has been that all parties, all persons even, believed that they could inherit the aristocratic mantle, and conflict thus arose between the people and M. Decazes, the people and M. de Villèle, the people and M. de Polignac, and the people and M. Guizot. This conflict of petty proportions educates us on constitutional matters. On the day we become sufficiently emancipated nothing will prevent us from taking hold of the reins of management of our affairs, for the fall of our great antagonist, the aristocracy, will have preceded our political education.

The English people, on the contrary, are growing in stature and becoming proficient and enlightened through the struggle itself. Historic circumstances which it is pointless to recall here have paralyzed the use of physical force in its hands. It has to have recourse to the power of public opinion alone, and the first condition for making public opinion a power in itself was that the people should enlighten itself on each particular question until unanimity was achieved. Public opinion will not have to be formed after the conflict; it has been formed and is formed during, for, and by the conflict itself. It is always in Parliament that victory is won and the aristocracy is forced to sanction it. Our philosophers and poets shone before a revolution which they prepared, but in England it is during the struggle that philosophy and poetry do their work. From within the popular party come forth great writers, powerful orators, and noble poets who are completely unknown to us. Here we imagine that Milton, Shakespeare, Young, Thompson, and Byron encompass the whole of English literature. We do not perceive that, because the struggle is ongoing, the chain of great poets is unbroken and the sacred fire inspires poets such as Burns, Campbell, Moore, Akenside, and a thousand others, who work unceasingly to strengthen democracy by enlightening it.

Another result of this state of affairs is that aristocracy and democracy confront each other with regard to all questions. Nothing is more likely to perpetuate and aggravate them than this. Something that elsewhere is just an administrative or financial debate is in this instance a social war. As far as one can tell, hardly a single question has sprung up in which the two great protagonists have not been at loggerheads. Henceforth, both sides make immense efforts to form alliances, to draft petitions, and to distribute pamphlets through mass subscription, far less over the issue itself than for the ever-present and living principles involved. This was seen, not only with regard to the Corn Laws, but regarding any law that touched on taxes, the church, the army, political order, education, foreign affairs, etc.

It is easy to understand that the English people have thus had to become accustomed, with regard to any measure, to going back to first principles and to basing discussion on this wide foundation. This being so, in general the two parties are opposite and mutually exclusive. It is a case of *all or nothing,* because both sides feel that to concede something, however small, is to concede the principle. Doubtless, when it comes to voting, bargains are sometimes struck. Reforms have naturally to be adapted to the times and circumstances, but in debates no one gives way and the invariable rule of democracy is this: take everything that is given and continue to demand the rest. And it has even had occasion to learn that its most certain course is to demand *everything,* for fifty years if necessary, rather than content itself with *a little* at the end of a few sessions.

Thus, the most rabid anglophobes cannot deceive themselves that reforms in England carry a quotient of radicalism, and therefore of grandeur, which astonishes and enthralls the mind.

The abolition of slavery[13] was won in a single step. On a particular day, at

13. The bill abolishing slavery was voted in 1833, and it was to come into effect fully in 1838.

a particular time, the irons fell from the arms of poor blacks in all the possessions of Great Britain. It is related that, during the night of 31st July 1838, the slaves were gathered together in the churches of Jamaica. Their thoughts and hearts, their entire life seemed to be hanging on the hands of the clock. Vainly did the priest try to fix their attention on the most imposing subjects capable of capturing the human mind. Vainly did he speak to them of the goodness of God and their future destiny. There was but a single soul in the congregation and that soul was in a fever of expectation. When the gong sounded the first chime of midnight, a cry of joy such as the human ear had never heard before shook the rafters of the church. These poor creatures did not have enough words and gestures to express the exuberance of their joy. They rushed weeping into each other's arms until, their paroxysm now calmed, they were seen to fall to their knees, raise their grateful arms to heaven, and cover with blessings the nation that had delivered them; the great men, Clarkson and Wilberforce, who had embraced their cause; and the Providence that had shone a ray of justice and humanity into the heart of a great people.

While fifty years were needed to achieve absolute personal freedom, a bargain, a truce, on political and religious freedom was reached more quickly. The *Reform Bill* and the Catholic Emancipation bill,[14] which at first were supported as principles, were delivered as matters of *expediency*. Thus, England has still two major troubles to overcome, the people's charter and the revocation of the established church as the official religion.

The campaign against protectionism is one of those that has been led by the leaders under the safeguard and authority of *principle*. The principle of freedom of trade is either true or false, and has to triumph or fall in its entirety. To strike a bargain would have been to acknowledge that property and liberty are not rights but, depending on the time and place, ancillary circumstances, whether useful or disastrous. To accept discussion on this ground would have been to deprive oneself of everything that constitutes authority and strength; it would have been to renounce having on one's side the sense of justice that lives in every human heart. The principle of the freedom to trade has triumphed and has been applied to the things that are

14. The First Reform Act of 1832 allowed middle-class people to vote for the first time in England. The Catholic Emancipation Act of 1829 removed many but not all restrictions on Catholics in the United Kingdom.

necessary to life, and it will soon be applied to everything that can be traded internationally.

This cult of the absolute has been transferred to questions of a lesser order. When it was a matter of postal reform, the question was raised as to whether individual communications of thought, the expression of friendship, maternal love, or filial piety, were *taxable matters*. Public opinion replied in the negative and from that time on a radical, absolute reform has been pursued, with no worry as to whether the treasury would be embarrassed or in deficit in any way. The cost of carrying letters has been reduced to the smallest English coin, since this is enough to pay the state for the service rendered and reimburse it for its costs. And since the post still makes a profit, there should be no doubt that the cost of carrying letters would be reduced still further if there were in England a coin smaller than a *penny*.[15]

I admit that in this audaciousness and vigor there is a touch of greatness which causes me to follow with interest the debates in the English Parliament and, even more, the popular debates that take place in associations and meetings. This is where the future is worked out, where long discussions end up with the question "Are we hitting a fundamental principle?" And if the answer is affirmative, we may not know the day of its triumph but we can be sure that such triumph is assured.

Before returning to the subject of this chapter, anglomania and anglophobia, I must first warn the reader against a false interpretation that may insinuate itself into his mind. Although the conflict between aristocracy and democracy, ever present and lively at the center of each question, certainly gives heat and life to debates; although by delaying the solution and pushing it further away it contributes to the maturing of ideas and shapes the political habits of the people, it should not be concluded from this that I consider it an absolute disadvantage for my country not to have the same obstacles to overcome and consequently not to feel the same spur, not to enjoy the same mixture of vivacity and passion.

Principles are no less involved in our country than in England. The only thing is that our debates have to be much more general and *humanitarian* (since the word is sacred), just as, in our neighbor's country, they have to be more national. The aristocratic obstacle, in their eyes, occurs in their country. For us, it is worldwide. There is nothing, of course, to prevent us from

15. The Uniform Penny Post system was introduced throughout the United Kingdom in 1840.

taking principles to a height that England cannot yet reach. We do not do this, and this is a result solely of our inadequate degree of respect and devotion for principles.

If *anglophobia* were only a natural reaction in us against English oligarchy, whose policy is so dangerous to the nations and in particular to France, this would no longer be anglophobia but, and may I be forgiven for such a barbarous word (which is more than apposite since it combines two barbaric ideas), *oligarcophobia*.

Unfortunately, this is not so and the most constant occupation of our major newspapers is to arouse national sentiment against British democracy, against the working classes, who are demanding work, industry, wealth, and the development of their faculties and the strength necessary for their emancipation. It is precisely the growth of these democratic forces, the perfection of work, industrial superiority, the extension of the use of machines, commercial aptitude, and the accumulation of capital, it is precisely an increase of all of these forces, I say, that is represented to us as being dangerous, as being opposed to our own progress and implying as of necessity a proportional decrease in similar forces in our country.

This is the *economic sophism*[16] I have to combat and it is through this that the subject I have just dealt with is linked to the spirit of this book and which may up to now have appeared to be a pointless digression.

First of all, if what I call here a *sophism* was a truth, how sad and discouraging it would be! If the progressive movement which is making an appearance in one part of the world caused a retrograde movement in another part, if the increase in wealth in one country was achieved at the expense of a corresponding loss spread over all the others, there would obviously be no progress possible overall and, in addition, all national jealousy would be justified. Vague ideas of humanity and fraternity would certainly not be enough to lead a nation to rejoice at progress achieved elsewhere, since such progress would have been attained at its expense. The enthusiasts of fraternity do not change the human heart to that extent, and according to the hypothesis I envisage, it is not even desirable. What element of honesty or delicacy would have me rejoice at one people's elevation to having more than they need if, as a result, another people has to descend to below what they need? No, I am not bound either morally or religiously to carry out such an act of selflessness, even in the name of my country.

16. *Economic Sophisms.*

This is not all. If this sort of *pendulum* was the law governing nations, it would also be the law governing provinces, communes, and families. National progress is no different from individual progress, from which it can be seen that if the axiom with which I am concerned were a truth and not a sophism, there would not be a man on earth who would not constantly have to strive to stifle the progress of all the others, only to meet in others the same effort made against himself. This general conflict would be the natural state of society and Providence, in decreeing that *the benefit of one is the loss of another,* would have condemned mankind to an endless war and humanity to an invariably primitive condition.

There is no proposition in social science, therefore, that it is more important to elucidate. It is the keystone of the entire edifice. It is absolutely necessary to grasp the true nature of progress and the influence that the progressive condition of one people has on the condition of other peoples. If it were demonstrated that progress in a given constituency has as its cause or effect a proportional depression in the rest of the human race, nothing would remain to us but to burn our books, abandon all hope in the general good, and enter into the universal conflict with the firm determination to be crushed as little as possible while crushing the others as much as we can. This is not an exaggeration; it is the most rigorous logic, that which is the most often applied. A political measure that is so close to the axiom that the profit of one person is the loss of another, because it is the incarnation of this, the Navigation Act of Great Britain was situated openly in the quotation of the famous words of its preamble: *It is necessary for England to crush Holland or be crushed by her.* And we have seen, *La Presse* quotes the same words to have the same measure adopted in France. Nothing is simpler, as soon as there is no other alternative, for peoples, as for individuals, than to crush or be crushed, from which we can see the point at which error and atrocity achieve fusion.

But the sad axiom that I mention is well worth being opposed in a special chapter. It is, in effect, not a matter of opposing vague declamations on humanity, charity, fraternity, and self-sacrifice to it. It needs to be destroyed by a demonstration that is, so to speak, mathematical. While being determined to devote a few pages to this task, I will pursue what I have to say about anglophobia.

I have said that this sentiment, insofar as it is linked to this Machiavellian policy which the English oligarchy has caused to weigh for so long on

Europe, was justifiable, with its own raison d'être, and should not even be labeled anglophobia.

It deserves this name only when it envelops in the same hatred both the aristocracy and that part of English society that has suffered as much as or more than we from oligarchic predominance and resisted it, the working class, which was initially weak and powerless but which grew sufficiently in wealth, strength, and influence to carry along in its wake part of the aristocracy and hold the other in check, the class to which we should be holding out a hand, whose sentiments and hopes we should share if we were not restrained by the deadly and discouraging thought that the progress it owes to work, industry, and commerce is a threat to our prosperity and independence, and threatens it in another form but as thoroughly as do the policies of the Walpoles, Pitts, etc., etc.

This is how anglophobia has become generalized, and I admit that I can view only with disgust the means that have been used to maintain and arouse it. The first means is simple but no less odious; it consists in taking advantage of the diversity of languages. Advantage has been taken of the fact that English is little known in France to persuade us that all English literature and journalism consisted only of outrages, insults, and calumnies perpetually vomited out against France, from which France could not fail to conclude that, on the other side of the Channel, she was the object of general and inextinguishable hatred.

In this we were marvelously served by the boundless freedom of the press and speech which exists in this neighboring country. In England, as in France, there is no question on which opinion is not divided, so that it is always possible, on every occasion, to uncover an orator or a newspaper that has covered the question from the point of view that hurts us. The odious tactic of our newspapers has been to extract from these speeches and writings the passages most likely to humiliate our national pride and quote them as an expression of public opinion in England, taking very good care to keep under wraps everything said or written giving the opposite view, even by the most influential newspapers and the most popular orators. The result has been what it would be in Spain if the press of that entire country agreed to take all quotations from our newspapers from *La Quotidienne*.

Another means, which has been employed very successfully, is silence. Each time a major question has caused organized resistance in England and was likely to reveal whatever existed in that country in the way of life, enlightenment, warmth, and sincerity, you could be sure that our newspapers would be determined to prevent the fact reaching the general public in France, by their silence, and when they have thought it necessary, they have imposed ten years of silence on themselves. As extraordinary as it may seem, English *resistance* against protectionism bears this out.

Finally, another *patriotic fraud* that has been widely used is false translation, with the addition, removal, and substitution of words. This ability to alter the meaning and the spirit of the discourse has meant that there is no limit to the indignation that can be aroused in the minds of our fellow countrymen. For example, when they found *gallant French* meaning "brave Frenchmen" ("gallant" being the word *vaillant* which was transferred to England and to which the only change made was that of the initial *V* to *G,* as opposed to the inverse change made to the words *garant,* "warrant"; *guêpe,* "wasp"; *guerre,* "war"), it was enough to translate it thus: "effeminate, philandering, corrupt nation." Sometimes they went so far as to substitute the word *hatred* for the word *friendship* and so on.[17]

On this subject, may I be allowed to relate the origin of the book I published in 1845 under the title of *Cobden and the League.*

I was living in a village in the heart of the Landes. In this village, there is a discussion group, and I would probably greatly surprise the members of the Jockey Club if I quoted here the budget of our modest association. However, I dare to believe that there reigns there an uninhibited gaiety and zest that would not dishonor the sumptuous salons of the boulevard des Italiens. Be that as it may, in our circle we do not only laugh, we also discuss politics (which is quite different), for please note that we have two newspapers there. This shows that we were strong patriots and anglophobes of the first order. As for me, as steeped in English literature as one could be in the village, I had seriously suspected that our newspapers were exaggerating somewhat the hatred that, according to them, the word *French* aroused in our neighbors and I sometimes happened to express doubts in this regard.

17. (Paillottet's note) One might plead an attenuating circumstance on behalf of French newspapers. It was, I think, particular ignorance, defensiveness, or inadvertence rather than calculation which figured in the majority of the misdeeds for which Bastiat reproaches them. If we examine, for example, the letters which he had to send to two of the leaders of Parisian journalism, the editors of *La Presse* and *Le National,* it will be clear that these two papers did not grasp either the progress or the importance of the debate on the Corn Laws in England. See letters to the editors of *La Presse.* [*OC,* vol. 7, p. 143, "Au redacteur de *La Presse*"; and p. 152, "Au redacteur du *National.*"]

"I cannot understand," I said, "why the spirit that reigns in journalism in Great Britain does not reign in its books." But I was always defeated, proof in hand or no.

One day, the most anglophobic of my colleagues, with eyes alight with fury, showed me the newspaper and said, "Read this and see." I read in effect that the prime minister of England had ended a speech by saying, "We will not adopt this measure. If we adopted it, we would fall, like France, to the lowest rank of all the nations." A patriotic flush rose to my cheeks.

However, on reflection, I said to myself, "It seems very extraordinary that a minister, the leader of a cabinet, a man who because of his position has to speak with such reserve and measure, would allow himself to utter an uncalled-for insult, which nothing has motivated, provoked, or justified. Mr. Peel does not think that France has fallen to the lowest rank of all the nations and, even if he thought that, he would not say so, in open Parliament."

I wanted to be sure of my facts. The same day, I wrote to Paris to subscribe to an English newspaper,[18] asking for the subscription to be backdated one month.

A few days later, I received about thirty issues of the *Globe*. I hurriedly searched for the unfortunate statement by Mr. Peel and I saw that it was as follows, "We could not adopt this measure without descending to the lowest rank of all the nations." The words *like France* were missing.

That put me on the right track and I have been able to ascertain since then a number of other *pious frauds* in our journalists' method of translating.

But that is not all I learned from the *Globe*. For two years, I was able to follow the development and progress of the *League*.

At that time, I was an ardent supporter, as I am today, of the cause of free trade, but I considered it to be lost for centuries, since it is no more spoken of in our country than it probably was in China in the last century. Imagine my surprise and joy on learning that this great question *had grabbed people's attention* across the length and breadth of England and Scotland, and on reading about this uninterrupted succession of huge *meetings*,[19] and the energy, perseverance, and enlightenment of the leaders of this admirable association!

But what surprised me even more was to see that the League was spreading, growing, and spilling floods of light over England, monopolizing the

18. The *Globe and Traveller.*
19. In English in the original.

attention of ministers and Parliament, without a word of mention in our newspapers!

Naturally I suspected that there was some correlation between this absolute silence on such a serious matter and the system of *pious frauds* in translation.

Naively thinking that it was sufficient for this silence to be broken just once for it not to persist any longer, I decided, trembling, to become a writer, and I sent a few articles on the League to *La Sentinelle* in Bayonne. However, the Paris newspapers paid not the slightest attention to them. I set about translating a few speeches by Cobden, Bright, and Fox and sent them to Paris newspapers themselves; they did not print them. "It is not to be tolerated," I said to myself, "that the day on which free trade is proclaimed in England should surprise us in our ignorance. I have only one course, that is to write a book. . . ."

---

6. Proposition for the Creation of a School for Sons of Sharecroppers

> [The following paper was presented in 1844 to the Chamber of Agriculture of the Landes, after being presented to a Catholic foundation that rejected it for lack of sufficient resources. From the private collection of Jean-Claude Paul-Dejean.]

I am going to put before you, sirs, the plan of the institution that I am proposing by telling you how the thought came to me. Since I am the owner of an estate, perhaps one of the most suited to major crop rotation in the country, I have tried out this project in the past, but it did not take long for me to realize that it was beyond my powers. As I am of uncertain health, I was constantly being warned that it was possible that I would not be able to continue this work, and I recoiled from any decision that by launching me definitely into this career would have obliged me to burn all my boats. With a certain hesitation I decided to make some preliminary expenditures which were bound to be written off if I had to stop the work and, as you know, in an enterprise that demands faith and strength, you have already lost if you have an eye constantly on retreating.

For a while I had the idea of finding someone to work with me and throwing myself into the very risky business of full-time farming. But I soon realized how risky this resolution was. Our region of sharecropping farms does not provide opportunities for large-scale farming; the only workers you find are the class of inhabitants known as "idlers," the dregs of the working population, who have been turned off sharecropping farms because of their laziness and bad behavior. It was therefore a question of nothing less than importing managers, workers, equipment, cattle, and seed from afar. How many mistakes might such farming entail, made up as it would be of oddments, without any form of trial and that preliminary testing without which a successful transition from small-scale to large-scale farming cannot be effected.

And then, would this operation have been genuinely useful? For reasons that I will not go into here, it is doubtful whether the managers would have made the interest from their capital that any other form of industry would have yielded and, as for the country, I think that its form of farming devoted to sharecropping would have gained little from the example of a large-scale farm, even supposing that the example had been totally positive.

There was just one avenue open to me. This was to improve the estate using the means it offered me, that is to say by enlightening the sharecroppers and by seeking to attract them to my ideas. I did not even try this. Apart from the huge difficulty of the enterprise and the constant state of conflict into which it would have put me vis-à-vis the smallholders, a conflict which I would be almost sure to lose through open resistance and even more by the force of inertia, I would feel guilty if I forced these good workers to abandon their method of farming. Whatever my total belief in the superiority of crop rotation, I could not keep from myself the fact that, when it comes to attempts directed by the willing but inexperienced and carried out by the ill-intentioned, the immediate results might be extremely dangerous. What right had I to bring possible losses on men incapable of supporting them? I congratulate myself now that I drew back from these various schemes (and if) I now tell the story of my disappointments, it is because I think that in almost all cases they relate to those overardent friends of progress, in too much of a hurry to achieve the promises of science without taking sufficient account of the difficulties that arise from a farming system and a series of habits evolved for a very different set of circumstances. Overcoming obstacles is doubtless proof of strength, but avoiding them in order not to be overcome is proof of wisdom.

What would therefore be most useful, philanthropic, and at the same time most practical would be to act with regard to the class of sharecroppers themselves, that is to say, on the young generation, to educate them, renew them, and raise them through intelligence and dignity to the level of the middle classes of society.

Among the projects that came to my mind, there is one that pleased me,

I must admit, more than all the others. It seemed to me to be worthy of occupying the life of a man who did not want to depart from this earth without leaving some trace of his passing and a few honorable memories in the minds of good men. It is the foundation of a school for sharecropping, for a nursery of good sharecroppers with whose help I would in the long run carry out on my estate this farming revolution that people long for so, in a way that would be most advantageous to me and my region. But since it has not been granted to me to make this institution my work, I hasten to set out the plan for it to you, having removed from it the personal aim that I might have had in a former time.

Admission. In order to gain entry to the school for sharecroppers, the candidate has to belong to the class of sharecroppers and to a family of good reputation; to be aged fourteen; to know how to read, write, and do calculations; to have proof of intelligence, activity, and an ordered and open mind at primary school; and to have a good physical constitution. These conditions would be imposed on us in any case by the limited resources that we will probably have at our disposal, which would not allow us to have at our school very young children who are incapable of earning even part of their subsistence and whose early education would require the intervention of an elementary teacher; we should be happy that they are not incompatible and they are even in total harmony with the object of our wishes, which is to train as quickly as possible and at the lowest possible cost a certain number of hard-working, well-instructed, and upright sharecroppers.

At the age of fourteen, a child is able to take part in all farming work; he is close to the age at which he can turn his hand to the plough and I do not see why one would reclassify a special school so as to overload it with the care of imparting the general primary education which our legislation has provided for. None of you, sirs, could fail to be interested in the efforts that have been made in various locations to preserve children from vagrancy. Like you, I admire these noble attempts. Who is able to read without emotion the account of his visit to the Hofwill that Mr. Feutrier has included in *Les Annales de Roville.*[20] However, the aim we have set ourselves is essentially different.

20. The agronomist Mathieu de Dombasle had created a model farm with a school in the village of Roville, in the *département* of La Meurthe. The farm published an agricultural journal, *Les Annales de Roville.* Hofwill (in Switzerland), as well as the French villages of Petit-Bourg and Mettray, mentioned below, also had agricultural schools.

In the philanthropic institutions to which I refer, the need has been felt to admit only children who are six years old. If they were older, they would introduce the seeds of immorality and evil tendencies into the schools. People preferred to have them institutionalized a few years longer rather than to expose young smallholders to the contagion of vice and insubordination. However, I repeat, the aim of Hofwill, Petit-Bourg, and Mettray differs from ours. It is directed exclusively to vagrants, beggars, and that precocious corruption which threatens society. We, on the other hand, are looking for exceptional natures, children gifted with naturally happy dispositions, which have been developed through the care of their families and community teachers. We are therefore able and are even obliged to postpone the age of admission, a fortunate circumstance that enables us to count on the actual work of these young people to contribute to the cost of their board and lodging.

Work at the School. If, after studying and discussing this project, the society believes it could implement it, I would be able to place at its disposal a conveniently situated sharecropping farm of twenty hectares of cultivable land and land that could be given over progressively to cultivation. The society will judge whether the school would continue to give me one-third of the produce or whether it would not be more appropriate to set an estimated rental price.

It is not yet time to talk about the system of cultivation that should be followed. I will say just a word while waiting to go into more detail if the occasion warrants this. I would like the cultivable land to be planted with mulberry bushes in wide rows. The number of these rows will permit the adoption of any form of rotation considered suitable and the submission of the estate, so to speak, to market gardening. In this way, the school would satisfy three essential conditions: 1. it would give the young pupils the experience of raising a great variety of plants, 2. it would supply manpower in proportion to the overall number of hands by definition at the disposal of the manager, 3. it would bring into the region market gardening, which fits in so well with the small acreage of our sharecropping farms and is, moreover, the only system that, through the abundance of its produce, enables competition between small- and large-scale farming enterprises.

The same divisions would be adopted in the second sector of the rural economy, the raising of stock. The production of milk and wool and the raising of calves and beef cattle would be carried out simultaneously. The results of all these operations, either in the fields or in the barns, would have to be carefully recorded in strict accounts. I do not know, sirs, whether I am exaggerating the usefulness of accounts, but I am one of those who think that no operation that is at all complicated can do without them. I dare to point out that there is no farmer, even among those who keep their accounts with the greatest care but who do not use the *double entry* system, who can establish with accuracy the cost price of his wheat, fodder, milk, fertilizer, and how much his working day or hour produces, what his teams and vehicles, plowing or hoeing cost, and still less if this or that harvest or occupation is more lucrative than another. There is also in accounting "a very vigorous, moralizing principle." A farmer who keeps his books knows exactly what each of his practices is worth or costs him. His books tell him in irrefutable figures and repeat this to him each time he opens them. Is it to be believed that a sharecropper would attend markets so much if he were obliged to note as a loss each hour of the time he wastes, according to a strict evaluation?

There is another reason that makes the use of accounting indispensable. Crop rotation certainly greatly complicates the relationships between sharecroppers and their owners; as long as it is only a question of sharing the sheaves and heads of corn on the spot, it is not essential to know their cost accurately. But when *rye* and *corn* are no longer the only and perhaps not the largest sources of income, when the master's capital and the work of the smallholder become intimately associated in the production of fodder, milk, butter, meat, and wool, only strict accounting can show the most appropriate agreements and make it easy to carry them out. Perhaps it will be thought that in this respect sharecropping seems to be incompatible with advanced cultivation. I admit that I consider their combination as necessarily leading to much more direct cooperation on the part of owners, and this certainly will be no bad thing. However, if the difficulties become too great, tenant farming would seem here to be a resource the adoption of which our school might even greatly facilitate.

Graduating from the School. Let us now move forward in thought, sirs, to the time at which your establishment will start to provide people for agriculture. Four pupils, now become men, will leave the school. Six years of study and practice have made them familiar with the most advanced farming methods. Accounting has made the most varied combinations easier for them and they are able to work in line with the views of enlightened owners. One will take up a sharecropping farm with his family. Others, while waiting for one to become available, may join together in association and take up a joint operation. They themselves will need young colleagues and will thus disseminate the education they have received. Will this not be so many subsidiaries for the mother school? From neighbor to neighbor, it will be easy for the most advanced owners, those who do not retreat in the face of progress, to propel their estates to the highest degree of perfection. The region will see the rise of a race of men combining knowledge with experience. We will no longer have to deplore the unbridgeable distance that now appears to separate the thinking class from the active class. Work, enlightenment, land, and capital will all combine and advance, and our society itself will be strengthened by an element, which it must be agreed it rather lacks, I mean the contribution of men who do things.

I will not hide, sirs, that an institution like this seems to me to go deeply into the depths of the major problems that we have to solve. I think that it meets more closely the needs of the region than what we call experimental farms, model farms, or farming institutes, and if we look at these closely we will be convinced that these expensive establishments are genuine vicious circles. Some may give us good lessons and others good examples, but what good are these lessons and examples to us, who are unable to apply them ourselves, or to our sharecroppers, who can benefit from neither?

On the other hand the project that I have the honor of submitting to you may in practice introduce four sharecropping farms each year into the orbit of crop rotation. Each of these in turn will train new adepts in the class of sharecroppers itself. Practical example and dissemination are in line and go hand in hand, and it seems to me that our school will perhaps require fifty years of existence to accomplish this major farming and social revolution in our region which, without it, would not appear to be possible in a hundred years.

I must now tell you of the difficulties which this project may encounter.

The Master. The first and by far the greatest lies in the choice of a master. What eminent qualities are not required for functions like these? The person called upon to assume them has to have a wide-ranging practical and theoretical farming education, his moral stature must be irreproachable, and he must have the gift of training and directing young minds. He must like children and give them only good lessons and examples and must submit himself to sharing their lives, studies, and work. No, we will not be asking him to cooperate as a mercenary but to undertake a task of total selflessness, sublime charity, devotion, and sacrifice.

These considerations led me to contact the Foundation of Saint-Antoine to find out whether we might count on the cooperation of one or more brothers from this order. Perhaps you know, sirs, that it is very similar to the Order of the Brothers of the Christian Doctrine. The difference between them is that the Christian Brothers devote themselves to general primary education while the foundation is devoted to imparting a farming education to orphans and vagrants. The reply I received and which I submit to the society does not give us hope for the cooperation I had counted on.

May I be allowed to say that the venerable priest who manages the Foundation of Saint-Antoine does not perhaps appreciate[21] the stature of the institution I am proposing when he considers it a powerful instrument for production? "While it is desirable to practice good farming methods," he said, "and prepare a generation that is intelligent and capable through a greater development of farming products, it is also good to make some effort to cure the plague of beggary and eliminate the seeds of vagrancy that are so detrimental to the peace of society."

Please God, how could I ever undermine the usefulness and merit of such work!

---

21. What Bastiat himself did not appreciate, as we know from other documents, is that the foundation did not feel able to do both jobs: the salvation of the dropouts and the training of the most gifted.

Section 2

Political Manifestos[1]

1. To the Electors of the *Département* of the Landes[2]

November 1830   [vol. 1, p. 217]

A people is not free simply because it has liberal institutions; it also needs to know how to put them into practice, and the same legislation that plucked from the ballot box such names as La Fayette and Chantelauze, Tracy, and Dudon can, depending on the wisdom of the electors, become the palladium of public freedom or the most unyielding instrument of total oppression, the one exercised over a nation by the nation itself.

In order for an electoral law to be a genuine guarantee for the public one condition is essential: electors must know where their interests lie and be determined to achieve their triumph. They must not allow their vote to be swayed by issues that are foreign to the election nor view this solemn act as a mere formality or at the very most as a matter between an elector and his candidate. They must not totally overlook the consequences of a bad choice. In a word, the public itself must know how to use the sole repressive means at its disposition, and show hatred and scorn for those voters who sacrifice it through ignorance or offer it up to their greed.

It is really strange to listen to the naive views of certain electors.

One will vote for a candidate through personal gratitude or through friendship, as though it were not a genuine crime to settle his debt at the

---

1. Bastiat's original French for "political manifestos" is *professions de foi,* which is literally translated as "professions of faith." We have chosen instead to translate *professions de foi* as "political manifestos," which better conveys his true intention in these pieces, namely, the expression of his beliefs and political program to his electors if he were to be elected.

2. (Paillottet's note) In support of the candidature of M. Faurie.

expense of the public and to make an entire people the victim of individual affection.

Another will yield to what he calls *the recognition due to major services rendered to the country,* as though the office of deputy were a reward and not a mandate; as though the Chamber were a pantheon which we have to people with cold, inanimate figures and not the arena in which the fate of peoples is settled.

One person would think he was dishonoring his region if he did not send a deputy born in the *département* to the Chamber. Out of fear that some candidatures will be deemed invalid, he encourages the belief that the electors are stupid. He considers that he shows more intelligence in choosing an idiot from his own region rather than an enlightened man from a nearby district and that it is better reasoning to have oneself oppressed by the representation of someone who lives in the Landes than to be released from one's chains by that of an inhabitant of the Basses Pyrénées.

Another wants a deputy who is versed in the art of lobbying; he hopes that our local interests will benefit and does not think that an independent vote on municipal law may prove to be more advantageous to all the regions of France than the lobbying and obsessions of a hundred deputies might be to a single one.

Lastly, yet another is obstinately determined to reelect the 221[3] indefinitely.

It is useless for you to put forward the most soundly based objections and his only reply will be: "My candidate is one of the 221."

What is his past record? "I have forgotten, but he is one of the 221."

But he is a member of the government. Do you think he will be ready to restrict the power he shares or to reduce the taxes on which he lives? "That does not worry me because he is one of the 221."

Just think that he will contribute to passing laws. Do you not realize the consequences of a choice made on grounds that do not relate to the goal you ought to set yourself? "That's all the same to me. He is one of the 221."

But it is above all the *moderation* which plays a major role in this army of sophisms that I wish to review briefly.

Everyone wants *moderates* at any price; we fear extremists above all and how can we judge the category to which our candidate belongs? We do not

---

3. To a threatening speech from the throne, 221 deputies replied with an address strongly condemning the government chosen by the king.

scrutinize his opinions but the place he occupies, and since the center is definitely between the right and the left, we conclude that this is where *moderation* lies.

Were those who each year voted for more taxes than the nation could bear *moderates*? What about those who never found the contributions to be sufficiently heavy, emoluments sufficiently huge, and sinecures sufficiently numerous? What about those who engaged in an odious traffic with all governments in the betrayal of the confidence of their constituents, a betrayal through which, in reward for dinners and positions, they accepted the most tyrannical institutions in the name of the nation: double voting,[4] *lois d'amour,*[5] or laws on sacrilege?[6] What of those who, in a word, have reduced France to breaking the chains they spent fifteen years in forging through a coup d'état?

And are those who want to prevent the return of such excesses *extremists*? I mean those who want to inject a dose of moderation into spending; those who want to *moderate* the action of the people in power and who are not *immoderate,* that is to say, insatiably seeking high salaries and sinecures; those who do not want our revolution to become just a change in surnames and color; those who do not want the nation to be exploited by one party rather than another and who wish to prevent the storm which will inevitably break if electors are rash enough to give a majority to the *center right* of the Chamber?

I will not go further in examining the reasons for supporting a candidate for whom the general opinion does not hold out much hope. What use would it be to spend more time refuting sophisms which are used only to delude oneself?

I think that electors have just one way of making a reasonable choice; they first need to know the general aim of the national representative body and then to gain an idea of the work that the future legislature will have to carry out. It is in fact the nature of the mandate which should decide the choice of a representative for us and, in this respect as in others, we will ex-

4. A law of 1820 specified that at each election of deputies one-fourth of the electors, those paying the most taxes, would be allowed to vote twice.

5. In 1824 the ministry of justice introduced laws limiting the freedom of the press, which the ministry presented as "laws of justice and love." They were derisively called *les lois d'amour* (the laws of love).

6. A law voted in 1825 inflicted the death penalty on authors of sacrileges. It was never enforced.

pose ourselves to great disillusionment if we adopt the *means,* leaving aside the *aim* we intend to achieve.

The general objective of national representative bodies is easy to understand.

In order to be able to carry out safely all the modes of activity in the course of private life, taxpayers need to be administered, judged, protected, and defended. This is the aim of government. Government is made up of the king, who is the supreme head, ministers, and an army of agents who report to one another and who envelop the nation as if it were in a huge network.

If this vast machine always kept itself within the limits of its responsibilities, elected representatives would be superfluous. However, the government is a living body at the center of the nation, which, like all organized entities, tends strongly to preserve its existence, to increase its well-being and power, and to expand indefinitely its sphere of action. Left to itself, it soon exceeds the limits which circumscribe its mission. It increases beyond all reason the number and wealth of its agents. It no longer administers, it exploits. It no longer judges, it persecutes or takes revenge. It no longer protects, it oppresses.

This would be the way all governments operate, the inevitable result of this law of movement with which nature has endowed all organized beings, if the people did not place obstacles in the way of governmental encroachments.

The electoral law is precisely this brake on the encroachments of government, a brake which our constitution hands over to taxpayers themselves. It tells them, "Government will exist from now on not for its own purposes but for yours. It will administer only to the extent that you feel the need to be administered. It will embark only on the development that you consider necessary for it to undertake. You will be the masters in expanding or tightening its resources. It will adopt no measure without your involvement. It will draw money from your purse only with your consent. In a word, since it is from you and for you that power exists, you may at will monitor it and contain it if need be, supporting its views when they are useful or reining in its action if it causes damage to your interests."

These general considerations impose on us, as electors, a primary obligation not to seek our representatives from among the ranks of government; rather, we should entrust the responsibility of resisting government to those over whom it is exercised and not to those by whom it is exercised.

Would we in fact be so foolish as to hope that, when it is a question of abolishing jobs and salaries, this mission will be properly carried out by civil servants and paid staff? When all our ills result from the excesses of those in power, would we entrust to a representative of that power the task of reducing it? No, no, a choice must be made. Let us nominate a civil servant, a prefect or a *maître des requêtes*[7] if we do not think the burden is sufficiently heavy, if we are not weary from the weight of the state billions,[8] if we are persuaded that government does not take an undue interest in things that ought to be outside its responsibilities, if we want it to continue to interfere in matters of education, religion, commerce, or industry or to allocate us doctors, lawyers, snuff, tobacco, electors, and jurors.

If we wish, however, to restrict the action of the government, let us not appoint employees of the government. If we wish to decrease taxation, let us not appoint those people who live off taxation. If we wish to obtain good municipal law let us not appoint a prefect. If we want freedom of education, let us not appoint a rector.[9] If we want to eliminate the *droits réunis*[10] or the Council of State, let us not appoint either a councillor of state or the director of the *droits réunis*. Individuals cannot independently represent those who pay them, and it is absurd to have a function kept in check by the very person bound by it.

If we examine the work of the future legislature, we see that it is of such importance that it can be regarded as a constituent body rather than as a purely *legislative* body.

It will have to provide us with an electoral law, that is to say, one that establishes the limits of sovereignty.

It will promulgate a municipal law of which each word must have an influence on the well-being of local regions.

It will be the body that debates the organization of the National Guard, which has a direct bearing on the integrity of our frontiers and the maintenance of public order.

Education will claim its attention and it will doubtless be called upon to open that education to the free competition of teachers and the choice of subjects to the care of parents.

Ecclesiastical affairs will require our deputies to have wide-ranging knowl-

---

7. A civil servant in charge of initiating appeals against the state.

8. A reference to the amount of the state budget.

9. Government-appointed head of all public education in an *académie* (a group of departments in the context of public education).

10. These were a combination of taxes introduced by Napoléon.

edge, great prudence, and unshakeable firmness. Perhaps, in line with the wishes of the supporters of justice and enlightened priests, the question will be raised as to whether the expenses arising from each faith should not be borne exclusively by those who take part in it.

Many other weighty matters will also be raised.

However, it is above all with regard to the economic part of the Chamber's work that we should be scrupulous in selecting our deputies. Abuses, sinecures, exorbitant pay, irrelevant pos itions, damaging jobs, and administrative structures substituted for competition will have to be strictly investigated; I have no fear in stating that this is the worst plague from which France is suffering.

I apologize to the reader for the digression into which I feel I am being irresistibly drawn, but I cannot stop myself from seeking to have the depths of my thoughts on this grave question understood.

If I considered excessive expenditure to be evil only because of the portion of wealth of which it deprives the nation for no good reason, if the only results I noted were the weighty burden of taxes, I would not raise the subject so often. I would say, with M. Guizot, that *liberty should not be bargained over,* that it is an asset so precious that no price is too high for it and that we should not regret the millions it costs us.

Such language implies that prodigality and liberty can go hand in hand. However, if I am deeply convinced that they are incompatible, that grossly overpaid jobs and the proliferation of positions not only exclude liberty but also undermine public order and peace and compromise the stability of governments, as well as polluting the ideas of peoples and corrupting their morals, no one will be surprised that I attach so much importance to the selection of deputies who will enable us to hope for the elimination of abuses like these.

But where can there be liberty when the government, in order to sustain enormous expenditures and forced to levy huge fiscal contributions, must resort to the most offensive and burdensome taxation, the most unjust monopolies, the most odious demands; to invade the sphere of private industry, to narrow incessantly the circle of individual activity, to make itself merchant, manufacturer, postman, and teacher, not only pricing its services at the highest level but also removing any competition which might threaten to reduce its profits, by means of punishments intended for crimes? Are we free if the government spies on all our movements in order to tax them, subjects all its activities to the goal of enlarging its cohort of employees, hampers all businesses, constrains all faculties, interferes with all commercial exchanges in order to restrain some people, hinder others, and hold almost all of them to ransom?

Can we expect *order* from a regime that places millions of enticements to greed all around the country and constantly gives the whole of a huge kingdom the appearance offered by a large town on the day of *free handouts*?

Do we believe that the stability of power is assured when, having been abandoned by people who have been alienated by its exactions, it remains without defense in the face of attack by the ambitious, when portfolios are fiercely assailed and defended and when those laying siege rely on rebellion just as those being besieged rely on despotism, the one in order to achieve power and the others to retain it?

Inflated salaries result not only in restrictions, a lack of order, and the instability of government; they also distort people's ideas by strengthening the barbarous prejudice that work is to be scorned and jobs in the public sector are the only ones worthy of honor. They corrupt morals by making careers in industry burdensome and government employment flourish; by enticing the entire population to abandon manufacturing in favor of careers in the state sector, work in favor of political intrigue, manufacturing in favor of sterile consumption, ambition to control things in favor of ambition to control men; and, in sum, by increasingly spreading a mania for governing and a zeal for domination.

Do we want then to free government from the plotters who pursue it in order to share out the spoils, from factions who undermine it in order to capture it, and from the tyrants who strengthen it in order to control it? Do we want to achieve order, freedom, and public peace? Let us above all take care to reduce excessive remuneration, remove the enticements if we fear greed, and eliminate the seductive prizes linked to the end of a career if we do not want careers beset with antagonism. Let us wholeheartedly embrace the American system, in which top civil servants are indemnified and not richly endowed, where positions lead to a great deal of work and little profit, where civil service jobs are a burden assumed and not the means to a fortune and do not give glory to those holding them nor arouse envy in those who do not.

Once we have understood the object of national representation, once we have examined the work to be carried out by the future legislature, we will find it easy to know what qualities and guarantees we have to require from our deputy.

It is clear that the first thing we have to look for in him is knowledge of the subjects he will be called upon to discuss, in other words his *ability* in the fields of political economy and legislation.

We cannot deny that M. Faurie fulfills this first condition. The ease with which he has managed his individual affairs is a guarantee that he will be capable of administering public matters. His knowledge of finance might be of great use in the Chamber. In short, throughout his life he has devoted himself with dedication to the study of moral and political science.

The *ability* to do well is not enough for our representative; he also needs *determination,* and this determination can be guaranteed only by a constant past record, total independence of character, wealth, and social position.

In all of these respects, M. Faurie should meet the requirements of the most stringent elector.

No inconsistency in his past gives us anxiety as to the future. His probity in private life is well known and virtue in M. Faurie is not a vague sentiment but a well-defined system that is invariably practiced, which means that it would be difficult to find a man whose conduct and opinions are more in harmony. His political probity is most scrupulous; his wealth places him beyond any form of enticement, just as his courage puts him beyond all forms of fear. He does not want positions and cannot desire them; he has neither sons nor brothers in whose favor he might, to our detriment, compromise his independence. In sum, the force of his character will make him for us not an intrepid lobbyist (it is good to note that he is this) but a stubborn defender when needed.

If, along with just ideas and high sentiments, we required a talent for oratory as a condition that is, if not essential, at least desirable, I would not dare to claim that M. Faurie possesses the passionate eloquence to rouse popular masses in a public arena, but I consider him perfectly capable of putting forward in the Chamber the observations his upright mind and conscientious intentions generate and it is accepted that, where it is a matter of debating laws, the eloquence which appeals only to reason for its enlightenment is less dangerous than that which appeals to passions in order to sway them.

I have heard an objection to this candidate which I consider to have little foundation, the comment "should we not fear that, as he comes from Bayonne, he will work harder for Bayonne than for the *département* of the Landes?"

My answer will not be that no one dreamed of raising this objection to M. d'Haussez; that the link that is forged between a representative and the electors is as powerful as that which binds a man to the region in which he was born; finally, that as M. Faurie's property lies in the *département* of the Landes, he may to some degree be regarded as a fellow countryman of ours.

There is another answer which, in my view, removes any basis for the objection.

To hear the language used by these farsighted men, would it not seem that the interests of Bayonne and the *département* of the Landes are so far opposed that nothing can be done for one that does not invariably run counter to the good of the other? But if we reflect a little on the respective positions of Bayonne and the Landes, we will perceive that, on the contrary, their interests are inseparable and identical.

In effect, in the ordinary course of events, a commercial town situated at the mouth of a river can have an importance only proportional to that of the region through which the river flows. If Nantes and Bordeaux are more prosperous than Bayonne, it is because the Loire and the Garonne flow through regions that are much richer than those the Adour traverses, areas that are capable of producing and consuming more. This being so, as the trade relating to this production and consumption is carried out in the town situated at the mouth of the river, it ensues that the trade in this town grows or is restricted depending on whether the surrounding regions prosper or decline. Were the banks of the Adour and its tributaries fertile, the moors cleared, the Chalosse given means of communication, our *département* crossed by canals and inhabited by a significant and rich population, then Bayonne would be assured of trade by the nature of things. If our deputy wants to make Bayonne flourish, he will first have to attract prosperity to the *département* of the Landes.

If different constituency boundaries brought Bayonne into our *département,* is it not a fact that we would not object? Well then, has a line drawn on a scrap of paper changed the nature of things? Does the fact that on a map a town is separated from the countryside surrounding it by a red or blue line divide their mutual interests?

There are some who fear compromising the proper order of things by selecting as deputies men who are clearly liberal. "For the moment," they say, "we need order above all. We need deputies who do not want to go too far too fast!"

Well! It is precisely in order to maintain order that good deputies should be appointed! It is through a love of order that we should seek to ensure that the chambers are in harmony with France. If you want order, are you going to strengthen the *center right,* at a time when it grates on France, a time when, with her most cherished hopes dashed, she is anxiously awaiting the election results? And do you know what she will do if she sees that, once again, her final hopes have evaporated? For my part, I do not know.

Electors, let us take up our stations, let us remember that the future legislature will bear within it the entire destiny of France, that its decisions must either snuff out for good or indefinitely prolong this struggle that has existed for so long between the France of yesteryear and modern France! Let us recall that our destiny is in our hands and that we are the masters on whom it falls to strengthen or dissolve this monstrous centralization, this gallows structure built up by Bonaparte and restored by the Bourbons in order to exploit the nation, once they had garroted it. Let us not forget that it is an illusion to count on colors and proper names to improve our lot; let us rely only on our independence and our resolve. Do we want the government to take more of an interest in us than we take in ourselves? Are we expecting it to restrain itself if we strengthen it and become less active if we send it reinforcements? Do we hope that the spoils it can take from us will be refused if we are the first to offer them? What! Should we expect a supernatural nobility of spirit or a chimerical impartiality in those who govern us, while for our part we are incapable of defending, through a simple vote, our dearest interests!

Electors, be careful! We will not be able to retrieve the opportunity if we let it slip. A major revolution has taken place; up to now, how has it improved your existence? I know that reforms take longer than a day, that we should not ask for the impossible nor criticize at random through bad temper or habit. I know that the new government needs strength and I believe it to be imbued with the best intentions, but ultimately we should not shut our eyes to the evidence nor should the fear of going too fast reduce us to immobility nor, worse, remove from us any hope of making progress. And, if there has been no material improvement, have we at least been given any reason for hope? No, they tear up those intoxicating proclamations which in the heat of the moment would have made us spill the last drop of our blood. Each day brings us closer to that past which the three glorious days should have cast back to a remote century. Is it a question of communal law? The Martignac[11] project is being exhumed, which was drawn up under the influ-

11. The comte de Martignac (J. B. Gay), minister of the interior from 1828 to 1829, planned to have the members of the general councils (councils of the *département*) and

ence of an officious court with no confidence in the nation. Is it a question of a mobile National Guard? Instead of these popular choices which ought to make it a moral force, they throw us as a consolation prize the election of subalterns, and their distrust of us is such that all our leaders are imposed on us. Is the question that of taxes? They clearly state that the government will not lower them by a cent; that if they make a *sacrifice* in one sector of the revenue, they will recover it from another; that the billion must remain intact indefinitely; that if some economy is achieved, taxpayers will not be relieved thereby; that eliminating one form of abuse would entail eliminating them all and that they do not wish to go down that road; that taxing drink is the fairest and most equitable of taxes,[12] the one which is least offensively collected and least costly, a fine ideal of fiscal design which must be maintained, with no attention paid to the *clamor* of an overburdened populace, and that if they agree to alter it, it is with reluctance and on condition that instead of one iniquity they will make us suffer two; that all forms of transport will be taxed without any problem or inconvenience resulting for anyone; that luxury goods should not be made to pay but rather that redoubled contributions should be imposed on useful objects; that France is beautiful and rich and can be counted upon; that it is easy to bring her round to reason; and a hundred other things which bring back comte de Villèle in the person of Baron Louis[13] and which confound you to such a dizzy extent that you do not know whether you are waking up in the reign of Philippe or that of Bonaparte.

But, people will say, these are only projects; our deputies still have to debate and adopt them.

Doubtless, and it is for this reason that we need to be scrupulous in our choices and to give our vote only to men who are independent of all governments, both present and future.

Electors, Paris has given us liberty with its blood; are we going to destroy its work with our votes? Let us go to the elections solely for the general good. Let us close our ears to all fallacious promises and close our hearts to all personal affection or even gratitude. Let us bring forth from the ballot

---

of the city councils elected by an appropriate electoral college instead of being appointed by the king.

12. Taxes on wine and spirits were especially opposed by Bastiat, as he came from and represented a wine-growing region.

13. Joseph-Dominique Louis.

the name of a man who is wise, enlightened, and independent. If the future brings us a better fate let us have the glory of having contributed to it; if it hides yet more storms, let us have nothing to reproach ourselves for.

———————

2. To the Electors of the District of Saint-Sever

1846   [vol. 1, p. 461]

My dear Fellow Countrymen,

Encouraged by a few of you to stand at the forthcoming elections, and wishing to ascertain the degree of collaboration on which I could rely, I have spoken to a number of electors. Alas! one finds me too *progressive,* another not enough; my anti-academic opinions are rejected by one, my aversion to the Algerian enterprise by another, my economic convictions by a third, my views on parliamentary reform by yet another, etc.

This proves that the best policy for a candidate is to hide his opinions, or, for even greater security, not to have any, and to confine himself to the hackneyed platform: "I'm for freedom without licentiousness, order without tyranny, peace without shame, and economizing without endangering any service."

Since I have not the slightest intention of deceiving your trust, I shall continue sincerely to make my ideas known to you, even if this should further alienate many votes from me. I beg you to excuse me if the need to pour forth convictions that weigh upon me drives me to overstep the limits that are customarily set to *political manifestos.*

I have met with many conservatives, I have conversed with many members of the opposition, and I think I can positively assert that neither of those two great parties that divide parliament is satisfied with itself.

They wage battles in parliament with soft balls.[14]

The conservatives have the official majority; they reign, they govern. But they feel in a confused way that they are leading the country, and themselves, to ruin. They have the majority, but, in the depths of their conscience, the manifest fraud of the polls raises a protest that bothers them. They reign, but they can see that, under their reign, the budget increases year by year, that the present is deep in debt and the future already tied up, that the first emergency will find us without resources, and they are well aware that financial

———

14. The black and white balls the deputies would drop into an urn for voting.

difficulties have always been the occasion for revolutionary outbursts. They govern, but they cannot deny that they govern people through their evil passions, and that political corruption is making its way into all the arteries of the electorate. They wonder what the consequences of such a serious state of affairs will be, and what is to become of a nation where immorality has pride of place and where faith in the political system is an object of mockery and contempt. They worry on seeing the constitutional regime perverted in its very essence, to the point where the executive power and the legislative assembly have publicly exchanged their responsibilities, with the ministers surrendering to the members of parliament the job of appointing people to all posts and the members of parliament relinquishing their share of legislative power to the ministers. As a result, they see civil servants overcome with deep discouragement, when favor and electoral submissiveness alone entitle you to promotion and when the longest and most devoted services are held of no account whatsoever. Yes, the future of France troubles the conservatives; and how many among them would not go over to the opposition, if only they could find there some guarantees for that peace at home and abroad of which they are so fond?

On the other hand, as a party, can the opposition rely on the strength of the ground on which it has placed itself? What does it demand? What does it want? What is the mainspring of its action? What is its program? Nobody knows. Its natural role would be to watch over the sacred deposit of the three great conquests of civilization: *peace, freedom, justice.* And it breathes out nothing but war, domination, and Napoleonic ideas. It is neglecting freedom of work and of trade along with freedom of thought and of education. And, in its conquering zeal, with regard to Africa and the South Seas,[15] there has never been any instance of the word *justice* passing its lips. It is aware that it is working for the ambitious and not for the public, that the multitude will gain nothing from the success of its scheming. We once saw an opposition party with only fifteen members supported by the enthusiastic assent of a great people. But today the opposition has not rooted itself in the sympathies of the people; it feels cut off from that source of strength and life, and, apart from the zeal with which personal designs fire its leaders, it is pale, confused, discouraged, and most of its sincere members would go over

15. Bastiat has in mind Algeria and Tahiti.

to the conservative party were they not loath to associate themselves with the perverse course the latter has given to affairs of state.

A strange sight indeed! How is it that whether in the center or at either extreme in the House, decent souls feel ill at ease? Could it not be that the conquest of ministerial offices, which is the more or less acknowledged aim of the battle they are engaged in, interests only a few individuals and remains a matter of complete indifference to the masses? Could it not be that they lack a rallying principle? Maybe it would be sufficient to toss into the heart of that Assembly one simple, true, clear, fertile, practical idea to see what one seeks there in vain suddenly emerge: a party exclusively representing, in all its scope and entirety, the interests of the *governed,* of the *taxpayers.*

I see that fertile idea in the creed of certain renowned political writers whose words have unfortunately gone unheeded.[16] I will try to sum it up before you.

There are things that can be done only by collective force or *established authority,* and others that should be left to private activity.

The fundamental problem in political science is to know what pertains to each of these two modes of action.

Public administration and private activity both have our good in view. But their services differ in that we suffer the former under compulsion and accept the latter of our own free will, whence it follows that it is reasonable to entrust the former only with what the latter is absolutely unable to carry out.

For my part, I believe that, when the powers that be have guaranteed to each and every one the free use and the product of his or her faculties, repressed any possible misuse, maintained order, secured national independence, and carried out certain tasks in the public interest which are beyond the power of the individual, then they have fulfilled just about all their duty.

Beyond this sphere, religion, education, association, work, exchanges, everything belongs to the field of private activity, under the eye of public authority, whose role should be one only of vigilance and of repression of disorder.

---

16. Bastiat is probably alluding to the works of Adam Smith, Jean-Baptiste Say, Charles Comte, and Charles Dunoyer, whose writings on economics and social theory had a profound impact on his thought, especially Comte and Dunoyer's theory of industrialism.

If that great and fundamental boundary were thus established, then authority would be *strong,* and it would be appreciated, because it would make felt a tutelary action only.

It would be *inexpensive,* because it would be confined within the narrowest limits.

It would be *liberal,* for, on the one condition that he or she did not encroach on the freedom of others, each citizen would fully and completely enjoy the free exercise of his or her physical, mental, and moral faculties.

I might add that, once the power of perfectibility that is within society had been freed from all regulating constraint, society would then be in the best possible position to develop its riches, its education, and its morality.

But, even if there were agreement on the limits of public authority, it is no easy matter to force it and maintain it within those limits.

Government power, a vast, organized, and living body, naturally tends to grow. It feels cramped within its supervisory mission. Now, its growth is hardly possible without a succession of encroachments upon the field of individual rights. The expansion of government power means usurping some form of private activity, transgressing the boundary that I set earlier between what is and what is not its essential function. Government power departs from its mission when, for instance, it imposes a particular form of worship on our consciences, a particular method of teaching on our minds, a particular finality for our work or for our capital, or an invasive drive on our international relationships, etc.

Gentlemen, I would bring it to your attention that government becomes all the more costly as it becomes oppressive. For it can commit no encroachments otherwise than through salaried agents. Thus each of its intrusions implies creating some new administration, instituting some fresh tax, so that our freedom and our purse inevitably share a common destiny.

Consequently, if the public understands and wishes to defend its true interests, it will halt authority as soon as the latter tries to go beyond its sphere of activity; and for that purpose the public has an infallible means, which is to deny authority the resources with which it could carry out its encroachments.

Once these principles are laid down, the role of the opposition, and I would even say that of parliament as a whole, is simple and clearly defined.

It does not consist in hindering the government in its essential activity, in denying it the means of administering justice, of repressing crime, of paving roads, of repelling foreign aggression.

It does not consist in discrediting or debasing the government in the public eye, in depriving it of the strength it needs.

It does not consist in making government go from hand to hand by changing ministries, and less still, by changing dynasties.[17]

It does not even consist in ranting childishly against the government's tendency to intrude; for that tendency is inevitable, incurable, and would manifest itself just as much under a president as under a king, in a republic as in a monarchy.

It consists solely in *keeping the government within its limits;* in preserving the sphere of freedom and of private activity as completely and extensively as possible.

So if you were to ask me: "What will you do as a member of parliament?" I would reply: "Why, what you yourselves would do as taxpayers and subjects."

I would say to those in power: "Do you lack the means to maintain order within and independence without? Well, here is money, here are men; for order and independence are to the advantage of the public and not of the government.

"But if you think you have the right to impose on us a religious cult, a philosophical theory, an educational system, a farming method, a commercial trend, a military conquest, then there will be neither money nor men for you; for in that case we would have to pay, not to be served but to be serfs, not to preserve our freedom but to lose it."

This doctrine can be summed up in the following simple words: Let everything be done for the majority of citizens, both great and humble. In their interest, let there be good public management of what can unfortunately not be carried out otherwise. In their interest also, let there be complete and utter freedom in everything else, under the supervision of established authority.

One thing will strike you, gentlemen, as it strikes me, and it is this: for a member of parliament to be able to express himself in this way, he must be part of that public for whom the administration is designed and by whom it is paid.

17. Bastiat is referring to the opposition of many members of parliament to the government of the prince de Polignac, prime minister in 1829 (under Charles X). This opposition led to the fall of the Bourbon dynasty and to the accession of the Orléans dynasty with Louis-Philippe, which ruled from 1830 to 1848.

It must be acknowledged that it is entirely up to the public to decide *how, to what extent, and at what cost* it means to have things managed; otherwise representative government would be nothing but a deception and the sovereignty of the people a meaningless expression. Now, having recognized the tendency of any government to grow indefinitely, when it questions you through the polls on the subject of its own limits, if you leave it to the government itself to reply, by entrusting its own civil servants with drawing up the answer, then you might as well put your wealth and your freedom at its disposal. To expect a government to draw from within itself the strength to resist its natural expansion is to expect from a falling stone the energy to halt its fall.

If the election regulations were to stipulate: "The taxpayers will have themselves represented by civil servants," you would find that absurd, and you would understand that there would no longer be any limit to the expansion of the powers that be, apart from riot, or to increase in the budget, apart from bankruptcy; but are the results any different when electors voluntarily make up for such a regulation?

At this point, gentlemen, I must tackle the serious question of *parliamentary conflicts of interest.*[18] I will not say much about it, reserving the right to address myself at greater length to M. Larnac. But I cannot entirely pass over it in silence, since he has thought fit to circulate among you a letter of which I have not kept a copy, and which, not being intended for publication, only touched on that vast subject.

According to the way that letter has been interpreted, it appears that I would demand that all civil servants be banned from parliament.

I do not know whether such an absolute meaning is perceptible in my letter. In that case, my expression must have gone beyond my thought. I have never considered that the Assembly in which laws are drawn up could do without magistrates, or that it could deal constructively with maritime problems in the absence of seamen, with military problems in the absence of soldiers, or with financial problems in the absence of financiers.

What I said and what I uphold is this: as long as the law has not settled the position of civil servants in parliament, *as long as their interests as civil servants are not, so to speak, effaced by their interests as taxpayers,* the best we electors can do is not to appoint any; and, I must admit, I would rather

18. Here Bastiat is referring to the problem of the conflict of interest that occurs when a civil servant continues to work for the government and sits in parliament as well.

there were not a single one of them in the House than see them there as a majority, without cautionary measures having been taken, as the good sense of the public requires, in order to protect *them* and to protect *us* from the influence that hope and fear must exercise over their votes.

This has been construed as petty jealousy, as mistrust verging on hatred toward civil servants. It is nothing of the sort. I know many civil servants, nearly all my friends belong to that category (for who doesn't nowadays?), as I do myself; and in my essays on economics, I maintained, contrary to the opinion of my master, M. Say,[19] that their services are productive just as private services are. But it is nonetheless true that they differ in that we take of the latter only what we want, and at an agreed price, whereas the former are imposed on us as well as the payment attached to them. Or, if it is claimed that public services and their payment are voluntarily approved by us, because they are formulated by our representatives, it must be acknowledged that our approval stems only from that very formulation. It is therefore not up to civil servants to see to the formulation. It is no more up to them to decide on the extent of the service and the price to be paid than it is up to my wine supplier to decide on the amount of wine I should take and the sum I should spend on it. It is not of civil servants that I am wary, it is of the human heart; and I can respect those who make a living out of collecting taxes, while considering that they are hardly qualified to vote them, just as M. Larnac probably respects judges, while considering their duties as incompatible with those of the National Guard.

My views on parliamentary reform have also been presented as tainted with excessive radicalism. And yet I had taken care to point out that, in my opinion, reform is even more necessary for the stability of the government than for the preservation of our liberties. As I said then, the most dangerous men in the House are not the civil servants, but those who aim at becoming civil servants. The latter are driven to waging, against whatever cabinet may be in power, an incessant, troublesome, seditious war, which is of no

19. Jean-Baptiste Say took the more radical position that all coercive government activities were "unproductive." Only voluntary exchanges could be called truly "productive." According to Say, all government activities were "ulcerous" and thus harmful to the free market and civil society. This view was taken up and further developed by Charles Comte (who married Say's daughter) and Charles Dunoyer, two theorists who considerably influenced Bastiat's intellectual development. However, on this issue, the magistrate Bastiat broke with his teachers. Gustave de Molinari (1819–1912) continued the Say-Comte-Dunoyer tradition, thus placing Bastiat in the middle ground on this matter.

use whatsoever to the country; they make use of events, distort questions, lead public opinion astray, hinder public affairs, disturb the peace, for they have only one aim in mind: to overthrow the ministers in order to take their places. To deny the truth of this, you would have to have never set eyes on the historical records of Great Britain, you would have to deliberately reject the teachings of our constitutional history as a whole.

This brings me back to the fundamental idea underlying my address, for, as you can see, the concept of *opposition* may take on two very different aspects.

The opposition, such as it is now, *the inevitable result of deputies being admitted to power,* is reduced to the disorderly struggle of ambitions. It violently attacks individuals, but only weakly attacks corrupt practices; that is natural, since corrupt practices make up the greater part of that which it is striving to control. It does not contemplate limiting the sphere of administrative action; rather, it seeks only to eliminate a few cogs from the vast machine it longs to control. Besides, we have seen it at work. Its present leader was once prime minister; the present prime minister was once its leader. It has governed under either banner. What have we gained from it all? Throughout these developments, has the upward trend of the budget ever been suspended even for a minute?

Opposition, as I see it, is the organized vigilance of the public. It is calm and impartial, but as permanent as the reaction of a spring under the hand that holds it down. So that the balance may not be upset, must not the force of resistance of the governed be equal to the force of expansion of those that govern? This opposition has nothing against the men in office: it has only to replace them, it will even help them within the sphere of their legitimate duties, but it will mercilessly confine them within that sphere.

You might think that this natural form of opposition, which has nothing dangerous or subversive about it, which attacks the government neither in those who hold office, nor in its fundamental principle, nor in its useful action, but only in its exaggeration, is less distasteful to the ministers than seditious opposition. Don't you believe it! It is precisely this form of opposition that they fear most of all; they hate it, they deride it in order to bring it to naught, they prevent it from emerging within their constituencies, because they can see plainly that it gets to the bottom of things and pursues evil to its very roots. The other kind of opposition, personal opposition, is less to be dreaded. Between those men who fight over ministerial portfolios, however bitter the struggle, there is always a tacit agreement, under which the vast edifice of government must be left intact. "Overthrow me if you can," says the minister, "I will overthrow you in your turn; only, let us take care that the stake remains on the table, in the shape of a budget of fifteen hundred million francs." But if one day a member of parliament, speaking in the name of taxpayers and as a taxpayer himself, rises from his seat in the House to say to present or prospective ministers: "Gentlemen, fight among yourselves over power, all I seek to do is restrain it; wrangle over how to manipulate the budget, all I wish to do is reduce it," ah! be sure that those raging fighters, apparently so bitterly opposed, will very soon pull together to stifle the voice of that faithful representative. They will call him a utopian, a theoretician, a dangerous reformer, a man with a fixed idea, of no practical value; they will heap scorn upon him; they will turn the venal press against him. But if taxpayers let him down, sooner or later they will find out that they have let themselves down.

I have spoken my mind, gentlemen; I have laid it before you plainly and frankly, while regretting not being able to corroborate my opinion with all the arguments that might have carried your convictions.

I hope to have said enough, however, for you to be able to appreciate the course I would follow if I were your representative, and it is hardly necessary to add that, with regard to the government and the ambitious in opposition, I would first make a point of placing myself in that position of independence which alone affords any guarantee, and which one must impose on oneself, since the law has made no provision in that respect.

Having laid down the principle which should, as I see it, govern the whole career of your parliamentary representatives, allow me to say a few words about the main subjects to which it seems to me this principle should be applied.

You may have heard that I have devoted some energy to the cause of free trade, and it is easy to see that my efforts are consistent with the fundamental idea that I have just set forth concerning the natural limits of government authority. As I see it, anyone who has created a product should have the option of *exchanging* it, as well as of using it himself. Exchange is therefore an integral part of the right of property. Now, we have not instituted and we do not pay government in order to deprive us of that right, but on the contrary in order to guarantee us that right in its entirety. None of the government's encroachments has had more disastrous consequences than its encroachment on the exercise of our faculties and on our freedom to dispose of their products.

First of all, this would-be protective regime, when closely examined, is based on the most flagrant plunder. Two years ago, when measures were taken to restrain the entry of oil-producing seeds, it was indeed possible to increase the profits on certain crops, since the price of oil immediately went up by a few pence a pound. But it is perfectly obvious that those excess profits were not a gain for the nation as a whole, since they were taken gratuitously and artfully from the pockets of other citizens, of all those who grow neither rapeseed nor olive trees. Thus, there was no creation, but simply an unjust transfer, of riches. To say that in so doing you supported one branch of agriculture is saying nothing at all as regards general welfare, because you gave it only the sap that you took from other branches. And what crazy industry might not be made lucrative at such a cost? Suppose a shoemaker takes it into his head to cut shoes out of boots, however unsound an operation; just give him a preferential license, and it will become an excellent one. If growing rapeseed is in itself a sound activity, there is no need to give any supplementary profit to those who practice it. If it is unsound, the extra income does not make it sound. It simply shifts the loss onto the public.

Plunder, as a rule, transfers wealth but does not destroy it. Protectionism transfers wealth and furthermore destroys it, and this is how: as oil-producing seeds from the north no longer enter France, there is no longer any way of producing here the wherewithal to pay for it, for example, a certain quantity of wine. Now, if, regarding oil, the profits of the producers and the losses of the consumers balance, the sufferings of the vine growers are an unjustified and unalleviated evil.

Many of you no doubt are not quite clear in your minds as to the effects of a protectionist regime. Allow me to make a remark.

Let us suppose that this regime were not forced on us by law, but directly by the will of the monopolists. Let us suppose that the law left us entirely free to purchase iron from the Belgians or the Swedes, but that the iron-masters had servants enough to prevent the iron from passing our frontiers and to force us thereby to purchase from them and at their price. Would we not complain loudly of oppression and injustice? The injustice would indeed be more obvious; but as for the economic effects, it cannot be said that they would be any different. After all, are we any the fatter because those gentlemen have been clever enough to have carried out by customs officers, and *at our expense,* that policing of the frontier that we would not tolerate were it carried out at their own expense?

The protectionist system bears witness to the following truth: a government that goes beyond its normal assignments draws from its transgressions power only that is dangerous, even for itself. When the state becomes the distributor and regulator of profits, all sectors of industry tug at it this way and that in order to tear from it a shred of monopoly. Have you ever seen free home trade put a cabinet in the predicament in which regulated foreign trade put Sir Robert Peel? And if we consider our own country, is it not a strong government indeed that we see trembling before M. Darblay? So, as you can see, by restraining the government you consolidate rather than endanger it.

Free trade, freedom of communication between peoples, putting the varied products of the world within everyone's reach, enabling ideas to penetrate along with the products into those regions still darkened by ignorance, the state freed from the contrary claims of the workers, peace between nations founded on intertwining interests—all this is undoubtedly a great and noble cause. I am happy to believe that this cause, which is eminently Christian and social, is at the same time that of our unhappy region, at present languishing and perishing under the pressure of commercial restrictions.

Education is also bound up with the same fundamental question that precedes all others in politics: Is it part of the state's duties? Or does it belong to the sphere of private activity? You can guess what my answer will be. The government is not set up in order to bring our minds into subjection or to absorb the rights of the family. To be sure, gentlemen, if it pleases you to hand over to it your noblest prerogatives, if you want to have theories, systems, methods, principles, textbooks, and teachers forced on you by the government, that is up to you; but do not expect me to sign, in your name, such a shameful abdication of your rights. Besides, you must not shut your eyes to the consequences. Leibnitz used to say: "I have always thought that whoever was master of education, would be master of mankind." Maybe that is why the head of our state education is known as *Grand Master.* The monopoly of teaching cannot reasonably be entrusted to any but an authority recognized as infallible. Otherwise, there is an unlimited risk that error be uniformly taught to the people as a whole. "We have made a republic," Robespierre would say; "it now remains for us to make republicans of everyone." Bonaparte wanted to make soldiers of everyone, Frayssinous wanted only religious devotees, M. Cousin would turn people into philosophers, Fourier would have only "harmonians," and I suppose I would want economists. Unity is a wonderful thing, but only on condition that you are in the right, which again amounts to saying that academic monopoly is compatible only with infallibility. So let us leave education free. It will perfect itself through trial and error, example, rivalry, imitation, and emulation. Unity is not at the starting point of the efforts made by the human mind; it is the result of the natural gravitation of free intellects toward the center of all attraction: truth.

That does not mean to say that the powers that be should withdraw in complete indifference. As I have already said, their mission is to supervise the use and repress the misuse of all our faculties. I accept that they should accomplish this mission to the fullest extent, and with even greater vigilance regarding education than in any other field; that the state should lay down conditions concerning qualifications and character references; that it should repress immoral teaching; that it should watch over the health of the pupils. I accept all that, while yet remaining convinced that its solicitude, however scrupulous, can offer only the very slightest guarantee compared with that instilled by nature in the hearts of fathers and in the interest of teachers.

I must make myself clear on one vast subject, more especially as my views probably differ from those of many of you: I am referring to Algeria. I have no hesitation in saying that, unless it be in order to secure independent frontiers, you will never find me, in this case or in any other, on the conqueror's side.[20]

To me it is a proven fact, and I venture to say a scientifically proven fact, that the colonial system is the most disastrous illusion ever to have led nations astray. I make no exception for the English, in spite of the specious nature of the well-known argument *post hoc, ergo propter hoc.*[21]

Do you know how much Algeria is costing you? From one-third to two-fifths of your four direct taxes, including the extra cents. Whoever among you pays three hundred francs in taxes sends one hundred francs annually to evaporate into the clouds over the Atlas mountains or to sink into the sands of the Sahara.

We are told that the money is an advance and that, a few centuries from now, we shall recover it a hundredfold. But who says so? The very quarter-

---

20. The French invaded Algeria in 1830, and their rule lasted until Algeria achieved independence in 1962, after eight years of civil and guerrilla war. Bastiat, like Cobden with regard to British colonialism, opposed the French conquest and colonization of Algeria. However, the conservative liberal Alexis de Tocqueville was a convinced defender of France's *mission civilatrice* in Algeria.

21. "After that, therefore because of that."

master general's department that swindles us out of our money. Listen here, gentlemen, when it comes to cash, there is but one useful piece of advice: let each man watch his purse . . . and those to whom he entrusts the purse strings.

We are further told: "The money spent helps to support many people." Yes, indeed, Kabyle spies, Moorish moneylenders, Maltese settlers, and Arab sheikhs. If it were used to cut the "Grandes-Landes" canal,[22] to excavate the bed of the Adour River and the port of Bayonne, it would help to support many people around us, too, and moreover it would provide the country with an enormous capacity for production.

I have spoken of money; I should first have spoken about men. Every year, ten thousand of our young fellow citizens, the pick of our population, go to their deaths on those consuming shores, and to no useful purpose so far, other than to extend, at our expense, the field of the administrative services, who are naturally all in favor of it. In answer to that, there is the alleged advantage of ridding the country of its *surplus.* A horrible pretext, which goes against all human feeling and which hasn't even the merit of being materially true, for, even supposing the population to be overabundant, to take from it, with each man, two or three times the capital which could have supported him here, is far from being any relief to those who remain behind.

But I must be fair. In spite of its liking for anything that increases the size of its administration, it seems that at the outset the government shrank from that abyss of bloodshed, injustice, and distress. The nation chose to go ahead; it will long suffer the consequences.

What carried the country away, besides the mirage of a *great empire,* of a *new civilization,* etc., was a strong reaction of national feeling against the offensive claims of the British oligarchy. England's veiled opposition to our designs was enough to persuade us to go ahead with them. I appreciate that feeling, and I would rather see it go astray than die out. But, on the other hand, is there not a danger that it should place us under the very domination that we hate? Give me two men, the one submissive and the other contrary, and I will lead them both on a leash. If I want them to walk, I will say to

22. The idea of a canal linking the Garonne and Adour rivers dated back to 1808 and was designed to serve and bring fresh life to the vast forest region of the Landes. Bastiat was in favor of the project. The final layout was drawn up in 1832, but the project was never carried out owing to dissension within the *département* of the Landes.

one: "Walk!" and to the other: "Don't walk!" and both of them will do as I wish. If our sense of dignity were to take that form, then all *perfidious Albion* would have to do, in order to make us do the most stupid things, would be to appear to oppose them. Just suppose, and it is certainly very allowable to do so, that England sees in Algeria the ball and chain that tie us down, the abyss which could swallow up our power; then would that country have only to frown, take on a haughty and angry air, in order to make us pursue a dangerous and insane policy? Let us avoid that pitfall; let us judge by ourselves and for ourselves; let no one lay down the law to us either directly or in a roundabout way. The problem of Algiers is unfortunately not isolated. We are bound by precedents; the past has committed the future, and there are precedents that must be taken into account. Let us, however, remain master of decisions to come; let us weigh the advantages and drawbacks; and let us not disdain to add a measure of *justice* to the balance, albeit toward the Kabyles. If we do not begrudge the money, if *glory is not to be haggled over,* let us at least attach some importance to the grief of families, the sufferings of our fellow countrymen, the fate of those who fall, and the disastrous habits of those who survive.

There is another subject that deserves all the attention of your representative. I am referring to *indirect taxation.* In this case the distinction between what is and what is not within the competence of the state does not apply. It is obviously up to the state to collect taxes. However, it may be said that it is the inordinate expansion of its power that makes the state have recourse to the most hateful tax inventions. When a nation, the victim of its own excessive timidity, dares do nothing by itself and is forever begging for state intervention, then it must resign itself to being mercilessly ransomed; for the state can do nothing without finance, and when it has drained the ordinary sources of revenue dry, it has no alternative but to turn to the strangest and most oppressive forms of extortion. Thus we have indirect taxation on alcohol. The suppression of these taxes therefore depends on the answer to the eternal question that I never tire of asking: Does the French nation want to be forever in tutelage and to call on its government to intervene in every matter? In that case, it should no longer complain about being overburdened and can even expect to see things get worse.

But, even supposing that the tax on alcohol could not be abolished (which I am far from conceding), it seems clear to me that it could be largely modified, and that it would be easy to cut out its most distasteful elements. All that would be necessary would be to induce the owners of vineyards to give up certain exaggerated ideas on the extent of their right of property and the inviolability of their domicile.[23]

Allow me, gentlemen, to end with a few personal observations. You must excuse me for doing so. For I, personally, have no active and devoted canvasser at a salary of three thousand francs plus four thousand francs in office expenses to busy himself with promoting my candidacy from one side of the constituency to the other, and from one end of the year to the other.

Some people say: "M. Bastiat is a revolutionary." Others: "M. Bastiat has thrown in his lot with the government."

What precedes answers that dual assertion.

There are those who say: "M. Bastiat may be a very decent fellow, but his opinions have changed."

As for me, when I consider how I have persisted in defending a principle that is making no progress in France, I sometimes wonder if I am not a maniac possessed with a fixed idea.

To enable you to judge whether I have changed, let me set before you an extract from the declaration of policy that I published in 1832, when a kind word from General Lamarque attracted the attention of a few voters in my favor.

"In my view, the institutions that we have already obtained and those that we can obtain by lawful means are sufficient, if we make enlightened use of them, to raise our country to a high degree of freedom, greatness, and prosperity.

"The right to vote taxes, in giving citizens the power to extend or restrain the action of the government as they please, isn't that management by the public of public affairs? What might we not achieve by making judicious use of that right?

"Do we consider that ambition for office is the source of many contentions, intrigues, and factions? It rests with us alone to deprive that fatal passion of its sustenance, by reducing the profits and the number of salaried public offices."

. . . .

23. Bastiat, always a staunch defender of property rights, was attempting to convince the wine growers to accept a politically achievable compromise to reduce the number and complexity of taxes while maintaining some government controls.

"Do we feel that industry is shackled, the administration overcentralized, education hampered by academic monopoly? There is nothing to prevent us from holding back the money that facilitates those shackles, that centralization, those monopolies.

"As you can see, gentlemen, I shall never expect the welfare of my country to result from any violent change in either the forms or the holders of power; but rather from our good faith in supporting the government in the useful exercise of its essential powers and from our firm determination to restrict it to those limits. The government has to be firm facing enemies from within and from without, for its mission is to keep the peace at home and abroad. But it must leave to private activity everything that is within the latter's competence. Order and freedom depend on those conditions."

Are those not the same principles, the same feelings, the same fundamental way of thinking, the same solutions for particular problems, the same means of reform? People may not share my opinions; but it cannot be said that they have varied, and I venture to add: they are invariable. It is too coherent a system to admit of any alterations. It will collapse or it will triumph as a whole.

My dear fellow countrymen, please forgive the length and the unusual form of this letter. If you grant me your votes, I shall be deeply honored. If you grant them to another, I shall serve my country in some less eminent sphere, better suited to my abilities.

Mugron, 1 July 1846

---

3. On Parliamentary Reform

1846   [vol. 1, p. 480]

To M. Larnac, Deputy for the Landes
Sir,

You have considered it appropriate to circulate a letter which I had the honor of sending you and your reply to it. I do not reproach you for this. No doubt you assumed that at the elections we would meet in opposing camps, and if my letter revealed to you a man who professed mistaken and dangerous opinions, you had the right to warn the general public. I allow that you took this decision with this sole preoccupation with the general interest in mind. Perhaps it would have been more fitting to choose between absolute silence and total publicity. You have preferred something that is neither of these, pompous yet hard to pin down scandalmongering about a letter of which I have not kept a copy and whose terms, consequently, I cannot explain nor defend. So be it. I have not the slightest doubt about the accuracy of the copyist responsible for reproducing it and that is enough for me.

However, sir, is this enough to achieve your aim, which is doubtless to enlighten the beliefs of the electors? My letter relates to a particular fact, followed by a political doctrine. I have scarcely touched on this fact, and this is simply explained, since I was addressing someone who was aware of the full circumstances. I sketched the doctrine as one can do in letter form. This is not enough detail for the general public, and since you have involved them in this matter, allow me to address them in my turn.

I find it too distasteful to introduce actual names into this debate to underline particular facts. Only the need to defend myself personally could make me decide to do this and I hasten to come to the major political question which is the subject of your letter, the conflicts of interest of a legislative mandate with work in the civil service.

I make it clear at the outset, I am not actually asking for civil servants to be excluded from the House; they are citizens and should be able to enjoy the rights of citizenship, but they should be admitted to it only as citizens and not as civil servants. If they wish to serve the nation over which the law reigns, they cannot be the executors of the law. If they wish to represent the general public which pays the government, they cannot be the salaried agents of that government. I consider that their presence in the Chamber be subordinated to a measure which I will indicate later; and I unhesitatingly add that, in my eyes at least, there are many more disadvantages in admitting them to the Chamber unconditionally than to excluding them unremittingly.

"Your thesis is truly immense (you say); if I were dealing a priori with the question of conflicts of interest, I would begin by castigating this tendency to suspiciousness, one which appears very illiberal to me."

But sir, what is the body of our laws if not a series of precautionary measures against the dangerous tendencies of the human heart? What is the constitution? What are all these checks and balances and the counterbalancing of powers if not a system of barriers to possible and even fatal encroachments in the absence of any restraint? What is religion itself, at least in one of its essential aspects, if not a source of grace intended by Providence to remedy native and therefore *foreseen* weakness in our nature? If you would remove from our symbols, charters, and law codes all that which has been placed there by what you call suspicion and I call prudence, you would make the task of legislators very easy, but make the fate of men quite precarious. If you believe man to be infallible, burn the laws and charters. If you consider him to be fallible, in that case, when it is a matter of conflicts of interest or even a particular law, the question is not to know whether it is founded on suspicion but whether that suspicion is an impartial, reasonable, enlightened one, in other words on a prediction unfortunately justified by the indelible infirmity of men's hearts.

This reproach made to suspicious tendencies has so often been directed against anyone who petitions for parliamentary reform that I feel obliged to repel it with some insistence. When we are very young and have just escaped from the atmosphere of Greece and Rome, where the university compels us to absorb our initial impressions, it is true that the love of liberty is too often mistaken in us with impatience in the face of any rules, of any government, and consequently with a puerile aversion to public office and civil servants. For my part, age and reflection have totally cured me of this aberration. I acknowledge that, except in instances of abuse, whether in public or private life, each person provides society with similar services. In one case, he satisfies the need for food and clothing, in another the need for order and security. I therefore do not take up arms against public office or suspect any civil servant individually. I have esteem for very many of them and I am a civil servant myself,[24] although one of very modest rank. If others have pleaded the cause of *conflicts of interest* under the influence of a narrow and bitter jealousy or of an alarmist version of democracy, I can pursue the same goal without associating myself with these sentiments. Of course, without exceeding the boundaries of reasonable caution, it is permissible to take account of man's passions or rather the nature of things.

However, sir, although public office and private industry have in common that both render similar services to society, it cannot be denied that they differ in one circumstance which it is essential to note. Each person is free to accept or refuse the services of private industry and receive them insofar as they suit him and to discuss their price. On the other hand, anything that concerns public office is regulated in advance by law and removed from our free will. It prescribes for us the quantity and quality we have to consume (pardon this rather too technical language) as well as the remuneration that

24. On 28 March 1831, Bastiat was appointed a justice of the peace of Mugron County.

will be attached. For this reason, it would seem that it is up to those for whom and at whose expense this type of service is established to approve at least the law which determines its particular purpose, its scope, and the salaries involved. If the field of hairdressing were regulated by law, if we left to wig makers the job of making the law, it is likely (and I would not at all wish to ruffle the feelings of wig makers, nor to display a tendency to illiberal suspiciousness but simply to base my reasoning on the knowledge we have of the human heart), it is likely, I repeat, that we would soon be inordinately well groomed, indeed to the point of tyranny and the emptying of our purses. In the same way, when the electors have laws passed which regulate the provision of public safety and the salaries thereby entailed, or those of any other governmental product, by civil servants who earn their living from this work, it would seem to me to be indisputable that these electors run the risk of being *administered* and *taxed* beyond all reasonable measure.

Obsessed by the idea that we are prey to illiberal suspiciousness, you add: "In periods of intolerance, we would have said to candidates, 'You must not be either a Protestant or a Jew'; these days, we say, 'Do not be a civil servant.'"

In that case we would have been absurd, whereas now we are being rational. Jews, Protestants, and Catholics, regulated by the same laws and paying the same taxes, are voted for by us as equals. How can a religious creed be a motive justifying exclusion for anyone among us? However, with regard to those who apply the law and earn a living from taxation, the prohibition against voting for them is not at all arbitrary. Administrative authority itself acts in accordance with this principle and thus demonstrates that it is common sense. M. Lacave-Laplagne does not have the accounts audited by the accountants. It is not him personally, it is the very nature of these two orders of functions that causes conflicts of interest. Would you not find it laughable for the minister to base it on religious creed, the length of the nose, or the color of hair? The analogy you offer is of this nature.

"I think that you need very serious, patently clear, and proven reasons for asking that an exception should be made of someone. In general, this idea is bad and retrograde."

Do you mean to satirize the Charter? It lays down that anyone who does not pay five hundred francs of taxes should be excluded on the simple *conjecture* that anyone who is not rich is not independent. Am I not aligning myself with its spirit when, since I have only one vote to allocate and am obliged to *reject* all the candidates except for one, I include among those I *reject* one who perhaps has financial resources but who, since he has gained them from the minister, seems to me to be more dependent than if he had none?

"I am in favor of the progressive adage *sunt favores ampliandi, sunt odia restringenda.*"[25]

Sunt favores ampliandi! Ah, sir, I very much fear that under this dispensation there are too many people. Be that as it may, I ask whether deputation has been created for the deputies or for the general public? If it is for the general public, show me how they benefit by delegating civil servants. I can well see that this tends to *expand* the budget, but not without *restricting* the resources of taxpayers.

Sunt odia restringenda! Useless functions and expenditure, these are the *odia* that need to be restricted. Tell me how, therefore, we can expect this of those who carry out the first and gobble up the second?

In any case, there is one point on which we agree. This is on the extension of electoral rights.[26] Unless you classify these among the *odia restringenda*, you have to include them in the number of the *favores ampliandi*, and your generous aphorism tells us that electoral reform can count on you.

"I have confidence in the workings of our institutions (in particular, I dare say, in the one which is the subject of this correspondence). I believe it to be conducive to the production of morality. This condition of society lies essentially in the electors; it is summed up in its representatives, it passes through the votes of majorities, etc."

This is certainly a most touching picture, and I like this morality which rises from the base to the summit of the edifice. I could trace a less optimistic picture and show the political immorality that descends from the summit to the base. Which of the two would be more true to life? What! The disorderly placement of the voting and execution of laws and the voting and control of the budget in the same hands produces morality? Logically, I have difficulty understanding this. Evidentially, I have even greater difficulty.

You invoke the adage *Quid leges sine moribus?*[27] I am doing nothing else. I have not called the law to account but the electors. I have uttered the hope

25. "Favors ought to be extended; disagreeable things ought to be restricted."

26. Reference to a proposed electoral reform intended to widen the electorate by lowering the required level of tax payment and admitting candidates exercising certain professions previously restricted.

27. "What are laws without customs?"

that they will get themselves represented by deputies whose interests are in harmony with and not in opposition to theirs. This is very much a matter of mores. The law does not forbid us to elect civil servants but it does not oblige us to do so either. I do not hide the fact that it would seem to me to be reasonable for it to contain a few precautions in this respect. In the meantime, let us take them ourselves: *Quid leges sine moribus?*

I said, "Whether right or wrong, it is a deep-seated idea of mine that deputies are the controllers of *power.*"

You jeered at the words *whether right or wrong.* So be it. I give way to you on this. Let us substitute this sentence: I may be mistaken, but I have the conviction that deputies are the controllers of *power.*

"What power?" you ask. Obviously *executive power.* You say: "I acknowledge only three *powers:* the king, the Chamber of Peers, and the Chamber of Deputies."

If we return to abstract principles, I will be forced to differ in opinion from you, as I fundamentally acknowledge only one power: national power. All the others are delegated, and it is because executive power is delegated that the nation has the right to control it. And it is in order that this control is not derisory that the nation, in my humble opinion, would be wise not to place in the same hands both power and control. Assuredly it is free to do so. It is free to draw down on itself, as it does, various impediments and taxes. In this it seems to me unwise and even less wise to complain about the result. You think that I hold a serious grudge against the government; not at all, I admire it and find it very generous, when the general public is so obliging, to limit itself to a budget of 1.4 to 1.5 billion. For the last thirty years taxes have scarcely doubled. This is something to be surprised at and it should be acknowledged that the avidity of the taxman has remained well below the rashness of the taxpayers.

You find the following thought vague: "The mission of deputies is to delineate the arena in which power should be exercised." "This arena," you say, "is clearly delineated; it is the Charter."

I have to say that, in the Charter, I do not know of a single clause which relates to the question. It must clearly be the case that we do not understand each other, so I will endeavor to explain my thoughts.

A nation may be more or less subject to government. In France and under the dispensation of the Charter, there are a multitude of services which may leave the scope of private industry and be entrusted to public authority and vice versa. In past times, spirited arguments were held to find out in which of these two modes of activity the railway system would remain. Even more heated is the question concerning to which of these two education should belong. One day, perhaps, the same doubts will arise with regard to religions. There are countries, such as the United States, in which the state does not interfere and they are all the better for this. Elsewhere, in Russia or Turkey, for example, the contrary system has prevailed. In the British Isles, as soon as the conflict over freedom of trade is settled in favor of the latter, another conflict is in the offing in favor of the *voluntary system* in religious matters or the disestablishment of the established church. I mentioned freedom of trade; in our country, the government has made itself, through variations in tariffs, the regulator of industry. Sometimes it favors agriculture over manufacturing and sometimes manufacturing over agriculture, and it has even the singular pretension to make all the sectors of production prosper at the expense of each other. It is exclusively the government that operates the carrying of mail, the handling of snuff and tobacco, etc., etc.

There is therefore a division to be made between private activity and collective or governmental activity. On the one hand, many people are inclined to increase the attributions of the state indefinitely. The most eccentric visionaries, such as Fourier, come together on this point with the most practical of the men of state, such as M. Thiers. According to these powerful geniuses, the state must, under their supreme management, naturally, be the great administrator of justice, the great pontiff, the great teacher, the great engineer, the great industrialist, and the people's great benefactor. On the other hand, many sound minds espouse the opposite view; there are even those who go so far as to want the government to be limited to its essential functions, which are to guarantee the security of people and property, to prevent and repress violence and disorder, to ensure for all the free exercise of their faculties and the proper reward for their efforts. It is already not without some danger, they say, that the nation entrusts to a hierarchically organized body the redoubtable responsibility for the police force. This is indeed necessary, but at least the nation should refrain from giving this body more jurisdiction over moral, intellectual, or economic life, if it does not wish to be reduced to the status of so much property or of a mere thing.

And it is for this reason that there is a Charter. And it is for this reason that in this Charter there is Article 15: "All tax laws must be first passed by the Chamber of Deputies." For, note this well, every invasion by public authority into the field of private activity implies a tax. If the government claims that it will take over education, it will need paid teachers and therefore a tax. If it aspires to subjecting our moral life to some religion or other, it will need clergy and therefore a tax. If it has to operate the railways and canals, it will need capital and therefore a tax. If it has to make conquests in Africa and Oceania, it will need armies, a navy, and therefore a tax. If it has to *weight* the profits of various industries through the action of tariffs, it will need a customs service and therefore a tax. If it is responsible for providing work and bread for all, it will need taxes and even more taxes.

However, for the very reason that, according to our national law, the nation is not the property of its government and that it is for the nation and not the government that religion, education, industry, the railways, etc., exist, it is up to the nation, not the government, to decide which services should be entrusted to or removed from government. Article 15 of the Charter gives the nation the means to do this. It just needs to refuse a tax to acquire liberty by this very action.

But if it abandons to the state and its agents, to executive power and its instruments, the task of establishing this great divide between the fields of collective and private industry, if in addition it delivers Article 15 of the Charter to it, is it not likely that the nation will shortly afterward be administered to death, that an indefinite number of functions will be created to substitute forced service for voluntary service in each sector and also the taxes to finance these functions? And is it possible to perceive any end to this series of encroachments and taxes which are mutually necessary, for, without wishing to attack individuals nor exaggerate man's dangerous leanings, can we not state that it is in the nature of any constituted and organized body to try to expand and absorb all forms of influence, power, and wealth?

Well, sir, the meaning of the sentence you found vague is this: when the nation nominates deputies, part of the mission it gives them is to circumscribe the government's sphere of action, to establish the limits which this action must not exceed and to remove from it any means of taking over the liberties the nation intends to retain, through a perspicacious use of Article 15 of the Charter. It will inevitably fail in this objective if it abandons this restrictive power to the very people in whom there resides the force for expansion that needs to be contained and restricted. May you, sir, not find the commentary less clear than the text.

Finally, there is in my letter another sentence which must lead me into lengthy explanation, since it appears to have shocked you particularly and it is this:

"From the moment the deputies have the possibility of becoming ministers, it is a simple fact that those who are ambitious seek to carve themselves out a route to the minister's position through systematic opposition."

Here, sir, I am no longer blaming those who occupy office, but, on the contrary, those who seek it; not civil servants but clearly those who wish to supplant them. I hope that in your eyes this will be irrefutable proof that I am not imbued with any bitter jealousy of a particular individual or class.

Up to now, I have dealt with the question of the *eligibility of civil servants to become deputies* and, adopting the taxpayers' point of view, I have tried to prove that they could scarcely (to use the expressions you quote with such insistence) hand over control to those being controlled without risking both their wealth and liberty.

The passage I have just quoted leads me to discuss the *eligibility of deputies for public office* and envisage the relationship of this wide-ranging question with government itself. In this way, the loop of the forms of *conflicts of interest* will come full circle.

Yes, sir, I regard the eligibility of deputies for public office, in particular in government, as essentially destructive of all effectiveness, stability, and consistency of governmental action. I do not think it possible to imagine a combination more adverse to the interests of the monarch and those who represent him or a pillow more lumpy for the king's head or those of his ministers. Nothing in the world seems more likely to me to arouse the spirit of partisanship, fan the flames of factions, corrupt all the sources of information and publicity, distort the action of the tribune and press, mislead public opinion after having aroused it, hinder administration, foment national hatred, provoke external war, wear out and scorn those in government, discourage and corrupt those being governed, and, in a word, throw out of alignment all the springs of the representative system. As far as I am concerned, I know of no social plague that compares with this. Since this side of the question has never been discussed or even noticed by the partisans of parliamentary reform, as far as I know, since in all their draft laws, if Article 1 raises the principle of *conflicts of interest,* Article 2 swiftly creates exceptions in favor of governments and their ministries, embassies, and all of what are known as *high political positions,* I am obliged to develop my thoughts at some length.

Above all, I must reject your preemptively seeking to define my argument out of court. You state that my case contradicts the Charter. Not at all. The

Charter does not prohibit a conscientious deputy from refusing a portfolio or prudent electors from selecting candidates from those who renounce this illogical pluralism. If it is not farsighted, it does not prohibit us from being farsighted. That having been said, I continue:

One of the predecessors of the current prefect of the Landes did me the honor of paying me a visit. The elections were close and conversation turned naturally to conflicts of interest and in particular on deputies' noneligibility for government office. Like you, the prefect was astonished that I dared to profess a doctrine which appeared to him, as to you, to be excessively rigid, impractical, etc.

I told him: "I think, sir, that you would do justice to the General Council of the Landes by acknowledging that you found a highly independent spirit there with no personal and systematic opposition. The measures you put forward are examined *on their own merit*. Each member votes for or against, depending on whether he considers them good or bad. Each person takes account of the general interest as he perceives it and perhaps local or personal interest, but there is no one who can be suspected of rejecting a useful proposal from you just because it comes from you."

"Never," said the prefect, "has the notion crossed my mind."

"Well, let us imagine that a regulation in the following terms were to be introduced into the law governing these councils: 'If a measure proposed by the prefect is rejected, he will be dismissed. The Council member who raised the opposition will be appointed as prefect and he will be able to distribute all the leading positions, such as general tax collection, the management of direct and indirect contributions, etc., in the *département* to his chance companions.'

"I ask you, is it not probable or even certain that such an article would completely change the spirit of the Council? Is it not certain that this Chamber, in which independence and impartiality currently reign, would be transformed into an arena of intrigue and faction? Is it not likely that ambition would be fueled in line with the sustenance offered it? And whatever good opinion you have of the virtue of Council members, do you think that they will avoid succumbing to this test? In any case, would it not be highly imprudent to attempt this dangerous experiment? Can we doubt that each of your proposals would become a battlefield of personal strife, that they would no longer be examined for their relevance to the public good but solely from the point of view of the opportunities they would create for the parties?

And now, you surely agree that there are newspapers in the *département*. It is clear that belligerent militants would not fail to attract them to their cause and their entire polemics would be infused with the passions engulfing the Council. And when election day arrives, corruption and intrigue, fanned by the flames of attack and defense, will know no limits."

"I confess," said the prefect to me, "that in such a state of affairs, I would not wish to retain my office, even for twenty-four hours."

Well, sir, is not this fictional constitution of a general council which so frightened a prefect the genuine constitution of the Chamber? What difference is there? Just one. The arena is vaster, the theater higher, the battlefield wider, the feeding of passion more exciting, the prize for the combat more coveted, the questions used as the text or pretext for the combat more burning, more difficult, and therefore more apt to mislead the sentiments and judgment of the multitude. It is disorder organized on the same model but on a vaster scale.

Men have filled their minds with politics, that is to say, they have dreamed of grandeur, influence, wealth, and glory. Suddenly the winds of election blow them into the legislative enclosure, and what does the constitution of the country say to them? To one it says: "You are not rich. The minister needs to swell his ranks; all the positions are in his gift and none of them is forbidden to you by law. The decision is yours." To a second it says: "You feel you have talent and daring. There is the ministerial bench. If you remove them, the place is yours. The decision is yours." To a third: "Your soul is not up to this level of ambition but you promised your electors to oppose the government. However, there is still an avenue to the region of power open to you; here is a party leader, link your fortune to his."

Then, invariably, this muddle of mutual accusations begins, these outrageous efforts to attract the power of transitory popularity to one's side, this ostentatious display of unachievable principles when one is on the attack and abject concessions when one is on the defensive. These are just traps and countertraps, mines and countermines. You can see the most disparate elements forming alliances and the most natural alliances dissolving. People bargain, stipulate, sell, and buy. Here the party spirit enters into a coalition, there subterranean ministerial cunning causes another to fail. Any event that arises, even if it bears in its wake general conflagration, is always seized upon by the assailants if it offers ground on which the boarding ladders can rest. The public good or general interest is just words, pretexts, or means. The essential point is to draw from a question the power which will help one party to overthrow the government and walk over the body. Ancona,[28] Tahiti,[29] Syria,[30] Morocco,[31] fortifications, or visiting rights are all good pretexts. All that is needed is the proper arrangements for putting them into practice. At this point we are drenched in the eternal stereotyped lamentations; internally, France is suffering, anxious, etc., etc.; externally, France is humiliated, scorned, etc., etc. Is this true, is it untrue? No notice is taken. Does this measure bring us into conflict with Europe? Does it oblige us to maintain five hundred thousand troops on constant alert? Will it stop the march of civilization? Will it create obstacles for future administrations? This is not what it is all about; just one thing is of interest, the fall and the triumph of two names.

And do not think that this sort of political perversity pervades only base souls in the Chamber, those hearts consumed by low ambition or the prosaic lovers of highly paid positions. No, it also and above all attacks elite souls, noble hearts, and powerful intellects. To quell and subdue them, it just has to awaken in the secret depths of their consciences, in place of the following trivial thought: *You will achieve your dreams of wealth,* another no less attractive: *You will achieve your dreams of public good.*

We have a remarkable example of this. There is not in France a man's head on which as many accusations, verbal abuses, and flagrant insults have been heaped as on that of M. Guizot. If the language used by the parties contained bloodier epithets than *turncoat, traitor,* or *apostate,* they would not have been spared him. However, there is one reproach that I have never

28. In order to stop disturbances in the papal states, Pope Gregory XVI called upon Austria for assistance. On 28 June 1832, Austrian troops entered Bologna, Italy. For reasons of diplomatic balance, a French garrison was sent to the seaport of Ancona, about 120 miles southeast of Bologna. The garrison remained in Ancona until 1838.

29. In 1842 Tahiti was a French protectorate. Following incidents with English ships, Admiral Dupetit-Thouars transformed it into a territory of "direct sovereignty." This created tension between London and Paris. The latter disavowed the admiral on 24 February 1844.

30. France supported Mehmet Ali, pasha of Egypt, over Syria, part of the Ottoman Empire. England and Russia supported the sultan.

31. A brief conflict arose between France and Morocco in 1844 because Morocco refused to sign the Treaty of Tangiers, allowing cruisers of the signatory states to control merchant ships in order to ascertain the absence of slaves. This "right of search" did not fail to raise trouble between France and England for a while, as English cruisers, outnumbering those of other nations, exerted a de facto policing of the seas.

heard formulated or even insinuated against him, that of having used parliamentary success to boost his personal wealth. I acknowledge that he pushes probity to the point of self-sacrifice. I accept that he will never seek personal triumph other than the better to ensure the triumph of his principles. This is, moreover, a form of ambition that he has formally admitted.

So, we have seen this austere philosopher and man of principle in opposition. What did he do there? Everything that might suggest a thirst for power. For example, he displayed democratic views that are not his own, he adopted a mantle of fierce patriotism of which he does not approve, he caused embarrassment to his country's government, he contrived obstacles to the most important negotiations, he fomented coalitions, and he formed leagues with any individuals, even enemies of the throne, provided that they were enemies of some minister. Being out of office, he opposed matters he would have supported within office. He supported the direction of the batteries of Ancona against M. Molé, just as M. Thiers directs the batteries of Morocco against him. In short, he conjured up a ministerial crisis with all his determination and might and deliberately created for his own future government the difficulties that result from such precedents. That is what he did, and why? Because in the Charter there is an Article 46, a tempting serpent which told him:

"You will be equal to the gods; achieve power, by whatever route, and you will be the savior of the country!" And so the deputy, beguiled, made speeches, set out doctrines, and carried out acts which his conscience condemned, but he said to himself: "This is necessary to reach office; once I have reached it, I will adopt once more my genuine philosophy and true principles."

Is there any need for further examples? My God, the history of the war for portfolios is the entire history of parliament.

I am not attacking anyone in particular; I am attacking the institution. If the prospect of power is offered to deputies, it is impossible for the Chamber to be other than a battlefield.

Let us see what is happening in England. In 1840 the government was on the point of bringing about free trade. However, there was one man in the opposition, imbued with the doctrines of Smith,[32] a man who couldn't sleep at the thought of Canning's and Huskisson's glory, who wished at all costs to be the instrument of this vast revolution. It was going to be accomplished

32. Adam Smith.

without him. What did he do? He declared himself the protector of protection. He aroused every shred of ignorance, prejudice, and egoism in the country. He rallied the terrified aristocracy and aroused the popular classes who were so easy to mislead. He combated his own principles in Parliament and on the hustings. He ousted the reforming government. He came to office with the express mission of closing the ports of Great Britain to foreign goods. As a result, a deluge of ills, unprecedented in the annals of history and which the Whigs had hoped to avert, swamped England. Production stopped; inactivity desolated both town and country, escorted by its two faithful satellites, crime and illness. Everyone with intellect or heart rose up against this frightful oppression and Mr. Peel, in betrayal of his party and the majority, came to Parliament to admit: "I made a mistake, I was wrong, I renounce protection and give my country free trade." No, he was not mistaken. He was as much of an economist in 1840 as he was in 1846. But he wanted glory and for that he delayed the triumph of truth, through countless calamities, for six years.

There are therefore very few deputies whom the prospect of positions and portfolios does not cause to swerve from the line of rectitude in which their constituents hope to see them walk. It would not be so bad if the harm did not go beyond the walls of the Palais Bourbon! But, as you know, sir, the two armies who dispute power carry their battlefield outside. The warlike masses are everywhere; only the leaders are in the Chamber and it is from there that they issue orders. They are fully aware that, to reach the center of the fort, they have to conquer the outer works, the newspapers, popularity, public opinion, and electoral majorities. It is thus fatal for all these forces, to the extent that they enroll under the banner of one of the line commanders, to become imbued and permeated with the same insincerity. Journalism, from one end of France to the other, no longer discusses the measures; it pleads their cause and not from the point of view of whether they contain good or evil points in themselves but from the sole viewpoint of the help they can temporarily provide to one or the other leader. It is well known that there are few eminent journalists whose future will not be affected by the outcome of this portfolio war. What policy is the prime minister pursuing in Texas,[33] Lebanon, Tahiti, Morocco, or Madagascar? It does not matter.

---

33. In 1844 the U.S. Congress accepted the entrance of Texas into the Union. The French and English governments had advised the Texas governor against it.

The progovernment press has a single motto, *È sempre bene;*[34] while the opposition press espouses what the old woman in the satire had written on her petticoat for us to see: *Argumentabor.*[35]

It would need a more experienced pen than mine to recount all the harm done in France by the partisan press, who (mark my words, this is the core of my thesis) disseminate their views solely to serve *a particular deputy who wants to become a minister.* You have access to the king, sir, I don't like to involve him in these discussions. However, I am able to say, since this is the opinion held by Europe, that he has contributed to maintaining world peace. But perhaps you have witnessed what sweat in the form of moral exertions is needed to wrench out of him this success worthy of the acclaim of nations. What is the reason for all this sweat, these problems, this resistance to such a noble task? Because at a given moment, peace was not supported by public opinion. And why was it not supported? Because it did not suit certain newspapers. And why did it not suit certain newspapers? Because it was unwelcome to a particular deputy. And why finally was it unwelcome to this deputy? Because peace was the policy of the ministers, and therefore war was necessarily that of those deputies who wished to become ministers. Indubitably, this is the root of the evil.

Shall I make mention of Ancona, the fortifications of Paris, Algiers, the events in 1840, visiting rights, tariffs, anglophobia, and so many other questions in which journalism led public opinion astray, not because it was itself led astray but because this was part of a coldly premeditated plan whose success was of importance to a particular ministerial alliance?

I prefer to quote here the admissions that were themselves proclaimed by journalism in the most widely distributed of its outlets, *La Presse* (17 November 1845).

"M. Petetin describes the press as he sees it, as he prefers to dream it. In all good faith does he believe that, when *Le Constitutionnel, Le Siècle,* etc., attack M. Guizot, when in turn *Le Journal des débats* confronts M. Thiers, these broadsheets are campaigning uniquely on philosophical grounds, for truth as provoked by the interior needs of conscience? To define the press in these terms is to paint it as one imagines it, not as it really is. It does not cost us anything to state this, since while we are journalists, we are less so by vocation than by circumstance. Every day we see newspapers in the service of

34. "It is always good."
35. "I shall prove it."

human passion, rival ambition, ministerial alliances, parliamentary intrigue, and political calculations of every hue, the most violently opposed and the least noble, and we see them closely involved in this. However, we rarely see them in the service of ideas, and when by chance a newspaper happens to espouse an idea, *this is never on its own merits, it is always as a MINISTERIAL instrument with which to defend or attack.* He who is penning these lines is speaking from experience. Every time he has attempted to draw journalism out of the rut of party politics and introduce it to the field of ideas and reforms, to the path of wholesome applications of economic science to public administration, he found himself alone and had to acknowledge that outside the narrow circle traced by the assembled letters of four or five names, there was no possibility of discussion. There was no policy. What good does it do to deny this evil? Does it stop it existing? When newspapers do not ally themselves with special interests, they ally themselves with passions and when these are themselves examined closely, in the majority of cases these passions are merely selfish interests. This is the truth of the matter."

What, sir, are you not scandalized, not appalled by this terrible admission? Or do you still have some doubt as to the cause of a situation so fraught with humiliation and peril? It is not I who am speaking. It is not a misanthropist, a republican, or a seditionist. It is the press itself that has unveiled its secret and is telling you to what depths this institution whose morality inspires such confidence in you has reduced it. The place where laws are supposed to be debated has been transformed into a battlefield. The destiny of the country, war and peace, justice and iniquity, order and anarchy count for nothing, absolutely nothing in themselves; they are instruments of combat that are taken up and put down according to one's own imperatives. What does it matter that at each turn of this impious struggle upheaval is experienced throughout the country? It has scarcely returned to calm when the armies change position and the combat is once more engaged with even more fervor.

Finally, do I have to demonstrate the existence of partisan spirit, this insidious worm, this devouring cancer which draws its life and strength from the eligibility of deputies for executive power, within the electoral college? I am not speaking here of opinions, passions, and political errors. I am not even speaking of the faintheartedness or venality of certain consciences; it is beyond the power of the law to make men perfect. I am targeting only the passions and vices which directly result from the cause I am discussing, which is linked to the portfolio war engaged in within the Chambers and waged over the entire range of the newspapers. Is it really so difficult to calculate its effect on the electoral body? And when, day after day, the tribune and press make a point of preventing anything but false glimmers, false judgments, false quotations, and false assertions reaching the public, is it possible to have any confidence in the verdict pronounced by the grand national jury thus misled, circumvented, and impassioned? What is it called upon to judge? Its own interests. Never does anyone speak of these to it, for ministerial battle is waged at Ancona, Tahiti, in Syria, wherever the public is not to be found. And what does it know of what is going on in these far-off regions? Only what it is told by orators and writers who, on their own admission, do not utter a single word either orally or in writing that is not inspired by the intense desire for personal success.

And then, suppose I wished to raise the veil that covers not only the errors but the turpitudes of the electoral urn! Why does the elector ensure that his vote is so valued, require it to be sought, and consider it as a valuable object of commerce? Because he knows that this vote contains the fortune of the fortunate candidate who is soliciting it. Why, for his part, is the candidate so flexible, so crawling, so generous with his promises, and so little concerned with any shred of dignity? Because he has ulterior motives, because the position of deputy is a stepping-stone for him, because the constitution of the country enables him to see in the distance, should he succeed, intoxicating prospects, positions, honors, wealth, power, and this golden cloak which hides all shame and absolves all base acts.

So, where are we now with all this? Where are the electors now? How many of them dare to remain and show themselves to be honest? How many will honestly deposit a ballot in the urn which faithfully expresses their political beliefs? Oh! They would be afraid of being seen as idiots and dupes. They are careful to trumpet loudly the bargain they have made of their vote and they will be seen to deposit their own ignominy at the door of the church rather than to cast doubt on their deplorable cunning. If there are still a few virtues that have survived this major shipwreck, these are negative virtues. They believe nothing, hope for nothing, and keep themselves from being contaminated, in the words of some poet or another:

> A calm indifference
> is the surest of virtues.[36]

36. Source unknown.

They let things happen, that is all. In the meantime, ministers, deputies, and candidates sink under the burden of promises and undertakings. And what is the result? This. The government and the Chamber change roles. "Do you wish to let me dispose of all jobs?" say the deputies. "Do you wish to let me decide on the laws and the budget?" reply the ministers. And each abandons the office for which he is responsible for one which does not concern him. I ask you, is this representative government?

But it does not stop there. There are other things in France than ministers, deputies, candidates, journalists, and electors. There is the general public, thirty million men who are being accustomed to being counted for nothing. They do not see this, you may say, and proof of this is their indifference. Ah, do not become confident in this seeming blindness. While they do not see the cause of the evil, they see its effects, the budget constantly increasing, their rights and titles trampled underfoot, and all favors becoming the price of electoral bargains from which they are excluded. Please God that they learn to link their suffering to its true cause, for irritation is growing in their hearts. They are seeking the means of enfranchising themselves and woe to the country if they make a mistake. They are seeking, and *universal suffrage* is taking hold of all minds. They are seeking, and *communism* is spreading like wildfire. They are seeking, and while you are drawing a veil over the hideous wound, who can count the errors, the theories, or illusions in which they think they have found a remedy for their ills and a brake against your injustices?

In this way, everyone is suffering from a state of affairs so profoundly illogical and vicious. However, if the full extent of the evil is appreciated somewhere, it must be at the summit of the social scale. I cannot believe that such statesmen as M. Guizot, M. Thiers, or M. Molé can be in contact with all these turpitudes for so long without having learned to recognize them and calculate their terrifying consequences. It is not possible for them to have been in turn in the ranks, facing systematic opposition, assailed by personal rivalry, and forced to struggle against artificial obstacles placed in their way by the urge to topple them, without saying to themselves that things would be different, administrative authority would be more steady, and the task of government much lighter *if deputies could not become ministers.*

Oh! If ministers were to deputies what prefects are to general councillors, if the law eliminated in the Chamber those prospects which foment ambition, I consider that a calm and fruitful destiny would be open to all the elements of the social body. The depositories of power might well still encounter errors and passions but never these subversive alliances for which any means are permitted and whose only aspiration is to overthrow one cabinet after another with the support of a fallacious and transitory unpopularity. Deputies could not have interests other than those of their constituents. Electors would not be made to prostitute their votes to selfish views. The press, freed from any links with leaders of parties which would no longer exist, would fulfill its proper role of enlightening public opinion and providing it with a mouthpiece. The people, wisely administered with consistency and economy, and who are happy or who cannot hold the authorities responsible for their sufferings, would not let themselves be beguiled with the most dangerous utopias. Finally the king, whose thoughts would no longer be a mystery to anyone, would hear during his lifetime the judgment that history reserves for him.

I am not unaware, sir, of the objections that may be made to parliamentary reform. There are disadvantages to it. But, my goodness, everything has its disadvantages. The press, civil liberty juries, and the monarchy have theirs. The question is never to see whether a reformed institution has disadvantages, but whether that institution without reform does not have even greater ones. And what calamities might emanate from a Chamber of taxpayers that are not equal to those which are disseminated over the country by a Chamber of ambitious deputies who are fighting each other for the possession of power?

It is said that such a Chamber would be too democratic, driven by passions that are too popular. It would represent the nation. Is it in the nation's interest to be badly administered, invaded by foreigners, such that justice is not rendered?

The strongest objection, unceasingly repeated, is that the Chamber would lack enlightenment and experience.

There is a lot to say on this subject, However, if the exclusion of civil servants gives rise to dangers, if it appears to violate the rights of honorable men who are also citizens, if it circumscribes the liberty of electors, would it not be possible, while opening the gates of the Palais Bourbon to the agents of government, to circumscribe their presence with precautions dictated by the most elementary prudence?

You are not expecting me to formulate a draft law at this point. However, I consider that public good sense would approve a measure drafted in terms of this sort:

"All French citizens, without distinction of profession, are eligible (except for exceptional cases in which a high official position would imply direct influence on voting, such as that of prefect, etc.).

"All deputies would receive suitable, uniform remuneration.

"Elected civil servants would resign their functions for the period of their mandate. They would not receive payment. They may neither be dismissed nor promoted. In a word, their life in the administration would be totally suspended and start again only once their legislative mission has expired.

"No deputy may be called upon to fill a public position."

Finally, far from admitting, as Messrs. Gauguier, Rumilly, Thiers, and others have done, that exceptions would be made on the principle of conflict of interest in favor of ministries, embassies, and all those functions known as *political positions,* it is exactly those that I wish to exclude, mercilessly and in the first place, since it is clear to me that it is the aspiring ambassadors and ministers who upset the world. Without wishing in the least to offend the leaders of parliamentary reform who put forward exceptions like these, I dare to say that they do not perceive or wish to perceive the millionth part of the evils that result from the eligibility of deputies for public office, that their so-called reform does not reform anything, and that it is just an underhand measure, one that is limited, with no social purchase, dictated by a narrow sentiment of base and unjust jealousy.

But, you say, what about Article 46 of the Charter? I have no answer to this. Is the Charter made for us or are we made for the Charter? Is the Charter the final expression of human wisdom? Is it a sacred Koran descended from heaven, whose effects may not be examined however disastrous they may be? Should we say: Let the country perish rather than change a comma in the Charter? If this is so, I have nothing to say, other than: Electors! The Charter does not forbid your using your vote for deplorable purposes, but it does not order you to do so either. *Quid leges sine moribus?*[37]

In ending this all too long letter, I should reply to what you tell me of your personal position. I will refrain from doing so. You consider that the reform, if it takes place, cannot affect you since you do not depend on responsible power but in fact on irresponsible power. Good for you! The legislature has decided that this position does not lead to legal incapacity. It is up to the electors to decide whether this does not constitute the clearest imaginable form of moral incapacity.

I am, sir, your faithful servant.

37. See note 27, p. 371.

4. To the Electors of the Landes

   Mugron, 22 March 1848   [vol. 1, p. 506]

My dear Fellow Countrymen,

   You are going to entrust the destiny of France and perhaps that of the world to the representatives of your choice, and I have no need to tell you how much I would be honored if you judged me to be worthy of your confidence.

   You cannot expect me to set out here my views on the many and serious tasks which will have to be dealt with by the National Assembly. I hope you will find in my past record some form of guarantee for the future. I am also ready to provide answers, through the newspapers or in public meetings, to any questions I may be asked.

   Here is the spirit in which I will support the Republic with wholehearted devotion:

   War waged against all forms of abuse: a people bound by the ties of privilege, bureaucracy, and taxes is like a tree eaten away by parasite plants.

   Protection for all rights: those of conscience like those of intelligence; those of ownership like those of work; those of the family like those of the commune; those of the fatherland like those of humanity. I have no ideal other than universal justice; no motto other than that on our national flag, LIBERTY, EQUALITY, FRATERNITY.

   I remain your devoted fellow countryman.

---

5. Letter to a Group of Supporters

   1849   [vol. 1, p. 507]
   To MM Tonnelier, Degos, Bergeron, Camors,
   Dubroca, Pomede, Fauret, etc.

My Friends,

   Thank you for your gracious letter. The constituency can dispose of me as it wishes; your enduring confidence will be an encouragement . . . or a consolation to me.

   You say that I am being painted as a *socialist*. What can I answer? My writings are there. Have I not countered the Louis Blanc doctrine with *Property and Law*, the Considérant doctrine with *Property and Plunder*, the Leroux doctrine with *Justice and Fraternity*, the Proudhon doctrine with *Capital and Rent*, the Mimerel committee with *Protectionism and Communism*, paper money with *Damned Money*, and the Montagnard Manifesto with *The State*? I spend my life combating *socialism*. It would be very painful for me to have this acknowledged everywhere except in the *département* of the Landes.

My votes have been depicted as close to the *extreme left*. Why have the occasions on which I have voted with the *right* not equally been mentioned?

But, you will say, how have you been able to be alternatively in two such opposing camps? I will explain this.

For a century, the parties have taken a great many names and adopted a great many pretexts; basically, it has always been a matter of the same thing, the struggle of the poor against the rich.

Now, the poor demand *more* than what is just and the rich refuse *even* that which is just. If this continues, *social war,* of which our fathers witnessed the first act in '93, and of which we witnessed the second act in June, this frightful fratricidal war[38] is not nearing its end. The only possible conciliation is on the field of *justice,* in everything and for all.

After February, the people put forward a host of iniquitous and absurd pretensions mingled with some well-founded claims.

What was needed to avert social war?

Two things:

To refute in written form the iniquitous claims and rebuff them legally.
To support the well-founded claims in written form and allow them legally.

That is the key to my conduct.

At the start of the revolution, popular hopes were highly exalted and knew no bounds, even in our *département,* and I remind you that I was not considered to be sufficiently *red.* It was much worse in Paris; the workers were organized, armed, and masters of the terrain, at the mercy of the most fiery demagogues.

The initial action of the National Assembly had to be one of resistance. It was concentrated above all in the *finance committee,* made up of men belonging to the rich class. Resisting mad and subversive demands, rebuffing progressively increasing taxes, paper money, the taking over of private industry by the state, and the suspension of national debts: such was its laborious task. I played my part, and I ask you, citizens, if I had been a *socialist,*

38. The revolution of 1848.

would this committee have selected me eight times in a row to be its vice president?

Once the work of *resistance* was completed, the work of *reform* remained to be carried out in the 1849 budget. So many unevenly shared taxes needed to be changed! So many restrictions needed to be removed! Just take this business of conscription, for example (they have since renamed it "recruitment"), a tax of seven years on lives, *drawn from a hat!* Given these *droits réunis*[39] (now known as indirect contributions), a regressive income tax affecting the poor disproportionately, are these not *well-founded complaints* from the people? After the days in June when anarchy was defeated, the National Assembly considered that the time had come to enter resolutely and spontaneously this avenue of reparation dictated by equity and even by prudence.

The finance committee, through its composition, was less inclined to this second task than the first. New people had been introduced into it by bielections,[40] and it was constantly being said that, far from changing taxes, we would be very happy if we could have reestablished the situation just as it had been before February.

For this reason, the Assembly entrusted to a commission of thirty members the task of preparing the budget. It charged another commission with harmonizing the tax on drink with the principles of liberty and equality enshrined in the constitution. I was a member of both and, much as I ardently rebuffed utopian demands, I was equally ardent in carrying out just reform.

It would take too long to relate here how the good intentions of the Assembly were paralyzed. History will reveal this. But you can understand my line of conduct. What I am reproached for is precisely what I am proud of. Yes, I have voted with the right against the left when it was a matter of resisting the excesses of mistaken popular ideas. Yes, I have voted with the left against the right when the legitimate complaints of the poor, suffering classes were being ignored.

Because of this, I may have alienated both parties and will remain crushed in the center. No matter. I am conscious of having been faithful to my commitments, logical, impartial, just, prudent, and in control of myself. Those who accuse me doubtless feel strong enough to do better. If this is so, let the constituency nominate them in my place. I will endeavor to forget that I

---

39. See "To the Electors of the *Département* of the Landes," p. 341, and note 10, p. 345.

40. A so-called bielection is an election held in a district to replace a deputy who died or resigned.

have lost its confidence by remembering that I obtained it once, and it is not a slight tremor of self-love that will efface the profound gratitude I owe it.

I remain, my dear fellow countrymen, your faithful servant.

---

6. Political Manifestos of April 1849

[vol. 7, p. 255]

My dear Fellow Countrymen,

You have given me a mandate which is drawing to its close. I have carried it out in the spirit in which it was given to me.

Do you remember the elections in 1848? What did you want?

Some of you had welcomed with delight the coming of the Republic, others had neither provoked nor wanted it, and yet others feared it. However, with an admirable surge of good sense, you united under this twin aim:

to maintain the Republic and give it a chance loyally;
to engage it in the path of order and security.

History will show that the National Assembly, in the face of immense dangers, has been faithful to this program. By dissolving itself it leaves anarchy and reaction conquered, security reestablished, subversive utopias made impotent, a steady government, a constitution that allows later ameliorations, peace established, and finances that have escaped the greatest dangers. Yes, although it has often been battered by storms, *your* Assembly has been the expression of *your* will. It seems to me to be an unexpected miracle of universal suffrage. To calumniate it is to calumniate yourselves.

For my part, I have always steeped myself in the spirit which imbued you all in April 1848. Very often when, under the pressure of terrible difficulties, I saw the flame which should have guided me flicker, I evoked the memory of the many meetings at which I appeared before you and I said to myself: "I have to want what my constituents have wanted, an honest Republic."

Fellow countrymen, I am obliged to speak of myself and will limit myself to the facts.

On 23 February, I did not take part in the insurrection. By chance, I happened to find myself present during the gunfire at the Hôtel des Capucines. While the crowd fled in panic, I advanced against the current, and facing the battalion whose rifles were still hot, with the help of two workers, I gave help during this unhappy night to those who were mortally wounded.

As early as the 25th, I managed to guess at the subversive ideological excesses soon to be concentrated on the Luxembourg Palace.[41] To combat them I founded a newspaper. Here is the judgment given of it by a review which I have come across, one which is not suspect, entitled *A Catholic Bibliography Intended for Priests, Seminaries, Schools, etc.* "*La République française,* a broadsheet which appeared soon after the Revolution, written with talent, moderation, and wisdom, opposed to socialism, the Luxembourg Palace, and circulars."

There followed what has been called with reason the *rush for positions.* Several of my friends were very influential, including M. de Lamartine, who had written to me a few days before, "If ever the storm carries me to power, you will help me to achieve the triumph of our ideas." It was easy for me to achieve high position; I have just never thought about it.

Almost unanimously elected by you, I entered the Assembly on 5 May. On the 15th, we were invaded. On that day, my role was limited to remaining at my post, like all my colleagues.

I was nominated as member and vice president of the finance committee, to which committee it was soon clear that we would have to fight against an extremely seductive proposal much vaunted at the time. On the grounds of satisfying popular demand, some people wanted to bestow an inordinate degree of power on the revolutionary government. They wanted the state to suspend the reimbursement of the savings bank and treasury bonds and take over the railways, insurance, and transport systems. The government was pushing in this direction, which does not appear to me to be anything other than *theft regularized by law and executed through taxes.* I dare to say that I have contributed to preserving my country from such a calamity.

However, a frightful collision was threatened. The genuine work carried out by individual workshops was replaced by the bogus production of national workshops.[42] The organized and armed people of Paris were the plaything of ignorant utopians and fomenters of disorder. The Assembly, forced

41. The Luxembourg Palace in Paris was the seat of the Government Commission for the Workers, created on 28 February 1848 to improve the condition of the workers. It consisted of 242 worker delegates and 231 employer delegates and was chaired by the socialist Louis Blanc. The commission was dissolved on 28 March 1848.

42. The national workshops were created on 27 February 1848 ostensibly for the purpose of employing retired workers. The workers received two francs a day, soon reduced to one franc because of the tremendous increase in their numbers (29,000 on 5 March; 118,000 on 15 June). Struggling with financial difficulties, irritated by the inefficiency of the workshops, the Assembly dissolved the workshops on 21 June.

to destroy these deceptive illusions one by one through its votes, foresaw the storm but had few means of resisting it other than the moral strength that it received from you. Convinced that voting was not enough—the masses needed to be enlightened—I founded another newspaper which aimed to speak the simple language of good sense and which, for this reason, I entitled *Jacques Bonhomme*. It never stopped calling for the disbanding of the forces of insurrection, whatever the cost. On the eve of the June Days, it contained an article by me on the national workshops. This article, plastered over all the walls of Paris, was something of a sensation. To reply to certain charges, I had it reproduced in the newspapers in the *département*.

The storm broke on 24 June. One of the first to enter the Faubourg Saint Antoine following the removal of the formidable barricades which protected access to it, I accomplished a twin and difficult task, to save those unfortunate people who were going to be shot on unreliable evidence and to penetrate into the most far-flung districts to help in the disarmament. This latter part of my voluntary mission, accomplished under gunfire, was not without danger. Each room might have hidden a trap, each window or basement window a rifle.

Following victory, I gave loyal assistance to the administration of General Cavaignac, whom I hold to be one of the noblest characters brought to the fore by the Revolution. Nevertheless, I resisted anything I considered to be an arbitrary measure as I know that any exaggeration about success compromises it. Self-control and moderation in every sense have been my rule or rather my instinct. In the Faubourg Saint Antoine, I disarmed insurgents with one hand and saved prisoners with the other. This has been the symbol of my conduct in parliament.

Around this time, I was stricken with a chest ailment which, combined with the huge size of our debating chamber, barred me from the tribune. I did not remain idle for all that. The true cause of society's ills and dangers lies, in my opinion, in a certain number of mistaken ideas, in favor of which those classes who have number and strength on their side unfortunately became enamored. There is not one of these errors that I have not combated. Of course, I knew that the action that one seeks to exercise over causes is always very slow and that such action is inadequate when the danger explodes. But can you reproach me for having worked for the future, after having done for the present all that I possibly could?

To the doctrines of Louis Blanc I opposed a treatise entitled *Individualism and Fraternity*.

When the very principle of ownership was threatened and efforts were made to direct the legislation against it, I wrote the brochure *Property and Law*.

The form of individual property which consists in the individual appropriation of land was under attack. So I wrote the brochure *Property and Plunder*, which, according to English and American economists, shed some light on the vexatious question of *rent from land*.

People wished to found fraternity on legal constraint. I wrote the brochure *Justice and Fraternity*.

Rivalry was stirred up between labor and capital; the population was deluded with the illusion of *free credit*. I wrote the brochure *Capital and Rent*.

Communism was overwhelming us so I attacked it in its most practical manifestation, through the brochure *Protectionism and Communism*.

The purely revolutionary school wanted the state to intervene in every matter and thus bring back a continuous increase in taxes. I wrote the brochure entitled *The State*, which was particularly directed against the manifesto of the Montagnards.

It was proved to me that one of the causes of the instability of government and the disorientating intrusion of false politics was the struggle for office. I wrote the brochure *Parliamentary Conflicts of Interest*.

I was convinced that almost all the economic errors that plague this country arise from a false concept of the functions of money. I wrote the brochure *Damned Money*.

I saw that financial reform was going to be carried out using illogical and inadequate procedures. I wrote the brochure *Peace and Liberty or the Republican Budget*.[43]

In this way, through action in the street or appealing to the mind through controversy, as far as my health allowed, I did not let a single opportunity slip to combat error, whether arising from socialism or communism, the Montagne or the Plaine.[44]

This is why on some occasions I had to vote with the left and on others with the right; with the left when it defended liberty and the Republic, with the right when it defended order and security.

And if I am criticized for this so-called double alliance, my answer is: I

---

43. *OC,* vol. 5, p. 407, "Paix et liberté ou le budget républicain."
44. The deputies without any strong ideology.

have not allied myself with anyone nor joined any coterie. On each question, I have voted according to my conscience. All those who have read my pamphlets carefully, whenever they were published, know that I have always had a horror of habitual majorities and oppositions.

The time came for the election for the president of the Republic. We still faced grave dangers, among which was foreign war. I did not know what we might expect from Napoléon, though I knew what we might expect from Cavaignac, who had made a declaration in favor of peace. I had my preferences and expressed them loyally. It was my right and even my duty to say what I was doing and why I was doing it. I limited myself to this. Universal suffrage proved me wrong. I rallied as I ought to its all-powerful wish. I challenge anyone to identify a systematic opposing vote of mine to the person elected on 20th December. I would consider myself to be a seditionist if, through ridiculous resentment, I blocked the grand and useful mission he had received from the country.

As a member of the finance committee and later of the budget commission, as far as our finances allowed, I worked to pursue the reforms which, as you know, have always been the object of my efforts. I contributed to reducing the taxes on salt and the post. I was a member of the commission on drink, which prepared a radical reform which the limited time of the Assembly postponed to a later date. I strongly campaigned for reducing the numbers of the army, and I would have liked to achieve a softening of the severe law on recruitment.

On the question of the dissolution of the Assembly, my views have never varied. We must pass fundamental laws indispensable for putting the constitution into practice, no more, no less.

Fellow countrymen, these have been my actions, which I subject to your impartial scrutiny.

If you think it appropriate to reelect me, I declare to you that I will persevere in the path you traced for me in April 1848, *to maintain the Republic and lay the basis for security.*

If, under the influence of the unhappy days you have endured, you have conceived other ideas and other hopes, if you wish to pursue a new goal and try new adventures, then I can no longer be your representative. I will not abandon the work we undertook together just when we are about to gather the fruit of our efforts. Security is without doubt the primary need of our era and the signal priority in any age. However, I cannot believe that it can be given a solid basis by triumphalist abuses, interference and harassment, violence and reactionary fury. The man you honor with your vote is not the representative of one class but of all classes. He should not forget that there is great suffering, destitution, and blatant injustice in the country. To hold things in check constantly is neither just nor even prudent. To search for the causes of suffering and produce all the remedies that are compatible with justice is a duty as sacred as that of maintaining order. Doubtless, truth must not be trifled with; false hopes must not be encouraged; popular prejudice must not be yielded to, even less when it is expressed through insurrection. My acts and writings are there to prove that, in this respect, I cannot be reproached. However, I should not be asked either to yield to outbursts of anger and hate against brothers who are unhappy and misguided, whose ignorance only too often exposes them to perfidious suggestions. The duty of a national assembly which results from universal suffrage is to enlighten them, to bring them back, to listen to their wishes, and to leave them with no doubt as to its strong sympathy. TO LOVE IS THE ONLY LAW, as a great apostle said. We are in an era in which this maxim is as true in politics as in morals.

> I remain, dear fellow countrymen,
> your devoted servant.

---

7. Letter on the Referendum for the Election of the President of the Republic

> [Article published in *Le Journal des Landes,*
> 13 August 1848. From the private collection
> of Jean-Claude Paul-Dejean.]

We are called upon to elect the president of the Republic. I do not aspire to influence your votes, but since I have been in a position, as a result of your votes, to study both men and matters at close quarters, I am able to say frankly what I myself would do without exceeding my rights and duties.

I will not vote for Louis-Napoléon Bonaparte. To place at the helm a man about whom we know nothing, who has provided no proof of his abilities, whose intentions and projects are unknown, whose entire past record lies in two ludicrous dynastic ventures, appears to me to play fast and loose with voters' rights and place in jeopardy the destiny of the country much beyond what can be done in all conscience. Whether his candidature is based on the cult of a name or on a secret desire to open the way for a new revolution, neither of these reasons could give me reason to support him.

I will vote for Cavaignac. This is not because, in my view, mistakes have not been made during his administration. I have never approved, and my voting record bears witness to this, the prolonged exceptional measures taken after the June Days, which went beyond the requirements of the conflict. But I will vote for him because I consider him to be a capable and trustworthy man, because he has resisted the undertow of warlike passions, because he has kept the government in harmony with the wishes of the people as shown in general elections, and because he wants to preserve loyally the charge entrusted to him, that is to say, the Republic. Because he has understood that a republic, which is the government of a country by the country, cannot be directed by extreme minorities without injustice and risk, because he bravely accepted the dreadful responsibility of power at a time of crisis, and finally because I would be afraid that if it did not acknowledge all these services rendered, the nation would end up discouraging all forms of such commitment.

Fellow countrymen, you may not share my judgment. But I do not want you to be able to doubt my impartiality. For this reason I think it would be relevant to say that I have never spoken to Cavaignac except during the June Days when, like all my colleagues, I had to make my report to the commander in chief on returning from the barricades.

Your devoted fellow countryman.

Section 3

Electoral Principles

1. Electoral Sophisms

[vol. 7, p. 271]

I have made my commitments.

I am not supporting M. So and So because he has not asked for
my vote.
I am voting for M. So and So because he has done me a good turn.
I am voting for M. So and So because he has rendered service to
France.
I am voting for M. So and So because he has promised to do me
a favor.
I am voting for M. So and So because I would like a position
with him.
I am voting for M. So and So because I am worried about keeping
my job.
I am voting for M. So and So because he comes from the region.
I am voting for M. So and So because he does not come from
the region.
I am voting for M. So and So because he *will speak up.*
I am voting for M. So and So because if he is not elected, our prefect
or subprefect will be dismissed.

Each of these sophisms has its own particular nature, but at the base of
each of them there is a common thread which needs to be disentangled.
They all are based on this twin premise:

The election is being run in the interest of the candidate.
The elector is the exclusive owner of one thing, that is to say, his vote,
which he is free to use as he pleases and in favor of whomever he wishes.

The error of this doctrine and its daily application will be made clear by our examination.

1. I AM NOT VOTING FOR M. A—— BECAUSE HE HAS NOT ASKED FOR MY VOTE.

This sophism, like all the others, is based on an attitude which, in itself, is not reprehensible, the sense of personal dignity.

When men seek encouragement in pursuit of some bad action, it is rare for the paradoxes with which they deceive themselves to be totally false. Such paradoxes make up a fabric. It is a fabric in which there are always a few threads of good sense to be seen. They always contain a grain of truth and this is why they impress. If they were totally false, they would not delude so many people.

The meaning of the one we are examining is as follows:

"M. A—— aspires to becoming my deputy. Being a deputy is the road to honors and wealth. He knows that my vote can contribute to his election. This is the least of what he is asking of me. If he behaves proudly, I in turn will behave proudly, and when I agree to use something as precious as my vote in someone's favor, I am determined that he should show gratitude to me, that he should not disdain coming to my house, entering into a relationship with me, shaking my hand, etc., etc."

It is very clear that the elector who reasons thus will make the twin mistakes we have pointed out.

    1. He believes that his vote is cast to be useful to the candidate.
    2. He thinks that, when it comes to helping people he is free to do so to whomever he chooses.

In a word, he disregards all the public good and evil which may result from his choice.

For, if he considered that the aim of the entire electoral mechanism is to send to the Chamber of Deputies those who are conscientious and devoted, he would probably reason in a contrary manner and say:

"I will vote for M. A—— for this reason, among others, that he has not asked for my vote!"

In fact, in the eyes of anyone who does not lose sight of the object of the function of deputies, I do not think that there can be a stronger presumption against a candidate than his insistence on seeking votes.

For, in the end, what drives this man to come and torment me in my own house, to endeavor to prove to me that I ought to give him my confidence?

When I know that so many deputies, holding two balls,[1] have dictated the law to ministers and have obtained good positions, should I not fear that this candidate has no other aim in view when he comes—sometimes from the other end of the kingdom—to beg for the trust of people he does not know?

One can doubtless be betrayed by the deputy one has freely selected. But if we, the electors, go to seek out a man in his retirement (and we can go to seek him out only because his reputation for integrity is perfectly established), if we drag him away from his solitary life to confer on him a mandate which he has not requested, do we not give ourselves the best possible chance of handing over this mandate into pure and faithful hands?

If this man had wanted to make a business out of being a deputy, he would have sought it. He has not done so and therefore has no base ulterior motives.

What is more, he to whom the mandate of deputy is freely given, as free evidence of general confidence and universal esteem, would feel so very honored, so grateful for his own reputation, that he would hesitate to tarnish it.

And, after all, would it not be natural for things to happen thus?

What are we discussing? Is it a question of rendering service to M. So and So, favoring him or setting him on the road to wealth?

No, it is a question of giving ourselves a representative who has our trust. Would it not be very simple to take the trouble to look for him?

Once there was a case of an important trusteeship. A family council of many members had met in the court. A man arrived out of breath, covered in sweat, having worn out several horses. No one knew him personally. All that was known was that he managed, somewhere far away, the properties of underage children and that he would soon have to account for these. This man begged them to appoint him as trustee. He spoke to the relatives on the father's side and then to those on the mother's side. He sang his own praises at length, speaking of his probity, wealth, and connections. He uttered prayers, promises, and threats. Deep anxiety could be read on his features, as well as an immoderate desire for success. Vain objections were raised

---

1. In order to vote for or against a law, deputies used to put a white or a black ball in an urn. (See also Letter 110, note 230.) Therefore, the reference to "holding two balls" implies that the deputy is withholding his vote in order to get political favors.

that the trusteeship was a weighty burden, that it would take up much of the time and wealth of the person to whom it was entrusted and override his other businesses. He brushed aside each difficulty. He asked no more than to devote his time to serving the poor orphans. He was prepared to sacrifice his wealth, so heroic was the disinterestedness he felt in his heart! He would view with stoicism his businesses' decline, provided that those of the under-age children prospered in his hands! "But you manage their property!" "All the more reason, I will account to myself for this and who is more equipped to examine these accounts than he who has set them up?"

I ask you, would it be reasonable for the family council to entrust to this earnest lobbyist the functions he requested?

Would it not be wiser to entrust this task to a relative known for his probity and scrupulousness, especially if it were the case that the interests of this relative and the underage children were identical to the extent that he could not do anything to their advantage or disadvantage without similarly affecting his own situation?

. . . .

2. I AM VOTING FOR M. A—— BECAUSE HE HAS DONE ME A FAVOR.

Gratitude, it is said, is the only virtue that cannot be abused. This is wrong. There is a very common method of abusing it, and that is to settle the debt imposed on us by it *at the expense of others*.

I acknowledge that an elector, who has received frequent acts of kindness from a candidate whose opinions he does not share, is put in an extremely delicate and embarrassing position if this candidate is bold enough to ask for his vote. Ingratitude is itself a repugnant characteristic; to go so far as to make an official display of it, in so many words, can become genuine tor-ment. In vain will you paint this defection in the colors of the most reasoned of political motives; in the depths of universal understanding there is an instinct that will condemn you. This is because political mores have not achieved nor been able to achieve the same progress as private mores. The public will always see your vote as a property of which you can dispose and it will censure you for not allowing it to be directed by a virtue as popular and honorable as gratitude.

However, let us examine this.

The question facing the electoral body, as raised in France, is in most cases so complex that it leaves great latitude in moral awareness. There are two candidates, one for the government, the other for the opposition. Yes, but if the government has committed a great many faults, so has the opposition. In addition, look at the manifestos of the two opponents: one wants order and liberty; the other demands liberty with order. The only difference is that one puts in second place what the other puts first; in essence they want the same thing. It was not worth the trouble, for such subtle differences, to betray the rights to your vote for one of the candidates because of the benefits received. You have no excuse for this.

But let us suppose that the question put before the electors is less vague and you will see that not only the rights but also the popularity and even the claim to gratitude are weakened.

In England, for example, long experience of representative government has taught electors that they should not pursue all types of reform simultaneously, but pass on to the second when the first has been carried out and so on.

As a result, there is always a central question facing the public on which all the efforts of the press, associations, and electors are focused.

Are you for or against electoral reform?
Are you for or against Catholic emancipation?
Are you for or against the emancipation of slaves?

At the moment, the sole question is:

Are you for or against free trade?

When this has been settled, doubtless this other question will be raised:

Are you for or against voluntary arrangements with regard to religion?

As long as there is *campaigning* with regard to any of these questions, everyone takes part, everyone seeks enlightenment, and everyone takes one side or another. Doubtless, the other major political reforms, although relegated to the shade, are not totally neglected. However, this is a debate which is engaged within each party and not between one party and the other.

Thus, at the present time, when *free traders* have to oppose a candidate to those supporting monopoly, they hold preparatory assemblies in which a person is proclaimed their candidate who, beyond the conformity of his principles with those of the *free traders* in matters of trade, is also more in line with the majority because of his opinions on Ireland or the Maynooth[2] bill, etc., etc. However, on the day of the great combat, the only question put to candidates is this:

Are you *free traders*? Do you support monopoly?

Consequently, it is on this alone that the electors will be called upon to vote.

It is thus easy to understand that a question couched in such simple terms will not allow any of the sophisms dealt with in this book to creep into the parties, in particular that of gratitude.

Let us say that in private life I have done an elector some notable favors. However, I know that he is in favor of free trade, while I am standing as a candidate for the partisans of protection. It would not cross my mind to expect him, through gratitude, to sacrifice a cause to which I know that he has devoted all his efforts, one to which he has subscribed and in favor of which he has allied himself with powerful interests. If I did this, his reply would be clear and logical and it would obtain public approval not only from his party but also mine. He would say to me: "I have personal obligations to you. I am personally ready to carry these out. I do not expect you to ask me for them and I will take every opportunity to prove to you that I am not ungrateful. There is, however, a sacrifice I cannot make to you, that of my conscience. You know that I am committed to the cause of free trade which I consider to be consistent with public interest. You, on the other hand, uphold the opposite view. We have met here to ascertain which of these two principles is upheld by the majority. On my vote may depend the triumph or defeat of the principle I support. In conscience I cannot raise my hand for you."

It is clear that, unless he were dishonest, the candidate would not be able to insist on proving that the elector is bound by a benefit received.

The same doctrine should prevail in our midst. Only, as the questions are very much more complicated, they give rise to a painful contest between the benefactor and the person in his debt. The benefactor will say: "Why are you refusing me your vote? Is it because a few shades of opinion separate us? But do you think in exactly the same way as my opponent? Do you not

2. In 1845 Robert Peel proposed a subsidy of thirty thousand pounds to rebuild the Irish college of Maynooth for young priests. The bill was adopted in spite of numerous petitions against it.

know that my intentions are pure? Do I, like you, not want order, liberty, and the public good? Are you afraid that I will vote for such and such a measure of which you disapprove; who knows whether it will be brought before the Chamber during this session? You can see perfectly well that you do not have sufficient reason to forget what I have done for you. You are just seeking a pretext to avoid offering any token of gratitude."

I think that the English method, that of pursuing just one reform at a time, without considering one's own advantages, also has the considerable advantage of invariably classifying the electors, sheltering them from bad influences, and preventing sophisms from taking hold, in short of shaping frank and firm political mores. This is why I would like it to be adopted in France. In the event, there are four reforms which are competing for priority.

1. Electoral reform
2. Parliamentary reform
3. Freedom of education
4. Trade reform

I do not know to which of these questions my country will give preference. If I have a voice in the matter in this respect, I would designate *parliamentary reform* as being the most important and urgent, the one for which public opinion is best prepared and which is most likely to lead to the triumph of the three others.

For this reason, I will say a few words about it at the end of this book.

. . . .

3. I AM VOTING FOR M. A—— BECAUSE HE HAS RENDERED
GREAT SERVICE TO THE COUNTRY.

Once upon a time, an elector's vote was sought for a general of great merit. "Who in the region," it was said, "has given greater service to the country? He has shed his blood on countless battlefields. All his promotions in rank have been due to his courage and military talent. He is a self-made man and, what is more, he has raised to senior positions his brothers, nephews, and cousins."

"Is our district threatened?" asked the elector. "Is there a mass uprising? Is it a matter of selecting a military leader? My vote is assured for the honorable general since all you tell me of him and what I know give him an irrefutable right to my trust."

"No," said the lobbyist, "it is a question of voting for a deputy, a legislator."

"What will his functions be?"

"To make laws; to revise the civil code, the code on procedures, and the penal code; to restore order to the finances; and to supervise, contain, restrain, and if necessary indict ministers."

"And what do the massive sword strokes made against the enemy by the general have to do with legislative functions?"

"That is not the question; it is a question of awarding him, through the office of deputy, a worthy recompense for his services."

"But if, through ignorance, he passes bad laws and if he votes for disastrous financial plans, who will suffer the consequences?"

"You and the general public."

"And can I in all conscience invest the general with the right to make laws if he is liable to make bad ones?"

"You are insulting a man of great talent and noble character. Do you think he is ignorant and of evil intent?"

"God forbid! My supposition must be that having been concerned all his life with the military training he is very knowledgeable on strategy. I am sure he insists on tip-top inspections and parades. But, here again, what is there in common between this area of knowledge and the kind required by a representative, or rather those being represented?" . . .

---

2. The Elections

[vol. 7, p. 280]

Dialogue Between a Convinced Political Writer and a Countryman

THE POLITICAL WRITER At long last you are going to benefit for the first time from one of the finest outcomes of the Revolution. You are going to assume a part of sovereignty itself; you are about to exercise one of the greatest of human rights.

THE COUNTRYMAN I am quite simply going to give my vote to the man I believe most capable of managing the portion of my affairs that is common to all Frenchmen.

THE POLITICAL WRITER No doubt. But this is to view the case from the most trivial point of view. No matter. I am assuming that you have given consideration to the solemn act you have come to carry out.

THE COUNTRYMAN It seems to me to be so simple that I did not think I needed to devote much time to considering it.

THE POLITICAL WRITER Is that what you think? Is it a simple matter to vote for a legislator? You clearly do not know how complicated our foreign policy is, how many mistakes our government has made, how many factions seek in a variety of ways to lead it astray. Selecting from among the candidates the man most able to grasp so many complexities, to reflect on the many laws we lack, and to distinguish the most patriotic of the parties in order to have it triumph over the others is not as easy a task as you might believe.

THE COUNTRYMAN Fine. However, I have neither the time nor the capacity necessary for examining so many things.

THE POLITICAL WRITER In that case, defer to those who have considered them. Come and dine with me at General B.'s house and I will tell you for whom you should cast your vote.

THE COUNTRYMAN I beg to accept neither your offers nor your advice. I have heard it said that General B. is standing for office. I cannot accept his dinner as I am firmly resolved not to vote for him.

THE POLITICAL WRITER That is very odd. Here, take this leaflet on M. B. . . . It is biographical. You will see how much he deserves your vote. He is a commoner like you. He owes his success solely to his bravery and his sword. He has rendered exceptional service to France. It is up to Frenchmen to reward him for this.

THE COUNTRYMAN I do not query this. If he has rendered genuine service to France, let France give him medals, or even a pension. However, I do not see that I have to give him a mandate for matters for which I consider him to be unsuitable.

THE POLITICAL WRITER The general not suited to attend to matters! He who has commanded army battalions, has governed provinces, has a profound knowledge of the politics of all the cabinets, and who is as eloquent as Demosthenes!

THE COUNTRYMAN All the more reason I should not vote for him. The greater his capacity, the more he is to be feared by me, as I am convinced that he would use it against my interests.

THE POLITICAL WRITER Are not your interests those of your country?

THE COUNTRYMAN Probably. But they are not those of the general.

THE POLITICAL WRITER Explain yourself. I do not understand you at all.

THE COUNTRYMAN There is no difficulty about my explaining myself. As a farmer, I belong to the peaceful laboring class and I propose to have myself represented by a peaceful working man and not by a man whose career and habits have projected him toward power and war.

THE POLITICAL WRITER The general insists that he will defend the cause of agriculture and industry.

THE COUNTRYMAN Fine, but when I do not know people, their word is not enough for me. I need a more solid guarantee.

THE POLITICAL WRITER What sort of guarantee?

THE COUNTRYMAN Their material interests. If I vote for a man who is a farmer and taxpayer like me, I will be sure that he will defend my interests in defending his.

THE POLITICAL WRITER The general is a landowner like you. Do you think he will make a sacrifice of ownership to power?

THE COUNTRYMAN A general is above all a soldier. His interests as a taxpayer cannot be equated with his interests as a tax beneficiary.

THE POLITICAL WRITER And when this happens, is not his devotion to his country well known? Is he not a child of the Revolution? He who has shed his blood for France, will he betray her for a handful of gold?

THE COUNTRYMAN I admit that the general may be a perfectly honest man. But I cannot believe that a man who has done nothing in his life other than command and obey, who has risen only through the political stairway, and who has become rich only by way of taxes paid by others can perfectly represent a taxpayer. I think it absurd that when I find government overbearing I should vote for a man who is part of it, that when I find taxes too burdensome I should entrust the duty of reducing them to a man who lives off them. The general may have a great deal of self-denial, but I do not want to take the risk of testing this. In short, you are asking me to commit an absurdity which I am not prepared to do.

A Country Elector, a Parish Priest

THE PARISH PRIEST Well, my friend, you have given me great satisfaction. I have been assured that you have nobly refused to give your vote to the candidate of the liberal faction. You have shown good sense in doing this. Is it possible that when the monarchy is in danger, when religion in distress stretches out its suppliant hands to you, you would agree to give new strength to the enemies of religion and the king?

THE COUNTRYMAN Pardon me, Father, but if I refused to vote for the general, it was not because I considered him to be an enemy of religion or of the king. On the contrary, it is because I was convinced that his position did not allow him to maintain a just balance between the means of the taxpayers and the needs of government.

THE PARISH PRIEST Your motives are not important. What is certain is that you were right to distrust the ambition of this man.

THE COUNTRYMAN You do not understand me, Father. I am not passing judgment on the character of the general. I merely say that I consider it risky to entrust my interests to a man who could not defend them without sacrificing his own. This is a risk that no reasonable man would needlessly run.

THE PARISH PRIEST I repeat that I am not scrutinizing your motives. You have just given proof of your devotion to the king. Well, finish your work. You have driven away an enemy and that is well worthwhile. However, it is not enough. Give the king a friend. He himself has designated him; vote for the worthy president of the college.

THE COUNTRYMAN I think I would be committing an even greater absurdity. The king has the power of initiative and sanction with regard to the laws; he appoints the Chamber of Peers.[3] Since the laws are made for the nation, he wanted the nation to contribute to making them, and so why then should I go on to vote for those whom the government

---

3. There existed a Chamber of Peers in France between 1814 and 1848. It had the same role as the English House of Lords.

designates? The result would be an absolute monarchy behind a constitutional facade.

THE PARISH PRIEST Do you suppose, then, that the king would abuse his position and make bad laws?

THE COUNTRYMAN Listen, Father, let us speak of things in their true light. The king does not personally know the 450 candidates he designates; it is the ministers who in fact submit them to our vote. Now the government's interest lies in increasing its power and wealth. However, it can increase its power only at the expense of my liberty and its wealth at the expense of my purse. If I wish to prevent it from doing this, therefore, I have to vote for a deputy who is a taxpayer like me, who will supervise it and set limits to its encroachments.

THE PARISH PRIEST In other words a deputy from the opposition?

THE COUNTRYMAN None other. Between one who lives off taxes and one who pays them, the opposition appears to be natural to me. When I buy something, I endeavor to buy it cheaply, but when I sell I set the highest price on my goods. Between the buyer and seller there is inevitably some dispute. If I wanted to have a cart at cost price, would I give a mandate to the maker to set it?

THE PARISH PRIEST Such a political outlook is small-minded and self-regarding. The issues are reduced to buying and selling, prices and producers. What nonsense! I am talking about the king, his dynasty, the peace of nations, and the upholding of our holy religion.

THE COUNTRYMAN Indeed, and I still maintain my opinion that it is a matter of selling and prices. Government is constituted by men, and the clergy is also made up of men who form a body. Government and clergy are two bodies made up of men. Now, it is in the nature of all bodies to endeavor to expand. Taxpayers would be mad if they did not also form a body to defend themselves against the expansion of government and the clergy.

THE PARISH PRIEST Wretched fellow! And if this latter body triumphs would you destroy the monarchy and religion? Goodness me, what is the world coming to!

THE COUNTRYMAN Do not worry, Father! The people would never destroy government, because they need it. They would never overthrow religion because it is indispensable to them. They would simply contain both within the limits which they cannot exceed without endangering everyone.

In the same way as I covered my house with a roof to shelter myself from the sun and rain, I want to pay magistrates and police officers to protect me from wrongdoers. In the same way as I willingly engage a doctor to care for my body, I would engage a minister of religion to care for my soul. But also, in the same way as I ensure that my roof is built as economically and sturdily as possible and discuss the cost of the payment with my doctor, I want to discuss the cost of their services with the clergy and government since, thank God, I have the ability to do this. And when I cannot do this myself, you would surely agree, Father, that I should mandate a man who has the same interests as I and not someone who belongs, whether directly or indirectly, to the clergy or established government.

A Country Elector, a Constitutional Candidate

THE CANDIDATE I do not think I have arrived too late to ask for your vote, sir, since I am convinced that you have not decided to give it to those who have preceded me. I have two opponents whose talent I acknowledge and whose personal character I honor but who, because of their position, I do not consider to be your natural representatives. I am a taxpayer like you; like you I belong not to the class that exercises power but that over which power is exercised. I am deeply convinced that what currently undermines order, liberty, and prosperity in France is the extravagant dimensions of government. Not only do my opinions make it a duty for me but my interests require me to make every effort to set limits to this terrifying expansion of the actions of government. I therefore consider that I would be useful to the cause of taxpayers if I joined their ranks; and if you share my ideas, I hope you will give me your vote.

THE COUNTRYMAN I am firmly resolved to do so. I share your opinions and your interests are a guarantee to me that you will act according to your opinions, and you may count on my vote.

3. Fragment

[vol. 7, p. 289]

As I wandered idly through the streets of one of our major towns, I met a friend of mine who seemed to be in a bad mood. "What is wrong with you," I asked him, "to make you paler than a rentier faced with a decree that cuts off a quarter of his income?" (Under the Great King,[4] a quarter of income was cut off.) At this, my friend drew from his pocket a bunch of papers; "I am," said he, "a thousandth *shareholder* in a business project to build a canal. We have entrusted the execution of the business to a clever man who sends us his accounts each year. Each year, he makes fresh calls for funds, he increases the number of his agents, and the work does not progress. I am going to a meeting in which all the shareholders will elect a commission to check, verify, approve, or rectify our man's accounts." "And doubtless," I replied, "you will pack this commission with your entrepreneur's men and make its leader the entrepreneur himself." "You are joking," he replied; "no man on earth would be capable of such stupidity." "Oh! Oh!" I said, "do not judge so quickly; in my country, this happens more than a hundred times a year."

---

4. Letter to a Candidate

[vol. 7, p. 298. According to Paillottet's
note below, this letter dates to about 1822.]

LETTER TO M. ——

[In reply to his letter dated 12th January[5]]

Dear Sir,

I have received the letter, dated the 12th of this month, which you did me the honor of writing to me, with the aim, in your own words, *of requesting my vote and those of my friends.*

I cannot speak, sir, for the intentions of my friends; I do not hide from them how I intend to cast my vote but I do not seek to influence theirs.

---

4. Presumably Louis XIV (1638–1715), the Sun King.

5. (Paillottet's note) There was a fair copy made of this letter, written in an exercise book about thirty years ago, and sent to its recipient, whose name I have suppressed. I am not sure, but I think it useful to reproduce it if only to show once again how seriously Bastiat took representative government and how much he liked to align his acts with his theories. I follow it with a letter addressed a few years later to M. Dampierre.

As for mine, it does not belong to me to the extent that I can commit it. Public interest will determine it and up to the time it drops into the ballot box, my only commitment is to the public and my conscience.

Public opinion attributes to General Durrieu, your opponent, views that are favorable to the present government and as a result unfavorable, in my opinion, to the interests of France and, in particular, southern France. No action on his part requires me to consider public opinion mistaken in this respect; on the contrary his personal position leads me to consider him a very bad representative of our interests, whether general ones or with respect to viniculture.[6] This means that I will not be giving him my vote.

However, for the same reason, I cannot give it to a candidate who, scarcely a year ago, *called very earnestly for the candidature of General Durrieu,* and still less if this same man now displays contrasting opinions, since either he was not sincere then or he is not now.

You tell me, sir, that the votes of the government *will slip away from you.* You have probably let them *slip away;* you sought them last year so earnestly that you did not shirk from influencing civil servants by means of those two drastic weapons, *fear of dismissal* and *hope of advancement.* I have in front of me a letter in which you solicited a civil servant's vote *under the auspices of his superior* (which amounts to a threat) and in which you spoke of your influence in Paris (which amounts to a promise). Today, your promises are addressed to independent men; either those of today or those of yesterday are not sincere.

And then, what are you promising us? *Favors.* Favors do not conduce to the public good but to public disadvantage; otherwise they would not be *favors.*

The next thing is that to oblige the *favorites,* you have at least to want to do so while you say that you do not *desire* anything from ministers.

Finally, sir, in the last few days during which the electors have been exchanging the letters with which you are favoring them, we see some addressed to ministerialists and patriots, nobles and commoners, Carlists, Philippists, etc. In all of them, you solicit the electors' goodwill, you ask for votes as one would request a service. We can be forgiven for thinking that, by voting for you, we would be rendering service to the candidate rather than the public.

---

6. After 1840 there was sporadic campaigning in the wine country of southern France to protest against tariffs on exports of wine.

5. Letter to Roger Dampierre

3rd July 1846   [vol. 7, p. 300]

M. Dampierre,

Like you, I regret not having been at home when you did me the honor of coming to see me and I regret it all the more since I received your kind letter dated 30th June. I cannot thank you enough for all the nice things you say; my only fear is that the efforts I have been able to devote to what I considered to be the good of the country have been highly exaggerated. I will limit myself to answering what you say with regard to the forthcoming elections and I will do so with the frankness I owe to the sincere tone with which your letter is imbued.

I have decided to issue my declaration of principles as soon as the Chamber is dissolved and abandon the rest to the electors whom this concerns. I have to say to you that, as I do not solicit their votes for myself, I cannot commit them to the alliance of which you speak. As for my personal conduct, I hope that you will find the reason for it in the brochure I am sending you with this letter.[7] Allow me to add a few explanations here. An alliance between your opinion and mine is a serious thing that I cannot agree to or reject without setting out for you, perhaps somewhat at length, the reasons that govern my decision.

You are a legitimist, sir, you say so frankly in your declaration of principles; and consequently I am more distant from you than from true conservatives.

Thus, if we had at the forthcoming elections a *conservative* candidate in opinion but who is independent by position, such as MM Basquiat, Poydenot,[8] etc., etc., I could not entertain for a moment the thought that, should my party fail, I would join yours. The prospect of determining a ministerial crisis would not cause me to decide and I would prefer to see an opinion with which I differ only subtly triumph, than that from which I differ because of my principles.

I must admit to you, furthermore, that these alliances of extreme parties appear to me to be trickery artificially arranged by ambitious people for their own benefit. I situate myself exclusively at the standpoint of the taxpayer, the person being administered, and the general public and I wonder what they

---

7. See "To the Electors of the District of Saint-Sever," p. 352.
8. Local personalities.

have to gain from alliances whose sole aim is to pass power from one hand to another. Allowing the success of an alliance between the two schools of opinion, to what can it lead? Obviously, they agree only for a moment by glossing over the points on which they differ and abandoning themselves to the only desire common to them: to overthrow the cabinet. But what happens next? When M. Thiers or anyone else is at the helm, what will he do with a minority of the left which will have been a majority only for a moment with the help of the legitimists, help which will henceforward be refused to them? I can see from here a new alliance forming between the right and M. Guizot. At the end of all this, I can see confusion, ministerial crises, administrative trouble, and satisfied ambition, but I do not see any benefit for the public.

For this reason, sir, I do not hesitate to say to you that I could not under any circumstances join you if it was genuinely a conservative opinion that would be presented at the forthcoming elections.

But this is not so. I see in a secretary under orders the representative not of a political opinion but of an individual thought and of this very thought to which electoral law should serve as a barrier. A candidature like this would remove us from a representative regime; it is more than a deviation from it, it casts derision on it, and it seems that by putting it forward, the government has resolved to see just how far the simplemindedness of the electoral body[9] will go. Without having any personal objection to M. Larnac, I have such a serious one against his position that I will not vote for him, whatever happens, and, what is more, if necessary, I will vote for his opponent, even if he is a legitimist.

Whatever the secret thought of the partisans of the senior branch of royalty may be, I fear it less than the intentions of the present government as witnessed in the support it gives to such a candidature. I hate revolutions, but they take a variety of forms and I consider as a revolution of the worst kind this systematic invasion of national representation by the agents of government and, what is worse, of irresponsible government. If therefore I am faced with the cruel alternative of choosing between a secretary under orders and a legitimist, my mind is made up: I would choose the legitimist. If the ulterior

9. (Paillottet's note) It is easy to infer from this passage and several others that Bastiat made two judgments on what is known today as *official candidatures*. 1. He would have seen in it scorn for the representative regime. 2. This scorn would have appeared to him more sad than new.

motives attributed to this party are in any way the case, I deplore this, but I do not fear it, for I am convinced that the principle of national sovereignty has enough life in France to triumph once more over its adversaries. But with a Chamber peopled with the creatures of government, the country, its wealth and liberty, are defenseless and there is in this a germ of revolution that is more dangerous than that which your party can contemplate.

To sum up, sir, as a candidate I will limit myself to issuing a declaration of principles and attending public meetings if I am invited to them. As an elector, I will first vote for a man of the left; failing that, for an independent conservative; and failing that again, for a frank and loyal legitimist, such as you, rather than for a secretary under the orders of the duc de Nemours.

I remain, sir, etc., . . .

Articles on Politics

1. On a New Secondary School to Be Founded in Bayonne

> [vol. 7, p. 4. According to Paillottet, this article, probably extracted from a copybook of Bastiat's, and written by him, was published in a Bayonne newspaper in 1834.]

The question was raised in the municipal council of providing Bayonne with a secondary school.[1] But what can you do? You cannot do everything at once; the most pressing needs must be met and the town has ruined itself in order to provide a theater. Pleasure first; education can wait. Anyway, is not the theater also a school and even more a school of morals? Ask anyone in vaudeville or musical comedy.

As it happens, Bayonne's fiscal capacity represents the high point of civilization and we can properly hope that the question of finance will prove no obstacle. Confident of this, I beg leave to submit a few ideas on public instruction to the city.

When I first heard of the municipal project, I asked myself if a secondary school whose curriculum focused on science and work which would dispense *scientific and industrial* instruction would not have some small chance of success. There is no lack of establishments close to Bayonne that teach or, to be more accurate, pretend to teach Greek, Latin, rhetoric, or even philosophy. Larresole, Orthez, Oléron, Dax, Mont-de-Marsan, Saint-Sever, and Aire provide classical education. There, the young generation which will succeed us behind the counter or in the workshop, in the fields and vineyards, in the night watch, and on the upper deck, is preparing to take on its rough task by being bored to death with the declension and conjugation of

---

1. Secondary education took place in royal "colleges" (former Napoleonic *lycées*), or municipal "colleges." The construction cost of the latter was borne by the town. The Theater of Bayonne had been built in 1840.

languages which were spoken some two or three thousand years ago. There, our sons, while waiting for machines to operate, bridges to build, moorland to clear, ships to deliver to the four corners of the earth, or strict accounts to keep, are learning to chant nicely using the tips of their fingers . . . *Tityre, tu patuloe recu,* etc.[2] Let us be just, however; before sending them out into the world and as they approach their majority, they should be given a vague idea of counting and even perhaps a glimpse or two of natural history in the form of commented texts from Phaedrus and Aesop, it being understood, of course, that they will not miss a comma of the *Lexicon* and the *Gradus ad Parnassum*.[3]

Let us suppose that, through an unheard-of singular occurrence, Bayonne in fact followed an opposite method, that it made *science,* the knowledge of *what exists* and a study of *cause and effect,* the founding principle and the reading of the ancient poets an accessory and ornament of education, do you not think that this idea, as ridiculous as it may appear at first glance, might prove attractive to many heads of families?

What is it basically that we are discussing? The composition of intellectual baggage which will nourish these children during their harsh journey through life. Some of them will be called upon to defend, enlighten, and teach morals; to represent and administer the people; to develop and perfect our institutions and laws, with the greater number by far having to seek through work and industry the means of earning a living for themselves and of supporting their wives and children.

And tell me, is it in Horace and Ovid that they will learn all of this? To be good farmers, do they have to spend ten years learning and reading the *Georgics*? To win their stripes in the army, do they need to wear out their youth in deciphering Xenophon? To become statesmen, to become imbued with the mores, ideas, and needs of our time, do they need to immerse themselves for twenty years in Roman life, make themselves the contemporaries of Lucullus and Messalina, and breathe the same air as Brutus and the Gracchi?

Not only does the long period of childhood spent in the past not initiate them into the present, but it inspires dislike of it in them. It warps their judgment and prepares only a generation of orators, seditionists, and idlers.

---

2. Virgil's first Eclogue begins, "Tityre, tu patulae recubans sub tegmine fagi." ("Tityrus, reclining beneath the cover of a spreading beech tree.")

3. "Steps to Parnassus" (title).

For what is there in common between ancient Rome and modern France? The Romans lived from plunder and we live from production, they scorned and we honor work, they left to slaves the task of producing and this is exactly the task for which we are responsible, they were organized for war and we aim for peace, they were for theft and we are for trade, they aimed to dominate and we tend to bring peoples together.

And how do you expect these young men who have escaped from Sparta and Rome not to upset our century with their ideas? Will they not, like Plato, dream of illusory republics; and like the Gracchi, have their gaze fixed on the Aventine Mount; and like Brutus, contemplate the bloody glory of sublime devotion?

I would countenance a literary education if we were, like the Athenians, a people of idlers. To talk at length on metaphysics, eloquence, mythology, fine arts, or poetry is, I believe, the best use of their leisure that a people of patricians can make, as they move above a host of slaves.

But for those who have to create the *nutritium,* the *vestitum,* and the *tectum*[4] for themselves, what is the use of the subtleties of the school and dreams of the seven sages of Greece? If Charles has to be a ploughman, he has to learn what water, the earth, and plants are *in reality* and not what Thales and Epicurus said about them. He needs the physics of facts and not the physics of poetry, science and not erudition. Our century is like Chrysale:

> He lives off good soup and not fine language.[5]
> I can hear Belise[6] protest: Is it possible to encounter a man as
> prosaic and as vulgar as this,
> A spirit composed of such bourgeois atoms?

And is it not sad to see, to use the current jargon (which rather resembles that of Belise), *facts smothering ideas?*

I would reply that the idea of the heroic age, that of domination, plunder, and slavery, is neither greater nor more poetic than the idea of the industrial age, with its concept of work, equality, and unity, and I have the authority of two great poets, Byron and Lamartine, on my side.

---

4. "Nourishment," "clothing," "housing."
5. From Molière's *Les Femmes savantes.*
6. Belise was one of "les femmes savantes" (the learned ladies).

Be that as it may, if man does not live by bread alone, he lives still less by ambrosia and I dare to say (asking you to forgive the play on words) that in our system of education it is the idea, and a false idea, that smothers facts. It is the idea that perverts our young people, which closes off the avenues to wealth to them and impels them toward a career by way of various positions or a desperate idleness.

And tell me, my native town, you whom corrupt laws (also the offspring of erroneous education) have stripped of your trade, you who are exploring new trade routes, who spin wool and linen, who smelt molten iron, dig up kaolin from your native soil, and do not know how to use it, you who build ships, maintain a model farm, and, in a word, you who draw power from a little boiling water and seek light in a little jet of gas, if you need hands to accomplish your undertakings and intellects to direct them, are you not obliged to call upon the children of the north for help, while your own sons, so full of courage and sagacity, walk the cobbles of your streets because they have not learned what it is essential to know today?

But let us allow that a classical education is really the most useful. We will at least agree that this is so only if it puts buyers in possession of the goods it produces. However, are these dead languages so generally taught widely known? You who are reading this, and who were perhaps first in your class, do you often walk on the banks of the Nive and the Adour[7] with a work of Perseus or Sophocles in your hand? Alas! In the fullness of our age, after such lengthy studies we are scarcely left with enough knowledge to decipher the meaning of a simple epigraph. I remember that in a large meeting once, a woman actually dared to ask what the famous motto of Louis XIV, *Nec pluribus impar*,[8] meant. The *construction* was worked out, followed by a *word for word* translation; a discussion was held on the force of the two negatives; each person had his own interpretation; no two were identical.

And it is for this result that you weary children. You saturate them with syntax for ten hours a day and for seven years in succession. You suffocate them with declensions and conjugations, you make them insipid and out of breath, you give them nausea, and then you say: "My son is charming, full of intelligence; he understands and catches half meanings, but he is frivolous, lazy, and *does not want to take an interest*." Poor little boy! Why is he

7. Bayonne is located at the confluence of the Adour and Nive rivers.
8. "No unequal match for many."

not wise enough to reply: "You see, nature gave me the taste and need for diversion, it made me curious, with a questioning mind ready to learn everything and what have these precious dispositions become in your hands? You enslaved all my moments to a single study, a study that was repellent and arid, one that explained nothing to me, taught me nothing, neither the origin of the sun that moves, the rain that falls, the water that flows, and the seed that germinates, nor what force supports ships in the water or birds in the sky, nor whence comes the bread that feeds me and the clothes I wear. No facts have entered my head. Words, just words, hour after hour, day after day, always and forever, from one end of my childhood to the other! To be determined that my noble will should be wholly concentrated on these miserable formulae, determined that I should not watch the butterfly that flutters by, the grass that grows green, or the ship that moves with neither oar nor sail, determined that my young instincts should not seek to penetrate the mystery of these phenomena, the food of my sensations, and substance of my thoughts, is to exact more than I can give. Oh, my father, if you tried this experiment on yourself, if you imposed this *straitjacket* on yourself, just for one month, you would see that it cannot be suitable to the energetic activities of childhood."

Therefore, if Bayonne were to establish a secondary school in which Latin occupied one hour a day, which befits a useful accessory, in which the rest of the time was devoted to mathematics, physics, chemistry, history, living languages, etc., I think that Bayonne would be meeting a widely felt social need and that the current administration would deserve the benediction of the coming generation.

---

2. Freedom of Teaching

[vol. 7, p. 231. According to Paillottet, this essay was originally published in *La République française,* 4 March 1848.]

All the acts of the provisional government relating to public education are designed, we are annoyed to say, in a spirit that supposes that France has abandoned freedom of teaching.[9]

9. On 29 February 1848, a High Commission for Education was set up to help the minister of education.

The circular from the minister to the rectors convinces us of this.

Here is a decree that creates a commission for scientific and literary studies.

Out of the twenty members who make it up, fifteen of them at least, if we are not mistaken, belong to the university.

In addition, the final article of the decree lays down that this commission will add another ten members, chosen by itself, as it says, *from civil servants in primary and secondary education.*

We cannot help noticing here that, of all the branches of national activity, that which has made perhaps the least progress is the teaching profession. It is still approximately at the stage it was in the Middle Ages. The idylls of Theocrates and the odes of Horace are still the basis of the instruction we give to the youth of the nineteenth century. This appears to indicate that there is nothing less progressive and more immutable than that carried out by government monopoly.

In France, there is a large school of opinion that thinks that, apart from legal repression or abuse, every citizen should have the free exercise of his faculties. This is both the prerogative of progress and its necessary condition. This is how they view liberty in the United States, and empirically this experiment is just as revealing as our experiences with monopoly in Europe. It should be noted that none of the men who belong to this school, known as the *économiste* school, has been called upon to join any of the commissions that have just been organized.

It is not surprising that they have been kept away from paid public office. They have kept themselves away and they had to, since their ideal is to reduce the number of positions to those that are essential for maintaining order, internal and external security, respect for persons and property, and, at the very least, the creation of a few projects of national importance.

However, that their contribution to simple surveys is systematically overlooked is a significant eventuality; it proves that we are being swept along by a hypertrophy of government, one which threatens an endless diminution of true liberty.

3. Freedom of Trade

[vol. 7, p. 14. According to Paillottet, this was an unpublished article that appears to have been intended for a newspaper in the south of France. It dates from 1844.]

During the session on 29th February last, M. Guizot said: "We constantly speak of the weakness of the king's government with respect to England. I cannot allow this calumny.

"In Spain,[10] no one can say that we have merely supported what England has done or simply got rid of the same things as she.

"There has been talk of a treaty on trade which is to be imposed by England; has this happened?

"Did we not revoke the regulations which have changed trade relations between England and France with respect to linen thread and cloth?

"Did not the prime minister pass a law on Algerian tariffs which has materially harmed in more than one respect real British interests?"

From all of this it results that, if the authorities are not under the yoke of England, they are certainly under the yoke of monopoly. All this shows that while the government may not be England's creature it is certainly a creature of monopoly.

Is the public really not going to open its eyes finally to this shameful misrepresentation and duplicity?

A few years ago, one might have thought that protectionism had very few years left to live.

Theoretically in ruins, it slipped into our legislation only as a transitory measure. The very minister who did most to let it linger on, M. de Saint-Cricq, constantly warned us that these *mutual taxes,* which workers paid each other, were basically unjust and, to the little extent that they were reasonable, were so only on the grounds of their supporting infant industries. Indeed, even the beneficiaries of these arrangements saw them not as a prerogative but as an essentially temporary privilege.

The actions being accomplished in Europe were such as to increase the hopes of the lovers of freedom.

Switzerland had opened its frontiers to products of all origins and this was working well.

10. Spain was the setting for several Franco-British rivalries.

Sardinia[11] also went down this road and found no reason to regret it.

Germany[12] had replaced a host of internal barriers with a single ring of customs posts based on a moderate tariff.

In England, the most vigorous effort ever attempted by the middle classes was on the point of overthrowing a system of restrictions which in that country represented another aspect of feudal power.

Even Spain seemed to understand that its fifteen agricultural provinces were unjustly sacrificed in favor of one manufacturing province.

Lastly, France was preparing for free trade by way of negotiating treaties of transition and by joining a customs union with Belgium.[13]

Thus was labor to be set free. Wherever on the globe that fate had caused them to be born, men were going to reconquer the natural right to exchange with each other the fruits of their labors and we were reaching the moment of seeing the achievement of a holy alliance of nations.

How did France allow herself to be turned away from this path? How did it come about that its children, who took pride in being the leaders of civilization, were suddenly seized with Napoleonic ideas and embraced the cause of isolation, antagonism between nations, theft carried out by its citizens one against the other, restrictions laid down on the right of ownership, in short, all that is barbarous in the bosom of protectionism?

To seek an explanation of this sad phenomenon, it would seem that we have to move away from our subject for a moment.

If, within a General Council, a member succeeded in creating a majority against the administration, it would not necessarily follow that the prefect would be dismissed and still less that the leader of the opposition would be appointed prefect in his place. In the same way, although general councillors are made of the same clay as deputies, their ambition is not satisfied by the maneuvers of systematic opposition, which explains why these maneuvers are not seen to happen in these meetings.

This is not the case in the Chamber. It is a maxim of our public law that if

11. In 1843 France signed a trade treaty with the kingdom of Sardinia.

12. A customs union, the Zollverein, was constituted after 1818 at the initiative of Prussia. In 1834 it comprised thirty-four German states.

13. A customs union between Belgium and France was contemplated as a counterbalance to the Zollverein but never realized. Instead, a less ambitious Franco-Belgian commercial treaty was ratified in 1845.

a deputy is cunning enough to mount a majority in opposition to a government, he will himself ipso facto become minister and will deliver the government as a prey to his colleagues who allied themselves to his undertaking.

The consequences of such an organization leap to the eye. The Chamber is no longer an assembly of *those governed,* who come to take note of measures projected by *those who govern,* to admit, modify, or reject these measures in line with the public interest which they represent; it is rather an arena in which government, dependent on the support of members' votes, is competed for.

Therefore, to overturn the government it is necessary only to remove its majority. To remove its majority, it is necessary to discredit it, make it unpopular, and debase it. The law itself, aided and abetted by the irremediable weakness of the human heart, has arranged things thus. It is useless for M. Guizot to cry: "Will we never learn to attack each other, combat each other, and *overthrow* each other without attributing shameful motives to each other?" I must say that I find these complaints puerile. You allow that your adversaries aim to replace you and yet you advise them charitably to neglect the means of success! In this respect, M. Guizot, the leader of the opposition, would do to M. Thiers, the minister, what M. Guizot, the minister, reproaches M. Thiers, the leader of the opposition, for doing.

We have therefore to admit that our mechanism of representation is organized in such a way that the opposition and all forms of opposition united have not and cannot have other than one single aim, namely to discredit the government, whichever one it is, in order to overthrow it and replace it.

But the most certain way, in France, to discredit the government is to represent it as treacherous, cowardly, in the pay of foreigners, and forgetful of national honor. Against M. Molé, this was the tactic used by M. Guizot in coalition with the legitimists and the Republicans; against M. Guizot, this was the tactic of M. Thiers, in coalition with the Republicans and the legitimists. One used Ancona[14] as the other used Tahiti.[15]

14. In order to quell disturbances in the papal states, Pope Gregory XVI called upon Austria. On 28 June 1832, Austrian troops entered Bologna, Italy. For reasons of diplomatic balance, a French garrison was sent to Ancona, southeast of Bologna. In 1832 the Austrian troops left Bologna and the French troops left Ancona.

15. In 1842 Tahiti was a French protectorate. Following incidents with English ships, Admiral Dupetit-Thouars transformed it into a territory of "direct sovereignty." This

However, opposition parties do not limit themselves to acting within the Chamber. They also feel the need to take some account of public opinion and the views of the electorate. All the opposition newspapers are thus obliged to work in concert, to exalt, irritate, and mislead national feeling, to represent the country as having descended to the lowest level of degradation and opprobrium as a result of the work of the government; and it has to be said that our national susceptibility to the memory of Empire and to the wholly *Roman* education which has prevailed among us gives this parliamentary tactic considerable chances of success. This being the situation, it is easy to predict all the gains that pampered lines of production would inevitably extract from it.

At a time when monopoly was about to be cast aside and the free communication of peoples gradually established, what could the cosseted groups do? Waste their time establishing protectionist principles at the very heart of their outlook, opposing such principles to the *theory of free trade*? It would have been a fruitless venture; on the soil of free and fair discussion, error stands little chance against truth.

No, the privileged groups had a clearer view of what might prolong their existence. They understood that they could continue peacefully to pick the pockets of the public so long as contrived antagonisms would prevent the drawing together and merging of nations. This being so, they harnessd their forces, influence, capital, and activity to *national hatred*. They, too, adopted the mask of patriotism. They bribed such newspapers as had not yet adopted the banner of false national honor, and it may rightly be said that this monstrous alliance stopped the march of civilization.

In these strange circumstances, the local press, especially in the south, might have been of great service. However, either because it did not perceive the motive behind these Machiavellian intrigues or feared to *appear* weak in the eyes of the enemy, the fact is that it foolishly added its voice to those of the newspapers funded by the privileged groups and today may well fold its arms at the sight of us, the men of the south, robbed and exploited, *doing its work,* the work it should have done itself, and devoting all the resources of our intelligence and all the energy of our feelings to consolidating the shackles and perpetuating the extortions it inflicts on us.

---

created tension between London and Paris. The latter disavowed the admiral on 24 February 1844.

This weakness has borne fruit. To repudiate the accusations heaped on it, the government had one thing only to do and it did it: it sacrificed us.

The words of M. Guizot, which I quoted at the beginning, did they not mean in essence:

"You say that I am subjecting my policy to that of England, but consider my actions.

"It was just to return to French citizens the *right to trade,* appropriated by a few privileged people. I wished to go down this path through trade treaties, but there were shouts of *Treason!* and I broke off negotiations.

"I thought that if French citizens needed to buy linen thread and cloth abroad, it was better to obtain more rather than less for a given price, but there were shouts of *Treason!* and I created differential dues.

It was in the interest of our young African colony to be provided with everything at a low cost in order to grow and prosper. However, there were shouts of *Treason!* and I handed over Algeria to monopolistic interests.

"Spain aspired to shake off its submission to a single province. This was in its interest. It was in ours and also in that of the English. There were shouts of *Treason!* and, to stifle this inopportune cry, I *maintained* what England wished to *overturn,* the exploitation of Spain by Catalonia."

This is our present position. The engine of war of all the parties is the *hatred of foreigners.* Left and right alike use it to disparage the government; in the center they go further, translating it into action to prove their independence and the monopolists fasten on to this uncertain outlook, fanning discord in order to perpetuate their situation.

Where will all this lead us? I do not know, but I believe that this game by the parties hides danger and I ask myself why, in a period of total peace, France maintains four hundred thousand men under arms, increases its navy, fortifies its capital city, and pays a billion and a half in taxes.

---

4. The Parisian Press

[vol. 7, p. 226. According to Paillottet, this
article was originally published in
La République française, 1 March 1848.]

The Parisian press offers a spectacle that is no less extraordinary or less imposing than the population on the barricades.

What has happened to the burning and often brutal controversy of late?

The lively discussions will doubtless return. But is it not very consoling to see that at the moment of danger, when the country has an overwhelming need for security, order, and confidence, all forms of bitterness are forgotten and even the most eccentric doctrines endeavor to present themselves in a reassuring light?

Thus, *Le Populaire,* the communist newspaper, shouts "Respect for ownership!" M. Cabet reminds his followers that they should seek triumph for their ideas only through discussion and by convincing the public.

La Fraternité, the workers' newspaper, publishes a lengthy program that economists might adopt in its entirety, except perhaps for one or two maxims that are more illusionary than dangerous.

L'Atelier, another newspaper edited by workers, beseeches its brothers to stop the ill-considered movement that in the first instance led them on to smash machinery.

All the newspapers vie with one another in trying to moderate or anathematize another barbarous sentiment that unfortunately the partisan spirit had worked for fifteen years to bolster: chauvinism. Apparently a single day of revolution has caused this engine of war incarnate, to which all the opposition parties have recourse, to disappear, simply by making it irrelevant.

External peace, internal order, confidence, vigilance, and fraternity: these are the watchwords for the entire press.[16]

---

5. Petition from an Economist

> [vol. 7, p. 227. According to Paillottet,
> this article was originally published in
> *La République française,* dated 2 March 1848.]

At the moment a petition is being signed that asks for: *A Ministry of Progress or for the Organization of Production.*[17] On this subject, *La Démocratie pacifique* has this to say:

"In order to organize production in French society, you have to know how to organize it at the village level, in the living and breathing workshops of the

---

16. (Paillottet's note) From the second issue of *La République française,* that of 27 February, until the fifth dated 1 March 1848, Bastiat's name figures on the last line of the newspaper with the names of its other editors. This is no longer the case in the following issues. Bastiat no longer gave his signature to the newspaper, but limited himself to signing his own articles.

17. The title of the petition was "A Ministry of Progress, Work Organization, and Abolition of the Exploitation of Man by Man."

nation. Any serious doctrine of social development must therefore succeed at the level of the basic workshop and be tried out initially on a small parcel of land. Let the Republic therefore create a Ministry of Progress and Organization of Production whose function will be to examine *all the plans put forward* by the various socialist doctrines and to favor over them a local, free, and voluntary experiment carried out in a territorial unit, the *square league*."

If this idea is put into practice, we will ask that we too be given our square league to try out our ideas. Why, after all, should the various socialist schools of thought be the only ones to have the privilege of having at their disposal square leagues, basic workshops, and everything which constitutes a locality, in short, villages?

They say that it is a matter of *free and voluntary* experiments. Are we to understand that the inhabitants of the commune who will be subjected to socialist experimentation will have to agree to it and that, on the other hand, the state should not take part with revenue raised from other communes? If so, what is the use of the petition, and what prevents the inhabitants of communes from carrying out freely, voluntarily, and at their own expense social experiments on themselves? Or is the intention that the experiment be forced or at the very least supported by funds raised from the entire community?

This in itself will provide a highly inconclusive result for the experiment. It is quite clear that having all the nation's resources at our disposal, we might squander a great deal of welfare on a square league of land.

In any case, if each inventor in the field of social organization is called upon to carry out his experiment, let us register ourselves and formally request a commune to organize.

Our plan is otherwise very simple.

We will claim from each family and through a single tax a very small part of its income, in order to ensure the respect of persons and ownership, the elimination of fraud, misdemeanors, and crimes. Once we have done this, we will carefully observe how people organize themselves.

Religion, teaching, production, and trade will be perfectly free. We hope that, under this regime of liberty and security, with each inhabitant having the facility, through free trade, to create the largest sum of value possible, in any form which suits him, capital will be built up with great speed. Since all capital is intended to be used, there will be fierce competition between capitalists. Therefore earnings will rise; therefore workers, if they are farsighted and thrifty, will have a great opportunity to become capitalists; and therefore it will be possible to create alliances or associations whose ideas are conceived and matured by themselves alone.

As the single tax will be modest in the extreme, there will be few civil service posts and few civil servants, no wasted efforts, and few men withdrawn from production.

As the state will have very restricted and well-defined powers, its inhabitants will have total freedom to choose their work. Here it should be noted clearly that any wasteful civil service post is not only a burden on the community but an infringement of the freedom of citizens. About the public services imposed without debate on the citizens, there are no half measures; either they are useful or else essentially *harmful;* they cannot be neutral. When a man exercises an action *with authority,* not over things but over his fellow men, if he does not do them good, he must necessarily do them harm.

With taxes thus reduced to the minimum required to procure *security* for all, lobbyists, abuses, privileges, and the exploitation of laws for individual interests will also be reduced to a *minimum.*

Since the inhabitants of this experimental commune will have, through free trade, the opportunity of producing the maximum value with the minimum work, the square league will provide as much welfare as the state of knowledge, activity, order, and individual economy allows.

This welfare will tend to spread out in an ever-more egalitarian manner, since, as the highest paid services will be the most sought after,[18] it will be impossible to amass huge fortunes, especially since the minimum level of tax will not allow great public contracts, loans, nor speculation, all sources of the scandalous fortunes we see accumulating in a few hands.

Since this small community will be interested in attacking no one and all the others will have an interest in not attacking it, it will enjoy the most profound peace.

Citizens will feel loyal to the country because they will never feel slighted or held back by the agents of the government, and to its laws because they will recognize them as based on justice.

In the conviction that this system, which has the merit at least of being simple and respecting human dignity, is all the better if it applies to a wider territory and a greater number of people, since it is there that the most se-

---

18. (Paillottet's note) In the sense that they attract competition the most.

curity is obtained with the least taxes, we conclude that if it succeeds in a commune, it will succeed at the level of the nation.

------

6. Article in *La République française*

[vol. 7, p. 223. According to Paillottet,
this article was originally published in
La République française, dated 1 March 1848.]

A newspaper does not achieve high circulation figures without echoing a few ideas dominant in the country. We acknowledge that *La Presse* has always been able to speak to the interests of the moment and even that it has often given good advice; in this way it has been able to sow in the soil of the country, along with the good grain, a great deal of chaff which will take a long time to remove.

Since the Revolution, it must be said, its attitude has been frank and resolute.

We are in complete agreement, for our part, with the two clarion calls which it is broadcasting today, No diplomacy! No rush for positions!

No diplomacy! What has the Republic to do with this institution, which has done so much harm and which perhaps has never done any good, where *sharp practice* is so traditional that it is used in the most simple matters and where sincerity is considered foolishness? It was by a diplomat and for diplomacy's sake that it was first observed that speech was given to man to disguise his thoughts.

One of the purest English democrats, Mr. Cobden, on a visit to Madrid, was visited by Mr. Bulwer. He said to him: "Ambassador, in ten years Europe will no longer need you."

When on principle nations are the property of kings, diplomacy and even diplomatic trickery are conceived. Events must be prepared well in advance, as must alliances and wars to expand the domain of the master.

However, what does a people which belongs to itself have to negotiate? All its diplomacy is carried out in the open in deliberating assemblies; its traders are its *negotiators,* the diplomats of union and peace.

It is true that, even for free peoples, there is a territorial question of the highest importance, that of *natural borders.* But does this question require the intervention of diplomacy?

Nations know full well that it is in the common interest and in the interest of order and peace that each should have borders. They know that if France withdrew within its limits, that would be one more guarantee of security for Europe.

What is more, the principle that peoples belong to themselves guarantees that, if there has to be a merger, it will take place with the free consent of those involved and not by armed invasion. The Republic has only to proclaim its rights, wishes, and hopes in this respect. There is no need for either ambassadors or trickery to do this.

Without ambassadors and kings, we would not in recent times have had the question of Spanish marriages. Has anyone ever given attention to the marriage of the president of the United States? As for the *rush for positions,* our desire echoes that of *La Presse.* We would have liked France in February not to give the world this sad and disgusting spectacle. But we have little hope of this, as we have no illusions about the weakness of the human heart. The means of reducing the *rush* is to reduce the number of positions themselves. It is puerile to expect lobbyists to restrain themselves; it is up to the public to restrain them.

For this reason, we must constantly repeat: Let us eliminate all superfluous positions. We advise children to think twice before saying something rash. We, for our part, say to the government: Break thirty quills before endorsing the creation of new positions.

A sinecure eliminated will thwart its holder but not enrage him. A sinecure passed from hand to hand exasperates him who has lost it, disappoints ten would-be placemen, and angers the public.

The most difficult part of the task handed down to the provisional government will probably be resisting the flood of requests for such sinecures.

All the more so because several schools of thought, which today are much in favor, hope to increase indefinitely the scope of the government, by repeated taxation, and to have the state do everything.

Other people say: The state needs to spend a great deal in order to provide a living for a great many people.

Is it therefore really so difficult to see that, when the government spends taxpayers' money, it is not the taxpayers who spend it?

7. The Scramble for Office

[vol. 7, p. 232. According to Paillottet,
this article was originally published in
La République française, dated 5 March 1848.]

All the newspapers, without exception, are speaking out against the scramble for office of which the Town Hall[19] is given a sad example. Nobody could be more indignant about, or more disgusted by, this frenzied greed than we.

But at the end of the day we have to find the cause of the evil, and it would be puerile to expect the human heart to be other than it has pleased nature to make it.

In a country in which, since time immemorial, the labor of free men has everywhere been demeaned, in which education offers as a model to all youth the mores of Greece and Rome, in which trade and industry are constantly exposed by the press to the scorn of citizens under the label *profiteering, industrialism,* or *individualism,* in which success in office alone leads to wealth, prestige, or power, and in which the state does everything and interferes in everything through its innumerable agents, it is natural enough for public office to be avidly sought after.

How can we turn ambition away from this disastrous direction and redirect the activity of the enlightened classes toward productive careers?

Obviously by eliminating a great many public posts, limiting government action, leaving a wider, freer, and more prestigious role to private activities and reducing the salaries for high public office.

What should our attitude be then to those theories, so fashionable currently, which propose the transfer into the world of paid public service, of activities still in the realm of private industry? *La Démocratie pacifique* wants the state to provide insurance, public transport, and haulage, and also to handle the trading of wheat, etc., etc., etc.

Do these ideas not provide fresh fuel for this disastrous mania which so offends honest citizens?

We do not want to discuss the other disadvantages of these proposals here. Examine one after the other all the industries managed by the state and see if these are not, indeed, the ones through which citizens are the most badly and most expensively served.

19. The Town Hall of Paris was the seat of the temporary government after the "three glorious days" of February 1848.

Take education, obstinately limited to the study of two languages dead these two thousand years.

See what kind of tobacco is provided to you and at what price.[20]

Compare in terms of regular supply and proper market price the distribution of printed matter by the public authority in the rue Jean-Jacques Rousseau with that by individual enterprises in the rue de la Jussienne.

However, setting aside these considerations, is it not evident that the *scramble for office* is and will always be proportional to the enticement to it?

Is it not evident that having industry run by the state is to remove work from honest activity in order to deliver it to lazy and indolent intrigue?

Finally, is it not clear that it will make the disorder which the Town Hall exemplifies, a disarray which saddens the members of the provisional government, permanent and progressive?

---

8. Impediments and Taxes

> [vol. 7, p. 234. According to Paillottet,
> this article was originally published in
> *La République française,* dated 6 March 1848.]

While a movement, possibly an irresistible one, is pushing us toward the hypertrophy of the state, and an increase in the number of taxes as well as of the irritating encumbrances such an increase inevitably entails, a very pronounced change in the opposite direction is apparent in England, one which will perhaps lead to the fall of the government.

There, every experiment and every effort to achieve good through the intervention of the state results in disappointment. It will soon be realized that good is not being achieved and that the experiment leaves behind it just one thing: *tax.*

Thus, last year, a law was passed to regulate the work of factories and the execution of this law required the creation of a body of civil servants.[21] Today, entrepreneurs, workers, inspectors, and magistrates agree in acknowl-

---

20. The sale of tobacco products was a state monopoly in France.

21. On 3 May 1847, the Whig government of John Russell adopted the Factory Bill (Ten Hours' Bill), which limited the work of women and young people under eighteen to ten hours on weekdays and eight hours on Saturday.

edging that the law has encroached upon all the interests in which it has interfered. Only two things remain: disorder and *taxes*.

Two years ago, the legislature dashed off a constitution for New Zealand[22] and voted for considerable expenditure to implement it. In spite of this, the said constitution collapsed badly. The only thing that did not fall, however, was *taxation*.

Lord Palmerston believed he had to intervene in the affairs of Portugal.[23] He thus brought down on the name of England the hatred of an allied nation, and that at a price of fifteen million francs, or a hefty *tax*.

Lord Palmerston persists in seizing Brazilian ships[24] engaged in the slave trade. To do this, he endangers the lives of a considerable number of English sailors, subjects British subjects living in Brazil to affronts, and makes a treaty between England and Rio de Janeiro impossible; all this damage is paid in ships and legal actions, that is to say, in the form of *taxes*.

The result is that the English are paying, not for receiving benefits, but for suffering damages to England.

The conclusion that our neighbors appear to wish to draw from this phenomenon is this: that the people, after having paid what is necessary to their political masters to guarantee their security, *keep the rest for themselves*.

This is a very simple thought, but it will sweep the world.

---

9. Freedom

[vol. 7, p. 235. According to Paillottet, this article was originally published in the first issue of *Jacques Bonhomme,* dated 11–15 June 1848.]

I have lived a long time, seen a great deal, observed much, compared and examined many things, and I have reached the following conclusion:

Our fathers were right to wish to be FREE, and we should also wish this.

---

22. By the treaty of Waitangi, the Maoris acknowledged English sovereignty but did not accept the constitution.

23. The queen of Portugal, Maria II, was threatened by rebels. Palmerston imposed a compromise that was not observed.

24. In 1845 Brazil had not yet abolished slavery. Palmerston decided that suspicious Brazilian ships would be inspected, even in territorial waters, and that guilty shipowners and captains would be prosecuted by British tribunals (Aberdeen Bill). The bill was applied.

It is not that freedom has no disadvantages, since everything has these. To use these disadvantages in argument against it is to say to a man trapped in the mire: Do not get out, as you cannot do this without some effort.

Thus, it is to be wished that there be just one faith in the world, provided that it is the true one. However, where is the infallible authority which will impose it on us? While waiting for it to manifest itself, let us maintain the *freedom of discussion and conscience.*

It would be fortunate if the best method of teaching were to be universally adopted. But who has it and on what authority? Let us therefore demand *freedom of teaching.*

We may be distressed to see writers delight in stirring up all forms of evil passion. However, to hobble the press is also to hobble truth as well as lies. Let us, therefore, take care never to allow the *freedom of the press* to die.

It is distressing that man should be reduced to earning his bread by the sweat of his brow. It would be better for the state to feed everyone, but this is impossible. Let us at least have the *freedom to work.*

By associating with one another, men can gain greater advantage from their strength. However, the forms of association are infinite; which is best? Let us not run the risk that the state imposes the worst of these on us; let us seek the right one by trial and error, and demand the *freedom of association.*

A people has two ways of procuring something. The first is to make it; the second is to make something else and trade it. It is certainly better to have the option than not to have it. Let us therefore demand the *freedom to trade.*

I am throwing myself into public debate; I am trying to get through to the crowd to preach all the *freedoms,* the total of which make up *liberty.*

---

10. Laissez-faire

> [vol. 7, p. 237. According to Paillottet, this article
> was originally published in the first issue of
> *Jacques Bonhomme,* dated 11–15 June 1848.]

Laissez-faire! I will begin by saying, in order to avoid any ambiguity, that *laissez-faire* is used here for honest things, with the state instituted precisely to *prevent* dishonest things.

This having been said, and with regard to things that are innocent in themselves, such as work, trade, teaching, association, banking, etc., a choice must be made. It is necessary for the state to let things be done or *prevent them from being done.*

If it lets things be done, we will be free and optimally administered most economically, since nothing costs less than *laissez-faire.*

If it *prevents things from being done,* woe to our freedom and our purse. Woe to our freedom, since *to prevent things* is to tie our hands; woe to our purse, since *to prevent things* requires agents and to employ agents takes money.

In reply to this, socialists say: "Laissez-faire! What a disaster!" Why, if you please? "Because, when you leave men to act, they do wrong and act against their interests. It is right for the state to direct them."

This is simply absurd. Do you seriously have such faith in human wisdom that you want universal suffrage and government of all by all and then you proclaim these very men whom you consider fit to govern others unfit to govern themselves?

------

11. Under the Republic[25]

[vol. 7, p. 210. According to Paillottet,
this article was originally published in
La République française, dated 27 February 1848.]

No one can say what the repercussions of the Revolution will be in Europe. Please heaven that all the peoples will be able to withdraw from the sad necessity of launching an attack on each other at a signal from the aristocracy and their kings.[26]

25. (Paillottet's note) In vol. 2, pp. 459 to 465, is shown the contingent supplied by Bastiat to the *Petites affiches de Jacques Bonhomme.* [*OC*, vol. 2, p. 459, "Petites affiches de Jacques Bonhomme"; and p. 462, "Circulaires d'un ministère introuvable."] Through the kindness of M. G. de Molinari, we are now able to reproduce short articles written by Bastiat for two other public broadsheets, which had a short existence in 1848, *La République française* and *Jacques Bonhomme.*

26. At the outset of the revolution of February 1848, the memory of the Revolution of 1789 was still very fresh, at least in the literature. In this article and the two following ones, Bastiat betrays the fear that the proclamation of the Republic will trigger a resumption of wars on the part of the monarchies. Later on, he wholeheartedly approves a subtle note sent to French embassies by Lamartine, the great poet and statesman, then minister of foreign affairs of the provisional government, aimed at soothing foreign concerns.

But let us suppose that the absolutist powers retain their means of acting abroad for a short time.

I put before you two facts which seem to me incontestable and whose consequences will then be seen:

1. France cannot take the initiative of disarming.
2. Without disarmament, the revolution[27] can fulfill the hopes of the people only imperfectly.

These two facts are, as we say, incontestable.

As for disarmament, the greatest enemy of France could not advise her to do this as long as the absolutist powers are armed. There is no point insisting on this.

The second fact is also obvious. Keeping oneself armed so as to guarantee national independence is to have three or four hundred thousand men under the flag and thus to find it impossible to make any significant cuts in public expenditure such as would permit a restructuring of the tax system immediately. Let us allow that, by means of a tax on luxury articles, we might reform the salt tax and a few other exorbitant ones. Is this something that might content the French people?

Bureaucracy will be reduced, they say. This may be so. However, as we said yesterday, the probable reduction in revenue will outweigh these partial reforms, and we should not forget that the last budget[28] ended in a deficit.

But if the revolution finds it impossible to restructure an iniquitous tax system whose incidence is unfair, and which oppresses the people and paralyzes work, it will be compromised.

However, the revolution has no intention of perishing.

Here are the necessary consequences of this situation with regard to foreigners. We, of course, will never advise wars of aggression, but the last thing that can be asked of a people is to commit suicide.

For this reason, if the armed bellicosity of foreigners forces us to keep three or four hundred thousand men in a state of readiness, even if they do not attack us directly, it is as though they were asking us to commit suicide.

In our view, it is perfectly clear that if France is placed in the situation we

27. The revolution of 1848.
28. The 1847 budget foresaw 1,357,253,000 francs of revenues and 1,458,725,000 francs of expenses, out of which 335,898,000 were for the army and 108,315,000 for the navy.

have just described, whether she wishes to or not, she will scatter the lava of revolution across Europe.

This will be the only way to create embarrassment for kings within their own territory, which will enable us to breathe more freely at home.

Let foreigners understand this clearly. They can escape danger only by taking the initiative and disarming straightforwardly. This advice will seem foolhardy to them. They will hasten to say, "This is rash." And we, for our part, say, "This is the most consummate prudence."

It is this which we will undertake to demonstrate.

-----

12. On Disarmament[29]

   Paris, 27 February 1848   [vol. 7, p. 215]

Today, *Le National* is looking at our situation with regard to the outside world.[30]

It asks, "Will we be attacked?" and, after having taken a look at the problems faced by Austria, Prussia, and Russia,[31] it answers in the negative.

We agree entirely with this opinion.

What we fear is not being attacked but that the absolutist powers, with or without premeditation and *simply through maintaining the military status quo,* will reduce us to seeking the salvation of the revolution[32] in armed propaganda.

We do not hesitate to repeat what we have said, since we wish to be understood both here and elsewhere. What we say with total conviction is this: We cannot take the initiative of disarming, and yet the simple military status quo gives us the alternative of perishing or fighting. It is for the kings of Europe to calculate the consequences of this fatal alternative. There is just one salvation for them: *to disarm themselves first and immediately.*

Readers will perhaps allow us a little useful fiction.

-----

29. This piece was untitled in the original.

30. Bastiat's letter is dated 27 February (1848). On 23 February the prime minister, François Guizot, resigned and a number of demonstrators were shot. On 26 February the liberal opposition organized a provisional government and declared the Second Republic, leading to the abdication of King Louis-Philippe.

31. The Austrian empire, ruled by Metternich under the nominal authority of Ferdinand I; Prussia of Frederick William IV; and the Russian empire of Tsar Nicholas I were the three great absolutist powers in Europe.

32. The revolution of 1848.

Let us imagine a small island, for many years more exploited than governed, with countless taxes and life insufferably curtailed, economically and politically. The nation is bent under the weight of this taxation and what is more it has to withdraw a significant part of its healthy population from the labor force to defend the realm and arm and feed it.

Out of the blue, this nation overthrows its oppressive government, with the aim of freeing itself from burdensome taxes and intolerable politics.

But the government, as it falls, leaves it with a huge burden of debt.

Initially, then, aggregate expenditure increases.

In parallel, however, all sources of revenue have diminished.

Now taxes are so odious that it is morally and materially impossible to maintain them, even provisionally.

Faced with this situation, the great and the good, who run all the nearby islands, anxiously entreat caution on the fledgling Republic:

"We hate you but we do not wish to attack you, in case we suffer harm ourselves. We will make do with surrounding you with a ring of soldiers and guns."

At this the young Republic is forced to come up with many soldiers and guns in like measure.

It cannot cut back on taxes, even the most unpopular ones.

It cannot keep any of its promises to its people.

It cannot fulfill any of the hopes of its citizens.

It flounders about in its financial straits, increasing taxes with all the burden that that entails. No sooner is the people's capital—the source of all paid employment—accumulated than it confiscates it.

In this desperate situation, nothing in the world could prevent our government from replying, "Your so-called moderation is killing us. Forcing us to maintain huge armies at the ready is to propel us toward social upheaval. We do not wish to perish and, rather than suffer this, we will stir up within your borders all the elements of disaffection that you have engendered in your own people, since you leave us no other path to salvation."

This illustrates rather precisely our position with regard to the kings and aristocracies in Europe.

We fear that the kings will not understand this. When have we ever seen them save themselves through prudence and justice?

Nevertheless, we should tell them this. They have just one resource, to act justly toward their people, relieve them from the weight of oppression, and *immediately take the initiative* and disarm.

Other than this, their crowns run the risk of a huge and prolonged struggle. This is not a question of revolutionary fever, but of historical understanding and the actual nature of the things which conduce to such fever.

The kings will say, "Is it not our right to remain armed?"

Probably so, but at their own risk and peril.

They will also say, "Does not simple prudence require us to remain armed?"

Prudence requires them to disarm immediately and today rather than tomorrow.

In fact all considerations which will impel France to break her bounds, if she is forced to arm, will retain her within them if she is put into a position to reduce her military forces.

In this event the Republic will have a good reason for swiftly eliminating the most odious of the taxes, allowing the people to breathe, giving capital and labor the opportunity to develop, and abolishing the restrictions and encumbrances that are inseparable from heavy taxation.

It will welcome with joy the chance to put into practice the great principle of *fraternity* it has just emblazoned on its flag.

---

13. The Kings Must Disarm

[vol. 7, p. 221. According to Paillottet,
this article was originally published in
La République française, dated 29 February 1848.]

If only the kings of Europe were prudent, what would they do?

England would freely renounce the right of search.[33] She would freely recognize that Algeria is French. She would not wait for these burning questions to be raised, and she would disband half her navy and use these savings to benefit her people by reducing the duties on tea and wine accordingly.

The king of Prussia would liberalize the half-baked constitution of his country,[34] and by giving notice to two-thirds of his army he would ensure the devotion of the people by relieving them of the weight of taxes and military service.

---

33. Under the honorable pretext of fighting the trade in slaves, the "right of search" in practice gave control of the seas to England. See "On Parliamentary Reform," note 31, p. 378.

34. In fact, the kingdom of Prussia did not have a constitution but a set of laws.

The emperor of Austria would quickly evacuate Lombardy and by reducing his army would put himself in a position to increase Austria's proverbial power.

The tsar would return Poland to the Poles.

All this done, France, no longer anxious as to her future, would concentrate on internal reform and let moral considerations take charge.

The kings of Europe, however, would expect to lose out if they followed this policy, the only one that can save them.

They will do exactly the opposite; they will want to stifle liberalism. So they will arm and the republics will arm too. Lombardy, Poland, and perhaps Prussia will become the theater of war. The alternative laid down by Napoléon, that *Europe will be Republican or Cossack,* will have to be resolved to the sound of guns. In spite of her ardent love of peace, expressed unanimously by the newspapers, but forced by her evident interest, France will not be able to avoid throwing her sword into the balance and . . . *kings perish but nations do not.*

---

14. Articles in *La République française* on the Political Situation[35]

26 February 1848   [vol. 7, p. 212]

When we go through the streets of Paris, which are scarcely wide enough to contain the throngs of people, and remember that in this immense metropolis at this moment there is no king, no court, no municipal guard, no troops, and no civil administration other than that exercised by the citizens over themselves, when we reflect that a few men, only yesterday emerged from our ranks, are taking care of public affairs on their own, then, judging by the joy, the sense of security, and the confidence shown on every face, our initial feelings are admiration and pride.

We soon return to the past, however, and say to ourselves, "So popular self-government is not as difficult as certain people tried to persuade us it was, and economy in government is not utopian."

There is no getting round the fact that in France we have become accustomed to excessive and grossly intrusive government. We have ended up believing that we would tear each other to pieces if we had the slightest liberty and if the state did not regulate all our movements.

---

35. We have grouped the following four articles under the new title, "Articles in *La République française* on the Political Situation."

This great experiment reveals indestructible principles of order within the hearts of men. Order is a need and the first of the needs, if not of all, at least of the vast majority. Let us be confident therefore and draw from this the lesson that the great and extravagant government machine which *those involved* called indispensable can and should be simplified.

27 February 1848   [vol. 7, p. 213. According to Paillottet,
                                    this article was originally published in
                                    La République française, dated 28 February 1848.]

Let us share this thought in *La Presse:*

What we need to ask a provisional government,[36] those men who devote themselves to public salvation amid incalculable difficulties, is not to govern in exact accord with all of our ideas, but to govern. We should help it, support it and make its rough task easy, and postpone any doctrinal discussion. The agreement of all the newspapers on this will not be among the least glorious events in our revolution.

We can all the more render to ourselves this homage to abnegation in favor of the common cause, because it is deep within us.

In a few of the decrees which follow one another, we see signs of the application of a doctrine which is not ours. We have combated this and will do so again when the time permits.

Two systems are confronting one another, both of which are born of sincere convictions and both having the common good as their objective. But, it has to be said, they emanate from two quite different ideas, which moreover oppose one another

The first, more seductive and popular, consists in taking a great deal of the people's earnings, in the form of taxes, in order to spread largesse among the people by way of philanthropic institutions.

The second wants the state to take very little, give very little, guarantee security, and give free rein to the honest exercise of every faculty; one consists in expanding indefinitely, the other in restricting as far as possible, the pre-

---

36. A provisional government was formed on 24 February 1848 and presided over by Jacques Charles Dupont de l'Eure, who was a liberal deputy under the restoration and a minister of justice under the July Monarchy. Among the government's most famous ministers were Lamartine (Foreign Affairs), Ledru-Rollin (Interior), Cremieux (Justice), and two socialists without portfolios: Alexandre Martin (called Albert) and Louis Blanc.

rogatives of power. The one of these two systems to which we are attached[37] through total conviction has few outlets in the press; it could not have had many representatives in government.

However, full of confidence in the rectitude of the citizens, to whom public opinion has entrusted the mission of building a bridge between our fallen monarchy and our burgeoning and well-ordered republic, we are willing to postpone the manifestation of our doctrine, and we will limit ourselves to sowing ideas of order, mutual trust, and gratitude to the provisional government.

27 February 1848   [vol. 7, p. 218]

All our cooperation, all our poor portion of influence, is devoted to the provisional government.

Certain of the purity of its intentions, we do not need to discuss all its measures in detail. It would be extremely demanding and even unjust, we might say, to demand perfection in emergency measures whose weight almost exceeds the limits of human strength.

We find it perfectly natural, at a time when the municipality needs so many resources, that local taxes be maintained, and it is an obligation for all citizens to ensure that this revenue is used wisely.

We would have liked the provisional government, however, not to appear to prejudge a major question with these words, "This tax must be revised and it will be shortly; it must be modified so as to make it less burdensome for the laboring classes."

We consider that we should not seek to modify the city toll but aim to eliminate it.

Paris, 28 February 1848   [vol. 7, p. 218. According to Paillottet,
                                            this article was originally published in
                                     La République française, dated 29 February 1848.]

The general good, the greatest sum possible of happiness for everyone, and the immediate relief of the suffering classes are the subjects of every desire, every wish, and every preoccupation.

Such, moreover, constitute the greatest guarantee of order. Men are never

---

37. (Paillottet's note) Here and elsewhere the use of the plural shows that Bastiat was speaking for his colleagues as well as himself. At this time, his signature appears in the paper as a mark of solidarity.

better disposed to help one another than when they are not suffering, or at least when they cannot accuse anyone, especially not the government, of those sufferings inseparable from human imperfection.

The revolution[38] began with a cry for *reform*. At that time, this word was restricted just to one of our constitutional arrangements. Today, it is still *reform* that we want, but of the fundamental kind, reform of our economic organization. The people, their complete freedom restored, are going to govern themselves. Does this mean the realization of all their hopes? We cannot bank on this chimera. The people will choose the measures that appear best suited to their purposes, but choice entails the possibility of error. However, the great advantage of government of the nation by the nation is that it has only itself to blame for the results of its errors and that it can always benefit from its experience. Its prudence now should consist in not allowing system builders to experiment too much on it and at its expense.

So, as we have said, two systems, discussed at length by polemicists, now confront one another.

One aspires to create the happiness of the people through direct measures. It says: "If someone suffers in any way, the state will be responsible for relieving him. It will give bread, clothing, work, care, and instruction to all those who need it." If this system were possible, one would need to be a monster not to embrace it. If somewhere, on the moon perhaps, the state had an always accessible and inexhaustible source of food, clothing, and remedies, who could blame it for drawing on it with both hands for the benefit of those who are poor and destitute?"

But if the state does not have in its possession and does not produce any of these things, if they can be created only by human labor, if all the state can do is to take them by way of taxation from the workers who have created them in order to hand them over to those who have not created them, if the natural result of this operation must be, far from increasing the mass of these things, to discourage their production, if from this reduced mass the state is obliged to keep a part for its agents, if these agents who are responsible for the operation are themselves withdrawn from useful work, and if, finally, this system which appears so attractive at first sight, generates more misery than it cures, then it is proper to have doubts and seek to ascertain whether the welfare of the masses might not be generated by another process.

The one we have just described can obviously be put into practice only

38. The revolution of 1848.

by an indefinite extension of taxes. Unless we resemble children who sulk when they are not given the moon when they first ask for it, we have to acknowledge that, if we make the state responsible for spreading abundance everywhere, we have to allow it to spread taxes everywhere, since it cannot give what it has not taken.

However, major taxes always imply major restrictions. If it were only a question of asking France to provide five or six hundred million, you might conceive an extremely simple financial mechanism for gathering it. But if we need to extract 1.5 to 1.8 billion, we need to use all the ruses imaginable in the operation of the tax laws. We need the town taxes, the salt tax, the tax on drink, and the exorbitant tax on sugar; we need to restrict traffic, burden industry, and limit consumers. An army of tax collectors is needed, as is an endless bureaucracy. The liberty of the citizens must be encroached upon, and all this leads to abuse, a desire for civil service posts, corruption, etc., etc.

It can be seen that, if the system of abundance drawn by the state from the people in order to be spread over the people by it, has its attractive side, it is also a medal that has its reverse side.

We, for our part, are convinced that this system is bad, and that there is another for achieving the good of the people, or rather for the people to achieve their own good; this consists in our giving the state all it needs to accomplish its essential mission, which is to guarantee internal and external security, respect people and property, the free exercise of faculties, and the repression of crime, misdemeanors, and fraud, and, after having given this liberally to the state, *in keeping the rest for ourselves*.

Finally, since the people are called upon to exercise their right, which is to choose between these two systems, we will often compare these before them, in all their political, moral, financial, and economic aspects.

---

15. To Citizens Lamartine and Ledru-Rollin

[vol. 7, p. 246. According to Paillottet, this
article was originally published in the third issue of
Jacques Bonhomme, dated 20–23 June 1848.]

Dissolve the national workshops. Dissolve them with all the care that humanity requires, but *dissolve them*.

If you want a reborn confidence, dissolve the national workshops.

If you want production to revive, dissolve the national workshops.

If you want shops to empty and fill, dissolve the national workshops.

If you want factories to reopen, dissolve the national workshops

If you want the countryside to become peaceful, dissolve the national workshops.

If you want the National Guard to have some rest, dissolve the national workshops.

If you want the people to bless you, including one hundred thousand workers out of the one hundred and three thousand in these workshops, dissolve the national workshops.

If you have not concluded that the stagnation of business followed by the stagnation of employment, followed by poverty, followed by starvation, followed by civil war, followed by desolation will become the Republic's funeral procession, dissolve the national workshops.

If you have not decided to ruin the finances, crush the provinces, and exasperate the peasants, dissolve the national workshops.

If you do not want the entire nation to suspect you of deliberately having the specter of riots hanging over the National Assembly, dissolve the national workshops.

If you do not want to starve the people after having demoralized them, dissolve the national workshops.

If you do not want to be accused of having imagined a means of oppression, fright, terror, and ruin which exceeds anything the greatest tyrants have ever invented, dissolve the national workshops.

If you do not have the ulterior motive of destroying the Republic by making it hated, dissolve the national workshops.

If you do not want to be cursed in the present and if you do not want your memory to be reviled from generation to generation, dissolve the national workshops.

If you do not dissolve the national workshops, you will draw down onto the country every plague simultaneously.

If you do not dissolve the national workshops, what will happen to the workers when you have no more bread to give them and private production is dead?

If you retain the national workshops with sinister intent, posterity will say of you, "It was doubtless by cowardice that they proclaimed the Republic, since they killed it by treason."

16. Report Presented to the 1849 Session of the General Council of
    the Landes, on the Question of Common Land

[vol. 7, p. 263]

Sirs,

You have referred the question of common land to your third commission. It has charged me with making its report to you. I beg leave to regret that it was not possible for this work to be completed by the colleague of yours[39] who, last year, began it so well.

Two diametrically opposed ideas have always dominated this question.

Some people, struck by the spectacle of infertility widely offered by these withered fields known as *heath* or *common land* and knowing, moreover, that what belongs to everyone is properly exploited by all, but taken care of by no one, are in a hurry to see the common domain become part of the private domain and invoke the help of the law to bring their system to fruition.

Others point out to us that agriculture, and consequently all the means of existence of this country, rest on common land. They ask what would become of the private domain without the resources of the common domain. Unless we find a system of crop rotation which enables us to do without fertilizer (an agricultural revolution that is not within sight), they consider alienation a public calamity and, in order to prevent it, they also invoke the help of the law.

Your commission considered that neither of these conclusions took enough account of a fact that dominates the entire subject and considerably simplifies the task of the legislator. This fact is property, before which the legislator himself has to give way.

In effect, does not the question whether the law should *force* or *prevent* alienation begin by giving communes property rights?

We have been struck by the lack of attention paid to this right, either in the questions asked by the ministers or in the replies given by the Council before the February revolution.[40]

This is how the ministerial circular set out the problem in 1846:

"What is the best use to which common land should be put? Should it

39. Victor Lefranc.
40. The revolution of 1848.

be left as it is today? Or should it be let under a short or long lease? Should it be shared or sold?"

Is this a question that could be asked when it is a matter of a given property, short of its status as such being denied?

And what was the answer from the Council?

After speaking in justificatory and almost laudatory terms of the ancient means of appropriation, such as confiscation or usurpation, means which do not exist today, it concluded with the necessity of alienating, adding:

"The consent of municipal councils, which will nevertheless always be consulted, would not be absolutely essential for alienating common land which is either heath land or vacant. . . ."

And further on:

"The Municipal Council would be consulted on the necessity of alienation, and, *whatever its opinion,* would the proposal, *communicated* to the District Council, submitted to the General Council, and approved by it, legitimate the order authorizing the act of sale?"

It must be admitted that this dialogue between the minister and the Council totally misunderstood the rights of property. However, it is dangerous to let it be thought that this right is subordinate to the wish of the legislator. Doubtless, reasons of public good and progress were invoked, but do not those whom we have since seen take such little note of private property also invoke these reasons?

And here it was all the more worrying that the right of the commons was lost to sight, since it is precisely in this right that the solution to a number of the difficulties linked to the question of common land is to be found.

What is, in fact, the most notable of these difficulties? It is the extreme difference observed between the situations and the interests of the various localities. We would like to draw up a general law, but when we turn our hand to it, we seem to be pitting ourselves against the impossible and begin to understand that, in order to satisfy all requirements, we would have to draw up as many laws as there are communes. Why is this? Because each commune, depending on its antecedents, agricultural methods, needs, customs, the condition of its communications, and the market value of the land, has different interests with regard to its common land.

The deliberation of the General Council in 1846 accepted this in the following terms:

"The development of a policy entailing consultation as to the situation of individual interests for each *département* and each village would be going too far. Here, we are content to state that nothing is possible if this first law is not observed, and it is above all in this matter that local custom must play an important part in the law and that the main arrangements of the law itself must leave a great deal of liberty and authority to the electoral bodies which are responsible for representing or protecting the commune."

The impossibility of drawing up a general law comes out in each page of the report made to you last year by M. Lefranc.

"Among the purposes that we may allot to our communal assets," he said, "in each *département* it is necessary to choose the one which will allow one place to be dried out and irrigated, another to provide easy and prompt transport, sowing and plantation in the Landes, advanced agriculture in the Chalosse, etc."

In fact, it seems to me that this means: since there are as many separate interests as there are communes, let us leave each commune to administer its common land. In other words, what should be done is not to violate common property but respect it.

Therefore, the one that has common lands only, which are essential for the grazing of livestock or for making fertilizer, will keep them.

The one that has more heath land than it needs will sell it, lease it out, or enhance its value depending on the circumstances and opportunity.

Is it not a good thing that, on this occasion, as on many others, respect for the law, in harmony with public utility, is in the end the best policy?

This policy may appear very simple, perhaps too simple. These days, we are inclined to want to carry out experiments on others. We do not allow them to decide for themselves, and when we have fathered a theory, we seek to have it adopted in order to go faster, using coercive means. To leave communes to dispose of their common land would seem to be folly both to partisans and to opponents of improvement. Communes are people of habit, the first will say; they would never want to sell. They are improvident, the others will say, and will not be able to keep anything.

These two fears are mutually destructive. Besides, nothing justifies them.

In the first place, the facts prove that communes do not oppose alienation absolutely. In the last ten years, more than fifteen thousand hectares have moved into the private domain and we can predict that this movement will accelerate with the improved viability, the growth of the population, and the rise in the market value of the land.

As for the fear of seeing the communes hurry to strip themselves of their wealth, this is even more of an illusion. Each time that administrative zeal has been directed to alienations, has it not met with resistance from the communes? Is it not this resistance, allegedly customary, that constantly provokes the legislator and all our deliberations? Did not M. Lefranc remind you last year that the Convention itself was not able to put across in this country a method of alienation truly attractive to people in the communes: *sharing!* I cannot stop myself from quoting the words of our colleague at this point:

"In order for a legislator, as powerful in his deeds and radical in his determination as the legislator of 1793, to have hesitated both to prescribe sharing in a uniform manner and to do violence to what he called the retrograde ideas of the provinces, he must have had a deep and irresistible sense of some sacred right, some imperative necessity hidden under the routine of tradition. In order for populations so violently dragged into the revolutionary current not to have found almost unanimously within their ranks a third of the votes favorable to the new procedure, eager for immediate and personal satisfaction and forgetful, given the price proffered, of the common interests and duties attaching to this common land, individuals determined, in the face of resistance, to introduce a standard, uniform law, the state of things that they wanted to destroy must have had its raison d'être elsewhere than in routine and ignorance."

From the above, sirs, you will guess the conclusion: that the interfering law should be limited to acknowledging communal rights of property with all their consequences.

But communal property is not placed under the sole safeguard of the municipal councils. These councils are frequently renewed. A majority may occur in one of them that is the result of a momentary upset, especially under the effect of a brand-new law which is, so to speak, at the experimental stage. An intrigue ought not to result in irremediable damage for the commune. Even though the municipal councillors are the natural administrators of the commons, your commission considered that with regard to important measures, such as alienation, the General Council might be armed with a temporary veto, without the right of property being compromised. It would have the right to adjourn the execution of the Municipal Council's conclusions until an election had given the inhabitants of the commune the opportunity of making their own opinion on the importance of the measure known.

We cannot end this report without drawing your attention to the opinion issued by the prefect,[41] not that we share all of his views, but because they are imbued with the most generous sentiments toward the poor classes and show all his care for the public good.

The prefect bases great hope on the common lands, not as a means of increasing the wealth of the region, since he agrees that personal appropriation would achieve this aim better, but as a means of rendering it more equal.

I have to say I find it difficult to understand how it can be the case that the exploitation of common lands, although this produces less wheat, less wine, less wool, and less meat than personal appropriation, nevertheless achieves the result that the whole community, even the poor, is better provided with all these things.

I do not wish to discuss this conception here, but I have to make the following remark: the belief of the prefect in the power of the common land is such that he is in favor, not only of absolute inalienability, but even of the setting up of common land where it no longer exists. What next? Are we now going down the path of moving land from the private to the common domain when so many years have been spent by the government in moving land from the common to the private domain?

Nothing is more likely, it seems to me, to give us confidence in the solution we have put before you than a respect for property with all its consequences. The law must stop at the point where it encounters the rights it is responsible for maintaining and not destroy them. For lastly, if for a few years the law forces common lands to be alienated because of the prevalence of the idea that common land is harmful, and if for another few years the law forces common land to be restored because it is thought to be useful, what will become of the poor inhabitants of the countryside? Will they have to be pushed in opposite directions by external forces, in line with the theory of the moment?

Note that the question is worded wrongly when you are asked, "What should be done with common lands?" It is not up to the legislator but the owner to dispose of it.

However, the commission is in full agreement with the views of the prefect when he speaks of the usefulness to the communes of adding value to the heath land that is not needed by agriculture. The council will probably second his efforts in this direction and the region will reward him with gratitude.

41. (Paillottet's note) M. Adolphe de Lajonkaire.

For these reasons, the third commission has charged me with submitting to you the following draft proposal:

The General Council considers that a law on common lands cannot do other than recognize properties of this type and regulate the method by which they are administered;

It considers it natural that the Municipal Council should be charged with this administration in the name of the inhabitants of the commune;

It is of the opinion that, should the Municipal Council vote for a land sale, the General Council should have the right to suspend the implementation of this vote, if it considers this to be appropriate, until it is confirmed by the Municipal Council at the next election.

---

17. National Assembly

> [vol. 7, p. 237. According to Paillottet, this article was originally published in the first issue of *Jacques Bonhomme,* dated 11–15 June 1848.]

"Master Jacques, what do you think of the National Assembly?"

"I think it is excellent, well intentioned, and devoted to the good. It is a product of the people; it loves the people and wants them to be happy and free. It brings honor to universal suffrage."

"But how hesitant it is! How slow! How many storms in a teacup there are! How much time wasted! What good has it done? What evils has it prevented? The people are suffering, production is failing, work is at a standstill, the treasury is ruining itself, and the Assembly spends its time listening to boring speeches."

"What are you saying? The Assembly cannot change the nature of things. The nature of things is at variance with nine hundred people governing with a will at once determined, logical, and swift. This being so, you must see how the Assembly is waiting for a government that will reflect its thought, how it is ready to give it a compact majority of seven hundred votes in favor of democratic ideas. However, no such government is in the offing at present and could hardly be so in the interim situation in which we find ourselves."

"What should the Assembly do?"

"Three things: deal with the emergency, draw up the constitution,[42] and make itself scarce."

---

42. The Constituent Assembly, elected on 23 April 1848, adopted the Constitution on 4 November and dissolved itself by the end of April 1849.

18. Parliamentary Conflicts of Interest

[This letter and the next one were sent to *La Sentinelle des Pyrénées*, which published them on 21 and 25 March 1843, respectively. We have grouped them under the new title, "Parliamentary Conflicts of Interest." From the private collection of Jean-Claude Paul-Dejean.]

We draw the attention of our readers to the following letter, which has been sent to us by one of our friends from the *département* of the Landes. This letter seems to us to envisage from an accurate viewpoint the current composition of our Chamber of Deputies, to which so many people bring just one preoccupation, that of climbing the greasy pole to power.

The Chamber has been presented for the third time with a huge question: the incompatibility of civil service functions with the function of a deputy or rather the *inaccessibility* of high positions to members of the National Assembly. Would you be willing, sir, to open the columns of your journal to a few reflections on this most serious matter? Above all, I would like to identify the class of readers to which these are addressed.

Two ideas are embossed on the July flag, and it will forever give shade to two major political parties, one which prefers to devote itself to the word *freedom* and the other which has made itself the principal defender of *public order*.

Parliamentary reform forms a natural part of the views of the Progressive Party. "How is it," they say, "that public freedoms are not in danger when they are entrusted to men whose existence is at the mercy of the authorities? How can we count on the independence of deputies who are civil servants when an independent vote may lead to their ruin? Is it wise to put men in the position where they have to choose between their interest and their duty? Besides, if we hand over the purse strings to the hands that take from the contents of the purse, should we expect the purse to be well managed? If we entrust the right to create positions of power to those who will be occupying them, should we not fear that the number of these will increase unreasonably? And what is the extension of the field of civil service functions if not a restriction of the field of private activity, in other words a restriction of freedom itself? Is it reasonable to expect deputies who are engineers, customs officers, or members of the university staff to hand back to us the *freedom* to oversee major public works, the *freedom* to trade, and the *freedom* of education?"

From the Progressives' point of view, these ideas seem to me to be too clear and obvious for it to be worth my while developing them. I would therefore like to address the *Conservatives* and examine with them whether *public order* is not as concerned with parliamentary reform as *freedom* itself, whether the principal cause of the *instability* they deplore and which rightly worries them is not *the easy access to positions of power of those who control power.*

What is the Chamber, as it is constituted at the present time? An arena in which the parties, or rather cliques, combat each other for public power. To lay siege to ministerial portfolios and to defend them, that is the sole business of parliamentary tactics.

A deputy comes to the Palais Bourbon. What is the attractive image that meets his gaze? It is power, flanked by its shining cortege of wealth, authority, influence, reputation, and consideration; I would be happy if these assets did not undermine his stoic virtue, but even if this man has no ambition, he has at least an idea which he wants to have accepted and it will not be long before he seeks advancement, if not in his own individual interest at least in the interest of his political beliefs. Our constitution has made power accessible to him and our parliamentary customs show him two avenues for achieving it. One is easy and regular: he just has to give his allegiance to a government and he will be rewarded with a good position for his pains. The other is steep and rough, but it leads higher and suits powerful ambitions; he must attack the government, place obstacles in its path, hinder its administration, decry its actions and make it unpopular, whip up the press and public opinion against it until at length, with the assistance of those who have hitched themselves to his star, he finally achieves a majority for a day and enters into the council of the crown as a victor.

But the conflict does not abate for all that; the roles merely change. He who was a defender the day before becomes an assailant in his turn. On leaving his position, he discovers the weapons that were used against him and takes control of them; it is his turn to make pompous speeches, seek popularity, paint a picture of France being shamefully propelled toward an abyss, revive in the depths of people's souls the ancient love of freedom and national independence and mislead them if necessary, and finally turn all these powerful missiles against his enemy. For his enemy, the aggressor of yesterday, is now on the defensive. All he can do is to struggle painfully against constantly renewed attacks and abandon attention to business to devote himself wholeheartedly to parliamentary conflict. His fragile majority soon escapes him. To achieve it he did not bargain with promises; to retain it, he has to be able to avoid bargaining with demands. Little by little the

cliques distance themselves and go to swell the ranks of the besieging coalition. In this way, as with the famous routs in our military celebrations,
power is taken over and retaken perhaps up to twenty times in the space of
ten years.

Is this order? Is this stability? And yet I challenge anyone to accuse me
of having drawn a fanciful picture. These are facts, this is history, and even
our constitutional history is nothing other than a narrative of conflicts like
these.

And can it be otherwise? Our constitution can be summed up in these
words: "Power is in the hands of deputies who know how to take hold of it.
Those of them who are clever enough to seize the majority from the government will become ministers and will distribute all the high positions in the
army, the treasury, the law, and the bench to their followers."

Is this not indeed a species of organized war, anarchy, and disorder? In
another article, I will examine how parliamentary reform might change this
order of things.

I am, sir, your obedient servant

F. B.

Dear Editor,

In a previous letter, I endeavored to point out the vice that is degrading
our national representation. With regard to freedom, handing over positions to those who finance them, and with regard to order, handing over
the reins of government to those who overturn it, these are concepts, as I
have said, whose twin danger leaps to the eye. I would add that this line of
reasoning is borne out by experience. If the limits of a journal allowed this,
I would now tell the tale of our countless *ministerial crises;* with *Le Moniteur* in my hand, I would compare M. Thiers, the chairman of the council,
with M. Thiers, the leader of the opposition; and M. Guizot, the instigator
of the coalition, with M. Guizot, the minister of foreign affairs. We would
see whether these assaults on ministerial portfolios, these formal sieges that
we call questions to the government, reintroduced several times a year, are
motivated by a love of the public good or a thirst for power. We would see
whether or not this determination to overturn in order to rebuild retreats
in the face of any contingency, whether it does not welcome auxiliaries to
the point where a general conflagration becomes likely, and whether this is
not provoked where necessary. We would finally see whether this constant
struggle, not of opinions but of rival ambitions, is not overshadowed by risk,

which, while weakening the country, causes it in the profoundest peace to be forever ready for war.

There are, however, several objections to parliamentary reform.

Ambition, it is said, is innate in the hearts of men, and reform will not uproot it.

Faith probably cannot destroy ambition, but it can destroy what gives it sustenance.

The members of general councils are sons of Adam just as the deputies are; why then does ambition not give rise to the same crises in these councils as it does in the Chamber? Solely because it finds nothing to feed on.

But if you introduce into the law that governs them an article with the following wording:

"If the prefect loses his majority in the General Council, he will be replaced by the leader of the opposition, who will distribute to his followers all the leading positions in the *département,* the headships of financial services, general and individual tax collecting, and seats on the bench and in the public prosecutor's department. These new civil servants will continue to be members of the Council and will retain their positions until a new majority snatches these from them."

I ask you, will a disposition like this not transform these deliberating bodies that are now so calm into hotbeds of intrigue and cliques? Will it not remove any spirit of continuity from the administration and any freedom of action from the prefect, and in sum all stability from the authority?

And what reason do we have for thinking that what would cause trouble in the sphere of the prefecture does not throw the governmental sphere into disarray? Is it because the stage is larger or because the passions whipped up by more powerful bait grow with more energy on it?

The objection having been voiced against reform that human ambition is an irremediable ill, reform is rejected because ambition in the Chamber is not even admissible.

Support for this reform, it is said, would be a condemnation of parliament; it would be a calumny pronounced against itself and would imply that there existed base passions in this Assembly that should not have access to it. In a word, it would be a law of suspects.[43]

In the first place, however, I do not see that the fact that the law declares

---

43. The *lois de suspects* (law of suspects), passed 12 August 1793 and enlarged by the decree of 17 September 1793, made way for the Terror phase of the Revolution. Directed

two functions incompatible by nature must sully those who occupy them. Mayors cannot be national guards, judges do not participate in juries, and nobody has heard it said that in these instances of incompatibility there is any form of personal discredit wished upon them by the law.

All that might be said is that the law takes account of the incurable and incontrovertible weaknesses in human nature.

And, to tell the truth, is the entire structure of the law anything other than a set of precautions taken against the weakness and perversity of mankind? We require guarantees from ministers and from the king, and the charter is merely a series of obstacles put in the path of possible encroachments and rivalries in the major offices of the state. And would society not be allowed to require the most rational of guarantees from its direct representatives?

It has to be agreed that parliamentary reform, as understood by the absolute prohibition for any civil servant to achieve national representation, presents two major disadvantages.

The first is that it restricts the rights of election and eligibility.

The second is that it lessens the consultative experience of the nation.

Would it not be dangerous in fact, at least in the current state of our legislative structure, to exclude magistrates, financiers, soldiers, and sailors from an assembly that is principally concerned with legislation, finance, and military and naval organization? Would a reform like this have any chance of being accepted?

This being so, does the problem consist not in setting out particular exclusions but in establishing general guarantees?

It may be formulated in these words:

"Placing the representatives of the nation in a situation in which they have no *personal* interest in giving their allegiance to a government or in overturning it."

If it is true that a well-phrased question is halfway to being resolved, a law that satisfies this double requirement should not be difficult to find.

It is not in my brief to go further and I will end this by noting that M. de Sade is far from facing up to the problem. He does not seem to have even noticed it. What is he proposing? To forbid deputies from taking up civil service appointments . . . except for ministries, embassies, general departments, etc.

---

at first toward the nobility, it allowed the immediate arrest of suspects, without cause or proof of a crime.

He thus accepts that high positions must continue to arouse the cupidity of the nation's representatives, that they can continue to dispute the possession of power among themselves, even if the conflict reduces this power to shreds. But it is precisely in this that the danger lies. And can we embellish with the title of parliamentary reform a measure that, while it restricts the domain of a few minor ambitions, leaves the way open to ambitions that throw the world into disarray?

I am, sir, your obedient servant.

F. B.

---

19. Parliamentary Reform

[vol. 7, p. 289. According to Paillottet, this outline, as Bastiat describes it in the margin and which survives as a fragment, is later than 1840.]

The July revolution has placed the soil of the country under a flag on which are emblazoned two words, *liberty* and *order.*

If we set aside certain completely eccentric theories, apocalypses of our modern luminaries, what forms the basis of common desires and general opinion is the longing for the simultaneous realization of these two goods, *liberty* and *order.* They include, in fact, everything that man must ask of government. The eccentric schools of which I was just speaking go much further, it is true. They require governments to provide riches for all, morality, education, well-being, happiness, and who knows what else? As if the government were itself anything other than a product of society and as if government, far from being able to give society wisdom and instruction, were not itself more or less wise and enlightened, in proportion to the virtue and enlightenment of society.

Be that as it may, the point on which the majority of men agree is this: allow any reform that extends liberty at the same time as it consolidates order; reject any innovation that compromises both one *and* the other of these benefits.

But what forms the greatest gulf between minds is the preference, or rather the preeminence, they give to either liberty or order. I have no need to say that I am not at all discussing the men who rally behind doctrines to satisfy their ambition. These make themselves the apostles of order or liberty, depending on whether they will gain or lose by a particular innovation. I am referring only to those minds that are calm, impartial, and which, after all, form public opinion. I am saying that what these minds have in common is that they all want liberty and order; they differ on one point, however: some concentrate more on liberty and others are concerned above all with order.

For this reason parliamentary debating chambers have centers, extreme rights and lefts, the liberals and the conservatives, the progressives and those who have been inaccurately labeled the "narrow-minded."

We should note in passing that the mutual accusations between those conscientious men who, for the most part, fix their gaze on just one of the words of the July motto are really puerile. Among the friends of liberty, there are none who would agree to a change in the law if it were shown that this change would result in disorder in society, especially if this was permanent. On the other hand, within the party of order, there is no one so narrow-minded that he would not welcome a reform that favored the development of liberty if he were totally reassured that order would be maintained and all the more if he thought that it would also have the effect of rendering government even stronger, more stable, and more capable of fulfilling its mission and guaranteeing the security of both people and property.

Thus, if among the reforms on which the public mind has been so concentrated in the last few years, there had been one which might satisfy both these twin conditions whose manifest result was first to limit government to its genuine prerogatives, tearing from its hands everything it held by way of encroachments on public freedoms, and second to restore to this properly limited authority a stability, a permanence, a freedom of action, and a popularity that it does not have today, this reform, I am emboldened to say, might well be rejected by those who benefit from the political wrongs whose reversal is the issue, although it should be welcomed by conscientious men on all the benches of the House and, in the public arena, by all the sectors of opinion that these men represent.

I consider parliamentary reform to be constituted thus:

To know what liberty and order would have to gain or lose from this reform, we need to examine how they are affected by the current state of affairs.

Under our electoral dispensation, about a hundred and fifty to two hundred civil servants entered the legislative chamber, and this number may be increased still further. It remains to be seen what influence this will have on liberty.

What is more, this legal dispensation also means that deputies who are not civil servants and who, by virtue of their backgrounds or their commitments to the electors, cannot become such, by allying themselves to a government, may break into the circle of government through another route, that of opposition. We will ponder the result of this state of affairs in connection with the stability of government and the question of social order.

We will examine the objections made to the principle of conflicts of interest.

Lastly, we will endeavor to put forward the grounds of a proper legal arrangement, taking account of those objections which have some foundation. . . .

On the Influence on Liberty of the Eligibility of Deputies for Public Office

In the eyes of the class of men who call themselves liberals, who are far from believing that all the progress made by society toward liberty is made at the expense of public order, who, on the contrary, are convinced that nothing is more suited to strengthening peace, security, respect for property and rights, than those laws which conform to absolute justice, for this class of men, I say, the proposal which I have to substantiate here appears so obvious that it seems unnecessary to lay much stress on its demonstration.

What is, in fact, the basis of representative government? It is that the men who make up a people are not the property of a prince, a family, or a caste; they are their own masters. It is that the government has to be carried out, not in the interest of those who govern, but in the interest of those who are governed. It is that the taxpayers' money should be spent for the benefit of the taxpayers and not for the benefit of the agents among whom this money is distributed. It is that the laws should be made by the mass who are subject to them and not by those who lay them down or who apply them.

It follows from this that this huge section of the nation which is governed has the right to keep an eye on the small section to whom government is entrusted, that it has the right to decide in what direction, within what limits, and at what price it wants to be governed, to stop government when it usurps prerogatives, either directly by rejecting those laws which shape these prerogatives or indirectly by refusing to make any payments to the agents by whom these pernicious prerogatives are exercised.

As the nation as a whole cannot exercise these rights, it has this done by its representatives. It chooses from within its ranks deputies to whom it entrusts this mission of control and supervision.

Does it not plainly follow that this control risks becoming totally ineffective if the electors choose as deputies the very men who administer, manage, and govern, that is to say, if power and control are placed in the same hands?

Our total tax burden exceeds 1.5 million and there are 34 million of us. We therefore pay an average of 45 francs each, or 225 francs for each family of five people. This is certainly exorbitant. How have we come to this in peacetime and under a regime in which we are supposed to hold all the purse strings? Heavens, the reason is simple; it is that if we, the taxpayers, are supposed to hold the purse strings, we do not genuinely hold them. We have them in our fingers for a moment in order to unfasten them very kindly and, once this has been done, we put them into the hands of those who draw on them. What is funny is that we are then astonished to find the purse lighter each day. Are we not like the cook who, as she went out, said to the cat, "Take good care of the buntings and, if the dog comes along, show him your claws."

What I have said about money applies equally to liberty! To tell you the truth, and even though this seems a bit prosaic, money and liberty are just the same. Let us develop this idea . . .

Suppose I am the king. Suppose that, as I have been led by events to provide a constitution for my people, I nevertheless want to retain as much influence and power as possible, what should I do?

I would begin by saying, "Deputies will not be paid any fee." And in order to have this article passed I would not hesitate to be sentimental, to vaunt the moral beauty of self-sacrifice, devotion, and sacrifice. However, in fact, I would understand perfectly that the electors could send only two classes of men to the Chamber, those who have a *considerable fortune,* as M. Guizot[44] says, and these are always willing to ally themselves with the court, and then a host of adventurers incapable of resisting the allure of Parisian life, the dazzle of riches, positioned between their inevitable ruin and that of their family and an assured ascension to the upper realms of fortune and prestige. I am aware that a few exceptional natures would emerge triumphant from the test, but in the end, a disposition like this would enable me to hope at least for considerable influence over the shaping of majorities.

But how could I attract these deputies? Should I offer them money? But

44. Since 29 October 1840, Guizot, then minister of foreign affairs, had been the key man of a government whose prime minister was Marshal Soult.

it should be acknowledged at once, to the credit of our country, that corruption in this form is not practicable at least on a wide scale—anyway, a civil list would not be sufficient for this. It is much cleverer and more amusing to have corruption paid for by the very people who suffer from it and to take from the pockets of the public what is needed to purchase the apostasy of its defenders. It will therefore suffice for a constitution to include these two strategies:

The king decides on all appointments
Deputies are eligible for all posts

I would have to be very clumsy or human nature of surpassing sophistication if, given these two lines in the charter, I were not master of the parliament.

Note, in fact, how slippery the step is for the deputy. It is not a question here of abject corruption, votes formally bought and sold. "You are skillful, M. Deputy; your speeches reveal a wide knowledge of diplomacy. France would be only too happy to have you represent her in Rome or Vienna." "Sire, I have no ambition; what I like most of all is retirement, rest, and independence." "Sir, one has a duty to one's country." "Sire, you are imposing on me the hardest of sacrifices." "The whole nation will be grateful to you."

Another fellow is a simple justice of the peace in his town and is content with this.

"Really, sir, your position is scarcely befitting to your legislative mandate. The procurator of the king who is now flattering you may be criticizing you tomorrow." "Sire, I value my modest position; it was the sole ambition of the great Napoléon." "You must, however, leave it. You must become a counsellor to the royal court." "Sire, my interests will suffer; there is all the travel, expenses. . . ." "You have to know how to make sacrifices," etc.

Sentimentality is all in vain; you have to have no knowledge of the human heart, to have never examined yourself sincerely, to have never followed the advice of the oracle: *Nosce te ipsum,*[45] and to know nothing of the subtleties of passions to imagine that *deputies,* who are called upon to cut a certain figure in the world, on whom all eyes are fixed and of whom exceptional liberality is required, would constantly reject the means to provide themselves with comfort, wealth, influence, the wherewithal to raise and introduce their sons, all this by an opening carefully presented to them as honorable and

45. "Know yourself."

meritorious. Do we need to spell out here the secret argument that in the depths of their heart dooms them to fall?

It is said that we should have confidence in those who govern. This position is puerile. If caution is not admissible, what good is representative government? Political writers of great talent, among them M. de Lamartine, have rejected parliamentary reform and the conflict-of-interest rule, on the pretext that France is a country of honor, generosity, and disinterestedness, such that it cannot be supposed that a deputy, *qua* deputy, would extend the authority invested in him as a civil servant or seek larger emoluments, that the conflict-of-interest rule would constitute a new law of suspicion, etc.

Oh really! Is there in our seven codes a single law which is not a law of suspicion? What is the Charter if not a whole system of barriers and obstacles to possible encroachments by the king, the peers, and ministers? Was the law on forced tenure made for the convenience of judges or in view of the dreadful consequences which their dependent position might have?

I must say I cannot accept that instead of scrupulously examining a measure we should repudiate it with flowery words and sonorous sentences which are, in any case, in flagrant contradiction of the entire set of acts constituting our private lives. I would very much like to know what M. de Lamartine would say to his steward if this man tried to talk this kind of language to him: "I have brought you the accounts of my stewardship but bad faith is not presumed. Consequently, I hope that you will leave me to check the accounts on my own and to have them checked over by my son."

You really need to close your eyes deliberately to the light, and refuse to see the human heart and the motives for our actions, such as they are, to say that since honor, delicacy, and virtue should always be presumed, it makes no difference if the control over government is assumed by government itself. It would be much simpler to eliminate the control. If you are so confident, take this confidence to the limit. This would still be a good calculation since, and I say this with the utmost sincerity, we would certainly be less misled by men who were fully responsible for their acts than if they were able to say to us, "You had the right to stop me and you let me continue. I am not the really guilty person."

Now I ask whether, once the majority has achieved power, not by free competition or the reasoned consent of the deputies, but because the latter has been successively enrolled in the ranks of government, can one still say sincerely that we have a representative government?

Imagine a particular law, running against the interests and ideas of those it is intended to govern. They are called upon to declare through the mediation of their representatives whether they accept or reject it. Obviously they will reject it if these representatives represent in fact *those whom the law is intended to govern.* But if they represent those who are proposing it, supporting it, and who are called upon to execute it, it will be accepted without difficulty. Is this representative government?

---

20. Letter to an Ecclesiastic

  Mugron, 28 March 1848   [vol. 7, p. 351. According to Paillottet, this
                                letter was published in *L'Économiste belge,*
                                dated 14 January 1860.]

Sir and Honorable Fellow Countryman,

When I arrived from Bayonne, I found your letter dated the 22nd in which you tell me that your vote in my favor will be subject to an issue you are now raising with me. At the same time I am put to the same test in the Maransin.[46]

I would be a very odd representative if I entered the National Assembly after rejecting, indeed because I had in fact rejected, freedom of trade and religion. The only remaining thing I would need to do to win a few other votes is to disavow freedom of teaching. In any case, my dear sir, I thank you for believing in the sincerity of my answer. You want to know my opinion on the emoluments given to the clergy; I must not disguise my thoughts even to gain votes I might legitimately be proud of.

It is true that I have written that each person should contribute *freely* to support the religion he professes. I have expressed this opinion and I will support it as a political writer and as a legislator, although not in any spirit of obstinacy, until good reasons make me change my mind. As I have said in my statement of principles/election manifesto,[47] my ideal is *universal justice.* The relations between the church and the state do not appear to me to be currently based on justice: on the one hand Catholics are forced to pay the pastoral stipends to the Protestant and Jewish religions (before long you will perhaps be paying Abbé Chatel, and that will upset a few sensibilities); on the other hand, the state takes advantage of whatever part of your budget it controls to intervene in the affairs of the clergy and to exercise an influence

---

46. A part of the Landes.
47. See "To the Electors of the Landes," p. 387.

to which I am opposed. It plays a part in appointing bishops, canons, and parish priests, though of course the Republic can take this sort of direction, even if fetters like this put some of us out of sorts. It seems to me, for instance, contrary to freedom and likely to increase the number of points of conflict between the temporal and spiritual powers.

I believe, furthermore, in a future merger of all the Christian religions or, putting it another way, in the absorption of the dissenting sects by Catholicism. For this to happen, however, the churches must not be political institutions. It is undeniable that the roles attributed to Victoria in the Anglican Church and to Nicholas in the Russian Orthodox Church are a serious obstacle to the reuniting of the entire flock under a single shepherd.

As for the objection arising from the situation in which thirty thousand priests would be placed by a measure such as the elimination of their payments[48] by the state, you are arguing, I believe, on the assumption that this step would be taken violently and not in a spirit of charity. As I see it, it implies the total independence of the clergy and, moreover, in decreeing this, we would have to take account of the treaty concluded in '89, one which you will remember.

I would need a whole volume to develop my thesis, but, after having expressed my views so frankly and in a way intended to preserve all my independence as a legislator and political writer, I hope that you will not cast doubt upon the sincerity of what remains for me to tell you.

I believe that the reform which I am discussing with you must and will be a subject for discussion rather than a matter for legislation, for many years and perhaps for many generations to come. The forthcoming National Assembly will have the straightforward mission of conciliating minds and reassuring consciences, and I do not think it will want to raise and even less to resolve the question you are putting to me in any way that will offend public opinion.

Take note, in fact, that even if my opinion is correct, it is held only by a very small number of men. If it triumphed now in the sphere of legislation, this would be so only at the price of alarming and arousing the opposition of the vast majority of the nation. It is, therefore, for those who share my

---

48. In 1789 the National Assembly put the properties of the church "at the disposal of the Nation." In exchange, the nation took over the payments to the clergy.

views a belief to be defended and propagated and not a measure amenable to immediate realization.

I differ from many others in that *I do not think I am infallible.* I am so struck by the native infirmity of individual reason that I neither seek nor will ever seek to impose my ideas. I set them out and develop them. As to their realization, I wait for public reason to pronounce its verdict. If they are right, their time will certainly come; if they are wrong, they will die before I do. I have always thought that no reform can be considered mature, with deep roots, and therefore useful, unless a lengthy debate has brought mass public opinion round to it.

It is on this principle that I have acted with regard to free trade. I have not addressed myself to those in power but to the general public and I have striven to bring it round to my opinion. I would consider free trade a lamentable gift if it were decreed before a reasoning public had called for it. I swear to you on my honor that if I had left the barricades as a member of the provisional government, with an unlimited dictatorship, I would not have taken advantage of it, as did Louis Blanc, to impose my personal views on my fellow citizens. The reason for this is simple: in my view, a reform introduced in this way, by surprise, has no solid foundation and will fall at the first test. This is also true for the question you put to me. If it depended on me, I would not accomplish the separation of the church and state violently, not because this separation does not seem to me to be a good thing in itself, but because public opinion, which is the queen of the world according to Pascal, still rejects it. This is the opinion that needs to be won over. On this question and on a few others, it will cost me nothing to remain, perhaps for the rest of my life, in an obscure minority. The day will come, I believe, when the clergy itself will feel the need to regain its independence through a new agreement with the state.

In the meantime, I hope that my opinion, which may be considered purely speculative and which in any case is far from being hostile to religion, will not lose me the honor of your vote. If, however, you feel obliged to withdraw it from me, I will in no sense regret that I have replied sincerely to you.

I remain your devoted fellow
countryman.

21. On Religion[49]

[vol. 7, p. 355]

I always thought that the religious question would continue to move the world. The legitimate religions of today, however, retain too much of the spirit and methods of exploitation to be reconciled with the inevitable progress of enlightenment. On the other hand, corrupt religious practice will put up a long and terrible resistance, being based on, nay confused with, the greatest need of humanity, that is to say with religious morality.

It appears, therefore, that humanity has not done with this sad pendulum swing which has filled the pages of history. On the one hand religious abuse is attacked, and in the heat of the conflict people are led on to dislodging religion itself. On the other hand, people stand as the champions of religion, and in the zeal of defense abuses are justified.

This long tearing apart was decided upon on the day a man used God to make another man his intellectual slave, the day one man said to another, "I am the minister of God. He has given me total power over you, your soul, your body, and your heart."

But, leaving aside these general reflections, I want to draw your attention to two facts referred to by the newspapers of today which prove how far from resolution are the problems surrounding the unity or separation of the spiritual and the temporal.

It is said that it is this complete separation which will solve all the difficulties. Those who put forward this assertion should begin by proving that the spiritual and the temporal can follow independent destinies and that the master of the spiritual is not the master of all.

Be that as it may, here are the two facts, or perhaps there is only one fact.

His Lordship, the Bishop of Langres, having been chosen by the electors of the *département* of —— to represent them, did not think he had to regard this election as sufficient, or even rely on his own decision. He has a superior who is neither French nor in France and, it should be said, who is at the

---

49. (Paillottet's note) This draft article indicates its date itself. [There are references in this piece to Pope Pius, who was pope from 1846 to 1878. Also there is a reference to "His Lordship, the Bishop of Langres" (Pierre-Louis Parisis), who was elected to the Constituent Assembly of 4 May 1848. Thus, we estimate that this article could be dated sometime in mid-1848.]

same time a foreign king. It is to this superior that His Lordship the Bishop of Langres refers. He says to him, "I promise you full and gentle obedience; will I do well to accept?" His spiritual superior (who is at the same time a temporal king) replies, "The state of religion and the church is so alarming that your services may be more useful on the political stage than in the midst of your flock."

At this, His Lordship of Langres lets it be known to his electors that he accepts their mandate. As a bishop he is obliged to leave them, but they will receive in compensation an apostolic blessing. Thus all was arranged.

Now, I ask you, is it to defend religious dogmas that the pope confirmed the election of ——? Is his Lordship of Langres going to the Chamber to fight heresies? No, he is going there to pass civil laws and to occupy himself exclusively with temporal matters.

What I want to point out here is that we have fifty thousand people in France, all highly influential in character, who have sworn total and gentle obedience to their spiritual leader, who is at the same time a foreign king, and that the spiritual and temporal are so intertwined that these fifty thousand men can do nothing even as citizens without consulting this foreign king whose decisions are unquestionable.

We would shudder if someone said to us, "We are going to endow a king, whether Louis-Philippe, Henri V,[50] Bonaparte, or Leopold,[51] with spiritual power." We would think that this might establish a boundless despotism. However, whether you add spiritual power to temporal power or superimpose one upon the other, is it not the same thing? How is it that we would not consider without horror the usurpation of the government of souls by the civil authorities while we find quite natural the usurpation of civil government by priestly authority?

After all, His Holiness Pius IX is not the only man in Europe in whom is vested this twin authority. Nicholas is both tsar and pope and Victoria is queen and female pope.

Let us suppose that a Frenchman professing the Anglican faith is elected as a representative. Supposing that he writes and has published in the newspapers a letter that goes as follows:

50. The name given by the absolutists to the count of Chambord, son of Charles X. He never reigned.
51. Leopold I.

Gracious sovereign,

I owe you nothing as queen, but as you are placed at the head of my religion, I owe you my total and gentle obedience. Please would you let me know, after consulting your government, if it is in the interests of the state and the Church of England for me to be a legislator in France.

Let us suppose that Victoria replies and has her reply published as follows:

My government is of the opinion that you should accept the office of deputy. Through this you would be able to render great service directly to my spiritual power and, consequently, indirectly to my temporal power, for it is very clear that each of these serves the other.

I ask you, could this man be considered a loyal and sincere representative of France? . . .

---

22. On the Separation of the Temporal and Spiritual Domains
    (an unpublished outline)

[vol. 7, p. 357. According to Paillottet,
this extract from one of Bastiat's notebooks
was probably written in 1849.]

"Is there a possible solution to the affairs of Rome?"[52] "Yes." "What is it?" "If we met a pope who says, 'My kingdom is not of this world.'" "Do you think that would be the solution to the Roman question?" "Yes, and to the Catholic question and to the religious question."

If in 1847 someone had proposed to abolish the Charter and invest Louis-Philippe with absolute power, there would have been a general outcry against such a proposal.

If, in addition, someone had proposed to give Louis-Philippe spiritual power in addition to temporal power, the proposal would not have been slain by a mere outcry but by the utter disdain it would provoke.

Why? Because we consider that the right to govern men's acts is already

52. Following a political crisis in Italy, Pope Pius IX took refuge in Gaeta, in the kingdom of Naples. The Italian Republic was proclaimed in 1849. To please the French Catholics and to prevent Austria from intervening, the National Assembly sent troops to restore the pope in Rome while protecting the new republic. The new Roman republic fell nevertheless after a month of fighting. See also "Pius IX" in the Glossary of Persons.

great enough and that we should not add to it that of dictating to their consciences.

What? Is giving spiritual power to a man with temporal power really so very different from giving him who is the spiritual leader temporal power? And is not the result absolutely the same?

We would rather let ourselves be chopped into pieces than let such a combination be imposed on us, and yet we impose it on others!

Dialogue

"But, see here, this state of things that you are criticizing has been going on for centuries!"

"That is true, but it ended by inducing the Romans to revolt."

"Do not speak to me of the Romans. They are brigands, assassins, degenerate, cowardly, without virtue, good faith, or enlightenment, and I do not see how you can take their side against the Holy Father."

"And I, for my part, cannot understand how you can side with an institution that has made a people become what you have described."

The world is full of honest people who would like to be Catholic and who cannot. Alas! They scarcely dare to appear to be.

Not being allowed to be Catholic, they are nothing. They have a root of faith within their heart, but they do not have faith. They aspire to a religion but don't have a religion.

What is worse is that this desertion is growing day by day. It pushes everyone out of the church, beginning with the most enlightened.

In this way, faith is dying out with nothing to replace it and the very people who, for political reasons or because they are terrified of the future, defend religion, have no religion. To any man whom I hear declaiming in favor of Catholicism, I ask this question: "Do you go to confession?" And he bows his head.

Of course, this is a situation that is not natural.

What is the reason for it?

I will tell you frankly, in my opinion it is entirely due to the union of both fields of power in the same person.

From the moment the clergy has political power, religion becomes a political instrument for it. The clergy no longer serves religion; it is religion that serves the clergy.

And soon the country will be covered with institutions whose aim, religious in appearance, is in fact material interest.

And religion is profaned.

And no one wants to play the ridiculous role of letting himself be exploited right to the depths of his conscience.

And the people reject what truth there is in religion along with the errors mingled in with it.

And then the time comes when priests cry in vain, "Be devout!"; people do not even want to be pious.

Let us suppose that the two powers were separate.

Religion would then not be able to procure any political advantage.

The clergy would then not need to overload it with a host of rites and ceremonies likely to stifle reason.

And each person would feel the root of faith, which never dries up completely, sprout in the depths of his heart.

And since religious forms would no longer be degrading, priests would not have to struggle against human respect.

And the merger of all the Christian sects into one communion would encounter no obstacles.

And the history of humanity would present no finer revolution.

But the priesthood would be the instrument of religion; religion would not be the instrument of the priesthood.

That says it all.

One of the greatest needs of man is the need for a moral code. As a father, husband, master, and citizen, man feels that he has no guarantee if a moral code does not form a brake for his fellow men.

Because this need is generally felt, there are always people inclined to satisfy it.

At the origin of each society, the moral code was encapsulated in a religion. The reason for this is simple. The moral code, in the correct sense of the term, is something which one is obliged to reason over; people have the right to put their maxims into quarantine. In the meantime, the world[53]——. Religion appeals to people most in a hurry. It speaks with authority. It does not advise, it imposes. "Thou shalt not kill. Thou shalt not steal." "Why?"

---

53. (Paillottet's note) The next word is missing in the manuscript. It is possible that the insertion of *would perish* would be in line with the thinking of the author.

"I have the right to say it," replies religion, "and I have the right not to say it, because I speak in the name of God, who neither makes mistakes nor is mistaken."

The basis of religion is therefore the moral code. In addition it has dogmas, facts, a history, ceremonies, and finally ministers.

Within the bosom of the people, ministers of religion are very influential men. Independently of the respect they attract as interpreters of the will of God, they are, in addition, the distributors of one of the things of which man has the greatest need, a moral code. . . .

Are things in religion not the same as in political economy?[54] And are we not mistaken in seeking the solution in a unity that is false, imposed, intolerant, persecuting, socialist, and in addition incapable of producing its right to domination and its proofs of truth?

Unity in all things is the supreme consummation, the point toward which the human spirit gravitates and will eternally gravitate, without ever attaining it. If it were to be achieved in humanity, it would be only at the end of all spontaneous social evolution.

It is variety and diversity which are at the beginning, the origin, and the point of departure of humanity, for the diversity of opinions must be all the greater if the treasure of truths acquired is smaller and the spirit of man has reached agreement, through science, on a smaller number of points. . . .

---

23. The Three Pieces of Advice

> [vol. 7, p. 361. According to Paillottet, this
> outline was published in *L'Économiste belge,*
> 3 June 1860. Based on internal evidence in the
> text, it was probably written in early 1850.]

"When the country is in danger, each individual owes it the tribute of what he may have acquired of enlightenment and experience."

This is how every giver of advice begins. A tax on advice! Is there any tax more abundant or more spontaneous?

I also wish to pay this tax, as well as all the others, in order not to be in debt in any way to my country.

Although the millions and millions of pieces of advice it receives differ

---

54. This paragraph and the preceding two paragraphs were found on a separate piece of paper.

from one another, they do have a point in common. Each has the pretension of saving society and those who give advice limit themselves to saying, "This is my approach; everything would be marvelous if everyone thought as I do." All this means that if we all agreed, we would come to an agreement.

"Let us all enter a phalanstery,"[55] says one, "and all our disputes will stop." "That's all very well, but 9,999 out of 10,000 Frenchmen have a horror of phalansteries." "Let us organize a social workshop in unanimous concert," says another, "and society will run like clockwork." "Doubtless, but those whom we are aiming at would sooner go to jail." "Let us bow down to the constitution," cries a third; "even if it is bad, if everyone carries it out it will be good." There is no truer word and I believe that this is the wisest and most plausible solution. But how do we persuade those who, although they detest the constitution, submit to it when anarchy threatens them and threaten it as soon as order raises their morale?

Some people say, "Evil arises as a result of the extinction of faith. Let us be good Catholics and social wounds will heal over." "You say this because you yourself are a Catholic . . . and yet. But what do we do to make those who are not become Catholic?"

Others, depending on their tastes, will repeat, "Let us all unite with the republic!" "Let us all rally to the monarchy!" "Let us all by common accord return to the past!" "Let us all go forward with courage toward the future!"

In the end, everyone follows his own advice, nothing is more natural, and proclaims that the world will be saved if it is followed, and nothing is more certain.

But none of these wins the day nor can any of them triumph, for all these efforts cancel each other out and the status quo remains.

Among these myriads of doctrines, there is a single one—I do not need to say that it is mine—which would have the right to generate common agreement. Why is it the only one with this privilege? Because it is the doctrine of liberty, because it is tolerant and just toward all the others. Found a phalanstery if that is what you want, form a group in a social workshop if that pleases you, discuss the constitution as much as you want, demonstrate your preference for the republic or monarchy openly, go to confession if your heart so dictates, in a word make use of all the rights of the individual; provided that you acknowledge these same rights in others, I will be satisfied

55. A Fourier-type commune. See also "Fourier" in the Glossary of Persons.

and, such is my conviction, society, in order to be just, ordered, and progressive, asks nothing else of you.

But I do not presume now to develop this approach which ought, in my view, be adopted as soon as it is put forward. Is there anything more reasonable? We cannot agree on the doctrines, well then, let each of us retain and put forward our own and agree to banish all oppression and violence from among us.

Adopting the point of view that facts are as they are and the situation is as events have made it, let us suppose, as I must, that I am addressing people who above all want France to be at peace and happy. In which case I would like to issue three pieces of practical advice, one to the president of the Republic,[56] the second to the majority in the Chamber, and the third to the minority.

I would like the president of the Republic to go before the National Assembly and make the following solemn speech:

Citizen representatives,

The greatest plague at the present time in our country is the uncertainty of the future. Insofar as this uncertainty may concern my projects and my views, my duty is to eliminate it and this is also my wish.

People ask, "What will happen in two years' time? Before my country, under the eye of God, and by the name I carry, I swear that on —— May 1852, I will relinquish the chair of president.

I have received a mandate from the people by virtue of the constitution. I will hand this mandate back to the people in accordance with the constitution.

There are some who say, "But what if the people choose you again?" To this I reply, "The people will not do me the injury of electing me against my wishes, and if a few citizens forget their duty to this extent, I will in advance consider null and void the votes that bear my name at the next election."

Others, considering themselves to be much wiser, think that my presidency can be prolonged by changing the constitution in accordance with the forms it has itself established.

It is not up to me to impose limits on the legal exercise of the rights of the Assembly. However, if it is the mistress of its regular resolutions, I am master of mine, and I formally declare that, should the constitution be modified, my first presidency would not immediately be followed by a second.

56. Louis-Napoléon.

I have thought about this and this is the basis of my opinion:

The rule governing our action is contained in these words, *France before all*. What ails France? Uncertainty. If this is the case, citizens, is calling everything into question a way of removing uncertainty? Good God! The constitution is just one year old and already you would hurl this burning question, do we need to draw up a new constitution? If your reply is negative, will the passions outside be calmed? If it is affirmative, another constitution will need to be convoked, the foundations of our national existence will once more be disturbed, we will rush headlong into a new unknown and, in a few months, undergo three general elections.

This extreme option appears to me to be the height of folly. I have no right to oppose it other than by declaring in the most decisive manner that it will not profit my followers, since, I repeat, I will not accept the presidency in whatever form or in whatever manner it happens to me.

This is my first resolution. I have taken it out of duty; I proclaim it with joy since it may contribute to the tranquillity of our country. I will be sufficiently rewarded if it provides me with a successor who is an honest republican who brings to the first function of the state neither bitterness nor utopia nor commitment to the political parties.

I now have a second resolution to put before you. Through the will of the people I must carry out *executive power* for two years more.

I understand the meaning of the words *executive power* and I am resolved to restrict myself to it absolutely.

The nation has handed down two delegations. On its representatives it has conferred the right to make laws. To me, it has entrusted the mission of having them executed.

Representatives, make the laws you consider to be the best, the most just, and the most useful to the country. Whatever they are, I will carry them out to the letter.

If they are good, their execution will prove this; if they are bad, their execution will reveal their faults and you will reform them. I have not the right and do not accept the responsibility of judging them.

I say all this in accordance with the faculty attributed to me by Article —— of the constitution.

I will execute your decrees, therefore, without distinction. There are some, however, to which I consider myself to be bound, by national wish, to give particular attention. These concern the repression of misdemeanors and crimes, order in the streets, respect for persons and property, using this word *property* in its widest meaning, which includes both the free exercise of faculties and labor and the peaceful enjoyment of acquired wealth.

So, representatives, make laws. Let citizens discuss all the political and social questions in meetings and in the newspapers. But let no one disturb the order reigning in the city, peace within families, and the security of industry. At the first sign of revolt or uprising, I will be there. I will be there together with all good citizens and with the true republicans. I will be there with the brave Republican Guard and with our admirable army.

Some people say, "Can we count on the zeal of the National Guard and on the loyalty of the army?"

Yes, in the path I have just traced we can count on them. I trust them as I trust myself, and no one has the right to insult our armed forces by believing that they would take sides with the disturbers of public peace.

I wish, and I have the right to wish, since the people have given me this express mission, and my will in this is the same as theirs, I wish order and security to be respected everywhere. I want this and it shall be so. I am surrounded by loyal soldiers and tested officers. I have on my side force, the law and public common sense, and if I did not fear to wound the just susceptibilities of those of whose assistance I am assured by appearing to doubt them, I would say that even defection would not make me hesitate. Legal order will reign, if it costs me the presidency and my life.

This, citizens, is my second resolution. And here is the third.

I wonder what is the cause of these incessant and passionate conflicts between the nation and the government it gave itself.

Perhaps it should be attributed to the ingrained habit of opposition. Combating power is to give oneself a role considered to be heroic because in the past it might have been glorious and dangerous. I know that there is no other remedy for this than time. But, as these perpetual conflicts and the language of hate and exaggeration that they generate are one of the great plagues of our Republic, I have had to examine whether they had causes other than irrational tradition, in order to eliminate any cause over which I had any power.

I sincerely believe that the legislative and executive powers mix up and confuse their roles too much.

I am resolved to limit myself to mine, which is to see that the laws you have voted are executed. In this way, I would have only a restricted responsibility, even in the eyes of the most susceptible. If the nation is badly governed, they will not be able to blame me, provided that I execute the laws.

The government and I will be blameless in the debates in the tribune and in the press.

I will choose my ministers outside the Assembly. In this way there will be a logical separation between the two powers. In this way, I will put an end to the alliances and portfolio wars within the Chamber which are so disastrous to the country.

My ministers will be my direct agents. They will come to the Assembly only when they are called, in order to answer questions asked in advance by means of regular messages.

In this way, you will be perfectly free and enjoy perfectly impartial conditions in which to draft laws. My government will not exercise any influence on you in this respect. For your part, you will have none over their execution. You will doubtless have to check them, but their execution as such is my responsibility.

This being so, citizens, is it possible to imagine a collision? Would you not have the greatest interest in seeing that only good laws result from your deliberations? Could I have any other interest than ensuring their proper execution?

In two years the nation will be called upon to elect another president. Its choice will doubtless fall upon the most worthy, and we will not fear any attack on freedom and the laws from him. In any case, I will have the satisfaction of leaving him precedents that will bind him. When the presidency is not set on the name of Napoléon, on the person elected by seven million votes, is there anyone in France who is able to dream of a coup d'état in his favor and aspire to empire?[57]

Let us therefore banish vain fears. We will live through a first, second, and third presidency free from danger....

57. The irony is that Louis-Napoléon seized power in a coup d'état in December 1851 and was made emperor in December 1852.

Glossary of Persons

ABD EL-KADER (1808–83). Algerian poet, diplomat, and soldier who directed the revolt against the French from 1832. He gave himself up in 1847, was imprisoned in France, and was freed in 1852.

AFFRE, ROMAIN. Close friend of Bastiat's and son-in-law of Mme Marsan (Marie-Julienne Badbedat).

ALFIERI, VITTORIO (1749–1803). Italian playwright who also wrote a short treatise, *De la tyrannie* (1802).

ANISSON-DUPERRON, ALEXANDRE (1776–1852). French politician and director of the Royal Printing House.

ARAGO, FRANÇOIS (1786–1853). French astronomer and physicist. Elected deputy from 1830 to 1852. In 1848 he was a member of the executive commission and the provisional government.

ARNAULT, LUCIEN (1787–1863). Diplomat and civil servant during the First Empire; the restoration put an end to his career. He later became a playwright, writing several tragedies, but is largely forgotten today. He was appointed a prefect during the July Monarchy (1830–48).

ARRIVABENE, GIOVANNI, count (1787–1881). Italian aristocrat. He was forced to flee the Piedmont revolution of 1821 and was condemned to death in absentia for his role in the uprising. He settled in Belgium and wrote extensively on the conditions of the working class in such books as *Sur la condition des laboureurs et des ouvriers belges* (1845). He also translated works by James Mill and Nassau Senior into French.

ASHWORTH, HENRY. Head of a successful manufacturing family in Bolton and one of Richard Cobden's closest personal friends.

AUGIER, ÉMILE (1820–84). Poet and novelist.

BADBEDAT, MARIE-JULIENNE (Mme Marsan) [dates unknown]. The only known woman with whom Bastiat fell in love. There was gossip that they had had an affair, but Bastiat denied it very strongly and indignantly.

BAINES, EDWARD (1774–1848). A leading radical journalist who owned the *Leeds Mercury* newspaper in England. He was active in numerous reform issues, such as antislavery, Catholic emancipation, the disestablishment of the Church of England, and the removal of the Corn Laws. Although he was a close ally of Richard Cobden over the Corn Laws, he split with him over the question of compulsory education. Baines was a strict voluntaryist on the matter.

BARBEYRAC, JEAN (1674–1744). French eighteenth-century writer on natural law; he also annotated and translated works by Hugo Grotius and Samuel Pufendorf, which were much used by French jurists and lawyers.

BASTIAT, JUSTINE. Frédéric's aunt. She raised him after his parents' death and was responsible for ensuring that he received an excellent education.

BASTIDE, JULES (1800–1879). French minister of foreign affairs and editor of the newspaper *Le National.*

BENOIST D'AZY, PAUL (1824–98). Industrialist in the metallurgical field who favored protectionism.

BÉRANGER, PIERRE-JEAN (1780–1857). French poet and author of patriotic and liberal songs.

BERRYER, PIERRE ANTOINE (1790–1868). French lawyer and liberal politician.

BERTIN, EDOUARD (1797–1871). Artist. Son of François Bertin, founder of *Le Journal des débats.* He took over the paper after the death of his brother.

BILLAULT, ADOLPHE (1805–63). Lawyer, mayor of Nantes, France. Deputy and twice minister under Napoléon III.

BLAISE, ADOLPHE GUSTAVE (1811–86). A regular contributor to *Le Journal des économistes* and other periodicals. With Joseph Garnier he edited a series of lectures by Blanqui, *Cours d'économie industrielle* (1837–39), which Blanqui had given at the Conservatoire national des arts et métiers.

BLANC, LOUIS (1811–82). French journalist and historian active in the socialist movement. Blanc founded the journal *Revue du progrès,* publishing articles that later became the influential pamphlet *Organisation du travail* (1840). During the 1848 revolution he became a member of the temporary government, promoted the national workshops, and debated Adolphe Thiers on the merits of the right to work in *Le Socialisme; droit au travail, réponse* à *M. Thiers* (1848).

Blanqui, Jérôme Adolphe (1798–1854). Liberal economist and brother of the revolutionary socialist Auguste Blanqui. Blanqui became director of the prestigious École supérieure de commerce de Paris and succeeded Jean-Baptiste Say to the chair of political economy at the Conservatoire national des arts et métiers. He was elected deputy, representing the Gironde from 1846 to 1848. Among Blanqui's many works on political economy and sociology are the *Encyclopédie du commerçant* (1839–41), *Précis élementaire d'économie politique* (1842), and *Les Classes ouvrières en France* (1848).

Bonaparte, Louis-Napoléon (1808–73). Nephew of Napoléon Bonaparte, he was raised in Italy and became active in liberal Carbonari circles. Louis-Napoléon returned to France in 1836 and 1840 to head the Bonapartist groups seeking to install him on the throne. On both occasions he was unsuccessful. In 1848 he was elected president of the Second Republic. In 1851 he dissolved the Assembly and won a plebiscite that made him emperor of the Second Empire. Louis-Napoléon was popular for his economic reforms, which were a mixture of popularism and liberalism. A free-trade treaty with England was signed in 1860 during his reign by Cobden and Chevalier. A socialist uprising in 1870 and a disastrous war with Prussia in 1871 led to the ignominious collapse of his regime.

Boyer-Fonfrède, Henri (1788–1841). Liberal publicist, economic journalist, and supporter of the July Monarchy. He founded the *L'Indicateur* and wrote *Questions d'économie politique* (1846).

Bright, John (1811–89). Manufacturer from Lancashire and leading member of the Anti–Corn Law League. Elected to the Commons in 1843, he pleaded for the equality of religions under the law, criticized the privileges of the Church of England, supported the separation of church and state, and asked for the right for Jews and atheists to swear a non-Christian oath and to be allowed to be elected to Parliament. Later, in 1869, he became minister of the Board of Trade in the Gladstone Cabinet.

Broglie, Victor, duc de (1785–1870). Prime minister in 1835 and 1836 and son of an aristocrat guillotined during the Revolution. He negotiated an agreement with Britain to abolish slavery and another with the United States to compensate the United States for losses during Napoléon's continental blockade.

Buffet, Louis Joseph (1818–98). Lawyer, deputy, and minister of agriculture and commerce from December 1848 to October 1849.

Bugeaud, Thomas, marquess de Piconnerie, duc d'Isly (1784–1849). Governor of Algeria, marshall of France, and deputy.

BULOZ, FRANÇOIS (1802–77). Editor of *La Revue des deux mondes,* which covered arts, literature, politics, and society.

BULWER, HENRY (1801–72). British ambassador to Spain 1843–48.

BURSOTTI, GIOVANNI [dates unknown]. Italian economist and author of *Biblioteca di commercio* (1841–42) and *Esposizione della tariffa doganale per lo regno delle Due Sicilie* (1854).

CABET, ETIENNE (1788–1856). Lawyer, historian, journalist, and author of the book *Voyage in Icarie,* in which he expounded communist theories tinged with spiritualism. He left for the United States in February 1848, where he tried without success to found a communist community, first in Texas, then in Illinois. He came back to France in 1851 but in 1852 returned to the United States, where he spent the rest of his life.

CALMÈTES, VICTOR-ADRIEN (1800–1871). Born in Spain of French parents, he established a friendship with Bastiat at the Sorèze School. After Sorèze, he practiced law. In 1827 he joined the society Aide toi, le ciel t'aidera ("help yourself, heaven will help you"), led by Adolphe Thiers. Calmètes became a judge in Montpellier in 1830 and later president of the court. He was elected a general councillor in 1840 and deputy in 1869.

CANNING, GEORGE (1770–1827). British politician who inspired a group of young Tory members of Parliament eager for reforms (the Canningites).

CAREY, HENRY C. (1793–1879). American economist who argued that national economic development should be promoted by extensive government subsidies and high tariff protection. The proofs of his book *The Harmony of Interests, Agricultural, Manufacturing, and Commercial* (1851) were sent to Bastiat in November 1850, before the book appeared in print. After the publication of Bastiat's *Economic Harmonies* (1851), Carey accused him of plagiarism; and a bitter debate in *Le Journal des économistes* ensued.

CASTAGNÈDE [first name and dates unknown]. A local notable and colleague of Bastiat in the General Council.

CAUSSIDIÈRE, MARC (1801–61). Deputy and former worker, he was active in the revolutions of 1830 and 1848. He was accused, with Louis Blanc, of being an agitator in the "conspiracy" of 15 May.

CAVAIGNAC, EUGÈNE (1802–57). French general, deputy, minister of war, head of the executive. He crushed the workers' uprising of June 1848. He was a candidate in the presidential election of 10 December 1848 but obtained only 1,448,000 votes against 5,434,000 for Louis-Napoléon Bonaparte.

Changarnier, Nicolas Anne Theodule (1793–1877). French general who had a meteoric rise in the French army, with successes in various military campaigns in North Africa. During the revolution he assisted the provisional government in restoring order in Paris, was elected to the General Assembly to represent the Seine *département,* and was placed in command of the National Guard in Paris. For his opposition to Louis-Napoléon he was arrested and banished.

Chantelauze, V. (1787–1850). Magistrate, deputy, and minister of justice during part of the last government of Charles X. He prepared the ordinances that triggered the three revolutionary days of July 1830 and the proclamation of Louis-Philippe (duc d'Orléans) as "king of the French."

Charles Albert (1798–1849). King of Sardinia (1831–49).

Chateaubriand, François René, vicomte de (1768–1848). Novelist, philosopher, and supporter of Charles X. Minister of foreign affairs from December 1822 to June 1824. Defender of freedom of the press and Greek independence, Chateaubriand refused to take the oath to King Louis-Philippe after 1830. He spent his retirement writing *Mémoires d'outre-tombe* (1849–50).

Chatel, Ferdinand (1795–1857). Ordained a Roman Catholic priest in 1821, he served as a military chaplain. Chatel professed liberal and Gallican ideas, which led to his exclusion from the church. In 1830 he founded the French Catholic Church, a dissident church that adopted French for the liturgy and eliminated confession, fasting, and celibacy for priests. The church was closed by the police in 1842.

Chénier, André (1762–94). French poet and revolutionary. He was guillotined for protesting the excesses of the Terror.

Cheuvreux, Hortense (née Girard) (1808–93). Married Casimir Cheuvreux, a wealthy merchant, in 1826. M. and Mme Cheuvreux and their daughter Louise became good friends of Bastiat's. In 1877 Mme Cheuvreux published Bastiat's letters to her family in *Lettres d'un habitant des Landes.* (The sister of Casimir, Anne Cheuvreaux, had married Jean-Baptiste Say's son Horace in 1822, thus making the Cheuvreaux family part of the Say family.)

Cheuvreux, Louise. Daughter of Casimir and Hortense Cheuvreux.

Chevalier, Michel (1806–87). Liberal economist and alumnus of the École polytechnique. Minister of Napoléon III. Initially a Saint-Simonist, he was imprisoned for two years (1832–33) in France. After a trip to the

United States, he published *Lettres sur l'Amérique du Nord* (1836), *Histoire et description des voies de communications aux États-Unis et des travaux d'art qui en dependent* (1840–41), and *Cours d'économie politique* (1845–55). He was appointed to the chair of political economy at the Collège de France in 1840 and became senator in 1860. An admirer of Bastiat and Cobden, Chevalier played a decisive role in the 1860 treaty on free trade between France and England (Chevalier was the signatory for France, and Cobden the signatory for England).

CLARKSON, THOMAS (1760–1846). With William Wilberforce he was one of the leading figures in the campaign to abolish the slave trade (1807) and slavery itself (1833).

CLÉMENT, AMBROISE (1805–86). Economist and secretary to the mayor of Saint-Étienne for many years. Clément was able to travel to Paris frequently to participate in political economy circles. In the mid-1840s he began writing on economic matters and so impressed the publisher Gilbert-Urbain Guillaumin that the latter asked him to assume the task of directing the publication of the important and influential *Dictionnaire de l'économie politique* in 1850. Clément was a member of the Société d'économie politique from 1848, was a regular writer and reviewer for *Le Journal des économistes,* and was made a corresponding member of the Académie des sciences morales et politiques in 1872. He wrote the following works: *Recherches sur les causes de l'indigence* (1846), *Des nouvelles idées de réforme industrielle et en particulier du projet d'organisation du travail de M. Louis Blanc* (1846), and *La Crise économique et sociale en France et en Europe* (1886), as well as an early review of Bastiat's *Economic Harmonies* for *Le Journal des économistes* (1850), in which he praised Bastiat's style but criticized his position on population and the theory of value.

COBDEN, RICHARD (1804–65). Founder of the Anti–Corn Law League. Born into a poor farmer's family in Sussex, he was trained by an uncle to be a clerk in his warehouse. At twenty-one, he became a traveling salesman and was so successful that he was able to set up his own business by acquiring a factory making printed cloth. Thanks to his vision of the market and his sense of organization, his company became very prosperous. Nevertheless, at the age of thirty, he left the management of the company to his brother in order to travel. He wrote influential articles in which he defended two great causes: pacifism, in the form of nonintervention in foreign affairs; and free exchange. From 1839 he devoted himself exclusively to the Anti–Corn Law League and was elected member of Parliament for Stockport in 1841.

Toward the end of the 1850s, he was asked by the government to negotiate a free-trade treaty with France; his French counterpart was Michel Chevalier (*see above*).

COBURG, FREDERICK OF SAXE-COBURG (1737–1815). General in the Austrian army, who symbolized in the eyes of Frenchmen the first coalition in the war against the French Revolution.

COMTE, CHARLES (1782–1837). Lawyer, liberal critic of Napoléon and then of the restored monarchy, son-in-law of Jean-Baptiste Say. One of the leading liberal theorists before the 1848 revolution, he founded, with Charles Dunoyer, the journal *Le Censeur* in 1814 and *Le Censeur européen* in 1817 and was prosecuted many times for challenging the press censorship laws and criticizing the government. He encountered the ideas of Say in 1817 and discussed them at length in *Le Censeur européen*. After having spent some time in prison he escaped to Switzerland, where he was offered the Chair of Natural Law at the University of Lausanne before he was obliged to move to England. In 1826 he published the first part of his magnum opus, the four-volume *Traité de législation,* which very much influenced the thought of Bastiat, and in 1834 he published the second part, *Traité de la propriété.* Comte was secretary of the Académie des sciences morales et politiques and was elected a deputy representing La Sarthe after the 1830 revolution.

CONSIDERANT, VICTOR PROSPER (1808–93). Follower of the socialist Fourier and advocate of the "right to work" program, which so enraged Bastiat. He was author of *Principes du socialisme: Manifeste de la démocratie au XIXe siècle* (1847).

CONSTANT, BENJAMIN (1767–1830). Novelist, politician, and political theorist. Born in Lausanne, Constant was a close friend of Germaine de Staël and accompanied her to Paris in 1795. He was a supporter of the Directory and a member of the Tribunat but came to oppose the loss of political liberty under Napoléon. He became a staunch opponent of Napoléon, but in spite of this he was approached by him during the Hundred Days (period between Napoléon's return from exile on Elba to Paris on 20 March 1815 and the restoration of King Louis XVIII on 8 July 1815) to draw up a constitution for a more liberal, constitutional empire. Constant became a deputy in 1819 and continued to defend constitutional freedoms until his death. He is best known for his novel *Adolphe* (1807) and for *Principes de politique applicables à tous les gouvernements* (1815); *De l'esprit de conquête et de l'usurpation, dans leurs rapports à la civilisation européen* (1814); and *Cours de politique constitutionelle* (1820).

CORCELLE, CLAUDE TINGUY DE (1802–92). A Liberal, he held the post of deputy several times between 1839 and 1873. Corcelle was also a friend of Tocqueville's. His wife's grandfather was La Fayette, whose memoirs he published.

COUDROY, FÉLIX (1801–74). Son of a doctor from Mugron. He read law in Toulouse and Paris; however, a long illness prevented him from practicing. He lived in Mugron and established a strong and lasting friendship with Bastiat. He published a number of brochures and articles in *La Chalosse, Le Mémorial bordelais,* and *Le Journal des économistes.*

COUSIN, VICTOR (1792–1867). Philosopher and politician who at the time of the restoration sided with the liberal Doctrinaire party. He was also the leader of a spiritualist school of thought (*l'école spiritualiste éclectique*).

CUSTINE, ASTOLPHE, marquis de (1790–1857). French aristocrat known mostly for his perceptive writings about his travels, most notably to Russia.

DAIRE, EUGENE (1798–1847). A tax collector who revived interest in the heritage of eighteenth- and early nineteenth-century free-market economics. He came to Paris in 1839, met Gilbert-Urbain Guillaumin, discovered the works of Jean-Baptiste Say, and began editing the fifteen-volume *Collection des principaux économistes* (1840–48). It included works on eighteenth-century finance, the physiocrats, Turgot, Adam Smith, Malthus, Jean-Baptiste Say, and Ricardo.

DAMPIERRE, ROGER DE (1813–96). Landowner from the Landes. An unsuccessful candidate in 1842 and 1846, he was elected deputy in 1848 and 1849.

DARBLAY, AIMÉ-STANISLAS (1794–1878). French industrialist, active in the grain trade. He introduced the cultivation of oil-producing plants into the Brie region and set up one of the first factories for the extraction of seed oil.

DAVID, FÉLICIEN (1810–76). Composer from Aix-en-Provence. He moved to Paris in 1830, where he came under the influence of the Saint-Simonians.

DECAZES, ELIE, duc de Glücksberg (1780–1860). Minister of the interior between 1815 and 1820. He was appointed prime minister in November 1819 but had to resign in 1820, following the murder of the duc de Berri, heir to the throne. However, Louis XVIII made him a peer and sent him to London as ambassador. In 1826 he created an important mining and metallurgical company modeled after those he had seen in Britain.

Decazes, Louis Charles, duc de Glücksberg (1819–86). Son of Elie Decazes. Diplomat and minister of foreign affairs under the Third Republic.

Delavigne, Casimir (1793–1843). French dramatist who was fashionable during his life but is largely forgotten today.

Destutt de Tracy, Antoine (1754–1836). Tracy was one of the leading intellectuals of the 1790s and early 1800s and a member of the ideologues (a philosophical movement not unlike the objectivists, who professed that the origin of ideas was material—not spiritual). In his writings on Montesquieu, Tracy defended the institutions of the American Republic, and in his writings on political economy he defended laissez-faire. During the French Revolution he joined the third estate and renounced his aristocratic title. During the Terror he was arrested and nearly executed. Tracy continued agitating for liberal reforms as a senator during Napoléon's regime. One of his most influential works was the four-volume *Éléments d'idéologie* (first published in 1801–15) (Tracy coined the term *ideology*). He also wrote *Commentaire sur l'ésprit des lois* (1819), which Thomas Jefferson translated and brought to the United States. In 1823 he published his *Traité d'économie politique,* much admired by Jefferson and Bastiat.

Dombasle, Joseph Alexandre Mathieu de (1777–1843). An agronomist, he wrote a number of works dealing with agriculture, especially the sugar-beet industry, including *De l'impôt sur le sucre indigène: Nouvelles considerations* (1837). Inspired by British agriculture, he introduced the practice of triennial crop rotation (cereals, forage, vegetables), which Bastiat tried in vain to carry out in his own sharecropping farms.

Domenger, Bernard (1785–1865). Mayor of Mugron (1834) and friend of Bastiat's.

Donato, Nicolò (1705–65). Venetian diplomat and author of *Uomo de Governo* (The Statesman), which was translated into French.

Droz, Joseph (1773–1850). Moral philosopher, economist, literary critic, and father-in-law of Michel Chevalier. Some of his notable publications include *Lois relatives au progrès de l'industrie* (1801); *Économie politique, ou, Principes de la science des richesses* (1829); and *Applications de la morale à la politique* (1825). He was appointed to the Académie française in 1813 and to the Académie des sciences morales et politiques in 1833.

Duchâtel, Charles Tanneguy (1803–67). Liberal writer, author of several books, and minister of the interior.

DUDON, J. F. (1778–1857). Magistrate and deputy. He served as minister of state in the last government of Charles X.

DUFAURE, ARMAND (1798–1881). A lawyer, he was elected deputy in 1834 and became minister of public works in 1839. Twice minister of the interior under the Second Republic, he resigned after the coup of Louis-Napoléon. He returned to politics in 1871 and became prime minister in 1876.

DUFFOUR-DUBERGIER, MARTIN (1797–1860). Mayor of Bordeaux and defender of liberal ideas.

DUMAS, JEAN-BAPTISTE ANDRÉ (1800–1884). Chemist, professor at the Sorbonne and at the École polytechnique, and minister of agriculture and commerce from 31 October 1849 to 9 January 1851.

DUNOYER, BARTHÉLÉMY-PIERRE-JOSEPH-CHARLES (1786–1862). Dunoyer was a journalist; an academic (a professor of political economy); a politician; the author of numerous works on politics, political economy, and history; a founding member of the Société d'économie politique (1842); and a key figure in the French classical liberal movement of the first half of the nineteenth century, along with Jean-Baptiste Say, Benjamin Constant, Charles Comte, Augustin Thierry, and Alexis de Tocqueville. He collaborated with Comte on the journals *Le Censeur* and *Le Censeur européen* during the end of the Napoleonic empire and the restoration of the Bourbon monarchy. Dunoyer (and Comte) combined the political liberalism of Constant (constitutional limits on the power of the state, representative government); the economic liberalism of Say (laissez-faire, free trade); and the sociological approach to history of Thierry, Constant, and Say (class analysis and a theory of historical evolution of society through stages culminating in the laissez-faire market society of "industry"). His major works include *L'Industrie et la morale considérées dans leurs rapports avec la liberté* (1825), *Nouveau traité d'économie sociale* (1830), and his three-volume magnum opus *De la liberté du travail* (1845). After the revolution of 1830 Dunoyer was appointed a member of the Académie des sciences morales et politiques, worked as a government official (he was prefect of L'Allier and La Somme), and eventually became a member of the Council of State in 1837. He resigned his government posts in protest against the coup d'état of Louis-Napoléon in 1851. He died while writing a critique of the authoritarian Second Empire; the work was completed and published by his son Anatole in 1864.

DUPÉRIER [first name and dates unknown]. A colleague of Bastiat's in the General Council of the Landes.

DUPIN, CHARLES (1784–1873). A deputy, an alumnus of the École polytechnique, a naval engineer, and a professor of mechanics at the Conservatoire national des arts et métiers (where he taught courses for working people). He is one of the founders of mathematical economics and of the statistical office (Bureau de France).

DUPRAT, PASCAL (1815–85). Deputy from the Landes.

DURRIEU, SIMON (1775–1862). A French general born in Saint-Sever and a deputy of the Landes (1834–45). He was raised to the peerage in 1845 by Louis-Philippe.

DUSSARD, HYPPOLITE (1791–1879). A journalist, essayist, and economist. He was manager of *Le Journal des économistes* from 1843 to 1845, a collaborator of *La Revue encyclopédique,* and prefect of La Seine-Inférieure after the 1848 revolution.

DUVAL [first name unknown] (1807–93). Magistrate who married the daughter of Jean-Baptiste Say in 1830. He was elected senator in 1871.

EICHTHAL, GUSTAVE, baron d' (1804–86). Member of the Saint-Simonian socialist group, which also included Olinde Rodriguez, Prosper Enfantin, Auguste Comte, and Michel Chevalier. There was some contact between Comte and Saint-Simon and the liberal group of Charles Comte (no relation), Charles Dunoyer, and Augustin Thierry in the 1820s. Both groups were interested in the impact that "industry" (*see* Note on the Translation, pp. xvi–xvii) would have on the progress of society. The socialist group believed the state could and should assist in the development of industry. The liberal group rejected that view.

ELLIOT, EBENEZER (1781–1849). Elliot was known as the "free-trade rhymer." He played an important role in the propaganda efforts of the Anti–Corn Law League. His ideas are reflected in his *Corn Law Rhymes* (1830) and *The Splendid Village* (1844). The following comes from *The Ranter* (1830). The "bread tax" is a reference to the corn laws:

> In haste she turns, and climbs the narrow stair,
> To wake her eldest born, but, pausing, stands
> Bent o'er his bed; for on his forehead bare,
> Like jewels ring'd on sleeping beauty's hands,
> Tired labour's gems are set in beaded bands;
> And none, none, none, like bread-tax'd labour know'th
> How more than grateful are his slumbers brief.
> Thou dost not know, thou pamper'd son of sloth!

Thou canst not tell, thou bread-tax-eating thief!
How sweet is rest to bread-tax'd toil and grief!

EVANS, WILLIAM [dates unknown]. Chairman of the Emancipation Society and one of the pallbearers at Richard Cobden's funeral.

FALLOUX DU COUDRAY, ALFRED PIERRE (1811–86). Deputy and minister of education (20 December 1848–31 October 1849). Author of a bill on freedom of education.

FAUCHER, LÉON (1803–54). Journalist, writer, and deputy for the Marne. He was twice appointed minister of the interior. During the July Monarchy he became an active journalist, writing for *Le Constitutionnel* and *Le Courrier français,* and was one of the editors of *La Revue des deux mondes* and *Le Journal des économistes.* Faucher was appointed to the Académie des sciences morales et politiques in 1849 and was active in the Association pour la liberté des échanges. He wrote on prison reform, gold and silver currency, socialism, and taxation. One of his better-known works was *Études sur l'Angleterre* (1856).

FAURIE, FRANÇOIS (1785–1854). Merchant from Bayonne. Elected deputy of Bayonne from 1831 to 1837, he then gave up all political activity after two election failures.

FEUTRIER, FRANÇOIS-JEAN-HYACINTHE (1785–1830). An ecclesiastic who, as minister of ecclesiastic affairs, took a deep interest in educational matters. He became bishop of Beauvais in 1826.

FIX, THEODORE (1800–1846). Swiss by birth, he came to France to work as a land surveyor and soon moved to Paris to work as a translator of German texts. After becoming interested in economics, he and Sismondi began in 1833 a short-lived journal, *La Revue mensuelle d'économie politique,* which lasted only three years. One of the notable aspects of Fix's works was his fluency in both German and English, which allowed him to write with authority for a French-speaking audience on the economics works published in those languages. In the course of his work Fix met many well-respected French political economists, such as Rossi and Blanqui; wrote several articles for *Le Journal des économistes;* and became the chief economics writer for the periodical *Le Constitutionnel.* Before he died at a young age from heart disease, he published one book, *Observations sur l'état des classes ouvrières* (1846).

FONTENAY, ANNE PAUL GABRIEL ROGER DE (1809–91). Economist and devoted disciple of Bastiat. He wrote the preface to the Guillaumin edition of Bastiat's works.

FONTEYRAUD, HENRI ALCIDE (1822–49). Fonteyraud was born in Mauritius and became professor of history, geography, and political economy at the École supérieure de commerce de Paris. He was a member of the Société d'économie politique and one of the founders of the Association pour la liberté des échanges. Because of his knowledge of English, he went to England in 1845 to study at first hand the progress of the Anti–Corn Law League. During the 1848 revolution he campaigned against socialist ideas with his activity in Le Club de la liberté du travail and, along with Bastiat, Coquelin, and Molinari, by writing and handing out in the streets of Paris copies of the broadside pamphlet *Jacques Bonhomme.* Sadly, he died very young during the cholera epidemic of 1849. He wrote articles in *La Revue britannique* and *Le Journal des économistes,* and he edited and annotated the works of Ricardo in the multivolume *Collection des principaux économistes.* His collected works were published posthumously as *Mélanges d'économie politique,* edited by J. Garnier (1853).

FORBES, CHARLES, comte de Montalembert (1810–70). Journalist and politician. He was the leader of the liberal Catholics.

FOURIER, FRANÇOIS-MARIE-CHARLES (1772–1837). Socialist and founder of the phalansterian school (Fourierism). Fourierism consisted of a utopian, communistic system for the reorganization of society. The population was to be grouped in "phalansteries" of about eighteen hundred persons, who would live together as one family and hold property in common.

FOX, WILLIAM JOHNSON (1786–1864). Journalist and renowned orator, one of the founders of the *Westminster Review.* He became one of the most popular speakers of the Anti–Corn Law League and delivered courses to the workers on Sunday evenings. He served in Parliament from 1847 to 1863.

FRAYSSINOUS, DENIS (1765–1841). A member of the French Academy and appointed a grand master (1822–24). He became minister of state education and religious worship (1824–28) under the French restoration.

GANNERON, AUGUSTE (1792–1842). Manufacturer, banker, and deputy of Paris.

GARNIER, JOSEPH (1813–81). Garnier was a professor, journalist, politician, and activist for free trade and peace. He traveled to Paris in 1830 and came under the influence of Adolphe Blanqui, who introduced him to economics and eventually became his father-in-law. Garnier was a pupil, professor, and then director of the École supérieure de commerce de Paris, before being appointed the first professor of political economy at the École des Ponts et caussées in 1846. Garnier played a central role in the burgeoning free-market school of thought in the 1840s in Paris. He was one of the founders of the Association pour la liberté des échanges and the chief editor of its journal, *Le Libre échange;* he also was active in the Congrès de la paix. A founder, along with Guillaumin, of *Le Journal des économistes,* he became chief editor in 1846. Additionally he was one of the founders of the Société d'économie politique, along with being its perpetual secretary, and he was one of the founders of the 1848 liberal broadsheet *Jacques Bonhomme.* Garnier was acknowledged for his considerable achievements by being nominated to join the Académie des sciences morales et politiques in 1873 and to become a senator in 1876. He authored numerous books and articles, including *Introduction à l'étude de l'économie politique* (1843), *Richard Cobden, les ligueurs et la ligue* (1846), and *Congrès des amis de la paix universelle réunis à Paris en 1849* (1850). He edited Malthus's *Essai sur le principe de population* (1845), *Du principe de population* (1857), and *Traité d'économie politique sociale ou industrielle* (1863).

GAUGUIER, JOSEPH (1793–1855). Industrialist and deputy (1831–42). He unsuccessfully proposed a parliamentary reform in 1832 and 1834.

GAY, J. B., comte de Martignac (1778–1832). Minister of the interior from 1828 to 1829.

GÉRARD, ETIENNE (1773–1852). Volunteer in the French revolutionary wars in 1792; appointed general in 1812 and field marshal in 1830. He was elected deputy in 1822 and served as prime minister (18 July–29 October 1834).

GIOBERTI, VINCENZO (1801–52). Italian philosopher and politician.

GIRARD, EDOUARD [dates unknown]. Brother of Mme (Hortense) Cheuvreux.

GIRARD, Mme [first name and dates unknown]. Mother of Mme (Hortense) Cheuvreux.

GLÜCKSBERG, duc de. *See* Decazes, Elie, *and* Decazes, Louis Charles.

GRIVEL, JEAN-BAPTISTE (1778–?). Vice admiral, nominated deputy peer of France in 1845 after a distinguished military career. Senator during the Second Empire.

GUILLAUMIN, GILBERT-URBAIN (1801–64). Orphaned at the age of five, Guillaumin was brought up by his uncle. He arrived in Paris in 1819 and worked in a bookstore before eventually founding his own publishing firm in 1835. He was active in liberal politics during the 1830 revolution and made contact with the economists Adolphe Blanqui and Joseph Garnier. In 1835 he became a publisher in order to popularize and promote classical liberal economic ideas, and the firm of Guillaumin eventually became the major publishing house for liberal ideas in the mid-nineteenth century. Guillaumin helped found *Le Journal des économistes* in 1841 with Horace Say (Jean-Baptiste's son) and Joseph Garnier. The following year he helped found the Société d'économie politique. His firm published scores of books on economic issues, making its catalog a virtual who's who of the liberal movement in France; it included works by Bastiat. Guillaumin also published the following key journals, collections, and encyclopedias: *Journal des économistes* (1842–1940), *L'Annuaire de l'économie politique* (1844–99), the multivolume *Collection des principaux économistes* (1840–48), *Bibliothèques des sciences morales et politiques* (1857–), *Dictionnaire d'économie politique* (1852) (coedited with Charles Coquelin), and *Dictionnaire universel théorique et practique du commerce et de la navigation* (1859–61).

GUINARD, AUGUSTE (1799–1874). Political agitator for the republican cause. Elected deputy in 1848 but not in 1849.

GUIZOT, FRANÇOIS (1787–1874). A successful academic and politician whose career spanned many decades, he was born to a Protestant family in Nîmes. His father was guillotined during the Terror. As a law student in Paris, the young Guizot was a vocal opponent of the Napoleonic empire. After the restoration of the monarchy Guizot was part of the "doctrinaires," a group of conservative and moderate liberals. He was professor of history at the Sorbonne from 1812 to 1830, publishing *Essai sur l'histoire de France* (1824), *Histoire de la revolution d'Angleterre* (1826–27), *Histoire générale de la civilisation en Europe* (1828), and *Histoire de la civilisation en France* (1829–32). In 1829 he was elected deputy and became very active in French politics after the 1830 revolution, supporting constitutional monarchy and a limited franchise. He served as minister of the interior, minister of education (1832–37), ambassador to England in 1840, and then foreign minister and prime minister, becoming in practice the leader of the government from 1840 to 1848. He promoted peace abroad and liberal conservatism at home, but his regime, weakened by corruption and economic difficulties, collapsed with the monarchy in 1848. He retired to Normandy to spend the rest of his days writing history and his memoires such as *Histoire parlementaire de France* (1863–64) and *Histoire des origines du gouvernement représentif en Europe* (1851).

HALÉVY, JACQUES (1799–1862). Parisian composer, mostly of opera and ballet.

HARCOURT, FRANÇOIS-EUGÈNE, duc d' (1786–1865). Liberal politician, president of the Association pour la liberté des échanges in Brussels in

1841, and ambassador to Rome. He wrote *Discours en faveur de la liberté du commerce* (1846).

HAUSSEZ, CHARLES D' (1771–1854). Prefect, counsellor of state, and deputy. He became minister of the navy in August 1829.

HICKIN, JOSEPH. Secretary of the Anti–Corn Law League.

HUMANN, GEORGES (1780–1842). Businessman and liberal politician. Twice minister of finance.

HUSKISSON, WILLIAM (1770–1830). President of the Board of Trade (1823–27). He reformed the Navigation Act, reduced duties on manufactured goods, and repealed some quarantine duties.

JOBARD, JEAN-BAPTISTE-AMBROISE-MARCELLIN (1792–1861). He wrote *Nouvelle économie sociale* and coined the phrase *Le Monautopole* (meaning "monopoly of oneself"), which referred to the natural right of an inventor to be the sole disposer of his or her own work.

JOINVILLE, FRANÇOIS-FERDINAND-PHILIPPE-LOUIS-MARIE D'ORLÉANS, prince de (1818–1900). A son of Louis-Philippe.

JOUY, VICTOR ETIENNE DE (1764–1846). French playwright and author of librettos.

KNATCHBULL, SIR EDWARD (1781–1849). Member of Parliament for the county of Kent and author of *The Speech of Sir E. Knatchbull* (1829).

LACAVE-LAPLAGNE, JEAN-PIERRE (1795–1849). French politician and deputy from 1834 to 1849. Minister of finance from 1837 to 1839 and again from 1842 to 1847.

LAFARELLE, FÉLIX DE (1800–1872). French lawyer and economist. He was deputy of La Garde de 1842 in the revolution of 1848 and correspondent of the Académie des sciences morales et politiques in 1846. He was author of *Du progrès social au profit des classes populaires nonindigentes* (1847).

LA FAYETTE, MARIE JOSEPH, marquis de (1757–1834). A French aristocrat, he was a general in the American War of Independence. After the war La Fayette returned to France and played an important role in the early phases of the French Revolution. He served in the Estates General, and later the National Constituent Assembly. He attempted to guide the Revolution along a more moderate course, joining the Feuillants, who wanted France to become a constitutional monarchy. Ultimately, overwhelmed by the excesses of the Terror, he fled France in 1792 and was considered a traitor for his efforts to save the constitutional monarchy. Imprisoned in Prussia for five years as a "revolutionary," he returned to France and lived in semiretirement on an estate belonging to his wife. Elected deputy in 1818, he reentered the political scene to fight for individual liberties.

Laffitte, Jacques (1767–1844). Born in Bayonne. Banker, entrepreneur, and friend of the Bastiat family. He was elected deputy in 1816 and served as prime minister from 1831 until March 1832.

Lamarque, Jean-Maxilien (1770–1832). French general under Napoléon. Exiled in 1815 for three years, he translated the ten-thousand-odd verses of the *Ossian Poems,* by James Macpherson, into French. In the Landes, he showed a great interest in agricultural methods and in means of communication. He was elected deputy of the Landes in 1828 and 1830. In parliament, he was an influential speaker. He died of cholera in Paris and was given a national funeral, during which a popular uprising against the monarchy was repressed by General Lobau. The event is described by Victor Hugo in *Les Misérables.*

Lamartine, Alphonse de (1790–1869). Poet and statesman. As an immensely popular romantic poet, he used his talent to promote liberal ideas. He was a member of the provisional government and minister of foreign affairs in June 1848. After he lost the presidential election of December 1848 to Louis-Napoléon, he retired from political life and returned to writing.

Lamennais, Félicité, abbé de (1782–1854). Priest, deputy, and journalist; known for his four-volume *Essai sur l'indifférence en matière de religion* (1821–23). Lamennais was a strong critic of the Gallican Church and an ardent defender of the pope. By 1832, he resented the lack of encouragement from the Vatican in the face of violent attacks from Gallicanism and progressively distanced himself from Rome. He became active in journalism and, like Bastiat, was elected to the legislative assembly of 1848.

Larnac, Marie Gustave (1793–1868). Tutor to Louis-Philippe's son, the duc de Nemours. Larnac later became the duke's secrétaire des commandements (head of the private cabinet). As the candidate sponsored by the government, Larnac was elected deputy of the district of Saint-Sever in 1845 and reelected in 1846, defeating Bastiat. He gave up political life after the revolution of 1848.

Laromiguière, Pierre (1756–1837). Member of the doctrinaires (*see* Guizot, François). He taught humanities and philosophy while pursuing medical studies. His Ph.D. dissertation on property rights and taxation,

"Le Droit de propriété est violé toutes les fois que les impôts sont levés arbitrairement," was a criticism of the ancien régime. He left the clergy in 1792 to become professor of philosophy at the Sorbonne. His *Leçons de philosophie; ou, Essai sur les facultés de l'âme* (1815), which had six consecutive editions between 1815 and 1844, greatly influenced Bastiat as well as generations of students.

LATOUR-MAUBOURG, Mme de [first name and dates not known]. Wife of Victor Nicolas de Fay, vicomte de Latour-Maubourg (1768–1850) and former minister of war.

LAURENCE, A. M. Colleague of Bastiat's in the General Council of the Landes.

LEDRU-ROLLIN, ALEXANDRE (1790–1874). Lawyer, deputy (1841–49), owner of the newspaper *La Réforme,* minister of the interior of the provisional government of February 1848, and then member of the executive commission. He had to yield his powers to General Cavaignac in June 1848. In 1849 Ledru-Rollin organized a demonstration against the foreign policy of Louis-Napoléon, the new president of the republic. He was exiled and came back to France only in 1870.

LEFRANC, VICTOR (1809–83). Lawyer and deputy from the Landes.

LEOPOLD I (1790–1865), king of Belgium (1831–65). He was elected king by the Belgian National Congress.

LEROUX, PIERRE (1798–1871). Prominent member of the Saint-Simonian group of socialists. Like Bastiat, he was a journalist during the 1840s and was elected to the Constituent Assembly in 1848 and to the Legislative Assembly in 1849. His most developed exposition of his ideas can be found in *De l'humanité* (1840) and also in *De la ploutocratie, ou, Du gouvernement des riches* (1848).

LHERBETTE, ARMAND (1791–1864). Lawyer and attorney of the king. Elected deputy in 1831.

LOBEAU [LOBAU], GEORGES MOUTON, comte de (1770–1838). Bastiat's spelling is wrong; the correct spelling is "Lobau." Volunteer in 1792, general in 1805. Elected liberal deputy in 1828. Nominated Maréchal de France by Louis-Philippe in 1831. Lobau repressed the uprising that followed the funeral of Jean-Maxilien Lamarque.

LOUIS, JOSEPH-DOMINIQUE, baron (1755–1837). Politician and diplomat. He was minister of finance under the two restorations and the July Monarchy and made a peer of France in 1832.

Louis-Philippe, duc d'Orléans (1773–1850). Louis-Philippe was the last French king during the July Monarchy (1830–48), abdicating on 24 February 1848. He served in the French army before going into exile in 1793. His exile lasted until 1815, when he was able to return to France under the restoration of the monarchy (King Louis XVIII was his cousin). During his exile he visited Switzerland, Scandinavia, the United States, and Cuba before settling in England. When the July revolution overthrew King Charles X in 1830, Louis-Philippe was proclaimed the new "king of the French." Initially, he enjoyed considerable support from the middle class for his liberal policies, but he became increasingly conservative and was ousted in the February 1848 revolution.

Malthus, Thomas Robert (1766–1858). Malthus is best known for his writings on population, in which he asserted that population growth (increasing at a geometric rate) would outstrip the growth in food production (growing at a slower arithmetic rate). Malthus studied at Jesus College, Cambridge, before becoming a professor of political economy at the East India Company College (Haileybury). His ideas were influential among nineteenth-century political economists. His principal work was *An Essay on the Principle of Population* (1st ed., 1798; rev. 3rd ed., 1826).

Manuel, Jacques Antoine (1775–1827). Liberal deputy (1815–27) in the Chamber that followed Napoléon's abdication. Manuel formed an alliance with Constant and La Fayette.

Marmont, Auguste de (1774–1852). Appointed field marshall and duke of Ragusa by Napoléon, whom he betrayed. His defection in 1814 made Napoléon's abdication inevitable.

Marsan, Julie [dates unknown]. Daughter of Marie-Julienne Marsan (née Badbedat). *See* Badbedat, Marie-Julienne.

Mauguin, François (1785–1852). Lawyer and deputy (1848 and 1849).

Mendizabal, Juan (1790–1853). Prime minister (13 June 1835–15 March 1836), later minister of finance of Spain.

Mignet, François-Auguste-Alexis (1796–1884). Liberal lawyer, journalist, historian, and an editor of *Le Courrier français* and *Le National* (edited by Mignet, Thiers, Carrel, and Passy). In 1830 he joined other journalists in protesting the restrictive press laws. He secured a job as director of the Archives of the Foreign Ministry, from which position he was able to publish many historical works. He lost his job as a result of the 1848 revolution and took early retirement to continue writing works of history. He became a member of the Académie des sciences morales et politiques in 1832, assuming the post of permanent secretary in 1837, and became a member of the Académie française in 1836. His main works were *Histoire de la Révolution française* (1824), *Histoire de Marie Stuart* (1852), and *Notices et mémoires historiques* (1843), which contains many eulogies of important political economists and historians.

MILL, JOHN STUART (1806–73). English philosopher, political theorist, and economist who became one of the most influential thinkers of the nineteenth century. He worked for the East India Company before becoming a member of the British Parliament (1865–68), where he introduced many proposals for reform legislation, such as women's suffrage. Mill went to France in 1820 and met many of the leading liberal figures of the day, such as Jean-Baptiste Say. He had a great interest in French politics and history and wrote many essays and reviews on these topics. His best-known books include *System of Deductive and Inductive Logic* (1843), *Principles of Political Economy* (1848), *On Liberty* (1859), *Utilitarianism* (1861), and *The Subjection of Women* (1869).

MILLEVOYE, CHARLES HUBERT (1782–1816). French poet, author of the poem *The Fall of the Leaves.*

MOLÉ, LOUIS MATHIEU, comte de (1781–1855). Former prefect and minister of justice under Napoléon and under Louis XVIII. Rallying to Louis-Philippe, he was head of the government and minister of foreign affairs in 1836. Accused by some deputies of being little more than a spokesman for the king, he resigned in 1839 and led a moderate opposition against Guizot. He served as deputy in 1848 and 1849 but quit political life after the coup of 1851.

MOLESWORTH, WILLIAM, Sir (1810–55). British politician and member of the Anti–Corn Law League.

MOLINARI, GUSTAVE DE (1819–1912). Born in Belgium but spent most of his working life in Paris, where he became the leading representative of the laissez-faire school of classical liberalism in France in the second half of the nineteenth century. His liberalism was based on the theory of natural rights (especially the right to property and individual liberty), and he advocated complete laissez-faire in economic policy and an ultraminimal state in politics. In the 1840s he joined the Société d'économie politique and was active in the Association pour la liberté des échanges. During the 1848 revolution he vigorously opposed the rise of socialism and published shortly thereafter two rigorous defenses of individual liberty in which he pushed to its ultimate limits his opposition to all state intervention in the economy, including the state's monopoly of security. During the

1850s he contributed a number of significant articles on free trade, peace, colonization, and slavery to the *Dictionnaire de l'économie politique* (1852–53) before going into exile in his native Belgium to escape the authoritarian regime of Napoléon III. He became a professor of political economy at the Musée royale de l'industrie belge and published a significant treatise on political economy (*Cours d'économie politique,* 1855) and a number of articles opposing state education. In the 1860s Molinari returned to Paris to work on the *Journal des débats,* becoming editor from 1871 to 1876. Toward the end of his long life, Molinari was appointed editor of the leading journal of political economy in France, *Le Journal des économistes* (1881–1909). Molinari's more important works include *Les Soirées de la rue Saint-Lazare* (1849), *L'Évolution économique du dix-neuvième siècle: Théorie du progrès* (1880), and *L'Évolution politique et la révolution* (1884).

MONCLAR, EUGÈNE DE (1800–1882). Priest and first cousin of Bastiat. Like Bastiat, he worked in the family commercial firm, which he left to study law. Shortly after becoming a lawyer, he studied for the priesthood. Once ordained, he became a member of the Company of Priests of Saint-Suplice, devoted to the education of ecclesiastics, and taught in different cities. He traveled to Italy and while in Naples learned that his cousin Bastiat was in Rome and was able to be with him in his final hours.

MONJEAN, MAURICE (1818–?). A member of the editorial board of *Le Journal des économistes* from 1841 to 1845. He also edited Malthus's *Principles of Population* and *Definitions of Political Economy* in the series *Collection des principaux économistes* (1846).

O'CONNELL, DANIEL (1775–1847). Irish campaigner, member of Parliament, mayor of Dublin.

ODIER, ANTOINE (1766–1853). Businessman, deputy (1827–37), then *pair de France* (a peer of the realm). Member of the liberal opposition. Father-in-law of General Cavaignac.

ORLÉANS, DUC D'. *See* Louis-Philippe.

ORTOLAN, JOSEPH (1802–73). Professor of law.

PAILLOTTET, PROSPER. Political writer and the editor, friend, and legal executor of Bastiat. (See also the General Editor's Note and the General Introduction.)

PALMERSTON, HENRY JOHN TEMPLE, third viscount (1784–1865). Whig leader and minister of foreign affairs (1830–41 and 1846–50). Palmerston was prime minister of Britain during the Crimean War and a liberal interventionist. He worked to limit French influence in world affairs.

PASSY, FRÉDÉRIC (1822–1912). Nephew of Hippolyte Passy. He was a supporter of free trade and the ideas of Richard Cobden and Bastiat. Passy was a cabinet minister and then professor of political economy at the University of Montpellier in France. He wrote an introduction to one of the Guillaumin editions of the works of Bastiat. Active in the French peace movement, he helped found the Ligue internationale et permanente de la paix. For his efforts he received the first Nobel Peace Prize (1901, with Henri Dunant, one of the founders of the Red Cross). He wrote many books on economics and peace, including *Notice biographique sur Frédéric Bastiat* (1857), *Pour la paix: notes et documents* (1909), and *La Démocratie et l'instruction: Discours d'ouverture des cours publics de Nice.*

PASSY, HIPPOLYTE (1793–1880). Cavalry officer in Napoléon's army and French economist. After the restoration of the monarchy, Passy traveled to the United States and there discovered the works of Adam Smith. Upon his return to France, he wrote for several opposition papers, such as the liberal *National* (with Adolphe Thiers and François-Auguste Mignet), and published a book, *De l'aristocracie considérée dans ses rapports avec les progrès de la civilization* (1826). Passy was elected as a deputy from 1830 on, serving as minister of finance in 1834, 1839–40, and 1848–49. In 1838 he became a member of the Académie des sciences morales et politiques, in which he served for some forty years, and was particularly active in developing political economy. He criticized the colonization of Algeria and advocated free trade. He cofounded the Société d'économie politique (1842), wrote numerous articles in *Le Journal des économistes,* and authored several books, including *Des systèmes de culture et de leur influence sur l'économie sociale* (1848) and *Des causes de l'inégalité des richesses* (1848).

PAULTON, ABRAHAM. Free-trade lecturer and radical journalist recruited by Richard Cobden for the Anti–Corn Law League.

PAVÉE DE VANDŒUVRE, baron de (1808–?). Minister of Louis XVIII and president of the General Council of the *département* of l'Aube. Peer of France.

PEEL, SIR ROBERT (1788–1850). Leader of the Tories and former minister in the government of the Duke of Wellington. In 1841 he became prime minister and took measures aimed at alleviating the most severe poverty, thus giving some satisfaction to the free traders while at the same time trying to broaden the outlook of the aristocracy. He accomplished the repeal of the Corn Laws on 26 May 1846 by obtaining a composite majority, but not without adverse consequences. The Tory Party was irreparably divided, and on that same evening, Peel lost a vote of confidence on his Irish policy and had to resign.

PERGOLESI, GIOVANNI BATTISTA (1710–36). Neapolitan composer.

PÉRIER, CASIMIR (1777–1832). French entrepreneur, deputy, and influential member of the liberal opposition. Prime minister from March 1831 until his death.

PETITTI, CARLO ILARIONE, conte di Roreto (1790–1850). Italian economist, academic, counsellor of state, and senator. Petitti wrote numerous works, including *Saggio sul buon governo della mendicità, degli istituti di beneficenza e delle carceri* (1837), *Delle strade ferrate italiane e del miglior ordinamento di esse: Cinque discorsi* Capolago (1845), and *Considerazioni sopra la necessità di una riforma de' tributi con alcuni cenni su certe spese dello Stato* (1850).

PEUPIN, HENRI (1809–72). French clockmaker. Wrote liberal articles in workers' magazines.

PITT, WILLIAM (the Younger) (1759–1806). British politician. Son of prime minister William Pitt the Elder, he was himself twice prime minister (1783–1801 and 1804–6). A Tory and a strong opponent of the French Revolution.

PIUS IX (Cardinal Giovanni Ferretti) (1792–1878). Pope from 1846 to 1878. He started out as a liberal but became more conservative after the 1848 revolution. He took refuge in Gaeta, in the kingdom of Naples, for a brief time in 1848 and lost the papal states permanently to Italy in 1870.

POLIGNAC, AUGUSTE-JULES-ARMAND-MARIE, prince de (1780–1847). Childhood friend, then prime minister, of Charles X. Polignac was an ultraroyalist politician who served in various capacities during the restoration of the Bourbon monarchy after 1815. He was appointed ambassador to England in 1823, minister of foreign affairs in 1829, and prime minister by Charles X just prior to the outbreak of the July revolution in 1830. He was responsible for issuing the Four Ordinances (designed to weaken the constitution), which was the immediate trigger for the outbreak of the revolution. After the revolution he was imprisoned at Ham, amnestied in 1836, and finally exiled from the country. During his imprisonment he wrote *Considérations politiques sur l'époque actuelle* (1832).

PRINCE-SMITH, JOHN (1809–74). Liberal economist, born in London, where he worked as a parliamentary reporter before moving to Hamburg in 1828 to write for an English-language newspaper there. He was an ardent supporter of Bastiat. In 1831 he was employed as an English teacher at a local gymnasium. While in Hamburg Prince-Smith discovered economics and began writing about British economic developments for his German readers. In 1846 he settled in Berlin, where he published *John Prince-Smith über die englische Tarifreform und ihre materiellen, sozialen und politischen Folgen für Europa,* a small book on tariff reform in Britain and its likely impact on Europe, a work that reflected his interest in Cobden, Bastiat, and the Anti–Corn Law League. He also published works on banking and currency issues. In 1846 he founded a German free-trade association and was elected deputy representing Stettin in the Prussian parliament. Between 1870 and 1874 he was head of the Congress of German Economists. His collected works, published shortly after his death, were titled *John Prince-Smith's Gesammelte Schriften* (1877–80).

PROUDHON, PIERRE JOSEPH (1809–65). French political theorist, considered to be the father of anarchism. Proudhon spent many years as a printer and published numerous pamphlets on social and economic issues, often running afoul of the censors. He was elected to the Constituent Assembly in 1848 representing La Seine. In 1848 he became editor in chief of several periodicals, such as *Le Peuple* and *La Voix du peuple,* in which he wrote articles critical of the government. These views got him into trouble again with the censors, for which he spent three years in prison, between 1849 and 1852. He is best known for *Qu'est-ce que la propriété? Ou recherches sur le principe du droit et du gouvernement* (1841), *Système des contradictions économiques* (1846), and several articles published in *Le Journal des économistes.* His controversy with Bastiat on the subject of capital and interest appears in the form of letters between Bastiat and Proudhon (*OC,* vol. 5, p. 94, "Gratuité du crédit").

PUYRAVAULT, AUDRY DE (1773–1852). French businessman and deputy (1822–37).

QUESNAY, FRANÇOIS (1694–1774). Surgeon and economist. He taught at the Paris School of Surgery and was personal doctor to Madame Pompadour. As an economist he is best known as one of the founders of the physiocratic school, writing the articles "Fermiers" and "Grains" for Diderot's *Encylopédie* (1756). Quesnay also wrote *Le Tableau économique* (1762) and *Physiocratie, ou constitution naturelle de gouvernement le plus avantageux au genre humain* (1768).

QUIJANO, GARCIA. Member of the Société d'économie politique and occasional contributor to *Le Journal des économistes.*

RASPAIL, FRANÇOIS (1794–1878). A self-taught French botanist, chemist, and hygienist who made major contributions to cell theory and pioneered the use of the microscope in the study of cell tissue. He turned to radical politics after the 1830 revolution and was jailed for his role as president of the Society of the Rights of Man. During the 1848 revolution he was imprisoned for participating in the demonstration of 15 May 1848 but was later released from prison by Napoléon III only to spend the years until 1863 in foreign exile. Raspail unsuccessfully stood for president in the 1848 election. He was elected a deputy from Lyon in 1869. During the Third Republic he was an outspoken and popular republican deputy.

RENOUARD, AUGUSTIN-CHARLES (1794–1878). French lawyer with an interest in elementary school education. He was secretary general of the minister of justice and an elected deputy. He also was vice-president of the Société d'économie politique and wrote or edited a number of works on economic and educational matters, including *Mélanges de morale, d'économie et de politique extraits des ouvrages de Franklin, et précédés d'une notice sur sa vie* (1824); and "L'Éducation doit-elle être libre?" in *Revue encyclopédique* (1828).

REYBAUD, LOUIS (1798–1879). French businessman, journalist, novelist, fervent antisocialist, politician, and writer on economic and social issues. In 1846 he was elected deputy representing Marseilles, but his strong opposition to Napoléon III and the empire forced him to retire to devote himself to political economy. He became a member of the Académie des sciences morales et politiques in 1850. His writings include the prizewinning critique of socialists, *Études sur les réformateurs et socialistes modernes: Saint-Simon, Charles Fourier, Robert Owen* (1840); the satirical novel *Jérôme Paturot à la recherché d'une position sociale* (1843); and *Économistes contemporains* (1861). Reybaud also wrote many articles for *Le Journal des économistes* and the *Dictionnaire de l'économie politique* (1852).

RICARDO, DAVID (1772–1823). English political economist, born in London of Dutch-Jewish parents. Ricardo joined his father's stockbroking business at a young age and made a considerable fortune on the London Stock Exchange. In 1799 he read Adam Smith's *Wealth of Nations* (1776) and developed an interest in economic theory. He met James Mill and the Philosophic Radicals in 1807, was elected to Parliament in 1819, and was active politically in trying to widen the franchise and to abolish the restrictive Corn Laws. He wrote a number of works, including *The High Price of Bullion* (1810), on the bullion controversy; and the treatise *On the Principles of Political Economy and Taxation* (1817).

RIDOLFI, COSIMO (1794–1865). Descendant of a very wealthy and learned Florentine family who distinguished himself in chemistry and agronomy. In 1841 he chaired the Congress of Italian Scientists, which took place in Florence.

ROSSI, PELLEGRINO (1787–1848). Italian politician. Born in Tuscany, Rossi lived in Geneva, Paris, and Rome. He was a professor of law and political economy, as well as a poet, ending his days as a diplomat for the French government. He moved to Switzerland after the defeat of Napoléon, where he met Germaine de Staël and the duc de Broglie. He founded, with Sismondi and Etienne Dumont, *Les Annales de législation et des jurisprudences*. After the death of Jean-Baptiste Say, Rossi was appointed professor of political economy at the Collège de France in 1833, and in 1836 he became a member of the Académie des sciences morales et politiques. In 1847 he was appointed ambassador of France to the Vatican but was assassinated in 1848 in Rome. He wrote *Cours d'économie politique* (1840) and numerous articles in *Le Journal des économistes*.

RUMILLY, LOUIS GAUTHIER DE (1792–1884). French lawyer and deputy (1830–34 and 1837–40). Unsuccessfully presented a project for parliamentary reform in 1840.

RUSSELL, JOHN, first Earl Russell (1792–1878). English Whig and liberal member of Parliament. He was prime minister twice, in 1846–52 and in 1865–66. As leader of the opposition in 1845, Russell favored the repeal of the Corn Laws and advised the prime minister, Sir Robert Peel, to take a similar stance.

SAINT-CHAMANS, AUGUSTE, vicomte de (1777–1860). Deputy (1824–27) and mercantilist economist.

SAINT-CRICQ, PIERRE DE (1772–1854). French politician, deputy, general manager of customs, and president of the Trade Council. Favorable to protectionism.

SAINT-HILAIRE, JULES BARTHÉLEMY (1805–95). French businessman, journalist, and writer. Professor of Greek and Latin philosophy at the Collège de France. Elected senator for life in 1875.

SALVANDY, NARCISSE ACHILLE DE (1795–1856). Former soldier of Napoléon, he became active in politics from 1830. He was the French ambassador in Madrid and Turin and author of novels and political writings.

SAY, HORACE ÉMILE (1794–1860). Son of Jean-Baptiste Say. Married Anne Cheuvreux, sister of Casimir Cheuvreux, whose family were friends of Bastiat's. Say was a businessman and traveled in 1813 to the United States and Brazil. A result of his trip was *Histoire des relations commerciales entre la France et le Brésil* (1839). He became president of the Chamber of Commerce of Paris in 1834, was a counsellor of state (1849–51), and headed an important inquiry into the state of industry in the Paris region (1848–51). Say was also very active in liberal circles: he participated in the foundation of the Société d'économie politique, the Guillaumin publishing firm, *Le Journal des économistes,* and *Le Journal du commerce;* and he was an important collaborator in the creation of the *Dictionnaire de l'économie politique* and the *Dictionnaire du commerce et des marchandises.* In 1857 he was nominated to the Académie des sciences morales et politiques but died before he could formally join.

SAY, JEAN-BAPTISTE (1767–1832). The leading French political economist in the first third of the nineteenth century. Before becoming an academic political economist late in life, Say apprenticed in a commercial office, working for a life insurance company; he also worked as a journalist, soldier, politician, cotton manufacturer, and writer. During the Revolution he worked on the journal of the idéologues, *La Décade philosophique, littéraire, et politique,* for which he wrote articles on political economy from 1794 to 1799. In 1814 he was asked by the government to travel to England on a fact-finding mission to discover the secret of English economic growth and to report on the impact of the revolutionary wars on the British economy. His book *De l'Angleterre et des Anglais* (1815) was the result. After the defeat of Napoléon and the restoration of the Bourbon monarchy, Say was appointed to teach economics in Paris, first at the Athénée, then as a chair in "industrial economics" at the Conservatoire national des arts et métiers, and finally as the first chair in political economy at the Collège de France. He is best known for his *Traité d'économie politique* (1803), which went through many editions (and revisions) during his lifetime. One of his last major works, the *Cours complet d'économie politique pratique* (1828–33), was an attempt to broaden the scope of political economy away from the preoccupation with the production of wealth, by examining the moral, political, and sociological requirements of a free society and how they interrelated with the study of political economy.

SAY, LÉON (1826–96). Grandson of Jean-Baptiste Say and son of Horace Say. He had a career as a banker and administrator of the Chemin de fer du nord. Say wrote a number of articles for *Le Journal des débats* and was a prominent popularizer of free trade and other economic issues. After 1871 he had a distinguished political career as a deputy for La Seine and then as minister of finance in the Third Republic, where he pursued policies of reducing taxation, deregulating internal trade, and opposing the Méline Tariff. In 1880 he was appointed ambassador to England. Say was elected to the Académie

des sciences morales et politiques and also to the Académie française. He
was a key editor of and contributor to the *Nouveau dictionnaire d'économie
politique* (1891–92). Many of his writings on finance can be found in *Les
Finances de la France sous la troisième république* (1898–1901).

SCHWABE. The Schwabes were English friends of the Cheuvreux family
and of Bastiat. Their daughter, Mrs. Salis-Schwabe, a writer, was married
to a Frenchman. She wrote *Richard Cobden: Notes sur ses voyages,
correspondences, et souvenirs* (1879).

SCIALOJA, ANTONIO (1817–77). Italian economist and professor of political
economy at the University of Turin. He was imprisoned and exiled during
the 1848 revolution. His major economic works were *I principi della
economia sociale esposti in ordine ideologico* (1840), later translated into
French as *Les Principes de l'économie exposé selon des idées* (1844); *Trattato
elementare di economia sociale* (1848); and *Lezioni di economia politica*
(1846–54). He also wrote many works on law.

SCRIBE, EUGÈNE (1791–1861). French dramatist and author of opera libretti.

SENIOR, NASSAU WILLIAM (1790–1864). British economist who became
a professor of political economy at Oxford University in 1826. In 1832
he was asked to investigate the condition of the poor and, with Edwin
Chadwick, wrote the *Poor Law Commissioners' Report* of 1834. In 1843 he
was appointed a correspondent of the Institut de France. He returned to
Oxford University in 1847. During his lifetime he wrote many articles for
such review journals as the *Quarterly Review,* the *Edinburgh Review,* and
the *London Review.* His books include *Lectures on Political Economy* (1826)
and *Outline of the Science of Political Economy* (1834).

SIMON, RICHARD (1638–1712). Oratorian monk. In 1678 he published *Une
Histoire critique de l'Ancien Testament,* which was condemned by the
French bishop Bossuet and destroyed. He was excluded from his order.

SMITH, ADAM (1723–90). Scottish moral philosopher and a leading figure
in the Scottish Enlightenment. He was one of the founders of modern
economic thought with his work *The Wealth of Nations* (1776). Smith
studied at the University of Glasgow where one of his teachers was the
philosopher Francis Hutcheson. In the late 1740s Smith lectured at the
University of Edinburgh on rhetoric, belles-lettres, and jurisprudence;
those lectures are available to us because of detailed notes taken by one
of his students. In 1751 he moved to Glasgow, where he was a professor
of logic and then moral philosophy. His *Theory of Moral Sentiments*
(1759, translated into French in 1774) was a product of this period of his

life. Between 1764 and 1766 he traveled to France as tutor to the Duke of Buccleuch. While in France, Smith met many of the physiocrats and visited Voltaire in Geneva. As a result of a generous pension from the duke, Smith was able to retire to Kirkaldy to work on his magnum opus, *The Wealth of Nations,* which appeared in 1776 (French edition in 1788). Smith was appointed in 1778 as commissioner of customs and was based in Edinburgh, where he spent the remainder of his life. An important French edition of the *Wealth of Nations* was published in 1843 by Gilbert-Urbain Guillaumin, with notes and commentary by leading French economists such as Blanqui, Garnier, Sismondi, and Say.

SMITH, JOHN BENJAMIN (d. 1879). Member of the Manchester Chamber of Commerce and a supporter of the Anti–Corn Law League.

SOULT, NICOLAS, duc de Dalmatie (1769–1851). Field marshall under Napoléon. After the empire fell, he went into business and then into politics during the July Monarchy. He was minister of war and thrice prime minister.

SOUSTRA [first name and dates unknown]. Member of the Bayonne city council.

STAËL, ANNE-LOUISE-GERMAINE DE (1766–1817). Née Germaine Necker, the daughter of the Swiss-born financier Jacques Necker, who served as controller-general under Louis XVI from 1776 to 1781 and again from 1788 to July 1789. She married the Baron de Staël-Holstein (1766–1817). Staël is best known today as a writer of novels, such as *Corinne, ou l'Itale* (1807), and for her analysis of German literature and character in *De l'Allemagne* (suppressed by Napoléon so that it did not appear until 1813). She also played an important role in developing a liberal movement around the exiles and enemies of Napoléon, first in a salon in Paris and then at her residence, Coppet, on the shores of Lake Geneva. In 1794 she started a long-lasting though stormy liaison with Benjamin Constant. Her book *Considérations sur les principaux événements de la Révolution française* (1818) was one of the first major histories of the French Revolution and the economic policies of her father, whose attempts to reform French finances on the eve of the Revolution failed.

STANHOPE, PHILIP, Earl of Chesterfield (1694–1773). English aristocrat, politician, and writer. Member of the Commons (1718–26) and later a member of the House of Lords. His *Letters Written by the Late Right Honourable Philip Dormer Stanhope, Earl of Chesterfield, to His Son* (1774) was translated into French in 1877, long after Bastiat's death.

THIERS, ADOLPHE (1797–1877). French lawyer, historian, politician, and journalist. While Thiers was a lawyer he contributed articles to the liberal journal *Le Constitutionnel* and published one of his most famous works, the ten-volume *Histoire de la révolution française* (1823–27). He was instrumental in supporting Louis-Philippe in July 1830 and was the main opponent of Guizot. Thiers defended the idea of a constitutional monarchy in journals like *Le National*. After 1813 he became successively a deputy, undersecretary of state, minister of agriculture, and minister of the interior. He was briefly prime minister and minister of foreign affairs in 1836 and 1840, when he resisted democratization and promoted restrictions on the freedom of the press. During the 1840s he worked on the twenty-volume *Histoire de consulat et de l'empire,* which appeared between 1845 and 1862. After the 1848 revolution and the creation of the Second Empire he was elected deputy representing Rouen in the Constituent Assembly. Thiers was a strong opponent of Napoléon III's foreign policies and after his defeat was appointed head of the provisional government by the National Assembly. He then became president of the Third Republic until 1873. Thiers wrote essays on economic matters for *Le Journal des économistes,* but his protectionist sympathies did not endear him to the economists.

THOMPSON, THOMAS (1783–1869). English political writer and owner of the *Westminster Review.* He was an active member of the Anti–Corn Law League. In 1811 he became governor of Sierra Leone, where he fought slavery.

TRACY. *See* Destutt de Tracy, Antoine.

TRÉLAT, ULYSSE (1795–1879). French physician and liberal politician. He was minister of public works between 12 May and 19 June 1848.

TURGOT, ANNE-ROBERT-JACQUES, baron de L'Aulne (1727–81). Economist of the physiocratic school, politician, reformist bureaucrat, and writer. During the mid-1750s Turgot came into contact with the physiocrats, such as Quesnay, Dupont de Nemours, and Vincent de Gournay (who was the free-market intendant for commerce). Turgot had two opportunities to put free-market reforms into practice: when he was appointed Intendant of Limoges in 1761–74; and when Louis XVI made him minister of finance between 1774 and 1776, at which time Turgot issued his six edicts to reduce regulations and taxation. His works include *Eloge de Gournay* (1759), *Réflexions sur la formation et la distribution des richesses* (1766), and *Lettres sur la liberté du commerce des grains* (1770).

TURPIN, ETIENNE (1802–73). French landowner and deputy.

VERNES, CHARLES (1786–1858). Founder of the Banque Vernes. Sous-gouverneur of the Bank of France (1832–58) and author of a report on the Algerian war.

VILLÈLE, JEAN-BAPTISTE, comte de (1773–1854). French statesman and leader of the ultralegitimists. He became prime minister in 1822 but had to resign after the victory of the liberals in 1828.

VILLERMÉ, LOUIS RENÉ (1782–1863). French military surgeon, then civilian doctor. He was a member of the Académie des sciences morales et politiques. He wrote on public-health issues such as prisons, mortality rates, population growth, and the condition of workers. On the latter he wrote *Tableau de l'état physique et moral des ouvriers employés dans les manufactures de coton, de laine, et de soie* (1840), which became a basis for labor regulations.

VILLIERS, GEORGE, Earl of Clarendon (1800–1870). Diplomat and politician. Succeeded his father in the House of Lords. Influential member of the Whig opposition to Robert Peel. Advocate of the repeal of the Corn Laws. His brother, a member of Parliament since 1835 and an active member of the League, presented a motion at each session of Parliament aimed at repealing the Corn Laws.

VINCENS SAINT-LAURENT, MARC-ANTOINE (1764–1860). French high-ranking civil servant. He wrote several books that were praised in *Le Journal des économistes.*

VIVIEN, ALEXANDRE (1799–1854). French high-ranking civil servant, deputy (from 1833), minister of justice under Thiers. Minister of public works under Cavaignac, he resigned from all positions after the coup of Louis-Napoléon Bonaparte.

WALPOLE, ROBERT, Earl of Oxford (1676–1745). One of the leaders of the Whigs and twice chancellor of the exchequer. He controlled the country's politics between 1715 and 1742 and laid the foundations for the parliamentary regime of the United Kingdom.

WILBERFORCE, WILLIAM (1759–1833). British politician. One of the leading figures in the campaign to abolish the slave trade (1807) and slavery itself (1833).

WILSON, GEORGE (1808–70). British businessman whose main business interests were the management of railways and telegraphs. He had a long involvement in the liberal politics of Manchester and later became chairman of the Anti–Corn Law League.

WILSON, JAMES (1805–60). Born in Scotland, he founded the *Economist* in 1843 and was elected a member of Parliament in 1847. His books include *Influence of the Corn Laws* (1839) and *Capital, Currency, and Banking* (1847), which was a collection of his articles from the *Economist*.

WOLOWSKI, LOUIS (1810–76). Lawyer, politician, and economist of Polish origin. His interests lay in industrial and labor economics, free trade, and bimetallism. He was a professor of industrial law at the Conservatoire national des arts et métiers, a member of the Académie des sciences morales et politiques from 1855, serving as its president in 1866–67, and a member and president of the Société d'économie politique. His political career started in 1848, when he represented La Seine in the Constituent and Legislative Assemblies. During the 1848 revolution he was an ardent opponent of the socialist Louis Blanc and his plans for labor organization. Wolowski continued his career as a politician in the Third Republic, where he served as a member of the Assembly and took an interest in budgetary matters. He edited *La Revue de droit français et échange* and wrote articles for *Le Journal des économistes.* Among his books are *Cours de législation industrielle: De l'organisation du travail* (1844) and *Études d'économie politique et de statistique* (1848), *La question des banques* (1864), *La Banque d'Angleterre et les banques d'Ecosse* (1867), *La Liberté commerciale et les résultats du traité de commerce de 1860* (1869), and *L'Or et l'argent* (1870).

Glossary of Places

ADOUR. A river flowing through the Landes. It allowed the transportation of goods from the Chalosse, the part of the *département* in which Bastiat lived, to the port of Bayonne, from which they could be exported. Eventually, sand deposits made navigation on this river more and more difficult.

LES BAGNÈRES. Spas in the Pyrenees. Bastiat went to these spas as often as he could in order to cure an affliction of the throat, an illness that would eventually kill him.

LE BUTARD (The Butard Wood). A former hunting lodge of Louis XIV, located in the woods west of Versailles, close to the Château de la Jonchère. Owned by the state, it was rented by a M. Pescatore, a friend of the Cheuvreux family and an admirer of Bastiat. Pescatore made it available to Bastiat whenever he wanted to use it in order to rest from the hustle and bustle of Paris. In this solitary, charming place, the writer composed the first chapters of *Economic Harmonies*.

CHALOSSE. The part of the Landes in which Bastiat had his home. It covers several counties.

CROISSY. A small town near Paris.

LES EAUX-BONNES. *See* Les Bagnères.

GARONNE. A river in southwest France.

LANDES. A French *département* in southwest France, where Bastiat spent most of his life.

MUGRON. A small town in the Landes overlooking the Adour River, where Bastiat lived from 1825 to 1845. At the time it was a significant commercial center, with a port on the Adour River and about two thousand inhabitants (fifteen hundred now). Today, Mugron has a street, a square, and a plaza named after Bastiat.

PAU. A town in southwest France.

VÉFOUR. A famous Parisian restaurant, still in existence. The members of the Société d'économie politique held a monthly meeting there.

Glossary of Subjects and Terms

ACADÉMIE DES SCIENCES MORALES ET POLITIQUES. One of the five *académies* that compose the Institut de France (*see* Institut de France).

ANTI–CORN LAW LEAGUE. The Anti–Corn Law League, Corn League, or League, was founded in 1838 by Richard Cobden and John Bright in Manchester. Their initial aim was to repeal the law restricting the import of grain (Corn Laws), but they soon called for the unilateral ending of all agricultural and industrial restrictions on the free movement of goods between Britain and the rest of the world. For seven years they organized rallies, meetings, public lectures, and debates from one end of Britain to the other and managed to have proponents of free trade elected to Parliament. The Tory government resisted for many years but eventually yielded on 25 June 1846, when unilateral free trade became the law of Great Britain.

ASSOCIATION POUR LA LIBERTÉ DES ÉCHANGES. Founded in February 1846 in Bordeaux. Bastiat was the secretary of the board, presided over by François d'Harcourt and having among its members Michel Chevalier, Auguste Blanqui, Joseph Garnier, Gustave de Molinari, and Horace Say.

CAPITAL AND RENT (*OC,* vol. 5, p. 23, "Capital et rente"). This pamphlet first appeared in February 1849 and was a reply to the socialists Proudhon and Thoré.

LE CENSEUR. A journal founded by Charles Comte and Charles Dunoyer. From 1814 to 1815 its full name was *Le Censeur, ou examen des actes et des ouvrages qui tendent à détruire ou à consolider la constitution de l'État;* later, from 1817 to 1819, it was called *Le Censeur européen ou Examen de diverses questions de droit public et de divers ouvrages littéraires et scientifiques, considérés dans leurs rapports avec le progrès de la civilisation.* The journal was devoted to political and economic matters and was a constant thorn in the side of first Napoléon's empire and then the restored monarchy. It was threatened with closure by the authorities on several occasions and finally was forced to close in 1815. During this period of enforced leisure Comte and Dunoyer discovered the economic writings of Jean-Baptiste Say, and when the journal reopened, it tilted toward economic and social matters as a result. It was one of the most important journals of liberal thought in the early nineteenth century.

LE CENSEUR EUROPÉEN. See *Le Censeur.*

LA CHALOSSE. A weekly journal of the district of Saint-Sever.

CHARTER. *See* Constitutional Charter.

COBDEN AND THE LEAGUE (*OC*, vol. 3: *Cobden et la ligue: ou, L'Agitation anglaise pour la liberté du commerce*). First published in 1845 by Guillaumin as a separate book before it was reissued in Bastiat's *Œuvres complètes.* Bastiat was so impressed with the organization and tactics of the Anti–Corn Law League in Britain that he wished to emulate it in France. He was ultimately largely unsuccessful. As part of his efforts to inspire the French people to pressure the government for tariff reform he put together this collection of translations of many of the League's public speeches, newspaper reports of their meetings, and other documents of the campaign. He prefaced the book with a long introduction in which he outlined the League's goals and beliefs (see *OC*, vol. 3, p. 1, "Introduction").

COLLÈGE DE FRANCE. An institution created under François I in 1529 to deliver advanced teaching not yet available at the universities.

CONSERVATOIRE NATIONAL DES ARTS ET MÉTIERS. A public institution of higher education created by Abbé Grégoire in 1794. It was intended for people already engaged in professional life.

CONSTITUENT ASSEMBLY (Assemblée constituante). A body elected by universal suffrage to prepare a constitution. Its motions were prepared by two commissions and fifteen committees.

CONSTITUTIONAL CHARTER. Promulgated by Louis XVIII on 4 June 1814. It was a compromise between the principles of the ancien régime and the reforms brought about by the French Revolution.

CORN LAWS. Legislation introduced by Parliament in the seventeenth century to maintain a high price for corn (in the British context this meant grain, especially wheat) by preventing the importation of cheaper foreign grain altogether or by imposing a duty on it in order to protect domestic producers from competition. The laws were revised in 1815 following the collapse of wheat prices at the end of the Napoleonic Wars. The artificially high prices which resulted led to rioting in London and Manchester. The laws were again amended in 1828 and 1842 to introduce a more flexible sliding scale of duties which would be imposed when the domestic price of wheat fell below a set amount. The high price caused by protection led to the formation of opposition groups, such as the Anti–Corn Law League in 1838, and to the founding of the *Economist* magazine in 1843. Pressure for repeal came from within Parliament by members of Parliament, such as Richard Cobden (elected in 1841), and from without by a number of factors: the well-organized public campaigning by the Anti–Corn Law League; the writings of classical economists who were nearly universally in favor of free trade; the writings of popular authors such as Harriet Martineau, Jane Marcet, and Thomas Hodgskin; and the pressure of crop failures in Ireland in 1845. The Conservative prime minister Sir Robert Peel announced the repeal of the Corn Laws on 27 January 1846, to take effect on 1 February 1849 after a period of gradual reduction in the level of the duty. The act was passed by the House of Commons on 15 May and approved by the House of Lords on 25 June, thus bringing to an end centuries of agricultural protection in England.

COUNCIL OF STATE. A French institution giving advice on draft bills and acting as a court of final appeal on administrative matters. Its members were appointed by the king.

LE COURRIER FRANÇAIS. A daily paper, with a mildly Catholic, leftist, and monarchic slant. It ran from 1819 to 1851.

DAMNED MONEY (*OC,* vol. 5, p. 64, "Maudit argent"). The pamphlet *Maudit argent* first appeared in the April 1849 edition of the *Journal des économistes* and was written in response to a criticism of money expressed by an economist on the government's finance committee.

LA DÉMOCRATIE PACIFIQUE: JOURNAL DES INTÉRÊTS DES GOUVERNEMENTS ET DES PEUPLES. A Fourierist journal, launched by Victor Considérant, advocating the creation of "harmonious communities." It ran from 1843 to 1851.

DÉPARTEMENT. France is divided into ninety-five *départements,* which are the equivalent of counties and which enjoy a certain administrative autonomy.

DEPUTY. A member of the French parliament.

ECONOMIC HARMONIES (*OC,* vol. 6: *Harmonies économiques*). "Social Harmonies" was the original title Bastiat gave to what was eventually published as *Economic Harmonies.* The idea that all voluntary economic exchanges are "harmonious," mutually beneficial to both parties to the exchange, and conducive to social peace and order is a key insight of Bastiat and one that preoccupied him as he was dying. His chef d'œuvre and the only book-length work he ever wrote but left unfinished at his death was *Harmonies économiques*. It was published posthumously in a more complete version by his friends in Paris in 1851.

ECONOMIC SOPHISMS (*OC*, vol. 4: *Sophismes économiques*). Bastiat published two collections of essays under the general title *Economic Sophisms*. Originally published in *Le Journal des économistes* in 1845 and 1847, these essays were designed to refute common misconceptions about the free market, which Bastiat termed "sophisms." A first collection was published by Guillaumin in book form in 1846 as *Sophismes économiques*. Guillaumin also published further editions in 1847 and 1848. Very popular, they went through many editions and were quickly translated into Spanish, Italian, German, and English.

ÉCONOMISTE. See *Les Économistes*.

LES ÉCONOMISTES. In Bastiat's lifetime *Les Économistes* was the term used to refer to the free-trade school of economic thought.

FEBRUARY REVOLUTION. *See* Revolution of 1848.

FOURIERISM. *See glossary of names:* Fourier, François-Marie Charles.

GENERAL COUNCIL. A chamber in each French *département* that deliberates on subjects concerning the *département*. It has one representative per county (28 at the time for the Landes *département*, 31 today), elected for nine years then (six years today). Its functions have varied over time. Bastiat was elected general councillor in 1833 for the county of Mugron, a post he held until his death. At that time, the council deliberations had to be approved by the prefect.

HARMONIES. See *Economic Harmonies*.

L'INDICATEUR. Newspaper with a very liberal perspective.

INDIVIDUALISM AND FRATERNITY (*Individualisme et fraternité*). The unpublished sketch "Individualisme et fraternité" was written to refute the socialist interpretation of the first French Revolution that was expressed by Louis Blanc in his *Histoire de la révolution française,* the first volume of which appeared in 1847.

INSTITUT DE FRANCE. Academic institution covering the five *académies* (arts, literature, sciences, history and archaeology, and moral and political sciences).

JACQUES BONHOMME. A short-lived biweekly paper that seems to have lasted for only four issues (June–July 1848). It was founded and largely written by Bastiat, Alcide Fonteyraud, Charles Coquelin, and Gustave de Molinari. Its purpose was to counter socialist ideas during the 1848 revolution, and it was handed out in the streets of Paris.

LE JOURNAL DES DÉBATS. A journal founded in 1789 by the Bertin family and managed for almost forty years by Louis-François Bertin. The journal went through several title changes and after 1814 became *Le Journal des débats politiques et littéraires.* The journal likewise underwent several changes of political positions: it was against Napoléon during the First Empire; under the second restoration it became conservative rather than reactionary; and under Charles X it was in support of the liberal stance espoused by the doctrinaires. It ceased publication in 1944.

LE JOURNAL DES ÉCONOMISTES. *Le Journal des économistes: revue mensuelle de l'économie politique, des questions agricoles, manufacturières et commerciales* was the journal of the Société d'économie politique and appeared from December 1841 until the fall of France in 1940. It was published by the firm of Guillaumin, which also published the writings of most of the liberals of the period. *Le Journal des économistes* was the leading journal of the free-market economists (known as *Les Économistes*) in France in the second half of the nineteenth century. It was edited by Adolphe Blanqui (1841–42), Hippolyte Dussard (1843–45), Joseph Garnier (1845–55), Henri Baudrillart (1855–65), Joseph Garnier (1865–81), Gustave de Molinari (1881–1909), and Yves Guyot (1910–?). Many of Bastiat's articles for the journal were later published as pamphlets and books, and his works were all reviewed there. There are fifty-eight entries under Bastiat's name in the table of contents of the journal for the period 1841 to 1865.

LE JOURNAL DU COMMERCE. A business daily that appeared from 1795 through 1837 under various titles.

JULY MONARCHY. *See* Revolution of 1848.

JULY REVOLUTION. *See* Revolution of 1848.

JUSTICE AND FRATERNITY (*OC,* vol. 4, p. 298, "Justice et fraternité"). This essay first appeared in *Le Journal des économistes* on 15 June 1848 and was one of several essays Bastiat wrote during the 1848 revolution to counter socialist ideas. In this essay, Bastiat takes aim at socialists such as Fourier, Cabet, Owen, Proudhon, and Louis Blanc, who wished to use the law in order to bring about by force their ideal of fraternity. Bastiat contrasts this with the aim of political economists like himself, who saw the function of the law as one of achieving universal justice by protecting each individual's life, liberty, and property.

THE LAW (OC, vol. 4, p. 342, "La Loi"). Bastiat wrote two pieces titled "La Loi": the first was published as a pamphlet, *La Loi* (1850); the second was his only entry, "Lois," in the *Dictionnaire de l'économie politique* (1852), vol. 2, pp. 93–100, published posthumously. *The Law* is quite well known to English readers because it was quickly translated in 1853 and has been kept in print since 1950 by the Foundation for Economic Education, Irvington-on-Hudson, New York.

LEAGUE. *See* Anti–Corn Law League.

LE LIBRE ÉCHANGE. The weekly journal of the Association pour la liberté des échanges. It began in 1846 as *Le Libre-échange: Journal du travail agricole, industriel et commercial* but changed its name to the simpler *Libre échange* at the start of its second year of publication. It closed in 1848 as a result of the revolution. The first fifty-two issues were published as a book by the Guillaumin publishing firm under the title *Le Libre-échange, journal de l'association pour la liberté des échanges* (1847). The first sixty-four issues were published by Bastiat, the editor in chief, and Joseph Garnier; the last eight issues were published by Charles Coquelin. The journal's editorial board included Anisson-Dupéron (pair de France), Bastiat, Blanqui, Gustave Brunet (assistant to the mayor of Bordeaux), Campan (secretary of the Chamber of Commerce of Bordeaux), Michel Chevalier, Coquelin, Dunoyer, Faucher, Fonteyraud, Garnier, Louis Leclerc, Molinari, Paillottet, Horace Say, and Wolowski.

LE MÉMORIAL BORDELAIS. A newspaper that represented several political perspectives.

LE MONITEUR. See *Le Moniteur industriel.*

LE MONITEUR INDUSTRIEL. A periodical created in July 1835. It became the stronghold of protectionists and Bastiat's bête noire.

MONTAGNARD MANIFESTO. *See* La Montagne.

MONTAGNARDS. *See* La Montagne.

LA MONTAGNE (The Mountain). La Montagne comprised a group of deputies (Montagnards) favorable to a "democratic and social republic." The Montagnard Manifesto expressed their ideas. The name comes from the first general assemblies of the Revolution, in which the deputies professing these ideas sat in the highest part of the assembly, "the mountain."

LE NATIONAL. Liberal paper founded in 1830 by Adolphe Thiers to fight the ultrareactionary politics of the prince de Polignac. It played a decisive role during the "three glorious days" and contributed to the success of Louis-Philippe. Its readership considerably exceeded the number of its subscribers (around three thousand).

NATIONAL GUARD. A militia created in 1789, recruited mainly from among the bourgeoisie. It was responsible for keeping order jointly with the army. Dissolved in 1827, it was reestablished in July 1830. La Fayette took command of it, as he had forty years earlier, in 1789. It played an essential role under Louis-Philippe, and its desertion in 1848 marked the end of that regime.

NAVIGATION ACT. The act prevented merchandise from being imported into Britain if it was not transported by British ships or ships from the producer countries. The first act, adopted in 1651, applied to commerce within Europe and generated a war with Holland (1652–54). Extended to colonies in 1660 and 1663, it generated a second war with Holland (1665–67). It was repealed in 1849.

LA PATRIE. A political journal of no fixed political opinions.

PLUNDER AND LAW (OC, vol. 5, p. 1, "Spoliation et loi"). The pamphlet *Spoliation et loi,* published by *Le Journal des économistes* on 15 May 1850.

PREFECT. A representative of the executive branch in a *département* (see Glossary of Places: *département*). The prefecture is the location of the office of the prefect. In large *départements,* there are also administrative subdivisions called *sous prefectures,* which are headed by *sous préfets.*

LA PRESSE. A widely distributed daily newspaper, created in 1836 by the journalist, businessman, and politician Émile de Girardin (1806–81). Girardin was one of the creators of the modern press and author of, among many works, the brochure *Le Socialisme et l'impôt* (1849), in which he advocated a single tax on capital and revenue.

PROPERTY AND LAW (OC, vol. 4, p. 275, "Propriété et loi"). The pamphlet *Propriété et loi* appeared in the May 1848 edition of *Le Journal des économistes* and was written to defend a natural law theory of property.

PROPERTY AND PLUNDER (OC, vol. 4, p. 394, "Propriété et spoliation"). During the 1848 revolution Bastiat wrote an important pamphlet in the July 1848 edition of *Le Journal des débats.* It was a reply to socialist critics of property, such as Louis Blanc, Proudhon, and Considérant, especially the latter's *Théorie du droit de propriété et du droit au travail.* A key to understanding the social and economic ideas of the French *économistes* in general, and Bastiat in particular, is the contrasting notions of "property" and "plunder" (or "spoliation" in French). According to this view, there are two contrasting ways of acquiring and owning property. On the one hand there is "property" justly acquired through one's own hard work or by the peaceful exchange with other property owners on the free market. On the other hand there is "spoliation," or plunder, by which one uses violence oneself or uses the power of the state to act on one's behalf to take the justly acquired property of others through legislation, subsidies, tariffs, taxation, or other state-enforced means.

PROTECTIONISM AND COMMUNISM (*OC,* vol. 4, p. 504, "Protectionisme et communisme"). The pamphlet *Protectionisme et communisme* was written in response to a work by Thiers, *De la propriété.*

LA QUOTIDIENNE. A royalist journal, organ of the legitimists during the July Monarchy.

LA RÉPUBLIQUE FRANÇAISE. A newspaper launched by Bastiat, which lasted only a few days. The circumstances are explained in the letter to Félix Coudroy of 13 February 1848 (*see* Letter 89).

REVOLUTION OF 1848 (also called the February Revolution). Because France went through so many revolutions between 1789 and 1870, they are often distinguished by reference to the month in which they occurred. Thus, we have the "July Monarchy" (of 1830) (also called the revolution of 1830), when the restored Bourbon monarchy of 1815 was overthrown in order to create a more liberal and constitutional monarchy under Louis-Philippe; the "February Revolution" (of 1848), when the July Monarchy of Louis-Philippe was overthrown and the Second Republic was formed; the "June Days" (of 1848), when a rebellion by workers in Paris who were protesting the closure of the government-subsidized National Workshops work-relief program was bloodily put down by General Cavaignac; and the "18 Brumaire of Louis-Napoléon," which refers to the coup d'état that brought Louis-Napoléon (Napoléon Bonaparte's nephew) to power on 2 December 1851 and which ushered in the creation of the Second Empire—the phrase was coined by Karl Marx and refers to another date, 18 Brumaire in the revolutionary calendar, or 9 November 1799, when Napoléon Bonaparte declared himself dictator in another coup d'état. Bastiat was an active participant in the 1848 revolution, being elected to the Constituent Assembly on 23 April 1848 and then to the Legislative Assembly on 13 May 1849.

REVOLUTION OF 1830. *See* Revolution of 1848.

La Revue britannique. A monthly review founded in 1825 by Sébastien-Louis Saulnier (1790–1835), which contained many articles on economic matters. Its full title read *Revue britannique. Receuil international. Choix d'articles extraits des meilleurs écrits périodiques da la Grande-Bretagne et de l'Amérique, complété sur des articles originaux.* The issue of the 6th series, vol. 1, in 1846, contained a long essay on the Anti–Corn Law League, by Alcide Fonteyraud, "La Ligue anglaise," which was based on Bastiat's book *Cobden and the League* (1845). The *Revue* ceased publication in 1901.

La Revue des deux mondes. A review founded in 1829 by François Buloz that published essays on arts, literature, politics, and society. Its name was a reflection of its aim, namely, to bring France and the United States closer together. It ceased publication in 1944.

La Revue encyclopédique. A review founded in 1819 by M. A. Julien. During the restoration period it was quite liberal, with many articles and book reviews on economists such as Say, Dunoyer, and MacCulloch. It changed direction in 1831, when the son of the founder took it in a markedly Saint-Simonian direction. It ceased publication in 1835.

September Laws. Laws restricting liberties promulgated in September 1835, following an attempt against the life of Louis-Philippe.

Social Harmonies. See *Economic Harmonies.*

Société d'économie politique (Society of Political Economy) was founded in 1842, with the name Réunion des économistes, and began meeting regularly in October 1842. Summaries of the meetings were published by Joseph Garnier, the permanent secretary and vice president of the society, in *Le Journal des économistes.* The articles "Adresse au président de la ligue anglaise son adhésion sympathique aux principes de cette association," vol. 13 (December–March 1846), p. 19; "Réponse de M. Cobden au nom de la Ligue," vol. 14 (April–July 1846), p. 60; and "Banquet offert à M. Cobden," vol. 15 (August–November 1846), p. 89, show the very great interest the society had in Cobden's activities in England.

Sophisms. See *Economic Sophisms.*

The State (*OC,* vol. 4, p. 327, "L'État"). Originally published in *Le Journal des débats* in September 1848, "The State" was one of several essays which Bastiat wrote during the 1848 revolution in order to counter socialist ideas and proposals for increased economic interventionism. His criticism and sarcasm in this piece was directed toward the Montagnard faction (*see* La Montagne) in the Chamber. This group was promising the moon to

French citizens and was urging massive increases in the function of the state to achieve this. In this short essay Bastiat sarcastically offered his own definition of what the state was, namely "the great fiction by which everyone endeavors to live at the expense of everyone else."

LA VOIX DU PEUPLE. A newspaper launched by Proudhon on 30 September 1849 to replace *Le Peuple,* a paper that had ceased on 13 June 1849. *La Voix du peuple* ceased in May 1850.

WHAT IS SEEN AND WHAT IS NOT SEEN (OC, vol. 5, p. 336, "Ce qu'on voit et ce qu'on ne voit pas ou, l'économie politique en une leçon"). This was the last pamphlet Bastiat wrote, in 1850, before his death. It has a sad story, as Bastiat wanted to refute many of the bad economic arguments he had heard in the National Assembly. According to George de Huszar, the editor of Bastiat's *Selected Essays on Political Economy* (Irvington-on-Hudson, N.Y.: Foundation for Economic Education, 1964), in which this essay appears, Bastiat lost the original manuscript in a house move and so rewrote it. He was unhappy with the result, so he rewrote it again. The expression "what is seen and what is not seen" has become emblematic of Bastiat's approach to economic problems in that he wants to go beneath the apparent surface of economic phenomena, such as in the parable of the broken window. Some would see the broken window as an opportunity for the glass industry to expand its sales and create more work; others, like Bastiat, would see it as a loss because the old window has been destroyed and what is spent on replacing it might have been used to purchase something else. Bastiat spent the last decade of his life making arguments like this to a popular audience who did not seem to understand.

WINE AND SPIRITS TAX. Eliminated by the revolutionary parliament of 1789, the tax on wine and spirits was progressively reinstated during the empire. It comprised four components: (1) a consumption tax (10 percent of the sale price); (2) a license fee paid by the vendor, depending on the number of inhabitants; (3) a tax on circulation, which depended on the *département;* and (4) an entry duty for the towns of more than four hundred inhabitants, depending on the sale price and the number of inhabitants. Being from a wine-producing region, Bastiat had always been preoccupied by a law that was very hard on the local farmers.

List of the Correspondence by Recipient

To Victor Calmètes
1. Bayonne, 12 September 1819
2. Bayonne, 5 March 1820
3. Bayonne, 18 March 1820
4. Bayonne, 10 September 1820
5. Bayonne, October 1820
6. Bayonne, 29 April 1821
7. Bayonne, 10 September 1821
8. Bayonne, 8 December 1821
9. Bayonne, 20 October 1822
10. Bayonne, December 1822
15. Mugron, 12 March 1829
16. Mugron, July 1829
19. Bayonne, 22 April 1831
54. Bayonne, 4 March 1846

To Félix Coudroy
11. Bayonne, 15 December 1824
12. Bayonne, 8 January 1825
13. Bordeaux, 9 April 1827
14. Bayonne, 3 December 1827
17. Bayonne, 4 August 1830
18. Bayonne, 5 August 1830
20. Bordeaux, 2 March 1834
21. Bayonne, 16 June 1840
22. Madrid, 6 July 1840
23. Madrid, 16 July 1840
24. Madrid, 17 August 1840
25. Lisbon, 24 October 1840
26. Lisbon, 7 November 1840
27. Paris, 2 January 1841

28. Paris, 11 January 1841
29. Bagnères, 10 July 1844
30. Eaux-Bonnes, 26 July 1844
37. Paris, May 1845
38. Paris, 23 May 1845
39. Paris, 5 June 1845
40. 16 June 1845
41. 18 . . . [no month or year given]
42. Paris, 3 July 1845
43. London, July 1845
53. Bordeaux, 19 February 1846
56. Paris, 22 March 1846
60. Paris, 18 April 1846
61. Paris, 3 May 1846
62. Paris, 4 May 1846
63. Paris, 24 May 1846
67. Bordeaux, 22 July 1846
77. Paris, 11 March 1847
81. Paris, August 1847
85. Paris, 5 January 1848
87. Paris, 24 January 1848
89. Paris, 13 February 1848
94. Paris, 29 February 1848
101. Paris, 9 June 1848
102. Paris, 24 June 1848
108. Paris, 26 August 1848
110. Paris, 7 September 1848
115. Paris, 26 November 1848
116. Paris, 5 December 1848
120. Paris, 1 January 1849
130. Paris, 15 March 1849

133. Paris, 25 April 1849
142. Paris, 30 July 1849
155. Paris, 13 December 1849
158. Paris, January 1850
189. Paris, 9 September 1850
203. Rome, 11 November 1850

To A. M. Laurence
31. Mugron, 9 November 1844

To Richard Cobden
32. Mugron, 24 November 1844
36. Mugron, 8 April 1845
44. London, 8 July 1845
46. Mugron, 2 October 1845
48. Mugron, 13 December 1845
50. Mugron, 13 January 1846
51. Mugron, 9 February 1846
52. Bordeaux, February 1846
55. Paris, 16 March 1846
57. Paris, 25 March 1846
58. Paris, 2 April 1846
59. Paris, 11 April 1846
64. Paris, 25 May 1846
65. Mugron, 25 June 1846
66. Bordeaux, 21 July 1846
68. Paris, 23 September 1846
69. Paris, 29 September 1846
70. Paris, 1 October 1846
71. Paris, 22 October 1846
72. Paris, 22 November 1846
73. Paris, 25 November 1846
74. Paris, 20 December 1846
75. Paris, 25 December 1846
76. Paris, 10 January 1847
78. Paris, 20 March 1847
79. Paris, 20 April 1847
80. Paris, 5 July 1847
83. Paris, 15 October 1847
84. Paris, 9 November 1847
91. Paris, 25 February 1848
92. Paris, 26 February 1848
96. Mugron, 5 April 1848

98. Paris, 11 May 1848
100. Paris, 27 May 1848
103. Paris, 27 June 1848
106. Paris, 7 August 1848
107. Paris, 18 August 1848
151. Paris, 17 October 1849
152. Paris, 24 October 1849
157. Paris, 31 December 1849
185. Paris, 3 August 1850
186. Paris, 17 August 1850
188. Paris, 9 September 1850
199. Pisa, 18 October 1850

To Horace Say
33. Mugron, 24 November 1844
82. Mugron, Monday, October 1847
97. Mugron, 12 April 1848
146. Mugron, 16 September 1849
172. Mugron, 3 June 1850
182. Les Eaux-Bonnes, 4 July 1850
200. Pisa, 20 October 1850

To Charles Dunoyer, member of the Institute
34. Mugron, 7 March 1845

To Alphonse de Lamartine
35. Mugron, 7 March 1845.

To Mr. Paulton
45. Paris, 29 July 1845

To [D.] Potonié
47. Mugron, 24 October 1845

To Alcide Fonteyraud
49. Mugron, 20 December 1845

To Mrs. Schwabe
86. Paris, 17 January 1848
88. Paris, 27 January 1848
90. Paris, 16 February 1848
99. Paris, 17 May 1848
114. Paris, 14 November 1848
118. Paris, 28 December 1848
129. Paris, 11 March 1849

150. Paris, 14 October 1849

*To Marie-Julienne Badbedat
(Mme Marsan)*
93. 27 February 1848

To Bernard Domenger
95. Paris, 4 March 1848
109. Paris, 3 September 1848
122. Paris, 18 January 1849
125. Paris, 3 February 1849
126. Paris, 1849 [no month or day]
127. Paris, 21 March 1849
131. Paris, 25 March 1849
132. Paris, 8 April 1849
134. Paris, 29 April 1849
136. Paris, 1849 [no month or day]
140. Paris, Tuesday, 13 ... (Summer
      1849)
154. Paris, 13 November 1849
156. Paris, 25 December 1849
162. Paris, 18 February 1850
164. Paris, 22 March 1850
196. Pisa, 8 October 1850
205. Rome, 28 November 1850

To Julie Marsan (Mme Affre)
104. Paris, 29 June 1848

To Mr. Schwabe
105. Paris, 1 July 1848
111. Dover, 7 October 1848
112. Paris, 25 October 1848

To Mme Cheuvreux
113. Paris, November 1848
119. Paris, January 1849
123. Paris, February 1849
124. Paris, February 1849
128. Paris, Monday, March 1849
135. Paris, 3 May 1849
137. Brussels, Hôtel de Bellevue,
      June 1849
138. Brussels, June 1849

139. Antwerp, June 1849
143. Mont-de-Marsan, 30 August 1849
144. Mugron, 12 September 1849
147. Mugron, 18 September 1849
148. Paris, 7 October 1849
149. Paris, 8 October 1849
153. Paris, November 1849
159. Paris, 2 January 1850
160. Paris, January 1850
161. Paris, February 1850
163. Paris, March 1850
165. Paris, Friday, April 1850
166. Bordeaux, May 1850
168. Mugron, 20 May 1850
169. Mugron, 23 May 1850
170. Mugron, 27 May 1850
174. Les Eaux-Bonnes, 15 June 1850
176. Les Eaux-Bonnes, 23 June 1850
177. Les Eaux-Bonnes, 24 June 1850
181. Les Eaux-Bonnes, 4 July 1850
183. Mugron, July 1850
192. Lyons, 14 September 1850
194. Marseilles (on board the *Castor*),
      22 September 1850
195. Pisa, 2 October 1850
198. Pisa, 14 October 1850
202. Pisa, 29 October 1850
207. Rome, 14, 15, and 16 December
      1850

To the Count Arrivabene
117. Paris, 21 December 1848
201. Pisa, 28 October 1850

*To George Wilson, chairman of the
Anti–Corn Law League*
121. Paris, 15 January 1849

To Prosper Paillottet
141. Paris, 14 July 1849
167. Mugron, 19 May 1850
171. Mugron, 2 June 1850
175. Les Eaux-Bonnes, 23 June 1850
178. Les Eaux-Bonnes, 28 June 1850

179. Les Eaux-Bonnes, 2 July 1850
190. Lyons, 14 September 1850
197. Pisa, 11 October 1850
204. Rome, 26 November 1850
206. Rome, 8 December 1850

To M. Cheuvreux
145. Mugron, 16 September 1849
184. Mugron, 14 July 1850
193. Marseilles, 18 September 1850

To Louise Cheuvreux
173. Mugron, 11 June 1850
191. Lyons, 14 September 1850

To M. de Fontenay
180. Les Eaux-Bonnes, 3 July 1850

To the president of the Peace Congress in Frankfurt
187. Paris, 17 August 1850

From Prosper Paillottet to Mme Cheuvreux
208. Rome, 22 December 1850

To the Journal des économistes
209. Undated

Bibliography of Primary Sources

WORKS BY BASTIAT

The works by Bastiat listed below represent not only the sources used for this translation but also those frequently cited in the text, notes, and glossaries.

PUBLISHED SOURCES FOR THIS EDITION

Lettres d'un habitant des Landes, Frédéric Bastiat. Edited by Mme Cheuvreux. Paris: A. Quantin, 1877.

Œuvres complètes de Frédéric Bastiat, mises en ordre, revues et annotées d'après les manuscrits de l'auteur. Paris: Guillaumin, 1854–55, 1st ed.; 1862–44, 2d ed.; 1870–73, 3rd ed.; 1878–79, 4th ed.; 1881–84, 5th ed.; if there was a sixth edition, the date is unknown; 1893, 7th ed.

The editions of Bastiat's *Œuvres complètes* that were used in making this translation are as follows:

Vol. 1: *Correspondance et mélages* (2d ed. of 1862)

Vol. 2: *Le Libre-échange* (2d ed., 1862)

Vol. 3: *Cobden et la Ligue ou l'agitation anglaise pour la liberté des échanges* (2d ed., 1864)

Vol. 4: *Sophismes économiques. Petits pamphlets I* (3rd ed., 1873)

Vol. 5: *Sophismes économiques. Petits pamphlets II* (3rd ed., 1873)

Vol. 6: *Harmonies économiques* (2d ed., 1864)

Vol. 7: *Essais, ébauches, correspondance* (2d ed., 1864)

MAJOR PAMPHLETS AND ESSAYS
MENTIONED IN THE TEXT AND NOTES

Capital et rente. Paris: H. Bellaire, 1849. (See also Glossary of Subjects and Terms: *Capital and Rent.*)

Ce qu'on voit et ce qu'on ne voit pas. Paris, 1850. (See also Glossary of Subjects and Terms: *What Is Seen and What Is Not Seen.*)

L'État. Journal des débats (25 September 1848). (See also Glossary of Subjects and Terms: *The State.*)

Justice et fraternité. Journal des économistes (15 June 1848), vol. 20. (See also Glossary of Subjects and Terms: *Justice and Fraternity.*)

La Loi. Paris, 1850. (See also Glossary of Subjects and Terms: *The Law.*)

Maudit argent. Journal des économistes (April 1849), vol. 23. (See also Glossary of Subjects and Terms: *Damned Money.*)

Propriété et loi. Journal des économistes (15 May 1848). (See also Glossary of Subjects and Terms: *Property and Law.*)

Propriété et spoliation. Journal des débats (24 July 1848). (See also Glossary of Subjects and Terms: *Property and Plunder.*)

Protectionisme et communisme. Paris, 1849. (See also Glossary of Subjects and Terms: *Protectionism and Communism.*)

Spoliation et loi. Journal des économistes (15 May 1850). (See also Glossary of Subjects and Terms: *Plunder and Law.*)

PRIMARY SOURCES BY OTHER AUTHORS
CITED IN THE TEXT AND THE NOTES

We list here the works by other authors mentioned in the text, notes, and glossaries that play a significant role in the understanding of Bastiat's life and works. Although not exhaustive, this list cites many primary sources that were important during Bastiat's time.

Annales de la Société d'économie politique. Publiées sur la direction de Alphonse Courtois fils. 16 vols. Paris: Guillaumin, 1889–96.

The Anti–Bread Tax Circular. Published by the Anti–Corn Law League. Manchester, England: John Gadsby, 1841–43.

Arrivabene, Giovanni. *Sur la condition des laboureurs et des ouvriers belges, et sur quelques mesures pour l'améliorer: lettre adressée à M. le Vicomte Biolley, Sénateur.* Brussels: Méline, Cans, 1845.

Bibliothèques des sciences morales et politiques, Paris, Guillaumin, 1857–[no end date located].

Blaise, Adolphe Gustave. *Cours d'économie industrielle* (lectures give at the Conservatoire des arts et métiers, 1836–39). Paris and Versailles: L. Hachette, de L. Mathias & J. Angé, 1837–39.

Blanc, Louis. *Histoire de la révolution française.* Paris: Langlois et Leelereq, 1847–69.

———. *Organisation du travail.* Paris: Prévot, 1840.

———. *Le Socialisme; droit au travail, réponse à M. Thiers.* Paris: M. Levy, 1848.

Blanqui, Jérôme Adolphe. *Les Classes ouvrières en France.* Paris: Pagnerre, 1849.

———. *Encyclopédie du commerçant.* Paris: Guillaumin, 1839–41.

———. *Précis élementaire d'économie politique.* Paris: Guillaumin, 1857.

Bursotti, Giovanni. *Biblioteca di commercio.* 3 vols. Naples: C. Batelli, 1841–42.

———. *Esposizione della tariffa doganale per lo regno delle Due Sicilie.* Naples: G. Nobile, 1854.

Carey, Henry C. *The Harmony of Interests, Agricultural, Manufacturing, and Commercial*. Philadelphia: J. S. Skinner, 1851.

Chateaubriand, François René, vicomte de. *Mémoires d'outre-tombe*. 42 vols. Paris: Eugène et Victor Penaud Frères, 1849–50.

Chevalier, Michel. *Cours d'économie politique fait au Collège de France: La monnaie*. Vol. 3. La Haye: Les Héritiers Doorman, 1850.

———. *Histoire et description des voies de communications aux États-Unis et des travaux d'art qui en dépendent*. Paris: C. Gosselin, 1840–41.

———. *Lettres sur l'Amérique du Nord*. Paris: C. Gosselin, 1836.

———. *Lettres sur l'organisation du travail, ou, Études sur les principales causes de la misère et sur les moyens proposés pour y remédier*. Brussels: Méline, Cans, 1850.

———. *Les Questions politiques et socials*. Paris: Bureau de la Revue des Deux Mondes, 1850.

Clément, Ambroise. *La Crise économique et sociale en France et en Europe*. Paris: Guillaumin, 1886.

———. *Des nouvelles idées de réforme industrielle et en particulier du projet d'organisation du travail de M. Louis Blanc*. Paris: Guillaumin, 1846.

———. *Economic Harmonies* book review. In *Le Journal des économistes* 26 (June 15, 1850): 235.

———. *Recherches sur les causes de l'indigence*. Paris: Guillaumin, 1846.

Cobden, Richard. "Réponse de M. Cobden au nom de la Ligue." *Le Journal des économistes* 14 (April–July 1846): 60.

Collection des principaux économistes. 15 vols. Edited by Horace Say. Paris: Guillaumin, 1840–48.

Comte, Charles. "Considérations sur l'état moral de la nation française, et sur les causes de l'instabilité de ses institutions." In *Le Censeur européen* 1 (1817): 1–92.

———. "De l'organisation sociale considérée dans ses rapports avec les moyens de subsistance des peuples." In *Le Censeur européen* 2 (1817): 1–66.

———. *Traité de la propriété*. 2 vols. Paris: Chamerot, Ducollet, 1834. [Brussels edition, H. Tarlier, 1835. A second, revised edition was published in 1835 by Chamerot, Ducollet of Paris in 4 vols. to coincide with the publication of its sequel, *Traité de la propriété*. A revised and corrected third edition was published in 1837 by Hauman, Cattoir of Brussels.]

———. *Traité de législation, ou exposition des lois générales suivant lesquelles les peuples prospèrent, dépérissent ou restent stationnaire*. 4 vols. Paris: A. Sautelet, 1827; Paris, Chamerot, Ducollet, 1835 (2d ed.); Brussels: Hauman, Cattoir, 1837 (3rd ed.).

Considérant, Victor Prosper. *Principes du socialisme. Manifeste de la démocratie au XIXe siècle*. 2d ed. Paris: Librairie Phalanstérienne, 1847.

———. *Théorie du droit de propriété et du droit au travail*. Paris: Librairie phalanstérienne, 1848.

Constant, Benjamin. *Commentaire sur l'ouvrage de Filangieri*. Paris: P. Dufart, 1822–24.

———. *Cours de politique constitutionelle*. Paris: Pancher, 1820.

———. *De l'esprit de conquête et de l'usurpation, dans leurs rapports à la civilisation européen*. Paris: Le Normant, 1814.

———. *Principes de politiques applicables à tous les gouvernements*. Paris: Alexis Eymery, 1815. (Published as *Principles of Politics Applicable to All Governments*, 2003, by Liberty Fund.)

Courcelle-Seneuil, Jean Gustave. "Lois agraires." *Dictionnaire de l'économie politique*, 2:100–103. Edited by Charles Coquelin and Gilbert Guillaumin. Paris: Guillaumin, 1853.

Custine, Astolphe, marquis de. *L'Espagne sous Ferdinand VII*. 4 vols. 2d ed. Paris: Ladvocat, 1838.

Delavigne, Casimir. *Le Paria: Tragédie en cinq actes, avec des cœurs*. Paris: J.-N. Barba, 1821.

Destutt de Tracy, Antoine. *Commentaire sur l'esprit des lois*. Paris: Delaunay, 1819.

———. *Éléments d'idéologie*. 4 vols. Paris: Didot l'aîné, et al., 1801–15.

———. *Traité d'économie politique*. Paris: Bouguet et Lévi, 1823.

Dictionnaire de l'économie politique. Edited by Charles Coquelin and Gilbert-Urbain Guillaumin. 2 vols. Paris: Guillaumin, 1852–53.

Dictionnaire universel théorique et practique du commerce et de la navigation. 2 vols. Paris: Guillaumin, 1859–61.

Dombasle, Christophe Joseph Alexandre Mathieu de. *De l'impôt sur le sucre indigène: Nouvelles considérations*. Paris: Huzard, 1837.

Donato, Nicolo. *L'Homme d'état*. 3 vols. Liege: Clement Plomteaux, 1769.

Droz, Joseph. *Applications de la morale à la politique*. Paris: Chez Antoine-Augustin Renouard, 1825.

———. *Économie politique, ou, Principes de la science des richesses*. Paris: J. Renouard, 1829.

———. *Lois relatives au progrès de l'industrie*. Paris, 1801.

Dunoyer, Charles. *De la liberté du travail, ou simple exposé des conditions dans lesquelles les force humaines s'exercent avec le plus de puissance*. 3 vols. Paris: Guillaumin, 1845.

———. "Du système de l'equilibre des puissances européennes." In *Le Censeur européen* 1 (1817). Reprinted in *Notices d'économie politique,* vol. 2 of *Œuvres de Dunoyer,* ed. Anatole Dunoyer, pp. 1–25. 3 vols. Paris: Guillaumin, 1870, 1885, 1886.

———. "Esquisse historique des doctrines auxquelles on a donné le nom industrialisme, c'est-à-dire, des doctrines qui fondent la société sur l'industrie." In *La Revue encyclopédique* 33 (February 1827): 368–94.

———. *L'Industrie et la morale considérées dans leurs rapport avec la liberté*. Paris: A. Sautelet, 1825.

———. *Nouveau traité d'économie sociale*. Paris: A. Sautelet, 1830.

Economisti classici italiani. Scrittori classici italiani di economia politica. 50 vols. Edited by Pietro Custodi. Milan: G. G. Destefanis, 1803–16.

Elliot, Ebenezer. *Corn Law Rhymes. Sheffield Mechanics' Anti–Bread Tax Society.* Sheffield: Platt and Todd, 1830.

———. *The Splendid Village; Corn Law Rhymes, and Other Poems*. London: B. Steill, 1844.

Faucher, Léon. *Études sur l'Angleterre*. Paris: Guillaumin, 1856.

Fix, Théodore. *Observations sur l'état des classes ouvrières*. Paris: Guillaumin, 1846.

Fonteyraud, Henri Alcide. "La Ligue anglaise." In *La Revue britannique*, 6th series, vol. 1 (1846).

———. *Mélanges d'économie politique. La Ligue anglaise pour la liberté du commerce. Notice historique sur la vie et les travaux de Ricardo*. Edited by J. Garnier. Paris: Guillaumin, 1853.

Franklin, Benjamin. *Mélanges de morale, d'économie et de politique*. Précédés d'une Notice sur Franklin par A.-Ch. Renouard. Edited by Augustin-Charles Renouard. 2 vols. Paris: Renouard, 1824.

Garnier, Joseph. *Congrès des amis de la paix universelle réunis à Paris en 1849*. Paris: Guillaumin, 1850.

———. *Introduction à l'étude de l'économie politique*. Paris: Guillaumin, 1843.

———. *Richard Cobden, les ligueurs et la ligue*. Paris: Guillaumin, 1846.

Guizot, François. *Essais sur l'histoire de France*. Paris: Priere, 1824.

———. *Histoire de la civilisation en France*. Paris: Pichon et Didier, 1829–32.

———. *Histoire de la révolution d'Angleterre*. Paris: A. Leroux et C. Chantpie, 1826–27.

———. *Histoire des origines du gouvernement représentif en Europe*. 2 vols. Paris: Didier, 1851. (Published as *The History of the Origins of Representative Government in Europe*, trans. Andrew Scoble, 1861, by Liberty Fund, 2002.)

———. *Histoire générale de la civilisation en Europe*. Paris: Pichon et Didier, 1828.

———. *Histoire parlementaire de France*. Paris: Michel Lévy Frères, 1863–64.

Harcourt, François-Eugène, duc d'. *Discours en faveur de la liberté du commerce*. Paris: Guillaumin, 1846.

Janin, Jules Gabriel. *Pictures of the French: A Series of Literary and Graphic Delineations of French Character*. London: W. S. Orr, 1840.

Jobard, Jean-Baptiste-Ambroise-Marcellin. *Nouvelle économie sociale, ou, Monautopole industriel, artistique, commerciel et littéraire*. Paris: Mathias, 1844.

Knatchbull, Sir Edward. *The Speech of Sir E. Knatchbull, Bart. M.P. for the County of Kent, to Which Is Added the Speech of H. Bankes, Esq. M.P. for Dorsetshire, in Defence of the Protestant Constitution*. London: J. Chappell, 1829.

Lafarelle, Félix de. *Du progrès social au profit des classes populaires nonindigentes*. Paris: Guillaumin, 1847.

Lamennais, Félicité, abbé de. *Essai sur l'indifférence en matière de religion.* 4 vols. Paris: Méquiguon, 1820–23.

Laromiguière, Pierre. *Leçons de philosophie sur les principes de l'intelligence, ou sur les causes et sur les origines des idées.* Paris: H. Fornier, 1815.

League, The. The Exponent of the Principles of Free Trade, and the Organ of the National Anti–Corn Law League. London: National Anti–Corn Law League, 1844–46.

Ledru-Rollin, Alexandre Auguste. *De la décadence de l'Angleterre.* Paris: Escudier Frères, 1850. Translated into English as *The Decline of England.* London: E. Churton, 1850.

Leroux, Pierre. *De la ploutocratie, ou, Du gouvernement des riches.* N.p.: Boussac, 1848.

———. *De l'humanité,* 2d ed. Paris: Perratin, 1840.

Malthus, Thomas Robert. *An Essay on the Principle of Population.* 1st ed., London: J. Johnson, 1798; rev. 3rd ed., London: J. Murray, 1826.

———. *Observations on the Effects of the Corn Laws.* London: J. Johnson, 1814.

———. *Principles of Political Economy.* London: J. Murray, 1820. Appeared in French as *Principes d'économie politique,* with unpublished critical remarks by J. B. Say, preceded by an introduction and accompanying explanatory and critical notes by Maurice Monjean. Paris: Guillaumin, 1846.

Mignet, François-Auguste-Alexis. *Histoire de la Révolution française.* Paris: Didot, 1824.

———. *Histoire de Marie Stuart.* Paris: Paulin, L'Heureux, 1852.

———. *Notices et mémoires historiques.* Paris: Paulin, 1843.

Mill, John Stuart. *On Liberty.* London: J. W. Parker, 1859.

———. *Principles of Political Economy.* London: J. W. Parker, 1848.

———. *The Subjection of Women.* Longmans, Green, Reader and Dyer, 1869.

———. *A System of Deductive and Inductive Logic.* London: J. W. Parker, 1843.

———. *Utilitarianism.* London: J. Fraser, 1861.

Molinari, Gustave de. *Cours d'économie politique.* Paris: Guillaumin, 1855.

———. *L'Évolution économique du dix-neuvième siècle: Théorie du progrès.* Paris: C. Reinwald, 1880.

———. *L'Évolution politique et la révolution.* Paris: C. Reinwald, 1884.

———. *Les Soirées de la rue Saint-Lazare.* Paris: Guillaumin, 1849.

Nouveau dictionnaire d'économie politique. Edited by Léon Say and Joseph Chailley. Paris: Guillaumin, 1891–92.

Passy, Frédéric. *Notice biographique sur Frédéric Bastiat.* Paris: Guillaumin. 1857.

———. *Pour la paix: notes et documents.* Paris: Fasquelle, 1909.

Passy, Hippolyte. *De l'aristocracie considérée dans ses rapports avec les progrès de la civilization.* Paris: A. Bossange, 1826.

———. *Des causes de l'inégalité des richesses.* Paris: Pagnerre, 1848.

———. *Des systèmes de culture et de leur influence sur l'économie sociale.* Paris: Pagnerre, 1848.

Petitti, Carlo Ilarione, conte di Roreto. *Considerazioni sopra la necessità di una riforma de' tributi con alcuni cenni su certe spese dello Stato.* Turin: Giannini e Fiore, 1850.

———. *Delle strade ferrate italiane e del miglior ordinamento di esse. Cinque discorsi.* Capolago: Elvetica, 1845.

———. *Saggio sul buon governo della mendicità, degli istituti di beneficenza e delle carceri.* Turin: [publisher unknown], 1837.

Polignac, Jules August Armand Marie, duc de. *Considérations politiques sur l'époque actuelle: adressées à l'auteur anonyme de l'ouvrage intitulé* Histoire de la restauration, *par un homme d'état.* Paris: Pinard, 1832.

Potier, Jean-Pierre, and André Tiran, eds. *Jean-Baptiste Say: Nouveaux regards sur son œuvre.* Paris: Economica, 2003. "Tableau chronologique," pp. 740–60.

Potonié, D. *Note sur l'organisation facultative des débouchés de l'industrie parisienne abouchement direct du producteur et du consommateur: juillet 1848.* Paris: Guillaumin, 1848.

Prince-Smith, John. *John Prince-Smith's Gesammelte Schriften.* Berlin : F. A. Herbig, 1877–80.

———. *Über die englische Tarifreform und ihre materiellen, sozialen und politischen Folgen für Europa.* Berlin: J. Springer, 1846.

———. *Über Handelsfeindseligkeit.* Königsberg: Bei Theodor Theile, 1843.

Proudhon, Pierre Joseph. *Qu'est-ce que la propriété? Ou recherches sur le principe du droit et du gouvernement.* Paris: Prévot, 1841.

———. *Système des contradictions économiques.* Paris: Guillaumin, 1846.

Quesnay, François. *Physiocratie, ou constitution naturelle de gouvernement le plus avantageux au genre humain.* Paris: Merlin, 1768.

———. *Le Tableau économique.* Hamburg: Chréstien Hérold, 1762.

Renouard, Augustin-Charles. "L'Éducation doit-elle être libre?" In vol. 39 of *La Revue encyclopédique* (August 1828).

Report of the Proceedings of the Second General Peace Congress, Held in Paris, on the 22nd, 23rd and 24th of August, 1849. Comp. from Authentic Documents under the Superintendence of the Peace Congress Committee. London: Gilpin, 1849.

Report of the Proceedings of the Third General Peace Congress, Held in Frankfort, on the 22nd, 23rd, 24th of August, 1850. Comp. from Authentic Documents. London: C. Gilpin, 1851.

Reybaud, Louis. *Économistes contemporains.* Paris: J. Claye, 1861.

———. *Études sur les réformateurs et socialistes modernes: Saint-Simon, Charles Fourier, Robert Owen.* Paris: Guillaumin, 1840.

———. *Jérôme Paturot à la recherché d'une position sociale.* Paris: Paulin, 1843.

———. "Socialistes, socialisme." In vol. 2 of *Dictionnaire de l'économie politique,* pp. 629–41.

Ricardo, David. *The High Price of Bullion.* London: John Murray, 1810.

———. *On the Principles of Political Economy and Taxation.* London: J. Murray, 1817.

———. *The Works and Correspondence of David Ricardo.* Edited by Piero Sraffa, with M. H. Dobb. 11 vols. Indianapolis, Ind.: Liberty Fund, 2004.

Rossi, Pellegrino. *Cours d'économie politique.* Paris: Joubert, 1840.

Salis Schwabe, J. *Richard Cobden. Notes sur ses voyages, correspondences, et souvenirs. Recueillés par Mme Salis Schwabe, avec une préface de M. G. de Molinari.* Paris: Guillaumin, 1879.

Say, Horace Émile. *Histoire des relations commerciales entre la France et le Brésil.* Paris: Guillaumin, 1839.

Say, Jean-Baptiste. *Cours complet d'économie politique pratique.* Paris: Rapilly, 1828–33.

———. *De l'Angleterre et des Anglais.* Paris: A. Bertrand, 1815.

———. *Traité d'économie politique.* Paris: Déterville, 1803.

Say, Léon. *Les Finances de la France sous la troisième république.* Paris: C. Lévy, 1898–1901.

Scialoja, Antonio. *Lezioni di economia politica.* Turin: G. Pomba, 1846–54.

———. *I principi della economia sociale esposti in ordine ideologico.* Naples: G. Palma, 1840. [French edition: *Les Principes de l'économie exposé selon des idées.* Paris: Guillaumin, 1844.]

———. *Trattato elementare di economia sociale.* Turin: G. Pomba, 1848.

Senior, Nassau William. *Lectures on Political Economy.* [Place and publisher unknown], 1826.

———. *Outline of the Science of Political Economy.* London: B. Fellowes, 1834.

Smith, Adam. *The Glasgow Edition of the Works and Correspondence of Adam Smith.* 8 vols. Hardcover. Oxford: Oxford University Press, 1960. Paperback. Indianapolis, Ind.: Liberty Fund, 1982–87.

———. *An Inquiry into the Nature and Causes of the Wealth of Nations.* London: W. Strahan and T. Cadell, 1776. [French edition: *Recherches sur la nature, et les causes de la richesse des nations. Traduit de l'anglois de M. Smith.* Paris: Pierre J. Duplain, 1788.]

———. *The Theory of Moral Sentiments.* London: A. Millar; Edinburgh: A. Kincaid and J. Bell, 1759. [French edition: *Théorie des sentimens moraux. Traduction nouvelle de l'anglois de M. Smith, . . . par M. l'abbé Blavet.* Paris: Valade, 1774–75.]

Staël, Anne-Louise-Germaine de. *Considérations sur les principaux événements de la Révolution française.* Paris: Delaunay, 1818. (*Considerations upon the Principal Events of the French Revolution.* Edited by Aurelian Craiutu. Indianapolis: Liberty Fund, 2008.)

———. *Corinne, ou l'Itale.* Paris: H. Nicolle, 1807.

———. *De l'Allemagne.* London: John Murray, 1813.

Stanhope, Philip, Earl of Chesterfield. *Letters Written by the Late Right Honourable Philip Dormer Stanhope, Earl of Chesterfield, to His Son, Philip Stanhope, Esq.: Late Envoy Extraordinary at the Court of Dresden: Together with Several Other Pieces on Various Subjects.* London: J. Dodsley, 1774.

Thiers, Adolphe. *De la propriété.* Paris: Paulin, 1848.

———. *Histoire de consulat et de l'empire.* 20 vols. Paris: Paulin, 1845–62.

———. *Histoire de la révolution française.* 10 vols. Paris: Lecointe et Durey, 1823–27.

Turgot, Anne-Robert-Jacques, baron de l'Aulne. *Éloge de Gournay.* [Place and publisher unknown], 1759.

———. *Lettres sur la liberté du commerce des grains.* [Place and publisher unknown], 1770.

———. *Œuvres de Turgot.* Edited by E. Daire and Gilbert Guillaumin. Paris: Guillaumin, 1844.

———. *Réflexions sur la formation et la distribution des richesses.* [Place and publisher unknown], 1766.

Villermé, Louis René. *Tableau de l'état physique et moral des ouvriers employés dans les manufactures de coton, de laine, et de soie.* Paris: Jules Renouard, 1840.

Wilson, James. *Capital, Currency, and Banking.* London: Office of the Economist, 1847.

———. *Influence of the Corn Laws.* London: Longmans et al., 1839.

Wolowski, Louis. *La Banque d'Angleterre et les banques d'Écosse.* Paris: Guillaumin, 1867.

———. *Cours de législation industrielle. De l'organisation du travail.* Paris: Guillaumin, 1844.

———. *Études d'économie politique et de statistique.* Paris: Guillaumin, 1848.

———. *La Liberté commerciale et les résultats du traité de commerce de 1860.* Paris: Guillaumin, 1869.

———. *L'Or et l'argent.* Paris: Guillaumin, 1870.

———. *La Question des banques.* Paris: Guillaumin, 1864.

Index

Abd El-Kader, 201, 477

Aberdeen Bill, 433n24

abolition of slavery. *See* slavery and slave trade

Académie des sciences morales et politiques, 294n380, 511

Académie française, 294n380, 485, 496, 504

Academy, the, at Mugron, xxviii, 332

administrative decentralization, French need for, 184, 350

Adour River, 509; canal project, xxvii, 62, 364; Mugron on, xxviii, 509–10; navigability of, 314; sea pine forests of, 49n55; unspoiled nature of, 212

advertising, press reliance on, 63

advice, Bastiat on, 471–72

Aesop, 416

Affre, Romain (husband of Julie Marsan), 157, 198n270, 477

agriculture: Bastiat's interest in agricultural reforms, xxvi, xxviii, 23, 180n244, 485; in the Chalosse, 313–16; common land, report to the Landes on, 446–51; establishment of farm schools in each *département*, 183n247; existing farm schools in France and Switzerland, 336, 337; proposal of school for children of sharecroppers, xxviii, 334–40; socialism and agrarian law, 246. *See also* wine trade

Aide toi, le ciel t'aidera (society), 6, 480

Akenside, Mark, 326

Alboni, Marietta, 179

Alexandre, Mme (friend of Mme Cheuvreux), 218

Alfieri, Vittorio, 14, 18, 477

Algeria: England and, 141, 365, 421, 439; French colonization of, xxxiv, 141, 352, 353n15, 363–65; French postal reform and, 174n238; monopolistic interests in, 425; tariffs in, 421

ambassadors, 429–30

America: Bastiat's secondary school, Americans attending, xxv; Bastiat's works, American editions of, 103, 195; Cabet and, 480; Carey on landed property and, 299; Chevalier and, 481–82; civil servants in, 347; delegates to Frankfurt Peace Congress from, 265n353; democracy and aristocracy, English struggle between, 322, 325; Destutt de Tracy and, 485; economists and *économiste* school in, 76, 420; freedom of teaching in, 420; Indivision Treaty (1818) in Oregon, 90n119; La Fayette and, 492; liberal, meaning of, xvii; liberty as viewed in, 420; marriage of U.S. president, lack of public interest in, 430; Napoleonic blockade, compensation for, 479; Passy, Hippolyte, and, 498; political economy in, 20; religious freedom in, 373; *La Revue des deux mondes* and, 519; Say, Horace, and, 502; Texas's admission to United States, 381; War of Independence in, 123, 322, 325

Ancona, French garrison in, 378, 379, 381, 383, 423

anglophobia: Algerian question and, 365; "Anglomania, Anglophobia" (Bastiat, 1847), 72n92, 138, 198, 320–34; aristocracy and democracy, English struggle

anglophobia (*continued*)
between, 320–29; Coudroy's article on, 138; in journalism, 54, 331–33; in Ledru-Rollin's *De la décadence de l'Angleterre*, 138; means of disseminating, 331–34; mentioned in Bastiat's correspondence, 87, 95, 121, 133–34, 136, 141, 150; Peel's speech, mistranslation of, xxviii; progress of democracy in England, relationship to, 329–31

Anisson-Duperron, Alexandre, 477; in Bastiat's correspondence, 94, 96, 100, 102, 104, 109, 112, 114, 115, 137, 157; on editorial board of *Le Libre échange*, 516

Anti–Bread Tax Circular (Anti–Corn Law League, 1841), 88

Anti–Corn Law League, 511; banquet to celebrate final repeal of Corn Laws (1849), 176–79; Bastiat inspired by, xxiii, xxviii–xxix, xxx, xxxi, 6, 51; Bastiat's correspondence on, 4–5, 51, 54, 176–79; corn, definition of, xxix*n*3; Corn Law legislation, xxviii–xxxi, 512–13; founding of, xxxiv, 513; French press's grasp of issues, 332n17; Manchester meeting, 82, 84, 86; Masons, compared to, 70; repeal of Corn Laws (1846), xxxi, 107, 176n240, 323, 513. *See also* Cobden, Richard; *Cobden and the League*

Arago, François, 95, 207, 477

aristocracy: class divisions in France, 230–31, 388; English struggle between democracy and, 320–29; privileges of clergy and nobility, French suppression of, 321n6

armed forces, disarmament of. *See* disarmament

Arnault, Antoine-Vincent, 18

Arnault, Lucien, 18, 477

Arrivabene, Giovanni, 7, 171–72, 286, 477, 523

Articles of Paris, 77, 78, 89

Ashworth, Henry, 70, 80, 477

association, freedom of, 434

Association pour la liberté des échanges, xxxi, 93–103, 109–10, 112n162, 119n172, 511, 516

Atelier, L' (newspaper), 426

Augier, Émile, 215, 477

Australia, 226

Austria: authoritarian nature of, 321; Bologna, invasion of, 378n28, 423n14; Charles Albert of Sardinia defeated by, 185, 192n260; French fear of attack by, 437; Krakow annexed by, 122n176; in Lombardy, 185, 192n260, 440; revolution of 1848, French fear of attack after, 437; on Syria, position of, 42n46

Auxerrois gate, 179–80

Baccalaureate and Socialism (Bastiat, 1850), xxxiii

Bacon, Francis, 319

Badbedat, Marie-Julienne (Mme Marsan), 142–43, 157, 477–78, 523

Baines, Edward, 151, 478

Balmaceda, General, 32

banishment, laws of, 222

Barbeyrac, Jean, 311, 478

Barbier de Seville, Le (Beaumarchais), 248n332

Basque language, 211, 241, 305–8

Bastiat, Frédéric, xxiii–xxxv; agricultural reforms, interest in, xxvi, xxviii, 23, 180n244, 485; Anti–Corn Law League, inspired by, xxiii, xxviii–xxix, xxx, xxxi, 6, 51; childhood and education of, xxiv–xxv; chronology, xxxvi–xxxvii; *Complete Works* of (see *Complete Works* of Bastiat); correspondence of (*see* correspondence of Bastiat); electoral principles of (*see* electoral principles); England, travel to, xxx; family background, xxiii–xxiv; final illness and death of, xxxiii, xxxiv, xxxv, 3, 4, 8, 127n83, 231n312, 267n354, 269–70, 274, 277, 278, 279–80, 282, 284, 287–89, 291, 292, 294–97; on free trade (*see* free trade); homesickness of, 4, 6, 36, 66, 68, 116, 160, 223, 316; humor and wit of, 8–9; ill health of, mentioned in correspondence, 13, 43, 68, 119, 127, 129, 131–32, 138, 139, 142, 146, 160, 168, 174, 178, 180, 181, 183, 196, 205, 219, 225, 228, 231, 233,

235, 236, 237, 241, 242, 244, 251, 258–59, 261, 262, 263, 265, 267, 392; illustration of, iii; language proficiency of, 305n1; as local official, xxvii–xxviii, 85, 369; maps of France showing cities associated with or mentioned by, xxxviii, xxxix; marriage of, xxvii, 8; Masonic affiliation of, xxvi; mortality, awareness of, 8; parents, death of, xxiv, 8; Paris, reasons for moving to, 316–17; peace and free trade, on connection between, xxxiv; persistence of interest in, xixn1; on politics (see political economy, politics, and government; political manifestos); in revolution of 1830, xxvii; talkativeness of, 230, 237, 239, 243–44; as teacher, 130–32, 137, 139, 224; trade and commerce, interest in, 11–12, 14–15, 24; writings of (see specific titles and subjects); writing style of, xv

Bastiat, Justine (aunt): Bastiat raised by, xxii; biographical information, 478; chambermaid of, 8–9, 210–11, 215, 241, 246; failing health of, 242; mentioned in Bastiat's correspondence, 32–33, 35, 36, 40, 41, 42, 62, 66–68, 124, 125, 126, 208, 209, 210–11, 215, 229, 234, 242, 244n328, 251, 289; wife of Bastiat left in care of, xxviin1

Bastiat, Pierre (father), xxiii–xxiv

Bastiat, Pierre (grandfather), xxiii–xxiv, xxvi, 19

Bastide, Jules, 478

Batistant (winegrower), 44

Bayonne: Bastiat and Bastiat family in, xxiii–xxvi, 19, 305n1; Bordeaux to Bayonne railway line, letter to newspaper on, 312–16; in revolution of 1830, xxvii, 25n26, 26, 27, 28–30; secondary school, appropriate curriculum for, 415–19; theater, 415

beards, propensity of French for, 204

Beaumarchais, Pierre Augustin Caron de, 248n332

Beccaria, Cesare, 129n186

beer and wine drinkers contrasted, 247

beet sugar versus cane sugar, 23

Belgium: Bastiat's trip to, 200–205; Eco-nomic Harmonies in, 278n364; proposed customs union between France and, xxxi, 422; royalism in, 217

Bellini, Vincenzo, 167

Benoist d'Azy, Paul, 280, 478

Bentham, Jeremy, 115

Béranger, Pierre-Jean, 30, 59, 95, 97, 478

Bernardin de Saint-Pierre, Jacques-Henri, 18

Berri, duc de, murder of, 484

Berryer, Pierre Antoine, 95, 478

Bertin, Edouard, 276, 478, 515

Bertin, Louis-François, 478, 515

Bertin, Mme, 288

Biarritz, 115, 157n222, 198, 247

Billault, Adolphe, 187, 478

Blaise, Adolphe Gustave, 66, 478

Blanc, Louis, 478; Bastiat's association with, xxxii; Bastiat's writings in reply to, 387, 392, 517; Caussidière and, 480; Government Commission for the Workers, 391n41; Individualism and Fraternity written in opposition to, 188–89, 392, 514; Justice and Fraternity addressing ideas of, 515; mentioned in Bastiat's correspondence, 39, 141, 161–62, 164, 165, 188, 213, 214, 229; in provisional government, 441n36, 465; riots/conspiracy of 15 May (1848) and, xxxiii, 161–62, 164–65, 480; Wolowski's opposition to, 508

Blanqui, Auguste, 68, 479, 511

Blanqui, Jérôme Adolphe, 479; in Association pour la liberté des échanges, 511; Bastiat influenced by, 5; Blaise, Adolphe Gustave, and, 478; Fix, Theodore, and, 488; French edition of Wealth of Nations, notes and commentary in, 505; Garnier and, 489; Guillaumin and, 490; Le Journal des économistes edited by, 515; Le Libre échange and, 516; mentioned in Bastiat's correspondence, 5, 55, 93, 100, 102, 109, 118

Boislembert (deliverer of speech at unveiling of Girard's bust), 232

Bonaparte, Louis-Napoléon, 479; administrative appointments for supporters of, 240n35; Bastiat's advice to, 473–76;

Bonaparte, Louis-Napoléon (*continued*)
Bastiat's association with, xxxii; in
Bastiat's correspondence, 4, 174–75,
225n304; Changarnier's opposition to,
481; dictatorship seemingly foretold by
Bastiat, 175n239; 18 Brumaire of, 518; as
Napoléon III (emperor of France), 478,
481, 497, 501, 506; presidency of Second
Republic, election to, xxxii, 174–75,
179n241, 394, 395–96, 480, 493; seizure
of power by, 476n57
Bonaparte, Napoléon. *See* Napoléon I; Na-
poleonic wars
Bordeaux: Bastiat's plan to teach in, 132;
free trade campaign in, xxxi, 31–32, 51,
86–94, 98, 99; railway line from Ba-
yonne to Bordeaux, letter to newspaper
on, 312–16; in revolution of 1830, 27
Bordogni, Giulio Marco, 179
Bossuet, Jacques-Benigne, 69, 319, 504
bourgeoisie, Bastiat on, 230–31
Boyer-Fonfrède, Henri, 32, 479
Brazil, 433
Bright, John, 69, 70, 74, 79, 89, 104, 176,
334, 479, 511
Bright, Thomas, 79, 80
Brissot, Jacques Pierre, 220n296
Britain. *See* England
Broglie, Victor, duc de, 95, 96, 103, 258,
479, 502
Brunet, Gustave, 516
Brussels Peace Congress (1848), xxxiv,
226n305, 263n52
Brutus, 416, 417
Buffet, Louis Joseph, 183, 184, 191, 479
Bugeaud, Thomas, 206, 479
Buloz, François, 85, 239, 480, 519
Bulwer, Henry, 134, 429, 480
Burns, Robert, 326
Bursotti, Giovanni, 128, 480
business, Bastiat's interest in, 11–12, 14–15, 24
Bussières (member of Association pour la
liberté des échanges), 100
Butard Wood (Le Butard), 200, 205–6, 207,
208, 250, 259n348, 267n354, 277, 509

Butte Montmartre, 201
Byron, George Gordon, Lord, 24, 326, 417

Cabet, Etienne, 426, 480, 515
Calmètes, Victor-Adrien, 480; Bastiat's
correspondence with, 6, 11–18, 24–25,
30–31, 91–92, 521; joint school prize won
by Bastiat with, xxv; liberalism, involve-
ment with, 6
Campan, 516
Campbell, Thomas, 326
Canada, 90, 226
cane sugar versus beet sugar, 23
Canning, George, and Canningites, 379,
480
canuts, revolts of, 273n363
Cape Colony (South Africa), 226
capital, Fontenay's essay on, 267–68, 270
Capital and Rent (Bastiat, 1849), xxxiii,
181–82, 189, 387, 393, 511
Carey, Henry C., xxxiv, 290, 293, 297–300,
480
Carlists and Don Carlo (brother of Ferdi-
nand VII), 32, 38, 411
Carrel, Armand, 495
Carrière, Eugène, 17
Castagnède, 49, 480
Catholicism. *See* Roman Catholicism
Caussidière, Marc, 161, 480
Cavaignac, Eugène, 480; Bastiat's support
for administration of, 392; during June
Days, 518; Ledru-Rollin yielding powers
to, 494; mentioned in Bastiat's cor-
respondence, 4, 153n217, 156n221, 160,
162, 163, 169–70, 174, 181, 192; Odier,
Antoine, as father-in-law of, 497; presi-
dential elections, supported by Bastiat in,
394, 396
Censeur, Le/Le Censeur européen (periodi-
cal), 20, 22, 53–54, 56, 483, 486, 511–12
Chadwick, Edwin, 504
Chalosse, La (newspaper), xi, 59, 305, 309,
484, 512
Chalosse region, 509; agriculture in,
313–16; Basque country and, 305; Bas-

tiat family in, xxiii, xxiv; common land in, 448; in correspondence, 30, 50, 94, 110, 114, 183n247, 278; economy of, xxvi, xxvii–xxviii; means of communication needed in, 349; population of, 50, 313–15

chambermaid of Justine Bastiat, 8–9, 210–11, 215, 241, 246

Chamber of Peers, 407

Chambord, count of (son of Charles X, known as "Henri V"), 467

Changarnier, Nicolas Anne Théodule, 193, 481

Chantelauze, V., 341, 481

Charles II (king of Spain), 253n339

Charles X (king of France), xxvii, 25n26, 179n242, 356n17, 467n50, 481, 486, 495, 499, 515

Charles Albert (King of Sardinia), 185, 192n260, 481

Charter, constitutional, 370, 372–76, 379, 386, 456, 461, 462, 468, 512

Chateaubriand, François René, vicomte de, 258, 268–69, 481

Chatel, Ferdinand, 463, 481

Chaumel (Bastiat's doctor), 252

Chénier, André, 81, 274, 481

Chesterfield, Philip Stanhope, earl of, 16, 505

Cheuvreux, Anne (sister of Casimir; later Mme Horace Say), 202, 271, 285

Cheuvreux, Casimir (husband of Hortense), 481; Bastiat's correspondence with, 6, 212–13, 260–62, 274–75; mentioned in Bastiat's correspondence, 179, 202, 208, 209, 210, 211, 217, 218, 221–22, 230, 236–38, 240, 244, 254, 258, 272, 276, 278, 281, 288, 294, 524; mentioned in Paillottet's letter, 297; Say, Horace, relationship to, 502

Cheuvreux, Hortense Girard (Mme Cheuvreux), 481; Bastiat's close relationship to, 6–7, 8; Bastiat's correspondence with, 167, 173–74, 179–80, 185–86, 197–98, 200–205, 208–11, 215–19, 222,

229–32, 235–38, 240–45, 248–50, 251–54, 257–60, 273–78, 281–82, 287–88, 294–95, 523; on Bastiat's provincial appearance, xxix–xxx; childhood friend, loss of, 215, 260; letters of Bastiat collected by, xi, xxxn6, 3, 5, 481; mentioned in Bastiat's correspondence, 246, 262, 275; mother, illness and death of, 292, 295; Paillottet's letter to, 296–97, 524

Cheuvreux, Louise (daughter of Hortense and Casimir), 6, 481; Bastiat's correspondence with, 6, 246–48, 270–73, 524; marriage plans for, collapse of, 236, 238, 240, 242, 247; mentioned in Bastiat's correspondence, 174, 179–80, 185, 198, 200, 202, 203, 208–11, 215, 219, 231, 233, 234, 236–38, 240, 241, 242, 249, 250, 251, 254, 257, 258, 261, 275, 276, 277, 281, 288, 295; mentioned in Paillottet's letter, 297

Cheuvreux family: Bastiat's correspondence with, 6–7 (see also specific family members); Bastiat's friendship with, xxix, 481; Italy, trip to, 276–78, 281–82, 287–88; New Year celebrations at home of, 229–30

Chevalier, Michel, 481–82; in Association pour la liberté des échanges, 511; Droz, Joseph, and, 485; free-trade treaty between England and France, as signatory of, 479, 482, 483; Le Libre échange, on editorial board of, 516; mentioned in Bastiat's correspondence, 68, 100, 120, 149, 211, 221, 239, 254–55, 294; in Saint-Simonian socialist group, 487

cholera, 8, 166, 200, 212, 489, 493

Christian Brothers, 340

Christianity. See religion

chronology for Bastiat, xxxvi–xxxvii

church-state relations. See religion

Cincinnatus, 16

civil servants: ambassadors, 429–30; revolution of 1848, scramble for office following, 431–32 civil servants as elected officials, opposition to: in Bastiat's address to electors of Saint-Severs (1846), 357–59; in Bastiat's address to electors of the Landes (1830), 344–45, 347; Bastiat's argument from liberty regarding (after 1840), 457–63; in Bastiat's correspondence (1849), 187; Bastiat's letters to *La Sentinelle* on (1843), 452–57; Bastiat's political manifesto on (1846), 25n24, 75n100, 367–86; in Bastiat's "Three Pieces of Advice" (1850), 476; *Parliamentary Conflicts of Interest* (Bastiat, 1849), xxxiii, 189, 216, 293

Clarendon, George Villiers, earl of, 70, 89, 176, 507

Clarkson, Thomas, 327, 482

class divisions in France, 230–31, 388

classical education, Bastiat on, 415–19, 424, 431

classical world, Bastiat's references to, 16, 369, 417, 431

Clément, Ambroise, 23, 251, 256, 259, 293, 482

Club de la liberté du travail, 489

clubs, political, 148, 184, 192

Cobden, Mrs. (wife of Richard), 114, 116, 125, 131, 151, 152

Cobden, Richard: Ashworth, Henry, and, 477; Baines, Edward, and, 478; Bastiat's *Complete Works* and, xii; Bastiat's correspondence with, xxxi, 4–5, 6, 50–53, 58, 69, 71, 74–76, 79–81, 84–90, 92–93, 95–99, 104–36, 139–42, 146–47, 151–52, 155–56, 159–61, 220–21, 226–29, 262–64, 267–69, 282–83, 522; Bastiat's efforts to imitate career of, 3; Bastiat's meetings with, xxx, 6, 7, 64, 69–70, 165; Bastiat's use of English with, xvii, 69–70; biographical information, 482–83; Chevalier, Michel, and, 482; on diplomacy, 429; on Fonteyraud, 82; invited to visit Bastiat, 80; mentioned in Bastiat's correspondence, 78, 82, 165, 166, 173, 176, 186, 203, 208, 258; Passy, Frédéric, influenced by, 498; peace and free trade, belief in connection between, xxxiv,

6, 165; Prince-Smith and, 500; public fundraising campaign for, 107; Société d'économie politique and, 519; travel to Europe by, 110, 114–15, 116, 123, 125–26, 128, 129, 282–83. *See also* Anti–Corn Law League

Cobden and the League (Bastiat, 1845), 512; dedicated copies of, 69, 71; introduction to, 65, 94; mentioned in Bastiat's correspondence, 52–53, 54–55, 58, 61n77, 63n80, 65n82, 69, 72, 73n96, 89, 91, 92, 94n128, 107, 117; origins of, xxx, 332–34; publication of, 65; second edition of, 117; subject matter of, 323n9; title of, 58, 80, 87; translations of, 73

Coburg (Frederick of Saxe-Coburg), 119, 483

cod-liver oil, 167, 174

Collège de France, 68, 149, 254, 512

colonialism: Algeria, French colonization of, xxxiv, 141, 352, 353n15, 363–65; Bastiat's opposition to, xxxiv, 90, 107, 120, 221, 324, 363; free trade and, 177–78, 226–27

Columbus, Christopher, 57

Commerce, Le (newspaper), 113

commerce and trade, Bastiat's interest in, 11–12, 14–15, 24

common land, Bastiat's report to the Landes on, 446–51

communism. *See* socialism

Complete Works of Bastiat: editorial notes, xii; ellipses, use of, xiii; glossaries for, xiii; online resources for, xii; sources and editions used for, xi–xii, xix–xx; thematic arrangement of, xi; translation of, xv–xvii

Comte, Auguste, 487

Comte, Charles, 483; Bastiat influenced by, xxvi, 5, 21, 53, 55, 297, 319, 354n16; *Le Censeur/Le Censeur européen* founded by, 483, 511–12; Coudroy influenced by, 21, 55; Dunoyer and, 67, 483, 486, 511–12; government activities, nonproductiveness of, 358n19; industry, meaning of, xvi–xvii, 16n6; mentioned in Bastiat's correspondence, 5, 21, 53, 55, 67; notes

and papers of, Bastiat's access to, 69, 71;
Saint-Simonians and, 487; Say and, xxvi,
483, 512
Comte, Hippolyte (son of Charles), 69, 71
conflicts of interest, parliamentary. *See* civil
servants as elected officials
Congress of Verona (1822), 24n23
Congress of Vienna (1815), 122n176,
192n260
conservatives and opposition, mutual dissatisfaction of, 352–54
Conservatoire national des arts et métiers,
68, 512
Considérant, Victor Prosper, xxxiii, 229,
387, 483, 513, 517
conspiracy/riots of 15 May (1848), xxxiii,
161–62, 164–65, 480
Constant, Benjamin, 6, 21, 22, 317, 483, 486,
495, 505
Constituent Assembly, 512; Bastiat on
responsibilities of, 451; in Bastiat's correspondence, 4, 148, 153nn217–18, 179n241,
198n272, 214, 218; Bastiat's election to,
xxxii
constitutional Charter, 370, 372–76, 379,
386, 456, 461, 462, 468, 512
Constitutionnel, Le (periodical), 381, 488
Coquelin, Charles, 281, 489, 491, 514, 516
Corcelle, Claude Tinguy de, 100, 484
Corn Laws. *See* Anti–Corn Law League;
Cobden, Richard
correspondence of Bastiat: Bastiat's character as revealed in, 3–5; number of letters,
3; recipients of, 5–7, 521–24 (*see also specific recipients by name*); recurring themes
in, 7–9 (*see also specific themes*); sources
of letters, 3, 5; text of, 11–302
Coudroy, Félix: Bastiat's correspondence
with, xxix, 6, 18–23, 25–49, 59–71,
90–91, 100–103, 108–9, 113–14, 124–25,
131–32, 137–39, 143–45, 153–55, 161–65,
168–71, 174–75, 187–89, 193–95, 207–8,
223–25, 228–29, 269–70, 288–89, 309n2,
521–22; biographical information, 484;
influences on, 20, 21, 55; mentioned in
Bastiat's correspondence, 209n280, 210,

233n314, 234, 244; mentioned in Bastiat's
letter to *Le Journal des économistes,* 297–
98; reading shared with Bastiat, xxvi, 20,
21, 210; sister of, 36, 62, 113, 125, 139, 289;
writings of, 93, 103, 138, 309–12, 484
Council of State, 212, 225, 345, 486, 513
country life, in Bastiat's correspondence, 17
Courcelle-Seneuil, Jean Gustave, 246n331
Courrier français, Le (newspaper), 94, 99,
100, 115–16, 488, 495, 513
Cousin, Victor, 94, 362, 484
Cremieux, Adolphe, 441n36
Crimean War (1854–56), 134n191
Croissy, 212, 254, 509
Crumpsall House, Manchester, 167, 173,
186. *See also* Schwabe family
Curii and Manius Curius Dentatus, 16
Curzay, 27
Custine, Astolphe, marquis de, 34, 38, 41,
484
customs duties and tariffs. *See* taxation and
tariffs
Cuvier, Georges, 299, 312

Dabadie (monk native to Saint-Sever), 47
Daguerre (friend of Coudroy and
Bastiat), 94
Daire, Eugène, 59, 68, 484
Dalmatie, Nicolas Soult, duc de, 45,
460n44, 505
Damned Money (Bastiat, 1849), xxxiii, 189,
387, 393, 513
Dampierre, Roger de, 183–84, 193–94,
410n5, 412–14, 484
Danton, Georges Jacques, 78
Darblay, Aimé-Stanislas, 362, 484
David, Félicien, 271, 484
Decazes, Elie, duc de Glücksberg, 325, 484,
485
Decazes, Louis Charles, duc de Glücksberg,
134, 485
decentralization, French need for, 184, 350
"Declaration des principes" (Bastiat, 1846),
xxxi
De la décadence de l'Angleterre (Ledru-
Rollin, 1850), 138

De la liberté du travail (Dunoyer, 1845), 56n69, 60n75, 486

Delavigne, Casimir, 17–18, 485

democracy: anglophobia in France related to progress of democracy in England, 329–31; English struggle between aristocracy and, 320–29

Démocratie pacifique, La (periodical), 426–27, 431, 513

Demosthenes, 405

Despouys (winegrower), 44

Destutt de Tracy, Antoine, xxvi, 20, 66, 67, 341, 485

Dictionnaire de l'économie politique (1852), 130n187, 246n331, 260, 298n386, 482, 497, 501, 503, 516

diplomacy, 429–30

disarmament: Bastiat's peace policy based on, xxxiii–xxxiv, 5, 136, 140–41, 147, 152, 159, 160–61, 178; Bastiat's recommendation to European powers, 439–40; British reduction of forces, Bastiat and Cobden on, 5, 89–90, 122, 134–36, 140–42, 147, 152, 159, 160–61, 165; free trade leading to, 178; National Assembly's efforts regarding, 159; revolution of 1848 and, 435–40

doctrinaires, 491, 493, 515

Dombasle, Christophe Joseph Alexandre Mathieu de, 67, 336n20, 485

Domenger, Bernard: Bastiat's correspondence with, 6, 145–46, 163–64, 179–85, 189–93, 196–200, 205–6, 222–23, 225, 232–35, 278–79, 291–92, 523; biographical information, 6, 485; mentioned in Bastiat's correspondence, 34, 44, 137, 165, 179, 193

Donato, Nicoló, 126, 485

double entry accounting, 338

drama: cited in Bastiat's articles and addresses, 417; opera, in Bastiat's correspondence, 103, 117, 167–68, 179; referred to in Bastiat's correspondence, 17–18, 219, 231, 231n311, 248, 257, 290

Droz, Joseph, 294, 485

Dubarry, Mme (mistress of Louis XV), 205

Duchâtel, Charles Tanneguy, 68, 87, 108, 485

Dudon, J. F., 341, 486

dueling, 60, 61, 309–12

Dufaure, Armand, 170, 218, 486

Duffour-Dubergier, Martin, 90n120, 104–5, 107, 486

Dumont, Etienne, 502

Dunant, Henri, 498

Dunoyer, Barthélémy-Pierre-Joseph-Charles, 486; Bastiat influenced by, xxvi, 5, 21, 22, 46, 48, 53–54, 297, 319, 354n16; Bastiat's correspondence with, 7, 46, 48, 55–56, 61, 62, 522; *Le Censeur/Le Censeur européen* founded by, 486, 511–12; Comte, Charles, and, 67, 483, 486, 511–12; Coudroy influenced by, 21, 55; at dinner in honor of Bastiat, 59–60; government activities, nonproductiveness of, 358n19; industry, meaning of, xvi–xvii, 16n6; *Le Libre échange,* on editorial board of, 516; mentioned in Bastiat's correspondence, 5, 21, 22, 46, 48, 53–54, 59–60, 62, 63, 65, 68, 93, 95, 103; Saint-Simonians and, 487; Say's influence on, xxvi, 486, 512

Dupérier, 55, 101–2, 486

Dupetit-Thouars, Admiral, 378n29, 423–24n15

Dupeyrat, Aristide, 183–84, 191

Dupin, Charles, 21, 60, 218, 309–11, 487

Dupont de l'Eure, Jacques Charles, 441n36

Dupont de Nemours, Pierre Samuel, 506

Duprat, Pascal, 154, 157, 487

Durham Report (1839), 226–27n306

Durrieu, Simon, 45, 48, 411, 487

Dussard, Hyppolite, 55, 59, 65, 68, 487, 515

Duval (magistrate and senator), 487

Duval, Raoul (counselor at Rheims), 64

Dyer (English Anti–Corn Law League member), 80

Economic Harmonies (Bastiat, 1850), xxxiv, 513–14; basic ideas expressed in early correspondence, 25n25; Coudroy's copy of, Bastiat's address in, 18n9; draft preface in form of letter to author, 316–20; foreign editions of, 278; *Le Journal des économistes* and, xxxiv, 171n237, 251, 255, 293, 297–302, 482; Le Butard, early chapters composed at, 509; mentioned in Bastiat's correspondence, 3, 4, 8, 106, 131, 146, 160, 169, 171–72, 195n265, 206, 207, 210, 213, 216–17, 228, 229, 239, 249–52, 255–56, 259–62, 278, 289, 293–94, 294n381; plagiarism accusations of Henry Carey, xxxiv, 290, 293, 297–300, 480; preface to, 137n96; property and community considered in, 199n273; reviewed by Clément, 482; value, Bastiat's theory of, 171–72, 195, 215n290, 299

Economic Sophisms (Bastiat, 1845 and 1847), 514; "Anglomania, Anglophobia" intended for, 320, 329, 329n16; in Bastiat's correspondence, 59, 63–64, 67, 89n118, 103, 113, 117, 126, 131, 137, 138n199, 195n266; English and American translations of, 103; publication of, xxx

Economist (periodical), 513

Économiste belge, L', 463, 471

Economisti classici italiani (1803–16), 129n186

economists and *économiste* school: in America, 76, 420; black cloaks, tendency to wear, 8, 217; free-trade economists, as meaning of term, xv–xvi, 55n65, 514; High Commission for Education and, 420; liberty as viewed by, 420; social experimentation as designed by, 426–29

education: of Bastiat, xxiv–xxv; Bastiat as teacher, 130–32, 137, 139, 224; Bayonne secondary school, appropriate curriculum for, 415–19; classical, 415–19, 424, 431; establishment of farm schools in each *département*, 183n247; existing farm schools in France and Switzerland, 336, 337; freedom of education, xxxii, 345, 353, 362–63, 373, 403, 463, 488; freedom of teaching, 419–20, 434, 463; High Commission for Education, 419–20; sharecroppers' children, school for, xxviii, 334–40; state monopoly, Bastiat's political views on, xxxiin10

Eichthal, Gustave, baron d', 94, 96, 100, 487

electoral principles, 341–52, 397–414; aims and purposes, wise choices based on, 343–44, 345–46, 347; Bastiat's address to electors of the Landes on, 341–52; Bastiat's letters to candidates stating, 410–14; business metaphor for, 410; civil servants as elected officials, Bastiat's opposition to, 187, 344–45, 357–59; corruption of, 383; economics and taxation, importance of considering, 343, 346–47, 351; liberty, relationship to, 341, 346; moderation, valorization of, 342–43; order and security as considerations, 349–50; personal interests of electee, 348–49; political alliances, dangers of, 412–14; political position of electee, importance of voting based on, 404–9; qualifications of electee, 348; after revolution of 1830, 350–52; sophisms regarding voting choices, 341–42, 397–404

Elliot, Ebenezer, 233n315, 487–88

Enfantin, Prosper, 487

England: Algeria and, 141, 365, 421, 439; Bastiat in, 69–71, 77, 165, 223; Bastiat's plans to visit, 23, 42–43, 64, 141–42, 220–22; Catholic emancipation in (1829), 119, 123, 324, 327, 401; colonialism, Bastiat's opposition to, xxxiv, 90, 107, 120, 221, 324, 363; Corn Laws (*see* Anti–Corn Law League; Cobden, Richard; *Cobden and the League*); democracy and aristocracy, struggle between, 320–29; disarmament/reduction of armed forces, Bastiat and Cobden working for, 5, 89–90, 122, 134–36, 140–42, 147, 152, 159, 160–61, 165; established church in, 322, 323–24, 327, 373, 464, 467–68; free trade in, 327–28; French Revolution, resistance to, 322, 325; Greek harbor of Piraeus, British blockade of, 262n351, 268; liberty in, 52, 66, 71, 327; Navigation Act, 96, 134, 227, 330, 492, 517; *On the Influence of French and English Tariffs on the Future of the Two Peoples* (Bastiat, 1844), xxix, 46, 48, 51, 56; policies not aligned

England (*continued*)
with free-trade philosophy of, 133–35;
political economy of, 20–21; postal reform in, 328; Reform Bill (1832), 323, 327;
reformist mentality in, 326–28; reform
methodology in, 401–3; search, British
right of, 141, 433, 439; slavery, abolition
of (*see* slavery and slave trade); Spain,
Franco-British rivalries played out in,
421, 425; state interventions, taxation increased by, 432–33; on Syria, position of,
42n46, 378; weather in, 79; wine trade
with, 87, 110, 135. *See also* anglophobia
English language: Bastiat's praise for study
of, 18; Bastiat's use of, xvii, 69–70;
French lack of knowledge of, 331, 332–33
Epicurus, 417
Espartero, General, 32n38, 39, 40
established church, in England and Russia,
322, 323–24, 327, 373, 464, 467–68
Evans, William, 80, 488
executive power, 474–75

Fabricii and Caius Fabricius Licinius, 16
Factory Bill (Ten Hours' Bill) of 1847, England, 432
Falloux du Coudroy, Alfred Pierre, 202,
213, 488
fandango, 253
farming. *See* agriculture; wine trade
Faucher, Léon: biographical information,
488; *Le Libre échange,* editorial board
of, 516; mentioned in Bastiat's correspondence, 100, 102, 118, 121, 179, 180,
184n248, 197–98, 216
Faulkner (associate of Schwabe family),
165, 220
Faurie, François, 341n2, 348–49, 488
Fay, Victor Nicolas de, vicomte de
Latour-Maubourg, 494
February revolution. *See* revolution of 1848
Femmes savantes, Les (Molière), 417n5
Ferdinand I (emperor of Austria), 437n31
Ferdinand VII of Spain, 24n23, 32n38
Ferlus, François and Raymond-Dominique,
xxiv–xxv

Feuillants, 492
Feutrier, François-Jean-Hyacinthe, 336, 488
Filangieri, Gaetano, 22n19, 129n186
Fix, Theodore, 55, 65, 488
flag, tricolor, 28–30, 387
Florence, 269, 278, 283, 287, 290
Fontenay, Anne Paul Gabriel Roger de, 239,
251, 255–56, 267n357, 270, 291, 293, 294,
488, 524
Fonteyraud, Henri Alcide, 74, 76, 79,
81–84, 85, 111, 489, 514, 516, 522
Forbes, Charles, comte de Montalembert,
171, 489
Foundation of Saint-Antoine, 339–40
Fourier, François-Marie-Charles, and Fourierism (phalansterian school), 51, 106, 130,
319, 362, 373, 472, 483, 489, 515
Fourvières, 273
Fox, William Johnson, 64, 69, 70, 123, 319,
334, 489
France: Algeria, colonialization of, xxxiv;
Carey's dislike of, 299–300; class divisions in, 230–31, 388; maps, xxxviii,
xxxix; *On the Influence of French and
English Tariffs on the Future of the Two
Peoples* (Bastiat, 1844), xxix, 46, 48, 51,
56; Revolution of 1789 (*see* French Revolution); revolution of 1830 (*see* revolution
of 1830); revolution of 1848 (*see* revolution of 1848); Second Republic (*see*
Second Republic); Spain, Franco-British
rivalries played out in, 421, 425
Frankfurt Peace Congress (1850), 226n305,
263–66, 268
Franklin, Benjamin, xxvi, 22–23, 501
Fraternité, La (newspaper), 426
Frayssinous, Denis, 362, 489
Frederick of Saxe-Coburg (Coburg), 119,
483
Frederick William IV of Prussia, 437n31
free credit, 189, 224, 393
Free Credit (Bastiat, 1849), xxxiii, 224
freedom. *See* liberty
free trade: Anti–Corn Law League (*see*
Anti–Corn Law League; Cobden, Richard; *Cobden and the League*); Bastiat on

his failure to advance cause in Assembly, 154–55, 156, 158; Bastiat's correspondence on, 86–139, 176–79, 280; Bastiat's political views on, 126, 127, 360–62, 421–25, 465; Bordeaux, campaign in, xxxi, 31–32, 51, 86–94, 98, 99; chambermaid's support for, 8–9, 210–11; colonialism and, 177–78, 226–27; economists and *économiste* school, free-trade meaning of, xv–xvi, 54n65, 514; in England, 327–28; English policies not aligned with free-trade philosophy, 133–35; France turning away from, 421–25; laissez-faire principle of, 434–35; liberty, as element of, 434–35; Paris, campaign in, xxix–xxxii, 77–79, 83–84, 85, 89, 91, 96–103, 118; peace and, belief in connection between, xxxiv, 6, 20, 165, 178; policies and positions implied by, 168; social experimentation based on, 426–29; socialism as obstacle to, 129–31. *See also* Association pour la liberté des échanges; economists and *économiste* school; protectionism

French Catholic Church (dissident organization), 481

French Revolution (1789): abolition of slavery during, 220n296; aristocracy and democracy, struggle between, 325; Bastiat family's possible enrichment due to, 7; Bastiat's grandfather's opinion on, xxiv; Blanc, Louis, on, 189n254; English resistance to, 322, 325; La Fayette and, 492–93; nationalization of church property, 464n48; privilege as social principle extinguished by, 321; revolution of 1848 and memories of wars following, 435n26; Staël, Mme de, on, 505; the Terror, xxiv, 187, 455n43, 481, 485, 491, 492

Freppa, Mme (friend of Cheuvreux family), 254

friendship, Bastiat on, 15, 244, 257

Friends of Peace, 226n305

Gabrielle (Augier, 1849), 215n291

Galiani, Ferdinando, 129n186

Ganneron, Auguste, 97, 489

garbure (a soup), 211

Garnier, Joseph, 489–90; in Association pour la liberté des échanges, 511; Blanqui and, 478; at dinner in honor of Bastiat, 59; French edition of *Wealth of Nations,* notes and commentary in, 505; Guillaumin, Gilbert, and, 490, 491; *Le Journal des économistes* and, 490, 491, 515; *Le Libre échange,* as editor of, 490, 516; mentioned in Bastiat's correspondence, 5, 59, 74n98, 128, 202, 280, 284, 293, 298n386; Société d'économie politique meetings, summaries of, 519

Garonne River, 45, 313, 349, 364n22, 509

Gauguier, Joseph, 386, 490

Gay, J. B., comte de Martignac, 350, 490

General Council of the Landes, 514; common lands, Bastiat's report on, 446–51; mentioned in Bastiat's correspondence, 35, 46, 48, 164, 168, 183–84, 191, 209, 213

Gérard, Etienne, 26, 27, 490

Germany: free trade in, 422; influence of Bastiat in, 195, 229; revolution of 1848, 166

Gioberti, Vincenzo, 286, 490

Girard, Anna (Mme Girard), 211, 237, 275, 292, 295, 490

Girard, Edouard (M. Edouard), 232, 272, 275, 288, 490

Girard, Marguerite, 277

Girardin, Émile de, 517

glasses, Bastiat's loss of, 185

Globe and Traveller (newspaper), xxviii, 51, 333

Glücksberg, Elie Decazes, duc de, 325, 484, 485

Glücksberg, Louis Charles Decazes, duc de, 134, 485

Goethe, Johann Wolfgang von, 198n269

Gordon, George, Lord Byron, 24, 326, 417

Gournay, Vincent de, 298n386, 506

government. *See* political economy, politics, and government

Government Commission for the Workers, 391n41

Gracchi, 416, 417

Gradus ad Parnassum, 416
Great Britain. *See* England
Greece, ancient, 369, 417, 431
Greek harbor of Piraeus, British blockade of, 262n351, 268–69
Grégoire, Abbé, 220n296
Gregory XVI (pope), 378n28, 423n14
Grivel, Jean-Baptiste, 100, 490
Guenin, Jacques de, xiii, xxxv
Guillaumin, Gilbert Urbain, 490–91; Ambroise, Clément, and, 482; Daire, Eugène, and, 484; dinner given in honor of Bastiat by, 59; French edition of *Wealth of Nations* published by, 505; mentioned in Bastiat's correspondence, 5, 58, 59, 64, 82, 132, 202, 233, 236, 260, 293, 300
Guillaumin edition of *Œuvres complètes,* xi–xiii, 3, 5, 488, 498
Guillaumin et Cie, xi, 236, 491, 503, 505, 512, 514, 515, 516
Guinard, Auguste, 222, 491
Guizot, François, 491; Aide toi, le ciel t'aidera (society), 6; aristocracy and democracy, struggle between, 325; civil servants as ministers, Bastiat's opposition to, 454, 460; in correspondence, 4, 45, 62, 68, 87, 103, 115n164, 123; on free trade and protectionism, 421, 425; mentioned in Bastiat's political manifestos, 346, 378–79, 381, 384; Molé and, 496; on opposition party politics, 423; political alliances and, 413; resignation as prime minister, 437n30; Thiers, Adolphe, and, 506
Guyot, Yves, 515

Haiti, 220n296
Halévy, Jacques, 257, 491
happiness, Bastiat on, 16–17
Harcourt, François-Eugène, duc d', xxxi, 93, 96, 100, 102, 491–92, 511
Hart, David M., 9
Haussez, Charles d', 348, 492
Henri, count of Chambord (son of Charles X, known as "Henri V"), 467
Heron (friend of Schwabe family), 220

Hiard (correspondent of Bastiat), 170
Hiard, Clotilde (wife of Bastiat), xxvii, 8
Hickin, Joseph, 51, 52, 492
High Commission for Education, 419–20
Hodgskin, Thomas, 513
Hofwill (Switzerland), farm school in, 336, 337
Holland, Navigation Act and British wars with, 517
Horace (classical author), 195, 416, 420
Hugo, Victor, xxxii, 186, 226n305, 287–88, 316, 493
Humann, Georges, 43, 492
humor of Bastiat, 8–9
Huskisson, William, 379, 492
Huszar, George de, 520
Hutcheson, Francis, 504

Indicateur, L' (newspaper), 31, 479, 514
indirect taxation, 365–66
Individualism and Fraternity (Bastiat; unpublished), 188–89, 392, 514
Indivision Treaty (1818) in Oregon, 90n119
industry: meaning of term, xvi–xvii, 16n6, 21, 22; Say, Comte, and Dunoyer on, xxvi, 16n6, 21; socialists versus liberals on, 487
Institut de France, 87, 91, 94, 130, 514
insurance: Say's article for *Dictionnaire de l'économie politique* on, 260; Spain, Bastiat's intent to found insurance company in, 33–35
Ireland, 67, 81, 402
Isabella II (queen of Spain), marriage of, 115–16
Italy: Bastiat in, xxxv, 276–97; Bastiat's journey to, 269–76; Bologna, Austrian occupation of, 378n28, 423n14; Charles Albert (King of Sardinia) in, 185, 192n260, 481; Cheuvreux family's trip to, 276–78, 281–82, 287–88; Cobden in, 123, 125–26, 128, 129, 282–83; *Economic Harmonies* in, 278; influence of Bastiat in, 195; Lombardy, Austrian occupation of, 185, 192n260, 440; republic and republicanism in, 159, 185, 192–93, 468n52, 469; Sciajola, imprisonment of, 263;

subscribers to *Le Libre échange* in, 120. *See also* Rome

Jacques Bonhomme (biweekly paper), 144n206, 298n386, 392, 433, 434, 435n25, 444, 451, 489, 490, 514–15
Janin, Jules Gabriel, 210
Jefferson, Thomas, xxv, 485
Jobard, Jean-Baptiste-Ambroise-Marcellin, 60, 492
Jockey Club, 332
Joinville, François-Ferdinand-Philippe-Louis-Marie d'Orléans, prince de, 198, 492
Joseph (servant of Bastiat), 295
Journal des débats, Le, 515; in correspondence, 60, 95, 100, 161, 189, 231, 251; journalistic motivations and, 381; *Property and Plunder* published in, 517; *The State* originally published in, 519
Journal des économistes, Le, 515; Bastiat approached as manager for, 65–69; Bastiat's articles for, 3, 5, 46, 48, 51, 55, 515; Bastiat's letter to, 297–302, 524; Carey plagiarism scandal and, 290, 293, 297–300, 480; *Cobden and the League* preface in, 63; Cobden's articles in, 95, 135; *Damned Money* published in, 513; *Economic Harmonies* and, xxxiv, 171n237, 251, 255, 293, 297–302, 482; *Economic Sophisms* and, xxx, 63, 514; editors of, 515; founding of, 490, 491, 503, 515; Garnier and, 490, 491, 515; *Justice and Fraternity* published in, 515; Lamartine, Bastiat's open letter to, 56, 58n72; Ledru-Rollin's *De la décadence de l'Angleterre* reviewed in, 281n367; Molesworth's speech, Bastiat on, 160; *On the Influence of French and English Tariffs on the Future of the Two Peoples* published in, xxix, 46, 48, 51, 56; payment of employees by, 61; *Plunder and Law* published in, 239, 517; property, position taken on, 293–94, 300–302; *Property and Law* published in, 150, 517; Say, Horace, and, 245; self-government periodical spinoff, Bastiat's idea of, 214; Société d'économie

politique and, 519; subscribers, 60, 120, 132
Journal du commerce, Le, 20, 503, 515
journalism: advertising, reliance on, 63; anglophobia of, 54, 331–33; Anti–Corn Law League and, xxviii–xxix, 75; Bastiat's career in, xxiii, xxviii, 4, 121; corruption of, 128; freedom of the press, 163, 280, 323–25, 331, 343n5, 481, 506; June Days, suppression of press during state of siege following, 162, 163; political partisanship in, 380–83; provincial and Paris presses, relative influence of, 91; revolution of 1848, moderation in Paris press after, 425–26; signature requirements, 280; youthful dominance of, 128. *See also individual newspapers, journals, and reviews*
Jouy, Victor Etienne de, 18, 492
Julien, M. A., 519
July Monarchy/July revolution. *See* revolution of 1830
June Days, revolution of 1848, 155–59, 392
justice: in Bastiat's articles, 324, 353, 387, 388, 395, 428, 463; in Bastiat's correspondence, 7, 15–16, 83, 107, 121, 138, 177, 178, 196, 206, 231, 255, 298
Justice and Fraternity (Bastiat, 1848), 387, 393, 515

Knatchbull, Sir Edward, 87, 492
Krakow, invasion of (1846), 122

Labadie (Cheuvreux friend or servant), 216, 241
Labeyrie (winegrower), 44
Lacauchy (Bastiat's doctor), 294
Lacave-Laplagne, Jean-Pierre, 101n137, 370, 492
Lacordaire, Jean-Baptiste-Henri Dominique, xxxii
Lafarelle, Félix de, 100, 492
Lafaurie (Mugron hospice benefactor), 225
La Fayette, Marie Joseph, marquis de, 6, 26, 27, 317, 341, 484, 492, 495, 517
Laffitte, Jacques, xxvi, 26, 45, 493
La Fontaine, 237n320, 243

Lagelouze, 157
"Laissez-faire" (Bastiat, 1848), 298n386, 434–35
laissez-faire, laissez-passer: as expression, 298; principle of, 434–35. *See also* free trade
La Jonchère, Chateau de, 200, 203, 205, 208, 209, 211, 212, 217, 250–54, 257, 258, 267n354, 271, 272, 274, 275, 277, 509
Lajonkaire, Adolphe de, 450n41
Lamarque, Jean-Maximilien, 29, 31, 366, 493, 494
Lamartine, Alphonse de, 493; Bastiat's association with, xxxii; Bastiat's correspondence with, 7, 56–57, 58, 391, 522; Bastiat's meeting with, 60; civil servants as elected officials and, 462; on the industrial age, 417; mentioned in Bastiat's correspondence, 4, 55n67, 58, 60, 62, 94–95, 97, 100, 125, 139, 141, 142, 213, 214, 249; mentioned in draft preface to *Economic Harmonies,* 319; national workshops, Bastiat's call to dissolve, 444–45; in provisional government, 435n26, 441n36
Lamennais, Félicité, abbé de, 21, 319, 493
land. *See* property
Landes, the, 509; Bastiat and Bastiat family in, xi, xxiii; Bastiat's article on distribution of taxes in, 48n53, 49–50; Bastiat's homesickness for, 116, 160; Cobden in, 110; common land, Bastiat's report on, 446–51; electors, Bastiat's addresses to, 341–52, 387; population of, 50; sea pine forests of, 49. *See also* Adour River; Bayonne; Chalosse region; General Council of the Landes; Mugron
Langsdorf, M. de (chargé d'affaires in Baden), 72–73
Larnac, Marie Gustave, xxxii, 75n100, 102, 357, 358, 367–86, 413, 493
Laromiguière, Pierre, xxv, 12, 493–94
Last Days of a Condemned Man (Hugo, 1829), 287–88
Latour-Maubourg, Mme de, 257, 494
Latour-Maubourg, Victor Nicolas de Fay, vicomte de, 494

Laurence, A. M., 49–50, 494, 522
Law, The (Bastiat, 1850), xxxiii, xxxv 245n330, 249n335, 252, 254, 255, 516
Lebanon, 381
Leclerc, Louis, 516
Ledru-Rollin, Alexandre, 170, 281, 441n36, 444–45, 494
Lefranc, Victor, 146, 446n39, 448, 449, 494
Legislative Assembly, xxxii, 179n241, 198n272, 353, 518
Legitimists, 163, 179n242, 292, 412–14, 423
Le Havre, 96, 99, 112, 114, 115, 117, 252
Leibnitz, Gottfried, 362
Leopold I (king of Belgium), 467, 494
Leopold of Saxe-Coburg, 115n164
Leroux, Pierre, 229, 387, 494
Les Bagnères (Les Eaux-Bonnes), 241, 244, 247–50, 252, 253, 257, 258, 509
letters. *See* correspondence of Bastiat
Lherbette, Armand, 100, 494
liberal, as term, xvii
liberalization of trade. *See* free trade
liberty: association, freedom of, 434; civil servants as elected officials and, 457–63; *économiste* view of, 420; education, freedom of, xxxii, 345, 353, 362–63, 373, 403, 463, 488; electoral responsibilities and, 341, 346; eligibility of deputies for public office and, 459–63; in England, 52, 66, 71, 327; as foundational principle defended by Bastiat, xxxiii, 4, 51, 57, 66, 85, 184, 252n338, 318, 320, 324, 327, 387, 393, 403, 433–34, 472–73; freedoms contributing to, 434; free trade as element of, 434–35; limited government and, 356, 367, 435; order and security balanced with, 4, 26, 88, 162, 184, 192, 283, 369, 389, 393, 401, 403, 427, 457–59; parliamentary conflicts of interest and, 452–54; press, freedom of, 163, 280, 323–25, 331, 343n5, 481, 506; prodigality and, 346; religion, freedom of, 373, 472; as solution to social problem, 252n338; in Spain, 40; speech and thought, freedom of, 331, 353, 434; taxation encroaching on,

355, 444; teaching, freedom of, 419–20, 434, 463; as topic in *Economic Harmonies*, 131; use of "liberty" versus "freedom" as translation of *liberté*, xv; work, freedom to, 434

Libre échange, Le (periodical), 516; Bastiat as editor of, xxxi; Bastiat's articles in, 137, 324n12; Bastiat's establishment of, 98, 124n179; Garnier as editor of, 490, 516; initial publication of, 117; subscribers and distribution, 116, 120, 126, 132

limited government, Bastiat's espousal of, 354–57, 367, 372–74, 432–33, 435

Lind, Jenny, 172, 173

Lisbon, Bastiat's trip to, 41–43

Lobau (Lobeau), Georges Mouton, 26, 27, 493, 494

lobbyists and lobbying, 191, 198, 342, 348, 404, 428, 430

lois d'amour, les (1824), 343

lois des suspects (1793), 455

Loménie, Louis Léonard de, 111

London Peace Congress (1843), xxxiv

London Peace Congress (1851), 263n52

Louis, Joseph-Dominique, baron, 351, 494

Louis XIV (king of France), 205, 253n339, 410n4, 418, 509

Louis XV (king of France), 205n277

Louis XVI (king of France), 505, 506

Louis XVIII (king of France), 483, 484, 495, 496, 498, 512

Louis-Napoléon. *See* Bonaparte, Louis-Napoléon

Louis-Philippe (duc d'Orléans, later king of France), 495; Bastiat's eventual support for monarchy of, xxvii; Chantelauze and, 481; Chateaubriand's refusal to take oath to, 481; Lafitte, Jacques, as minister of finance and prime minister under, xxvi; Lobeau and, 494; Molé, Louis Mathieu, and, 496; National Guard in reign of, 517; overthrow of, 139n201, 473n56, 476n57, 507; in revolution of 1830, 25n26, 27n32; September Laws following attempt on life of, 106, 519; Thiers's support for, 506

Lucullus, 416

Lyons: Bastiat in, 270, 271, 273; free-trade campaign in, xxxi, 96, 118, 120, 127, 134, 227; sale of *Economic Harmonies* in, 278

Macpherson, James, 493

Madagascar, 381

Maintenon, Mme de (second wife of Louis XIV), 205

Malade imaginaire, Le (Molière), 290n373

Malthus, Thomas Robert, 67, 293, 299, 300, 302, 484, 490, 495, 497

Manchester: Anti–Corn Law meetings in, 82, 84, 86; Bastiat's visit to, 70, 79; Crumpsall House, 167, 173, 186 (*see also* Schwabe family)

Manin (mutual friend of Paillottet and Bastiat), 291

Manuel, Jacques Antoine, 317, 495

Marcet, Jane, 513

Maria II (queen of Portugal), 433n23

Maria Christina (queen of Spain), 32n38, 39n42

Marmont, Auguste de, 25n26, 27, 495

marriage: of Bastiat and Clotilde Hiard, xxvii, 8; Cheuvreux, Louise, collapse of marriage plans for, 236, 238, 240, 242, 247; Spanish marriages, 115n164, 430; U.S. president, lack of public interest in marriage of, 430

Marriage de Figaro, Le (Beaumarchais), 248n332

Marsan, Julie (Mme Affre), 156–57, 495, 523

Marsan, Mlle, 157

Marsan, Mme (Marie-Julienne Badbedat), 142–43, 157, 477–78, 523

Marseilles: Bastiat in, 273, 274, 275, 281, 287, 291; free-trade campaign in, xxxi, 96, 99, 110, 117, 118, 120, 121, 122, 127; sale of *Economic Harmonies* in, 278

Martignac, J. B. Gay, comte de, 350, 490

Martin, Alexandre (called Albert), 441n36

Martineau, Harriet, 513

Marx, Karl, 518

Masons: Anti–Corn Law League compared to, 70; Bastiat's affiliation with, xxvi

Matta, Commander (army medical officer), 231

Mauguin, François, 26, 495

Maynooth bill (1845), 402

McAleer, Kevin, 310n3

Médecin malgré lui, Le (Molière), 231n311

Mehmet Ali (pasha of Egypt), 42n46, 378n30

Méline Tariff, 503

Mémorial bordelaise, Le (newspaper), 516; Bastiat's articles in, xxxi, 87, 90n122, 91, 92, 115n163; Bastiat's letters to, 108, 312–16; in correspondence, 31n36, 59n73, 87, 90n122, 91, 93, 103, 108, 138; Coudroy's articles in, 93, 103, 484

Mendizabal, Juan, 37, 495

Messalina, 416

Metternich, Klemens Wenzel, prince von, 437n31

Mettray, farm school in, 336n20, 337

Mignet, François-Auguste-Alexis, 100, 495–96, 498

Mignon (Goethe, 1795), 198n269

Mill, James, 477, 501

Mill, John Stuart, 496

Millevoye, Charles Hubert, 235, 496

Milton, John, 326

Mimerel committee, 387

Ministry of Progress and Organization of Work, petition to create, 426–27

moderation, electoral valorization of, 342–43

Molé, Louis Mathieu, comte de, 235, 379, 384, 423, 496

Molesworth, William, 160, 496

Molière, 231n311, 257, 290n373, 417n5

Molinari, Gustave de, 496–97; in Association pour la liberté des échanges, 496, 511; Bastiat influenced by, 5; *Jacques Bonhomme,* role in, 489, 515; *Le Journal des économistes* edited by, 515; *Le Libre échange,* on editorial board of, 516; meaning of *economist* in works of, xvi; mentioned in Bastiat's correspondence, 280, 284; on nonproductiveness of government activities, 358n19; short articles provided to Paillottet by, 435n25

Monclar, Eugène de (first cousin of Bastiat), 91, 245n329, 286n371, 288, 295, 296, 497

Monclar, Henri (uncle of Bastiat), xxiv, xxv

Moniteur industriel, Le, 60, 63–64, 164, 224, 454, 516

Monjean, Maurice, 59, 66, 497

Montagne, La, and Montagnard Manifesto, 169, 170, 192, 218, 387, 393, 516, 519

Montalembert, Charles Forbes, comte de, 171, 489

Mont-de-Marsan, 190n258, 240, 415

Montespan, Mme de (mistress of Louis XIV), 205

Montesquieu Hall, Paris, 118, 119, 123

Montmartre, 201

Moore, D. C. (member of Anti–Corn Law League), 70

Moore, Thomas (Irish poet), 326

Morocco, 378, 379, 380

mortality, Bastiat's awareness of, 8

Mugron, 509–10; Academy and bourgeois life in, xxviii, 332; Bastiat and Bastiat family in, xxiii, xxviii, 19, 21; Bastiat as general counselor for, xxvii; Bastiat's aunt's chambermaid in, 8–9, 210–11, 215, 241, 246; Bastiat's descriptions of, 211, 212–13, 216, 242, 243–44; Bastiat's homesickness for, 4, 6, 36, 66, 68, 223; hospice, extension of, 225, 234

Mure (with Bastiat in Pisa), 288

music concerts, Bastiat's attendance at, 173–74, 180

Nantes, 96, 349

Napoléon I (emperor of France): centralized government created by, 350; Constant and, 483; 18 Brumaire of, 518; Marmont, Auguste de, and, 495; Molé, Louis Mathieu, and, 496; slavery reintroduced by, 220n296; Soult and, 505; Staël, Mme de, and, 505

Napoléon III (emperor of France), 478, 481, 497, 501, 506. *See also* Bonaparte, Louis-Napoléon

Napoleonic wars: Bastiat family fortunes affected by, xxiv; Say's experience of, xxvi;

United States compensated for blockades of, 479

National, Le (newspaper), 100, 281, 332n17, 437, 478, 495, 506, 517

National Assembly: balls used for voting in, 164, 352, 399; Bastiat's advice regarding, 474–76; in Bastiat's correspondence, 144, 149–51, 156, 158, 159, 189, 193, 214; Bastiat's voting record in, 389, 390; civil servants as elected officials in (*see* civil servants as elected officials); *What Is Seen and What Is Not Seen* as response to poor economic arguments in, 520. *See also* Constituent Assembly; Legislative Assembly

National Guard: Changarnier's command of, 481; in correspondence, 26, 27, 29, 142, 158, 161, 164; defined, 517; electoral responsibilities and, 345, 351; national workshops, Bastiat's call for dissolution of, 445

national workshops, 391–92, 444–45, 472, 518

Navigation Act (England), 96, 134, 227, 330, 492, 517

Necker, Jacques, 505

Nemours, duc de, 45, 414, 495

New Zealand, 227n306, 433

Nicholas I (tsar), 437n31, 440, 464, 467

Nobel Peace Prize, 498

nobility. *See* aristocracy

Nouveau dictionnaire de l'économie politique (1891 and 1900), 260n350

O'Connell, Daniel, 81, 497

Odier, Antoine, 26, 497

"On Parliamentary Reform" (Bastiat, 1846), 25n24, 75n100, 367–86

On the Influence of French and English Tariffs on the Future of the Two Peoples (Bastiat, 1844), xxix, 46, 48, 51, 56

opera, in Bastiat's correspondence, 103, 117, 167–68, 179

opposition party: Bastiat's advice regarding, 475–76; mutual dissatisfaction of conservatives and opposition, 352–54; political role of, 359–60, 423

order and security: electoral choice and, 349–50; liberty, balanced with, 4, 26, 88, 162, 184, 192, 283, 369, 389, 393, 401, 403, 427, 457–59

Ordre, L' (newspaper), 250

Oregon, 90

Orleanists, 179n242, 292

Orléans, duc d'. *See* Louis-Philippe

Ortolan, Joseph, 118, 497

ortolans, 216, 217, 218

Othon (king of Greece), 269

Ovid, 416

Owen, Robert, 501, 515

Oxford, Robert Walpole, earl of, 331, 507

Paillottet, Mme, 270

Paillottet, Prosper, 497; on "Anglomania, Anglophobia," 320; Bastiat's correspondence with, 7, 206–7, 238–40, 245, 250–51, 254–55, 270, 279–81, 290–91, 292–94, 523–24; Carey, Henry, and, 293n379; Cheuvreux, Mme, letter to, 296–97, 524; on draft preface to *Economic Harmonies*, 316; as editor and executor for Bastiat, xii, 3, 5, 7, 251n336, 294n381; on French press, 332n17; *Le Libre échange*, on editorial board of, 516; mentioned in Bastiat's correspondence, 244–45, 249, 276, 288, 289, 294, 295; in Rome at Bastiat's death, 295–97

Palmerston, Henry John Temple, third viscount, 115n164, 134, 258n346, 262, 269, 433, 497–98

papacy. *See* Roman Catholicism *and specific popes by name*

Pariah, The (Delavigne), 17–18

Paris: Articles of Paris, 77, 78, 89; Bastiat's reasons for moving to, 316–17; Butte Montmartre, 201; free-trade campaign in, xxix–xxxii, 77–79, 83–84, 85, 89, 91, 96–103, 118; Montesquieu Hall, 118, 119, 123; provincial presses compared to Paris press, 91; revolution of 1848, moderation in Paris press after, 425–26; Schwabe, Mrs., arrival of, 236; Véfour (restaurant), 60, 63, 510

Parisis, Pierre-Louis (bishop of Langres), 466–67

Paris Peace Congress (1849), 202n275, 226n305, 263n52

Parliamentary Conflicts of Interest (Bastiat, 1849), xxxiii, 189, 216, 293. *See also* civil servants as elected officials

passports, 200

Passy, Frédéric, 498

Passy, Hyppolite, 59, 72, 495, 498

Patrie, La (periodical), 100, 280, 284–85, 517

Patru, Olivier, 211

Pau, 110, 248, 510

Paul-Dejean, Jean-Claude, xi, xxxv, 3, 76, 142, 156, 305, 334, 395, 452

Paul et Virginie (Bernardin de Saint-Pierre, 1787), 18

Paulton, Abraham, 72–73, 79, 88, 96, 104, 498, 522

Pavée de Vandœuvre, baron de, 96, 100, 498

peace: Bastiat's letter to president of Frankfurt Peace Congress, 265–66; free trade and, belief in connection between, xxxiv, 6, 20, 165, 178; Friends of Peace, 226n305; Greek affair affecting chances for, 268; Peace Congresses, xxxiv, 202n275, 226n305, 263–66, 268. *See also* disarmament

Peace and Freedom, or the Republican Budget (Bastiat, 1849), xxxiii, 181n245, 182n246, 189, 393

Peel, Sir Robert, 498–99; in Bastiat's correspondence, 53, 72, 81, 87, 89–90, 96, 122; Corn Laws, repeal of, 513; free trade and protectionism, position on, 362, 379–80; on Indivision Treaty, 89–90; letter to Bastiat, quotation of, 72; Maynooth bill (1845), 402n2; mistranslation of speech of, xxviii, 333; Russell and, 502; Villiers and, 507

Pergolesi, Giovanni Battista, 238, 499

Périer, Casimir, 26, 499

Perseus, 418

Persiani, Mme (opera singer), 167–68

Pescatore (renter of Le Butard), 250, 509

Petetin (quoted by Bastiat from *La Presse*), 381

Petit-Bourg, farm school in, 336n20, 337

Petitti, Carlo Ilarioni, conte di Roreto, 499

Peupin, Henri, 118, 499

Phaedrus, 416

phalansterian school (Fourierism), 51, 106, 130, 319, 362, 373, 472, 483, 489, 515

Philippe d'Anjou (grandson of Louis XIV), 253n339

Philippists, 411

philosophy, Bastiat's interest in, 11, 13, 46

physiocrats, 195n264, 298, 484, 500, 505, 506

Pisa, 269, 270, 274, 278, 284, 287n372, 288, 291

Pitt, William, the Younger, 119, 331, 499

Pius IX (pope), 128–29, 171, 466n49, 467, 468n52, 499

plagiarism accusations of Henry Carey, xxxiv, 290, 293, 297–300, 480

Planat, Mme de, 185–86, 291

Plato, 222, 319, 417

Plunder and Law (Bastiat, 1850), xxxiii, 239n322, 245n330, 517

Plutarch, 232

Poland, 122, 154n220, 440

Polignac, Auguste-Jules-Armand-Marie, prince de, 25n26, 325, 356n17, 499, 516

political clubs, 184, 192

political economy, politics, and government: administrative decentralization, French need for, 184; Bastiat's discovery of political economy, xxv–xxvi, 11–12, 20–21; Bastiat's importance to French political economy, 195; Bastiat's political career, xxxii–xxxiv, 31, 45–46, 48, 52, 75, 92, 108–9, 148, 153–65, 168–71, 174–200, 206, 218, 219, 223–25; church-state relations (*see* religion); civil servants as elected officials, Bastiat's opposition to (*see* civil servants as elected officials); Cobden's advice on disseminating doctrines of, 75–76; conservatives and opposition, mutual dissatisfaction of,

352–54; electoral principles regarding (*see* electoral principles); free trade (*see* free trade); imposition of views, Bastiat's opposition to, 464–65; independence of representative, importance of, 360, 376–77; limited government, Bastiat's espousal of, 354–57, 367, 372–74, 432–33, 435; meaning of terms, xv–xvi; opposition party, role of, 359–60, 423; reform methodology in England, 401–3; true opinions, successful political candidates hiding, 352. *See also* free trade; peace; taxation and tariffs

political manifestos, 341–96; Bastiat's term for, 341n1; on civil servants as elected officials (1846), 25n24, 75n100, 367–86; on election of president of Second Republic (1849), 395–96; on electoral principles (1830), 341–52; explanation of voting record (1849), 387–90; statements of political convictions addressed to electors (1846, 1848), 352–67, 387; summary of political record and reelection bid (1849), 390–95

Pope, Alexander, 18, 19n11, 243

Populaire, Le (newspaper), 426

population, Bastiat on, xxxiv, 50, 67, 131, 251, 256, 312–16, 364, 448, 482

Porter, G. R., 103n142, 228

Portugal: Bastiat's trip to, 41–43; British intervention in, 433

postal system and postal reform, 105, 110, 174, 175, 328

Potonié, [D.], 76–79, 522

prefects, recall of, 193

presidency of Second Republic: Bastiat's advice regarding, 473–76; election of Louis-Napoléon to, xxxii, 174–75, 179n241, 394, 395–96, 480, 493

press, the. *See* journalism

Presse, La (newspaper), 92, 161, 199, 332n17, 429, 430, 441, 517

Primi, Mme, 286

Prince-Smith, John, 264, 499–500

privateering, 269

private versus public spheres of influence (limited government), 354–57, 367, 372–74, 435

property: Carey on, 299; common land, Bastiat's report to the Landes on, 446–51; *Le Journal des économistes,* position of, 293–94, 300–302

Property and Law (Bastiat, 1848), 150, 189, 252n338, 387, 393, 517

Property and Plunder (Bastiat, 1848), 189n255, 251, 252n338, 387, 393, 517–18

protectionism: anglophobia and, 136; Bastiat on French return to, 421–25; Bastiat's differentiation of free trade from, 280; Bastiat's family affected by, xxix; Corn Laws (*see* Anti-Corn Law League; Cobden, Richard; *Cobden and the League*); English campaign against, 327–28; meetings and associations formed for purposes of, 110, 114, 116–17; *Le Moniteur industriel* associated with, 516; during revolution of 1848, 153n219, 155–56; wages and, 119; in wine trade, xxviii

Protectionism and Communism (Bastiat, 1849), xxxiii, 189, 387, 393, 518

Proudhon, Pierre-Joseph, 500; Bastiat's association with, xxxii; Bastiat's writings in reply to, 189, 387, 511, 517; *Justice and Fraternity* addressing ideas of, 515; mentioned in Bastiat's correspondence, 189, 200, 223, 224, 225, 229, 234, 301; opposition of Bastiat to interventionist economics of, xxxiii; socialist school of, 130n187; *La Voix du peuple* launched by, 500, 520

Prussia: Bastiat on conditions in, 439, 440; Cobden's tour of, 110n156; disarmament in, 141, 439; French fear of attack by, 437, 440; Krakow as free town under protection of, 122n176; on Syria, position of, 42n46; Zollverein, 73, 422nn12–13

public versus private spheres of influence (limited government), 354–57, 367, 372–74, 435

Punch (British journal), 137

Puyravault, Audry de, 26, 500

Quesnay, François, 195, 500, 506
Quijano, Garcia, 251, 500
Quotidienne, La (periodical), 331, 518

Racine, Jean, 18, 112–13
railways: in Bastiat's correspondence, 105,
    201, 203–4, 281; Bordeaux to Bayonne
    railway line, letter to newspaper on,
    312–16
Ramel (recipient of assistance from minis-
    try of interior), 180
Raspail, François, 170, 500–501
reactionaries, 169–70, 183, 205–6, 234–35
Red Cross, 498
Reds or Red Republic, 163, 169, 170, 174,
    388. *See also* socialism
reform: of civil servants as elected officials
    (*see* civil servants as elected officials);
    as purpose of revolution of 1848, 443;
    reformist mentality in England, 326–28;
    reform methodology in England, 401–3
Reform Bill (1832), England, 323, 327
Reform Club, London, 70
Réforme, La (newspaper), 494
religion: abuses in name of, 466; Bastiat's
    interest in, 8, 13–14, 46, 47, 70, 202, 279,
    297; diversity of, at Bastiat's secondary
    school, xxv; England, established church
    in, 322, 323–24, 327, 373, 464, 467–68;
    freedom of, 373, 472; future merger of
    all Christian religions, Bastiat's belief
    in, 464; moral code as basis of, 470–71;
    nationalization of church property in
    France, 464n48; payments to clergy,
    state responsibility for, 346, 463–65;
    privileges of clergy and nobility, French
    suppression of, 321n6; Russia, established
    church in, 464; Spanish monastic houses,
    confiscation of, 36–38; spiritual and tem-
    poral power, value of separating, 466–71.
    See also Roman Catholicism
Renouard, Augustin-Charles, and family,
    59, 102, 212, 254, 501
République française, La (newspaper), 518;
    articles published in, 391, 419, 425, 426,
    429, 431, 432, 435, 439, 440, 441, 442;

in Bastiat's correspondence, 139n200,
    143n204; Bastiat's signature in, 426n16,
    442n37
Revolution of 1789. *See* French Revolution
revolution of 1830 (July Monarchy, July
    revolution), 518; actions of Bastiat dur-
    ing, xxvii, 25–30; Chantelauze and,
    481; circumstances leading to, 356n17;
    collapse of July Monarchy (*see* revolu-
    tion of 1848); electoral responsibilities
    following, 350–52; "three glorious days,"
    25–30, 350
revolution of 1848 (February revolution),
    518; abolition of slavery during, 220n296;
    actions of Bastiat during, xxxii, 3, 4, 7,
    390–92, 518; Bastiat's correspondence
    on, 3, 4, 139, 142–47, 153–59, 168–70;
    Bastiat's reflections on political situation
    in late February 1848, 440–44; Bas-
    tiat's statement of political convictions
    addressed to electors in wake of, 387;
    Bastiat's summary of his political record
    after, 390–95; Bastiat's voting record
    following, 387–90, 393–94; civil service
    positions, scramble for, 431–32; disarma-
    ment and, 435–40; fear of attack after,
    435, 437; French Revolution (of 1789),
    wars following, 435n26; June Days,
    155–59, 392; ousting of Louis-Philippe,
    139n201, 437n30, 495; Paris press, mod-
    eration of, 425–26; provisional govern-
    ment, formation of, 441n36; Reaction
    party during, 169–70; reform as purpose
    of, 443; riots/conspiracy of 15 May,
    xxxiii, 154, 161–62, 164–65, 480; siege,
    votes on state of, 162, 163; socialism dur-
    ing, 153–54, 155–56, 158, 163, 169–70,
    174
revolution of 1848, in Germany, 166
Revue britannique, La, 74, 84, 489, 519
Revue des deux mondes, La, 86, 188n253,
    239, 258, 480, 488, 519
Revue du progrès, 478
Revue encyclopédique, La, 21, 487, 501, 519
Revue mensuelle d'économie politique, La,
    488

Reybaud, Louis, 59, 62, 65, 130, 501
Ricardo, David, 293, 299, 300–302, 484, 489, 501
Ridolfi, Cosimo, 283, 501–2
right of search, British, 141, 433, 439
riots/conspiracy of 15 May (1848), xxxiii, 154, 161–62, 164–65, 480
Rodriguez, Olinde, 487
Roman Catholicism: in Bastiat's correspondence, 13–14, 34–35, 41–42, 47, 119, 123, 171, 214, 231; England, Catholic emancipation in (1829), 119, 123, 324, 327; French troops sent to Rome to restore papacy (1849), 468n52; future absorption of dissenting sects by, Bastiat's belief in, 464; Maynooth bill (1845), 402; Paillottet on Bastiat's final confession, 297; temporal power of papacy, 467, 468
Roman expedition, xxxiii, 222–23
Rome: Bastiat's final illness and death in, xxxv, 269, 278, 279, 286, 287, 288, 290–92, 296–97; Cheuvreux family visit to, 278, 286, 287, 292; Cobden in, 126; Italian Republic, proclamation of, 185n249, 468n52; Paillottet in, 295–97; Roman republic (1849), 468n52, 469
Rome, ancient, 16, 369, 417, 431
Ronconi, Giorgio, 179
Rossi, Pellegrino, 65, 68, 120, 293, 302, 488, 502
Rothschild, Jakob Mayer, 97
Rouen, 114, 278
Rousseau, Jean Jacques, 210
royal guards in revolution of 1830, 26
Rubens, Peter Paul, 205
Rumilly, Louis Gauthier de, 386, 502
Russell, John, first earl, 81, 86n112, 134n190, 432n21, 502
Russia: authoritarian nature of, 321; Cobden's tour of, 110n156; established church in, 464; French fear of attack by, 437; Krakow as free town under protection of, 122n176; Poland and, 440; religion in, 373, 464; on Syria, position of, 42n46, 378

Sade, M. de, 456–57
Saint-Antoine, Foundation of, 339–40
Saint-Chamans, Auguste, 280, 502
Saint-Cricq, Pierre de, 421, 502
Sainte Chapelle, 173, 179–80
Saint-Hilaire, Jules Barthélemy, 200, 502
Saint Louis d'Antin, Bastiat's report of medieval music concert at, 173–74
Saint-Sever, xxiv–xxv, 46, 94, 102, 109, 190, 314, 415
Saint-Simon, Claude Henri de Rouvroy, comte de, 487, 501
Saint-Simonians, 130n187, 481, 484, 487, 494, 519
Salis-Schwabe, Mrs., 504
Salvandy, Narcisse Achille de, 68, 502
Sardinia, 185n249, 422
Saulnier, Sébastien-Louis, 518
Say, Horace Émile (son of Jean-Baptiste), xxix–xxxn5, 503–4; in Association pour la liberté des échanges, 100, 511; Bastiat's correspondence with, 7, 53–55, 132, 148–49, 214, 245–46, 259–60, 284–85, 522; *Dictionnaire de l'économie politique* and, 260; at dinner in honor of Bastiat, 59; as economist, 5; French edition of *Wealth of Nations,* notes and commentary in, 505; *Le Journal des économistes,* founding of, 491; *Le Libre échange,* on editorial board of, 516; mentioned in Bastiat's correspondence, 59, 61, 62–63, 65, 67, 68, 69, 93, 100, 103, 112, 135, 157–58, 166, 179, 202, 211, 212, 217, 221, 233, 246, 254, 257, 258, 271
Say, Jean-Baptiste, xxixn5, 503; Bastiat at home of, xxix; Bastiat influenced by, xxiii, xxv–xxvi, 5, 12–13, 20, 21, 50, 53, 297, 319, 354n16; Comte, Charles, and, xxvi, 483, 512; Coudroy influenced by, 20, 55; Daire, Eugène, and, 484; *Dictionnaire de l'économie politique* and, 260n350; Dunoyer influenced by, xxvi, 486, 512; government activities, nonproductiveness of, 358; importance to French political economy, 195; *industry,* meaning of, xvi–xvii; Mill, John Stuart, and, 496; on

Say, Jean-Baptiste (*continued*)
property, 293, 300, 302; Smith, Adam, and, 195n264

Say, Léon (son of Horace, grandson of Jean-Baptiste), xxxn5, xxx, 158, 179, 221, 260n350, 285, 503–4

Say, Mme (wife of Horace; née Anne Cheuvreux), 202, 271, 285

Schonen (in provisional government), 26

schools and schooling. *See* education

Schwabe family: arrival of Mrs. Schwabe in Paris, 236; Bastiat's correspondence with, 6, 7, 137–39, 150–51, 157–59, 165–68, 173, 186–87, 219–20, 522–23; biographical information, 504; mentioned in Bastiat's correspondence, 152, 262, 269; name, pun on meaning of, 152; nature of Bastiat's relationship with Mrs. Schwabe, 8

Scialoja, Antonio, 128, 263, 504

Scott, Walter, 24

Scribe, Eugène, 257, 504

search, British right of, 141, 433, 439

Second Republic: Bastiat's advice regarding presidency of, 473–76; correspondence on, 4; election of Louis-Napoléon to presidency of, xxxii, 174–75, 179n241, 394, 395–96, 480, 493; establishment of, xxxii

security and order: electoral choice and, 349–50; liberty, balanced with, 4, 26, 88, 162, 184, 192, 283, 369, 389, 393, 401, 403, 427, 457–59

Sémélé, General, 27

Sengresse (Bastiat domain), xxiv, xxvi, xxvii

Senior, Nassau William, 70, 477, 504

Sentinelle des Pyrénées, La (newspaper), xi, 59, 334, 452

separation of church and state. *See* religion

September Laws, 106, 519

Shakespeare, William, 210, 326

sharecroppers: in the Chalosse, 313–16; school for children of, xxviii, 334–40

Siècle, Le, 100, 381

Simon, Julian P., 256n345

Simon, Richard, 69, 504

Sismondi, Jean Charles Léonard Simonde de, 488, 502, 505

slavery and slave trade: in ancient Rome, 417; Britain, French negotiation to abolish slavery with, 479; British campaign to abolish, 326–27, 482, 507; British right of search based on, 141, 433, 439; French abolition of, 220n296; oligarchies, extraction of abolition from, 119, 123; in Sierra Leone, 506; Tangiers, Treaty of (1844), 378n31

Smith, Adam, 504–5; Bastiat influenced by, xxv, 20, 26, 50, 297, 319, 354n16; Daire, Eugène, and, 484; Donato compared to, 126; French edition of *Wealth of Nations*, 505; liberal politics linked with classical liberal economics of, 26; Passy, Hyppolite, influenced by, 498; Peel influenced by, 379; on property, 293; Ricardo and, 501; Say, Jean-Baptiste, and, 195n264

Smith, John Benjamin, 80, 221, 222, 505

smocks, 253

Social Harmonies (Bastiat, planned but never written), xxxiv, 64, 161, 235n317, 513

socialism: agrarian law and, 246; Bastiat's voting record and charges of, 387–90; *Capital and Rent* as reply to, 189, 511; change equated with, 229; economist's social experimentation in reply to, 426–29; English socialists, Bastiat's debate with, 223; fallacies disseminated by, 51; free trade, as obstacle to, 129–31; *Justice and Fraternity* as counter to, 515; *laissez-faire* principle and, 435; popular growth of, 384; *Property and Plunder* as reply to, 517; *Protectionism and Communism* (Bastiat, 1849), xxxiii, 189, 387, 393, 518; provincial fears of, 148; revolution of 1848 and, 153–54, 155–56, 158, 163, 169–70, 174; Saint-Simonians, 130n187, 481, 484, 487, 494, 519; *The State* as counter to, 388, 519; youth attracted by, 106, 130–31, 199–200

Société d'économie politique, 3, 5, 88, 95, 97, 293n379, 515, 519

Society of the Rights of Man, 501

Socrates, 97n133, 287

Soirées de la rue St. Lazare, Les (Gustave de Molinari, 1849), xvi

Sonnambula, La (Bellini opera), 167

Sophocles, 418

Sorèze secondary school, Bastiat's attendance at, xxiv–xxv

Soult, Nicolas, duc de Dalmatie, 45, 460n44, 505

Soustra, 29, 35, 36, 505

South Africa (Cape Colony), 226

Spain: Bastiat's trip to, 32–41, 201; civil war (1833–40), 32n38, 39–41; Cobden's trip to, 114–16; Franco-British rivalries played out in, 421, 425; free trade and protectionism in, 421; liberal constitution of 1812, Ferdinand VII forced to restore, 24n23; monastic houses, confiscation of, 36–38; royal marriages in, 115n164, 430

Sparta, 320–21, 417

speech and thought, freedom of, 331, 353, 434

stability, Bastiat on, 273

Staël, Anne-Louise-Germaine de (née Germaine Necker), 210, 483, 502, 505

Stanhope, Philip, earl of Chesterfield, 16, 505

State, The (Bastiat, 1848), xxxiii, 388, 393, 519–20

state, the. *See* political economy, politics, and government

study, Bastiat's correspondence on, 11–12, 13–14, 15–16, 18–19, 23

Sturler (mentioned in letter to Mme Cheuvreux), 287

sugar, cane versus beet, 23

Switzerland: farm school in Hofwill, 336, 337; free trade in, 421

Syria, French support for, 42n46, 378, 383

Tahiti, 213, 353n15, 378, 380, 383, 423

Tangiers, Treaty of (1844), 378n31

taxation and tariffs: in Algeria, 421; *Anti–Bread Tax Circular* (Anti–Corn Law League, 1841), 88; disarmament and reduction of (*see* disarmament); early interest of Bastiat in customs reform, 20; electoral responsibilities with regard to, 343, 346–47, 351; government intervention increasing, 432–33; indirect taxation, 365–66; the Landes, Bastiat's article on distribution of taxes in, 48n53, 49–50; liberty encroached on by, 355, 444; *On the Influence of French and English Tariffs on the Future of the Two Peoples* (Bastiat, 1844), xxix, 46, 48, 51, 56; political ills related to, 147; poor and wealthy, taxation of, 196, 199; during revolution of 1848, 153n219, 155–56; wine and spirits tax, xxvii–xxviii, 43–44, 175, 223–24, 315, 351n12, 365–66, 411n6, 520; woollen cloth export subsidy, 153n219

Taylor, William Cook, 73

teachers and teaching. *See* education

Temple, Henry John, third viscount Palmerston, 115n164, 134, 258n346, 262, 269, 433, 497–98

Ten Hours' Bill (Factory Bill) of 1847, England, 432

Terror, the, xxiv, 187, 455n43, 481, 485, 491, 492

Texas's admission to United States, 381

Thales, 417

theater. *See* drama

Themis, 16

Theocrates, 420

Thierry, Augustin, xvi, 486, 487

Thiers, Adolphe, 506; Aide toi, le ciel t'aidera (society), 480; Blanc and, 478; civil servants as ministers, Bastiat's opposition to, 454; mentioned in Bastiat's correspondence, 45, 207, 235; mentioned in Bastiat's manifesto on civil servants as electors, 373, 379, 381, 384, 386; *Le National* founded by, 516; opposition of Bastiat to interventionist economics of, xxxiii; opposition party politics and, 423; Passy, Hyppolite, and, 495, 498; political alliances and, 413; *Protectionism and Communism* written in response to, 518; Vivien, Alexandre, and, 507

Thompson, Thomas, 64, 69, 70, 123, 176, 326, 506
Thoré, S., 511
"three glorious days" of revolution of 1830, 25–30, 350
timeline for Bastiat, xxxvi–xxxvii
tobacco products, state monopoly on, 432
Tocqueville, Alexis de, xxxii, 363n20, 484, 486
"To the Electors of the District of Saint-Sever" (Bastiat, 1846), xxxiin9, 108n151, 109, 352–67, 412n7
Tracy. See Destutt de Tracy, Antoine
trade and commerce, Bastiat's interest in, 11–12, 14–15, 24
trade liberalization. See free trade
trains: in Bastiat's correspondence, 105, 201, 203–4, 281; Bordeaux to Bayonne railway line, letter to newspaper on, 312–16
Traité d'économie politique (Treatise on Political Economy; Say, 1830), xxvi, 12, 503
Traité de législation (The Treatise of Legislation; Comte, 1827, 1835), xxvi, 21n16, 67, 71, 483
Trélat, Ulysse, 164, 506
tricolor (flag), 28–30, 387
tuberculosis, xxiv, xxxiin12, 3, 8, 127n183
Turgot, Anne-Robert-Jacques, 126, 298n386, 484, 506
Turkey, 155, 373
Turpin, Etienne, 506
221, the, 342–43

ultralegitimists, 20n14, 507
United Kingdom. See England
United States. See America
universal suffrage: in Bastiat's correspondence, 145, 147, 158, 175, 181, 219, 243n327; in Bastiat's political manifestos, 384, 390, 394, 395; in Bastiat's political writings, 435, 451; Constituent Assembly elected by, 512

value, Bastiat's theory of, 171–72, 195, 215, 299
Véfour (restaurant), 60, 63, 510

Vernes, Charles, 97, 507
Verona, Congress of (1822), 24n23
Verri, Pietro, 129n186
Victoria (queen of England), 464, 467–68
Vienna, Congress of (1815), 122n176, 192n260
Villèle, Jean-Baptiste, 325, 351, 507
Villeneuve de Marsan, 50
Villermé, Louis René, 66, 507
Villiers, George, earl of Clarendon, 70, 89, 176, 507
Vincens [de] Saint-Laurent, Marc-Antoine, 100, 507
Virgil, 416n2
Vivien, Alexandre, 170, 507
Voix du peuple, La (newspaper), 224, 225, 239, 500, 520
Voltaire, 505

wages, Bastiat's interest in, 119
Waitangi, Treaty of, 432n22
Walpole, Robert, earl of Oxford, 331, 507
Westminster Review, 489, 506
whale fishing, 241
What Is Seen and What Is Not Seen (Bastiat, 1850), xxiii, xxxiii, xxxv, 3, 250, 254, 520
Wilberforce, William, 327, 482, 507
Wilson, George, 69, 74, 79, 126, 176–79, 507, 523
Wilson, James, 96, 508
wine trade: Bastiat family involvement in, xxiv, xxv; beer and wine drinkers contrasted, 247; with England, 87, 110, 135; organization of local growers by Bastiat, xxviii, 44, 77; protectionism affecting, xxviii; southwestern France, barriers to trade in, 110; wine and spirits tax, xxvii–xxviii, 43–44, 175, 223–24, 315, 351n12, 365–66, 411n6, 520
wit of Bastiat, 8–9
Wolowski, Louis, 66, 100, 508, 516
women: Bastiat's relationship with, 7–8; bourgeois families, Bastiat's association

with, 4, 6–7; luggage, women's propensity for, 271; marriage of Bastiat, xxvii, 8; mother of Bastiat, death of, xxiv; politics, Bastiat on women and, 197, 218; rights and accomplishments of, Bastiat's support of, 8, 197, 233–34. *See also specific women by name*

Wood, Mr. (president of Manchester Chamber of Commerce), 86
work, freedom to, 434

Xenophon, 416

Zollverein, 73, 422nn12–13

This book is set in Adobe Garamond, designed by Robert Slimbach in 1989. The face is based on the refined array of the typefaces of French punchcutter, type designer, and publisher Claude Garamond. These faces combine an unprecedented degree of balance and elegance and stand as a pinnacle of beauty and practicality in sixteenth-century typefounding.

Claude Garamond (ca. 1480–1561), a true Renaissance man, introduced the apostrophe, the accent, and the cedilla to the French language.

This book is printed on paper that is acid-free and meets the requirements of the American National Standard for Permanence of Paper for Printed Library Materials, z39.48-1992. ∞

Book design by Barbara E. Williams
BW&A Books, Inc.
Durham, North Carolina
Typography by Graphic Composition, Inc.
Athens/Bogart, Georgia
Printed and bound by
Worzalla Publishing Company
Stevens Point, Wisconsin